PRAISE FROM OUR READERS

Mastering HTML 4

"This is THE book!! If you can't find what you are looking for or learn HTML from this book, then there is no hope. This is the most comprehensive HTML book I have ever seen! Well worth the money and time to read it!"
Martha Rich, Arkansas

"Fantastic, Comprehensive, Easy-to-Read! I've thumbed through, and read thoroughly, many HTML books, but this one just grabs your brain, rattles out your neurons and implants the goodies you need to slam-dunk a great Web site. The authors provide an easy-to-read format with just the right amount of examples and details that won't leave you asking more questions or bore you with too many arcane details."
Sabrina Hanley, North Carolina

Mastering FrontPage 98

"Best of the 9 FrontPage 98 books I own. Sybex does it again! I have been reading computer books for the last 10 years and Sybex has been a great publisher—putting out excellent books. After reading 3/4 of the book so far, I know that the publisher and the authors take pride in their product. It's a wonderful book!"
Mike Perry, New Jersey

"This is THE book for mastering FrontPage 98! I skimmed through 4 other books before deciding to buy this one. Every other book seemed like a larger version of the weak documentation that comes with the software. This book provided the insight on advanced subjects necessary for administering a web. A must buy for FrontPage users."
Richard Hartsell, Utah

Mastering CorelDraw 8

"I'm a computer graphics instructor (college level) and the 'Mastering' books have long been on my Highly Recommended list for students. As for Rick Altman, I've been using his Corel books for the last four versions. This is a reference book, and a beautifully complete one. This is for the artist who needs to truly understand an effect or feature and get back to work. It's also readable. Students can work through chapters, or even the entire book, and they certainly won't get bored. I love following an Altman book from start to finish."
Christine C. Frey, Maryland

SYBEX
www.sybex.com

MASTERING™
CORELDRAW™ 9

Rick Altman

SYBEX®

San Francisco • Paris • Düsseldorf • Soest • London

Associate Publisher: Amy Romanoff
Contracts and Licensing Manager: Kristine O'Callaghan
Acquisitions & Developmental Editor: Cheryl Applewood
Editor: Anamary Ehlen
Project Editor: Julie Sakaue
Technical Editor: Joe Donnelly
Book Designer: Franz Baumhackl
Electronic Publishing Specialist: Maureen Forys, Happenstance Type-O-Rama
Color Insert Design: Kate Kaminski
Project Team Leader: Lisa Reardon
Proofreaders: Richard Ganis, Bonnie Hart, Jeff Chorney, and Lindy Wolf
Indexer: Matthew Spence
Cover Designer: Design Site
Cover Illustrator/Photographer: Sergie Loobkoff, Design Site

SYBEX is a registered trademark of SYBEX Inc.

Mastering is a trademark of SYBEX Inc.

Screen reproductions produced with Collage Complete.
Collage Complete is a trademark of Inner Media Inc.

This publication includes images from CorelDRAW which are protected by the copyright laws of the U.S., Canada and elsewhere. Used under license.

This publication may also include images from the following third parties through CorelDRAW: Image Club Graphics Inc. at www.imageclub.com or 1-403-262-8008, One Mile Up Inc. at www.onemileup.com or 1-703-642-1177, and Techpool Studios Inc. at www.lifeart.com or 1-216-382-1234.

Microsoft, the Microsoft Internet Explorer logo, Windows, Windows NT, and the Windows logo are either registered trademarks or trademarks of Microsoft Corporation in the United States and/or other countries.

TRADEMARKS: SYBEX has attempted throughout this book to distinguish proprietary trademarks from descriptive terms by following the capitalization style used by the manufacturer.

The author and publisher have made their best efforts to prepare this book, and the content is based upon final release software whenever possible. Portions of the manuscript may be based upon pre-release versions supplied by software manufacturer(s). The author and the publisher make no representation or warranties of any kind with regard to the completeness or accuracy of the contents herein and accept no liability of any kind including but not limited to performance, merchantability, fitness for any particular purpose, or any losses or damages of any kind caused or alleged to be caused directly or indirectly from this book.

Library of Congress Card Number: 99-62996
ISBN: 0-7821-2520-4

Manufactured in the United States of America

10 9 8 7 6 5 4 3 2 1

To two ten-year anniversaries. My wonderful wife Becky has put up with me for 10 years. We got married right about the time that CorelDRAW version 1 was becoming the largest-selling graphic program ever seen under Windows.

Acknowledgments

I have two daughters, ages six and three. I feel as if I also have a son. He exhibits many of the tendencies and much of the behavior requisite of an offspring: he is constantly demanding of attention, he devises creative strategies to get his way, he has good days and bad days, and he has woven himself throughout my life in countless ways.

This son of mine is not flesh and blood, but instead bark and pulp. He's about 800 pages long, and you're holding him in your hands right now. Parenting this wayward child cannot be done in the traditional way—this is one of those times when both the Democrats and Republicans would agree that it really does take a village. As chief witch doctor, I am grateful for the assistance of my team of villagers.

Heading the list is our technical editor, Joe Donnelly, who represents perhaps the finest coup this book has ever enjoyed. We signed him up just one month after he decided to leave his post at Corel...*as CorelDRAW Product Manager!* He spent two years directing the team of engineers, determining which features would stay and which would go, and how they would be implemented. For two years, he *was* CorelDRAW.

We wondered how he would respond to the areas in this book where we are critical of Corel or the software. Would he take it personally? Well, in Chapter 2, when we wrote about being "underwhelmed and unimpressed by DRAW as a Web page creation tool," his quick retort was that we had misspelled *underwhelmed*.

Following very close behind is our primary contributor, Debbie Cook, whose star is rising steadily in the Corel community. She began making her mark with volunteer technical support on newsgroups and other online discussion venues for CorelDRAW users. She also has been a prominent member of the technical team at the annual CorelWORLD User Conference, and has most recently found prominence for the set of scripts she created for producing effects within PHOTO-PAINT. Her keen eye and persistent research graces our "What's New" chapter, and much of Part VII, "The CorelDRAW Freeway."

Returning for his sixth season is Wayne Kaplan, whose influence can be found throughout the book. As a "Tier 1 beta tester" (which means that Corel Corp. pays Wayne to test the product before its release), Wayne is as close to the program as is possible, without actually being one of the engineers.

Working with the team at Sybex was especially gratifying this year—from Acquisitions Editor Cheryl Applewood on down, it was clear that the people involved in this book came from a background or an interest in graphics. Julie Sakaue kept the ship afloat with unusual aplomb, and returning for a second year as copy editor, Anamary Ehlen lived up to her initials of A.C.E. Each member of the production team—Maureen Forys, Lisa Reardon, Richard Ganis, Bonnie Hart, Jeff Chorney, Lindy Wolf, and especially Kate Kaminski—contributed their special talents to turn the manuscript and art files into a book.

As always, I owe a debt of gratitude to the over 800 CorelDRAW users who have joined us at the annual CorelWORLD User Conferences since 1993. Your feedback, experiences, suggestions, positive attitude, and overall good humor and cheer continue to fuel our creative fire. We will be in Orlando in October of 1999 and would love for all our readers to join us there. For details about this and many other opportunities for DRAW users, visit us at www.altman.com.

And finally, a special thanks to Greg, Kathy, Sharon, and Steve, who make up the nucleus of the coed volleyball team that proved to be my sole refuge during book-writing season. We all met as new parents, and when we discovered a mutual affinity for the game, we joined a league and decided to name our team No D.I.N.K.S. Get it…?

—Rick Altman
Lead Author

Contents at a Glance

Table of Contents

Introduction

"Is this big book you're writing the reason that you can never play golf with me?" my father asked, with just the right amount of sarcasm to make me smile and feel guilty at the same time.

While the ideal retort might have been, "No, Dad, I'm scared to ride in the golf cart with you," the fact is that he was right.

"Is it another monster?" my father continued. "And does it have any of that Internet stuff in it?"

"Oh, yes. You can't write a book today without discussing the World Wide Web."

"Oy vey, the whole world's gone meshuga."

Repartee with my father is now a tradition here in the introduction, and we're quite sure that he is responsible for the first instance of the Jewish expression for "gone crazy" ever to appear in a CorelDRAW book.

Mastering CorelDRAW 9 is the sixth go-round of this special type of *mishigos* for me and my writing team, but in many ways it feels like the first. While it is fine to allow a chapter here and there to ride from one year to the next, we decided it was time for a true house-cleaning. The result is a book that is over 95-percent fresh material. I have the sore fingers to prove it.

What Is CorelDRAW?

Since its debut 10 years ago, CorelDRAW has been a clear and obvious leader among Windows-based drawing and illustration programs. But what is neither clear nor obvious is what exactly it means to be a drawing program. Is it a program that allows you to work with refined curves and objects to produce precise artistic effects? Is it a powerful typographic engine for the creation of logos and other text-based work? Is it a laboratory for manipulating photos and images? Is it the hub of a World Wide Web tool? Or does CorelDRAW continue to be, primarily, a tool for driving book authors...meshuga?

The fact that CorelDRAW is actually all of these things underscores the impression this program has made in its community. One way or the other, the applications in the box of software known as CorelDRAW assist you in the creation of modern-day graphics. They are the tools with which you can create:

- Full-color illustrations
- Complex drawings
- Logos
- Graphics for the World Wide Web

- Fancy headlines
- Photo-realistic images
- Surrealistic images
- Animation sequences
- Libraries of clipart
- High-quality drawings from low-resolution originals

CorelDRAW Is for Graphics

Be it for traditional media or for the Web, CorelDRAW is a graphics clearinghouse of tools. With it you can create illustrations from scratch, enhance clipart, use and embellish scanned photos, and send your finished work out one of many ways. This is the domain of the Big Two—DRAW and PHOTO-PAINT—and these are what users buy the software for. Many users occasionally turn to the services of Corel TRACE for help in converting a scanned image into more refined artwork, but day in and day out, DRAW and, increasingly, PHOTO-PAINT, are what see the most active duty.

This lopsided popularity is not lost on us, and the lion's share of this book is devoted to DRAW, the flagship product. But unlike in previous editions, where we confess to having virtually ignored PAINT, we devote six chapters to the creation of bitmap graphics, and two to the fundamentals of image editing.

For Whom Does This Book Toll?

As lead author, I like to think that any CorelDRAW user on the planet will enjoy the pages of this book. The fact that I won't try to convince you of that is a sure sign that I have no future as the marketer of books, only the writer of them. From our ongoing series of CorelDRAW seminars and conferences—at which I meet several hundred users every year—I have defined a clear profile of you, the mainstream user: You produce lots of one-page fliers, logos, small brochures, signs, banners, T-shirts, and increasingly, Web pages. You do not necessarily have a professional background in the arts; in fact, most of you do not. But even if you do, your primary aim is to develop a better under-standing of DRAW's tools and functions and learn the hidden treasures that allow for faster and more efficient operation.

This book is written with the following users in mind:

- Technical illustrators, who want to reduce the amount of busywork involved in producing diagrams, charts, and simple drawings.
- Amateur and budding designers, who strive to develop an eye for good, clean, simple designs.

- Web designers, who seek a powerful tool for creating graphics and who wonder exactly what role DRAW can and should play in their Web sites.
- Desktop publishers, who need a better understanding of DRAW's text-handling capabilities.
- Commercial artists, who might be auditioning this new version of DRAW for producing their next double-page advertising spread.
- Fine artists and illustrators, who will not tolerate a book that tries to teach them their business, but who want to sharpen their CorelDRAW skills and their understanding of its tools.
- Brand-new users looking for a book that neither talks down to them nor leads them laboriously by the hand, but rather arms them with information and gives them the practice they need to become self-sufficient.
- And prospective users, who want to get a sense of what CorelDRAW is all about before they make their purchase.

Your Roadmap

In this book, we include both tutorial and reference material, and when necessary, we specify right away any chapter that is either for beginners or more advanced users. Teachers and trainers will want to keep an eye out for the "Step by Step" sections that frequent many chapters, as they make for ideal training exercises.

Part I, "A Quick Tour of CorelDRAW," is an introduction to the software in general, and the elements that are new to the program. We know that many users play leapfrog with versions, and that many of you are coming to DRAW 9 from version 7. As a result, Chapter 2, our "What's New" chapter, details additions and improvements introduced in DRAW 8 and DRAW 9.

Part II, "Life in an Object-Oriented World," explores the lifeblood of DRAW: curves, nodes, object creation, fills, and outlines.

Part III, "Mastering Text," covers—you guessed it—your work with text in DRAW: paragraph and artistic, fancy and conservative, fast and slow, good and bad.

Part IV, "Effects and Affects," features the stellar performers found under the Effects menu, responsible for the more dramatic effects possible with DRAW.

Part V, "Drawing for Cyberspace," focuses on creating graphics for the World Wide Web. It covers in detail the creation of Web graphics, Web pages, image maps, hyperlinks, backgrounds, and much more. It offers many strategies for creating successful Web graphics, including frank discussions about DRAW's strengths and weaknesses.

Part VI, "The Bitmap Era," is a brand new section of the book dedicated to the wonderfully scary world of bitmap imagery. One of the chapters focuses on the services that DRAW can perform for imported photographs, and then two chapters explore PHOTO-PAINT.

Part VII, "The CorelDRAW Freeway," exposes DRAW as the expressway it is, with emphasis on its exits and entrances—namely printing, color and prepress theory, importing, and exporting. You won't want to miss Chapter 28, where we introduce the new Publish to PDF tool.

Part VIII, "Taking Control," explores the improved functions of styles, templates, object management, recordable scripts, and the amazing opportunities provided by DRAW's customizable interface.

N O T E   This book also has a companion Web site at www.sybex.com. There you'll find additional information that will help you master CorelDRAW 9. You'll find files that will help you get started with many of the tutorials, as well as drawings that you can reverse-engineer to learn more about special techniques and all that goes into a successful drawing. Just click the Catalog button on Sybex's home page (www.sybex.com), then use the search engine found on the Catalog page to arrive at the companion Web site for *Mastering CorelDRAW 9*. Once you reach this Web site, we suggest you bookmark it for your future visits.

The Foundation of CorelDRAW

I remember it as if it were yesterday—the day that CorelDRAW 1 was first released. Up until then, the closest things to illustration software were unremarkable paint programs and nongraphical applications that required you to describe the effect you wanted, instead of drawing it. ("Circle, 2-inch radius, create.") CorelDRAW was one of the first Windows-based drawing programs to take hold.

Today, over 10 years later, CorelDRAW is one of the giants of the industry, in terms of its customer base, its stature, and the depth and breadth of the programs that are included in this one product.

It is no mystery why this is so. From its inception, CorelDRAW has been one of the most approachable and most inviting of all graphics programs. Its army of users covers virtually all corners of the graphics community: from fine artists to illustrators to technical artists; from freelance designers to desktop publishers; book publishers and newsletter editors; sign-makers, T-shirt designers, and logo creators; secretaries turned designers; well-meaning but unartistic managers...and even my six-year-old daughter, Erica. Granted, becoming proficient with CorelDRAW might be a challenge; but more than two million users will attest to the fact that playing around with, developing a feel for, and even getting the hang of this program is not difficult at all.

Drawing vs. Painting

When we first started hosting the CorelWORLD User Conference—three days of seminars and workshops, dedicated to DRAW and PAINT—I was surprised to discover how many users did not understand the essential qualities of the two broad categories of illustration programs. Today, a good six years later, we still encounter hundreds of users who are unclear on the concept, because many electronic artists simply take for granted what these programs do in the background. When you get past all of the jargon about Béziers, pixels, halftones, clipping paths, and process colors, graphics programs produce art in one of two ways: they produce curves, lines, and other distinct shapes that are based on mathematics; or they produce dots. At the core of it all, everything that comes from graphics software is curves or dots.

The one characteristic that distinguishes vector-based drawing programs like DRAW, Xara, Adobe Illustrator, Macromedia Freehand, and others is their particular degree of intelligence. When you draw a circle in one of these programs, the circle has a set of properties—an identity, if you will. It has a radius from the center, a circumference, a set of x- and y-coordinates, an outline, and an interior color. If you change the appearance or size of the circle, DRAW still knows that the circle is a circle.

Painting programs, on the other hand—such as PHOTO-PAINT (included in the CorelDRAW box), Adobe PhotoShop, and PaintShop Pro—create graphics that are not nearly as smart. In fact, they're pretty dumb, but don't think of that as an insult. Their primary job is to lay down pixels on a screen, no questions asked, just as a painter would apply paint to a canvas. The circle you create in a paint program is simply a collection of pixels, perhaps millions of them, lined up in rows. Taken together, the dots might happen to look like a circle, but there are no properties identifying it as a circle, as there are in DRAW.

When You Have to Choose...

When buying graphics software, it's unlikely that you would choose *either* a vector-based *or* a paint program. Most businesses need the services of *both,* because whether dumb or smart, both types of software play important roles. That is precisely why every copy of CorelDRAW includes DRAW (the drawing program) and PAINT (the painting program).

If You Need Clipart   Turn to DRAW and the gaggle of prefab clipart images on the CorelDRAW CD. Because vector drawings can be edited so easily, DRAW is the perfect tool to produce simple art from scratch or to modify existing art.

If You Need to Scan Photos   That's a job for PAINT. The undying virtue of bitmap image editing is the extraordinary level of control you have. *You* decide how small each dot is to be (that is, how high the resolution is), and *you* can change the color of every dot that makes up the image.

If You're Creating Artwork for the Internet   Take your pick, or use them both. The revolution and the miracle that is the World Wide Web is fertile ground for both vector and bitmap software. Ultimately, graphics make their way to the Internet in bitmap form—as .gif or .jpg files—yet both DRAW and PAINT are capable of creating them. Within the bounds of good taste, all of DRAW's formatting prowess and special effects arsenal can be brought to bare on a Web site in search of a personality. Part V looks at the exciting and sometimes scary world of Internet graphics.

If You Need to Capture and Refine Computer Screen Images   Here, as well, give the nod to your paint program, coupled with a screen capture program (such as Corel CAPTURE, included in the CorelDRAW box). When you take a picture of your screen, it is stored as a bitmap. Although this bitmap is not as detailed as most photographs, you can still edit all the way down to the dot level.

If You Need to Set Lots of Type   Hightail it back to DRAW, where all the fidelity of your typeface format is honored, including letter spacing, tracking, kerning, and hinting.

If You're Producing Technical Drawings   Once again you're in DRAW's domain, where you can achieve utter precision, razor-sharp lines, and can scale, reshape, group, and duplicate individual objects.

If You're Creating Logos, Fliers, Brochures, or Ad Layouts   Chances are you're going to want both DRAW and PAINT, because today's electronic art often contains text and other vector-based objects integrated with scanned images. DRAW can be your Grand Central Station for such projects, because it allows you to import bitmap images into a drawing and even apply special effects to them.

The Magic of the Curve

We may be guilty of a bit of oversimplification, but the cornerstone to DRAW can be summed up in one plural noun: *curves*. The essence of DRAW is its ability to create curves, and this stands in stark contrast to what a paint program does. This bears repeating: paint programs do not "understand" that the millions of dots that they are storing are supposed to look like something—that happens practically by accident. DRAW understands the dynamics responsible for an object's shape; it knows about radiuses, angles, straight and curved lines, and all of the subtleties of typefaces.

As a result, vector art is quite lean. Bitmap images can get big in a hurry, with all of those dots to cart around, but vector art is marked by its tidy set of mathematical instructions for describing objects.

Figure 1 is a drawing of President Clinton's family, produced in DRAW. The curves and fill patterns that make up this image will require less than 100K of disk space, but if it were converted to a bitmap image, you'd be looking at a minimum of 500K for a low-resolution rendition, and as much as 5MB for one in full color.

No question about it, if you choose your paint program to produce work that is better suited for your drawing program, you'll hear about it from your hard drive. And if you decide to go all out and use a professionally scanned photograph of the Clintons *and* the First Feline (the cat—we're talking about the cat) standing in the Oval Office, you're talking about really high rent: 10MB to 40MB.

FIGURE 1

Rendered as vector art, the Clinton family is a lean, 100K DRAW file. Described as bitmap art, this same image grows to at least 500K and likely more.

You'll read a lot about curves throughout this text, especially the so-called *Bézier curve,* shown in Figure 2. It's named after the man who discovered the dynamic relationship that exists between a starting point, an ending point, and the two control points that determine the path taken by the curve from start to finish. You don't need to understand the intricacies—just know that Bézier curves get the credit for just about everything that CorelDRAW does right.

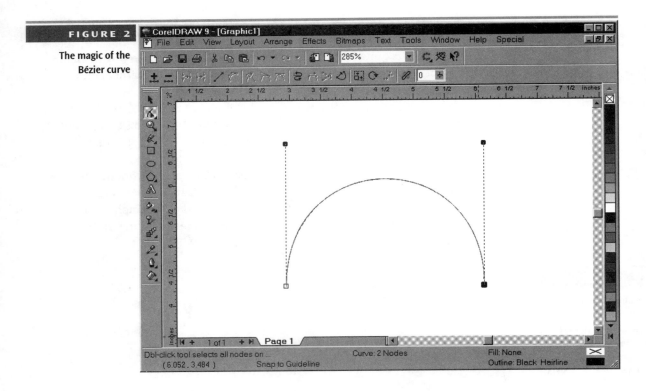

FIGURE 2

The magic of the
Bézier curve

CorelDRAW Is Greater Than the Sum of Its Parts

Like most sophisticated graphics programs, CorelDRAW hits its stride when you apply a few of its special effects to otherwise simple objects. Creating a few ellipses, like the ones shown at the left of Figure 3, may not be cause for celebration, but you will really begin to turn heads when you unleash the higher-octane features. There's Blend, which transforms one object into another, and Trim, the tool responsible for creating the sprocket in the center of Figure 3 from the four simple ellipses. There's Extrude, which produced the depth-defying effect for the finished sprocket. There's Radial Fill, which gently changes the fill color from one to another, and Rotate, Envelope, Weld, Distribute, Trim, PowerClip—the list goes on. As Figure 3 shows, the relationship between simple objects and powerful effects might be the marriage made in electronic heaven.

PART I

A Quick Tour of CorelDRAW

A Tour of the Tools

Featuring

CHAPTER

1

A TOUR OF THE TOOLS

Most long-term users are amazed at how different each version of CorelDRAW appears from the previous one. Corel's engineering team seems to work eight days a week through the entire calendar year to come up with a bevy of new features, and usually at least one entirely new application every 12 to 18 months. While Chapter 2 focuses on what has changed in versions 8 and 9, here you'll read about what has stayed the same. From one version to the next, CorelDRAW's essential look and feel—its heart and soul, really—have remained unswervingly consistent. This chapter is for new or occasional CorelDRAW users seeking an overview of the program, or for more experienced users who want to brush up on their fundamentals.

N O T E CorelDRAW 9 is a 32-bit application and will not run under Windows 3.*x*. It will run only on Windows 95, Windows 98, and Windows NT 4.0.

As with most 32-bit Windows programs (95 and later), all of the CorelDRAW modules consist of menus that you pull down, dialog boxes that you invoke, and tools that you click. Most of the functions, across all the CorelDRAW modules, can be accessed from both keyboard and mouse. We will likely harp a bit throughout the book on favorite hotkeys, as we believe them to be invaluable for those seeking efficiency and economy of motion. (And what's fair is fair, so we'll also complain a bit about some very strange key mnemonics, and others that are inexplicably absent.)

Surfing the Interface

This chapter is akin to the couch-potato activity of cruising via remote control every single television station offered by your cable provider. We won't stop long at any one of them—we'll surf.

Figure 1.1 shows the essential interface for DRAW, the main module of the CorelDRAW suite of programs. Veteran users will note that the DRAW 9 screen looks markedly similar to that of earlier versions, perhaps identical. On the other hand, your screen might look slightly different from the one shown here because video cards, color palettes, your preferred Windows Display Properties, and your screen resolution all affect the appearance of Windows applications.

FIGURE 1.1

DRAW may overwhelm you with its depth, but its interface has remained clean and uncluttered since version 1.

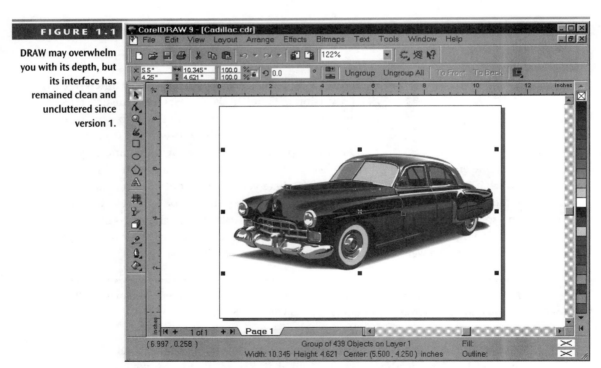

The 14 icons along the left side of the work area make up DRAW's *toolbox*, providing access to the most common commands and functions of the program. The *Standard toolbar* below the menus provides access to other frequently used commands, while the *property bar* below that offers context-sensitive controls. In other words, the icons and shortcuts on the property bar change as you use the program. If you are creating a rectangle, the property bar displays controls to edit the rectangle; if you are creating text, the property bar offers text-editing and formatting commands.

DRAW owes much of its success to its clean interface. Even if you have never used a drawing program, you can probably draw a blue circle in DRAW for the first time without too many wrong turns. And once you know the most basic of maneuvers—click on the tool, move to the page, click and drag, and click on a fill color—you are all set to create not just rectangles, but ovals, text blocks, lines, stars and other polygons, and free-form objects. In mastering this maneuver, you also automatically know how to zoom in on parts of your drawing, group and ungroup objects, and change the basic shape of curves.

All these operations result from one set of motions:

1. Click on the desired tool.

2. Move your cursor out over the drawing page.

3. Press and hold Button 1 on your mouse.

4. Drag the mouse across the page.

5. Let go of the mouse button.

NOTE   We try to avoid "dexteritism"—discrimination on the basis of one's dexterity, that is. So instead of "right-click" and "left-click," we would prefer "Button 1" (the primary mouse button, the left one for most users) and "Button 2" (the secondary mouse button). Unfortunately, Microsoft has officially coined and sanctioned "right-click" as the term for clicking with Button 2 to pull down a context-sensitive menu, and it will be hard for us to avoid it. Nonetheless, when it comes to plain old clicking or clicking-and-dragging, we'll use Button 1 and Button 2 to keep them distinct.

We're only exaggerating a little bit when we say that once you have learned this procedure, you have learned about 90 percent of the motions required to drive the program. Of course, knowing how to press on the accelerator doesn't give you license to drive a car, and this tool is not capable of creating fine art on its own. For that matter, total expertise with DRAW won't turn you into a fine artist if you weren't one already, and this is a point that we will continue to drive home throughout this book. Becoming a capable DRAW user requires vision, good judgment, experience, and lots of practice.

Couple that with a knowledge of the arts, and you're on your way to becoming a successful electronic illustrator.

The Supporting Actors

Many parts of DRAW's face are leased from Windows itself. Like practically every Windows program, all of the CorelDRAW modules include:

- A title bar listing the name of the application and/or the particular file opened, with Minimize/Maximize/Restore/Close buttons to control the DRAW window
- A menu bar that provides access to most of the program's functions and commands
- At least one row of icons for reaching the most frequently used commands
- Scroll bars for moving to other parts of a drawing, and page icons and tabs for scrolling through pages (if a drawing contains more than one)
- The DRAW balloon icon at the top-left corner of the screen, for quickly sizing and closing DRAW or the current window

It would be nearly impossible to find a Windows program today that *doesn't* offer File, Edit, and View as its first three menu choices, or that doesn't offer some sort of button or toolbar with icons that provide shortcuts to commands and functions. DRAW is no exception.

The Status Bar

The *status bar* displays by default at the bottom of the screen. Initially, you see two areas in the status bar: the coordinates on the left give you the screen position of the mouse pointer, and Fill displays the fill pattern or color of the selected object. In Figure 1.1, the status bar also displays information about the selected object(s); in this case, that it is a group consisting of 439 smaller objects.

The status bar can be one or two lines deep and positioned on the top or bottom of the CorelDRAW window. While you can move or size it by clicking and dragging interactively, the easier way is to right-click on the status bar and then use the context menu. From that context menu, you can reset the status bar to its original size and position and also customize it to show you various items of information, such as memory allocation and the status of CapsLock and NumLock. For details about customizing your system, refer to Chapter 34, "Your Very Own Interface."

The rectangle at the far-right end of the status bar changes dynamically to reflect the properties of the currently selected object. If the object were red, so would be the rectangle. And if the outline were red and three points thick, the line around the rectangle would change to reflect that. When objects overlap, sometimes the only way you can tell which object is selected is to watch this little box in the status bar. Continuing with the automobile analogy used earlier in this chapter, staying mindful of this representative box is akin to using your rearview mirror: it's an excellent habit to develop and will no doubt save you from major trouble some day.

The Scroll Bars

DRAW's *scroll bars* operate just like those in most other Windows programs, and the horizontal and vertical scroll bars operate identically. There are three ways to scroll the screen: You can scroll little by little, by clicking on the small arrow buttons on either end of the scroll bar. You can scroll a lot at a time, by clicking on the gray part of the scroll bar (on your system, the scroll bar may be a different color). Or you can scroll any amount you choose, by clicking and dragging the small rectangle (the *scroll button*) inside the scroll bar.

TIP   We consider scrolling to be a necessary evil, but an evil nonetheless. Little provides us with more tedium and more finger fatigue than having to click on those awful little boxes at the edges of the scroll bars. Therefore, we were delighted with the addition of on-screen panning, introduced in DRAW 7. With this handy feature, you can scroll the screen by using your keyboard arrow keys in conjunction with Alt. Try it for yourself—just press Alt and then an arrow key—and we think you'll agree it is a quicker and far less tedious way to move around.

The Color Palette

Along the right edge of the screen you'll find the *color palette,* which provides you with a very easy method for changing the interior fill or the outline color of a selected object. Because most color palettes have many more colors than can fit on the screen, the palette works like a scroll bar to give you access to all the palette's selections. To display additional color choices, click the down arrow at the bottom end of the color palette. Because of the number of colors available, you will scroll a long way to get to that last black box.

NOTE   In DRAW 9, you can open more than one color palette on the screen at a time.

The × button at the top end of the color palette is for the quick removal of a fill or outline. One palette serves both the outline and the fill, thanks to the fact that PC mice have two buttons. When hovering over a color, here are the four things you can do with the color palette and your mouse buttons:

Click Button 1	Change or remove the interior fill of a selected object
Click Button 2	Change or remove the outline of a selected object
Click and hold Button 1	Pop up a palette of shades of the color
Click, hold, and then release Button 2	Invoke the context menu for the color palette

The color palette, the status bar, the on-screen rulers, and the property bar can all be toggled on and off via the View menu. The toolbox, as well, is controlled on the View menu, using the Toolbars command (the toolbox is treated as a special toolbar). By controlling all these screen elements, you can make a dramatic change in DRAW's appearance, as shown in Figures 1.2 and 1.3.

FIGURE 1.2

The DRAW interface with all its essential parts intact

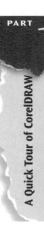

FIGURE 1.3

The DRAW interface without the property bar, status bar, Standard toolbar, rulers, color palette, toolbox, and page border

Understanding Dialog Boxes

When you issue commands for actions, such as removing the status bar or the color palette from the DRAW interface, you are performing the next most common maneuver in the program after the click-and-drag: pulling down a menu and then choosing one of its functions. Clicking on a menu choice will generally produce one of two results. It will either trigger an on/off toggle (as in showing and hiding the on-screen rulers), or it will activate a *dialog box* in which a collection of controls resides. (We use the term *dialog* for short.) The menu choices that invoke dialogs are all followed by … (an ellipsis), indicating there is more to the story. Figure 1.4 shows the result of choosing Text ➤ Format Text. You can also reach this point by clicking on the blue *F* on the property bar (with a string of text selected).

The tabbed dialog in Figure 1.4 is tried-and-true Windows. In version 8, DRAW made a departure from convention with dialogs that use a tree-like structure—point and click on the item you want to change, and the tree expands to reveal additional choices for you to make. Figure 1.5 shows the Options dialog box where first we chose Workspace and then Display. The controls on the right all affect display settings in some way.

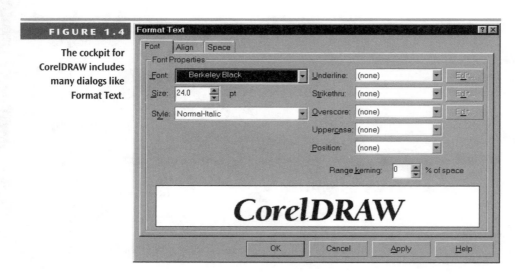

FIGURE 1.4

The cockpit for CorelDRAW includes many dialogs like Format Text.

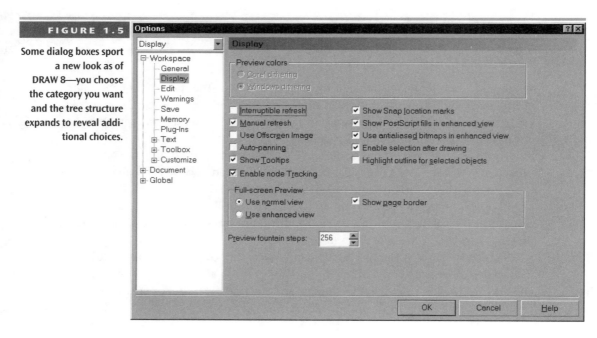

FIGURE 1.5

Some dialog boxes sport a new look as of DRAW 8—you choose the category you want and the tree structure expands to reveal additional choices.

Remember, it makes no difference to DRAW how you get to this dialog. You can use your mouse, clicking once on Tools in the menu bar and then on Options. Or you can press Alt+O for Tools and then O for Options. Or you can mix and match your keyboard and mouse actions; DRAW isn't particular.

Because the route to this Options dialog is heavily traveled by regular DRAW users, the developers assigned a *hotkey* to it: Ctrl+J. DRAW's hotkeys provide you with instant access to a dialog or command without having to pull down a menu. Whenever you want to access the Options dialog, pressing Ctrl+J will do it, no questions asked. Hotkeys are particularly handy if you just want to check a value for a setting without changing it. Ctrl+J opens the dialog box, and pressing the Esc key closes it, ignoring any changes you might have made. While experienced DRAW users had become used to the Ctrl+J/Esc shuffle, they don't use it as often anymore, now that so many of the options for a selected object remain visible on the property bar.

N O T E   All of DRAW's keyboard shortcuts to dialogs are shown on the menus with their functions. For instance, pull down the File menu and you'll see Ctrl+S associated with the Save command. A variety of "hidden" keystrokes also exist that have special jobs when used at specific times. All told, there are about 150 different hotkeys across the entire program—including such obscure gems as holding down the Shift key to erase a line drawn with the Freehand tool, and pressing Alt while moving an object to create a spray of objects. Furthermore, you can invent your own; Chapter 34 offers the details on that.

Understanding all of DRAW's controls can be tricky, but working them is easy. DRAW lets you navigate with the mouse or the keyboard within almost every dialog. As you can see in Figures 1.4 and 1.5, you can access every field, check box, and button with a keystroke (press Alt plus the underlined letter). So, for instance, to change the value for Preview Fountain Steps in Figure 1.5, you have three choices:

- Use the mouse to place the cursor in the entry box, press Backspace to erase the current value, and enter a new value.
- Press Alt+R to highlight the box and type the new value.
- Click on the little down-and-up arrow box to increase or decrease the value.

No surprise here—our preference is the second option, using the keyboard. Nothing is faster, or easier on your hands and wrists. Try all three and judge for yourself.

Exploring the Standard Toolbar

There was a time when we thought DRAW's Standard toolbar was not worth mentioning. We just couldn't get that excited about a little button that saves a drawing, since File ➤ Save or Ctrl+S both do that just fine. Vertical screen space on even a high-resolution display is far too valuable to waste on redundant controls, we thought.

But we've been singing a different tune since DRAW 6. You now have the ability to determine what goes on the Standard toolbar and where the toolbar resides. You can now position the Standard toolbar anywhere on the screen, add and remove functions, or drag tools from the toolbox to the toolbar.

This is also true for the property bar, which is potentially of even greater value, thanks to its context-sensitivity. Just remember this: once you set up your Standard toolbar, it will always look the same, no matter what you're doing in the program. However, the property bar is ever-changing, reflecting the set of controls that are most relevant to the particular task you are performing.

Working with Dockers

Introduced in version 8, *dockers* perform many of the same functions as conventional dialogs, but they are more interactive. For instance, they don't disappear as conventional dialogs do after carrying out a command. And because of their flexibility, you can place dockers right next to the object you are drawing for quick mouse action, or dock it (hence the name) to any of the four edges of the DRAW window. Dockers have been gradually replacing roll-ups, the old-style interactive control, and as of DRAW 9, that replacement is complete.

Different dockers relate to different tasks you may be working on, and DRAW lets you open only the ones you need at a given time. For example, when you are working with multiple objects in your illustrations, you can open the Object Manager docker window to help you keep track of the different objects on your pages.

Figure 1.6 shows one of the many dockers available to you in DRAW. This one enables you to choose the position of objects. Instead of clicking on an OK button to enact a change, you click on the Apply button. And instead of disappearing promptly, this docker can stick around, making a series of tweaks a friendlier task.

Note in Figure 1.6 the name of the docker, running vertically, and also that another docker, Shaping, is also available. You can open many dockers at once, and those that are not active lie in wait behind the one that is. To see a list of all dockers in the program, go to Window ➤ Dockers.

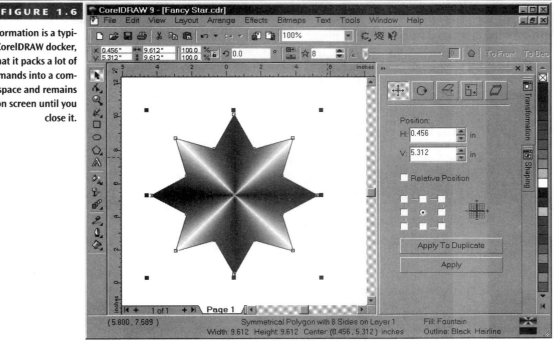

FIGURE 1.6

Transformation is a typical CorelDRAW docker, in that it packs a lot of commands into a compact space and remains on screen until you close it.

Exploring the Toolbox

The tools that make up the toolbox are the electronic lifeblood of DRAW. You can create hundreds of complete drawings using just these tools and no menu commands (except Save!). Following is a brief rundown on each tool.

The Pick Tool

The Pick tool acts as home base for DRAW. It is the tool that you use to select objects before altering them, and it is the active tool every time you start the program. You can select an object by clicking on it with the Pick tool, or by dragging across it with a *marquee* (see Chapter 3, "The Miracle of the Click").

TIP   When you drag a marquee around an object or group of objects, you must make sure to completely surround them—unless you know the secret shortcut, introduced in version 6: hold the Alt key while dragging your marquee, and you need only touch an object with the marquee to select it.

Once you've selected an object, you also use the Pick tool to move and/or resize it. Most advanced DRAW users take the Pick tool so much for granted that they may not even know its name. They might describe it as "that thing at the top that is always highlighted when you aren't using anything else. You know, the one that pretty much does everything." That about sums up the Pick tool.

Hotkey: the spacebar (except when you are editing text, then use Ctrl+spacebar)

The Shape Edit Flyout

The tools in this flyout, led by the Shape tool itself, preside over parts of an object, rather than the whole. While you would reach for the Pick tool to move or resize an entire curve or a whole string of text, the Shape tool and its brothers (the Knife, Eraser, and Free Transform tool) provide access to a part of the curve or one character in the text string. The parts of a curve are called *nodes* (the Shape tool is commonly referred to as the Node Edit tool), and by adjusting a node you can change the essential shape of a curve.

In addition to node-editing, the Shape tool can edit and kern selected text characters, crop bitmaps, round the corners of rectangles, and turn circles into arcs and pie slices.

Hotkey: F10

 N O T E   Note the downward-pointing triangle in the lower right of the icon. Seven of the tools display this, and it indicates the presence of a flyout menu. Click and hold the icon and the flyout appears.

The Zoom Flyout

The Zoom tool is one of the most essential aids to creating and editing illustrations because it lets you work in the optimum magnification. The toolbox offers you quick access to the Zoom In tool, which you can use to drag a marquee around the area you want to magnify. The flyout offers a panning tool as well, which we suspect you won't use too often, because the panning technique of using Alt and your arrow keys is faster and more convenient.

The other Zoom commands are available from the View Manager (reached from the Zoom toolbar, one of several toolbars that you can place on screen). All told, you can use zoom the following ways in DRAW:

- Zoom In allows you to define a marquee around the area you want to magnify.
- Pan enables you to pan around a drawing by dragging.

- Zoom Out enables you to reduce the view of a magnified area.
- Zoom Actual Size lets you display your drawing at its actual printing size.
- Zoom to Selected brings selected objects into the closest possible view.
- Zoom to All Objects brings all objects in a drawing into the closest possible view.
- Zoom to Page displays the entire page.
- Zoom to Page Width brings the width of the page into close view.
- Zoom to Page Height brings the length of the page into close view.

Hotkeys: F2 for triggering Zoom In mode, F3 for Zoom Out, Shift+F2 for Zoom to Selected, F4 for Zoom to All Objects, and Shift+F4 for Zoom to Page

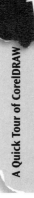

The Curve Flyout

If the Pick tool is the essential editing tool, then the Freehand tool is the essential creation tool. It is the electronic equivalent of the artist's sketching pencil. The Freehand tool's primary mission is to support *freehand drawing* and *Bézier drawing,* but several other types of drawing tools are part of this combined tool. Click on the tool and hold for a moment to access the flyout, and then hover your cursor over each one to see its name.

Freehand drawing really is like working with a pencil: to draw, you hold the mouse button down and move around the page. If you remember the old Etch-a-Sketch contraptions, you can get a good idea of the type of free-form (and sometimes dreadful) work this tool is capable of.

Bézier drawing creates the smooth curves required by fine art and illustration. When drawing in Bézier mode, you do not hold down the mouse button to create curves. Rather, you click once to define a starting point and then click again to define an ending point. The path that connects the two is treated as a curve or a line whose shape and position can be readily changed. Most of the attractive work you see produced with DRAW makes extensive use of Bézier curves. The Natural Pen tool might as well be called the Felt Pen. If you think of it that way, that's all the description you need.

The dimension tools feature lines that automatically calculate their distances and their angles, and lines that connect and stay connected for the purpose of creating flowcharts and organization charts.

Hotkey: F5

The Rectangle and Ellipse Tools

The first tools most new users reach for—the simple Rectangle and Ellipse tools—produce their respective shapes with simple click-and-drag maneuvers. Once created, these shapes inherit the default outlines and fills that are in effect for that DRAW session. With both the Rectangle and Ellipse tools, if you hold the Shift key while dragging, the object draws from the center out. If you hold the Ctrl key while dragging, you can create squares and perfect circles.

Hotkeys: F6 for Rectangle, and F7 for Ellipse

The Object Flyout

It must not have been a very inspiring day at Corel when the developers named this set of tools. From this rather drab-sounding flyout comes the rather exciting Polygon, Spiral, and Graph Paper tools. The Polygon tool does more than just create stars; it creates dynamic objects with multiple sides, all of which move as you move one of them. The spiral tool makes spirals (imagine that), and the Graph Paper tool makes grids of boxes, according to your specification. Nested in this tool are two other tools, one for making spirals and another for making grids.

Hotkey: None, but like all other parts of the interface, you can assign one to each of the three.

The Text Tool

This tool brings the written word to your drawings. By clicking once on the Text icon and then once on the page, you can create *artistic text*, the more versatile of the two text types. This text can be enhanced with all the special effects DRAW has to offer, such as extrusions, blends, and fitting to a path.

With the Text tool, you can also create *paragraph text,* ideal for creating blocks of copy. To use the Text tool to create paragraphs, you click the tool and then go to the page and click and drag to form a rectangular boundary for the text. When you do this, DRAW knows you want to create paragraph text instead of artistic text.

Hotkey: F8

The Fill Flyout

With this tool, you can make quick changes to fills and patterns without having to retreat to a dialog. It triggers its own property bar, with all of the primary fill patterns and controls present. The other tool on the flyout is the new Mesh tool, capable of creating freeform patterns with solid colors.

Hotkey: None

The Interactive Transparency Tool

With this tool, you can apply transparency to objects with on-screen controls. The most noteworthy distinction of this feature is its ability to apply transparency to *any* object, be it a vector object you create in DRAW or a bitmap image you import from elsewhere. Furthermore, transparency doesn't have to be flat and even; you can create graduated transparencies that more closely mirror life.

Hotkey: None

The Interactive Tool Flyout

Another uninspired name, if we do say so. This should have been called the Effects flyout, because it is now the primary residence of all of DRAW's amazing special effects. Blend gets top billing thanks to its position as leadoff hitter, but batting behind it are contour, distortions, envelopes, extrusions, and drop shadows.

Hotkey: None, but all can be given custom hotkeys.

The Eyedropper Flyout

This brand new pair of tools makes it very easy to determine colors used in an image or an object and apply them to other objects. The Eyedropper can sniff out a color in any type of object, including an imported bitmap, and it honors the type of color model used. We'll show you how these new tools operate in Chapter 6.

Hotkey: None.

The Outline Flyout

The Outline tool is a one-stop shop for assigning outline colors and widths to any selected objects, be they curves, rectangles, ellipses, or text characters. You can choose from six preset outline thicknesses and seven percentages of black. Or you can access the Outline Pen dialog or docker to treat yourself to a bevy of controls. Clicking on the × button removes any outline from a selected object (just like the × on the color palette).

If you use the Outline tool without first selecting an object, DRAW informs you that you are about to change the default, which will affect subsequently drawn objects.

Hotkeys: F12 to reach the Outline Pen dialog, and Shift+F12 for the Outline Color dialog

The Fill Flyout

Perhaps the richest of all the tools, the Fill tool can help you perform some simple chores, such as assigning a pure color to an object, as well as more exotic tasks, such as creating a fountain or textured fill. (For simple color fills, you might prefer to use the on-screen color palette or the Interactive Fill tool.)

When you assign a fill, it affects only the selected object, like the Outline tool. If no object is selected, the change is made to the default, filling all subsequent objects. And you can access other dialogs and dockers that bring the full power of this tool to your fingertips, just as you can with the Outline tool.

Hotkeys: F11 to reach the Fountain Fill dialog, and Shift+F11 for the Uniform Fill dialog

Figure 1.7 shows an effective use of DRAW's more exotic fill patterns: a bitmap pattern fill provides a nice backdrop for this sampling of traditional artist tools. The graphics all came from Corel's clipart collection (the paintbrush has undergone a bitmap effect), the ampersand started as a text character before it was embossed, and the background is one of many built-in patterns. As a result, this creation took our artistically challenged lead author less than 20 minutes to create.

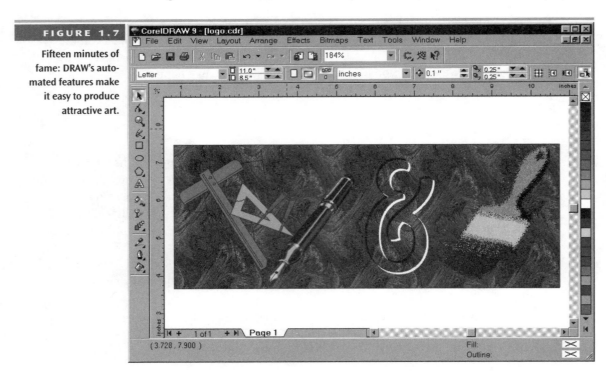

FIGURE 1.7

Fifteen minutes of fame: DRAW's automated features make it easy to produce attractive art.

We'll revisit this logo in Chapter 23. We don't hold it up as a masterpiece worthy of your admiration; rather, we want to show you how quickly and easily you can bring a few elements together into a simple, attractive piece.

Browsing the Menus

As mentioned earlier, it's possible to produce several simple drawings without having to access DRAW's pull-down menus—especially if you make a habit of using hotkeys such as Ctrl+S (Save) and Ctrl+P (Print). Whether you're a hotkey kind of person or not, though, it's important for you to understand how the menus are laid out and what kind of logical (and in some cases, illogical!) groupings the program employs for its commands.

The File Menu

This menu is DRAW's Grand Central Station, where all files enter and exit. This is the menu from which you open, save, import, export, and print files (just as it is in practically all Windows programs). Veteran users will notice a few new items: Print Preview is a shortcut to DRAW's new preview screen within the Print dialogs (added in version 8), and Publish to PDF might be one of the most significant additions to DRAW ever.

Note the underlines sprinkled throughout this menu indicating the keyboard alternatives for invoking commands and dialogs, as well as the plethora of hotkeys.

Drawings listed near the bottom of the menu (just above Exit) represent the most recently opened files. DRAW will list up to four recently opened files. If you wanted to reopen one of them, you could simply click on its name, instead of choosing File ➤ Open and then finding it.

Finally, the … (ellipsis) that follows many of the commands is there to tell you that a dialog or docker is lurking underneath. By contrast, commands that perform their entire functions as soon as you activate them—such as Save and Exit—don't have the ellipsis.

The Edit Menu

This menu is in charge of changing, duplicating, copying, deleting, cloning, undoing, redoing, and repeating just about anything. As it does in all OLE-compliant programs (that is, programs that support Windows Object Linking and Embedding), the Edit menu acts as the headquarters for all Clipboard activity coming from and going to other programs.

On this menu, the Paste and Paste Special commands are available, indicating that there is an object on the Clipboard, placed there by DRAW or another program. Also on the menu are Undo and Redo. You will also be happy with the Find and Replace command, which allows you to find and replace both objects and text.

The View Menu

The View menu takes charge of almost all on-screen activities. These controls let you specify which parts of the DRAW interface you want to make visible or keep hidden, as well as how much detail of your drawing's components you want displayed. Notice the viewing choices of Simple Wireframe, Wireframe, Draft, Normal, and Enhanced, and the large number of on-screen controls to toggle on and off. This is also the home of DRAW's snap controls—Snap to Grid, Guidelines, and Objects.

DRAW 8 introduced viewable guides to show you the printable area of the page, and new to DRAW 9 are guides to show you the "bleed" line—the extension off of the page (1/4 inch by default) to which you should size objects that are designed to be printed to the edge of the illustration. (Print shops ask you to take objects beyond the edge of the page to insure against an object not going far enough and leaving a small streak where the ink didn't get applied to the paper. By extending—bleeding—by an extra 1/4 inch, there is no chance of that happening.)

The Layout Menu

The Layout menu has shrunk considerably in DRAW 9, with the exodus of the snaps. We think it should have been renamed to the Page menu, as the seven commands that make up the menu all have to do with page controls—adding, deleting, and configuring pages, including the new Switch Page Orientation, which addresses the ability to have pages with different orientations, all in the same drawing.

The Arrange Menu

If it needs to be ordered, layered, aligned, collected, skewed, stretched, moved, taken apart, or put back together again, it's a job for the Arrange menu. Here you can insist that two objects be moved and sized together with the Group, Combine, or Weld commands, or coupled more exotically with the Intersection and Trim commands.

The drawings you create in DRAW will include many different shapes and objects layered in just the right way to create the effect you want. The Order flyout has the commands for moving objects to the front and back of the stack and for moving items forward and back one layer. Like many seasoned DRAW users, you will want to commit to memory the keyboard shortcuts for these commands, because they are nested somewhat inconveniently a level below the other functions in the Order fly-out. You'll find the key assignments displayed on the flyout itself.

New to the Arrange menu in DRAW 8 were the Lock commands—Lock Object, Unlock Object, and Unlock All Objects. You won't have to worry about those accidents that can knock your perspective out of whack—just lock the graphic up tight when you've got it the way you want it. And new to DRAW 9 is the way-cool Convert Outline to Object command, with which you can treat an object's outline as a separate object, allowing you to apply any fill or effect to it.

The Effects Menu

This used to be DRAW's most happening place, housing all of its special effects. But now it's a sparse house, with most of the celebrities having moved out and taken up residence on the flyout as interactive tools. Lens still lives there and so do PowerClip and Add Perspective. The other commands address bitmap transformations and controls for the Natural Media tool.

You'll probably head there most to access the Clear, Copy, and Clone commands that work on special effects.

The Bitmaps Menu

The Bitmaps menu introduces many of the powerful features found in PHOTO-PAINT, for use with imported bitmaps. For examples of the cooler effects, see Part VI, "The Bitmap Era."

The Text Menu

The Text menu is your supermarket for text formatting and editing, and a wide assortment of powerful tools can be found here. The Fit Text to Path command is perhaps the most widely used special effect in all of DRAW history.

On the other hand, Thesaurus, which is available on the Writing Tools flyout, might be the least-used command. As DRAW continues to increase its support for text-heavy documents, word processing features might see more action; as of now, however, they lie almost dormant (at least, so say demographic studies across thousands of DRAW 4 through 8 users). We will concede that Type Assist, also in the Writing Tools flyout, introduced to little fanfare in version 5, has found its niche and provides valuable services for typists looking for a few shortcuts or assurances of professional typography, such as true quotes and em-dashes.

DRAW 8 introduced HTML support—no big surprise there—so you can now turn the text you are typing into HTML-compatible text for linking, formatting, and displaying on the Web.

The Tools Menu

The Tools menu is the electronic equivalent of the tool shed you may have out back, or the large peg board hanging in your garage. Before embarking on a big project, make a stop here and pull down the various tools that you will need along the way. Most of these tools existed in previous versions but were scattered across various menus.

The Window Menu

This window has seen the most change in DRAW 9. Once the modest domicile for DRAW's Multiple Document Interface services, now all sorts of new tenants occupy it. Most notably, you can get a list of all palettes, dockers, and toolbars that DRAW offers.

The Help Menu

This menu is the conventional gateway to DRAW's Help system. CorelTUTOR offers step-by-step instructions and can also act like a Wizard, completing a given task on its own as you observe. If you have used earlier versions of DRAW and are upgrading to DRAW 9, check out CorelTUTOR to get an overview of new features and familiarize yourself with the newest offerings in the program.

WHAT'S NEW IN CORELDRAW

Featuring

WHAT'S NEW IN CORELDRAW

This is the sixth consecutive edition of *Mastering CorelDRAW* in which we are including this chapter—a comprehensive overview of the new features and additions in the latest versions of CorelDRAW. We first decided to write this chapter because Corel itself decided not to. In its user guides for DRAW 4 and 5—two robust upgrades—the documentation team devoted no space at all to new features. When we did here in these pages, it became immediately popular with our readership, and as a result, Chapter 2 is now our traditional What's New chapter. To its credit, Corel's current online help includes an overview of the new features of each release, and even though it reads like a flashy commercial, we're happy to see at least that much. But we're still including this chapter. After all, we started it...

We make two assumptions in this chapter. The first is that most users interested in the new features already know a bit about the old ones. We hope that all DRAW users will find value in our now-famous Chapter 2, but we direct it primarily to experienced users, ones who have some knowledge of and familiarity with prior versions.

Our second assumption is that there are a fair number of you who are making the jump from CorelDRAW 7 or earlier directly to 9, having decided to sit on the sidelines for 8. (Oh, yes—we know all about the legend of the even-numbered curse, and can show you deficient royalty checks in 1996 and 1998 as proof. This one better be a best-seller...)

Therefore, this chapter is divided into two parts: a section that describes changes and additions introduced in version 8, and a section on new features in 9. Those of you upgrading from version 8 might want to skim the first part of this chapter and go right to the section on new 9 features.

Finally, we offer our standard proviso: don't expect this chapter to be a dry and even-handed recounting of new features. We intend for this chapter—and really, the entire book—to reflect our respective roles as users of the software. So we don't hesitate to add commentary, and we won't waste your time with phrases like "in our opinion" and "if you were to ask us." We know that you didn't ask us, and you might not give a hoot about our opinions. But you did buy our book, so now you're stuck with us, bias and all.

CorelDRAW 8

Version 8 was not a revolutionary upgrade; it was an evolutionary one. Its emphasis is on increased usability, more intelligent use of tools, incremental performance enhancements, and a new feature or two for good measure. Here is a complete overview of all that was new in 8, divided into seven categories, and within each category, listed in order of our perceived value and importance.

More Interactivity

In the last three years, this has become the new buzzword of modern software. Funny, we thought that computer software, by its very nature, is interactive, but DRAW 7 and 8 helped to redefine the word.

And what is that definition? Issuing a command through a dialog and having to press OK to see the change...that's not very interactive. Using a series of on-screen tools and controls, in which each change is immediately applied to the selected object...that's interactive.

Here are the areas that saw their interactivity quotients raised in version 8.

The Color Palette

Two very significant additions have been made to the behavior of the on-screen color palette, an otherwise ho-hum member of DRAW's interface. You are used to clicking once with Button 1 to fill a selected object and once with Button 2 to outline the object. In version 8, if you press and hold for about one second on a color on the palette, you will be presented with a square array of different shades of that color, as shown in Figure 2.1. Once that array appears, you can either click Button 1 or Button 2 to choose a different shade of that color for your fill or outline.

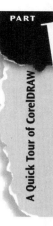

Choosing tints of a particular color is now performed interactively with the on-screen palette.

You can also interactively assign tints of another color to an object with a Ctrl+click, instead of a click. This is best shown by doing:

1. Create an object on screen. Any closed object will do, like a rectangle or an ellipse.

2. Assign a color to it, like blue.

3. If you were to click on yellow, you would replace the blue fill with the yellow fill. Instead, Ctrl+click on yellow. By doing that, you are not replacing the blue with yellow, you are adding 10% of the yellow to the blue. Each successive Ctrl+click adds 10% more yellow to the existing color.

This is an outstanding new feature for those creating Web graphics and on-screen presentations. It could be dangerous if used for traditional projects in which true color accuracy should only be entrusted to printed samples of the color. See Chapter 6, "Applying Fill Patterns," for more.

A Better Envelope

DRAW 7 users will remember, probably fondly, how transparency and fills received interactive controls. As of DRAW 8, Envelope joins the interactive era, and in so doing, makes huge strides in efficiency.

As powerful as it was, Envelope was kludgy. In all previous versions, you would make the adjustments to the envelope shape and then return to the Envelope roll-up to apply those adjustments. And to edit an existing envelope, you would have to open the Node Edit roll-up to access the needed tools…but then return to the Envelope roll-up just to click on the lousy Apply button.

With the Interactive Envelope tool—available from the Interactive flyout in the toolbox—once you move an envelope handle, the envelope is instantly applied. When applying an envelope, the property bar changes to offer all of the same controls that you would find in the Envelope roll-up. Except Apply…that ugly thing is history. Chapter 13 has more on Envelopes.

A Better Extrude

Extrude also wins a starting position on the Interactive team, making Figure 2.2 a possibility. Study the figure and you'll note that there is no Extrude roll-up or docker anywhere to be found. Instead, we chose the Interactive Extrude tool and performed an immediate click-and-drag. Figure 2.2 shows the dragging of the mouse up and to the left, with the corresponding extrusion taking effect. If you create extrusions regularly, you'll love this new interactive control.

See Chapter 15 for details on Extrude.

FIGURE 2.2

With version 8, you can create extrusions with your mouse and property bar.

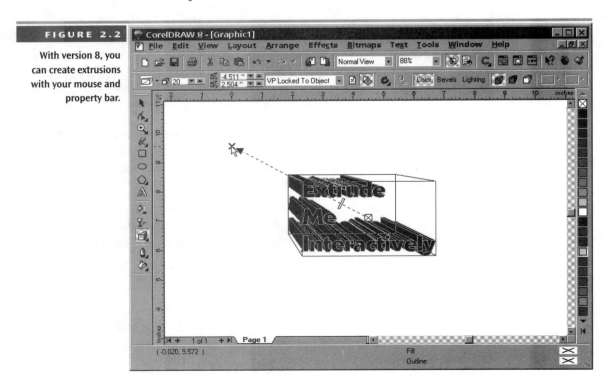

Automatic Drop Shadows

While envelopes and extrusions are a bit of a specialty, practically every DRAW user needs to create drop shadows from time to time, and we think that this one might be the most valuable of all of the new interactive features. Figure 2.3 shows how easy it is to create a drop shadow in 8: you choose the Drop Shadow tool from the Interactive flyout, you click and drag in the desired direction, and you count to about ten. The property bar provides complete control over placement, feathering, and opacity, with immediate results. These drop shadows are created from bitmaps, not blends or contours, and as a result, they are much more realistic and flexible. We really like this feature, and picked it as the version 8 Rookie of the Year. It gets an entire chapter to itself, Chapter 18.

FIGURE 2.3

The Interactive Drop Shadow feature is one of the stars of the version 8 show.

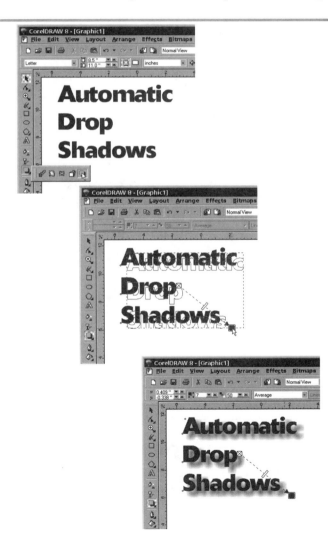

Other players on the Interactive team were introduced in version 8, and we introduce them throughout the book.

CorelDRAW 8's Interface

The most sweeping changes that debuted in version 8 are about how DRAW presents itself to us. Some of them are far-reaching in scope and implication; others have us scratching our heads and wondering about the point of it all. You be the judge...

Where'd All of the Modes Go??

One of the most significant, powerful, and invasive of all the changes is a move to modeless editing of objects. Once you learn the visual cues, you can create, size, move, and shape an object without taking a single trip to the toolbox to switch tools. Do this simple exercise to learn how it works:

1. Switch to the Freehand tool and draw a curve—any curve at all.

2. Compare your screen against Figure 2.4.

In particular, note how the cursor continues to notify you that you are in "drawing mode." In previous versions, all you could do at this point was create more freehand curves. But with modeless editing, you can also perform other tasks, and your cues are on screen. Note that you can see the six nodes that make up this curve; pass your cursor atop one of them, and the node will enlarge. At this point, you can perform basic node-editing, like altering the path, changing the node type, deleting the node, or adding another one next to it.

3. Now find the × in the middle of the object.

4. Drag right on the × to move the object, or click a second time to get rotation handles.

5. Use the handles as per usual to size the object. All the while if you click and drag anywhere else, you will create a second curve, because through it all, the Freehand tool is active. If the Ellipse tool were the active one, then a click-and-drag in open space would create an ellipse.

While this is a powerful interface addition, it might also get in the way. Therefore, you should know how to disable it, by going to Options ➤ Workspace ➤ Display and unchecking Enable Node Tracking. The × still appears in the middle and the nodes are still visible, but they won't grow when you pass over them.

Better Guideline Control

Another in a procession of subtle improvements, DRAW 8 treats guidelines as objects. That means you can delete them, copy and paste them, nudge them, select and move

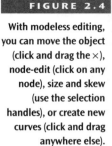

FIGURE 2.4

With modeless editing, you can move the object (click and drag the ×), node-edit (click on any node), size and skew (use the selection handles), or create new curves (click and drag anywhere else).

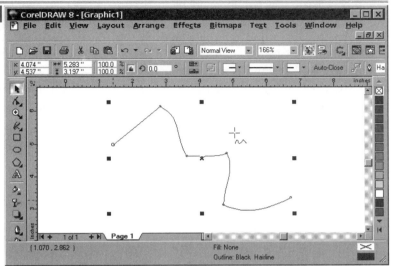

several at once, and rotate them around any center of rotation. Coupled with another new feature—the ability to lock any object—guidelines are much more flexible. We were never crazy about the fact that we had to lock all of our guidelines en masse when we often wanted to lock only some of them. Now, instead of locking the entire Guideline layer, we will just select a particular guideline and request that it be locked.

Your Own (Work)space

If you think of your workspace as your overall CorelDRAW environment, then you're on the right track. Position of toolbars...type of color palette...rulers visible...status bar one line...customized menus...nudge setting...and the list goes on and on. With version 8, not only can you save all of those settings (as with previous versions), you can also create more than one group of settings. Corel calls them *workspaces*, and you can create customized workspaces for particular users or projects.

A workspace is one of several version 8 designs that are at the same time powerful and potentially confusing. You might need to unlearn a few things before taking advantage of it, and we throw a blanket on the subject in Chapter 34.

Quick-Align Accelerator Keys

Let's say you want to align two objects so that their left sides are at the same vertical position. As most of you know, the traditional way would involve a trip to the Align and Distribute dialog where you would choose Left and then OK.

When objects are selected, there are plenty of hotkeys available for specific functions, like Ctrl+A, Ctrl+L, and Alt+F3. But pressing character keys by themselves in all previous versions didn't do anything; you could type the entire alphabet and get no response from DRAW. Corel engineers saw in this a golden opportunity to add more interactivity to the program. Why open a dialog to align objects when there are these perfectly good keys doing nothing at all? In one of the more ingenious displays of minimalist thinking, they added so-called *accelerator keys* to the alignment options. With two or more objects selected:

- Press L to left-align them.
- Press R to right-align them.
- Press T to top-align them.
- Press B to bottom-align them.
- Press C to center-align them vertically.
- Press E to center-align them horizontally.

You don't need to press anything else with these keys; it's not Ctrl+L or Alt+R or anything like that. Just press the key and the objects instantly align. This is definitely one of those Why-didn't-we-think-of-that features.

Dockers

No, these aren't pants; they are part of a new interface design, functioning like very flexible roll-ups. Go to Window ➤ Dockers to see a list of services that used to be handled by roll-ups and are now in the custody of dockers. They get their name because they can be floated like roll-ups, or docked on the sides of the application. What's more, if you open more than one docker, they all share the same space, as Figure 2.5 shows. We see a nice fit with owners of large displays; the jury might still be out as to how they are received by the 17-inch SVGA crowd.

New Line Styles

One of the true buried treasures in all previous DRAW versions was the method for changing the style of an outline. In earlier versions, there was an .ini file that stored line styles in what seemed to be a derivative of Morse code. Now there is the clean and simple dialog shown in Figure 2.6, where you can determine the precise pattern and its length.

You can read all about outlines in Chapter 7.

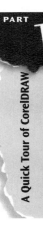

FIGURE 2.5

DRAW 8's new dockers let you pack many functions into one space. Here, Symbols share space with styles and the Object Manager.

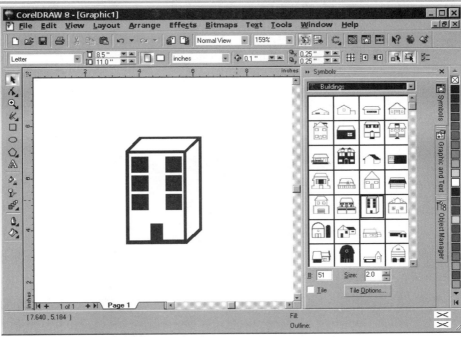

FIGURE 2.6

Creating a custom line style is now a simple matter of turning dots on or off.

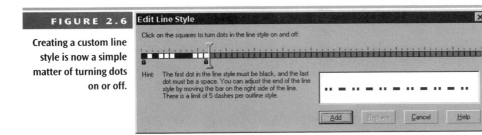

Options Shmoptions

DRAW has always had a lot of user-selectable options and defaults. We never realized just how many until they were all put into one place. This could be seen as a good thing or a bad thing: being all in one place makes them easier to browse, no doubt, but—good grief—the Tools ➤ Options dialog is now an encyclopedia!

Options have three main categories—Workspace, Document, and Global—and within those categories hide a dizzying array of subcategories. Figure 2.7 shows you one branch of the Workspace category, and when we created this screen image, we discovered with mild rejoicing the option to prevent symbol typefaces from appearing in standard font dialogs (we don't have many occasions to set text in the Animals or Building typefaces...). But we practically stumbled across it; would we have been able to find it otherwise? This remains an open question and one that your own personal style with the program will ultimately answer. But one thing is for sure: it wouldn't hurt at all for you to spend a good five or 10 minutes browsing the pages that make up this new and voluminous network of program options.

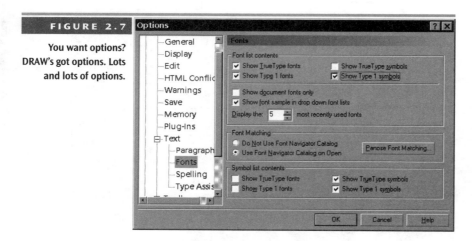

FIGURE 2.7

You want options? DRAW's got options. Lots and lots of options.

As mentioned earlier in this section, one powerful component to DRAW's approach to user settings is the ability to save practically any of them as defaults for new drawings.

Redesigned Print Engine

DRAW 8 uses a standard tabbed dialog to house all of the print options. In version 7, there was an Options button that appeared to take the user to an entirely different place. The new design is much cleaner. Chapter 26 includes chapter and verse on print features, new and old.

Size Graphic on Import

When you import a graphic, now you receive a prompt enabling you to place the graphic in the standard way (by just clicking once), or by determining the size of the graphic on the page (by clicking and dragging).

Custom Page Sizes

If you create a page size for a special job that doesn't fall into any conventional category, you can save the size as a custom size, assign a name to it, and easily retrieve it later.

Creation Tools

Most of the features discussed so far don't focus on creating new objects, but on improving access to existing tools. There are a handful of features that speak directly to new object creation, and this section explores them.

Drop Shadow

As this is an interactive tool, we already discussed it in the previous section. But we think it is one of the stellar features of this release, worthy of another mention. We know from our conferences how many users want to create shadows behind elements, and this new automated feature does it better and faster than all previous methods.

Duotones

A duotone is one of the most economical ways to add color to a low-budget print project or a photo that was originally black and white. Think of a duotone as "black plus one spot color," although the two colors can be any two spot colors at all.

From the Bitmaps menu, you can also create monotones, tritones, and quadtones. Monotones are excellent for applying a different ink color to a black-and-white photograph.

Distortions

This is the one gee-whiz feature added to version 8, but it hasn't proved to scratch many creative itches. With the Interactive Distortion tool, you can create truly bizarre variations of single objects or strings of artistic text. Figure 2.8 shows the three types of distortion that can be applied to objects: Push/Pull, Zipper, and Twister. Pull the electronic throttle a small amount to create the middle image of each of the three columns; lean on the throttle to create the unintelligible spikes, blobs, and twirls in the bottom images.

We don't devote much space to them. In fact, you just read our entire coverage of distortions.

Unbelievably, the text that is being so horribly disfigured in Figure 2.8 is still editable text.

FIGURE 2.8

Three types of distortion are now available to, uh, grace your illustrations.

Inflate Bitmap

This featurette was likely added solely to address one nagging problem with DRAW 7 and its support for bitmap effects. With version 7, if you applied a bitmap effect, like a blur, to an object with a fixed bounding box, the effect would get clipped off if it stretched beyond the bounding box. With the Inflate Bitmap option checked (from Bitmaps ➤ Inflate Bitmap), you can instruct DRAW to provide as much room as the bitmap effect requires.

Object Controls

In this category, we place any new functions that address the manipulation or selection of objects. This category has two very nice improvements, and a couple of klunkers, as well…

Object Manager

This roll-up was a powerful addition to version 7, yet was not used very often by most users. In version 8, now as a docker, it is guaranteed to be visited more often, because the Layers Manager has been rolled into it. The first few times, you will fumble around looking for the familiar Layers roll-up, and then you will remember. A few minutes of practice is all you'll need with this new integrated set of object services.

Digging

This curious term came about because this is what you now do: go digging for objects that are hiding under other objects. Prior to version 8, there was no way to select objects that were underneath others, except to press Tab repeatedly (and ad infinitum if your page contains many objects). Now you can Alt+click on an object to select the object underneath, the one underneath that one, etc., etc.

Once selected, you can resize the object with its selection handles, as always, and thanks to node-tracking and the × in the center of selected objects, you can also move an object and even node-edit it.

The Evolution of Trim, Intersect, and Weld

You probably are already aware of this triad of commands that looks at overlapping objects and causes one object to affect another. In the past, these three commands would only work on individual objects; now you can trim into, find the intersection of, and weld together groups of objects. Chapter 11 is devoted to these three tools.

Select All Grows Up, Too

We hope this will be seen as an improvement. The command Edit ➤ Select All gives you three choices: Objects (i.e., truly all), Text (all text objects), or Guidelines (which are now treated as objects). This is very handy in special circumstances; otherwise, it costs you an extra keystroke or mouse action to choose Objects. Advanced users ran right to Customize to create a hotkey or special icon for the traditional Select All command; in DRAW 9, Select All inherits Ctrl+A, and a fourth choice is added to Select All to select all nodes in an object.

Objects Can Be Locked

Mentioned earlier with reference to guidelines, any selected object can be made untouchable, even if the layer it resides on is editable. You lock an object from the Object Manager's context menu, or from the Arrange menu.

Witnessing the Move

If you want more detail as you move objects, version 8 can supply it. Click on an object and move it quickly—the action is the same as with previous versions. Click, pause, and then move, and the object displays in full color as it moves. You can disable the moving display of complex objects (textures, bitmaps, lenses, blends with many steps, etc.) from the Properties sheet of the Pick tool.

Filling Open Paths

With version 8, you can fill the interior of an object that is not closed. Why would you want to do this? We haven't a clue, but we're sure that somewhere, there is someone who has found some reason to do this. Figure 2.9 shows two examples of this, one plain and one dramatic. The top-left object is a square that is missing one of its corners. By all known laws of DRAW, this object cannot be filled...unless you first visit an impossible-to-find option (buried in Tools ➤ Options ➤ Document ➤ General ➤ Fill Open Curves) and check it. Once done, you can produce the top-right graphic—an object that is filled, even though not closed.

The lower image is even more logic-defying, as it is not at all clear which is the inside and which is the outside.

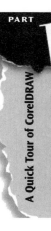

FIGURE 2.9

Don't stop the presses, but DRAW 8 can fill an object that isn't closed.

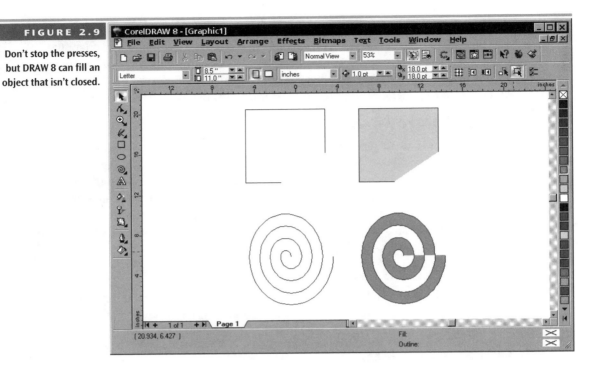

Text Features

Improvements and additions to DRAW's text handling abilities are few but significant. We count five new features, all but one of them likely to be helpful to your creative abilities or your workflow. See Chapters 8, 9, and 10 for our lengthy discussions on text creation, formatting, and manipulation.

In-Line Graphics

Your desktop publishing software can take a graphic and attach it to the flow of text; now DRAW can, too. Anything that is in the Clipboard can be pasted to the current cursor position. Figure 2.10 shows one light-hearted application for it, and you'll notice that this isn't just single-color line art. Full-color graphics and even photos can be inserted into artistic text strings and paragraph text frames. Once done, the graphic can be selected, sized, and even kerned, just like text.

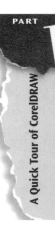

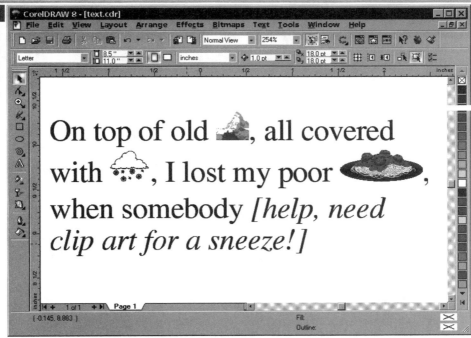

Automatic Text-Fitting

Another text feature that promises to be one of our favorites, this new command will resize the text within a frame so that all of the text fits. Figure 2.11 shows the simple dynamic, as the frame on the left does not contain all of the text that has been flowed into it (as evidenced by the little downward-pointing triangle at the bottom selection handle). But the one on the right has been set to Fit Text to Frame, and has had its text automatically sized down.

Two points of interest with this feature: (1) if you type more text into a fitted frame, you will have to reissue the Fit Text to Frame command; and (2) you can use this command in the opposite direction and instruct the text to be expanded to fill out the frame.

Easier Cursor Placement

One small but annoying flaw was corrected in version 8 that seems to make all the difference in the world to the text-editing process. To begin typing into a frame or string of text, you can double-click to place an editing cursor. You no longer have to press F8 or click the Text tool in the toolbox.

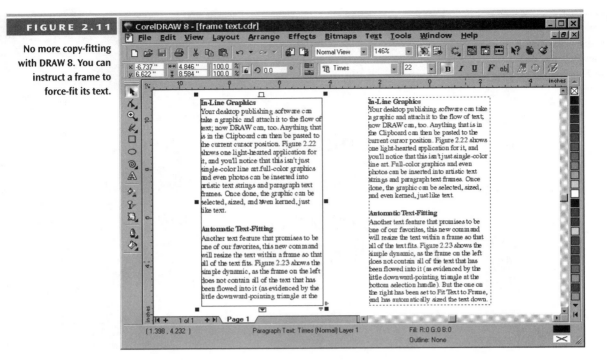

FIGURE 2.11

No more copy-fitting with DRAW 8. You can instruct a frame to force-fit its text.

Complex Text Linking

When Corel demo-meisters showed this feature, everyone oohed and aahed...while we shrugged our shoulders. You be the judge: Figure 2.12 shows two new capabilities of DRAW 8. The first is that the middle text looks like a conventional string of artistic text being fitted to a line. Actually, it is paragraph text. The second new item is that all three pieces of text are linked and flowing dynamically between the normal frame at the top, the text fitted to the line in the middle, and the frame shaped like an ellipse.

We are impressed with the technology, but where's the beef? Last edition we asked, "Please tell us, is this a feature that you think you might ever use?" We received exactly zero responses.

Internet-Specific Features

No question that DRAW 8 was developed with one eye on the World Wide Web. Entire DRAW pages can now be exported as HTML pages, there is a more robust JPEG export, better downsampling of 24-bit images to GIF format, and built-in FTP access from within DRAW itself. Also, PHOTO-PAINT is much more mature in its facility for creating animated GIF images.

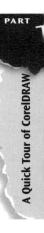

FIGURE 2.12

These three strings of text are all linked. Impressive? Definitely. Useful? Doubt it.

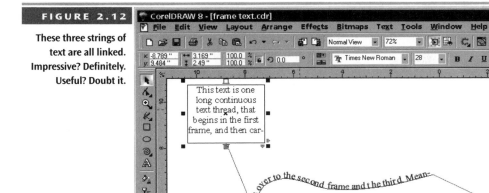

These features will be covered in depth in Part V with three chapters dedicated to the creation of graphics for the World Wide Web.

Font Navigator

Veteran DRAW users will remember a version of FontMinder that shipped with DRAW 5, much to the delight of all typeface enthusiasts. But Ares sold its fine typeface management program to Adobe the following year, and DRAW users had a lean season in the typeface management department. Meanwhile, the original developers of FontMinder went to work for Bitstream and produced FontNavigator, an evolution of FontMinder, a copy of which is included with the program. You would be hard-pressed to find a comparable typeface management utility.

Backgrounds

When you set up your page, you can ask to include a solid or a bitmap-tiled background. This is very handy for Web page developers, and you can determine whether the background will be included in any print jobs or export operations.

When All Is Said and Done...

The final piece of commentary to be made about DRAW 8 is the timing of its release. Many users pointed to the 18-month development cycle (stretched from 12 months) as the primary reason for the success of DRAW 7. The extra six months gave Corel engineers more time to solidify the product and it gave users time to prepare. By prepare, we mean emotionally—versions of DRAW tend to shellshock users with their annual assault. Corel returned to the 12-month cycle to release DRAW 8 at the end of 1997, and this did not sit well with many users. Summing up this sentiment was Rebecca Austin, a user from Chicago and loyal reader of these books. "Tell them to cool their jets," she writes. "If Corel really wants to keep us happy, they should stop making us run around in circles all the time. I just upgraded from 5 to 7, and I'm having a hard enough time getting all my hardware to adjust to the new version. I certainly don't want to (and won't) go through all of this again in a few months."

Austin has put her finger on the one point that DRAW users keep coming back to over and over again: they get overwhelmed with the constant upgrading and don't feel as if they ever get quality time to truly learn any one version. Irrespective of the intrinsic value of version 8, Corel's quick trigger-finger might cloud an otherwise positive impression that the program merits.

Otherwise, DRAW 8 should be seen as an evolutionary step, with some very significant productivity enhancements and a small handful of new features. Software continues to become more refined as the market matures, and version 8 is a clear indication of this thinking, with a streamlined interface, a central location for user settings, and a continual reliance on context-sensitivity to place the most important tools where they are most accessible.

CorelDRAW 9

If we had to choose one word to describe DRAW 9, it would be *refined*. This release is equal parts new features, redesigning, and problem-solving, and in all three departments, Corel seems to have kept a close focus on refinement of the finished product. As a result, we hold many aspects of this version in high regard.

One thing you won't find in DRAW 9: lots of new effects. At least not in the conventional "Oh wow, gee whiz" sense. There is no new Squiggle effect or Node Discombobulator tool, and that suits us just fine. The improvements to this version are more subtle...and that suits us fine, too.

CorelDRAW 9's Interface

Yes, another menu reorganization, and while that might anger some veteran users, this one doesn't seem as gratuitous as ones in versions past. Many familiar menu items have been moved (and in some cases *re*moved) from the default interface, and it feels like there is a method to the madness. Most of us on the writing team became comfortable with the new layout quickly. If you don't, rest assured there is a DRAW 8 workspace that you can activate.

Here are some of the more notable interface changes.

Roll-Ups Are History

The transition is complete—there are no more roll-ups in CorelDRAW. They either have been transformed into dockers or, in the case of most special effects, have been replaced with interactive tools with increased property bar functionality. If you became attached to roll-ups, the dockers can be individually torn off, resized, and rolled up.

More Logical Keystrokes

Corel has taken steps to bring the program's shortcuts more in line with other programs in the box, with the Macintosh version, and with Windows norms. For instance, Ctrl+A has been reassigned to Select All, and (finally!) Ctrl+E is Export, not Extrude.

As always, this all can be customized, but now the starting point is closer to what new users are likely to expect, based on their experiences with other programs.

Cleaner Property Bars

In DRAW 9, property bars play a greatly increased role—for many of the tools, that is now the only place to go to adjust settings. Happily, many of the property bars have been streamlined so that they take up less space and allow for extensive customization. Pop-up sliders and text alignment drop-downs are two specific examples. These new buttons are at least 50 percent smaller than their previous incarnations.

Smarter Guidelines

As in DRAW 8, guidelines are treated as objects; however, now any guideline (or group of guidelines) can have its own custom colors. Select a guideline and right-click on a color swatch to change the color of the selected guideline or drag a color from an on-screen palette. Figure 2.13 shows how helpful this can be. The left guideline is perfectly visible where you don't need it to be—i.e., in the blank space—but useless in the drawing, thanks to the dark background. But the right guideline has been colored yellow and is perfectly visible against the background.

You can Shift+select multiple guidelines to change their colors at once.

FIGURE 2.13

Guideline color is no longer an all-or-nothing proposition—you can color them individually.

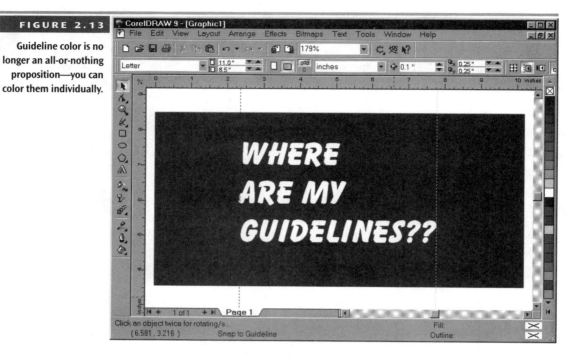

Furthermore, you can now create guidelines according to a number of presets, such as page borders, defined bleed area, inset margins, and others, as shown here.

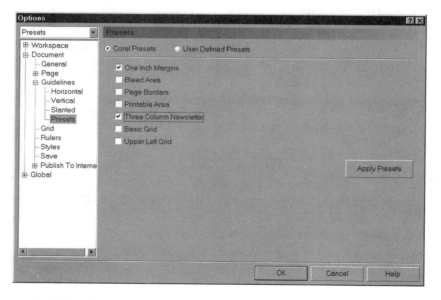

Guidelines have earned their own property bar, so you can make many basic changes to them instantly.

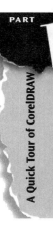

From Camera to DRAW

If you're tired of playing the software shuffle with your digital camera, you'll love DRAW 9's new Digital Camera Interface. With this new import feature, you can snap away and have images flow directly into DRAW or PAINT, without the need for any software to convert a proprietary image format. For regular users of digital photography, this could be the most significant development in DRAW 9.

Page Layout and Setup

DRAW 9 can now be started "empty"—in other words, without a new graphic open. We thought this was kind of a yawner, until we remembered all the times we were presented with a blank drawing when we had no intention of doing anything with it, proceeding instead to the File ➤ Open dialog.

Multiple page sizes are now allowed within one document file. This will be convenient for users who want to create, for example, corporate identities (letterhead, business cards, envelopes) and keep the items together in the same file. The letterhead page can be portrait, the envelope page landscape, and the business card page a label.

There is still no auto page numbering tool, although the Corel SCRIPT language now includes commands that will allow more elegant scripting for this function. See Chapter 33 for a step-by-step tutorial on creating this script.

Better Palette Control

The biggest news on this front is your ability to open more than one on-screen palette. Figure 2.14 shows four distinct color palettes open—the default palette, a browser palette, a Pantone palette, and the TruMatch palette. You'll want a large monitor before you get carried away, however…

Each palette is controlled individually and can be torn off, resized, and relocated. Colors can be dragged from the palettes and applied to objects as fills and outlines. You can also drag colors between nonfixed palettes to quickly create personalized palettes. This is much faster than going through the dialogs. In addition, you can now drag colors between nonfixed palettes to create the most customized palette ever!

The Palette Editor has been streamlined and should now be less confusing and frustrating for both new and experienced DRAW users alike. At least that's the theory, but there is controversy among beta testers. "I find the Palette Editor has taken 10 giant steps backward," argues Debbie Cook, a prominent tester and member of our writing team. "It's way too big, wastes too much space, and you can't even pick or edit colors directly from this dialog. Why not just add the Palette Editor as a new tab at the back of the Color dialog? In addition, it's far too easy to overwrite fixed palettes by just saving over them. I know. I tried it."

Finally, there is now support for the Pantone metallic and pastel spot color palettes using the standard naming conventions (CVC, CVU). In addition, the HKS model has been added as additional support for European artists.

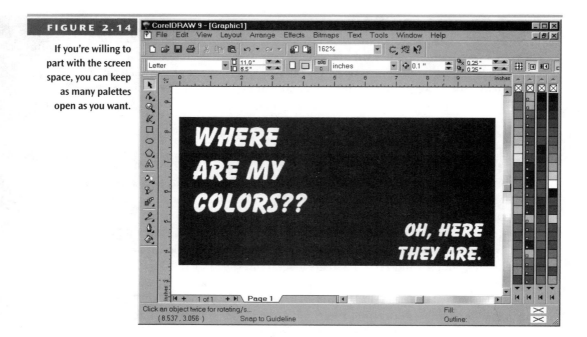

New Tools, New Functionality

Lots of little changes were made to existing effects and tools. Here is a laundry list, in general order of perceived importance.

The Return of PowerLines

Corel has been listening to those users wishing for the return of PowerLines. The Natural Pen tool has been renamed the Artistic Media tool and has been given increased functionality and options. Strokes are created with a much more manageable number of control points/nodes. They can be edited after being drawn, including curve direction and width. And they can be applied to existing lines and strokes—just like a powerline. Furthermore, pressure strokes really work now, even with a mouse (hold Up while drawing for more pressure, Down for less).

The Artistic Media tool offers custom brushes that you can make from any vector or bitmap objects. There is also a Spray mode, which makes Figure 2.15 simple to create. Speed and feel are both excellent.

Smoother Freehand Lines

The Freehand tool sports a new "smoothing" slider, which functions as an on-the-fly node-reducer. Even at the default value, the smoother allows much more natural line drawing without the hordes of nodes from past incarnations of this tool. For once, it is actually possible to create useful freeform shapes with the Freehand tool on the first try.

FIGURE 2.15

These footprints were
not drawn, they were
"sprayed."

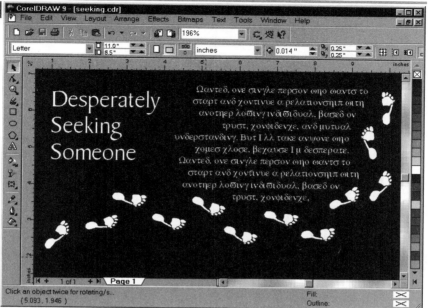

The Shape tool offers a similar control on its property bar. A pop-up slider there allows you to auto-reduce the nodes of a curve interactively.

On the subject of the Shape tool, double-clicking it now selects all the nodes in the selected object (which many users feel should have been the case for years). And the gradual advancement of accelerator keys makes its second stop at node-editing: pressing C while a node is selected toggles between a curve and a cusp, and pressing S toggles between symmetrical and smooth.

Finally, a new Flow Lines tool links objects together for creating organizational and flow charts. You can edit lines with the same options as normal outlines; you can add arrowheads, dashed lines, etc.

Rectangles Can Be Nonconformists

In DRAW 9, you can round individual corners, not just all four. You can do this from the property bar or interactively, by clicking twice on the desired corner.

Making Messes with Mesh

We're only half-kidding with the headline, as we can imagine some of the hideous experimentation that might go on in public with this tool. Nonetheless, the new Interactive Mesh Fill tool is very handy for creating gradient patterns in freeform directions and shapes. Meshed objects are output as bitmaps. We cover this tool in Chapter 6.

New Interactive Tools

Blend, Contour, and Extrude have joined their cousins Drop Shadow, Envelope, and Distort as interactive tools. The roll-ups have been removed and the dockers are buried in the bowels of the interface, so deep that only advanced users could find them. This was intentional, as Corel wants you to use the property bar and the new on-screen controls for all actions relevant to these tools. We adjusted very quickly, and we're wondering if you will greet these new controls the same way. We know that some traditionally inclined users will not be happy with the elimination of many dockers that used to perform important functions. Experienced users can rescue those dockers from banishment by going to the Customize dialog, and Chapter 34 has all the details.

The Interactive Drop Shadow tool has been enhanced to add perspective shadows. You can determine the orientation of a shadow after creating it or while creating it. We elaborate on Interactive Drop Shadow and all of these interactive controls throughout Part IV.

The Eyedropper

This new tool is terrific for picking up fill and outline colors from objects or bitmaps on the page. The selection can be from fill, a sampling of pixels, the outline, the middle of a fountain fill, or an imported bitmap image. DRAW recognizes the correct color model also, so colors from an RGB image will be picked up as RGB, and colors from a fountain fill of CMYK colors will be picked up as CMYK.

The Paintbucket tool is the partner for the Eyedropper tool, and it can be used to fill successive objects with the colors sampled with the Eyedropper. The user also has a modifier key (Shift) option for toggling the Eyedropper to Paintbucket action. Read more about this new tool in Chapter 6.

Changes to Text Handling

More subtleties mark the changes that can be found in the Text department, and again, the key word is "refinement." To wit:

Hunt and Peck   It is much easier to find a typeface from the drop-down list. To find Times New Roman, just start spelling it. You'll also find a Most-Recently-Used list of typefaces at the top of the drop-down.

Robust Wrapping   A new drop-down list shows all wrapping options for paragraph text, and text can be wrapped around other text.

Enhanced Fit Text to Path   Click anywhere on the path and text is fitted to the path beginning at that insertion point.

Smarter Import   Imported text retains more original formatting, such as columns, page size, and margins. We're not sure if this is a welcome addition or a hindrance. We can think of plenty of instances where we just want the text, not the formatting. We expect to be using Paste Special much more often.

Better Frame Editing   One editing mode fits all now, as you can adjust the size of the frame with your cursor still in the text.

Printing Improvements

Quite a bit of news in this department, as Corel continues to promote DRAW as a creator of professional-caliber output.

Support for PPD Files   When printing to a PostScript device, you can now opt to use an industry-standard PostScript Printer Description (PPD) file. This is especially valuable if you are creating print files for a particular and specialized output device. PPD files are free, available en masse, and easily distributed by service bureaus.

Support for Generic PostScript   You can also create the opposite—a plain, vanilla print file—by opting to generate a Device Independent PostScript file. This file ignores any driver-specific settings.

Better Preflight Checking   The new Issues tab in the Print dialog warns you to potential risks and output problems that might lie ahead. Figure 2.16 shows the kinds of circumstances that the Issues tab alerts you to. Notices are categorized as informational, warning, and "I wouldn't do that if I were you." You can decide for yourself which of the two dozen situations are worthy of warnings.

PART

A Quick Tour of CorelDRAW

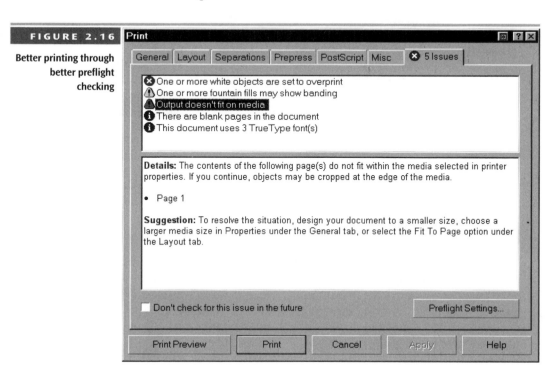

FIGURE 2.16

Better printing through better preflight checking

Interactive Preview   Most of us didn't notice it until late in the development phase, but a tiny little button at the top of the Print dialog produces a preview panel, attached to the side of the dialog, as shown in Figure 2.17.

Thumbs Up to N-Up   The N-Up and Signature tools have been combined into a new Imposition Layout tool for easier access. The popular imposition standards come as presets and you can name and save others. Furthermore, print styles are now stored as external files, and you can opt to have them contain imposition layouts. That means that you can transfer from system to system (and one CorelDRAW application to another) all of the intelligence of your print configuration.

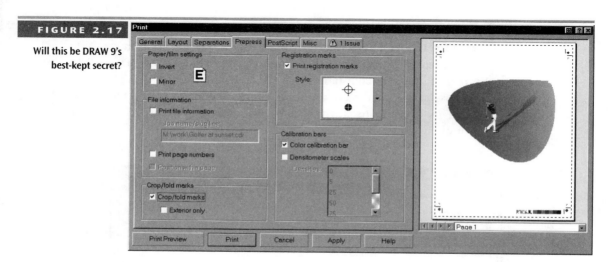

FIGURE 2.17

Will this be DRAW 9's best-kept secret?

Bitmap Safety Net   If you're not sure whether that cool effect will print, you can opt to rasterize the entire page. This is similar to converting a specific image to a bitmap, but with a global reach.

We show all of DRAW's printing prowess in Chapter 26.

Import/Export

We'll save the biggest news for the next section; still, there are a few items worthy of note with conventional importing and exporting. For starters, EPS export appears to be cleaner than ever and the two-tabbed EPS Export dialog is packed with useful options. As you can see in Figure 2.18, EPS export can double as a print-file creator—high time, seeing how so many service bureaus prefer that their clients send them EPS files instead of PostScript print files.

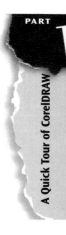

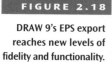

FIGURE 2.18

DRAW 9's EPS export reaches new levels of fidelity and functionality.

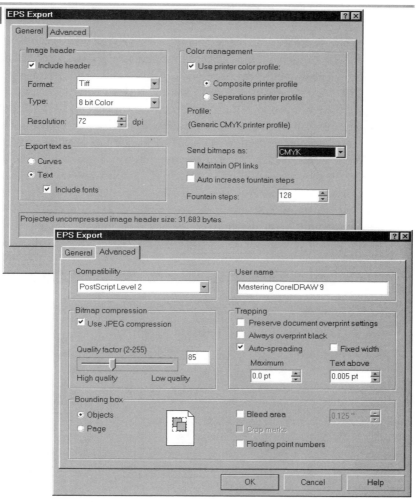

Corel also threw lots of programming time at DRAW 9's AI export capabilities, and we offer chapter and verse in Verse 30.

PostScript import has learned many new tricks, including:

- Support for color models that previously were converted to RGB
- Correct handling of monotone and duotone images from PhotoShop
- Better mapping of Type 1 fonts
- More accurate clipping path calculations

Various nickel-and-dime changes were made to DRAW's JPEG and GIF export, and you can read all about them in Part V, "Drawing for Cyberspace."

Publishing to PDF

Ah, we've buried the lead. To many, this will be worth the price of admission by itself. With version 9, Corel has announced full support for the creation of Adobe Acrobat files.

We're not talking about the barely-better-than-screen-capture freebie export filter thing that DRAW offered in previous releases. This is a complete clone of Adobe's commercial Acrobat product, built right into the DRAW and PAINT interfaces. As beta testers hammered away at it for months, they found output to be absolutely identical to using the commercial product. The only discrepancies anyone could find were file-size differences due to Corel's use of an alternate compression scheme.

Figure 2.19 shows one of the four tabs in the Publish to PDF dialog. All of the functionality of Acrobat Distiller is here, including featues new to version 4, such as job ticketing, preset styles, and automatic generation of hyperlinks and bookmarks that previously required Adobe Exchange.

Tune your dial to Chapter 28 for full coverage of the DRAW-to-PDF phenomenon.

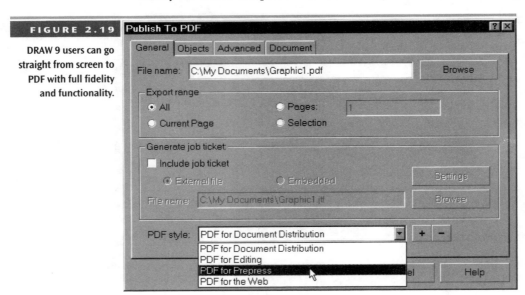

FIGURE 2.19

DRAW 9 users can go straight from screen to PDF with full fidelity and functionality.

Publishing to the Internet

The biggest news on this front is DRAW's ability to create pages with cascading styles, and optionally, an accompanying cascading style sheet file.

Other additions include a statistics page that can analyze and detail an HTML publishing job, more image output options when creating HTML pages, and several user-selectable options, including one to toggle on and off conditions that will trigger the HTML Conflict notices.

There is also a Link Manager docker, which tracks all links assigned in a drawing and can verify the legitimacy of them. Finally, the new Internet Bookmark Manager makes it easy to assign hyperlinks to objects within the drawing.

This new feature works fine. All of these additions work fine. Everything is fine. Yawn…

Forgive our sarcasm, but we continue to be underwhelmed and unimpressed by the notion that DRAW can function as a Web page creation tool. Any serious Webmaster is going to head straight for a real Web page editor, and anyone who isn't has much better options in JPEG export or the new PDF tool. We maintain that DRAW's best contribution to a Web site is its ability to create the graphics. It should leave page creation to other programs.

Other Things

Here is a round-up of all of the other miscellaneous additions, tweaks, and fixes found in version 9.

More Bitmap Effects

Pull down the Bitmaps menu and you'll think you were in PHOTO-PAINT. For examples of many of them, see what we do to President Clinton in Chapter 23.

Direct to Trace

If you want to convert a bitmap image to a vector object, you can launch CorelTRACE directly from within DRAW. When you are done, TRACE delivers a vectorized copy of the image to your drawing. Very clean. TRACE has more tracing options, and we think it's a bit smarter this year, too.

Degree of Rotation No Longer Brain Dead

We have complained about this for years, so we will take ownership of this being fixed. If you rotate an object, say, 25 degrees counterclockwise and then 10 degrees back the other way, the property bar will show that the object is rotated 15 degrees. In other words, rotation is now cumulative. In all previous versions, you only knew the degree of rotation from the object's previous position; now you can know it from its *original* position. Finally…

Enable Selection after Drawing

A subtle but potentially important new option, unchecking this option means that bounding box handles will not appear (i.e., get in the way!) as soon as you have completed drawing an object.

Enhanced View

With rendering speed so fast, this is now the default view. You can choose any of the other views from the View menu, and you can still toggle the last two with Shift+F9.

Unfortunately, that keystroke is no longer hard-wired to begin with a toggle between Wireframe and Normal/Enhanced. You have to do it manually the first time. Our lead author acknowledges that this is nitpicky, but he hates it and yells at it at least twice daily.

Enter Visual Basic

DRAW 9 ships with Microsoft Visual Basic for Applications, version 6. Those familiar with VBA can program in a more comfortable environment. Corel SCRIPT is still part of the program and is useful for recording a script.

Canto Cumulus Replaces MEDIA FOLDERS

While some of you will miss MEDIA FOLDERS, very few of you used it and most of you don't even know what we're talking about. Nonetheless, managing all of your media—your clipart, photos, Web images, etc.—is a crucial issue for any electronic designer, and there is a whole new breed of software to address this, called media asset management software.

Corel worked out a bundling agreement with Canto to include a lite version of its highly touted Cumulus Desktop media management program. With this program, you can track, thumbnail, and archive all of your media files, including DRAW files.

MEDIA FOLDERS can be added to Cumulus catalogs, so those of you who have invested time with it won't have to start over.

And Finally...

The winner of the Useless Feature of the Year award: you can assign sounds to CorelDRAW events, as you do with Windows events. Actually, our lead author did find use for this on April 1, when he infiltrated a colleague's machine and assigned `BreakingGlass.wav` to Delete Object, Mouse Over Node, Print, Undo, Redo, and Zoom. Poor guy—thought he had contracted the Melissa virus...

It's Soup

We refer you back to our final commentary on DRAW 8 earlier in this chapter, where we expressed our dismay over Corel's return to its harried and unpopular 12-month development cycle. No such haste prevailed over the DRAW 9 cycle, and it shows. In fact, every time Corel has taken its time, the result has been noticed by the user community, and we think that the same happy fate will grace this release. Corel's emphasis was on streamlining, cleaning up, and improving output—those are generally easier objectives than creating a sink full of new features.

We not only applaud the objective, but we applaud the result. We think this one's a winner.

PART II

LIFE IN AN OBJECT-ORIENTED WORLD

chapter 3

THE MIRACLE OF THE CLICK: MANEUVERING THE MOUSE

Featuring

THE MIRACLE OF THE CLICK: MANEUVERING THE MOUSE

e mentioned it in Chapter 1, and it bears repeating here: the manual skills required to operate DRAW are not hard to acquire. They consist mostly of clicking, double-clicking, and a bit of dragging. Now please don't infer from this that producing beautiful work in DRAW is easy; manual skills and design expertise are two entirely different things. We can help you only a little with the latter, and anyone who claims otherwise should be held in the same regard as those who peddle Internet-based get-rich-quick schemes. But we can get you up and running nicely with the manual skills, and that's what this chapter is all about.

Working with Objects

There are six ways to place an object into a DRAW file: you can create it yourself; you can import a piece of clipart; you can paste an object from another program by using the Clipboard; you can drag artwork from another application and drop it into DRAW; you can find an item in DRAW's online Symbols library; or you can get an object from DRAW's Scrapbook. Regardless of their origins, all these objects behave the same once they arrive. They are all subject to (drumroll, please) *Altman's Laws of DRAW*.

Altman's Laws of DRAW proclaim the following rights for objects:

- Thou shalt be selectable by the mouse.
- Thou shalt be at liberty to move about the page.
- Thou shalt be free to be resized, reshaped, and rotated.
- Thou shalt include an outline, which can be colored and thickened.
- If thou art a closed object, thou shalt accept an internal color, tint, or pattern.
- Thou shalt be disconnectable.

Only one type of object is exempt from these laws: bitmap images that are brought into DRAW or converted from existing artwork (discussed later in this chapter). Bitmap images cannot be filled, outlined, or taken apart, but they can be sized, shaped, and rotated. All other objects (all vector objects) follow the CorelDRAW fold.

Creating, Moving, and Changing Objects

If you have used Windows applications at all, you already know how to create an object, and as we said earlier in the book, you could probably get behind DRAW's steering wheel and drive your way to an ellipse or a rectangle on your first try. The simple *click-and-drag* maneuver is all that's required. Creating lines and Bézier curves is a bit more involved than creating ellipses and rectangles, and these techniques will get a starring role in subsequent chapters.

To get started with objects in DRAW, the only other things you need to know are how the click and double-click work: one click selects objects on the page or colors from the on-screen palette, and a double-click (two quick clicks) selects files from various dialogs (Open, Import, Save, Export, and so forth). You'll always know when an object in a drawing is selected because it exhibits all sorts of growths around its perimeter:

- The black squares outside of the object are its *handles*, and you use them to size the object.
- The smaller hollow squares on the edge of the object are its *nodes*, and you use them to change the shape of the object.

The click-and-drag technique is the handiest maneuver of all. It is responsible for accomplishing many tasks in DRAW:

- To move a selected object that is filled with a color (even white), click anywhere inside the object and drag it to its new home.
- To move a selected object that has no fill, click carefully on the object's outline and then drag it. If the object is obscured by another object, find the little × in the middle of the object, click it, and drag.

- To resize an object in height, width, or both, click one of its handles, hold the mouse button down, and drag the handle to another position.

- To rotate or skew an object, select it, click it a second time, and then click and drag one of the skew handles, as shown in Figure 3.1.

TIP If you find it difficult to click and drag on unfilled objects, then right-click the Pick tool, select Properties, and check Treat All Objects As Filled.

PART

Life in an Object-Oriented World

Click-and-drag is the most flexible way to move objects, but not the most precise. If you need more control over motion, there are a few other places to look. First, visit the Position option of the Transformation docker, reached through Arrange ➤ Transformation. This tool enables you to enter coordinates for an object's new position, providing far greater precision than you could accomplish with the mouse, or even a drawing tablet. Another strategy is to use the Ctrl key while dragging an object. When you hold Ctrl as you drag, an object is constrained to move either up and down or side to side, but not both at the same time.

The Ctrl key might become your best friend in DRAW because it provides precision in many different situations. For instance:

- Hold Ctrl while rotating an object, and rotation is constrained to 15-degree increments (15 degrees is the default setting; you can change the value at Tools ➤ Options ➤ Edit ➤ Constrain Angle).

- Hold Ctrl while sizing an object, and sizing is constrained to whole increments. You can double the size of the object, or triple it, and so on, but nothing in between.

- Hold Ctrl while using the Interactive Fountain Fill tool, and you constrain the fill angles to 15-degree increments (the default setting).

- Select an object, hold down Ctrl, click on a handle, and drag it back across the object to mirror it across the vertical or horizontal axis. To copy the object, click Button 2 once before releasing Button 1.

T I P   In DRAW, think of Ctrl as an abbreviation for CONstrain.

You've probably already realized it: DRAW can't do anything to an object on the page until you first select it. That's how you call the object to DRAW's attention. When you have a few simple objects on a page, selecting the objects is easy, but as your drawing board becomes more crowded, selecting will become more challenging. Chapter 32 offers a few strategies for selecting objects in crowded places.

Importing Objects

When it comes to incorporating files from other programs, DRAW will digest almost anything you throw at it. DRAW can accept text files from word processors, tables of numbers from spreadsheets, image files from paint programs, vector art from itself, completed drawings from competing programs, and print files produced by practically any other application. The key requirement is that you either tell DRAW what type of file it is, or give DRAW the opportunity to figure it out for itself. But if you try to import a .pcx file while telling DRAW to expect a Word for Windows file, you're asking for trouble. Mind-reading is promised in the millenium edition—then you probably won't even need to select objects before working on them.

The gateway to all importing is the File ➤ Import dialog shown in Figure 3.2. Like most programs, DRAW expects certain formats to have particular filename extensions, and it behooves you to follow standard naming conventions when you create your files.

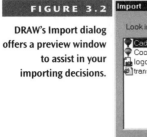

FIGURE 3.2

DRAW's Import dialog offers a preview window to assist in your importing decisions.

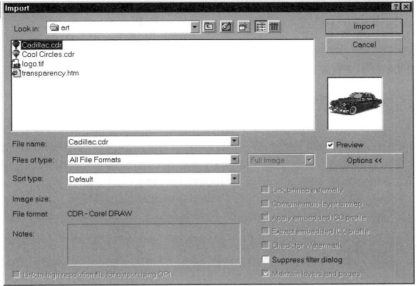

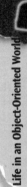

Notes about the Exercises

The following instructions will appear a lot throughout this book:

- We often tell you to use the Look In drop-down list to find a directory (see step 3 below). This list functions as a window to your entire system, including local and network drives and all items on your Desktop. You can click on any drive icon, and the directories for the selected drive appear automatically in the large window.

- When we tell you to "OK the box" (see step 5), remember that when you're choosing files from a list, there are three ways to OK your choice: highlight the file and click on the OK button, highlight the file and press Enter, or just double-click on the file. All Windows 9x and NT 4 dialogs that involve choosing files work this way.

Here are the steps for importing a file:

1. Choose Import from the File menu.

2. In the Import dialog, at the Files of Type box, choose All File Formats.

3. Using the Look In drop-down list, navigate your way to the directory that contains the file you want to use.

4. Choose one of the files in the File window.

5. OK the box.

Most of the time, DRAW does a pretty good job of figuring out the format of a file, meaning that you could keep the Files of Type field set to All File Formats. If DRAW tells you that a certain file you have tried to import is corrupted, don't believe it right away. Try to import it again, but this time set the file type explicitly (for instance, set it to TIFF bitmap for a `.tif` file).

Pasting Objects

DRAW's support for the Clipboard has always been robust, and version 9 continues the tradition. Just about anything that you place on the Clipboard can be brought into DRAW one way or the other (or both). One of the most helpful ways to see this in action is to copy a few paragraphs of text to the Clipboard and watch the ways that DRAW can accept them. Try the following little exercise:

1. Open your word processor or WordPad.

2. Create some text and format it with a few font changes.

3. Select the text and choose Edit ➤ Copy to place the text on the Windows Clipboard.

4. Switch back to DRAW (or open it if it's not already running).

5. Choose Edit ➤ Paste. The text will appear on the page, much like Figure 3.3, depicting the way that these five steps appeared in our word processor.

FIGURE 3.3

This text arrives across the Clipboard looking just like it did in our word processor.

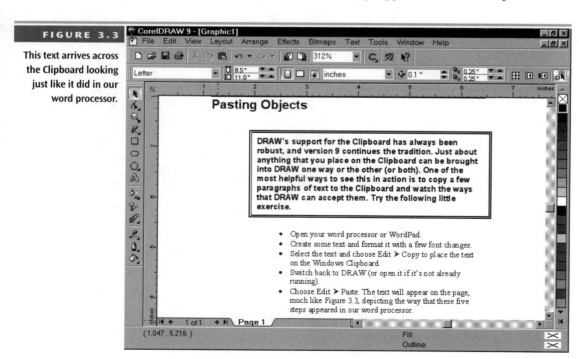

The Many Ways to Paste

Edit ➢ Paste, or Ctrl+V for short, instructs DRAW to paste the data from the Clipboard onto the page, using a default format. In this case, the default format is a picture of the text, the way it looked in the word processor. This is great for depicting the original format, but lousy for editing the text, and if you didn't know of any alternatives, you would declare the Clipboard a failure.

If you want more choices, choose Edit ➢ Paste Special. This presents a menu of format choices, with the default format listed first. The other choices for this text were:

Metafile   Pastes a group of artistic text strings, each line of text being its own string.

Rich Text Format (RTF)   Pastes the text as paragraph text, with typefaces and simple formatting retained from the original text.

Text   Pastes the text into DRAW with no formatting at all. All text takes on the prevailing style of Default Paragraph Text.

Each of these choices could be invaluable when used at the right time. If you needed to show text in its original format, you would paste the text as a picture (Metafile). If you wanted to preserve the format of the text, but be able to edit it in DRAW, you would choose RTF. And if you wanted the text to conform to the existing style established in your drawing, you would choose Text.

For a discussion of artistic and paragraph text, see Chapter 8, and for more on the Clipboard, see Chapter 29.

PART

Life in an Object-Oriented World

Dragging and Dropping Objects

Here is another way to import outside data into DRAW:

1. Open the Windows Explorer.

2. Search for a graphic file with an extension of .tif, .pcx, or .bmp. If you can't find any, navigate into the Windows directory where you will find various .bmp files used as Windows wallpaper.

3. Open or switch to DRAW and position its window so that you can see both DRAW and Explorer.

4. Now drag the file from Explorer into DRAW and drop it there.

Behind the scenes, the maneuver in this exercise is essentially the same as using the Copy-and-then-Paste maneuver, except that you don't get the menu of Paste Special choices. The default choice is automatically used. You can do something similar even if

DRAW is not running: find the graphic you want in Explorer, press Button 2, and choose Copy. Then start DRAW, open a new drawing, and choose Edit ➤ Paste.

Using the Symbols Library

For an easy starting point to creating a simple drawing, nothing beats DRAW's online Symbols library. To access it, choose Tools ➤ Symbols and Special Characters, or press Ctrl+F11. From there you can browse through several categories of symbols. When you find one that you like, click on it, then just drag it out of the docker and drop it on the page. Creating the army of candles shown in Figure 3.4 is quite easy:

1. Choose Household from the drop-down list of themes.

2. Check Tile Symbol/Special Character from the drop-down menu at the top-right of the docker (activated by the small right-pointing arrow next to Household).

3. Drag the desired symbol to the page. When you tile symbols, the one at the top-left is the master, and all others are clones of it. Any change you make to the master changes all the others.

4. Select the master object, click again, and rotate it slightly.

5. Using the on-screen color palette, select a color for the interior (Button 1) and for the outline (Button 2).

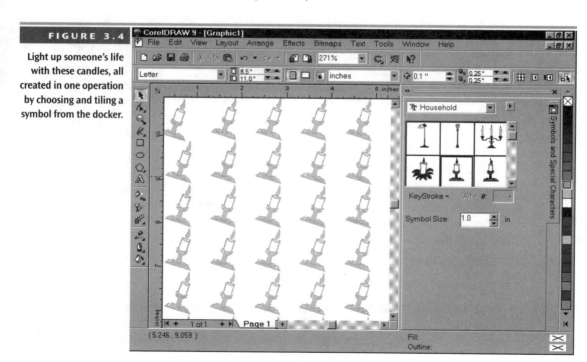

FIGURE 3.4

Light up someone's life with these candles, all created in one operation by choosing and tiling a symbol from the docker.

DRAW's Scrapbook

The Scrapbook helps you organize and access favorite elements you use often. Whether you have certain photos, clipart, 3D models, fills and outlines, or even FTP sites you use frequently, you can save them to DRAW's Scrapbook and then access them easily as you work. To start working with the Scrapbook, choose Tools ➤ Scrapbook and then choose the command you want from the submenu that appears. Figure 3.5 shows the dialog that appears when you choose the Browse command from the Scrapbook pop-up submenu.

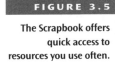

FIGURE 3.5

The Scrapbook offers quick access to resources you use often.

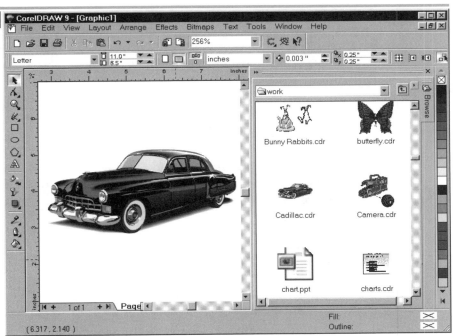

You can quickly open any file in the Scrapbook by double-clicking on its icon, or you can drag the icon into your current drawing to import the file. If you leave the Browse page set to the directory where you keep your current project, you will have instant access to those files.

The second tab of the Scrapbook, Clipart, takes you to the Samples directory. You may want to navigate to the Corel Clipart CD or some other directory or disk where you have additional clipart files. To change the location in which Corel looks for clipart, click the down-arrow beside the Look In box and choose the drive or folder from the displayed list. The Scrapbook provides preview images of clipart on the disk or in the directory you select. When you find the image you want, drag it into your drawing.

The Photos tab also opens to the Samples directory. You may want to change the directory in the Look In box to the Photos directory on the Corel CD. You can then navigate to the photo image you want and drag it to the Corel work area to add it to your current file.

The Favorite Fills and Outlines tab enables you to store your favorite fills and outlines for easy access when you want to reuse them. Details about this are found in Chapter 29.

The 3D Models tab enables you to store and select 3D models you create or import from other sources. Lastly, the FTP Sites tab gives you easy access to FTP sites you use to download files for use in your projects. Both the 3D Models tab and the FTP Sites tab were added to the Scrapbook in DRAW 8. Now you can connect directly to an FTP site from the Scrapbook and download files for use in your illustrations without needing or starting up a dedicated FTP client of your own.

Using Fills and Outlines

One of the first things that new DRAW users do to selected objects is apply fills and outlines, undoubtedly because the controls of the on-screen color palette are right there in front of their noses. Although the Outline and Fill dialogs and dockers have considerable depth, it's easy (as usual) to perform the basic moves. To apply a fill to a selected object, try this:

1. Open `Kiddy105.cdr` from the `\Collection\Sports\Baseball` subdirectory of CorelDRAW 9's CD No. 2.

2. Zoom in on and then select the glove on the boy's hand. Because the components of this clipart are grouped (as is the case with all of Corel's clipart), in order to select the glove, you need to hold Ctrl while you click it.

3. Find Dark Brown on the color palette at the right side of the screen, and click on it with Button 1 (see Figure 3.6). Voilà!

4. To create a red outline around the glove, click on red on the palette, using Button 2.

Any object can be outlined, but until version 8, only objects that were *closed* could be filled. A closed object is one whose outline begins and ends in the same place, such as a circle or a rectangle. Chapters 6 and 7 offer considerable detail on filling and outlining, respectively.

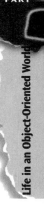
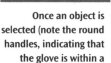

FIGURE 3.6

Once an object is selected (note the round handles, indicating that the glove is within a group), changing its appearance is easy with the on-screen palette.

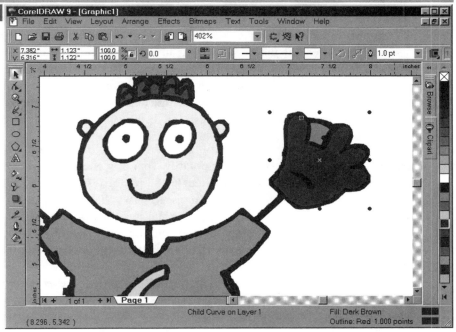

Selecting Multiple Objects

DRAW allows you to select literally thousands of objects at one time for the purposes of grouping, combining, welding, moving, duplicating, deleting, or mass editing of fills and/or outlines.

If the objects are in close proximity and are well defined, you can drag a *marquee* around them to select them. If you need to select certain objects amid others that you don't want to select, the trick is to use the Shift key, like this:

1. Select the first object.
2. Hold down the Shift key.
3. Click on another object. Now both objects are selected.
4. While still holding Shift, click on any other objects you want. As long as you continue to hold Shift, any previously selected objects will remain selected. If you click on an already selected object while holding Shift, you deselect that object.

N O T E   And you thought a marquee was just for displaying movie titles! In DRAWspeak, you create a marquee when you click and drag diagonally to outline a rectangular area. A marquee created with the Pick tool selects all objects that are completely inside the marquee. If you hold the Alt key down, the marquee also selects objects it touches in addition to the ones completely inside. You'll hear the term often, as in "drag a marquee" or "marquee-select several objects." Another use of marquees is with the Zoom tool, discussed later in this chapter.

If you expect to want to do anything to those objects, now or later, consider grouping them (discussed next), even temporarily. That way, they move as one, size as one, fill as one, etc. It's easy to ungroup them later, but not as easy to reselect all of them again, once you go off and do other things. To select all of the objects in your drawing, you can forget about marquees or Shift+clicks or any of that nonsense and head straight for Edit ➤ Select All, where you would then have a choice of all objects, text objects, or just guidelines. Ctrl+A is the new shortcut for selecting all objects. (Well, new shortcut for DRAW, old for Windows.)

If a drawing contains many overlapping objects—or if you ever want to get a better idea of the components of a drawing—a quick trip into Wireframe view would be a good idea. There, only outlines are displayed—no fills. (You toggle Wireframe with View ➤ Wireframe.) Figure 3.7 shows two renditions of the same toy (thanks to DRAW's ability, since version 6, to show two simultaneous views of the same drawing). Notice that it is easier to pick out the individual objects that make up this jack-in-the-box when it is displayed in Wireframe view.

From Traditional Art to Computer Art: Making the Shift

Wireframe view really helps drive home the point that working in DRAW is not like taking a pencil or a paintbrush and sketching. Each tube of Jack's mid-section is a separate object. Each component of his face...the crank...the handle...the flower...his hat...the brim of his hat—all separate objects, each with its own fill and outline characteristics.

Traditional artists who turn to the PC might initially prefer using a painting program, such as Corel PHOTO-PAINT, where the paradigms of brushes, strokes, and palettes still apply, and any spot on the canvas can be painted on. Using DRAW requires a shift in thinking, as objects have individual shapes, colors, and properties, and the creation process is more deliberate and methodical. But it is also more efficient and much more forgiving—two advantages that ultimately win over most users.

FIGURE 3.7

When you use Wireframe view, it is easy to see the shapes and lines that make up the foundation of your drawing.

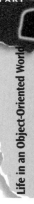

Turning Many Objects into One

DRAW offers three commands that, in some fashion or another, take multiple objects and lump them together so you can work with them all at once. When used correctly, each of these commands is enormously helpful in organizing the various elements contained in drawings. The three commands—Group, Combine, and Weld—are found under the Arrange menu. And once you get the objects the way you want them, three commands introduced in DRAW 8—Lock Object, Unlock Object, and Unlock All Objects—enable you to make sure they stay the way you've designed them, until you are ready to modify them later.

Grouping Objects

The most straightforward of the three "lump together" functions, Group uses an imaginary paper clip or rubber band to collect a set of objects. In other words, the objects are completely independent of one another; they are just held together so you can move, size, or color them in one step. Grouped objects can always be ungrouped—each maintains almost complete autonomy from the other members of its group.

Figure 3.8 includes a set of grouped objects (top-left); notice how the members of this group appear the most autonomous of the three sets.

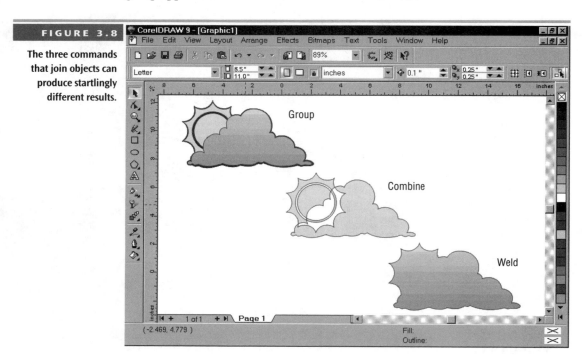

FIGURE 3.8

The three commands that join objects can produce startlingly different results.

If you apply a fill or an outline to a group, all the objects in the group will receive that fill or outline (except elements that are not closed, which will not be filled).

It's a good idea to get into the habit of grouping objects *after* their spatial relationship to one another has been established (you can continue to make changes to objects within a group). The two hotkeys for grouping and ungrouping, Ctrl+G and Ctrl+U, will come in handy.

Another command in the Arrange menu, Ungroup All, enables you to ungroup a collection of grouped items at once.

TIP   You can select an individual object within a group by holding down Ctrl and clicking on the desired object. You'll know you did it correctly when you see circular handles (instead of square ones) around the object. Once selected, you can edit a "child" object within a group just as if it were outside of a group. In DRAW 9, you can even delete a child within a group.

Combining Objects

Combining gives you a less flexible set of objects than does grouping. First, the objects that are combined lose their individual identities; in other words, rectangles, ellipses, and text characters become generic "curves" after being combined. The individual components still have their shapes and their properties, but they have become attached to one another.

Since combined objects become a single curve, they can have only one outline and one fill. Of all the objects in the combined set, the one selected last determines the outline and fill. Where areas overlap, a hole is created.

The middle image of Figure 3.8 shows the effects of Combine. The sun and the cloud are now one object. Notice where the sun and the clouds intersect—the many overlapping areas create a striking mosaic of filled and hollowed areas.

You can break apart an arrangement of combined objects with the Arrange ➤ Break Apart command (or press the hotkey Ctrl+K instead, if you choose). But don't expect the objects to remember how they used to be. Objects you break apart are just curves, and they each inherit the outline and fill of the combined object before it was broken apart. It's not terribly significant that a rectangle becomes a curve, because it still looks and acts the same. However, when *text* is combined with other objects and then broken apart, it loses all of its text properties. It may still look like text because even text characters are actually a collection of curves, but it can never be edited as text again.

Welding Objects

You can take the Weld command literally—it melts separate objects together. In welding, as in combining, the last selected object determines the outline and fill for the new object. Unlike Combine, however, Weld couldn't care less about the points at which welded objects intersect; Weld removes all overlapping areas. No holes are created, and overlapping objects lose their individual shapes entirely. As Figure 3.8 shows, Weld is determined to turn all selected objects into one big blob, and in so doing, removes all parts of objects that lie inside the new outline. When you use Weld, you perform radical surgery.

The Undo command will reverse the Weld effect altogether. Other than that, there is only one way that a Weld can be taken apart, and that is if the welded objects do not touch at all. In that case, Weld is the same as Combine, and the objects can be broken apart. But if they touch, welded objects become permanently fused and cannot be taken apart. They truly become one object.

The Fourth Dimension of Object Conversion

There is one more way that multiple objects can be turned into one: you can convert them to a bitmap. This is easy to do—select the object(s), go to Bitmap ➤ Convert to Bitmap, and choose a resolution and color depth—but impossible to undo (except t o actually use Undo). When you convert an object to a bitmap, you tell DRAW to forget anything it knew about those objects and convert everything to a bunch of dots of different colors. Shapes of rectangles...the radius of an ellipse...the typeface and size of text...the qualities of a fountain fill—they all get converted from intelligent vector objects to unintelligent pixels. They are no different than a bitmap image you created or acquired elsewhere and imported into DRAW.

Locking and Unlocking Objects

If you have ever spent an afternoon getting a drawing just the way you want it and then accidentally changed something that cost you time, effort, and frustration, you will appreciate the Lock command. Now you can ensure that an object stays the way you want it to be—no more accidental click-and-drags, rotations, or deletions.

To lock your object, select it and choose Arrange ➤ Lock Object. The handles around the object change to little lock symbols (see Figure 3.9). You cannot move, resize, recolor, or delete the object. It's there for the duration—until you unlock it with one of the other commands in the Arrange menu.

When you are ready to unlock the object, select it and choose Arrange ➤ Unlock Object, or Arrange ➤ Unlock All Objects if you have multiple locked objects you want to unlock all at once. Now you can modify, copy, or delete the object as needed.

Other Points of Interest

As you take your first few tours of DRAW, there are several other stops you will want to make. The following tasks are easily learned and performed, like all the other commands and functions discussed in this chapter.

Saving and Opening Files

Saving your work is arguably your most important task in DRAW—if you didn't, nothing would be permanent. We won't insult your intelligence by explaining how to do it. (The only time we have ever actually done that in a book or magazine article was in 1986, when our lead author attempted to show how to save changes in EDLIN. He reports that he no longer remembers the command...)

PART

Life in an Object-Oriented World

FIGURE 3.9

In the real world, this family would have lost its luggage six exits ago. With DRAW, however, you can lock the objects so that they don't move...or fall all over the road.

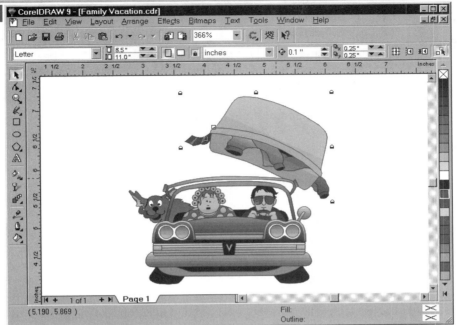

The key to effective saving is first to establish an organized directory structure. DRAW remembers the directories you last chose for saving and opening files. So if you are consistent with your use of files and directories, you will have far less navigating to do in DRAW's file windows.

Our only other advice: remember the hotkey Ctrl+S; it makes saving as routine as a Mark McGwire home run.

Zooming

The easiest way to zoom in on your drawing is to press F4. This hotkey takes into account all the objects in your drawing and chooses the closest magnification that still allows you to see them all.

If you need to zoom in on just a piece of your drawing, you've got two choices. To zoom on objects that are selected, click the Zoom tool, move to the page, click Button 2, and choose Zoom to Selection from the flyout. (Or better still, use the hotkey Shift+F2.) To zoom in on a particular collection of objects that may or may not be selected, click the Zoom tool and move to the page. Now any marquee you create on your drawing becomes the zoom area, and DRAW will automatically calculate the magnification.

TIP   Efficient DRAW users combine a bit of hotkeying and a bit of mousing to make zooming much faster and easier. If you let the mouse go solo, you would have to mouse all the way over to the toolbox, click the Zoom tool, and then mouse back to the page to create the marquee. Instead, get your nonmouse hand into the act: use it to press F2 (the hotkey for the Zoom tool) while your mouse hand begins to draw the marquee.

With DRAW's support for multiple drawings and multiple windows, you can open the same drawing in two different windows, keeping one of the windows zoomed out on the whole image while the other window is zoomed way in on a particular area. To open a drawing in a second window, go to Window ➤ New Window. Then use one of the Tiling commands, if you want, to arrange the windows.

Aligning Elements

Align and Distribute is a two-tab dialog reached through the Arrange menu. It gives you a variety of ways to automatically arrange objects in relation to each other or to the page. For example, you can use the Align tab to align the top edges of several objects to the center of the page—all in one operation. If you do not align to a part of the page, the last object selected will be the "anchor," and other objects will move to align to it.

The icons on the Align tab are fairly clear, but you may need to experiment to understand how multiple options relate to one another. For example, if you check Center of Page, then check the Left box, selected objects will be aligned with their left edges along the center of the page. They will also have their vertical centers aligned with the center of the page unless you uncheck that box.

The Distribute tab works similarly, but allows you to space objects equally across an area or the entire page. Both tabs have Preview buttons, so you can see the effect of your actions before you commit yourself.

Since DRAW 8, this dialog box has seen decreasing action, as many DRAW users have discovered the one-touch commands for aligning. With two or more objects selected, you can align objects with the press of one key:

T	Objects align along their top edges
B	Objects align along their bottom edges
E	Objects align along their horizontal midpoints
L	Objects align along their left edges
R	Objects align along their right edges
C	Objects align down their centers

Also, be sure to experiment with the Arrange ➤ Order commands of To Front, To Back, Forward One, Back One, Reverse Order, In Front Of, and Behind. Choosing either of the last two commands activates a heavy black arrow with which you choose the object that you want the selected objects to go "in front of" or "behind."

Using Undo

DRAW's Undo command has a very good memory, and you can make it even better. In Tools ➢ Options ➢ Workspace ➢ General, you can set the number of *levels* for Undo. Let's say you do the following to a circle: (1) change its color, (2) move it 2 inches away, (3) make it larger, and (4) delete it. You can undo each of those actions, starting with the most recent and working back in time. Each action is called a level, and the default number of levels for Undo is 99. That's a lot; it seems unlikely you could remember that many actions to know you would want to undo them. You might want to cut it down to a more reasonable number like 20 or 30, particularly if memory is in short supply on your computer.

DRAW 8 introduced a second Undo function, specifically for bitmap effects. The default value is 2, but you can also set it as high as 99. Remember, however, that Corel uses your system's RAM to store previous versions of objects, and keeping track of 99 incarnations of a bitmap will require a galaxy of memory. To keep your system memory from running out, keep the Undo setting for bitmap effects at a modest number.

For both regular and bitmap Undo operations, you cannot pick and choose the actions that you want to undo; they must be undone in precisely the reverse order in which they were done. For instance, in the example above, you cannot undo the color change without first undoing the move and the resize.

There are four actions that cannot be undone with Undo:

- Changes to View settings
- File operations such as Save, Save As, and Export (although DRAW does save backup files, so in the case of Save, you can retrieve the previous version under the name `Backup_of_Filename.cdr`)
- Selection of objects
- Printing (obviously)

By the way, our trusty technical editor reminds us that DRAW 8 and 9 can undo even after a save. Past versions would throw away the Undo list after a Save command.

Copying Properties

With two or more objects in a file, you can take the properties of one object and assign them to another using the Copy Properties From command on the Edit menu. To copy properties:

1. Select the object(s) you want to change.

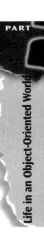

PART

Life in an Object-Oriented World

2. To invoke the Copy Properties dialog, select Edit ➤ Copy Properties From (or press Ctrl+Shift+A).

3. Choose the particular component(s) you want to apply—outline pen, outline color, fill pattern, or text properties—and OK the dialog.

4. When DRAW changes its cursor to an arrow, point to and click on the object that *already has* the attributes. The selected objects change immediately.

Quick Fix for Properties

DRAW offers a quicker way to copy the fill and outline properties from one object to another. Using Button 2, drag the object that already has the attributes and drop it on the object that needs them. You will get a menu with a number of options, including Copy Fill Here, Copy Outline Here, and Copy All Properties.

Using the Repeat Command

In conjunction with tedious tasks, such as applying special fill patterns or outlines to many objects, or even just careful placement of objects, nothing beats the Edit ➤ Repeat command and its Ctrl+R hotkey. Here is a good illustration of how Repeat can be used:

1. Create a small object.

2. Drag the object a short distance away, and click on Button 2 before releasing Button 1. This creates a duplicate.

3. Press Ctrl+R to repeat the action in step 2 over and over again.

Drag-and-Dupe (a.k.a. Leave Original)

The official name of this feature is Leave Original, but we prefer our own name, "drag-and-dupe." It refers to the popular technique of making a copy of an object while moving or reshaping it. Let's see how this works.

When you move, rotate, skew, size, or distort an object, it involves the following four basic steps:

1. Select the object.

2. Press and hold Button 1.

3. Perform the desired action.

4. Let go of Button 1.

To do a drag-and-dupe, tap Button 2 *before you let go of Button 1*, anytime after step 3. This automatically creates a copy of the object and applies the effect you are creating to the copy, not to the original. You can use this in many different ways:

- To make an enlarged copy of an object, select it, begin dragging one of the corner selection handles, and tap Button 2 before releasing Button 1.

- To rotate a copy of an object, select the object, click a second time to get the rotation handles, begin rotating the object, and tap Button 2 before releasing Button 1.

- To stretch a copy of an object, select it, drag a side handle, and tap Button 2 before releasing Button 1.

You get the idea here: any type of transformation can be performed on a copy instead of the original by tapping Button 2 during the transformation. Button 2 acts like a toggle: tap it again and you are then changing the original object. Your cue is the little plus sign that will appear and disappear at the cursor position with each tap of Button 2.

Right-Click 'til You Drop

Drag-and-dupe is one of many important uses for the second button on your mouse, track ball, or tablet. In normal use (i.e., not in the middle of a transformation), pressing Button 2 (or "right-clicking") activates a context-sensitive menu of functions and commands. If you have selected a rectangle, the context menu will be different than if you have selected a string of text.

Our advice to you is simple: right-click on everything! Corel has done a pretty good job of providing pop-up menus that include the important operations connected with each type of object or screen element. Just don't try to remember all the details. Instead, right-click on every possible screen element, every object, tool, and icon, and take note of the various options that appear.

NOTE When we give instructions throughout the book, most of the time we'll refer you to the traditional methods of invoking commands or clicking icons, and we'll let you know when a hotkey is available. You can take other routes as you like, such as using the context menu, going to a custom toolbar, or using a script.

Step by Step: Spyrograph Revisited

We're just starting out with DRAW, yet you already know enough to work the program and produce a simple piece of art. Try this:

1. Click the Ellipse tool in the toolbox and move out to the page.

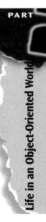

PART

Life in an Object-Oriented World

2. Create an ellipse of any size or shape. Notice that when you finish drawing the ellipse, the Ellipse tool is still active, enabling you to continue drawing ellipses.

3. Create a second ellipse, this time holding Ctrl while you drag. The result is a perfect circle.

4. Create another ellipse, this time holding Shift. Shift forces the ellipse to draw from the center out in all directions.

5. Create an ellipse while holding both Ctrl and Shift. The result is a perfect circle drawn from the center out in all directions. These two keys behave the same for rectangles and polygons.

6. Select all objects on the page (Edit ➢ Select All ➢ Objects, Ctrl+A, or double-click the Pick tool) and delete them.

7. Now draw one thin ellipse, as shown below.

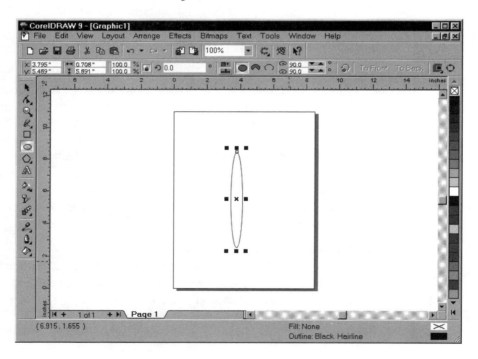

8. Color it blue, or some dark color other than black (the outline is black and it will look better if the interior is a different color).

9. Change to the Pick tool (use the toolbox or just press the spacebar), and click once on the ellipse to get the rotation handles.

10. Click on one of the corner rotation handles, and rotate the ellipse approximately 10 degrees. The property bar above the page will show you the degree of rotation as you move the handle. Don't release Button 1 yet…

11. While still holding down Button 1, tap Button 2. That creates a copy, as shown below.

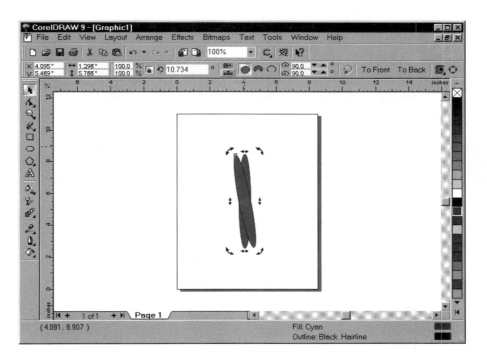

12. With the second ellipse still selected, press Delete to delete it.

13. Select the original ellipse, click again for the rotation handles, and begin rotating again.

14. This time, however, press and hold Ctrl while you rotate. As discussed earlier, this constrains the rotation to 15-degree increments. You'll get immediate confirmation of this as the ellipse snaps from one position to the next (the property bar will also confirm the constraint).

15. While still holding Ctrl and while still holding Button 1 (this is like an aerobic workout for your hands), tap Button 2 to make a copy.

Take your hand off the mouse for a moment to review (and rest your fingers!). In steps 12 through 15, you selected an object, began rotating it, constrained its rotation, and made a copy. DRAW sees all of those things as one maneuver. That means that it can be repeated easily. Watch:

16. Go to Edit ➤ Repeat Rotate (and note its shortcut of Ctrl+R). Suddenly, another ellipse appears.

17. Press Ctrl+R to make another one.

18. Keep pressing Ctrl+R as the ellipses make their way around the pattern. Stop when your screen looks like the one below.

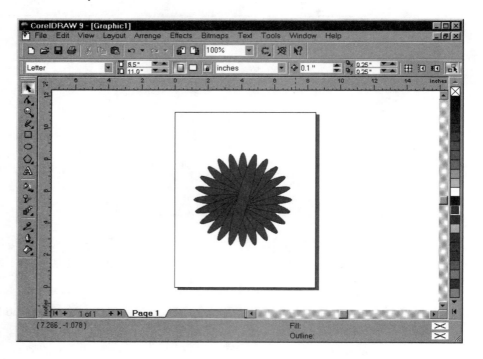

Now for the pièce de résistance.

19. Select all the ellipses, using any of the Select All commands noted in step 6, or just by drawing a marquee around them.

20. Choose Arrange ➤ Combine (or press Ctrl+L).

21. Press F4 to get a closer look and press Esc to remove all selection handles.

22. Save your drawing if you would like to keep it.

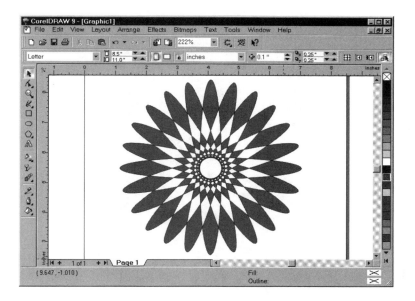

Remember the discussion earlier about how Combine turns many objects into one and cuts holes from overlapping areas? This is merely a dramatic example of that—each time an ellipse was on top of another, a hole was created.

Because this is all one object, you can easily experiment with different fill patterns, and the place to go for that would be the Interactive Fill tool from the toolbox (the one that looks like a paint bucket with paint pouring out). It provides access to each fill type that DRAW offers and all of the common controls. Going from a flat color to a gradient color (one that gradually changes from one to the next) is easy, as shown below.

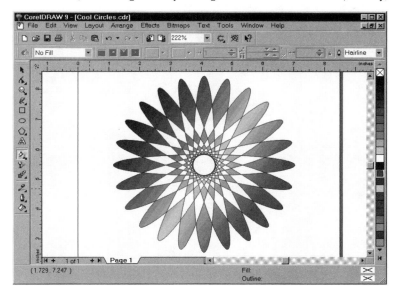

And applying a more exotic fill from Corel's Texture or Bitmap libraries is also easy.

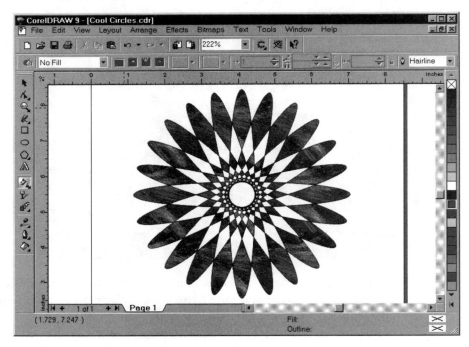

In all cases, the fill pattern displays where a closed shape is present, but disappears in the hollow areas where the Combine command cut holes in the shapes. You'll find this 30-second masterpiece as Cool Circles.cdr on the companion Web page for this book on the Sybex Web site, www.sybex.com.

As the Curve Turns

Featuring

As the Curve Turns

or five years now, we have looked at the title for this chapter and wondered if the time had come to replace this mildly clever double-entendre (you know...As the World Turns...that soap opera about life...curves are everything to CorelDRAW...as the curve turns, so turns life...oh, forget it).

But after close annual scrutiny, the title stays. The curve really is the lifeblood of everything that CorelDRAW does. Almost every shape you create in DRAW has curve-like properties. Rectangles and ellipses are really curves in disguise. Text characters have nodes, just like curves. Even straight lines are treated by DRAW as curves. The only type of object that DRAW doesn't try to define as a curve is an imported bitmap. In short, if it's a vector-based object, DRAW sees it as a curve.

A vector object always has a *path* that defines its shape. If the path is closed—that is, the start and end points are the same—the object also has an interior that can be filled with colors or patterns. (As of DRAW 8, you can fill open curves, but that falls under the category of knowing the rules well enough to break them; we'll start with the fundamentals here.) All paths created in DRAW contain two components: *segments* and *nodes*. Here is how DRAW defines these terms:

- A *path* represents the route from a start point to an end point. Simple closed objects, such as rectangles or ellipses, generally have a single path. If you combine several objects into one, the new object has multiple *subpaths*. Letters with holes, like *O*, are also made up of multiple subpaths. One subpath is the outer oval of the letter, and another forms the inner edge.

- A *segment* is a single section of a path. It can be either a line or a curve. Each side of a rectangle, for instance, is a segment. An ellipse is a single segment. A crooked line drawn with the Freehand tool could consist of many segments.

- A *node* is the little point that is the start or end point of a segment. A rectangle has four nodes; a circle has two, one on top of the other; your freehand line might have a dozen.

Every object you create in DRAW contains these three basic elements—paths, segments, and nodes—and in all cases, DRAW provides access to them for editing and reshaping. Sometimes, that access is not so straightforward, as is the case with text characters, but one way or the other, you can reach the quantum particle level of an object and see its paths, segments, and nodes in action.

When you draw with the Freehand tool, you are automatically creating lines or curves, end of discussion. But when you use the other four tools—Ellipse, Rectangle, Polygon, and Text—you create objects that DRAW treats with a bit more reverence. Ellipses, for instance, always have one continuous circumference, rectangles always have four sides, polygons maintain their symmetry, and text carries with it a host of special attributes such as typeface, style, spacing, and size.

Once you use DRAW's Convert to Curves command, however, DRAW strips those objects of their special status; they become just curves. You then are free to add a fifth side to a rectangle, turn circles into odd shapes, and commit all sorts of unspeakable crimes on text characters.

Let's start by looking at curves and lines; we'll cover ellipses, rectangles, polygons, and text characters later in the chapter.

The Science of Curves and Lines

To begin exploring the dynamics of curves, click on the Freehand tool and draw a curve. Any curve will do, like the one in Figure 4.1. If the Freehand tool isn't visible, click and hold the Curve flyout (the fourth button from the top of the toolbox). Choose the Freehand tool from the flyout.

With the object selected, you can count for yourself the number of nodes and segments that make up the curve. In Figure 4.1, 18 nodes were required, including the first and last ones, to represent the 17 segments of the curve. Notice that the curve intersects itself; that's okay.

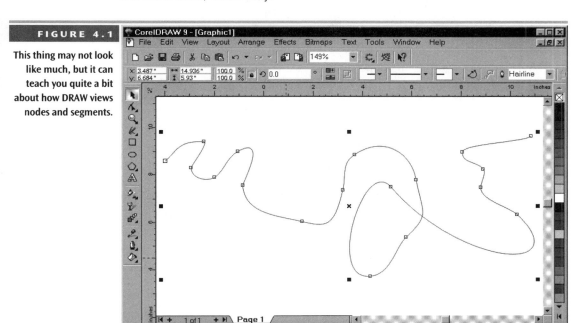

Because you used the Freehand tool, your object is already a curve and can be easily altered. Once you select the Shape tool, there are three ways to change the parts of a curve:

- Click and drag any node to move it.
- Click and drag any segment to change the path between two nodes.
- Click a node and then drag the control handles to change the shape of the path as it approaches that node.

Moving a segment often produces the same result as moving the control handles…but often not. The mechanics of nodes and segments make up a science that resides right next door to black magic, and trying to understand their true nature and behavior promises to be a fruitless venture. Far better for you to experiment with the three different ways to shape curves and develop a feel for them. Sometimes we suspect the developers themselves aren't entirely sure what kind of a Frankenstein monster they've created.

Screen Gems

DRAW goes out of its way to provide you with visual clues about what part of the curve you have selected, and picking up on these clues is crucial to your success as a curve shaper. Here are the important things to know about DRAW's on-screen behavior:

- You can perform some node-editing even if the Pick tool is active. As your cursor crosses over a node, the cursor grows, the node grows, and a four-headed arrow appears next to it. While working with the Pick tool, the only shaping you can perform is to pick up a node and move it elsewhere, but that is often good enough, and if it saves you from switching tools, you're ahead of the game. (This assumes that the Enable Node Tracking option is enabled. If it is not, then you will not be able to track over and move these nodes with the Pick tool.)

- With the Shape tool selected, DRAW not only tells you when you are atop a node (same visual cue), but also when you are atop a control point or along the path of the segment. DRAW presents the same four-headed arrow to indicate you are atop a control point, and offers up a small wavy line to tell you that you are on a segment, even if that segment is a straight line (remember, DRAW thinks everything is a curve).

- Clicking on nodes is an exacting, meticulous, and often tiresome and painful activity. We predict you will find it easier to marquee-select the node. Creating a marquee around a node is usually easier than clicking right on top of it.

 T I P   Experienced users might want to take time out to customize their status bars. Click on it with mouse Button 2, choose Customize, and then double-click Status Bar in the Toolbars list box. From selections displayed on the right side of the window, click and drag any status bar item (such as Object Details) to the status bar on the bottom of your screen display. Now watch as you select various nodes; DRAW refers to them as either *line* or *curve* nodes, and either type may be *smooth* or *cusp*. As you drew your curve, DRAW automatically decided which type of node to use at each turn.

DRAW uses smooth nodes where it finds a gradual transition from one segment to another and cusp nodes to make sharper turns. Figure 4.2 zeroes in on one of the cusp nodes of the curve we created for Figure 4.1. Notice how the curve makes a sharp downward turn. DRAW automatically used a cusp node to create this shape; we didn't have to tell it to. Also, if DRAW senses that you went from one node to another along a straight path, it will use a straight line segment between those two nodes, instead of a curve segment.

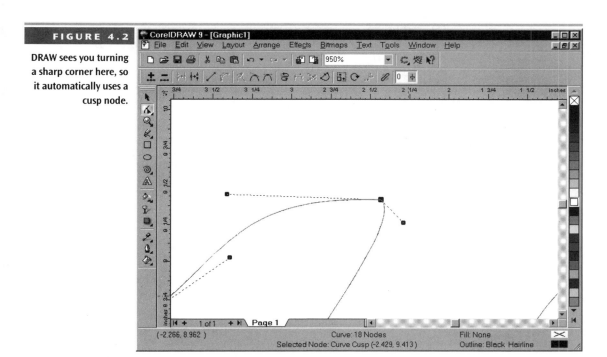

FIGURE 4.2

DRAW sees you turning a sharp corner here, so it automatically uses a cusp node.

What Are These Nodes?

Good question. It's entirely possible that you read and followed everything we've written so far and still do not understand what nodes are or what they do. Our advice is to forget about understanding what they are (we don't really know, either), and concentrate instead on what they do. Following is a close look at the five types of nodes: line cusp, line smooth, curve cusp, curve smooth, and curve symmetrical.

Try the following exercise to get a better idea of what nodes do.

1. Open a new drawing using File ➢ New. Create a large rectangle of any shape and fill it with any light color or shade.

To access the nodes of this rectangle, you must tell DRAW to stop thinking of it as a rectangle and consider it a plain old curve instead.

2. Click the Convert to Curves button near the right end of the property bar (or press Ctrl+Q).

3. Choose the Shape tool and select each node in turn while watching your status bar. For each node, it reports "Line Cusp." This rectangle started with four lines; therefore, its path is made up of straight lines and its nodes are all line cusps.

PART

Life in an Object-Oriented World

When working with nodes, the property bar will be a critical member of your team, providing access to all of the tools you would want to use with nodes, as described in the graphic below.

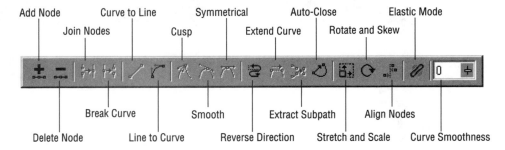

Add Node • Curve to Line • Symmetrical • Auto-Close • Elastic Mode
Join Nodes • Cusp • Extend Curve • Rotate and Skew

Break Curve • Smooth • Extract Subpath • Align Nodes
Delete Node • Line to Curve • Reverse Direction • Stretch and Scale • Curve Smoothness

4. Select the lower-right node of the rectangle and click the To Curve button on the property bar. This button converts the node from a straight line to a curve. If you did it right, the appearance of the line running down the right side will change (it will grow control handles).

NOTE Remember that DRAW uses "curve" in different ways. Convert to Curves takes the entire path of a "special" object, such as a rectangle, ellipse, or string of artistic text, and makes a generic curve out of it. Clicking the To Curve button converts a line segment of an object to a curve segment. In other words, a curve could be made up of a series of curves...and you have our permission to complain to Corel's developers about confusing syntax.

5. Click and drag the segment on the right and watch this former rectangle change shape drastically. Drag to the inside and your screen will look something like Figure 4.3. Notice that the status bar now calls the node a "Curve Cusp."

6. Instead of moving the segment, click the node and move it. Note the effect.

7. Now click and drag the control points that emanate from the selected nodes and watch what happens.

TIP Remember how Ctrl equals CONstrain? When holding Ctrl, any dragging of nodes, segments, or control points is constrained to purely vertical or purely horizontal movement.

What would happen if you were to turn this node back into a line segment? As you can probably guess, the curve that you created would instantly revert to a straight line. Try it. With the lower-right node selected, click To Line on the property bar, but then press Ctrl+Z to undo, because now we're moving on.

PART

Life in an Object-Oriented World

FIGURE 4.3

By changing a node from a line to a curve, you can dramatically reshape what started as a rectangle.

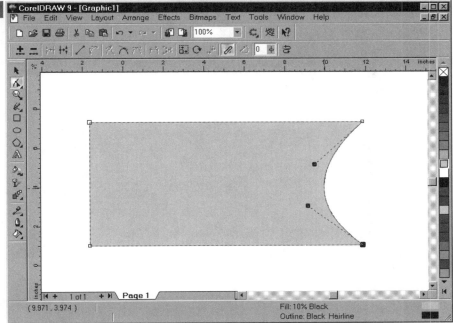

Smooth Operators

The curved path that you just created turns a very sharp corner because the other side of the node is still a straight line. By default, DRAW creates cusp nodes at sharp corners. Convert that lower-right node to a smooth node by selecting it and then clicking the Smooth button on the property bar. Figure 4.4 shows the result.

Now, select the lower-left node and convert it to a curve. Then reshape the segment along the bottom, and notice that the segment along the right changes too. With a smooth node, motion on one side of the node usually affects the other side. This can make working with smooth nodes frustrating (as you'll no doubt experience for yourself in the exercises later in the chapter), but it is responsible for the fidelity and accuracy you can achieve with them.

Node Symmetry

Many DRAW users misunderstand the dynamic of a symmetrical node. They think symmetry means that any shape on one side of the node must be the exact same on the other side. In fact, symmetry and mirroring are not the same. Have you ever worked out on one of those rowing machines? If so, you can imagine how when you pull your arms toward your body, you thrust your legs away from you. These actions are not identical, but they are symmetrical. Symmetrical nodes work much the same way.

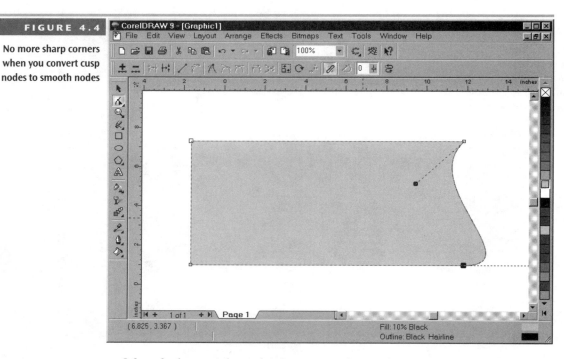

FIGURE 4.4

No more sharp corners when you convert cusp nodes to smooth nodes

Select the lower-right node of your now-distorted rectangle, and click the Symmetrical node on the property bar to turn it into a symmetrical node. Study the behavior of the node. Think of any movement as energy, and remember that axiom you learned in high school physics about every action having an equal and opposite reaction. Sorry for the obtuse analogies, but as you can see, we'll go to great lengths to avoid providing an actual definition of these curious little nodes.

Which Kind Is It?

To review, a segment of a curve can either be a straight line or a curve. If it's a curve, the nodes that control the segment can be one of three types: symmetrical, smooth, or cusp. If the segment is a straight line, there are only two options: smooth and cusp. Like we said, forget about definitions; think rules, instead. And DRAW has fairly strict rules for the behavior of its curve nodes, as follows.

How Do You Know It's a Symmetrical Node?

Symmetrical nodes have control points that must form a straight line through the node. Furthermore, the distance from one control point to the node must be the same as the distance from the other control point to the node (i.e., the two control points must be equidistant from their node). Figure 4.5 illustrates this: in image A, the lower control point for the selected node is about to be dragged downward. Because this is a symmetrical node, the upper control point moves away equally. The result, shown in image B, is a curve that behaves symmetrically with respect to the node.

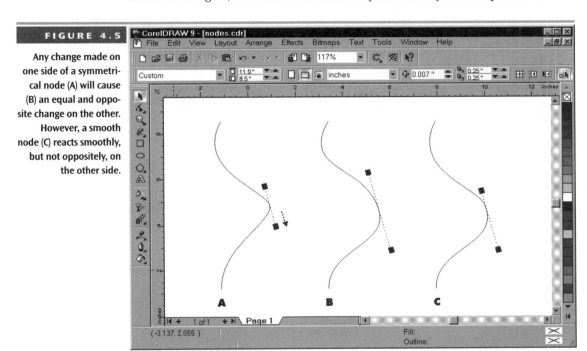

FIGURE 4.5

Any change made on one side of a symmetrical node (A) will cause (B) an equal and opposite change on the other. However, a smooth node (C) reacts smoothly, but not oppositely, on the other side.

Symmetrical nodes can be useful but exasperating because they change the shape of the adjacent segment whether you want them to or not. Candidly, you'll find few instances where a symmetrical node is required to depict a shape.

How Do You Know It's a Smooth Node?

Like a symmetrical node, a smooth node contains control points that form a straight line right through the node. But unlike a symmetrical node, there is no requirement of equidistance. One control point can be further from the node than the other. Figure 4.5, image C, illustrates the dynamics of a smooth node. As the control point is extended downward and at an angle, the opposite control point adjusts its angle, to maintain the straight line. However, this control point does not extend in the opposite direction. The curve adjusts to remain smooth (hence the node's name), but there is no symmetrical action.

Smooth nodes are useful in a variety of circumstances—in fact, you will probably use them the most when creating or shaping objects. But be aware that they, too, will change the shape of the path on both sides of the node.

How Do You Know It's a Cusp Node?

When a node has totally different routes on either side of it, it's a cusp node. Cusp nodes do not allow movement on one side to affect the other side. The two control points do not have to form a straight line with the node, and they can move independently. As Figure 4.6 illustrates, the upper control point doesn't react at all when the lower one is extended out and at a different angle. If you want a high degree of control over the segments of a curve, cusp nodes are the best choice.

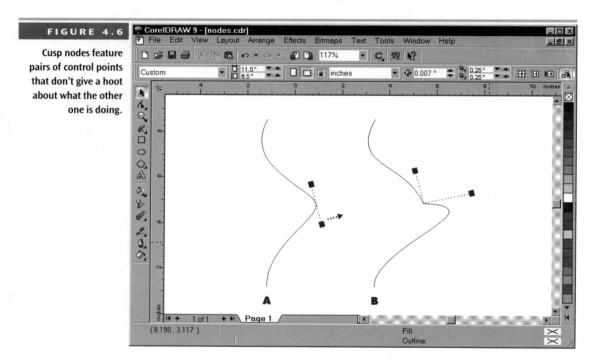

FIGURE 4.6

Cusp nodes feature pairs of control points that don't give a hoot about what the other one is doing.

Practice Makes Perfect

We think it likely that most of our readers may never have occasion to conscientiously create certain types of nodes as they are making a drawing. It is far more likely that you will need to change node types in the refinement process. That is why it is important that you recognize the behavior of the three types of nodes (four, counting straight lines).

So create another freeform curve and play with it. Change the curves to lines, change them from cusps to smooth nodes and from smooth to symmetrical nodes. Drag nodes, drag segments, and drag control points. Switch to the Pick tool and note the actions you can no longer easily perform, and the one action (node relocation) that you still can perform. Fiddle with the various buttons on the property bar. In particular, note the following:

- You can select two nodes at a time by selecting one and then Shift+selecting the other, or by marquee-selecting one, holding down Shift, and marquee-selecting the next one. The latter may be preferable because marquee-selecting is easier on your hand and carries little risk of inadvertently moving the node when you click on it.

- If you select the two end nodes, you can merge them into one (to close the curve) with the Join Two Nodes button on the property bar. You can connect the two end nodes with a new segment using the Auto-Close button without even selecting the nodes first.

- You can split any node into two using the Break Curve button. When you split a closed object, it becomes an open curve. If you break a curve that is already open, you create two subpaths within the one curve.

- Try creating new nodes. Click once on a segment and you'll see a small dot appear. Click the plus button on the property bar (or press the plus key on the numeric keypad) to create a new node at that spot. You can also create nodes by selecting an existing one and clicking the plus button (or pressing the plus key on your keyboard). DRAW places the new node between the selected node and the one before it on the curve.

- If you select more than one node, you can rotate or align them with those buttons on the property bar.

- If you prefer to right-click and use the context menu instead of the property bar (more clicking, less mousing), many of the same controls will appear. And note that you can access the node-editing context menu even if you are working with the Pick tool. Just make sure to hover over a node before right-clicking.

- And new to DRAW 9, if you hold Alt while marquee-selecting nodes, you can create a freehand shape around the nodes, instead of a standard rectangular shape. This makes intricate node selection much easier.

Draw Straight, Curve Later

Your curve was created by selecting the Freehand tool and clicking and dragging, but it will be easier for you—and ultimately better for your reputation as a desktop designer—if you learn the value of drawing straight lines. Instead of holding the mouse button and dragging through the entire curve, as you did previously, you leapfrog from one point to another to draw straight lines. Here are the actions a DRAW user takes when creating a series of straight lines:

1. Click to define a start point.

PART

Life in an Object-Oriented World

2. Move the mouse.

3. Click once to define the end point for the segment.

4. Click at the same place to define a new start point.

5. Move the mouse.

6. Click to define the end.

7. Click again at the same place to define a new start.

8. Repeat.

Figure 4.7 shows, in both dramatic and horrifying fashion, the value of creating straight lines for simple shapes. The top image shows the ease with which you can create a simple outline, like this building, with just a few clicks. On the other hand, as the lower image illustrates, it's not so easy to draw the building freehand.

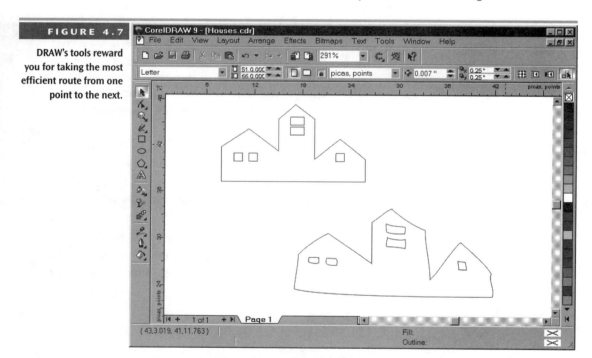

FIGURE 4.7

DRAW's tools reward you for taking the most efficient route from one point to the next.

This is not just another example of our lead author's undeveloped drawing skills—the most accomplished CorelDRAW artist couldn't do much better with instruments as clumsy as the Freehand drawing tool and a mouse. A drawing tablet, coupled with some of DRAW 9's new creation tools, would yield better results, but that misses the point, because that's not what DRAW is all about. When you work in a vector-based application, you are not a painter, and your physical drawing skills are secondary. Success in DRAW is determined first by your artistic vision, and second by your ability to manipulate vector objects to fit your vision. Much of this vector manipulation comes down to little more than a game of leapfrog where you hop from one point to the next.

Setting Thresholds with the Freehand Smoothing Tool

DRAW makes decisions about node placement and node type based on settings that you can control. Right-click the Freehand tool and choose Properties—you'll be greeted by the dialog shown here.

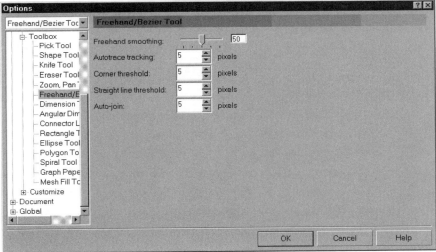

Brand new to DRAW 9, and a significant new tool, is the Freehand Smoothing setting, which can provide on-the-fly node reduction and curve smoothing. Higher values result in fewer nodes and smoother curves (although possibly at the loss of critical detail). The default of 50 results in practically every twist and turn of your mouse being translated into a smooth curve.

The threshold settings determine DRAW's tendency to use cusp nodes when turning corners and straight lines when going from node to node. The lower the number for the Corner threshold, the greater DRAW's tendency will be toward creating cusps. The lower the number for the Straight Line threshold, the greater DRAW's tendency will be toward drawing curves.

The other fields in this dialog also affect drawing. Click the Help button in the dialog to get descriptions of each field.

PART

Life in an Object-Oriented World

Drawing with a Not-So-Free Hand

Most DRAW users use the Freehand tool at least 75 percent of the time, and many DRAW users have never used anything but. Nonetheless, there are two other ways in which you can create curves in DRAW—using the Artistic Media tool and the Bézier tool—both of which are hiding behind the Freehand icon in the toolbox.

Artistic Media: the New Kid on the Block

With the ever-rising popularity of drawing tablets and other pen-type products, it makes sense that Corel would add tools that make it easier to sketch. The Artistic Media tool—the third icon in the Curve flyout—is designed to bring back some of the tactile feel of traditional drawing and sketching. While it is considered a drawing tool, technically speaking, the Artistic Media's output is quite unlike the other tools (elaboration forthcoming).

The first five icons on the Artistic Media property bar represent the five modes you can use with this tool:

Preset   Creates objects from a drop-down menu of two dozen shapes.

Brush   Allows you to draw lines made up of simple objects, like arrows, icons, ribbons, etc.

Sprayer   Creates multiple objects or colors along the creation path. With this tool, you'll feel as if you're using a can of spray paint; hence the name.

Calligraphic   Converts simple lines into calligraphic strokes.

Pressure   Object width is determined by action of pen or mouse.

Figure 4.8 shows the striking results possible with Artistic Media. The simple line at the left (A) was drawn with the Freehand tool, and there is nothing special about it. The next five lines were drawn the exact same way, mechanically speaking, but each with a different Artistic Media effect chosen.

In fact, these fancy lines are not lines at all, and that is what makes them quite different from basic lines. They are closed objects that have an interior fill and an outline. In each case, the line that you draw during creation acts as the path, along which the Artistic Media tool creates its special type of closed object.

Drawing with the Bézier Tool

Creating curves with the Freehand drawing tool is easy, if inelegant. It's not unlike using an Etch-a-Sketch, with which you move haphazardly from one point to another. Creating curves with the Bézier drawing tool is a truly different experience, both in the way the tool operates and in the results.

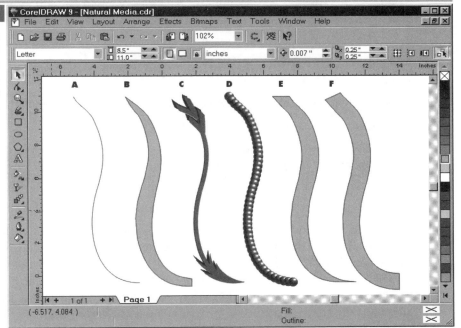

FIGURE 4.8

When is a line not a line? When it is: (B) a preset, (C) a brush stroke, (D) a spray, (E) calligraphy, or (F) a pressure-sensitive line.

After reading all of the books, scouring the CorelDRAW User's Manual, sifting through all of the magazine articles, and taking copious notes at CorelDRAW seminars, one conclusion seems inescapable:

It is impossible to teach anyone to use the Bézier drawing tool.

Drawing in Bézier mode is like sculpting with warm Jell-O. Every action has a reaction and you'll always feel like you're one jiggle too slow to keep up. You surely will gain little understanding of how the tool works by reading someone else's prose. The only way to learn is to experiment with the tool yourself. Nonetheless, our advice follows.

The Bézier tool doesn't trace every shake, rattle, and roll of your mouse through a path. It looks for a beginning point and an end point, and then connects them with one curve segment. When creating Bézier curves, you do not click and drag across the entire segment; rather, you click on the start and end points and drag *once* to shape the curve between the two points.

However—and this is one of several confusing aspects—you can choose *when* to perform the drag. You can do either of the following:

- Drag after laying down the start point, and then click once on the end point.
- Click once to create the start point, and then click and drag to the end point.

PART

Life in an Object-Oriented World

You were warned: this stuff is impossible unless you put hand to mouse or tablet. So open a new window and try the following two maneuvers:

1. From the Curve flyout, choose the Bézier tool (the second from the left).
2. Click once anywhere on the page.
3. Move the mouse elsewhere.
4. Click and drag. As you drag, you will be creating a smooth curve.

Press the spacebar twice to disconnect from the curve. Then try it this way:

1. This time, define the curve when you pick the start point. Click anywhere on the page, and then drag the mouse away from that point.
2. Release the mouse and move it elsewhere.
3. Click once. The path between the two points is automatically a curve.

You can also use Bézier mode to create a series of straight lines by clicking from one point to the next, and this we feel is the most efficient way to create shapes. It's easier than using the Freehand tool because you don't have to click twice in a row.

The important thing to understand here is that all curve segments in DRAW are in fact Bézier curves. (The Bézier curve is a science, not just a CorelDRAW feature. It was developed by French mathematician Pierre Bézier as a way of describing the dynamics of a parametric curve, for use in streamlining automobile design.) The essential difference between the Freehand tool and the Bézier tool is how you create the curves. With the Bézier tool, you do it explicitly; with the Freehand tool, you draw as if you had a pencil in your hand and you let DRAW figure out the details. And again, you can create straight lines with both tools, which, ultimately, is how we recommend you create many of your shapes.

Undrawing with Eraser and Knife

We like to refer to these two tools this way because they start their work only after you have already drawn something. As part of the toolset in the Shape Edit flyout, the Eraser and the Knife tools are as close as the DRAW user will get to sculpting: they allow you to create by removing elements.

Figure 4.9 began as a rectangle. Then we went to the Eraser tool and started undrawing. When used on a selected object, the Eraser tool eats into that object, chewing up and removing nodes and paths in its way. The Eraser tool is relatively crude, with no auto-smoothing. Creating the sun was easy—it's a simple shape—and so was the cloud. But the hills were difficult and the lightning bolt and rays of sunshine were agonizing, all requiring considerable cleanup and refinement with the Shape tool.

FIGURE 4.9

We used the Eraser tool to cut and chisel a rectangle to produce this simple picture.

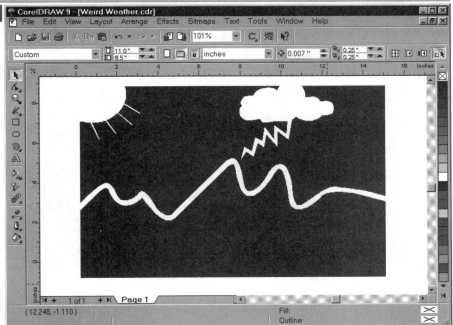

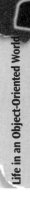

So it is not the process that is noteworthy with this drawing, which we acknowledge to be inefficient. And we don't consider it to be a piece of fine art; it rises to about the level of cute. But what makes our meteorologically confused drawing worthy of notice—and the reason you'll find it as `Weird Weather.cdr` on the companion Web page —is that the entire thing has been sculpted out of a rectangle. This drawing is not a dark backdrop with white-colored objects on top. There is only one object here, with one color, the dark background. Everything else has been cut from the background, with the Eraser tool making the big cuts and the Shape tool cleaning up after it.

Figure 4.10 adds a small stream, created with the Knife tool. The Knife can slice an object into two, and once done, the two pieces can be separated. So again, the river is not a white object; it is another gap between subpaths of this one object.

What is so important about this technique? After all, you could create the same look with white objects in front of the dark background, and if you needed it to be all one object, you could use Combine to do it. But the idea of erasing parts of an object is novel to vector drawing, and performing this feat manually—i.e., using the Shape tool and meticulously slicing up an object—would be so tedious and confounding as to be unthinkable. The Eraser and Knife tools provide a way to work with an object that would otherwise not be considered. You probably won't use the Eraser or Knife very often, but because no other tool works quite like these, when you do need them, you'll *really* need them.

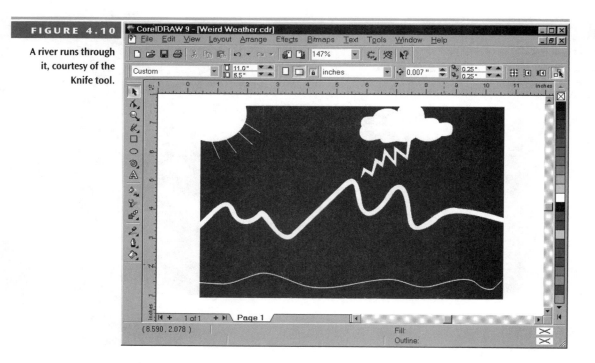

When a Curve Isn't a Curve (Yet)

Although it's true that all objects created in DRAW have paths and nodes, not all objects behave the same. As mentioned at the beginning of the chapter, ellipses, rectangles, polygons, and text strings are given special status. They have properties that DRAW considers sacred.

Draw a rectangle on your screen, and you'll notice a few things. First, in the status bar, the rectangle is called a rectangle, not just a curve. DRAW considers practically everything to be a curve (even a straight line is called a curve), but this object is special. Second, although this rectangle clearly contains four nodes, the property bar reflects only rectangle properties, even when you choose the Shape tool. *This rectangle cannot be shaped or node-edited.* With the exception of its corners, which can be rounded, the rectangle's shape is sacred.

Ellipses have the same status. The Shape tool cannot be used for node-editing, but by clicking on the node in an ellipse and dragging it around the circumference, you can create pie slices and semicircles.

And, as mentioned earlier, when you node-edit a polygon, you'll find total symmetry across all of its sides. Move a node, and the others move too; add a node, and another is automatically added to each side. (You can create some nice effects by selecting nodes of a polygon and spinning them.)

T I P   The essential properties of ellipses, rectangles, and polygons remain intact when you use the Shape tool. You can use the Pick tool to size or even skew them, but you cannot perform any node-editing.

Node-editing in text strings is somewhat more involved, but the techniques follow the same dynamic as with ellipses, rectangles, and polygons. Node-editing a character or group of characters is akin to local text formatting: you can adjust letter spacing, control baseline shift, and work with basic formatting, such as typeface, style, and size.

In Figure 4.11, the last few characters are crying out to be shifted to the left—a perfect job for the Shape tool. The figure shows that the string "erned" is already selected, and a simple drag or nudge to the left will close the gap between letters.

FIGURE 4.11

When used with text, node-editing can kern and format selected characters.

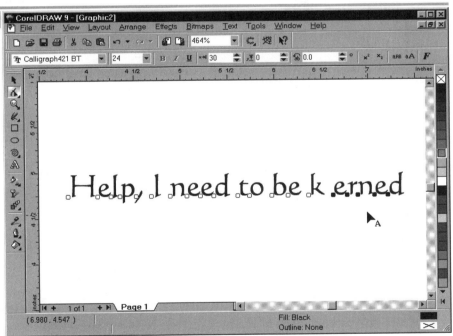

In none of these sacred objects can you add a node, shape the path between nodes, or change the basic properties of the object. Rectangles must have four corners, ellipses must have a single curve, and text strings must have a full character set and typeface formatting.

N O T E   If ever there's a time to use Nudge or the Ctrl+drag combination to constrain movement, it's when you're kerning characters. For instance, when moving the text string in Figure 4.11 closer to the other characters, it is of paramount importance that you keep it aligned to the baseline. You can ensure this by pressing Ctrl while you drag the characters to the left. If you forget to use Ctrl and you suspect that the selected characters have wandered off the baseline, make repairs using the Align to Baseline command from the Text menu.

Converting Objects to Curves

But my, how quickly the mighty can fall from grace. It takes but a single mouse click to knock these privileged classes down a peg. The command responsible for the demotion is Convert to Curves, on either the property bar or the Arrange menu. Apply this command to a selected rectangle, and you reduce it to a plain old curve. Haunt a circle with it, and you can then add a dozen nodes and disfigure the circle for life. Impose it upon a string of text, as shown in Figure 4.12, and you'll never again be able to edit the text.

W A R N I N G   Before you convert a text string into a collection of curves, make sure the text says what you want it to say. Once converted, there is no turning back (except with Undo).

In each of these events, the object (or string of text characters) becomes a collection of paths and nodes. As Figure 4.12 shows, former text characters get no respect. Once you use Convert to Curves, their basic shapes and outlines can be freely altered.

Step by Step: a Potpourri of Tracing Options

The most important lesson you can learn about the Shape tool may be this: *You don't need to make a curve perfect the first time!* Nodes and paths are forever editable and changeable and can always be reshaped later. It is usually better to rough out a general shape, and then go back and clean it up (especially if you use our recommended technique during the roughing-out phase). Trying to make it perfect the first time will likely take you much longer than it will to make two passes.

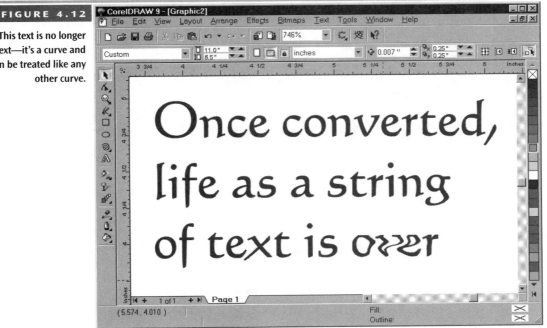

FIGURE 4.12

This text is no longer text—it's a curve and can be treated like any other curve.

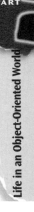

At this point, we want to remind you of the mission of this book: it's not to make you a master illustrator, but rather to help you add confidence and skill to your existing sense of design. Based on watching both new and experienced users fumble with node-editing and Bézier curve drawing, we believe the best course of action is a combination of the following three strategies:

- Lay down the basic shape of the curve as simply as you can.
- Concentrate on placing nodes correctly.
- Draw lines first; convert them to curves later.

Imagine an artist formulating an idea for a sketch. How fastidious do you think he or she would be at this early stage? Many artists use the back of an envelope or the margins of the daily newspaper to sketch out their ideas. When starting out, the artist wants merely to collect thoughts, dump ideas, and "catch the muse." Making the work perfect comes later. And so should it be with you, the DRAW user—even more so, as today's electronic tools make it easier than ever to change your mind and adjust elements.

In the following exercises, we look at several different strategies for tracing a shape. Tracing an existing shape is an essential activity in DRAW, not to mention an outstanding way to practice your skills. These exercises use the file `seagull.jpg` (see Figure 4.13) found on the companion Web page for this book on the Sybex Web site (www.sybex.com). Your mission is to re-create this bird, as faithfully as you can, using the tools covered in this chapter. When you import the seagull to DRAW, it will serve as a tracing template for you to place "underneath" your work.

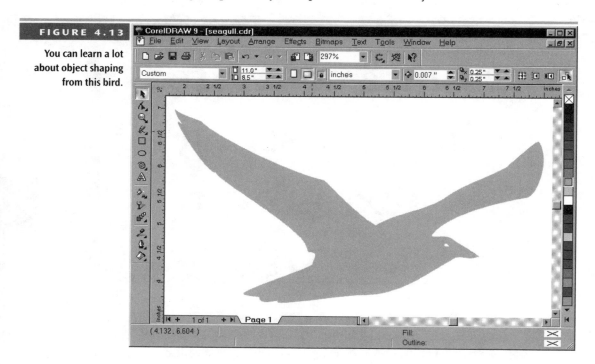

FIGURE 4.13

You can learn a lot about object shaping from this bird.

Where Do the Nodes Go?

To answer this question, we are reminded of the wonderful quote from Dr. Albert Einstein, who declared, with reference to nothing in particular, "All things in life should be as simple as possible, but no simpler."

This is gospel in the annals of freehand sketching or tracing. If you create too many nodes and curve segments, your sketch will be bumpy. If you don't use enough nodes, your sketch will lack accuracy and detail.

Your success as a sketch artist in DRAW rests significantly on your ability to recognize where nodes belong. You wouldn't be far off by concluding that a node needs to be placed at the points where a curve turns a corner, and indeed, many corners need a node. But to be technical, nodes belong at the points along a path where the shape changes direction, and by that we mean where it changes from clockwise to counterclockwise, and vice versa. If you choose the right node type, you can describe almost any type of shape, as long as it goes in just one direction.

Using the Bézier Tool: Not Quick, Just Clean

Most artists agree: when you need to trace or create a precise shape, the tool of choice is the Bézier, and that is what we will show you first.

1. After you have downloaded `seagull.jpg` and placed it in a known location on your system, go to File ➤ New to begin a new graphic and use File ➤ Import to retrieve the seagull. Click once to place the seagull on the page at full size.

2. Once the seagull is on your page, right-click on it and choose Lock Object. This way, you won't inadvertently move it. If you're going to trace it, you want it to sit still.

TIP   Experienced with Layers? If so, you could create a new layer, move the seagull to it, and lock the layer. More on Layers in Chapter 32.

3. Press F4 to move in as close as you can.

4. Activate the Bézier tool from the Curve flyout and start at the top-left corner of the bird.

On your own, see if you can identify the places where nodes belong. To place a node, simply click once with your mouse. Look for places where the shape turns a sharp corner and where the shape changes direction. (We'll give you a hint: this seagull can be completely described with 24 nodes.) Navigational skills are at a premium when you are doing close node work, so remember these maneuvers:

- Press F2 and draw a marquee to zoom in on any location.
- Press F3 to quickly zoom back out.
- Press F4 to show the entire drawing.
- Use Alt+arrow keys to scroll your screen without having to mouse down to the scroll bars.

Also keep in mind the following node-creation tips:

- If you place a node in the wrong place, don't worry. You can Undo with Ctrl+Z, switch to the Shape tool momentarily and relocate it, or just forget about it for now. You know you'll be refining it later.

- If you stop for any reason, you can pick up where you left off by clicking once on the last node you created. That tells DRAW to continue connecting the nodes.

- Your last click should be right on top of your first click. That is how you tell DRAW that you are done and that you want your curve to be a closed shape.

After 10 minutes of work, here is what our screen looked like.

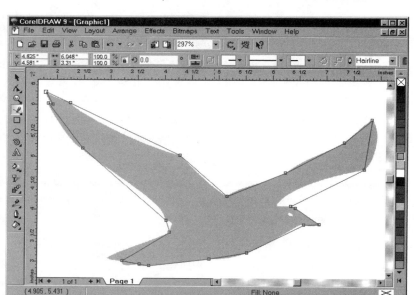

Our shape doesn't look at all like the bird, nor did we expect it to. Our sole focus was in placing nodes in the right places. There might be a few places were we were too ambitious. Can this swooping curve above the bird's beak be represented in just two nodes?

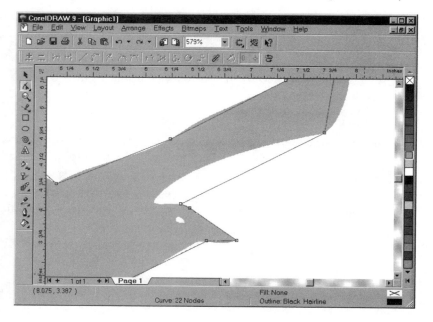

Perhaps not, but we know that we can always add more nodes if we have to. We would rather create too few than too many. Now you are ready to continue:

5. Switch to the Shape tool and go to Edit ➤ Select All ➤ Nodes (you can also press Ctrl+Home).

By default, paths that you create with single clicks begin as line segments, made obvious in the images shown earlier. Most of the nodes will be curves, however, and it is our experience that it is easier to turn everything into curves now and send some of them back to lines as you go.

6. With all nodes selected, click the Curve icon on the property bar, and then the Smooth icon. As soon as you do, all line segments will become smooth.

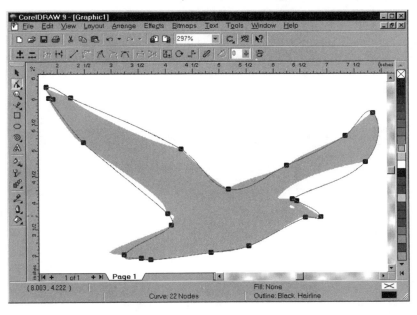

7. Now start shaping the nodes, trying to fit them to the contour of the bird. As you proceed at your own pace, keep in mind these things:

  • If a node isn't in the right spot, just pick it up and move it.

  • If you need another node, click on the line segment nearest it and click the plus icon on the property bar or press the plus key on your keyboard.

  • As you shape line segments, the other side of the node will move, also. This isn't a bug, it's a feature, but if you don't want that to happen, do one of these two things:

    • Convert the node to a cusp, using the property bar.

    • Use the control handles to shape the curve, instead of the path. The curve might still move on the other side of the node, but not by as much, and if you move directly toward or directly away from the node, the segment on the other side won't move at all.

Generally, the sharp corners will need to be described by cusp nodes, and we didn't find any places where symmetrical nodes were required.

To create the bird's eye:

8. Use the Freehand tool (or even just the Ellipse tool) to create the basic shape.

9. Node-edit to taste (if you use the Ellipse tool, convert the ellipse to curves and add a node or two as necessary).

10. Using the Pick tool, select both the eye and the body and go to Arrange ➤ Combine (or Ctrl+L) to turn them into one curve.

11. When you are done, select the bitmap, right-click to unlock it, and delete it.

12. Select your bird and shade or color it as desired.

We have no illusions that this will be a simple task. Shaping and manipulating nodes is not exactly an intuitive procedure, and it is unlikely that you can draw on past life experiences that would make it easier. This is probably uncharted territory for you. It took us a good 30 minutes to complete, and it could very well take you two, three, or four times longer.

Here is our version of the seagull, with 24 nodes—as simple as possible, but no simpler.

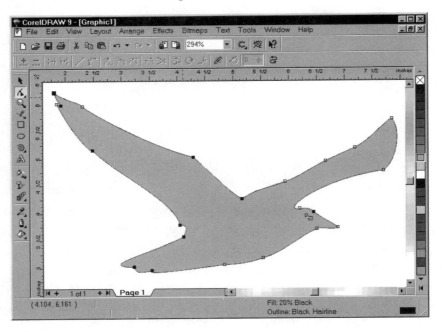

Of those 24 nodes, 10 of them are cusp nodes and the rest smooth. In the above graphic, we blackened the nodes that we turned into cusps, for your reference. Note that we were successful in describing the severe curve above the beak with just two nodes (even though it is a sharp angle, it doesn't change direction). On the other hand, we needed four nodes to depict the bird's tail, what with all those sharp angles.

This exercise really drives home the point, so we'll say it one more time: creating in DRAW is entirely different than actual drawing or painting, where you simply place ink or paint on a page.

You'll find `seagull.cdr`, our finished version, on the companion Web page for this book on the Sybex Web site.

Going Freeform: Head for the Hills!

One alternative to the Bézier route is the Freehand tool. First, let's distinguish between the two ways you can use it:

- If you click from point to point, you are essentially doing the same thing as you did in the Bézier exercises earlier in the chapter. The difference is that you have to click twice on each node to connect them.

- If you click and drag the Freehand tool, you are simulating use of a pencil.

There's just one problem: your mouse is no pencil, and even if you used a tablet, the screen is no sheet of paper. In short, tracing or creating a shape by dragging a cursor across the screen is, at best, a tedious affair, and at worst, a graphical disaster waiting to happen.

The only point that mitigates this is DRAW 9's new Freehand Smoothing tool (see the section "Draw Straight, Curve Later" earlier in this chapter), which does its best to eliminate unnecessary nodes and smooth over rough edges. Nonetheless, here is the best we could muster.

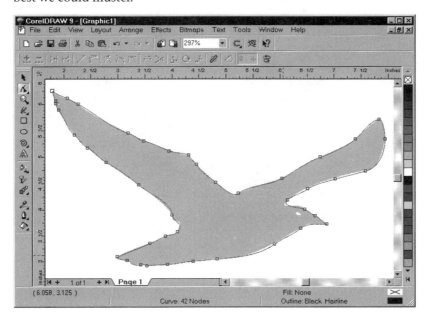

PART

Life in an Object-Oriented World

This drawing is significantly better than the pathetic chicken scratching we spewed forth using DRAW versions 8 and earlier, but even with Freehand Smoothing, it's unacceptable. The most damning point of all is what the status bar tells us: 42 nodes, almost twice as many as needed. To refine this graphic, you would have to first determine which nodes to eliminate and then move the surviving ones to their proper homes. Or not...you could leave them where they are...and settle for a lower fidelity image...and hope that nobody notices.

No, this is one of those times when going the extra mile pays off. By taking the time to place the nodes properly, you tell your audience that you know how to create high-quality shapes with DRAW.

Autotracing: You Might Get Lucky

The final avenue of object creation is akin to a get-rich-quick scheme: you might get lucky...but probably not. If you need to trace an object, and that object can come to you in the form of a monochrome bitmap, you could try DRAW's built-in autotracing module. Think of this as the microwave oven in the CorelDRAW kitchen. It can warm up a meal, but it won't cook it. Unfortunately, in the case of our seagull, it didn't even get it lukewarm.

We had a chuckle over the effort at the lower left: it's as if Autotrace started to head to the right to go behind the tail, then said to itself, "Nah, forget it," and turned back up the wing. We'd trade such consciousness for a bit of intelligence. Until then, you're not likely to get much satisfaction out of Autotrace.

And What about CorelTRACE?

There is one more place you can turn to as a tracing strategy—the *real* tracing utility. CorelTRACE is one of the applications in the CorelDRAW box, and it is more intelligent and skilled at converting bitmap art into vector.

Some say it's easier to use TRACE than to manually trace around an object. However, if you were to poll the *Mastering CorelDRAW 9* team of writers and artists, you would find no consensus on this question. Some believe that TRACE is an excellent starting point; others don't trust it.

Regardless of our collective or individual dispositions about TRACE, we don't think it's wise to depend on it for node-editing and curve creation. We think learning the manual skills is a necessary fundamental.

TRACE could be considered a viable tool as long as it used in tandem with a conscientious clean-up session in DRAW. It did produce a pretty good starting point.

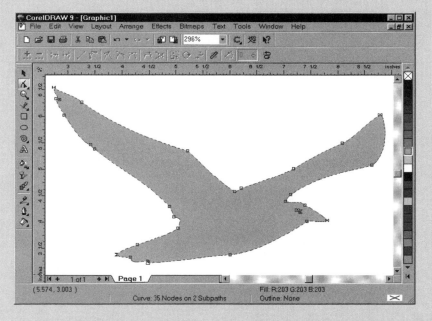

But as with the Freehand method, there are too many nodes, each extraneous node adding an unnecessary bump to the picture. Also, TRACE used cusp nodes throughout, resulting in a harsher image with coarser corners.

CorelTRACE can provide you with a workable starting point for bitmap images that you want to convert to vector, as long as you understand your role as cleaner-upper. And with clean-up promising to take longer with an autotraced image, we would just as soon see you hone your drawing skills and create the object yourself.

chapter 5

MAKING ARRANGEMENTS

Featuring

Making
Arrangements

s we leave the clubhouse turn in this part of the book, covering CorelDRAW fundamentals, you have already been exposed to much of the essence of vector-based drawing. This chapter completes the picture on ways that objects can be manipulated, and if you are in search of a course syllabus, then pull down the Arrange menu. To an item, those are the topics we'll cover here.

Transformations 101

Moving an object is easy—you've already learned that. You click and hold on it while you drag the mouse. Same with sizing, stretching, skewing, and rotating—they all can easily be done with your hand and your mouse.

But some actions must be carried out with precision, and for those times, you'll want to get up close and personal with the Transformation docker, available from Arrange ➤ Transformation. The five pages of this docker cover all of the types of basic actions that can be performed on objects or groups of objects. We define "basic" as meaning that the object still maintains its core identity, unlike if a special effect were applied to it. The five transformations are:

- Positioning
- Rotating
- Scaling and mirroring
- Sizing
- Skewing

All five of these transformations can be done by hand and mouse, but not with the precision possible from the docker controls. Figure 5.1 shows how you might move an object to the right by a prescribed amount. We are about to click Apply and make it happen; if we were to click Apply to Duplicate, that would be the same as the drag-and-dupe operation discussed in Chapter 3.

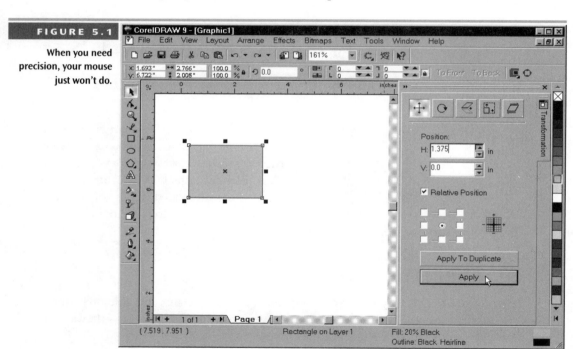

FIGURE 5.1

When you need precision, your mouse just won't do.

However, we must mince our words a bit. While these new docker windows are spiffy and powerful, we know from our surveys that many of you prefer to perform your precision operations from the property bar. And for good reason—if you study Figure 5.1, from left to right, you'll see all of the basic transformation controls present:

- Object Position
- Object Size

- Scale Factor (change just one of the two values to skew; click down the lock icon to prevent that)
- Angle of Rotation
- Mirror

We have nothing against Corel's dockers, but we see far less need to visit them these days. The dockers and the property bar handle basic services identically. In the following sections, we'll discuss the services that are available only in the dockers.

T I P To find out what an icon on the property bar does, hover your cursor over it for a moment, and a description will appear.

Working with the Transformation Dockers

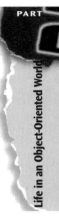

Working these docker windows is easy, so instead of a tutorial, here are a few rules of thumb.

Select the Object First!

If you don't have an object or a group selected, all five of these docker windows will be dormant, grayed out, and otherwise asleep.

Apply to Duplicate

All five of the Transformation dockers offer this button, providing *blank*-and-dupe services. You fill in the blank: drag, rotate, scale, size, skew. They all can be accomplished on screen with your mouse or through this group of dockers, the latter offering precision that your mouse, hands, and screen couldn't approach.

The property bar controls do not have Apply to Duplicate capability.

The Check Box and Tic-Tac-Toe

Each of these dockers offers a check box that you can click to further define the operation. In two of them—Position and Rotation—the option determines whether the values for horizontal and vertical placement describe the object's movement with respect to a fixed reference point (like the edge of the page), or relative to the current position of the object.

In the Scale & Mirror and Size dockers, you can provide for proportional operation, in which changing one direction (horizontal or vertical) will automatically cause the other to change by the same proportion. And in the Skew docker, the Use Anchor Point check box does nothing at all unless you also use the grid to indicate an anchor point other than the center.

This grid, which we like to call the tic-tac-toe controls, determines from which part of the object the transformation is to take place. If you use Position and you click the lower-left box in the grid, the object will move down and to the right. Click top-middle and the object moves straight up.

We have been writing about these check boxes and tic-tac-toe grids since 1993 and we still don't know them by heart (we always have to play with them before we write up this section). We could do a long, exhaustive treatise on them, but they are the kinds of tools that must be used to be understood.

So use them. Go to the Position docker and see how object placement differs with the different tic-tac-toe positions. See what Non-Proportional does to the sizing of objects. See how the anchor affects skewing.

You Say Potato, I Say Inches

DRAW maintains a link between the units of measure in all of the Transformation docker windows and the general settings for the drawing. For example, if you set the unit of measure to centimeters for your drawing, all docker windows will speak to you in centimeters.

This used to be a terrible flaw when the unit of measure was hidden in a dialog. In order to transform an object in a different unit of measure, you would have to go to a subdialog off of a flyout menu and change the measuring system for the entire drawing.

Now things are easier, for two reasons:

- To change the unit of measure for your drawing, you can deselect all objects and use the Drawing Units box on the property bar.
- You can enter any unit of measure you want, provided you know its abbreviation:

Inches	in
Millimeters	mm
Picas, points	pc
Points	pt
Ciceros, didots	cc
Didots	dd
Feet	ft
Yards	yd
Miles	mi
Centimeters	cm
Meters	m
Kilometers	km

Continued on next page

Knowing these abbreviations, you could, say, move a rectangle 6 points to its right, irrespective of the prevailing unit of measure for the drawing. You would enter 6pt as a value in the Position docker. DRAW automatically converts the number into the current unit of measure so, if your drawing were in inches, the docker would display .083 inch for 6 points.

You can use this technique not only in the Transformation dockers, but in the property bar and any place throughout the program that accepts values in the standard measurements.

Friendlier Degrees

In the eyes of many, DRAW 9 is finally starting to get it right in the rotation department. To best describe what Corel's engineers are now doing right, we'll first tell you what they have been doing wrong all these years.

"Want to louse up a perfectly level rectangle?" we asked in the last edition of this book. "Draw one and then open the Rotate or the Skew roll-up. Now apply the following degrees of change to it, one after the other: 17, -3, 38, 11, 16.6, -29, and 61. Okay, now return the rectangle to 0 degrees, so it's level again. We don't know how to spell the sound of 'Urrrghnt, Reject!' but that is the first thing that comes to mind."

Why couldn't you do it? Because DRAW did not keep track of the degree of change with respect to an object's original condition. There was no option to "remember original position," or any such safeguard. So each time you entered a rotation, DRAW added that change to the previous one.

This was true of the property bar and all of version 8's roll-ups (except Position with the Relative Position option unchecked). In all other cases, the only way to return the object to its original position was to Undo like crazy, manually reverse the operations by entering the opposite value for every number entered, or have your calculator close by and ready to figure out the object's exact percentage or degree of change at any given point.

Corel knows that this has driven its users nuts, and in version 9 they fixed the most egregious example: rotation. With DRAW 9, the Rotation value in the property bar tracks degrees of rotation with respect to the object's original position. So if you enter 15 degrees of rotation, the object moves counter-clockwise, and the value in the property bar stays at 15. If you then change it to 10, the object rotates clockwise back to 10 degrees.

This one little improvement will be responsible for fewer four-letter words uttered in CorelDRAW's presence.

Please note that this new behavior is only present for Rotation and only from the property bar; the dockers all continue to treat degrees of rotation and skew as cumulative values. Therefore, we continue to recommend the strategy of storing a copy of the object in the Clipboard before you begin transforming it. Then you can return the object to its original condition with Delete followed by Ctrl+V.

The Curse of the Scaled Outline

When stretching objects that have visible outlines, two things can happen to the outlines: absolutely nothing or nothing good. What determines this fate is a control within the Outline Pen dialog, called Scale with Image.

If Scale with Image is off, the object's outline stays set at the original thickness regardless of how much stretching, sizing, or skewing you do to the object. If you check Scale with Image, the outline scales with the image, *but only in the directions you stretch*. Figure 5.2 illustrates this. The original rectangle at top-left uses the default setting, with Scale with Image unchecked. The original rectangle at lower-left is set with Scale with Image checked on. As each rectangle is stretched in one direction, the results are obvious.

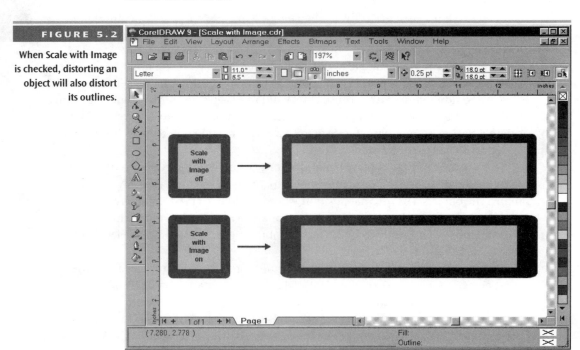

FIGURE 5.2

When Scale with Image is checked, distorting an object will also distort its outlines.

The Scale with Image option is crucial when an outline needs to be sized relative to the size of the object, but if you expect to be distorting the object, it would be better to keep Scale with Image off and size the outline manually.

Aligning with Aplomb

Object alignment is among the most crucial of activities for those who create precision drawing, and that is why we were so delighted to see such clever improvements in DRAW 8. The controls for alignment come alive anytime you select more than one object. Actually, that's not entirely true, because you can align single objects relative to the page—the controls treating the page itself as the second object.

Figure 5.3 shows many of the ways that a basketball can be aligned to its backboard. Because the horizontal and vertical controls can be combined, we would need about four complete pages to show all of the permutations. The lower image shows how the two can be combined.

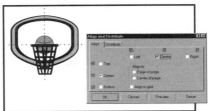

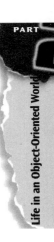

PART

Life in an Object-Oriented World

The Align and Distribute dialog is helpful for introducing the alignment controls, but it has effectively lost its job to the wonderful accelerator keys that control alignment. Introduced in Chapter 3, these shortcut keys are worth showing again. Select any two or more objects, and the following keystrokes swing into action:

L	aligns left
C	aligns center
R	aligns right
T	aligns top
E	aligns middle
B	aligns bottom

These keys can be used in succession, making CE the world's fastest way to align one object directly in the middle of another. This is awesome for creating text boxes: marquee-select the text and the container, press C and E, and you're done.

Distributed Thinking

The other page of the Align and Distribute dialog is—you guessed it—Distribute. You might not use it very often, but when you need it, it's like a gift from above. Its job description is simple: to make the space between objects even. You determine through the dialog (sorry, no accelerator keys) what part of the object is used for orientation—top, middle, bottom, left, etc.

The following succession of images shows the typical dilemma with distributing objects and the happy ending. In beginning a calendar, we set the days of the week as separate text strings, each one placed on the page according to random clicks with our mouse, with only a half-hearted attempt to place them.

These days of the week need to be evenly spaced from one guideline to the next, and without Distribute you would have to do one of the following: (1) set an elaborate grid, (2) get out your calculator, or (3) become lucky.

First off, aligning them to a common baseline is absolute cake: select them all and press B.

Now you need to think for a moment. If you distribute them according to the left of each text string, the longer days will knock into their neighbors.

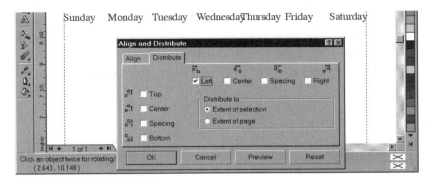

For that matter, using the text as a reference point won't work in any capacity. It's that darn Wednesday, being so much longer than the rest.

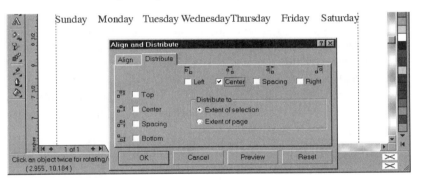

What you really want here is to even out the space between each day, rather than the starting positions of each day. And the Distribute tab of the dialog offers that very option.

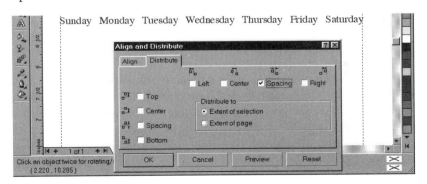

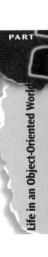

PART

Life in an Object-Oriented World

N O T E　Veteran users will discover soon enough that Ctrl+A has been usurped by the Select All command to bring DRAW in line with standard convention. First off, know that you can always reassign that keystroke back to Align and Distribute if you find such conformity loathsome. Second, the property bar offers quick access to the dialog when two or more objects are selected. Third, with those accelerator keys, you might find your trips to the dialog increasingly scarce. We wish there were a quick way to get to Distribute...

The Rest of the Team

The other commands on the Arrange menu are straightforward, so we will just describe them briefly. To see how they are used in various exercises throughout these chapters, consult our index.

Order

This is DRAW's gateway to creating stacking options of objects. Most drawing programs offer ways to place objects in front of all others and behind all others. DRAW does one better by allowing you to specify precisely which object the selected one should be placed in front of or behind. With an object selected, go to Arrange ➤ Order ➤ In Front Of (or Behind). DRAW offers you a pointing arrow, and once you click on an object on the page, DRAW instantly stacks the selected object accordingly.

It's good to know the hotkeys here:

Move to front	Shift+PgUp
Move to back	Shift+PgDn
Move up one place	Ctrl+PgUp
Move back one place	Ctrl+PgDn

You can also reach all of these commands from the context menu, the one that appears when you right-click on the selected object.

Group

There's not much to say about this venerable command. It throws a lasso around all selected objects. Ctrl+G and Ctrl+U have become second nature to keystroke lovers. Note the presence also, on both the Arrange and context menus, of an Ungroup All command. Many pieces of clipart come with groups inside of groups. This command will find the groups nested within other groups and ungroup them, too.

You can always select objects within groups by holding Ctrl as you click. DRAW will display rounded selection handles as your cue that you are working with objects within a group.

Combine and Break Apart

These two cousins are opposites. Combine takes selected objects and forces them into one curve. As we discussed in Chapter 3, overlapping objects appear as hollow cutouts. Meanwhile, Break Apart does the reverse, seeking out any subpaths to a curve and extracting them as separate objects.

The notable exception is with text. Two strings of artistic text, when combined, become one string of text, still editable. One string of text, when broken apart, becomes single-character individual letters. A double-deck headline, when broken apart, becomes two separate strings consisting of the first line and the second. The same in all of these cases goes for paragraph text.

If, however, you combine a string of text with a nontext object, DRAW shows no such reverence—it converts everything to a single curve.

Both commands are available via hotkeys (Ctrl+L and Ctrl+K, respectively) and from the context menu.

Lock and Unlock

Any object created or imported can be locked and made impervious to change. When you select a locked object, the selection handles look like little padlocks. No change can be made to a locked object until it is unlocked, from Arrange ➢ Unlock or from the context menu.

Shaping

This is the gateway to the three noteworthy commands for dealing with overlapping objects. Intersect, Trim, and Weld are the stars of Chapter 11.

Separate

It might sound like Break Apart, but this command is different. While you can use Break Apart on any object that contains subpaths, Separate is reserved for taking apart objects that have been altered with one of DRAW's special effects.

When you apply commands such as Fit Text to Path, Blend, Extrude, Contour, and Drop Shadow, you create a dynamic link between multiple objects. That link allows the effect to adjust as you move or edit one of the objects. For instance, if you move or recolor one of the objects of a blend, the entire blend adjusts. This link stays live until you kill it, and you do that with Separate.

This is not an Undo command—the appearance of the effect remains. You are telling DRAW to stop thinking of the objects as part of a dynamic effect, but rather just a collection of objects that happen to look like the effect.

Figure 5.4 shows the result of separating an extruded star. Until we moved the face of the extrusion, you wouldn't have known anything had happened. But once separated, each object that makes up the effect can be individually reached.

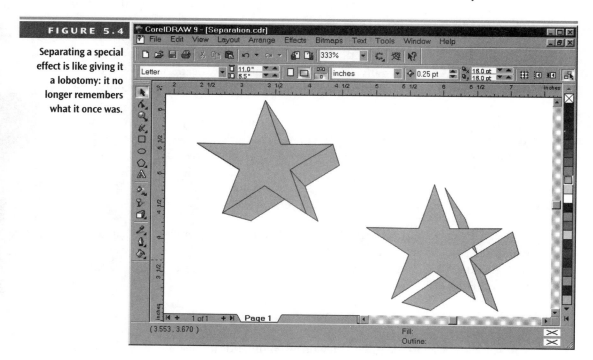

FIGURE 5.4

Separating a special effect is like giving it a lobotomy: it no longer remembers what it once was.

Convert to Curves

This is the command that strips VIP status from rectangles, ellipses, polygons, and strings of artistic text. In each of those objects, DRAW reserves a certain reverence. It will not allow conventional node-editing to them, using the Shape tool instead for different purposes (such as rounding corners of rectangles, making pie slices from ellipses, and kerning characters of text).

The Convert to Curves command is what makes the mighty fall. Once converted, these special objects become distinctly unspecial. Once converted, you can node-edit a rectangle as if it were just another common curve. Same with text.

Convert Outline to Object

This brand new command separates an outline that has been applied to an object and makes it its own object. It converts it to a closed shape, however thin, and that has enormous implications for designers who have long wanted to apply a pattern to an outline, instead of just a uniform color. Once an outline is converted to an object, it can take any fill pattern that DRAW offers. Creating fountain-filled outlines has historically been very difficult; now it is easy.

PART

Life in an Object-Oriented World

APPLYING FILL
PATTERNS

Featuring

APPLYING FILL
PATTERNS

We remember the good old days of, oh…about two years ago, when the concept of a filled object was quite simple. If the object was a closed shape, you could pour a color into it. If you wanted to get fancy, you could use a rainbow of colors, and for the nirvana of fill patterns, you could use a texture to fill a shape.

Well, what a difference a few years can make. Now you can fill objects with pictures, drag and drop colors onto objects, pick up existing colors, and oh yes, you can fill objects that aren't even closed. In few places is the war among vector drawing programs felt more than with the filling of objects.

Understanding Fills

Despite the shenanigans of the techno-age, there's nothing terribly complicated about the concept of applying fill patterns. In Chapter 4, "As the Curve Turns," we concerned ourselves with creating the outside edge of a shape; the *fill* is simply that which is placed inside the shape. Any color, shade, or pattern inside an object is considered a fill.

The following sidebar notwithstanding, all that is typically required to fill an object is closure of the shape. The Interactive Fill tool is the gateway to every type of fill available, most of which are represented in Figure 6.1.

FIGURE 6.1

A few of the countless types of fills available within DRAW

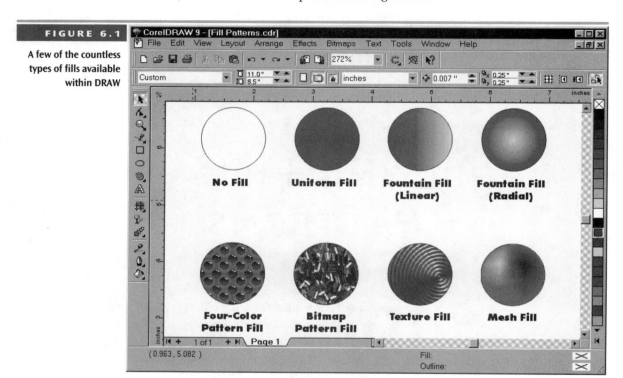

Death of a Sacred Cow: Filling Open Objects

As of DRAW 8, Corel took one of the fundamental rules of vector-based drawing and stomped all over it. Now you have the option of allowing DRAW to fill open curves. To do this, go to Tools ➢ Options ➢ Document ➢ General and check Fill Open Curves. Now apply the fill as you normally would.

When the selected object is an open curve, DRAW connects the first node to the last node using an imaginary line, and then applies the fill. What is this world coming to…

In editions past, we had to create full-page graphics, with lots of lines pointing hither and yon, just to show you the many tools, dialogs, and roll-ups that pertained to fills. The landscape is much cleaner now; in fact, you can satisfy all of your filling needs in two places:

- The Interactive Fill tool, from which you can apply every type of fill available in DRAW

- The Fill dialog, where you choose the color model and apply the specific color of a fill (DRAW 9 offers the Fill dialog as a docker, also.)

Not to imply that object fills make up a neat and clean science; they don't. A microcosm of CorelDRAW itself, fills are easy to apply but difficult to master. Underneath the controls lies a labyrinth of interrelated functions and dialogs, up to three levels deep in some cases. Nonetheless, at the risk of oversimplifying, DRAW's fill capabilities can be divided into five categories:

Uniform   A single color or shade covers the entire selected object.

Fountain   Colors or shades gradually change as they traverse the object. There are four types of fountains: *linear*, *radial*, *conical*, and *square*.

Patterns   A repeating pattern covers the object. There are four types of patterns: *two-color bitmap patterns*, *full-color vector patterns*, *full-color bitmap patterns*, and *PostScript textures*.

Textures   An artistic blend of bitmap images is poured into the object.

Mesh   Probably falls into one of the above categories, but these fills are so new that none of us is quite sure what to make of them just yet.

Applying Uniform Fills

It doesn't matter what type of fill pattern you are using—the tools behave the same. Let's say you have created a square on screen and you want to color it blue. Once you select it, here are the routes you could take.

Using the Dialog

Click the Fill flyout and choose the first icon, Fill Color (hotkey: Shift+F11).

- If you know the exact CMYK mixture, enter it. In this case you do: blue is defined as 100% of both Cyan and Magenta.

- If you seek a particular Pantone flavor of blue, click the Fixed Palettes tab and hunt for the specific name or number. If you want a Web-friendly blue, choose one of the Internet-ready palettes—Navigator or Explorer—from the drop-down list of this same tab.

- If you seek a blue from a custom palette, such as the default `coreldraw.cpl` palette, click the Custom Palettes tab, choose the desired palette, and find your blue.

The four faces of the Uniform Fill dialog—Models, Mixers, Fixed Palettes, and Custom Palettes—are shown in Figure 6.2.

FIGURE 6.2

The four ways to describe color in DRAW

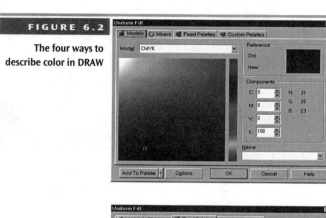
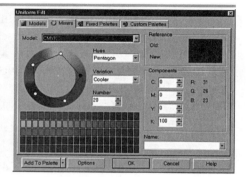
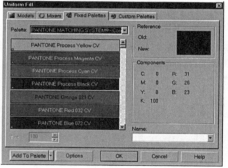
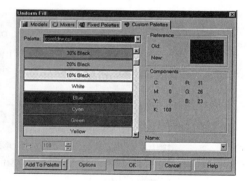

Setting a Default Fill

The very first time you create an object, it shows up on screen with a black outline and no fill at all (unless it's a string of text, in which case it is the opposite—black fill and no outline). You can change this. If you would rather have your newly created objects take on a light-gray fill, cyan, or even just solid white, you can change DRAW's defaults—either for the current session or for all time.

WARNING When working with color, if you trust your monitor's representation of the color that you'll get on the final printout, you're in for a rude and potentially costly surprise. To put it plainly, monitors lie. They emit light and display color very differently from a printing press that's applying ink to paper. DRAW has built-in features to compensate for monitor distortion; but during crunch time, when your color projects are on the line, you should trust only printed samples, like the color swatch books from Pantone and TruMatch. Both will show you exactly what a color will look like when printed. More on this in Chapter 27.

Using the On-Screen Palette

Find the color blue you want and click it *or* find the color blue and drag it on top of the object.

At first, we thought that this drag-and-drop-a-color feature, introduced in DRAW 8, was just a gimmick. After all, why would you want to perform a click-drag-and-drop to assign a color when you could just click? But then we discovered its value: when you have lots of objects to fill with different colors. The advantage that the drag-and-drop method enjoys over the conventional is its ability to fill an object that isn't selected. So, if you had five different objects that each needed its own color, you could do a bunch of drag-and-drops without having to stop and select each object. Having said that though, we find that to be its only virtue.

If you need to select a color that is not in the current palette, see the section, "All about Palettes."

Using the Color Docker

1. Go to Window ➤ Dockers ➤ Color.
2. Change the hue with the vertical slider.
3. Adjust the color values with the large square grid.

   or

   Enter the exact values directly, as shown in Figure 6.3.
4. Click Fill to apply the color.

NOTE   The Color docker will be of no use to you if you are picking colors from a fixed palette. You can dial in any combination of CMYK values, RGB, HSB, HLS, etc., but not specific palette colors such as Pantone 1271 or Focoltone 5016.

FIGURE 6.3

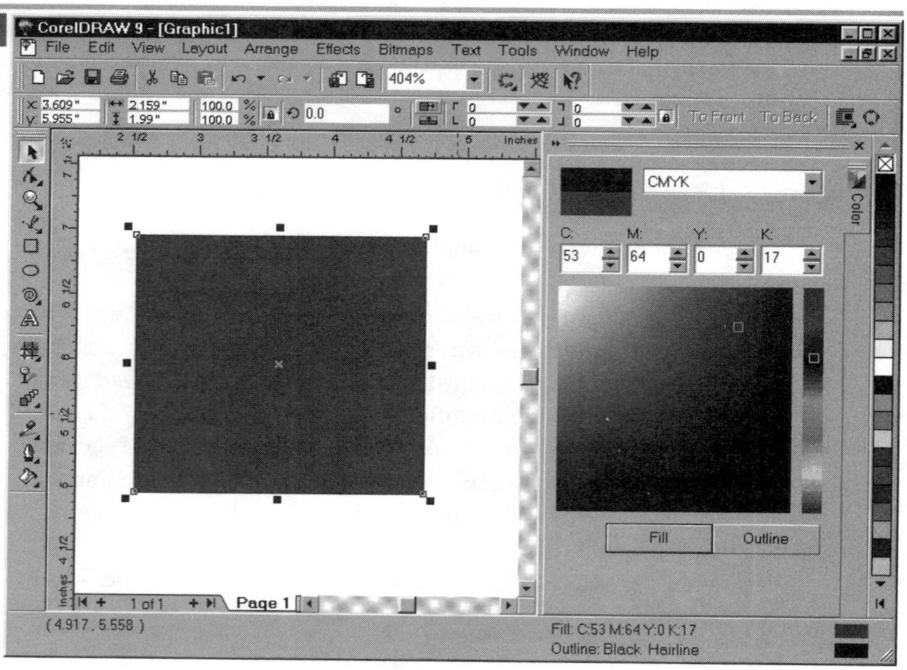

The new Color docker gives continuous access to the colors in a given color model.

The process is easy: you simply forget to select an object! Normally, you select an object before heading for one of the fill tools. But before invoking the Fill dialog or the Interactive Fill tool (discussed soon), make sure that no object is selected. DRAW offers you the dialog shown in Figure 6.4, and then once you OK your way through it, you are allowed to continue on your way. Whatever change you make will affect objects you create henceforth, be they graphics, strings of artistic text, or frames of paragraph text.

TIP   You can also change your default fill color just by clicking on one of the colors on the on-screen palette, after making sure that no object is selected.

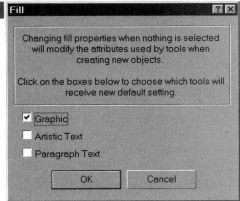

FIGURE 6.4

Forgetting something?
DRAW assumes not. If
you continue, you will
change the default for
any or all of the three
types of elements you
create with DRAW.

And now for the question that we receive perhaps more than any other: "I changed my default object color to cyan, but whenever I close and reopen DRAW, it's back to hollow. How do I make it permanent?"

We usually drip sarcasm all over our answer—like, "Well, you stand on one foot, wave a paper bag over your head, except on Tuesdays…" But we direct it at Corel's engineers, because they did seem to go out of their way to hide the control in the Options Jungle, as we like to call it. To make your new default permanent, go to Tools ➤ Options ➤ Document, check the box labeled *Save options as defaults for new documents*, and then check Styles. When you change the default fill, you are making a change to the so-called Default Graphic Style for that drawing. It is this Document page within Options that extends that change for all drawings you create from this point forward.

Knowing this, you could set your default fill to be one of the exotic fill patterns you'll be reading about next. Please don't…

Adding Flair with Fountains

One step removed from uniform fills, fountain fills (also known as *gradients*) describe an ever-changing pattern of colors, beginning on one side of the object and proceeding to the other. Those "sides" can be either left side to right side or inside to outside, and in either case, you define the transitions that comprise the fountain of color. You can also tell DRAW how abruptly or gradually to make the transition, and where to begin making the transition.

The absolutely simplest way to create a fountain fill involves two keystrokes:

1. Create a simple object on screen.

2. Press F11 and then Enter.

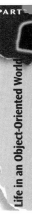

PART

Life in an Object-Oriented World

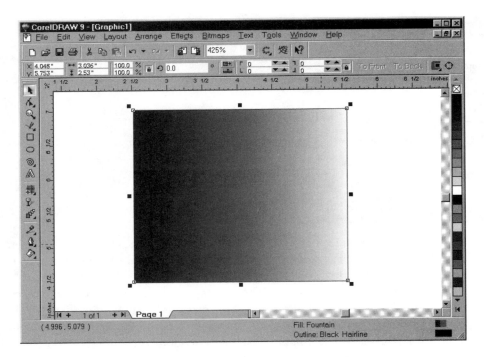

See, fountain fills are easy! Kidding aside, you were able to do that so fast because the Fountain Fill dialog has a hotkey (F11) and the dialog begins with a default pattern of black on the left side and white on the right. Pressing Enter simply accepted the default. You can also reach the Fountain Fill dialog by clicking on the second icon in the Fill flyout (although we're not sure why anyone would want to go to that trouble when F11 is so handy).

Let's return to the Fountain Fill dialog. Many of the following graphics show the result of the fountain along with the dialog that created it.

3. Change the Type of fountain from Linear to Radial.

4. Change the Center Offset either by entering values for Horizontal and Vertical, or better yet, by dragging the center in the preview at top-right.

5. Click the starting color (the "From" color) and change it from black to another dark color, like blue. Note that the little drop-down palette contains all of the colors in the current palette, and the Others button is the door to the Select Color dialog, where you can choose any color imaginable.

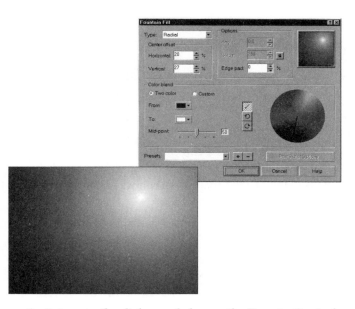

6. Return to the dialog and change the Type to Conical.

7. Adjust the offset as you did in step 4 above.

8. Hold Shift and then move about in the preview. Note that you are now changing the angle. (If you hold Ctrl also while operating the preview window, you constrain rotation or offset changes to 15 degrees and 10 percentage points, respectively.)

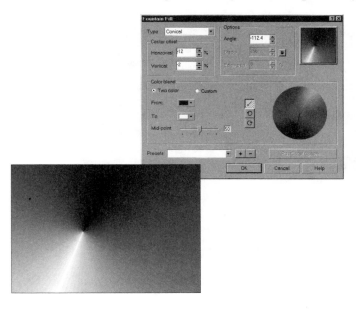

9. Change back to Linear and reset the angle to 0.

10. Dial up the number in the Edge Pad box and note in the preview window how the starting color waits longer before it begins to change and then changes faster. In essence, edge padding is the process whereby the start and end colors stay at their original colors longer, before transitioning.

To review, the default fountain is a linear fountain fill—one that flows evenly from one side of the object to the other. Radial fills change in concentric circles from the inside to the edge of the object. In a conical fill, each band of color extends from the center to the edge of the object. With the square fountain fill, the gradations of color are produced by small rectangles that work their way from the center to the outside.

Now things will start to get exciting…

11. Click on Custom and note that instead of simple From and To colors, you now have a continuum of colors.

12. Double-click somewhere in that continuum and note that a small triangle appears above it. You have now identified a new stop along the way between your start color and your end color. The triangle is solid, indicating that it is selected; you could select either of the end colors, and the small red square at the end color would become solid.

13. With the triangle still selected, click red on the palette. Your screen should look like this.

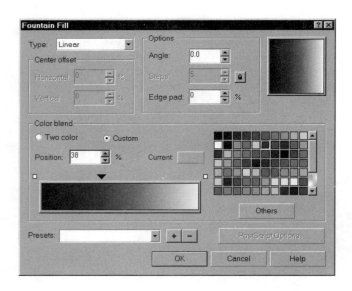

You can move your new midpoint color anywhere else in the continuum by dragging it or by entering a value for Position. And you can create new midpoints just by double-clicking. Create a few more, assign colors to them, and slide them around. After a few minutes of playtime, we produced this psychedelic specimen.

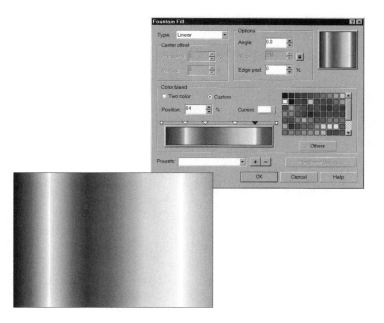

Please be advised that the technical limit of 99 intermediate colors far exceeds the limits of good taste.

Pop Quiz for Advanced Users

So you think you know your way around fountain fills? Answer this: What is the quickest way to create a fountain fill that spans the widest possible color range? Give up? You create a fountain with the same From and To colors. No, we are not under the influence of any mind-altering substances…you choose a color in From and you choose the same color in To. Oh…did we forget to tell you to click the little circular arrow? The one that sends the fountain all the way around the color spectrum?

Continued on next page

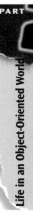

Life in an Object-Oriented World

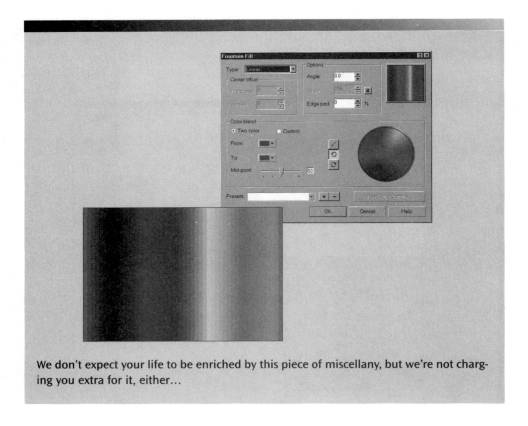

We don't expect your life to be enriched by this piece of miscellany, but we're not charging you extra for it, either...

Making Sense of Steps

There is one more option in the Fountain Fill dialog that can have a significant impact on your work: intermediate to advanced users will want to get a good understanding of exactly how the Steps field works. Steps (under Options in the Fountain Fill dialog, usually grayed out) controls the number of *bands* used to display and/or print the transition from one color to the other.

This can get confusing because there are two other places in the program where you can effect this change, and the three controls interact. Most of the time, you will probably keep the Steps field in its *locked* position (notice the little padlock to its right); when you do, Steps is determined by the value set under Tools ➢ Options ➢ Workspace ➢ Display ➢ Preview Fountain Steps (PFS). Locked, therefore, means the value is locked to the default value of the PFS setting. That setting is dynamic and global—change the PFS, and the display of all objects with fountain fills will adjust, as long as their Steps value is locked.

If you unlock Steps and enter a value in the Fountain Fill dialog, you are overriding the PFS default and establishing a permanent and fixed number of fountain steps for both displaying and printing that particular object.

This leads to the third place you can control the number of steps in a fountain fill: the Print or EPS Export dialog. If you change the Fountain Steps (FS) setting during printing or EPS export, you are setting the steps for any fountain fills whose Steps value remains locked, but an unlocked fountain fill retains its Steps value. Unlocking the steps of a fountain fill supercedes any other action. If you keep it locked, the FS setting controls its output and the PFS setting controls its display.

If this confuses you, follow this advice: Do nothing. Ignore all of this. Doing nothing usually works just fine, because both the FS and the PFS default to 256—a value more than sufficient for printing and displaying.

So when would you want to change these values? Here are our recommendations:

- Keep the Steps value in Fountain Fill locked, except when you want a particular fill to have a specific number of visible and printed steps. Figure 6.5 shows the outcome of changing the Steps value.

- Don't change the PFS setting in Tools ➢ Options ➢ Workspace ➢ Display unless your system slows down when displaying fountain fills. Most systems today are fast enough to render this point moot, but judge this for yourself. Radial fountains tend to be the most taxing, so create a bunch of radials on a page, press Ctrl+W to refresh the screen, and check performance.

- During printing and exporting, adjust the Fountain Steps setting as needed. But again, unless you are seeking a particular print effect, there is little reason to change this value.

NOTE For PostScript printing and EPS exports, use the Auto Increase Fountain Steps option. When checked, the optimum number of steps is calculated at printing time based on the resolution and screen frequency of the output device, and each fountain fill (or pair of colors in a custom fill) is increased to use that number of steps. Or, for faster output, use Optimize Fountain Fills, which reduces the number of steps to the maximum number that can be printed by the device.

Like a Fountain Fill? Bottle It

If you create a certain fountain fill over and over again, you can capture its settings as a *preset* and apply it to other objects. Simply create the fountain fill, type a name in the Presets field of the Fountain Fill dialog, and save it by clicking on the plus button at the right. Your new settings are then available to any object within any .cdr file. This holds true until you delete the preset (by selecting it in the Presets drop-down and clicking on the minus button).

PART

Life in an Object-Oriented World

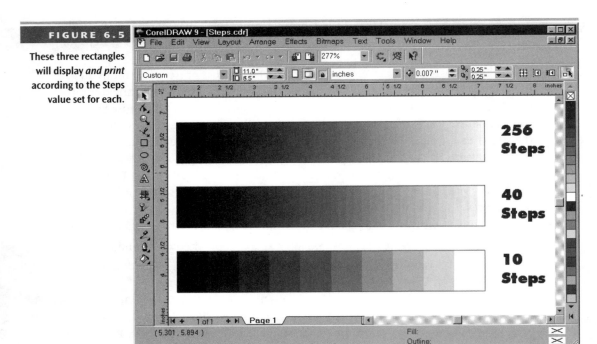

FIGURE 6.5

These three rectangles will display *and print* according to the Steps value set for each.

We recommend that you name your presets with a special character as the first letter, like &Sunset or %Gold Plating. That way, they will show up at the top of the Presets list. There are so many presets that Corel gives you, the ones you make will get lost in the shuffle unless you force them to the top.

A Word about Choosing Colors

Nothing is more fun and exciting than mixing many colors to produce rainbows and fountains on color displays. Printing them, on the other hand, is an entirely different matter, and mistakes can be costly. Before you go wild with fountain fills, you should know both your target output device and your budgetary constraints.

Printing to a color desktop printer

In this case you can go wild. Color laser printers, thermal transfer printers, and ink-based printers can create virtually any color. Use your imagination and (please!) your own good taste.

Continued on next page

Creating four-color separations

If you plan to create four negatives, one for each of the CMYK colors, then you can once again spread your wings. You can be confident that whatever colors DRAW uses, your four pieces of film negative will be able to represent them. But the important caveat is the unfortunate fact that your monitor will not accurately represent the colors that will actually appear in your printed piece. This is true in all cases, not just fountain fills; you should always confirm your color choices with a swatch book or reference of printed samples. The problem, however, is that it is difficult to know just what colors exist in the middle of a fountain fill. You need to have a pretty good idea that your start and end colors are complementary and will blend well, and ideas like that only come from practice. (Keep reading for a new DRAW 9 feature that addresses this.)

Creating spot-color separations

Here you must proceed with caution. Covered in detail in Chapter 27, spot-color printing is the method for adding just one or two extra colors to a project, not four. Instead of using the CMYK model, requiring four separate pieces of film, you designate specific colors—the spot colors—and your print house makes a print run for each color (typically black and one spot color).

You can create a fountain fill with spot colors, and DRAW will create transitions that are made up of just those two spot colors. But you are in treacherous waters, as it's anybody's guess what will actually come off press. The safest way to create fountain fills with spot-color jobs is to use one color and vary its tint:

1. In the Fountain Fill dialog, define the From color. Click on the First Fill button, then Others, then Fixed Palettes, and choose, say, Blue Pantone 072.

2. Use the same Blue 072 for the To color, but assign a different tint to it, like 30%. You can set a tint to any spot color.

This gives you a nice fountain, staying entirely within your Blue 072 color. The transition will be from 100 to 30%.

Going Interactive

The fountain fill has benefited from the move to interactive tools as much or more than any other feature in DRAW. The steps we outlined above for creating custom fountain fills aren't necessarily complicated, but they are unwieldy, what with all those trips to drop-down menus, dialogs, and subdialogs.

With the Interactive Fill tool, all of the controls are on the property bar, and instead of working in a little preview window, you manipulate the actual object on screen. The following images show how quickly you can turn a plain rectangle into a credible sunset.

This first graphic is your starting point—a rectangle with a default fountain fill of black on the left and white on the right. We used some mountains from Corel's clip-art library, just so we could have the sun setting behind something.

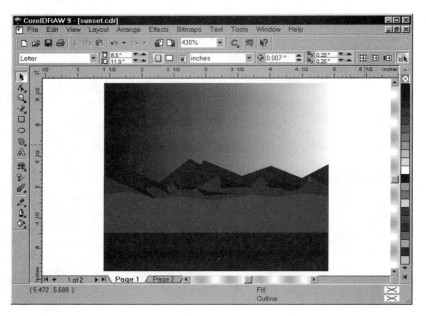

As soon as you select the rectangle and choose the Interactive Fill tool, the rectangle sprouts special control handles.

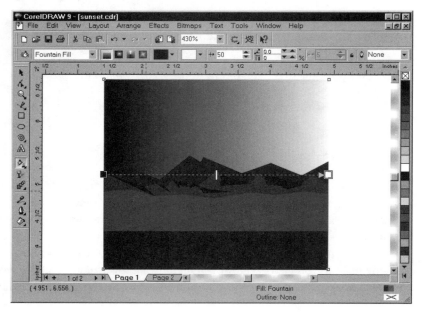

By simply grabbing the handles and moving them, you can change the angle of the fountain fill. You move the start handle up from the bottom, as most of the lower half of the rectangle is covered by the mountains.

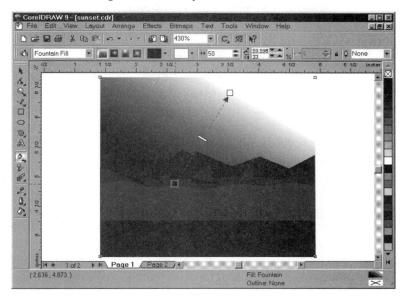

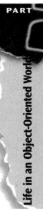

Changing the start and end colors and adding midpoint colors is the easiest of all: you simply drag and drop colors from the on-screen palette. You can drop colors on the start or end control points, or anywhere along the line. You drag yellow to the lower control handle and pink to the top handle. Then you deselect and admire your work.

The Last Word on Fountain Fills

Here is our parting thought concerning fountain fills: when in doubt, *don't use them!* If you are undecided about whether the use of a fountain fill will add any value to your drawing, then it probably won't. And it might very well detract.

In fact, if you output your final work on a 300dpi printer or reproduce your work on a photocopy machine, *never* use fountain fills with a high Steps value. Your laser printer or the down-the-street copy machine simply can't handle the density of the dot patterns, and you will look like an amateur designer who tried for too much. The only fountain fills you should attempt in this case are ones with low Steps values, designed to have blunt transitions, or ones with very coarse dot patterns. The 600dpi laser printers can produce credible results, provided you keep the From and To colors close together—for instance, from 15 to 45%.

If you expect to use fountain fills regularly for projects destined for film, read the discussions about setting PostScript halftone screens in Chapters 26 and 30.

When desktop publishing first struck it big, you could spot an amateur job from across the building: it had large Helvetica type inside a rounded rectangle with a gray background. Today, the dead giveaway of a bush-league electronic illustration is the misplaced fountain fill. If you want to help rescue the community of electronic designers from this collective notoriety, approach fountain fills with caution and restraint.

Applying Complex Fills

The next four fill tools—the ones that produce patterns—constitute the frills. In fact, these patterns often go largely unused, even by very talented and skilled DRAW users. Pattern fills are like Web page backgrounds—they tile across and down to fill the entire object. Here is a brief run-through of the four tools that produce patterns for your objects.

Two-Color Patterns

Three types of pattern fills are readily available from the property bar once you select the Interactive Fill tool. They are also combined in a single Pattern dialog, available from the third icon on the Fill flyout. The two-color fills include several dozen bitmap patterns that can be quickly applied to selected objects. Try this:

1. Create a closed object and make sure it is selected.
2. Select the Interactive Fill tool, then Pattern Fill in the drop-down list on the property bar.

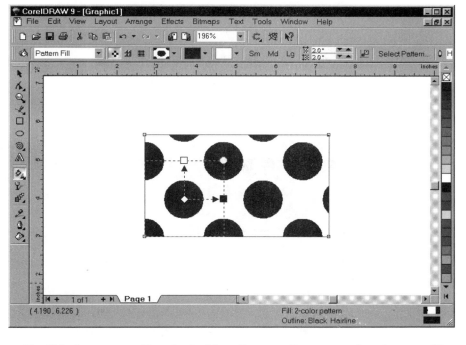

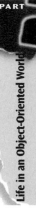

You'll feel at once as if you're inside a Gateway Computer advertisement (the ones with the cows and the big black spots). We wish for Corel to change the default pattern, as it doesn't exactly put the prettiest face on pattern fills. Be that as it may, the graphic above shows the effect of choosing patterns and the controls that DRAW offers. Experiment with all four handles that appear in the graphic:

- The one at bottom-left moves the center of the pattern.
- The white square on top sizes the pattern vertically and is also where you drop a color to change the background.
- The dark square on the right side sizes the pattern horizontally and controls the foreground color.
- The round button at the top-right sizes the pattern proportionally.

Most of the controls on the property bar are all obvious and intuitive, starting with the drop-down list, from which you choose the type of fill, to the three types of patterns available and the choices available in the current pattern, colors, and sizes:

Transform Fill with Object Determines whether the pattern sizes when the object is sized. The default is No, meaning that the pattern stays the same size and the object acts like a window to the pattern: open the window wide, see more of the pattern; close it, see less.

Select Pattern   We don't know why this isn't called Create Pattern, because that's what it does. With it, you can turn on-screen objects into a pattern.

Tiling   This governs how the pattern repeats. If you want to control the tiling of the pattern in more detail, you will want to work the controls in the dialog, available by clicking the far-left icon on the property bar.

Creating Your Own Patterns

If you can't find the pattern you want, you can always make your own. Any objects you create, paste, or import into DRAW can be turned into two-color bitmap patterns with the Tools ➤ Create ➤ Pattern command, or from the Select Pattern button on the property bar. Drag a marquee around the area, and DRAW will create a pattern from your objects and put it in the pattern preview box.

You can also create your own pattern from scratch with DRAW's built-in Pattern Editor, operating at the pixel level. Click Create from within the Pattern Fill dialog.

Full-Color Patterns

Because full-color images use the entire CMYK spectrum of colors, virtually any color can be represented in a full-color pattern. These are more useful for abstract work, where you want to use a more prominent background than a solid color. Figure 6.6 shows how one of these patterns could be used for a simple advertisement, and our example brings up an important point: sometimes these patterns detract rather than contribute. We like the cleaner ad better...

To create a new vector fill, use the Tools ➤ Create ➤ Pattern command in the same way as you do for two-color fills, but choose the Full Color option from the Create Pattern dialog before you marquee-select the area to be used for the pattern. You cannot change any of the colors in a vector pattern from the Pattern dialog. When making your own full-color patterns, you need to define all of your colors before you create the pattern.

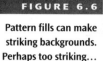

FIGURE 6.6

Pattern fills can make striking backgrounds. Perhaps too striking…

N O T E   Full-color vector patterns are saved as DRAW files, but with .pat instead of .cdr filename extensions. You can open and edit these files as you would any other DRAW file, or use any other existing DRAW file for a vector fill. The vector fill patterns supplied with DRAW are located in the Custom\Patterns directory. Any pattern you create within DRAW is saved there; any DRAW file that you create, name with a .pat extension, and place there will be available for pattern use.

Bitmap Patterns

Bitmap patterns are implemented like the other two pattern types, but they make it possible for you to place full-color photographs or other images within objects. You can import any bitmap image and use it as a pattern by using the Load button in the Pattern Fill dialog, but you cannot create bitmap patterns from selected objects. (Well, actually…you could export an object in DRAW to a bitmap file and then load that file back in.)

Although any external bitmap can be imported to use as a bitmap pattern fill, remember that all of DRAW's supplied fills are designed to create a seamless effect when tiled. So if the design of your imported file is not symmetrical, it will not produce an attractive fill pattern.

We think that we improved our ad by using the bitmap pattern shown in Figure 6.7.

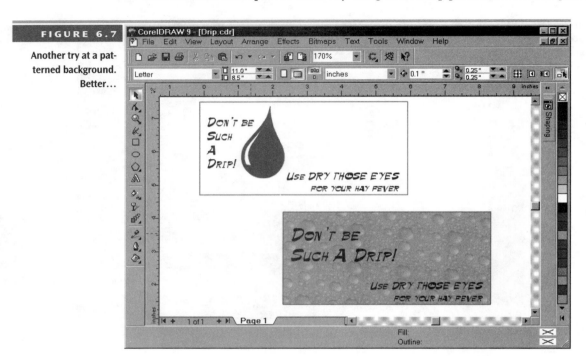

PostScript Patterns

These sophisticated fill patterns are, in essence, little programs written in the Post-
Script page-description language. Although you cannot add your own pattern, you
can alter the existing ones significantly using various controls provided in the
PostScript Texture dialog.

Because DRAW has a built-in PostScript interpreter, you *can* preview PostScript patterns on screen, provided you switch to Enhanced view by going to View ➤ Enhanced.
This is a tremendous time-saver, especially for anyone who customizes PostScript patterns. And that's not all: you can also output them to practically *any* printer, PostScript
or non-PostScript.

Texture Fills

Texture fills are bitmap images that will display on any screen and print to any laser
printer or imagesetter. Texture fill patterns are based on a library of bitmap images, all
produced according to an engine that allows individual aspects to be adjusted with
breathtaking precision.

N O T E   The Texture Fill dialog contains the same Tiling options as in the Pattern Fill dialog, including x- and y-axis controls; size, width, and height adjustments; skew and rotate angles; and percent row or column offset.

Figure 6.8 shows one of the more elaborate textures, a multicolored mineral fill, along with the dialog box that created it. Twelve individual properties make up this texture, and each component can be separately adjusted. The color selection buttons are gateways to the Select Color dialog.

FIGURE 6.8

This texture fill makes for a (warning, bad pun coming) rock-solid background.

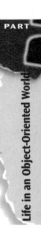

Texture fills have a decidedly video-game nature, and the Preview button is intended as a random generator of different textures. Each of this dialog's primary controls has a lock icon next to it, and this takes a bit of explaining. When you click on Preview, every element that is not locked will change randomly. The Softness % value might change from 83 to 17, the Brightness % from –22 to 60, the Texture # from 5742 to 28475, and the colors to just about anything in the spectrum.

But if you manually change a setting, the Preview button shows you the result of that change, without shuffling any other numbers. In other words, locking any element prevents it from being randomly changed, but you can always change an element manually, locked or not.

Wanted: More RAM, Larger Drives

These elaborate textures can devour memory, hard drive space, and printer resources. If you apply them to large objects or put many of them on a page, be prepared for some backtalk from your hardware. As a test, we created a rectangle and filled it two ways, with a simple fill pattern and with a texture. Here are the essential statistics of the two operations:

Fill Type	Size of File	Code Sent to Printer	Time to Print
Uniform	14K	26K	3 seconds
Texture	119K	291K	17 seconds

There are many different possible images for each texture. In the case of the mineral fractal, you can browse among 32,767 different variations.

Browse these textures for yourself, but we suggest you not get carried away. After all, let's say you wanted to see every possible permutation of one of the simpler ones—say Aerial Photography, which has controls for just Texture #, Softness %, Brightness ± %, and Background and Foreground colors. Let's see…32,768 textures, 0 to 100% for Softness, Brightness settings ranging from –100 to +100, and millions of possible values for the foreground and background colors. That's about 11,892,928,546,860,000,000,000,000,000 variations for just Aerial Photography. And among DRAW's various texture libraries, there are nearly 200 different texture fills, most of which have more permutations than this one. We think you can see our point…

DRAW's Newest Fill Tool

We await two different types of responses from the greater CorelDRAW community when the new Mesh Fill tool gets some mileage under its belt:

- Sheer glee at the wonderful fill effects it can produce
- Utter horror at the dreadful fill effects it can produce

Like any new special effects tool, there will be equal parts use and misuse, and we'll root for the former to prevail over the latter. Mesh fills have been requested for some time now, as a more flexible alternative to fountain or texture fills. When you reach for the Mesh Fill tool, DRAW places a grid over the selected object. Each quadrant of the grid can be filled with a color, and you do that with a simple drag-and-drop from any color palette. Different colors placed into neighboring quadrants will blend at the borders, creating the effect of the colors "meshing."

Continued on next page

A fountain fill works in only one direction, and even a custom fountain fill with multiple colors, set in a radial or a conical pattern, is really just a linear effect. But a mesh can move across a grid in any direction, changing colors on an electronic dime.

As you begin to work with mesh fills, you'll notice that the color placed most recently tends to predominate its neighborhood. This means that you'll want to be strategic not only in your color choices, but in the order you define them. And as with fountain fills, if you try to span too great of a color shift in a small area, you will create a very harsh look.

The best mesh fills (like fountain fills) are ones that produce the subtle color shifts that reflect the way light behaves in real life. They can produce a measure of realism beyond that of simple fountains or blends. Study the graphic below and you'll agree that the color shifts in the objects would require complex blends. In fact, each of them was created with a mesh fill.

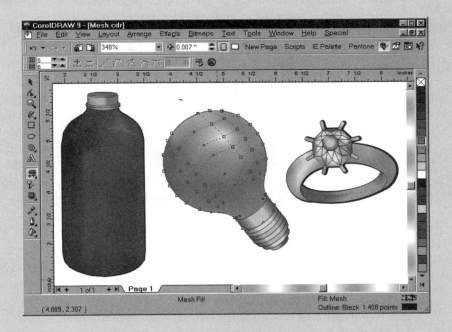

In the graphic, we selected the light bulb so you can see what the grid looks like. You can shape the grid as freely as you do nodes of any curve, providing even greater flexibility in the appearance of your meshed objects. You'll see another example of a mesh fill in Chapter 15, Figure 15.4.

The Appeal of the Palette

Of all the electronic metaphors for traditional artisan tools, none is quite as elegant as the palette. Even if you don't know which end of the paintbrush to use, you surely have an image in your mind of the painter, brush in one hand, palette in the other. The palette has all of those pretty little dots, each a different color. Each painting might use its own palette with an entirely new set of colors.

And so it is for CorelDRAW users, just not with the same tactile charm and allure. On the electronic side, a palette is a set of colors available for use on objects in a drawing. Typically, colors in a palette have a common bond, and that bond could be hues and shades (like a gray palette), type of usage (like a palette of eye or hair colors), or anticipated output (like a palette for Internet graphics).

While the science of palettes runs deep, you might glean all you need to know if you keep in mind the image of a traditional palette. There is really only one other paradigm that you need to understand...

The Concept of the Color Model

DRAW defines a color model as different from a color palette. While a palette has a fixed number of specific colors associated with it, a color model represents a formula used to produce colors. Usually millions of colors.

The most obvious example is the CMYK color model, used for identifying colors in traditional color printing. An exhaustive range of colors exists by mixing the right percentages of the four colors cyan, magenta, yellow, and black. *K* is for black rather than *B*, so that it's not confused with blue (which is actually not a primary color but a mixture of cyan and magenta). DRAW's default color palette, `coreldrw.cpl`, is based on the CMYK color model.

Okay, let's say that again, because these are important distinctions. There is a palette called `coreldrw.cpl` (all palettes have `.cpl` extensions). It consists of exactly 100 colors, and they all have names, such as Navy Blue, Deep Purple, Pale Yellow, Dusty Rose, etc. The *model* on which this palette is based is the CMYK color model, which is capable of producing millions of individual colors.

There are four reasons why `coreldraw.cpl` is used so extensively:

- As the default palette, it is the one that DRAW starts with, and many users feel no need to switch to a different one.

- Its color choices are very friendly, as it offers shades of gray in 10-percent increments, all of the standard rainbow colors (blue, red, green, orange, violet, etc.), the four process colors (cyan, magenta, yellow, black), and a host of other colors that look pleasing to the eye.

- Because it's based on the CMYK color model, you can check a color's components in a swatch book, like the TruMatch Color Finder.
- And it is a *custom palette*, meaning that you can add colors to it, remove colors from it, and edit colors in it.

If painters need a color that is not on their palettes, they can reach for other paints or they can mix two colors from their palette to create a new color. In DRAW, the metaphors for those two actions are:

- Open a different palette
- Go to the Select Color dialog or docker and mix a color

Remember, regardless of what palette is on screen, you can always go to the dialogs or the docker to mix or choose another color. And if you find a color that you want to use regularly, you can add it to your custom palette, using the Palette Editor shown in Figure 6.9. You can also assign your own name to a color. You can choose a technical name that describes the composition of the color, such as "C13M12Y88;" or one that is more descriptive of the color's use; or even, as in this case, one that reflects your opinion of it. Whatever name you choose will appear in the preview box on DRAW's status bar when you select an object that uses that color.

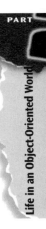

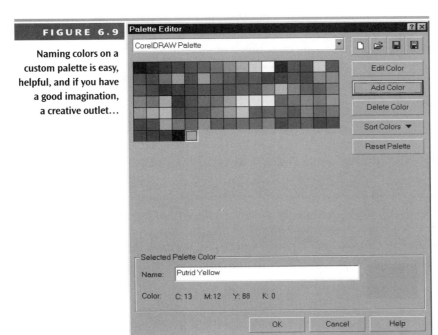

FIGURE 6.9

Naming colors on a custom palette is easy, helpful, and if you have a good imagination, a creative outlet...

If you are producing color-separated work, you should work with a palette that uses the CMYK color model, or choose CMYK-derived colors from the dialogs or docker. If you use a different model, DRAW will convert your color choices to CMYK anyway when you make separations. It's anybody's guess whether the conversion will be to your liking, so it's best to start with CMYK colors for your four-color printed work.

The other color model that you might use regularly is the RGB color model for work that is destined to remain on screen. The obvious application today is the Web site, and indeed, the two palettes for creating Web graphics, the Netscape Navigator and Internet Explorer palettes, are based on the RGB color model. All light sources transmit colors as components of red, green, and blue, and computer monitors are certainly light sources.

N O T E   For more detail on these and all of the other color models, consult the on-line Help where there are numerous explanations. Select Find and search for color, model, CMYK, or RGB.

Using Custom Palettes

Although most users rarely change from the default `coreldrw.cpl` palette, the program ships with several other palettes. To use a different palette as your default, go to Window ➤ Color Palette and choose one from the flyout menu. From that same menu, you can:

- Open the Color Palette Browser, which might make locating and choosing a palette easier

- Create a new palette, based on the color in your drawing or in selected objects of a drawing

- Open the Palette Editor, where you can edit any of the custom palettes

N O T E   New for 9: All palette operations are now under the Window menu. Go to Window ➤ Color Palettes for all operations relative to color palettes. Also, you can now open more than one on-screen palette. The more you choose, the more that will appear.

Creating Your Own Palettes

DRAW supplies palettes based on several different color models, but you can mix additional colors and add them to a palette, rename or change the definitions of existing colors, and create whole new palettes.

Once again, let's create a metaphor to the traditional medium: Imagine you are a painter working on a portrait. You probably have enough paint in your studio to create just about any color you might want, but as you approach a particular project, you choose a few colors in particular. You dab them on your palette and wield your brush. The palette is designed to make accessible to you *the specific colors you have chosen for this painting*. You know you can go get others, but these are the colors you expect to use now.

You can do the painter one or two better, because you can assign names to your colors, and you can choose colors that are from disparate color models. (The painter is stuck with paint, while you can have ink colors and computer monitor transmissions together on one palette.)

You can store your custom palettes in any directory on your hard disk, although it's best to keep them with the others so you can find them easily. All files will be saved as .cpl files.

Let's say you create a monthly newsletter. It uses black and one Pantone color (which you alternate monthly). You also create a Web site for the newsletter. You can create a custom palette for this job so you can have the colors you choose at the ready:

1. Go to Window ➤ Color Palette ➤ Palette Editor.

2. In the Palette Editor, select New, the first icon on the top-right.

3. Enter a filename for your new palette. DRAW automatically adds the .cpl extension.

4. Click on Add Color to be taken to the now-familiar Select Color dialog.

First, you grab black and the various shades of gray that you regularly use. These gray shades come from the CMYK color model, simply by dialing up or down the Black component. The simplest place to get them is from DRAW's colreldraw.cpl palette.

5. Click the Custom Palettes tab and choose black and the various gray shades you want. Click the Add to Palette button at the lower-left each time you find a desired shade.

6. Click on the Fixed Palettes tab, choose Pantone Coated (or Uncoated, depending upon your newsletter), and find the colors you want. If you know the number or general color you want, enter it in the Name box at lower-right and DRAW will help you find it. For instance, just typing **Blue** for Name took us to here.

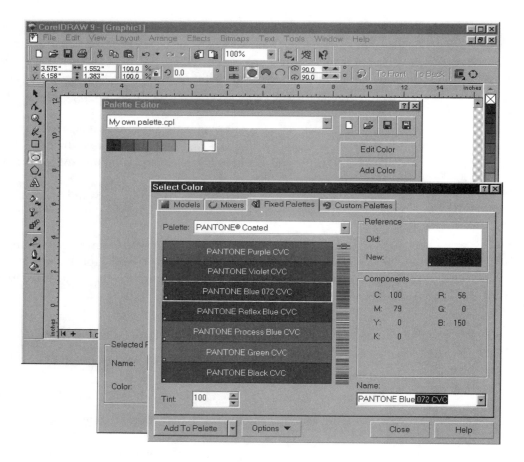

7. For your Web page, find the Internet palette of your choice, find the color you want to use, and click Add to Palette.

8. Click Close when you are done adding colors.

9. Optionally, rename any of the colors in your palette, as shown here.

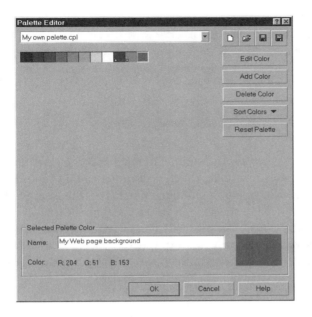

Your new palette won't show up on the flyout menu of palettes (those are all hard-coded in the program code), but you can get to it easily from the Color Palette Browser. As soon as you do, it becomes your default on-screen palette. What's more, because it is so small, you can tear it from its docked position and hover it right over your work, as we have done here.

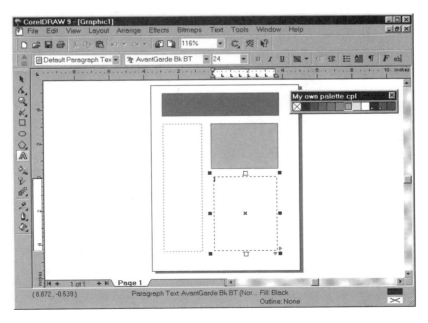

N O T E   When can you add colors to a palette? When it's a custom palette. You can't add a color to a fixed palette like the Pantone palette, unless you are the president of Pantone, Inc. and you are willing to wait until DRAW 2000. A custom palette includes colors that belong to other models or palettes.

Keep It Simple

Restricting yourself to a palette with a limited number of complementary colors is often the best way to produce visually effective documents. This "enforced discipline" is the idea behind the color palettes used in the templates of most presentation programs. However, if you need to spread your wings, remember that you can always use other colors, even if they are *not* on your palette. Just return to Uniform Fill and dial up any CMYK, RGB, or other value you want. Whenever a color isn't named in your custom palette, DRAW will refer to it on the status bar by listing the color model components. Name or no, DRAW will honor your mix of colors.

Make Palettes by Drawing

Thanks to a great new feature introduced in version 8, you can now create a palette of custom colors just by creating a drawing. Two powerful commands, Create Palette from Selection and Create Palette from Document, take the headache out of palette creation. You simply create objects on your page, assigning to them the colors you want in your custom palette. Then go to Window ➤ Color Palette ➤ Create Palette from Selection/ Document (your choice).

On-Screen Niceties

As we begin to wrap up this long chapter, we must point out two handy conveniences that will help you considerably as you manage your color choices. One of them was introduced in DRAW 8, and the other is brand new.

The Eyedropper

DRAW users have been coveting this helpful tool in PHOTO-PAINT for years, and Corel's engineers have finally figured out a way to bring it to the vector arena. With

DRAW's new Eyedropper tool (and its accompanying Paintbucket, which together share the third icon from the bottom of the toolbox), you can pick up the color from any object and apply it to any other object.

1. Activate the Eyedropper tool and head out to the page.

2. Click an object on screen (the color swatch on the status bar changes to reflect the chosen color).

At this point, you are in search of the color that you want to store in the Eyedropper. Any color you find will work. It can be a solid color, a color within a fountain, a color from a photo, even an outline color. If you click it, DRAW uses it.

3. Switch to the Paintbucket (hold Shift to toggle between the two).

4. Start clicking other objects that you have drawn. Each object you click gets filled with the stored color.

To be technical, the Eyedropper should have been called the Syringe. It doesn't drop a color down where you click; it picks the color up from where you click and applies it to the selected object. We're not trying to be obsessed with minutiae here; we just think you'll understand the tool better if you think of it that way.

The Eyedropper property bar is short and sweet: with it you can choose to apply the effect to the outline color of an object instead of the fill color, and you can determine how fine or how blunt to make the Eyedropper. For instance, if you choose the 1×1 size, you are zeroing in on the smallest possible unit, and the color chosen will be precise. On the other side of the spectrum, if you choose 5×5 as your size, you can click on an area that contains more than one color (like in a fountain or where an object's fill meets its outline). In that case, DRAW creates an intermediate color.

N O T E   We think the Eyedropper will find one of its most valuable uses in siphoning out colors that would otherwise be impossible to access. If you are wondering how dark the middle of a fountain fill will be, and whether it will provide sufficient contrast for a blue headline, the Eyedropper can tell you. And because it returns a CMYK value for the color extracted, you can then refer to a swatch book to see precisely the color that will be printed at that position of the fountain.

On-Screen Palette Tricks

Prior to DRAW 8, the personality of the on-screen palette was rather drab. You click on it with either Button 1 or 2 to set the fill or outline of a selected object. Ho hum. DRAW 8 changed all of that with two significant improvements in the way you can drive the palette. Both involve choosing shades and tints of colors that are on the palette.

Neighborhood Colors

If you create a rectangle and color it blue, you can easily try out other shades of that blue. Try this:

> With the object selected and colored blue, find Blue on the palette and click and hold Button 1 for a moment.

The little color grid that appears contains a range of colors related to the original color. A little bit less cyan...a shade of yellow...a touch of black. Each time you glide to a shade on the grid and release the mouse, that new color is applied to the selected object (or designated as the default, if no object is selected).

To return the object to the original color, just click the color on the palette. The swatch on the palette doesn't change to the new color on the grid, and that has been a source of confusion. Many DRAW users have thought that the color grid changes the color on the palette; it doesn't. If you want to edit a color on your custom palette, the Palette Editor can do it. But this technique is simply applying a variant of the color to an object.

Mixing Colors

If you create a blue rectangle and you would like to add a bit of yellow to it, try this:

1. Select the rectangle.
2. Color it blue.
3. Hold Ctrl and begin clicking Yellow on the palette.

With each Ctrl+click on Yellow, you take a small percentage of yellow and apply it in place of a similar percentage of the original colors. In the case of this blue-to-yellow transition, about seven percent of cyan and magenta are subtracted, in favor of seven percent of yellow.

 WARNING   These two features might be convenient, but they're also dangerous if used irresponsibly. You cannot trust that the various shades and hues that you mix will print desirably. If you are simply tinting back a color—by Ctrl+clicking on White—that's fine. But if you shade Blue to become C54M54Y32K5, that could become Puke Green when it comes off press. Make sure to consult a swatch book to examine the color you have produced. Do not trust your monitor to display accurate colors.

Step by Step

The following exercises will take you through the creation of a uniquely filled shape and a textured effect. Each of them is self-contained, and the finished files are available on the Sybex Web site.

A Colorful Star

Here is a short exercise that will give you practice with fountain fills and also introduce you to the Polygon tool.

1. From an untitled drawing, click the Polygon tool (seventh from the top in the toolbox) and create a polygon. This is the default shape when you use this tool, but it's not what we want.

N O T E   In the graphics shown here (and most of the graphics in this book), we are choosing not to display the page border. In the case of a simple logo, the page size is irrelevant and could be a distraction. To turn off the display of the page border, go to Tools ➤ Options ➤ Document ➤ Page and uncheck Show Page Border.

2. Delete the polygon from the page, right-click the tool, and choose Properties.

3. Increase the number of points to 8, and click Polygon As Star.

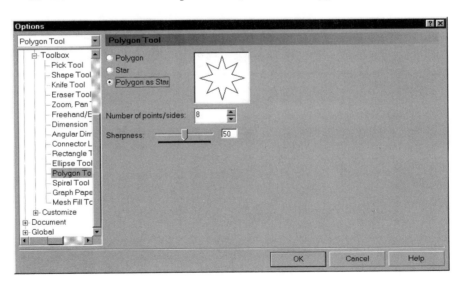

Note the sliding Sharpness meter; we'll get back to it later.

4. Okay the dialog and draw another polygon. This time, hold Ctrl while you draw it so it will be perfectly symmetrical.

5. When you're done drawing it, press F4 to zoom in.

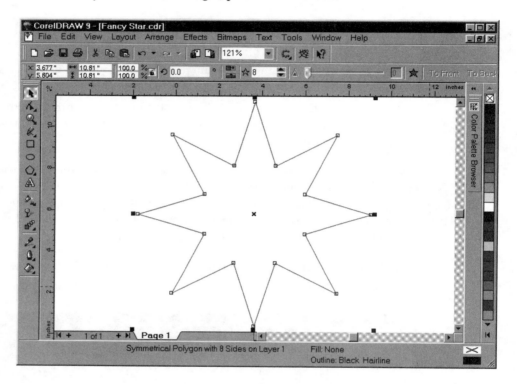

Polygons distinguish themselves from other objects in DRAW because they remain symmetrical, no matter what you do. If you adjust one point, they all adjust; add a node to one side, all sides get a node.

6. Move your cursor to one of the inside points and click and drag it toward the outside. Hold Ctrl while you do this to ensure that you don't skew the star (a nice effect when you mean to, but we don't).

This is the equivalent of reducing the Sharpness value by using the slider we saw on the Properties sheet.

7. Activate the Interactive Fill tool and choose Fountain Fill from the drop-down list.

8. From the four icons to the right of the list, choose Conical (the third one from the left).

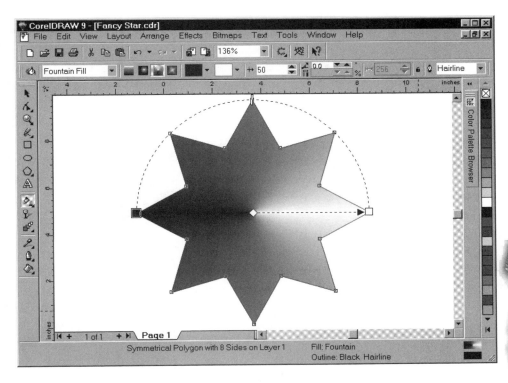

You'll recall from the earlier section about fountain fills, you can drag and drop colors onto the control handles to change the fountain. Polygons extend that capability. Watch:

9. From the on-screen palette, drag Black to the right-most control handle. As soon as you do, the entire star turns black (the fountain is now going from black to black).

10. Moving counterclockwise along the arc (shown in dashed blue), drag White to the next point, as shown in the top graphic on the next page. If the screen starts to pan, just press F4 to return to your desired zoom level.

11. Continue along the arc, dropping Black on top and White at the "10 o'clock" point. Leave the ending control handle as is.

12. Switch to the Pick tool (spacebar), deselect (Esc), and admire your work, as shown in the bottom graphic on the next page.

You can find this star as Fancy Star.cdr on the Sybex Web site.

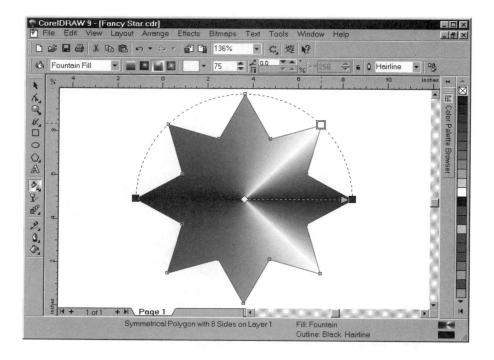

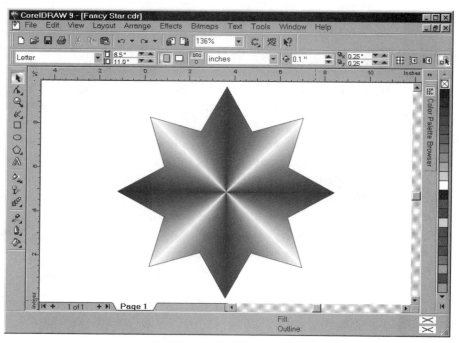

Textured Text

This exercise shows the kind of striking effect possible with CorelDRAW's Texture fills. If you are brand new to the program, some of the text formatting might be uncharted territory for you.

1. In a new drawing, create a rectangle.

2. Click the Interactive Fill tool and then choose Texture Fill from the drop-down menu of fill types.

3. Choose Samples 7 from the Texture Library drop-down and Concrete from the list of thumbnail textures.

How do you know which one Concrete is? Well, you don't. You might recognize it as the far-right choice on the second row, but if not, click Other. The full dialog shows the names of all of the textures.

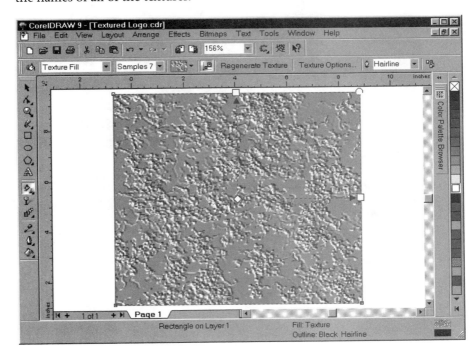

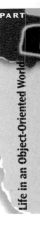

4. Save your drawing. Give it any name you want; we chose `Textured Logo.cdr`.

5. Choose the Text tool and click somewhere inside of the concrete rectangle.

6. Type the words **Etched in Stone**, pressing Enter after each word.

7. Find a typeface that is suitable for heavy text. We chose GeoSlab ExtraBold, from DRAW's typeface collection. It looks like it was made from rock.

8. Use the corner sizing handles and the × in the middle to size and position the text so that it is almost as big as the rectangle.

9. You'll need one trip to the Format Text dialog (Ctrl+T) to center the text and reduce the line spacing. Use the Align tab of the dialog for centering and the Space tab to set the space of the line to a percentage well below 100. Try 75%.

10. Click the Pick tool and press Esc to deselect the text.

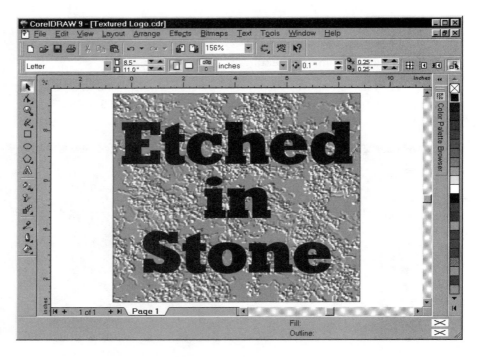

The trick now is to give the text nearly the same fill as the background, with just enough variation so that it barely can be discerned. We'll start with the exact same fill and then we'll vary it slightly.

11. Select the text and go to Edit ➤ Copy Properties From.

12. Choose Fill as the property to copy.

13. Press OK and then click once on the rectangle.

14. If you did it right, the text should practically disappear, save for the selection handles. It has the same fill type as the background rectangle.

15. With the text still selected, click the Interactive Fill tool.

16. Find the Regenerate Texture button and click it. When you do, DRAW will randomly regenerate the variables of the texture.

17. Keep clicking until you find one that offers a subtle change in the fill pattern. Here is what our screen looked like after we chose a pattern.

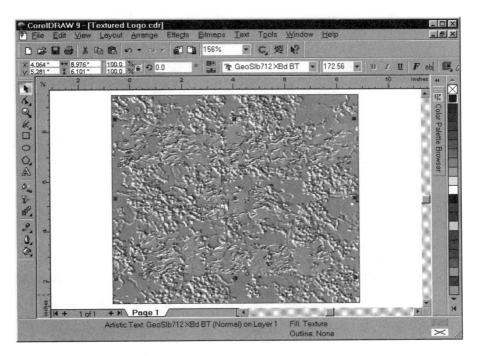

You can just barely make out a difference in tone where the text is. Talk about subtle!

At this point, you will be using some keyboard shortcuts to perform a few non-beginner moves in DRAW. In order to make this text appear as if it were chiseled out of the concrete, you need to create a shadow and a highlight. You can't use a fountain fill because the text already has a fill pattern. Instead, you will be using two copies of the text string, just barely offset from the original. Here goes:

18. To prepare, go to Tools ➤ Options ➤ Edit and set a Nudge value of 1 point. You can either change the unit of measure to points and enter **1** for a value, or simply enter **1pt** and let DRAW figure it out for itself. We'll explain this soon.

19. With the text still selected, press the plus key on your numeric keypad. The text will blink momentarily.

Pressing the plus key makes an instant copy of the selected object. So now there are two identical strings of text, one on top of the other. The new one on top of the original is currently selected. You want to change the one in back, and the easiest way to select it is to use the Tab key. Pressing Tab automatically cycles you through all objects in your drawing, selecting each one after the other. Here goes:

20. Press Tab to select the original string of text behind the copy. It won't appear as if anything has happened—you'll just have to trust DRAW that it has now selected the text in back.

21. Having taken this leap of faith, click Black or a dark color from the on-screen palette. You still won't see this black text, hiding behind the original text, but your status bar should now report that the selected object has a fill of Black (or whatever color you chose).

Now it's time to nudge. Moving this object a tiny distance would be next-to-impossible with a mouse or tablet. Instead, you will use Nudge, the handy feature whereby selected objects are moved as you press your keyboard arrow keys. Up, down, left, right…you press the key, DRAW moves the object. The distance is determined by the Nudge factor, which you set in step 18.

22. Press the down arrow a few times and the right arrow a few times until you begin to see the dark text behind the textured text appear as a sliver.

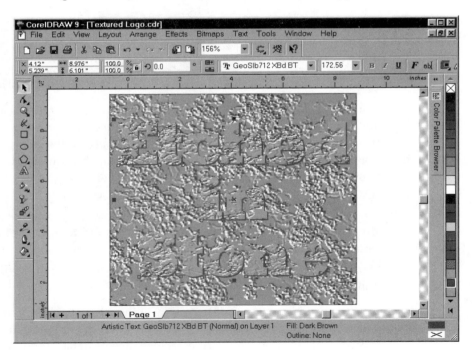

TIP   If you mistakenly placed the shadow text in front of the original text, press Ctrl+PgDn until it moves to the back.

23. Select the original text (you'll know you have done so when your status bar reports "Fill: Texture" at the lower-right).

24. Press the plus key to make another copy.

25. Press Tab to select the one behind the new one, and set its fill to White.

26. Nudge it up and to the left with the up and left arrows. Keep nudging until it displays as the same type of sliver as the shadow.

27. Press Esc to deselect. Save, and take a look.

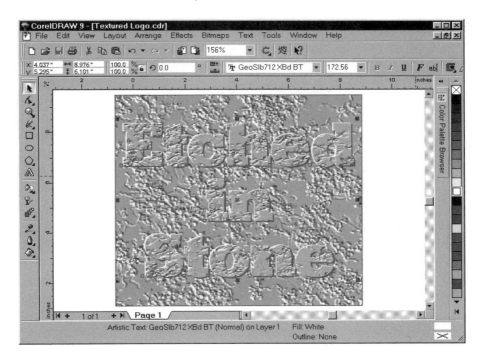

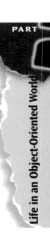

You'll find Textured Logo.cdr on the Sybex Web site.

UNDERSTANDING OUTLINES

Featuring

UNDERSTANDING
OUTLINES

While not quite as sensational as fill patterns, outlines are every bit as fundamental to the way that DRAW operates. Perhaps even more so—after all, you can place an outline around every single object you create in DRAW.

So first, let's define a few terms. Every object created in DRAW has an outer perimeter or path, but not necessarily an "outline." In DRAWspeak, the *outline* is the *visible line* that follows the path of an object, and the Outline Pen is the tool used to create or modify visible outlines. So even though all objects have outside edges to them, they only are said to have an outline if you can see it.

N O T E   A line or shape with no outline or fill? "What for?" you may ask. Although not a visible part of the drawing, this type of object can still be very useful. For instance, you might use an invisible rectangle to set the exact boundaries of a graphic whose elements must remain a particular size when imported or linked to another document. As you'll see in Chapter 10, invisible lines or objects are often used to fit text to a path. And when you're enveloping and creating powerclips (see Part IV), the possibilities become endless.

Accessing DRAW's Outline Tools

DRAW's controls for creating outlines have remained notably unchanged in the last few versions. That means that either Corel got it right the first time, or its engineers have run out of creative ideas for it. Kidding aside, outlining remains a straightforward operation.

To set the outline thickness for a selected object, do one of the following:

- From the Outline flyout, click the first icon to open the Outline Pen dialog (or just press F12), and adjust the value for Width, as shown in Figure 7.1.

- For any selected object that is considered a generic curve (i.e., not a rectangle, circle, polygon, or string of text), use the drop-down list of line widths on the property bar. You can choose one of the listed values, or type in your own.

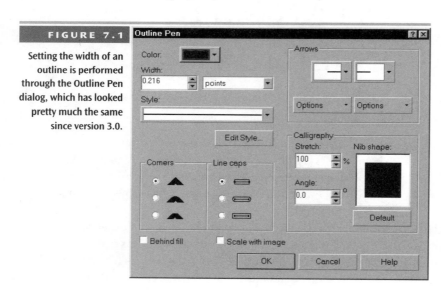

FIGURE 7.1

Setting the width of an outline is performed through the Outline Pen dialog, which has looked pretty much the same since version 3.0.

To set the color of an outline:

- Right-click the desired color on the on-screen palette.

- From the Outline flyout, click the second icon to open the Outline Color dialog (or press Shift+F12).

- From the Outline Pen dialog (where you set the width), click the drop-down Color list at top-left to pick a color from the current palette. Or click Other to head to the Select Color dialog.

TIP Advanced users and keystroke-lovers will find the third option to be the fastest. Watch how cleanly you can do it: after pressing F12 to reach Outline Pen, press the space-bar to open the drop-down Color list. Use your arrow keys to scroll the color choices, and when you find the right one, press Enter. Then press Tab to move to the Width setting.

Finally, you can reach width and color settings from the Properties sheet, accessible from the object's context menu.

The Outline flyout has seven preset outline widths, including no outline at all (shown as an ×). You can leave the Outline flyout connected to the toolbox, or you can detach, reshape, and move them into any desired position on the screen.

If you want to set the outline color of multiple objects, drag and drop a color from the on-screen palette to each outline. This is similar to your ability to drag and drop colors into objects to fill them, the difference being your drop point: as you approach the outline, the interactive cursor changes to a colored square outline, indicating that you will color the outline when you release the mouse.

Penning an Outline

While the property bar is handy, we predict that force of habit and more complete services will compel most users to journey to the Outline Pen dialog. That one dialog (thanks to the Color button) is a literal one-stop shop for outlining objects. Here are the settings offered there.

Outline Width

The Width settings give you total control over the thickness of an object's outline. You can designate anything from an impossibly thin 0.001 millimeter to an absurd 36 inches. And you can use any of DRAW's standard measuring units—inches, millimeters, picas and points, points, ciceros and didots, didots, feet, yards, miles (!), centimeters, meters, and kilometers. Additionally, our lead author whined and nagged and Corel's engineers added pixels to this list for those who produce Web-based graphics and want to keep all their measurements in units that make sense to the screen.

You can either dial up the numbers on the spin buttons next to the Width field, or place your cursor in the box and type the value yourself. To abbreviate the tip we gave to speed demons above, here is the fastest way:

1. Select an object and press F12 to invoke the Outline Pen dialog.

2. Tab once to select the Width field and highlight the current value.

3. Type in a new value.

4. Press Enter to OK the dialog.

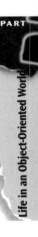

Regardless of the route you choose to get there and the way you enter the values, the Width field provides the most flexibility for setting Outline Pen widths.

Arrows

The two Arrows boxes provide access to 89 different arrow styles, ranging from a variety of normal-looking arrows to an airplane, a writing hand, and starbursts. The Arrows box on the left controls what will appear at the start of the line; the right box sets the arrow for the end of the line. Note that these are not based on direction: if you draw a line from right to left, the ending arrow will appear on the left side of the line. If you get confused and set the arrow on the wrong side, click Options and choose Swap (either Options button will do).

Do you see an arrow style here that you *almost* like? Maybe it would be just perfect if it were a little larger, or more elongated, or fatter? It's easy to create simple variations on arrow designs with the built-in Arrowhead Editor. From the property bar, choose Other from the drop-down list of arrows, or from the dialog, choose Options ➤ Edit.

WARNING   All the arrowhead style definitions are stored in a file called coreldrw.end, in the Custom subdirectory. Before editing any of the default arrow styles, make a backup copy of this file. Editing an arrow replaces its original version. Using your backup will be the only way to return to the default arrowheads, short of reinstalling the program.

For example, DRAW doesn't offer long and thin or short and squat arrows like the ones shown in Figure 7.2. But, using the Arrowhead Editor, you can create either of these arrows from an existing one. Just pick the arrow you'd like to use as your starting point and click on the Options button under the arrow selection box. Choose Edit to replace the chosen arrowhead, or New if you want to add your new design to the list. DRAW will bring up the Edit Arrowhead window, where you can resize and reshape your arrowhead and reposition it in relation to the end of the line.

You needn't concern yourself with keeping the arrow precisely in the center of its line—that's what the Center in X and Center in Y controls are for. (Remember your geometry? The x-axis runs along the horizontal and the y-axis along the vertical.) The Reflect buttons mirror the arrow along each axis. The Reflect in X button actually turns the arrow completely around, so it faces the line; pointing to where you've been rather than where you're going. The Reflect in Y button flips the arrow upside down.

The vertical line in the Edit Arrowhead window represents the end of the line to which the arrowhead will be applied. If the arrowhead extends past that line (as in the middle image in Figure 7.2), it will extend past the endpoint of the line to which it is attached.

FIGURE 7.2

The Arrowhead Editor is responsible for custom arrows like the ones shown here.

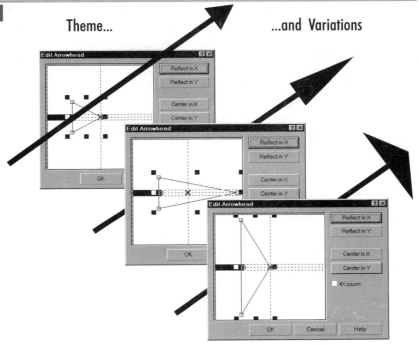

Theme...   ...and Variations

Line Style

This drop-down list offers you a choice of a solid line plus 27 other line styles. They are combinations of dots, spaces, and dashes. To use one of them, simply click on it and your selected object will inherit that line style. When this feature is used in conjunction with the Line Caps settings, several additional useful styles of dotted and dashed lines can be created.

You can also create your own pattern from the Edit Line Style dialog (see Figure 7.3). To open this dialog, select any line style other than solid, and then select the Edit Style button below the drop-down line style list.

NOTE   When you use (or create) a line style, the length of dots, dashes, and spaces scales with the line's width. A hairline will look solid unless you zoom to a high magnification. But make the same line 8 points wide, and you'll see the style clearly.

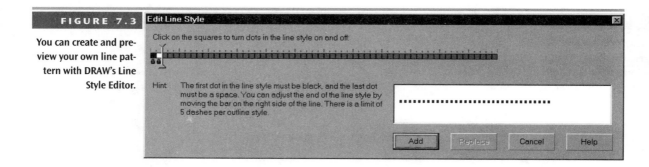

FIGURE 7.3

You can create and pre-
view your own line pat-
tern with DRAW's Line
Style Editor.

Color

Your handy entrance to all of the Outline Color controls is the Color drop-down box
in the Outline Pen dialog. Here you can choose among all the colors in the current
palette. And as we mentioned earlier, if that's not enough, click Others to reach the
Select Color dialog. From there, you can change palettes, choose spot colors, search
for names of Pantone colors, and mix your own CMYK, RGB, or HSB values. (For
more on color models and palettes, see Chapter 27.)

Corners

There are three choices for controlling how outlines are drawn on objects with sharp
corners. As Figure 7.4 demonstrates, these controls operate intuitively.

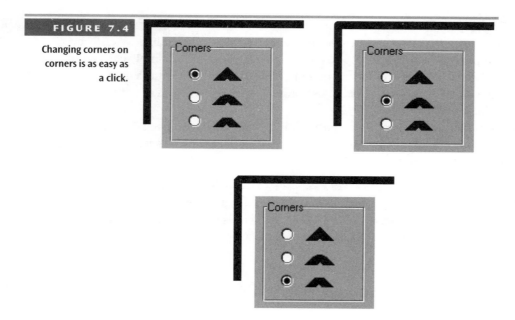

FIGURE 7.4

Changing corners on
corners is as easy as
a click.

Line Caps

These three options determine how the ends of lines are rendered. The first choice (the default) cuts the line off right at the end. The middle option draws round caps that extend beyond the end of the line, and the third control draws square caps that extend beyond the end of the line.

Figure 7.5 shows how a choice of line cap can affect lines that meet but do not share a node. Notice that with the default line cap (the first one), there is an obvious gap between the two lines, while the other choices produce the illusion that the lines meet.

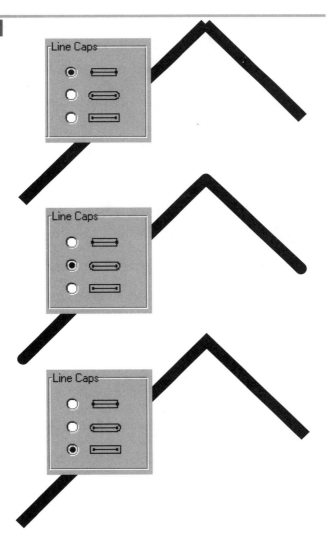

FIGURE 7.5

The influence of Line Caps on lines that have separate nodes where they meet

PART

Life in an Object-Oriented World

Calligraphy

Using these settings to control the shape and orientation of the Outline Pen is not unlike working with a pressure- and orientation-sensitive ink pen. By adjusting the size and angle of the pen, you can create realistic calligraphic effects. Figure 7.6 shows two such examples with their settings, along with an example of what is produced by the default settings (100% Stretch and 0 degree Angle).

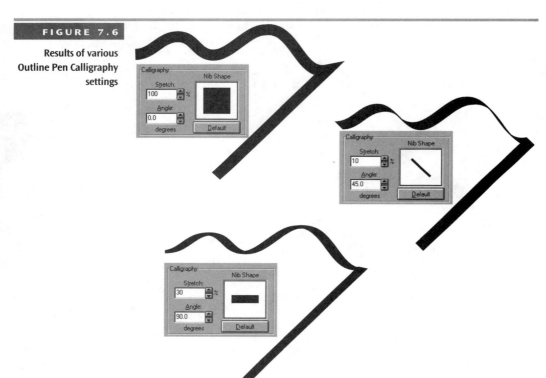

FIGURE 7.6

Results of various Outline Pen Calligraphy settings

Behind Fill

The position of the Outline Pen is either in front of a fill pattern (the default) or behind it. When an object has no fill, this control is of no consequence, which is why most users pay little or no attention to it. But the important thing to know about all of this is that DRAW places outlines in the center of an object's edge. In other words, half of the thickness of the outline is outside of the object's edge and half is on the inside.

This is also not normally front-page news, unless you do something like kern the heck out of a string of text and/or apply a thick outline, as shown in the top part of Figure 7.7. There simply isn't enough room for all of the outline!

Outline in front of fill:

WE COULD USE A LITTLE MORE BREATHING ROOM

Outline behind fill:

THANKS, THAT'S MUCH BETTER

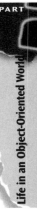

The solution is in one of the controls in the Outline Pen dialog, called Behind Fill. When this option is checked, the outline is placed behind the fill, so that only the outside part of the outline is shown. The lower half of Figure 7.7 shows the result—a nice effect of welded text.

Scale with Image

Let's say you create a rectangle and apply an outline to it. If you then scale the rectangle up by 200 percent or reduce it by 50 percent, the width of the outline will stay the same. This is fine if your spec calls for, say, a 2-point outline around all objects. However, if you need to create outlines that are proportional to their objects, you need to acquaint yourself with the Scale with Image option.

Don't turn the page, yet—there's more to the story. Scale with Image has its side effects. If you turn it on and you scale an object *disproportionately*—in other words, you make a rectangle wider, but not taller—two of the four sides will see its outlines grow, but two will not. This looks particularly unattractive when done with ellipses.

The ounce of prevention is simply for you to not scale objects with their side handles when you have Scale with Image on. Corner handles are okay, but side handles produce the disproportionate outlines. The pound of cure for objects that have already had their outlines distorted is to remove the outline (right-click the × on the on-screen palette) and reapply the outline and its width. You can keep Scale with Image on for this cure, because when you remove the outline and reapply it, DRAW forgets what the object once looked like and applies the outline evenly to all sides.

PART

Life in an Object-Oriented World

N O T E   When you scale arrowheads, they exhibit behavior similar but opposite to scaled outlines—that is, the size of the arrowhead increases or decreases as the thickness of the line changes. As with outlines, this may not always be what you want; unfortunately, there is no way to override this default condition with arrowheads.

The Outline Color Dialog

Except for the advanced technique of applying color trapping for offset color printing (discussed in Chapter 27), this dialog doesn't see a lot of action, either here or when invoked from within the Outline Pen dialog, where it goes under the pen name (get it?) of Select Color.

For most users, there is only so much you can do to a line around an object. All of the controls that make this such a robust dialog—choices of palettes, color models, percentages of color values, and custom names—are applicable to outlines as well as fills.

However, a new DRAW 9 feature gives outlines a new life. Called Convert Outline to Object, this command effectively separates an outline from the object to which it was attached. It lives on the Arrange menu, and once applied, turns the outline into its own closed shape. The significant implication of this is that the outline can now be filled with any fill pattern whatsoever. The image in Figure 7.8 doesn't look so complex, but in fact, without this new command, producing it would be difficult.

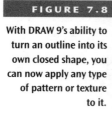

FIGURE 7.8

With DRAW 9's ability to turn an outline into its own closed shape, you can now apply any type of pattern or texture to it.

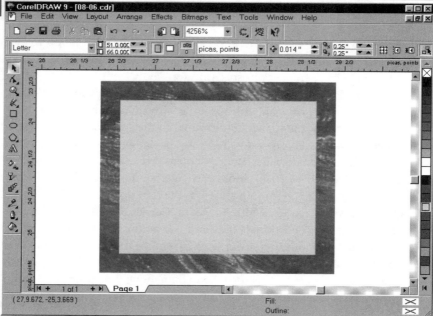

Setting the Outline Pen Defaults

By default, DRAW creates black outlines with a width of 0.2 point for all graphic objects and no outlines for text. Although it's rare that you'll want outlines around text characters, you might very well want a different default condition for outlines around graphic objects such as ellipses, rectangles, and curves.

To change one of DRAW's default outlines for the current drawing, you would do just as described in Chapter 6 for fills: make sure not to select anything before starting your trip to the dialogs or the property bar.

 N O T E   These changes only apply to the current document. Go to Tools ➤ Options ➤ Document to make permanent changes to the default styles.

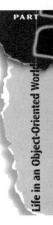

PART

Life in an Object-Oriented World

MASTERING TEXT

WORKING WITH TEXT

Featuring

WORKING WITH TEXT

With earlier versions of DRAW, dozens of book pages were required to explain how DRAW handled text and why it did it so differently than other Windows programs. The 32-bit versions of DRAW have cleaned up their acts. Now, DRAW 9 is a virtual master of type. Of DRAW's two distinct reputations in the electronic publishing and graphics community, one of them is now a distant memory. Still appropriate is the title of Typeface Giant, thanks to the always huge library of typefaces that ships with the program, but DRAW has pretty well lived down the rap that it is plagued with imprecise and poorly crafted typefaces. DRAW's typefaces now hold their own against all but the most finely crafted electronic typefaces in the industry, and they are available in both TrueType and Adobe Type 1 formats.

DRAW 9 Is Kosher for Windows

If you use Word, WordPerfect, Word Pro, WordPad, or just about any other word processor, Figure 8.1 will confirm that working with text in DRAW is now an intuitive affair. The only thing that you would need to know is how to get a text cursor, and that can be as simple as one click on the Text tool (Icon No. 8 in the toolbox) and one click on the page.

FIGURE 8.1

Like the toolbar in today's word processors, DRAW's property bar provides access to styles, typefaces, sizes, variations, and alignment.

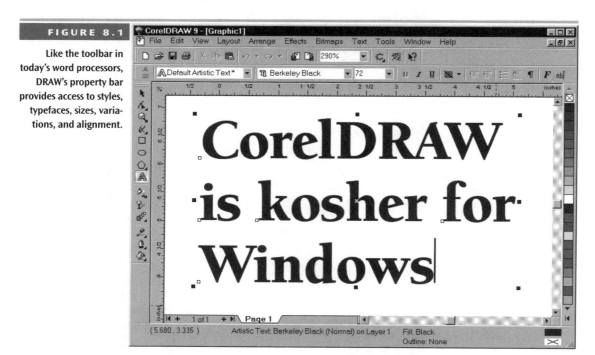

Watch Your Language!

Rarely are phrases mangled and misused more than the ones that describe type. We are guilty of lazy usage ourselves, sometimes using "font" in conversation when we mean "typeface." Just to set the record straight, there is a distinction between a *type family* (a collection of typefaces with a unifying design, such as Helvetica), a *typeface* (one in a collection, such as Helvetica Medium or Helvetica Bold), and a *font* (a typeface set in a specific size, such as 9-point Helvetica Italic).

We won't insult your intelligence by providing tutorials on the text-editing functions of the property bar. If you have used any word processor, you're home free. Place your cursor over a button on the property bar, and a pop-up will tell you what the button does. We will tell you that if you are new to DRAW, you might be confused at first by the presence of two distinct property bars for text—one for when a string of text is selected, and one for when your cursor is actually placed in the text. It's okay to be confused—we're still mystified by this and annually request that Corel streamline it.

While deaf ears seem to have been the only recipient so far of this request, Corel *is* listening to its users. Based on user feedback, the engineers simplified the text tools so that one tool can create either artistic or paragraph text: click once in the drawing area to create artistic text; click and drag to create paragraph text.

TIP   If you want a full-time, full-service toolbar for text, go to Window ➢ Toolbars and click Text. It won't function like a property bar—it will always be visible, consuming screen real estate—and that is either a good thing or a bad thing, depending upon your point of view (and monitor size!). Advanced users will want to consult Chapter 34 for how they can customize their interface and have the best of both worlds.

Artistic and Paragraph Text

Even brand new users can probably make an educated guess at the difference between DRAW's two types of text. If a picture is worth a thousand words, what would be the net worth of words that act like a picture? Artistic text is just such an animal. It is a string of text that can be manipulated like any other graphic object. It can be sized, shaped, distorted, filled, outlined, and even converted to curves and node-edited. Meanwhile, paragraph text is more like body copy—it can be flowed, indented, hyphenated, columnized, marginized, and probably a few other verbs that we could make up like the last two.

And as we said above, you create both types of text with the same tool (see Figure 8.2), and the hotkey for that tool is F8. The efficiency experts in the crowd will soon learn to use their nonmouse hand to press F8 and then their mouse hand to immediately click where they want to enter the text.

DRAW refers to a unit of artistic text as a *string* of text, and a unit of paragraph text as a *frame* of text. We will too, and in Chapter 9 you'll explore the differences between text strings and text frames. First, however, let's look at the similarities. Regardless of the type of text you create in DRAW, artistic or paragraph, you can do the following things to it.

PART

Mastering Text

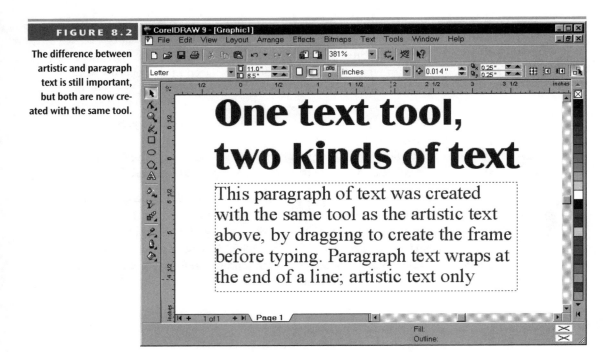

Change Its Size

You can set type as small as .001 point for the really fine print of a contract, or up to 3,000 points for a roadside billboard (roughly 30-inch-tall letters). You can resize text characters from the property bar or from the Format Text dialog, whose access is had from:

- Text ➤ Format Text
- The hotkey of Ctrl+T
- The context menu for selected text

You can also size text with the Pick tool, by clicking and dragging the corner selection handles. If you want to size paragraph text this way, you must press Alt while you drag. Otherwise you size the frame that holds the text, not the text itself.

With on-screen editing much faster now than in earlier versions, an editing window is not as important as it once was, and we don't encounter many users who regularly turn to this dialog anymore. Nonetheless, when you're working with large blocks of copy, a quick Ctrl+Shift+T will take you to the Edit Text dialog. This is helpful when on-screen text editing is difficult, like in the case of text that is fitted to a path or extruded.

Change Its Formatting

Both the property bar and the Format Text dialog provide full control of typeface selection, style (bold, italic, and so on), and size. You'll want to note how these controls behave in the three different settings in which they are used.

Setting	Formatting Action
With the entire string of text selected	Format changes affect all of the text.
With text selected within a string or frame	Only the selected text is changed.
With the editing cursor placed in text	Text that you type from that point forward uses the new formatting.

Change Its Alignment

As text alignment is a paragraph-wide setting, it makes no difference where your cursor is or what you have selected. If your cursor is in a paragraph or selection handles are around a paragraph, it's going to change when you set alignment. The problem is finding the controls to do this, as Corel has not done us any favors. In the Format Text dialog, you must navigate to the second tab, prompting many users to practice the Ctrl+Tab maneuver of switching tabs in a dialog. And as for the property bars, Corel has chosen to place alignment controls on the Editing bar (the one that appears when your cursor is placed) but not the Text bar (the one that appears when you have simply selected a string or frame of text). We've already complained about this earlier in the chapter so we'll shut up now…

Adjust Spacing

With DRAW's spacing tools, you can adjust the space between characters, between words, and between lines. You do all of this from the Space page of the Format Text dialog, shown in Figure 8.3. The controls work the same for artistic and paragraph text, except there are more of them for paragraph text, as space above and below a paragraph becomes relevant when you actually have paragraphs.

Line spacing (known in the industry as *leading*) can be set in exact measurements of points or by percentages of the text. The latter method is handy if you are resizing text with the Pick tool and you want line spacing to adjust proportionately.

PART

Mastering Text

FIGURE 8.3

Space...the final
frontier

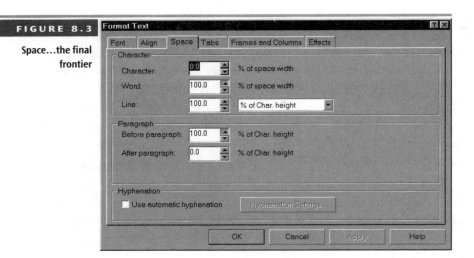

FIGURE 8.3

Space...the final
frontier

Figure 8.4 shows text set with various amounts of leading. You would think that 9-point text set with 10 points of leading would correspond to a percentage of *over* 100 percent, not *under* (97 percent). But in determining the percentage, DRAW uses the distance from the top of the *tallest character* to the bottom of the *longest descender,* rather than the actual point size.

FIGURE 8.4

DRAW can set line spacing in points or as a percentage of type size.

This is 9-point text
with 10-point spacing

This is 9-point text
with 11-point spacing

This is 9-point text
with 12-point spacing

This is 9-point text
with 13-point spacing

This is 9-point text
with 97% spacing

This is 9-point text
with 107% spacing

This is 9-point text
with 117% spacing

This is 9-point text
with 126% spacing

There is actually more to the story, because DRAW supports three different measuring systems for determining line spacing:

Percentage of Character Height   This option, shown in Figure 8.3, measures the spacing as a percentage of the character height—from the highest ascender to the lowest descender. Text set in 11 points and 100-percent character-height spacing would result in line spacing of almost 14 points.

Points   The traditional and largely preferred way to measure space between lines of type is in the fixed units of measurement known as points. If you have set a string of text in 11 points, you can establish the line spacing at precisely 13 points.

Percentage of Point Size   The old CorelDRAW measuring system, in which 11-point text set at 100-percent spacing would result in line spacing of 11 points (considered by most to be too tight).

Paragraph spacing can be set in exact measurements of points or by percentages of the text, both above and below the selected paragraph. This is particularly useful when you need to evenly distribute the amount of space between a set number of paragraphs on a given page, and it eliminates the need to resort to adding extra lines in between paragraphs.

Hyphenation also makes its home on the Space page.

Kern Individual Characters

Individual adjustment of characters is called *kerning*; the term is also used as a verb—to *kern* characters means to adjust the space between the characters. Capital letters, like the ones in Figure 8.5, often need manual kerning to look good. The sample at the top of the figure shows good, bad, and hilarious use of kerning.

FIGURE 8.5

Character kerning is especially helpful with text set in all caps.

NICE AND TIGHT

AVOID AWFUL KERNING

LOOSE, BUT NOT HORRIBLE

AVOID AWFUL KERNING

HORRIBLE

AVOID AWFUL KERNING

RIDICULOUS

AVOID AWFUL KERNING

There are three ways to kern:

- Select the characters you want to kern, open the Format Text dialog, and from the Font page, set a value for Range Kerning. Use the Apply button to keep the dialog open for fine-tuning.

PART

Mastering Text

- Select the entire string or frame of text, open the Format Text dialog, and from the Space page, enter values for Character and Word.
- Select the text, switch to the Shape tool, and drag the small thingamabob in or out, as shown in Figure 8.6.

Like most good typefaces, the ones in DRAW ship with built-in intelligence about which character combinations need more or less space between them—this is referred to as *kerning pairs*. Invariably, however, text set at large sizes or in all caps needs to be scrutinized for proper kerning.

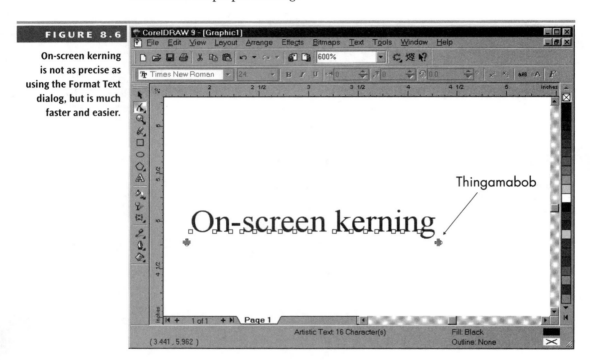

FIGURE 8.6

On-screen kerning is not as precise as using the Format Text dialog, but is much faster and easier.

Format Individual Characters

In addition to character kerning, DRAW supports character reformatting. To do this, you can reach for the Shape tool again and select the node in front of the character, or choose the Text tool and select characters by dragging across them. Either way, the property bar and the Format Text dialog are the gateways for reformatting characters.

The Text tool is more intuitive, providing a standard text cursor for selecting text, but the Shape tool has the advantage of allowing you to select noncontiguous characters. Select one character, hold Shift, and then select others anywhere in the string. You can also use the Shape tool to rotate individual characters with the Angle of Rotation control on the property bar.

WARNING   Individual character formatting is overridden by changes made to a text string's size or style. In other words, if you format characters using the Shape tool and then format the entire string in the conventional manner, your custom formatting will be lost for those attributes changed in the entire string. Rule of thumb: Global before local. Globally format the entire string first, and then locally format the individual characters.

Check for Spelling and Synonyms

Prominent typographical errors are the bane of publishing in any medium, and DRAW can help you keep them at bay. As Figure 8.7 shows, you can get copyediting help without having to send the text out to a word processor. Spell-checking is quite good; grammar-checking not as good.

- To check spelling, select a string or frame of text and choose Text ➤ Writing Tools ➤ Spell Check. You can spell-check an entire string or frame, or any portion of text that you have selected with the text cursor.

- To use the Thesaurus, select a word within a string or frame and choose Text ➤ Writing Tools ➤ Thesaurus.

- The Grammatik grammar checker is also reached by the Text ➤ Writing Tools route. Because the grammar checker also checks spelling, we often run it for both purposes.

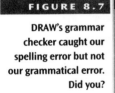

FIGURE 8.7

DRAW's grammar checker caught our spelling error but not our grammatical error. Did you?

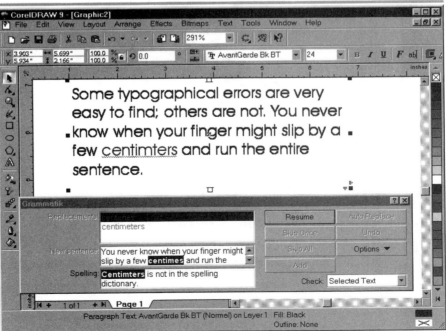

The Wonder of Artistic Text

The main thing you should know about artistic text is how…well, how artistic it is. You can treat it like an object—you can apply just about any special effect to it, any fill pattern, and unusual shaping to it. With artistic text, you can:

Size, Rotate, and Skew

Use any of its selection handles to configure and misfigure a string of text, just like you could with another shape. The text still retains all of its text properties, including your ability to drop a cursor into it and edit it.

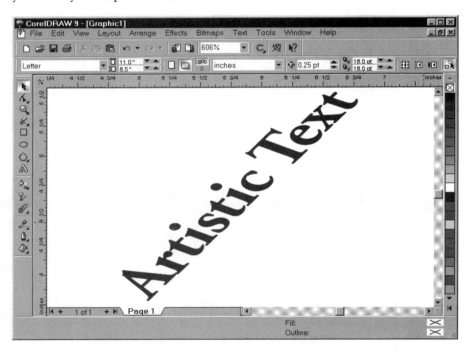

Fill with Any Pattern

A string of text is a closed shape, so it can accept any fill pattern that you and DRAW can conjure up, including little pieces of licorice.

Apply Special Effects

Again, if you can do it to an object, you can do it to a string of text. Here is a sneak preview of Part IV.

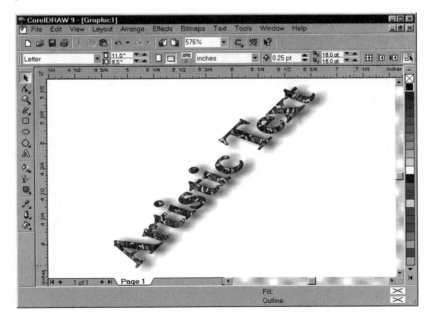

Shape around a Path

Artistic text can be enveloped, distorted, and made to have its baseline follow a specific path.

Node-Edit the Letter Forms

Once you convert the text to curves, you can do anything with it that you would to any other curve.

Do All of These at Once

As you can see from this progression, you can just keep heaping these effects onto text, one after the other. The only restriction is the conversion to curve process—after that, you cannot edit the text as text any longer. For instance, after converting to curves, if we decide that the *T* in Text should be lowercase, our only recourse is to use the Shape tool and electronically sculpt the *T* into a *t*. We wouldn't actually resort to that, in case you were wondering…

Setting Defaults

What, you don't set all of your artistic text in 24pt AvantGarde? For years now, we have snickered at Corel's insistence on using the outdated AvantGarde as its default typeface. "When is the last time anybody actually set type in it?" asked one skeptical beta tester during the development of DRAW 9.

Fortunately, artistic text has default settings, just like fills and outlines, and you can change them at will. All the same rules and techniques discussed in Chapter 6 and 7 apply:

1. Open the Format Text dialog but don't select any text first.

2. Make the change and OK the dialog.

3. Tell DRAW for which type of text you are changing the default.

4. To make the change permanent, go to Tools ➤ Options ➤ Document ➤ Save options… and check Styles.

There is only one difference in the procedure; with text, DRAW asks you to verify the action of changing the default on your way out of the dialog. With graphic objects, DRAW nags you on the way in.

PART

Mastering Text

WORKING WITH PARAGRAPH TEXT

Featuring

WORKING WITH
PARAGRAPH TEXT

I t has been one of computing life's little secrets. Up until DRAW 7, many DRAW users remained oblivious to "that other way to create text." Paragraph text has gradually, with each new version, become a legitimate tool for text-intensive projects. Many users of earlier versions were accustomed to creating art in DRAW and assembling the pieces of a brochure or an advertising layout in PageMaker or some other page-layout program. Now they do the whole thing in DRAW, thanks to the program's beefed-up support for setting, formatting, and editing large blocks of copy.

You create paragraph text inside a text frame, instead of directly on the page as you do artistic text. This distinction is clearer since DRAW 7, because the most direct way to create paragraph text is to drag the Text tool to create the frame before you begin to type.

The distinction is important because paragraph text has a different personality. Paragraph text uses *word wrap*, like the documents you create in your word processor, to create text that flows freely from one line to the next. The shape of the text flow is determined by the frame you establish when you first create it; the frame can be reshaped later and the text will flow to the new shape. Figure 9.1 shows renditions of the same paragraph of text, each one shaped differently.

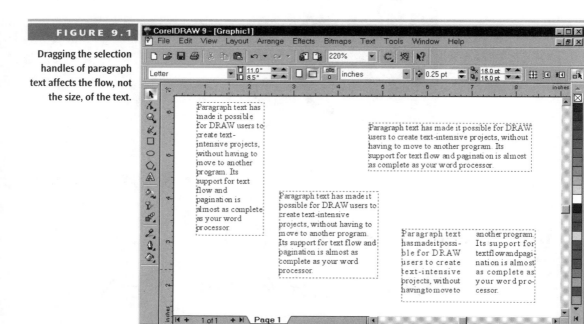

FIGURE 9.1

Dragging the selection handles of paragraph text affects the flow, not the size, of the text.

TIP   If you want to size your paragraph text with its frame, press and hold Alt as you drag one of the corner handles of the frame. But notice that line spacing will adjust when you do this *only if it is set as a percentage of type size.*

The Purpose of the Paragraph

One of the chief limitations of paragraph text is its indifference to most of DRAW's special effects. You cannot distort, skew, extrude, or do any of the other gee-whiz things to paragraph text. In reality, though, this is more of a safety measure than a flaw, because if you are trying to apply a special effect to a frame of text, one of two things is probably taking place:

- You are using a small amount of copy, so you could easily convert it to artistic text and then apply the effect.

- You are trying to apply a special effect to too large a block of copy, the results of which would probably be an aesthetic disaster.

The purpose of paragraph text is to allow you to set a lot of copy, not to create lots of artistic text. To this end, you'll find a treasure of features hidden within paragraph text, as described in the paragraphs that follow.

Better Redraw and Bigger Capacity

Paragraph text is much faster on the redraw than artistic text. When you change typeface, style, or size, paragraph text adjusts almost instantaneously, while artistic text may take a bit longer, especially if the string is long or effects have been applied to it.

While the capacity of both types of text has been greatly increased over the years, you will run into problems if you try to set huge blocks of copy in artistic text. However, there are no practical limits on the amount of text you can set with DRAW's paragraph text.

Better Text Control

Paragraph text offers the kinds of controls you would expect to find in a program that supports large quantities of text. You can set tabs and indents; create left and right margins; set space above and below a paragraph and between the lines of a paragraph; set up columns and adjust frame width; and specify bullet characters or drop caps at the beginning of paragraphs.

All of this is done through the Format Text dialog, the various pages of which are shown in Figure 9.2. With the text box selected, go to Text ➤ Format Text. Alternately, you can use the hotkey Ctrl+T, the property bar, or the Properties sheet that you can invoke by right-clicking on a frame of text.

Basic text-formatting functions are also available on the property bar; the range of such functions is greatest when working with the Text tool.

The Font page   The Font page of the Format Text dialog is essentially identical to the artistic text version discussed in Chapter 8. The only difference is that the Range Kerning control is not available for paragraph text, unless you first highlight a portion of the text. You can still adjust the spacing of individual characters, however, with the Shape tool, or on the Space page of the dialog.

The Align page   Alignment controls and hyphenation are here. The Character Shift controls at the bottom-right of the page allow you to move or rotate selected characters. The Indent controls are like those of most word processors. Figure 9.3 shows three of the most common Indent settings, along with their results. As with artistic text, if you want to do this with multiple noncontiguous characters, you are better off using the Shape tool and its property bar controls.

PART

Mastering Text

The many faces of
Format Text when used
with paragraph text.

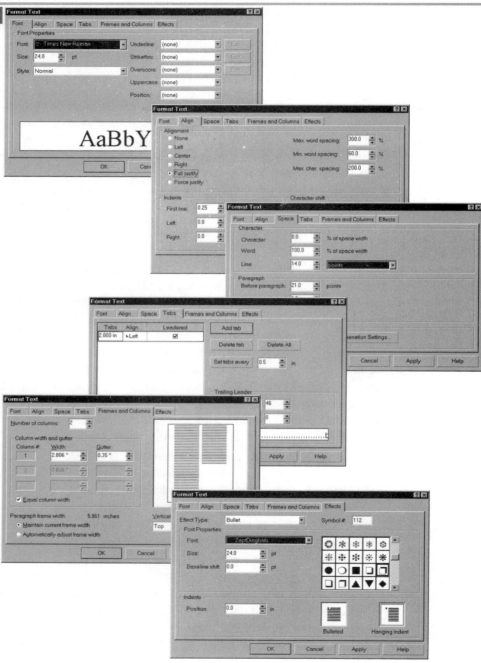

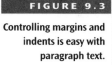

FIGURE 9.3

Controlling margins and
indents is easy with
paragraph text.

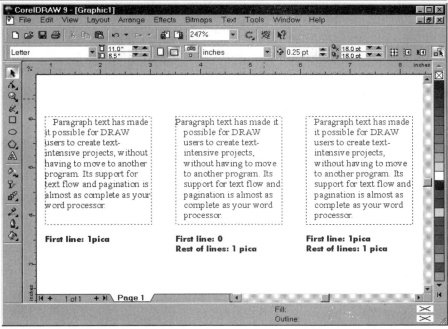

The Space page This page provides controls for space between characters, words, and lines within a paragraph (leading). You can also designate space above and below paragraphs (remember, you can have many paragraphs within one frame of text).

T I P Remember that you can insert *line breaks* into paragraphs—hard returns that do not signify the end of the paragraph. Unlike paragraph breaks, DRAW does not add any space above or below a line break. It simply drops down to the next line without waiting for the text to wrap at the end. You can insert these line breaks with Shift+Enter.

The Tabs page Tab controls work like every other tab function known to computing-kind. Leadered tabs can be set, using any character of any typeface you have installed. (Go easy on leadered smiley faces though, okay?)

The Frames and Columns page The controls on this page of the Format Text dialog allow you to specify how many columns you want within the current frame, how wide they should be, and how much space should be left between columns. You can tell DRAW to fit the columns into the existing frame width or to adjust the frame to fit the column widths you want.

PART

Mastering Text

The Frames and Columns page is also the home of Vertical Justification of text. The default setting is Top, which is what you are used to: the text begins at the top of the frame, uses the line spacing you specify, and ends wherever you run out of things to say. The other possibilities are Center, Bottom, and Full—the latter adjusting the line spacing automatically to fill the frame.

The Effects page   This set of controls enables you to precede any paragraph with a bullet or a drop cap. Any typeface that is identified as a "symbol" face (a property given to a typeface by its developer) will show up here in the font list when Bullet is the Effect Type. This means you can go way beyond the bounds of good taste when setting bullets, as clearly demonstrated by Figure 9.4.

FIGURE 9.4

There could come a time when a smiley face would be suitable as a bullet character. Then again, maybe not.

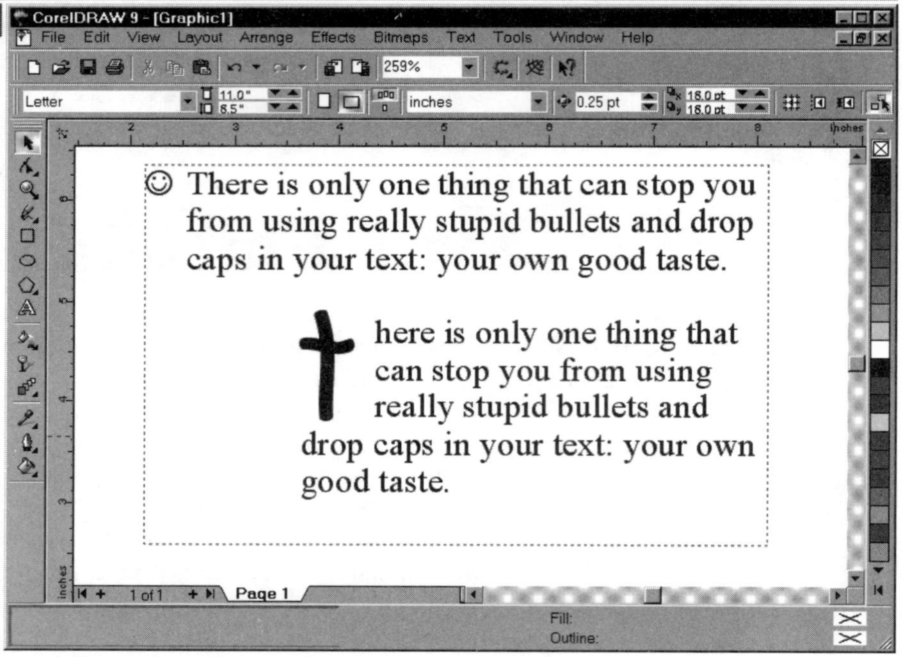

WARNING   Despite the ease of creating a drop cap, there's something else you should watch for. If you add a drop cap to a carefully sized text frame, it may take up more room than is available. When the middle selection handle below the frame turns into a downward-pointing arrow, DRAW is telling you that the text no longer fits in its entirety. Fixing it is easy—just extend the frame—but missing it is also all-too-easy, so keep an eye out for it.

Creating a drop cap is easier than choosing a bullet. Just choose Drop Cap from the Effect Type drop-down menu, choose Dropped or Hanging Indent placement, and click on OK. If you wish, you can then select the drop cap and change its font or other formatting as you would any other single character.

Irregular Text Wrapping

One of the most powerful special effects that can be applied to paragraph text is irregular text wrap. This is done in several different ways, including a handy new text-wrap tool. Figure 9.5 shows the result of wrapping text to follow the contour of an object. We'll cover this in detail in Chapter 10.

FIGURE 9.5

With the Envelope and Text Wrap feature, you can wrap text around and inside an object.

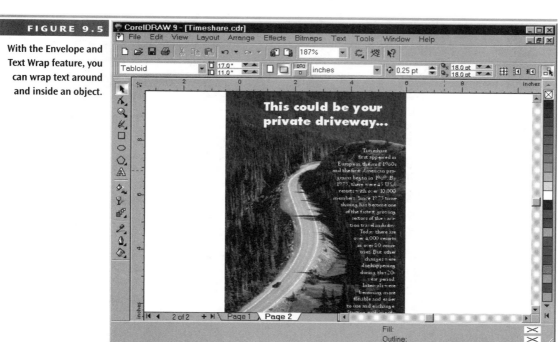

PART

3

Mastering Text

Navigating Your Way

There was a time when the only thing you could do in DRAW while your cursor was in a line of text was type. Now you can practically use DRAW as your word processor. Here are some of the reasons why.

On-Screen Controls

Not too long ago, DRAW didn't even have tabs. Now there is a full-featured dialog and fast and friendly on-screen controls in the ruler. As shown in Figure 9.6, when your cursor is in a frame of paragraph text, the rulers change to take the upper-left corner of the frame as their zero point. You can change tabs (using the marks in the ruler), indents (using the small triangular pointers), and column widths (using the vertical bars on the ruler). Just drag any of these symbols to a different position to change the setting. Tabs, columns, and indents are only relevant for paragraph text, and changing them will affect only the paragraphs that are selected. To change the settings for all paragraphs in a frame, either select all of them or select the frame with the Pick tool and use the controls in the Format Text dialog.

FIGURE 9.6

With paragraph text, you can set indents and tabs and check spelling without having to open any dialogs.

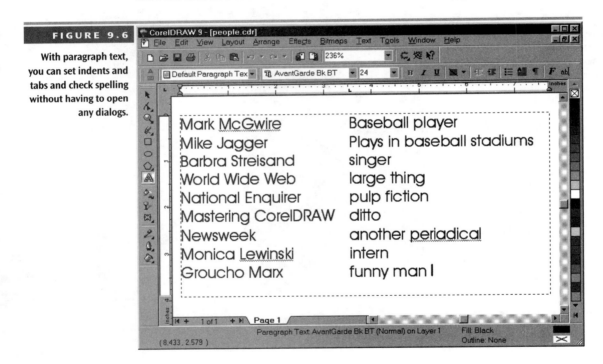

Proofreading

DRAW has benefited from having WordPerfect as its sibling, getting to use all of the latter's spelling and grammar tools. The spell checker, thesaurus, and Grammatik grammar checker come straight from WordPerfect, and with them, you get on-the-fly spell checking, with a red wavy underline to highlight questionable words, as you can see in Figure 9.6.

You reach the writing tools through Text ➤ Writing Tools. If you only want to check spelling, choose Spell Check or use the hotkey Ctrl+F12. Spell Check stopped at McGwire and Lewinski, and did indeed catch the typo of "periadical" that we planted. However, it did not cast any suspicion on the unusual but correct spelling of Barbra Streisand's first name.

If you choose Grammatik, DRAW will check both grammar and spelling, but you can expect mixed performance at best. When we set the text of a poem, a line that began with a lowercase letter was called an error by DRAW. That is forgivable—poetry is unusual—but check out the horrible sentence in Figure 9.7 that Grammatik barely raised an eyebrow over. Using the default of Quick Check, Grammatik didn't see anything wrong with it; only when we changed to the Very Strict setting did it even make the vague suggestion shown here.

FIGURE 9.7

Grammatik didn't seem to mind this example of glowing prose. In fact, it only suggested that we write more! Maybe we'll enter it in a writing contest…

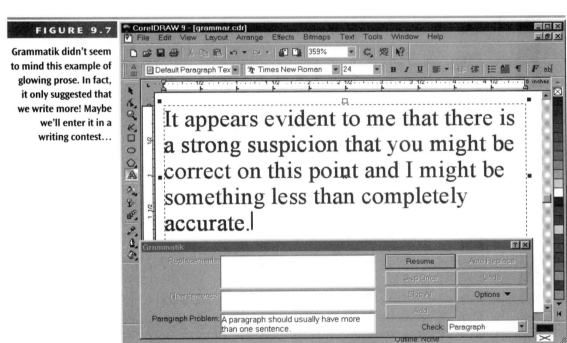

Full Alignment of Text

DRAW has long offered the standard choices (Left/Right/Center/Justify/None) for setting text alignment. These controls are on the Space page of the Format Text dialog. A sixth choice, Force Justify, determines the length of the longest line and forces all other lines in the text to extend to that point. As Figure 9.8 illustrates, you must use Force Justify with care.

FIGURE 9.8

Forced justification of
paragraph text must be
used with considerable
caution.

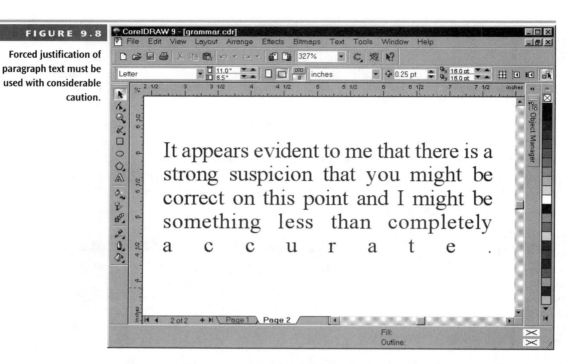

Where might you use Force Justify? Good question—and Figures 9.8 and 9.9 illustrate that use and misuse are first cousins: Figure 9.9 is the same text, with the frame width narrowed. The key to appropriate deployment of Force Justify is using lines of text that are similar in length to begin with, but we suspect you won't use it much. Fully justified text is an anachronism; text today usually isn't justified at all, let alone set so that even its last line is justified.

Editing Controls

There was no real value to having powerful editing controls in the early versions of DRAW because, most of the time, you weren't able to create text quickly enough or in sufficient volume to take advantage of them. Text rendering in DRAW 9 is quite speedy, so it will pay off for you to practice some of the in-line editing commands that DRAW offers. Odds are you already know many of them from the time you have put in with your word processor. Here is a summary:

What You Do	What DRAW 9 Does
Double-click	Selects the current word
Shift+click	Selects from the insertion point to the cursor
Ctrl+click	Selects the current sentence

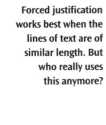

FIGURE 9.9

Forced justification works best when the lines of text are of similar length. But who really uses this anymore?

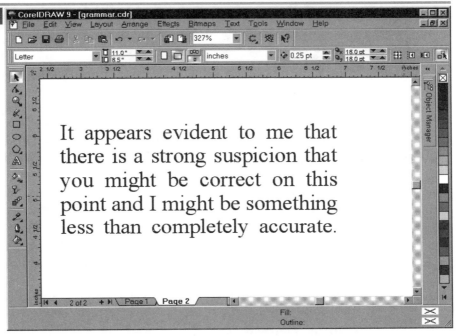

What You Do	What DRAW 9 Does
Ctrl+Right Arrow	Jumps one word to the right
Ctrl+Left Arrow	Jumps one word to the left
Home	Jumps to the beginning of the line
End	Jumps to the end of the line
Ctrl+Home	Jumps to the beginning of the text string or frame
Ctrl+End	Jumps to the end of the text string or frame
Shift+Right Arrow	Selects to the right of the cursor, character by character
Shift+Left Arrow	Selects to the left of the cursor, character by character
Shift+Home	Selects all text from cursor to beginning of line
Shift+End	Selects all text from cursor to end of line
Ctrl+Shift+Right Arrow	Selects to the right of the cursor, word by word
Ctrl+Shift+Left Arrow	Selects to the left of the cursor, word by word
Ctrl+Shift+Home	Selects all text from the cursor to the beginning of text string or frame
Ctrl+Shift+End	Selects all text from the cursor to the end of text string or frame

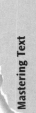

PART

Mastering Text

Choosing between Artistic and Paragraph Text

In some cases, it doesn't matter whether you choose artistic or paragraph text to set type. A standard headline of three or four words at the top of a newsletter is going to look the same regardless of which mode you use to create it. Other times, however, your decision will be crucial to your work flow. Here are some rules of thumb.

When Is Artistic Text the Best Choice?

Use artistic text in the following situations:

When you stretch and skew   Artistic text can easily be scaled and stretched—you just tug at the selection handles. (Paragraph text can be scaled with its frame by using the Alt key, but it cannot be stretched or skewed at all.)

When you mirror, extrude, envelope, or change perspective   These are effects that can be applied to artistic text only. The Envelope function can be applied to paragraph text, as shown in Figure 9.5, but when used with artistic text, Envelope and the other special effects actually bend the characters.

For editing character shapes   If you want to change the very shape of text characters by converting them to curves and then editing the nodes, you must use artistic text. If you try to choose Arrange ➤ Convert to Curves when working with paragraph text, DRAW just ignores you. In Chapter 10, we will take apart some characters and edit their shapes.

When Is Paragraph Text the Best Choice?

Use paragraph text in the following situations:

To set large blocks of copy   As appropriate as artistic text is for the headline of an article, so is paragraph text perfect for the article itself. Paragraph text can accommodate thousands of individual paragraphs, and you can create pages and pages of text.

To control text flow   Paragraph text can flow from frame to frame and from page to page. Also, you can easily change the length of each line in paragraph text, thanks to the soft returns it employs. (The only way to end a line of artistic text is to use a hard return.)

To control the baselines of text   A handy use for paragraph text is when you want to set text along an angle, as shown in Figure 9.10.

FIGURE 9.10

You may not need to set
text like this often, but
if you do, paragraph
text is the only
way to go.

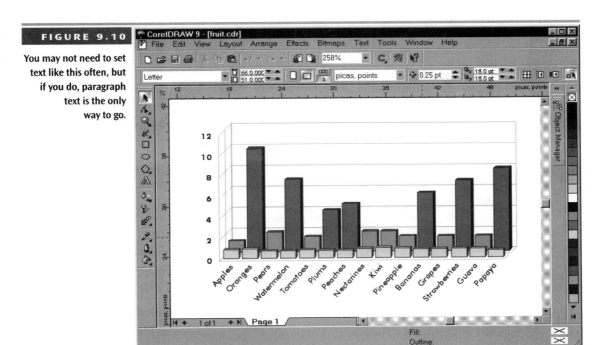

This is actually a pretty nice trick, because the alternative—lining up each one of
the fruits by hand—would take many times longer. To produce the text along the bottom axis, we set it as right-aligned paragraph text. Then we rotated the entire frame of
text 90 degrees counterclockwise, so that the text was appearing to hang down from
the top of the frame. Then we opened the Precision Skew docker and skewed the frame
by about –35 degrees, quickly and neatly angling all of the text.

Had this been artistic text, the characters themselves would have bent backwards,
and that is a fundamental distinction between the two types of text. When you select
a string of text, DRAW applies the chosen effect to the characters themselves; when
you select a frame of paragraph text, DRAW applies the effect to the frame. In Figure
9.10, DRAW skewed the baseline of text, not the text itself.

Switching from One to the Other

What happens when you create text in one form and discover that you really need it
to be in the other? The fix used to be complicated, but no more. Just right-click the
text and the first item on the context menu will be Convert to _____ Text (the blank
to be filled in by whatever the text is not).

PART

Mastering Text

Remember the Hotkeys

The hotkey shortcut can make text creation tasks much easier:

- Press F8 and click once to create artistic text.

- Press F8 and drag a frame to create paragraph text. Don't worry if you don't yet know what size or shape the frame should be. It's easy to change it later.

 TIP   If you have text currently selected, you can press F8 and immediately get a text cursor at the end of the string or frame. This is undoubtedly the easiest way to edit text. With one hand on the mouse and the other on the keyboard, select the text, press the hotkey, and you're ready to type. If the text is one of few objects on the page and the Pick tool is active, you don't need the mouse at all: press Tab until the text is selected, press F8, and start typing. Tab has a different function once the Text tool is active, so you can't use this last method to move among and edit multiple text objects.

Importing Text

DRAW is perfectly capable of receiving text from word processors and from the Clipboard. For details, see Chapter 29.

ADVANCED TEXT HANDLING

Featuring

ADVANCED TEXT HANDLING

I f you are hoping for one unifying theme to bring together all of the topics in this chapter, we should warn you that the chapter's title is as close as you'll get. As we once again open the overstuffed file folder entitled "Miscellaneous Text Stuff," we predict that this chapter will wander from one idea to the next, as it has in previous editions. It has always been one of our more enjoyable chapters, and we hope it will be one of yours, too. And in our best network television voice, may we say that this chapter is intended for our more mature readers; some material may not be suitable for new users.

Shaping Text to Objects

One of the litmus tests for graphics software today is its ability to wrap text around and inside an object. Before Corel added support for this a few versions ago, DRAW was widely regarded as "nice software, but it can't wrap text." DRAW provides this capability by extending its node-editing functionality to include both strings of artistic text and frames of paragraph text. Version 9 adds some nice automation to the latter.

In the following examples, you can watch or follow along as a piece of text is shaped around a curve in one of three ways:

- By controlling the shape of paragraph text in a frame
- By warping a string of artistic text
- By fitting text to a path

Flowing Text around an Object

Figure 10.1 may look rather complicated for a work-along exercise, but we are here to show you that it's not. If you want to follow along with the creation of this piece, you'll need some sample text and a globe—there are several in Corel's clipart library, or you can download Greenland.cdr from this book's companion Web site.

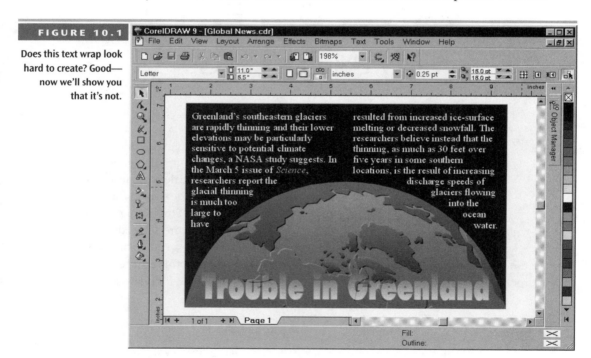

FIGURE 10.1

Does this text wrap look hard to create? Good—now we'll show you that it's not.

1. From a blank drawing, create a rectangle that is wider than it is tall. For reference, the one we drew is approximately 8 by 5¹/₄ inches. Save your drawing and give it a name.

2. Create a frame of text and type in some copy. Anything will do, but it's best if you use actual words and sentences, instead of "lorum ipsum, etc." We used an article from the NASA Web site about glacial melting.

3. Choose a typeface, pick an appropriate size, and then from Text ➤ Format Text set the frame to two equal columns. Position the text so that it has a comfortable margin on the top, left, and right.

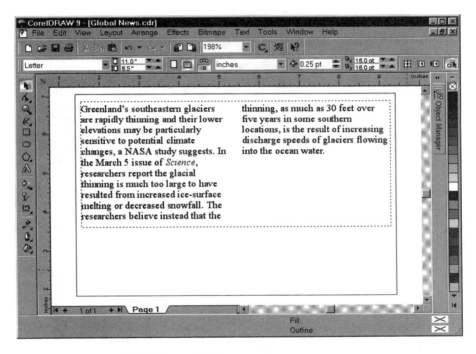

4. Import the globe of your choice onto the page.

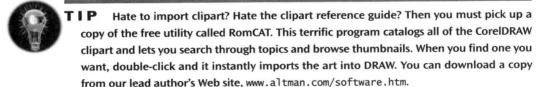

TIP Hate to import clipart? Hate the clipart reference guide? Then you must pick up a copy of the free utility called RomCAT. This terrific program catalogs all of the CorelDRAW clipart and lets you search through topics and browse thumbnails. When you find one you want, double-click and it instantly imports the art into DRAW. You can download a copy from our lead author's Web site, www.altman.com/software.htm.

5. Size and position the Earth so that it is as wide as the rectangle. There should be about 2 inches of space between the top of the Earth and the top of the rectangle.

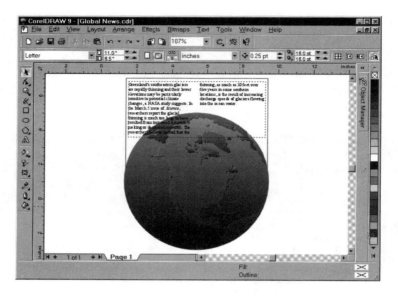

Now it's time for the actual text wrap, and before we show you the quick and easy way, we want you to know how to do it the manual way.

6. Select the text, open the Effects flyout (fourth icon from the bottom of the toolbox), and choose the Interactive Envelope tool (the fourth icon on the flyout).

Once you do this, the text frame will grow control handles that look like nodes. In fact, applying an envelope to paragraph text is just like node-editing the frame.

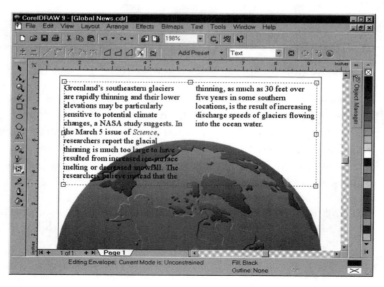

Your mission is to create a curve out of the bottom side of the frame, and remembering back to Chapter 4, "As the Curve Turns," it can be done with just two nodes and one path.

7. Select the lower-middle node (the one over the Earth) and delete it.

8. Click the path and drag it up over the Earth. As soon as you do, the text will instantly wrap within this new shape.

9. Optionally, you might want to add a node near each of the lower corners, as shown here.

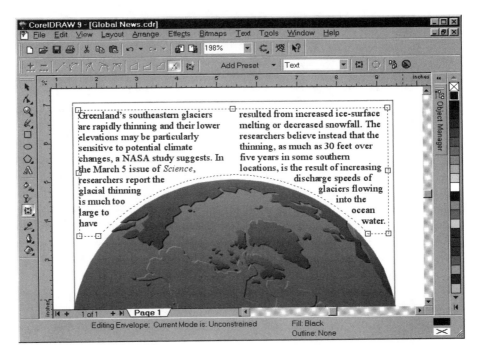

We made those new nodes cusp nodes so that the frame could turn a sharp corner—we want the path on the outside to be straight and the path on the inside to curve around the globe.

Automatic Text Wrapping

There is a reason why we didn't use the new auto-wrap feature, and we'll let you learn why for yourself soon enough. First, however, here is how you would apply an automatic text wrap.

1. Start from step 5 of the previous exercise. With the text selected, go to Effects ➢ Clear Envelope, or from the Interactive Envelope property bar, click the Clear Envelope button (the one with the line through it).

2. Select the Earth.

3. On the property bar, click the last button on the right to force any nearby paragraph text to wrap around it.

This tells DRAW to do automatically what you just did manually: create a new shape from the frame of text by adding and shaping nodes.

4. With the Earth still selected, right-click to get to the Properties sheet and note that the Wrap Paragraph Text box is checked (this is how DRAW 8 users did it before Corel added the nifty button to the property bar). For Text Wrap Offset, enter a value of .2 inch. This will give a bit more margin to the text where it wraps.

5. Save.

There is a high probability that you will need to fiddle with the text a bit to get it to wrap properly. Frequently, with text wraps that involve tight corners, words will break oddly and/or gaps between words will occur. You can either edit the text a bit or adjust the letter and word spacing. In our case, the text for this article originally read "...glacial thinning is too large to have resulted from..." But we had trouble with the break from the first column to the second, as the word "resulted" kept getting chopped in half. By simply adding the word "much" in front of "too large," we forced "resulted" to the top of column two and all was well.

The one big advantage of auto-wrapping is its dynamic nature. If the Earth shifts, the text wrap shifts with it. The manual wrap we performed earlier doesn't have a clue that it is wrapped around the Earth; it only knows what we told it—to place a node here, a node there, and make a curve from this point to that point.

The other shoe will drop soon...

Finishing the Drawing

The rest of this exercise is mostly a tangent, although we still owe you the other dropped shoe with auto-wrapping. We'll start with some recoloring. The defaults for rectangles and text are white and black, respectively. For this outer space-like feel, we want precisely the opposite:

1. Select the rectangle and fill it Black.

2. Select the text, which won't be so easy with the rectangle completely obscuring it. Press Tab if necessary and watch the status bar until it confirms that you have selected paragraph text.

3. Fill it White.

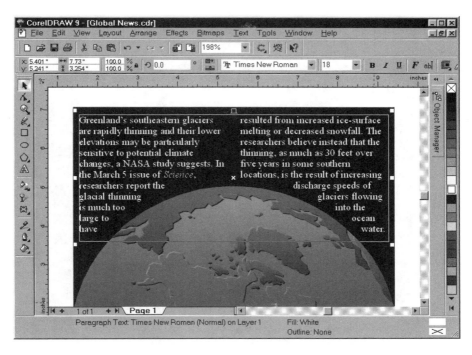

There is a good reason we waited until now to reverse out the text: it is no fun editing white text. See for yourself by dropping your text cursor into the frame and typing: DRAW creates white space around each line you change, instead of creating black space. You would need to constantly press Ctrl+W to refresh the screen, or retreat into Wireframe view. When we know we will be reversing text, we hold out as long as possible to make text editing easier.

Now…the Earth. It is hanging down below the black rectangle, when really it should be cropped to the shape of the rectangle. You'll be learning all about the PowerClip command in Chapter 19; here's a sneak preview.

4. First, go to Tools ➢ Options ➢ Edit and check the status of Auto-Center New PowerClip Contents. If it is checked, then uncheck it (we'll bore you with an explanation in Chapter 19).

5. Select the Earth.

6. Go to Effects ➢ PowerClip ➢ Place inside Container. DRAW will respond with a big pointing arrow.

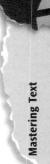

PART

Mastering Text

7. Click on the black rectangle (but not on the text). The mixed results appear below.

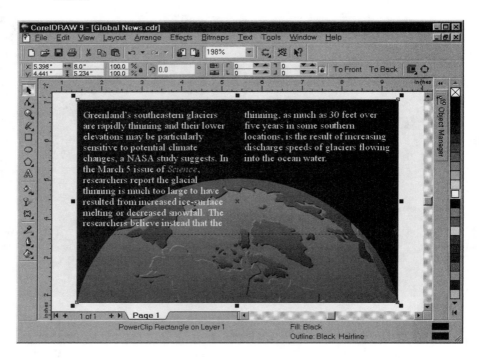

DRAW surely did crop (or clip, as DRAW calls it) the Earth into the rectangle, so no part of it is showing below the rectangle. This is one of the most powerful and popular of all CorelDRAW commands, but you can see one consequence of it right away: once the Earth is powerclipped, DRAW can no longer use it as the basis for an auto-wrap. We'll show you the workaround, but in the event that no workaround exists, it's good to know how to perform a manual wrap, and that is why we had you do it earlier in this project.

8. Zoom out a bit with F3 and draw an ellipse on top of the Earth. The ellipse probably defaults to a hollow interior and a black outline; if not, then use your on-screen palette to set it that way.

9. Shape and size the ellipse until it follows the contour of the Earth. This will take a few back-and-forth tugs and pulls on various selection handles, but eventually you'll get it.

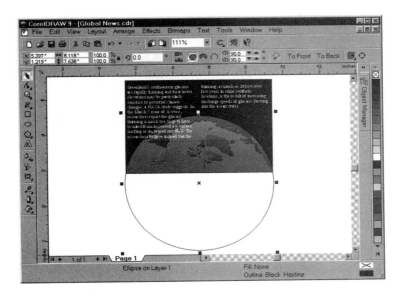

You can probably guess where we're going with this...

10. With the ellipse still selected, click the Wrap Paragraph Text button on the property bar to wrap the frame around this new ellipse.

11. Go to the Properties sheet of the ellipse and once again increase the offset to .2 inch.

12. Make the ellipse invisible by removing its outline.

13. Zoom in for a closer look—you're done.

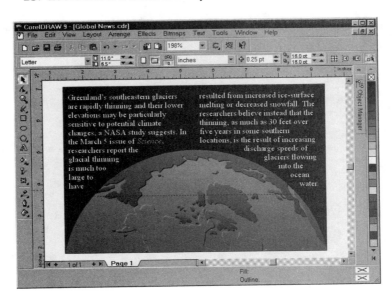

PART

Mastering Text

N O T E The dotted line you see in the preceding graphics is the boundary of the frame of paragraph text. You can choose not to display it by going to Tools ➤ Options ➤ Text ➤ Paragraph and unchecking Show Text Frames.

We'll return to this graphic in Chapter 17, "Through the Looking Glass," to produce the lettering. In the meantime, to see our finished file, check out Global News.cdr on the Sybex Web site.

Flowing Text within an Object

Flowing text inside of an object is trickier—rarely a one-step operation. Most of the time the ride on the inside of an object is a bit bumpier than the outside. Also, text inside of an object carries a higher *ugliness quotient*—defined by the probability that one false move results in an ugly drawing.

Figure 10.2 is a variation on the first Greenland article. This one flows within the outline of the country. It has fewer elements, but it probably took us twice as long to finish. And while we don't think it's ugly, we're not sure that we would use it for an actual project. Here is our journey.

1. We started with an outline of the country, shaded a light color.

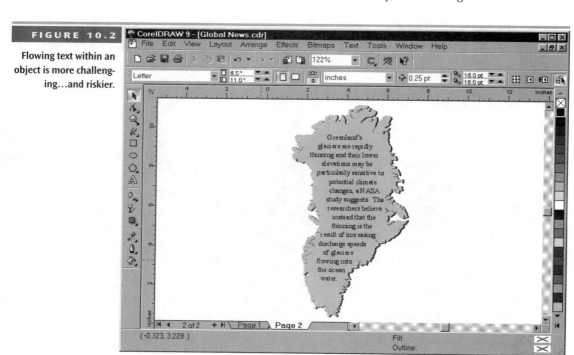

FIGURE 10.2

Flowing text within an object is more challenging...and riskier.

2. We copied the frame of text from the other design and pasted it nearby.

Flowing text inside an object is best done with a little-known maneuver that involves a "right-drag"—in other words, a click-and-drag maneuver with Button 2 instead of Button 1.

3. We selected the text, clicked and held Button 2, and dragged the text atop Greenland. Once we did, the cursor changed appearance, best described as the site of a rifle (we all agreed, even though none of us has ever actually looked through a rifle).

4. When we released the mouse, a menu appeared with several choices. We chose Place Text Inside.

5. About 45 seconds later, we saw this.

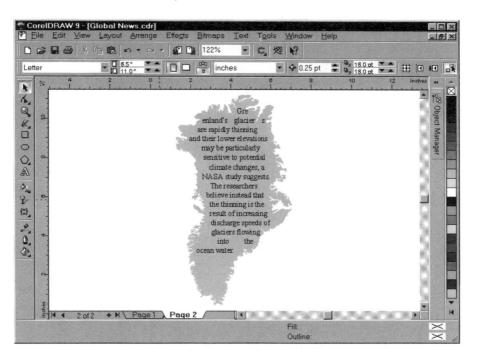

Visually speaking, the problems with this are obvious. Technically speaking, we made DRAW work way too hard. We asked it to try to flow this text inside of a shape that was full of jagged corners, sharp turns, and hundreds of nodes (which explains why the procedure took so long). And DRAW, the obedient creature it is, took us quite literally—it flowed the text into every little nook and cranny that it found.

PART

3

Mastering Text

The moral of this story is that you don't need to, and you shouldn't, try to make the text flow perfectly. We're not talking about a fill pattern here—you're not going to cover every pixel of the shape. The length of the words supercedes the directive to flow inside a shape. So give yourself a break and use a friendlier shape. Here's what we did:

6. We undid steps 3 and 4 with Ctrl+Z.

7. With the Pencil tool, we created a very simple shape—just six nodes.

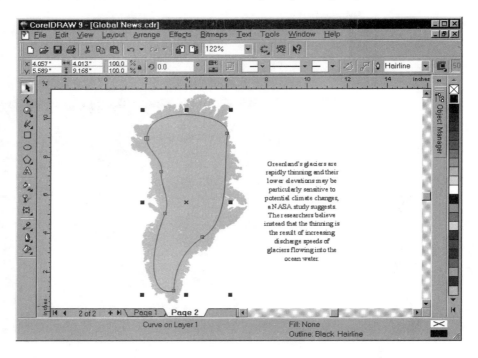

We didn't try to cover the jagged eastern coastline—we wouldn't want text to flow there, anyway.

8. We removed the curve's visible outline.

9. We repeated the right-drag maneuver atop this new curve.

10. When we released the mouse, within two seconds we saw this.

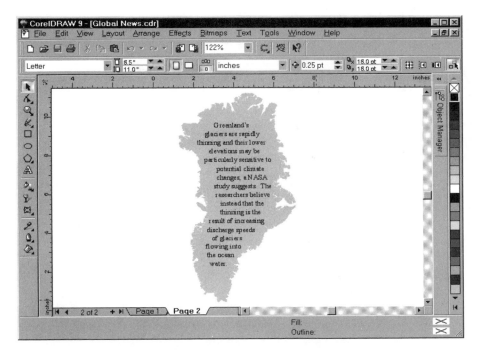

Much better. We created the drop shadow by making a copy of Greenland, moving it to the back, coloring it black, and nudging it over by a few points.

We must confess, though, that we did have to take some liberties with Greenland's coastline. We had particular trouble just to the right of "believe," where the jagged coast juts in. Well, if you study a map, you'll see that it juts in further than it does here. We had to perform a bit of Shape tool surgery to keep it from colliding with our text. We ask forgiveness of the gods of geography.

And incidentally, that right-drag business is a largely undiscovered jewel. Introduced in DRAW 8, it is a dramatic timesaver when performing operations that involve two objects. Check the context menu and see all of the things you can do when you right-drag-and-drop one object atop another.

Here are some things to think about concerning flowing text:

- Rarely will a wrap work the first time. Be prepared to edit the size, line spacing, character spacing, and even the text, if necessary.

- Set an appropriate offset. Often, the default of .1 inch is not enough. To adjust the offset, right-click and choose Properties.

- Consider using a third object to act as the shape to flow text around or within.

- Remember how to apply an envelope to the text (the manual method) for times when you can't use a shape.

PART

Mastering Text

Figure 10.3 is a soft and attractive piece that includes text gently wrapped around a graphic and flowed inside.

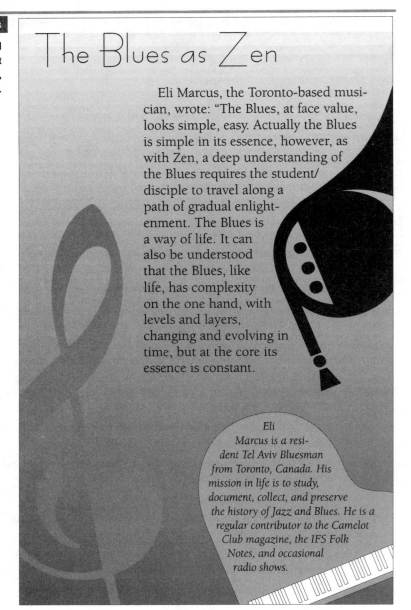

The Blues as Zen

Eli Marcus, the Toronto-based musician, wrote: "The Blues, at face value, looks simple, easy. Actually the Blues is simple in its essence, however, as with Zen, a deep understanding of the Blues requires the student/disciple to travel along a path of gradual enlightenment. The Blues is a way of life. It can also be understood that the Blues, like life, has complexity on the one hand, with levels and layers, changing and evolving in time, but at the core its essence is constant.

Eli Marcus is a resident Tel Aviv Bluesman from Toronto, Canada. His mission in life is to study, document, collect, and preserve the history of Jazz and Blues. He is a regular contributor to the Camelot Club magazine, the IFS Folk Notes, and occasional radio shows.

Warping Artistic Text

When you apply the Envelope tool to a string of artistic text, you end up with a drastically different effect than with paragraph text. Instead of just bending the frame in which the paragraph text flows, the Envelope tool actually bends the characters of artistic text. Figure 10.4 shows the result of enveloping artistic text. Although the effect is quite different from paragraph text, the same basic steps are used:

1. Select the text, open the Effects flyout, and choose the Interactive Envelope tool.

2. Shape the text as if it were a curve, shaping paths and tweaking and adding nodes as necessary.

The effects of enveloping artistic text and wrapping paragraph text are worlds apart, although the process is the same.

We captured Figure 10.4 with its node handles visible so you can see that it is just another exercise in shaping. We said it in Chapter 4 and it bears repeating: nodes speak to the core of CorelDRAW. From shaping a simple curve to wrapping a frame of paragraph text to the warping of artistic text shown here—the paradigm of nodes and paths is fundamental to the way that DRAW creates objects.

For details about applying envelopes, see Chapter 13.

PART

3

Mastering Text

Fitting Text to a Curve

There is yet a third way to alter text with respect to a curve: the Fit Text to Path command. To use it, create the curve that the text is to follow, and then do one of three things:

- With the Text tool activated, move the cursor to the curve. When the cursor changes to show an A with a wavy line below it, click once. Now any text you enter will adhere to the path. Your first click determines the text's origin.
- Create a string of text, go to Text ➢ Fit Text to Path, and when prompted by DRAW's big pointing arrow, click on the curve.
- Create a string of text, select it and the curve, go to Text ➢ Fit Text to Path, and watch as DRAW automatically fits the text to the path.

As with all other commands, the property bar offers you all of the controls to drive this feature.

We have reached a definite conclusion concerning Fit Text to Path: practically nobody knows by heart how to use it. There are many highly skilled DRAW users who produce brilliant work with it, but if you were to listen closely as they fine-tune fitted text, you'd probably hear something like this: "Okay, to move the text under the curve instead of over... Let's see, I think it's this one... No, how about this one... Well, maybe I should click here and then here... No, how about that one... Maybe I need to hum my mantra, too... There, got it!" And just when you think you understand the interplay between the controls on the property bar, DRAW turns your text inside-out or upside-down.

We're not going to waste a lot of paper describing every turn taken by the Fit Text to Path command—this is one set of controls that must be used to be learned. On the other hand, we can offer a few rules of thumb, and some good and bad examples of well-executed text fit to a path. Here is our starting text and curve.

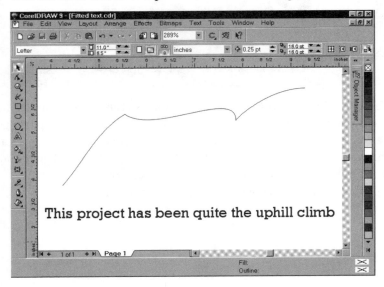

Choose Your Curve Wisely

Above all, text must be readable. If you lose the message in the medium, you've lost everything. A sure way to do that with the Fit Text to Path command is to choose the wrong path. If your path has sharp corners, the only way the Fit Text effect will work is if the text turns the corner between two words. In most cases, though, that would be blind luck. As you can see here, the result is disastrous, with the beginning of the word "uphill" falling into a canyon. *Moral*: Use rounded corners, not sharp ones.

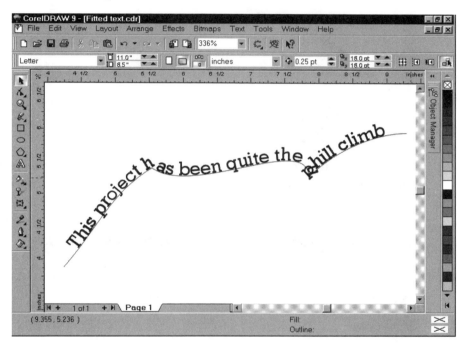

Choose Your Typeface Wisely

If you are pushing text along the contour of a crooked path, you need to choose a typeface with good shock absorbers. In the second effort at fitting text to a curve, the curve is much smoother than the previous one. But notice that the ostentatious Expo face can't handle even the slightest bump.

PART

3

Mastering Text

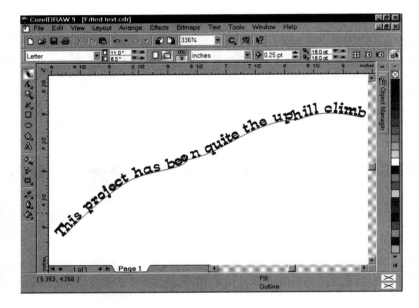

In the third try, we solved these two problems by switching to a more nimble type-face (Berkeley Book) and by smoothing out the curve even more. It was easy: with the Shape tool we selected each of the two sharply turning nodes, deleted one, and turned the other into a smooth node.

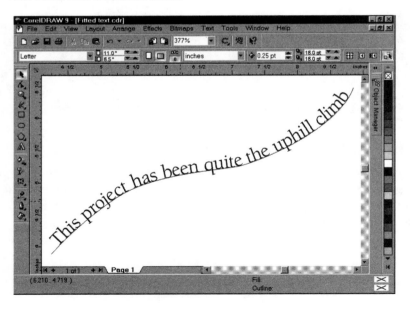

Keep Your Distance

What else is wrong with our fitted text? The text is sitting right on top of the curve—
very distracting. Either the text needs to be lifted off the curve, or the curve needs to
be removed altogether. (With many designs, the text simply becomes the curve, not
needing any other shape.)

So here's Take 4: we set the Distance from Path just enough to raise the descenders
up off the curve. You can see from the property bar where to set this—we chose a value
of .125 inch.

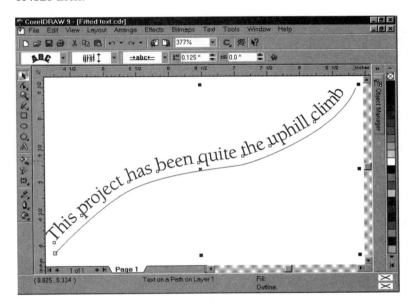

Incidentally, this little exercise pretty well typifies how most people use Fit Text to
Path: they fiddle, they fumble, they flounder, they futz, and eventually they get where
they want to go. Few people get there on the first try.

We considered removing the outline altogether. (Not the curve, but just its outline;
the curve must remain for the effect to stay dynamic.) But we decided instead to tint
it from solid black to a medium gray.

The final tweak—and you judge for yourself whether you prefer it or not—came at
the hands of the text orientation control, the one at the left end of the property bar.
The vertical skew and the slight upward rotation give the impression that the letters are
actually climbing up the curve. The control is included in the accompanying graphic
because, again, it's practically impossible to describe this text orientation control. But

PART

Mastering Text

since you asked: "You know the first drop-down box with the fat *ABC* letters? Click on it and choose the second set of fat letters." There.

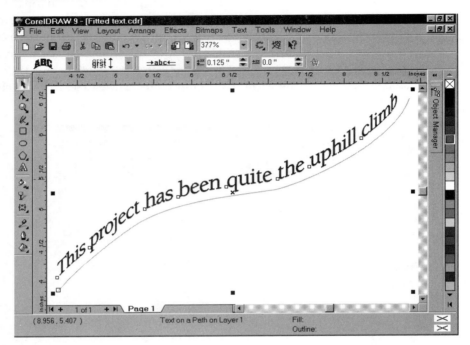

We carefully chose this example of text fitting, picking something that started out with big problems, to show you the pitfalls. Figure 10.5 is an example that has no problems. Corel's Technical typeface is perfect for text fitting because its letterforms are friendly and appear to be walking an uneven path, anyway. Also, the tree branch in this figure is an ideal path, with smooth and friendly curves. Finally, the text is comfortably positioned off the path, preserving the integration of the two elements while avoiding overcrowding.

Transparent Text

The next effect, and the one that follows it, is not at all difficult to produce, provided that you have prepared the text properly. In fact, it would be safe to say that in producing the transparent effect shown in Figure 10.6, preparation is the key to everything.

FIGURE 10.5

This fitted text is an unqualified success.

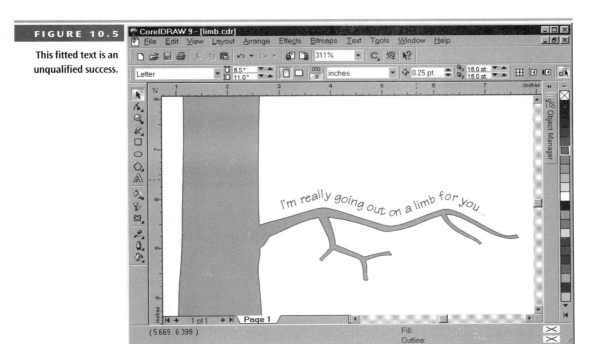

FIGURE 10.6

Transparent text is easy; preparing the text is tricky.

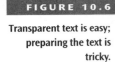

PART
3

Mastering Text

The wrinkle in all of this is the text's cozy condition: each of the letters overlaps its neighbors, and that carries its own set of issues and requirements. Let's step through this.

1. First, import the photograph. You can use 863057.wi from CD No. 3, in Photos\ Landscap. Press F4 to zoom tight.

2. Create a string of text. We chose the word *SUNSET* and we set it in Seagull Heavy from Corel's typeface collection. Thick faces work best.

3. Set the text to White and size and stretch it so that it is as big as the photo. Don't worry about sizing proportionally; symmetry adds nothing to the effect.

If your screen starts to pan when you size the text near the edge, just press F4 again. You could apply the transparent effect now and save yourself several minutes, but it will look much better if the text overlaps itself. It will be worth the following effort:

4. Switch to the Shape tool and drag the lower-right handle toward the middle of the text. As you do, the letters move closer to each other.

5. Continue until each letter overlaps the ones next to it.

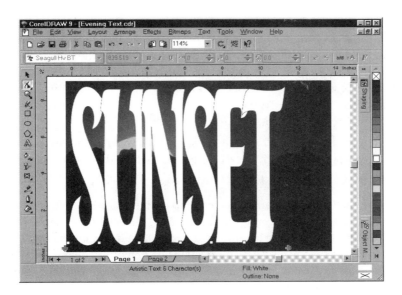

Some will overlap more than others, warranting a bit of individual kerning. For instance, in the graphic above, the *U* and *N* are barely touching, while the *E* and *T* overlap quite a bit. To fix this, select the node to the left of the *T* and bump it a bit to its right, using the Horizontal Shift value in the property bar.

6. Once kerned, switch back to the Pick tool and stretch the text back out so it fills the picture from left to right.

If you were to apply transparency to the text now, the effect would be deficient, because the areas where the characters overlap would become opaque gaps. You can see this easily enough just by selecting the text, activating the Interactive Transparency tool from the toolbox, and choosing any type of transparency from the property bar. We wish there were a text control called Remove Holes or something, whereby overlapping text would appear seamlessly. Because there isn't; you need to convert the text to curves and break apart the letterforms:

7. Convert the text to curves with Arrange ➤ Convert to Curves (or Ctrl+Q). As soon as you do, you'll see the effect we spoke of where the characters overlap.

8. Then break apart the letters with Arrange ➤ Break Apart (Ctrl+K).

With the letters broken apart, the overlap problem appears to be solved, because each letter is now its own curve. To be technical, instead of each letter being a subpath of one collective curve (producing the overlap effect), it is its own curve. But the fact remains that each character still overlaps its neighbor, meaning that the transparent effect won't be uniform (in the overlapping areas, there will be a second layer of transparent elements). Take a trip into Wireframe view (View ➤ Wireframe), and you'll see what we mean.

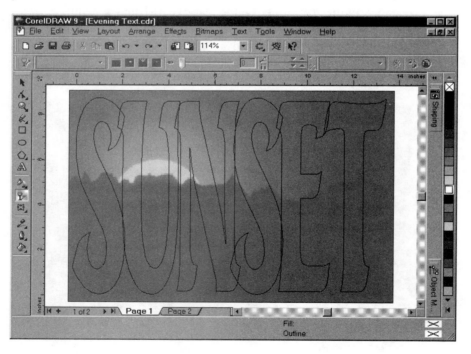

That's why you need to continue:

9. Select all six characters and go to Arrange ➤ Shaping ➤ Weld.

10. Click Weld To on the Shaping docker and head out to the page.

11. Click anywhere within the letters.

DRAW will think for a moment and blink at you once. Nothing else will appear to have happened, but actually, a significant transformation took place: DRAW looked for all of the places where the letters overlapped and it removed all nodes responsible for the overlap. Again, a trip to Wireframe view confirms this.

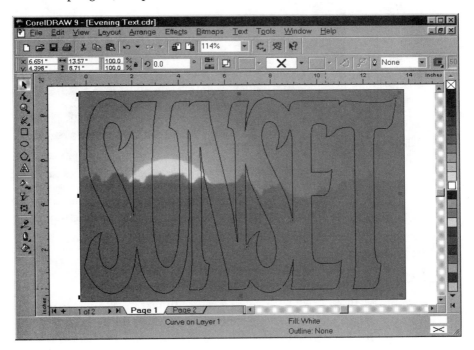

There are no paths in the interior of these letters—only exterior outlines. Now you are finally ready to create the transparent effect:

12. Select the text (which is no longer text, but one big curve) and activate Interactive Transparency.

13. Choose the type of transparency and the degree of transparency. We played it simple with a uniform transparency at its default values.

PART

Mastering Text

It would be tempting to experiment with exotic fill or transparency patterns, but we suggest you resist. The transparent effect is striking enough—further patterns could detract from the clean and simple effect.

Creating a Text Mask

Another attractive effect you can create with text in DRAW is that of looking through one object to see another object behind it. The technical term for this is *masking,* and DRAW has an automatic way of doing it, which you'll see in the following exercise.

But first let's talk about this word, *mask.* Our suspicion is that accomplished graphic artists use the term when they want to intimidate us amateurs. "Oh, we'll just mask off that image, cut an overlay, and do a burn on the plates." Yeah, right—and then we'll go on the Internet and discuss new radiation therapies with the doctors at Stanford Medical Center.

To understand masking, think of it literally, like a Halloween mask—an object with holes, through which elements behind the mask are visible (such as the eyes of the person wearing the mask). DRAW uses its own term, *powerclip,* but it is the same thing.

We will return to our sunset image to produce Figure 10.7.

The word *SUNSET* is acting as a mask for the actual sunset.

Most of this exercise has already been done for us, but we will have to undo a few things. Here's the easiest way:

1. Select both elements of the sunset and copy them to the Clipboard with Ctrl+C.

2. Press PgDn to create a second page in the drawing. Choose Landscape for orientation.

3. Paste the two elements with Ctrl+V.

4. Select the text, go to Interactive Transparency, and remove the effect.

Now you're ready…

5. Select the picture behind the text. As the text and picture are almost the same size, use the status bar to ensure you have selected the right thing. It should verify that you have selected a "color bitmap," instead of a curve.

6. Go to Effects ➢ PowerClip ➢ Place inside Container.

7. With the big pointing arrow, click once on the text.

8. Deselect to get a clean look at your masterpiece.

PART

Mastering Text

For good measure, we applied a drop shadow to the text, using the Interactive Drop Shadow tool that lives at the end of the Effects flyout in the toolbox. It took less than one minute to produce the effect.

You'll find Evening Text.cdr, containing both the transparent and masked text effects, on the Sybex Web site. We'll be offering considerable detail on both drop shadows and powerclips in Chapters 18 and 19, respectively.

Working with "Untext"

What do we mean by *untext*? It's text that is no longer text, stripped of its special status by the Arrange ➤ Convert to Curves command that you used earlier in the chapter. When you convert text to curves, you gain access to all of its nodes and paths, just like any other type of curve. This opens the door to many fascinating effects, with which you can personalize your text to a level beyond just what the typeface offers.

Unfortunately, whenever this feature is shown off in public at user group meetings or trade shows, the result always seems to look something like Figure 10.8. A guest at one of our recent seminars stood up and asked how to use the "Text Destroyer tool"—so closely identified is this tool with its potentially hideous results.

CorelDRAW 9 - [Text Uglifier tool.cdr]

File   Edit   View   Layout   Arrange   Effects   Bitmaps   Text   Tools   Window   Help

Letter   612.0 pt   792.0 pt   points   0.25 pt   18.0 pt   18.0 pt

Ugly Text

1 of 1   Page 1

(18.420, -210.198)   Fill:
                        Outline:

In many ways, working with converted text requires even more care than working with abstract objects, because readers know how a text character is supposed to look. If you distort a character too much, you can offend your readers' sensibilities; and if you don't change it enough, they might not notice the effect at all and decide instead that you are just using poorly crafted typefaces.

Figure 10.9 shows a couple of simple, yet effective, examples of text effects. What began as a string of Futura Black became four characters that stayed out in the sun too long. And the two lines of Brittanic Bold sacrificed their identities as text strings to create the logo at lower-right, using a single, crafted character to represent two letters at once.

PART

Mastering Text

When Type Effects Need Their Type

With many text effects, it is crucial that you use the right kind of typeface, and that is why many designers convert text to curves before sending a .cdr file to a colleague for review. If the desired typeface is replaced by another one because the recipient doesn't have it installed, the effect could be compromised.

But converting to curves is an inconvenient solution, making it impossible to edit or adjust the text. That is why Corel added a font-embedding capability to DRAW 8. If you are giving your .cdr file to someone who may not have the fonts you used in the file, check the Embed Fonts Using TrueDoc box in the File ➤ Save As dialog. If you have already saved the file without embedding the fonts and now want to embed them, issue a File ➤ Save As command, check Embed Fonts, and say Yes to overwriting the file.

Your fonts will be included in the file so it can be properly displayed (and even modified) on a computer that does not have the fonts installed. Each font will appear on the fonts list with an asterisk, indicating that it is available only within that document.

Not all typefaces can be embedded, but all of Corel's can.

PART IV

EFFECTS AND AFFECTS

WHEN OBJECTS COLLIDE

Featuring

WHEN OBJECTS COLLIDE

his chapter's title is perhaps more applicable to one of Carl Sagan's works, but CorelDRAW users also have reason to hold this topic in high regard. One of the core capabilities of vector-based drawing programs is the layering of objects. Consequently, the treatment and handling of objects that reside atop one another tell a lot about the application. DRAW is one of the most apt at dealing with objects that bang into each other, and that is the focus of this chapter.

The Shaping Triumvirate

They are now found on a docker instead of a roll-up, and Corel's architects improved access to them on the property bar. Nonetheless, the respective functions of Intersect, Trim, and Weld have remained the same since their inceptions in versions 4 (for Weld) and 5 (for the two others). These three commands study the areas where objects overlap and then do something at that overlap. What each command does, however, is quite different from one another. Together, the three make a very powerful team.

In the docker, the three commands share what we like to call the "Do It" button (its name changes between Intersect With, Trim, and Weld To, so we simply refer to it as Do It in all cases). In addtion, there are two check boxes that determine the status of the so-called *source* and *target objects*. Let's begin by defining these terms.

The Source Object

This is simply the object you select first. For trimming, the order in which you select objects is crucial; for the other two, it's not as important. But by definition, the object you select first is the source. And there can be more than one source; you can select several objects at once and call them all the *source*.

The Target Object

This is the object to which the effect gets applied. In other words, if you were to ask DRAW to find, say, the intersection between the oval and the star shown in Figure 11.1, you would go to Arrange ➤ Shaping ➤ Intersect, select one of the objects first, and click the Do It button. Then you would define the *target object* by clicking on it with the big fat arrow that DRAW presents you with.

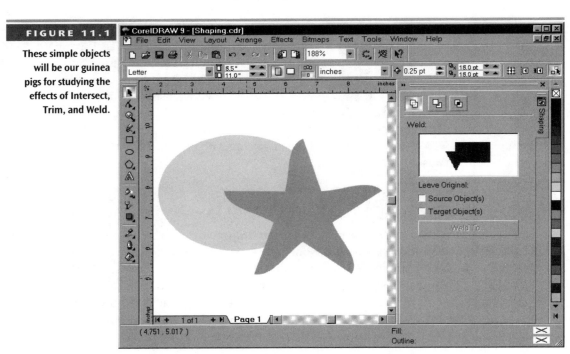

FIGURE 11.1

These simple objects will be our guinea pigs for studying the effects of Intersect, Trim, and Weld.

We wish that this term were better defined. When two objects are to be intersected, either one of them can be the intersector and the intersectee. It's not as if one of the objects does something to the other, as is the case with Trim—instead, the effect happens to both of them. So again, in many cases, it's arbitrary what object you define as the target. But, as with many other areas of DRAW, the object that you select *last*—the target object—is the one that determines the outline and fill for the new object created during the operation.

So for applying any of the shaping operations, you need to:

1. Select the source object(s) first.

2. Click the Do It button.

3. Click on the target object.

Leaving the Original

It is not immediately obvious what happens when you check or uncheck the two Leave Original boxes. Essentially, you can elect to use the objects just as a means for creating a new object (in which case you would ask DRAW to delete them when you're through) or keep the original objects on the screen after you create your new object.

Finding the Intersection

Our first audience will be with the Intersect function. Like the two others, Intersect studies the objects in question and determines the area where they overlap. It creates a new object that consists only of that overlap.

Create a few simple overlapping shapes like the ones in Figure 11.1 and fill them. Then do the following:

1. Select the oval. It is the so-called source object.

2. Go to Arrange ➤ Shaping ➤ Intersect to open the docker.

3. Make sure that both boxes in the Leave Original section of the docker are unchecked.

4. Click the Do It button, and then click on the star.

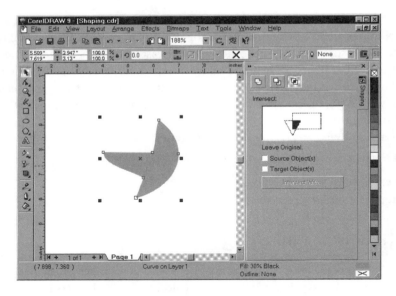

As you can see, the only thing left is the intersection of the two objects. Now do this:

5. Press Ctrl+Z to undo.

6. Select the oval again.

7. This time check both Leave Original boxes.

8. Perform the Intersect function again.

9. Using the on-screen palette, fill the new object with a different color (you'll only be able to see it because of its selection handles).

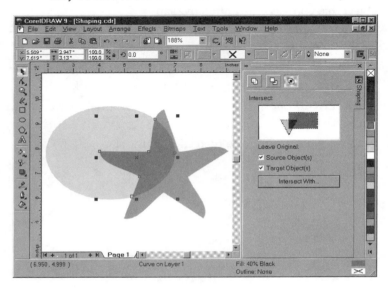

You can use this operation to produce realistic filtering and transparency of objects. You can experiment on your own by alternating between checking and unchecking each of the Leave Original boxes.

Intersect can be used effectively to focus on a particular part of an object. Figure 11.2 shows a detailed illustration of a camcorder, with a few buttons that need explaining. By using Intersect, we were able to create a cutaway and blow it up, to ease the process of pointing out and describing the buttons. Here's how we did it.

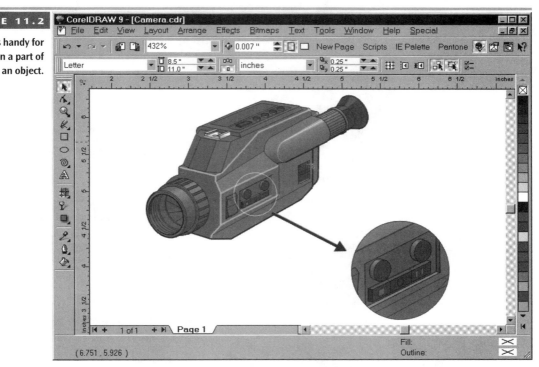

FIGURE 11.2

Intersect is handy for focusing on a part of an object.

1. We imported `camcord.cdr` from the `\Clipart\Leisure\Hobbies\` directory of the Corel clipart CD.

2. We made sure that the entire camera was grouped. You can define more than one object as the target, but because you only get one click, you need to group the objects.

3. We drew a white-outlined circle around the area of interest.

4. We opened the Intersect docker.

5. We wanted to keep the circle we drew, and of course, we wanted to keep the camera, so we made sure that both of the Leave Original boxes were checked.

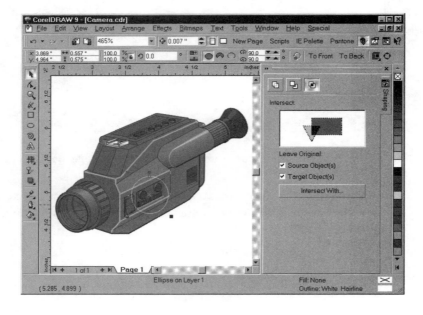

6. We clicked Do It, clicked once on the camera, and waited about five seconds.

7. We dragged the new group of objects to the side and enlarged it.

8. We added the arrow and saved.

N O T E The Intersect tool is always going to create the same objects—there can be only one intersection between objects—but the effect can look radically different, depending upon the order in which you select the objects. For instance, we wanted to see what would happen if we switched roles and selected the camera as the source and then chose the oval as the target. The result reminded us that the target always determines the outline and fill colors of the new intersected objects: with an oval that is hollow and outlined white, Intersect produced a group of objects all hollow and outlined white. Oops...

Cookie Cutters and Cookie Dough

In many ways, Trim is the exact opposite of Intersect. Where Intersect finds an overlap and creates an object in that space, Trim finds an overlap and carves it away. Intersect creates a new object; Trim removes part of an existing object.

The simplest way to view the Trim operation is to imagine yourself baking cookies of various shapes and sizes. You use cookie cutters to slice into the dough and create the shapes, trimming off the excess and eating it when nobody is looking. (Cathy of cartoon fame says those calories don't count because you weren't actually making cookies from that dough.)

This is exactly how Trim works, and Figure 11.3 illustrates this. The rabbit is the cookie cutter and the warped rectangle is our best effort at cookie dough. In the upper-right image, the cookie cutter is pressing its way through the dough. The lower image shows the result—a hole cut out from the dough, in the precise shape of the rabbit.

N O T E If the source is located entirely within the target, then Trim functions the same as Combine.

With Trim, the cutter is the source and the dough is the target. And to continue the analogy, just as you can cut multiple shapes into the dough with different cookie cutters, so too can you use more than one object as a source.

FIGURE 11.3

The best way to think of
Trim is to think of cut-
ting a shape out of
cookie dough.

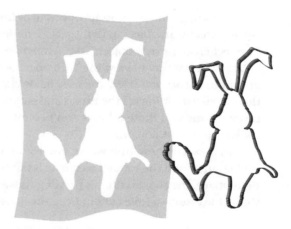

Trimming involves exactly the same procedure as intersecting: select the source, decide what to keep and what to throw out, click Do It, and choose the target. Returning to the oval and the star, here is a journey through the trim process. The star, already selected, is the source, and the docker shows that we intend to keep the source when we're done, but eliminate the original target.

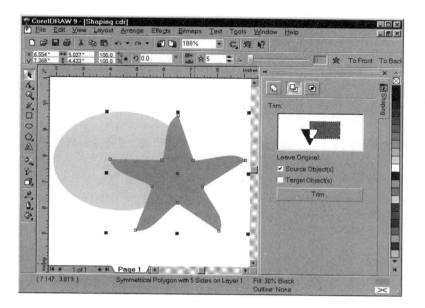

By clicking the Do It button and then clicking on the oval, the star is being asked to take a bite out of the oval. Because the bite is right underneath the star, you won't see it until you move the star over a bit.

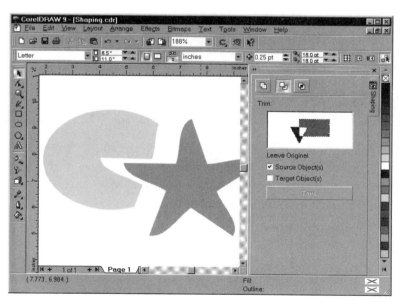

We generally regard Trim as the handiest of the three for its ability to shape objects so quickly and so radically. It does not have the deftness for creating shapes as the Pencil or Bézier tools, but it works very quickly. The gear in Figure 11.4 was created in less than five minutes, and while the shading and the extrusion might be what capture your attention, they're the easy part. The hard part is creating the teeth of the gear; imagine having to do it using only the Shape tool!

FIGURE 11.4

This gear was created in 10 minutes. Without Trim, it would have taken over an hour.

To create this gear, start with a big gray circle and a little circle and follow these steps. If you have not used the Blend command before, you might need to consult Chapter 14 before you can keep up with all of the steps.

1. Drag and dupe a copy of the small circle.

2. Use the Interactive Blend tool to blend between the two small circles.

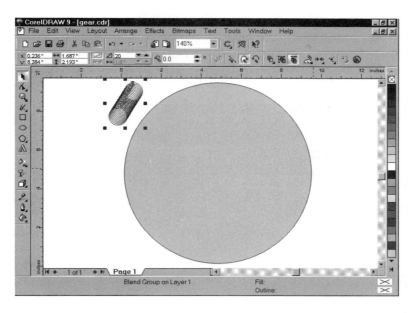

3. Click Path Properties on the property bar, choose New Path from the flyout menu, and click on the big circle.

4. Click Miscellaneous Blend Options and choose Blend along Full Path.

5. Use the Steps control to increase or decrease the number of blend steps so that the circles are not too crowded or too far apart.

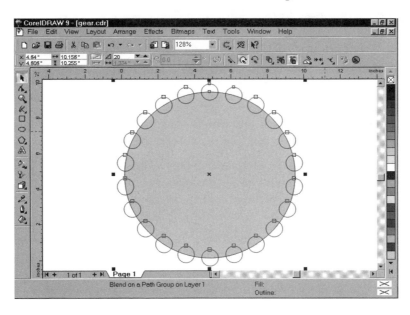

6. With the blended circles still selected, go to Arrange ➤ Separate (DRAW cannot use a Blend group as a source).

7. Open the Trim docker.

8. Uncheck both Leave Original boxes, click Do It, and click on the big circle.

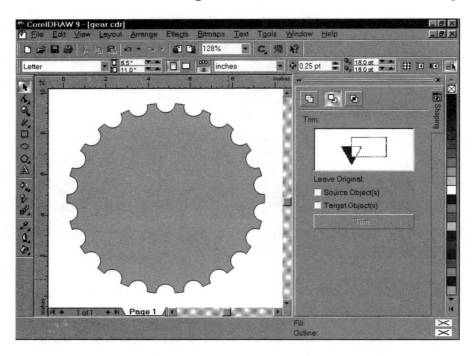

9. Create another circle and place it near the middle of the gear.

10. Select both the circle and the gear and center them by pressing C and E. Introduced in DRAW 8, these accelerator keys are the quickest way to align objects. See Chapter 3 for a listing of all of them.

11. Select the small circle and trim the gear with it (in other words, click Do It and click the gear). You can see the result on the facing page.

We'll finish this gear in Chapter 15 when we apply the extrusion to it. While we acknowledge that this required a little tango with the Blend tool, using Trim was many times easier than creating the shape manually.

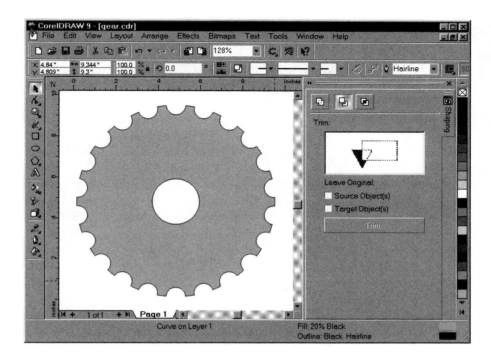

Melting Objects Together

The third member of the Shaping Triumvirate, Weld, produces the most radical results. It finds the areas where objects overlap and eliminates everything in that space. It has the power to reduce multiple objects to lifeless blobs that have nodes and paths only along the periphery, not in the interior. With Weld, like Intersect, it often doesn't matter which object you select as the source and the target. The target object's only role, once again, is to determine the outline and fill color of the resulting shape.

Figure 11.5 shows the reign of terror that Weld imposes on unsuspecting objects, as the star and oval have become permanently and mercilessly fused. Weld hunted down and eliminated every node and path that was in the interior, leaving only the outline around the periphery.

Weld's default is to not leave any original objects.

If Trim is the most useful of the three, Weld is not far behind. By eliminating their interiors, Weld simplifies objects, and that can be invaluable in numerous situations. Here are just a few.

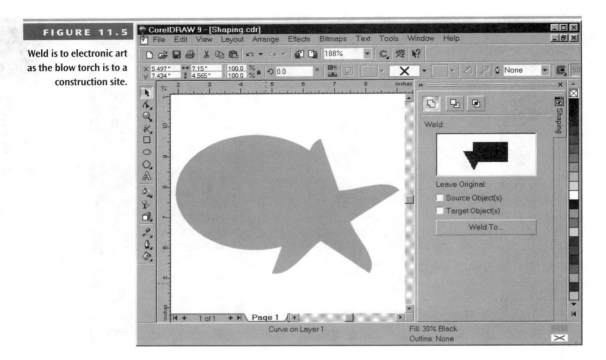

FIGURE 11.5

Weld is to electronic art as the blow torch is to a construction site.

Creating Silhouettes

If all you want is the form of an image but not the detail, Weld is your ticket. In Figure 11.6 you see how an image of famous pitcher Dennis Eckersley can be converted into a generic silhouette of an anonymous pitcher.

If you want to see an equally dramatic example of Weld in action, Figure 11.7 shows the original picture (left) of the bunny rabbit that we used as our cookie cutter (right) earlier in the chapter. It took us but a moment to separate the egg from the bunny and then nuke the poor bunny into welded oblivion.

This starts to sound a bit morbid, and we confess that the cool thing about Weld is how destructive you can be and how quickly you can destroy things. All you have to do is ungroup the objects, select them, and issue the Weld command. Like a tornado ravaging the countryside, everything is simply gone. There's just nothing left to all of the detail that, moments ago, defined the image. It's just gone.

FIGURE 11.6

Weld maintains an object's form while eliminating the detail.

FIGURE 11.7

Another example of the destructive force of Weld

Outlining Script Text

Turning to less violent pursuits, if you have occasion to create an outline around a string of fancy text, you might be frustrated to discover that many script typefaces don't truly connect their characters—understandable, given that they must be able to appear integrated with any other character in that face. This goes unnoticed with black text, but becomes terribly annoying with text that has an outline color different from its fill.

Figure 11.8 illustrates this dilemma. Looking at the line of BrushScript text at the top, you would never suspect any problem. However, the middle image shows what happens when you fill the interior a different color than the outline—the magnified part exposes overlapping subpaths. The bottom image has been welded. (You can weld a compound image, such as text, to itself by selecting it initially and then choosing it again for the target object.) Notice how the overlaps are now clean.

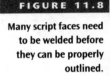

FIGURE 11.8

Many script faces need to be welded before they can be properly outlined.

The sacrifice is that the text is no longer text, so as with all other radical changes to text strings, edit it for content first.

Preparing for Sign Making

Printing your work on a laser printer is one thing; printing on a large sign-making device is quite another. If you print one object on top of another to your laser printer, you don't really care that both objects print, because one completely covers the other. On the other hand, when a vinyl cutter begins rendering an image, it will cut every location where it encounters a line. It can't go back and hide or uncut. So in the case of the script typeface, the cutter would render it quite poorly unless you modified the text first.

Weld has proven to be a great gift to DRAW users who send their work to vinyl cutters. Previously they had to manually remove all unwanted lines in the interior of an object. Now Weld does that automatically.

The Advanced Options

The Shaping docker is a friendly way to use Intersect, Trim, and Weld. It's also a bit tedious, having to click numerous times in different places. DRAW added the friendlier controls a few years ago (they were in a roll-up then), and advanced users got upset. "DRAW is becoming so friendly it's driving me nuts!" shouted one patron of our annual CorelWORLD User Conference during a wish-list session. "I want controls that let me get in and out quickly."

The answer is on the property bar that appears whenever more than one object is selected. On the right side, just left of Align, you'll see three icons, one for each member of the Triumvirate. These are one-stop shops, applying the respective effect to the selected objects according to the following rules:

- The objects selected first are the source(s) and the one selected last becomes the target.
- Intersect creates the intersecting object and leaves all other objects on the page.
- Trim slices up the target and leaves all other objects on the page.
- Weld melts all objects together, without leaving any original objects.

Advanced users will likely prefer these quick-attack icons. All you have to remember is the order in which you select objects, and then one click does the job. If these default settings leave unwanted objects on the page, just select them and delete them.

Step by Step: Turning Many Shapes into One

This is one of our favorite exercises for learning about shaping overlapping objects—the creation of a simple key. You'll see how very simple shapes can team up to create a plausible graphic.

1. Let's start with two simple rectangles. Create them as shown below. Select them both and press C to ensure that the top rectangle is centered above the lower one.

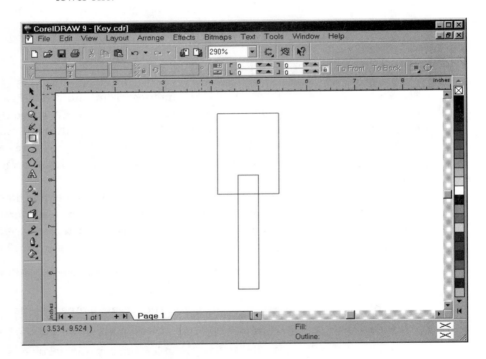

2. Select the top rectangle and switch to the Shape tool.

3. Choose any node and move it. You will see instantly how the Shape tool behaves when applied to a rectangle: all four corners become rounded.

4. Repeat step 3 for the longer, thinner rectangle.

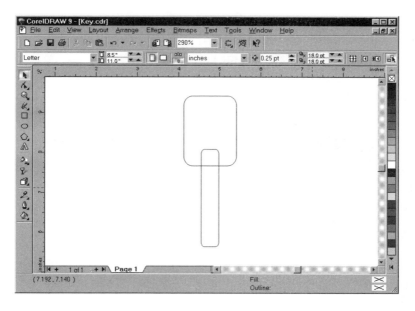

Watch how easy it is to weld with the property bar.

5. Select both rectangles.

6. Click the Weld icon on the property bar (the left-most of the three).

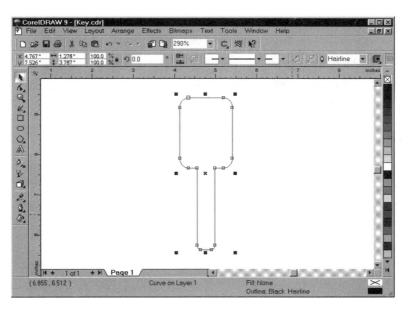

The jagged part of the key is a perfect opportunity to use Trim. The first step is to create the trimming tool. Here goes:

1. Switch to the Bézier tool and create a shape similar to the one shown below. It is important that your jagged shape be a closed object, so make sure that your very last click is right on top of your first click.

This shape becomes your trimming tool.

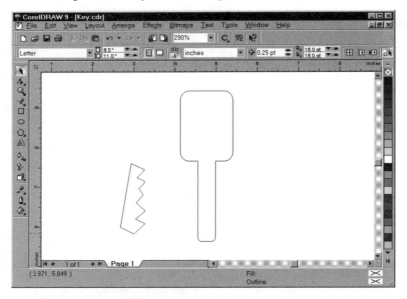

2. Move the trimming tool into position over the key.

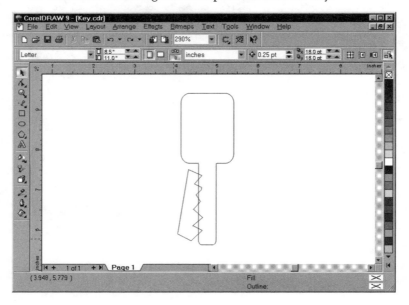

3. Select the trimming tool first and the rest of the key second.

4. Click Trim (the middle icon of the group of three on the property bar).

5. Select the trimming tool and delete it to see the result.

You're done.

Effects and Affects

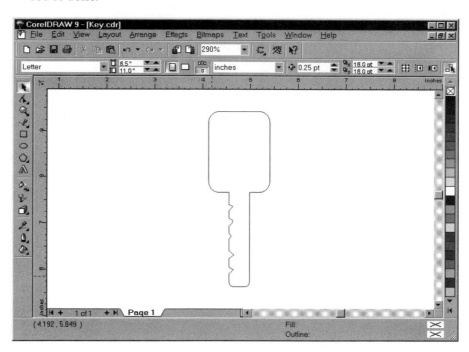

Three different objects teamed up to create this key: two rectangles and the trimming tool. But now, after Weld and Trim got involved, the key is just one object. Weld fused the two rectangles, and Trim created the jagged edge.

chapter 12

A MATTER OF PERSPECTIVE

Featuring

A MATTER OF
PERSPECTIVE

n this chapter, we introduce what will become a familiar refrain. Graphic drawing programs have become so sophisticated, it is all too easy to lose sight of one important fact: despite all the flash, sizzle, and power, the electronic drawing canvas remains a two-dimensional environment. Despite all illusions to the contrary, Corel-DRAW lives in a flat universe, in which objects can be either in front or in back, but nothing in between. Objects cannot go through other objects, and there is no such thing as an object being further away from another, or taller, or shorter, or fatter. There is just a height and a width and an "in front of" and a "behind."

Now that we have said that, we will also tell you that this chapter, and the six that follow, will do everything possible to make you believe otherwise. DRAW's special effects, when used strategically and wisely, can achieve stunning realism. They can make you believe that you are working in a three-dimensional CAD program. You know better, but you might be fooled sometimes.

This chapter looks at one of the tamer effects, to be frank. Perspective offers a method of distorting an object or group of objects to create the illusion of distance. The operative word is *illusion...*

Adding Perspective

Unlike blends and extrusions—two effects which actually add new elements to a drawing—perspective is a distortion to existing objects. Perspective is designed specifically to create a sense of dimension relative to a particular viewpoint.

To add a perspective, select an object or group and go to Effects ➤ Add Perspective. This is one of the few tools that has not been given a spot on the Interactive Effects flyout, but that's an unfair demotion: Add Perspective has been an interactive tool for years now. It was the first of the interactive tools. That's because it's so simple to use, that's all you do: work interactively with a few controls on screen.

If you know how to node-edit with the Shape tool, you know how to add perspective. In fact, you use the Shape tool for applying perspective, and as far as DRAW is concerned, all you're doing is a bit of node-editing. But instead of shaping the actual nodes and paths of an object, you are shaping its viewpoint. You are determining the angle from which the object is viewed. And when used capably, that can make all the difference in the world...even a two-dimensional world.

Adding perspective to a drawing is quite easy. Follow these steps and see for yourself:

1. In a new drawing, create one straight vertical line by using the Freehand tool and holding Ctrl while you draw. (You'll be using Ctrl a lot in this chapter, by the way.) Set the outline width to 2 or 3 points.

2. Switch to the Pick tool (spacebar) and drag and dupe a copy of the line just to the right of the original, holding Ctrl while dragging to make sure that the copy doesn't wander up or down.

3. Press Ctrl+R to make a third line.

4. Select the middle line, go to the Outline Style Selector button on the property bar, and choose a dotted line as the style.

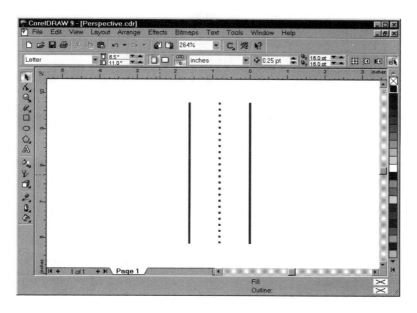

Effects and Affects

5. Select all three lines and group them with Ctrl+G.

6. Select Effects ➤ Add Perspective and DRAW will enclose your group in a perspective grid. Now hold Ctrl and drag the bottom-right handle off to the right.

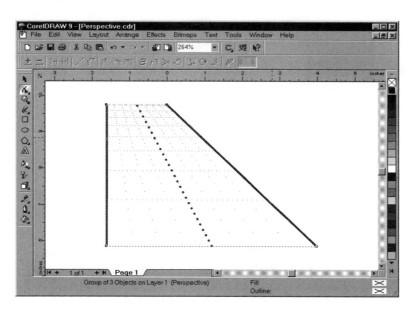

Thanks to Perspective, this view from above a road or airline landing strip appears much more realistic.

Undo the perspective with Ctrl+Z and try applying different perspectives.

- Drag the bottom-left handle off to the left and note the change.
- Drag both bottom handles to the outside.
- Do it again, without holding Ctrl.
- Try dragging the top handles, also.
- Move the "vanishing point"—the on-screen × that we'll explain shortly.
- Try everything.

WARNING   You cannot select several objects at once and apply a perspective to them. They must be grouped first.

One-Point Perspective

The simple roadway shown in the preceding exercise is an example of *one-point perspective*. One-point perspective gives the impression that the object is receding from view in a single direction. You create one-point perspective when you drag the perspective handles vertically *or* horizontally, but not both.

The × above the object is the hypothetical *vanishing point* that appears while you are applying or editing a perspective. Because this point represents the theoretical spot toward which the object is receding, it is normally very far away from the actual object. To see it, you might have to zoom out with F3 a few times. Once it is visible, you will see the vanishing point move as you drag the handles. You can also move the vanishing point itself, as an alternative to moving the handles.

TIP   To ensure that your drawings are constrained to one-point perspective, remember to use the Ctrl key. If you also hold Shift, the opposite handle will symmetrically mirror the movement of the handle you are dragging.

Two-Point Perspective

Remember that one-point perspective is maintained only if all handle-dragging is confined to either horizontal or vertical movements. You will still have a one-point perspective even if you move all four handles, *if they have all been moved along the same axis.* Two-point perspective involves motion along two planes, so objects appear to be receding in two directions at once. You can achieve this by dragging one handle up or down and another handle left or right, or by dragging one handle in a diagonal direction.

WARNING   Before you apply any perspectives, make sure your object is already shaped the way you want it. Once you apply a perspective to an object, you can't shape its nodes.

Figure 12.1 shows what is an all-too-common dilemma: two pieces of clipart that just don't quite work together (not the least of which is that space shuttles don't land on aircraft carriers, but we'll overlook that minor detail for now). You can see this for yourself by importing `carriert.cdr` from the `\clipart\collection\transpor\ships` directory and `shut10002.cdr` from the `\clipart\collection\space\shuttles` directory.

The aircraft carrier has a distinct perspective and the shuttle has a distinctly different one. Specifically, the carrier is horizontal—it's floating on the sea—but the shuttle looks like it is flying up into space, as shuttles are want to do. It is not receding into the distance like the carrier is. You cannot look at this shuttle and get any plausible impression that it is going to land on the carrier.

FIGURE 12.1

What's wrong with this drawing? If you can't quite put your finger on it…it's probably perspective.

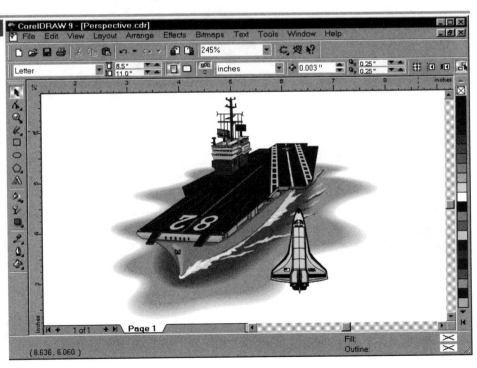

You might be tempted to try to rotate or flatten the shuttle to make it look better; that rarely works. And let's be frank, sometimes nothing works when you are trying to squeeze realism out of two-dimensional graphics. But before you give up, try perspective.

Figure 12.2 shows the result of applying two-point perspective: we tugged at the lower-right handle and tweaked the lower-left one a bit. The shuttle appears to be receding into the distance, and that is enough to give the impression that the shuttle is landing on the carrier. At least now the shuttle appears to be in the same dimension...sharing a similar perspective.

FIGURE 12.2

By adding two-point perspective, the shuttle is now plausibly landing on the strip, not flying into space.

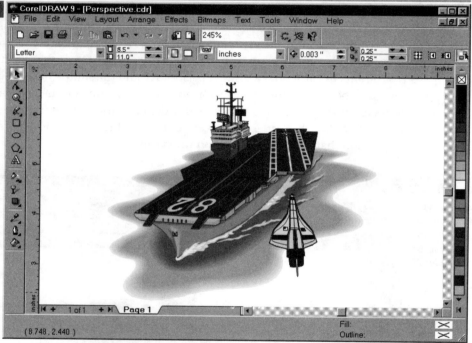

TIP   When adjusting perspective, make regular trips into Full Screen Preview with F9. Otherwise, the plane and grids that the Add Perspective tool places on screen will become annoying.

To drive home the difference between one- and two-point perspective, imagine that you are working a camera on a movie set, on one of those fancy cranes that allow you to move in all directions. If you swing around the set in either purely horizontal

PART

Effects and Affects

or purely vertical motions, your film will have a one-point perspective. But if you swing around in all directions at once, you'll get a two-point perspective (along with a queasy stomach).

The Fallacy of Copying Perspectives

Since version 2, DRAW has offered automatic copying of one object's perspective to another. Also since version 2, we have been searching for legitimate uses of this feature.

Copying a perspective sounds like a valuable operation (found at Effects ➤ Copy Effect ➤ Perspective From), and you might expect that you could use it to create nice three-dimensional scenes. However, this command simply copies the same relative distortion from one object to another. It rarely contributes to realism. Witness the poor street sign that gets massacred when the perspective of the road is applied to it.

Original objects

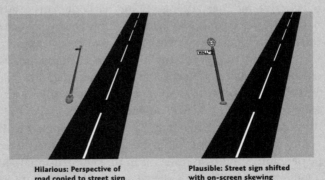

Hilarious: Perspective of
road copied to street sign

Plausible: Street sign shifted
with on-screen skewing

Continued on next page

Fixing it involved applying a perspective just to the sign, and one quite different than the one given to the road. Generally, spending a few minutes with the on-screen skewing controls produces much better results than the Copy Perspective command.

While copying perspectives is usually futile, adjusting perspective so two objects share the same vanishing point is often an excellent tactic. You can achieve this by making note of the vanishing point coordinates shown on the status bar when you are editing a perspective, or just by noting its on-screen position visually.

WARNING   Perspective can be a useful effect, but it has one important limitation: applying perspective does not scale object outlines, even if you enable Scale with Image in the Outline Pen dialog. If you use a thick outline as a border on an object, don't expect it to scale realistically when you add perspective. Neither do pattern fills scale according to the perspective.

Our Perspective on Perspectives

Two final thoughts on perspectives before a Step-by-Step exercise: First, though it is possible to group objects that already have a perspective and add a new perspective to the group, this isn't necessarily a good idea. You might end up creating a nice effect, but you lose control over it, because each perspective introduces a distortion on top of the previous distortion. So, if your intention is to add a totally different perspective to the objects, you're better off using Effects ➤ Clear Perspective to clear the existing perspective and then adding a brand-new one. This goes for single objects or groups of objects, although it is easier to control the appearance of single objects, lowering the risk of applying perspectives on top of perspectives.

The second thought is this: Add Perspective is good for applying simple visual effects to objects; don't expect more from it than it can deliver. When professional artists turn to DRAW to produce realistic work, they *don't* call on Add Perspective. A good case in point is the award-winning work shown in Figure 12.3, authored by Antonio De Leo of Rome, Italy. This piece is dripping with realistic perspective, and you can bet that Antonio did not use the Add Perspective command to create it. Instead, he determined his own horizons in three-dimensional space, created his own vanishing points, and created all objects so that they conform. In studying the drawing and his use of guidelines, we suspect he spent more time just on creating perspective lines than most of us spend on entire drawings.

For another excellent example, see St. Tropez Harbor in the Color Gallery.

FIGURE 12.3

This award-winning illustration by Antonio De Leo is a good example of an artist creating true perspective in a drawing.

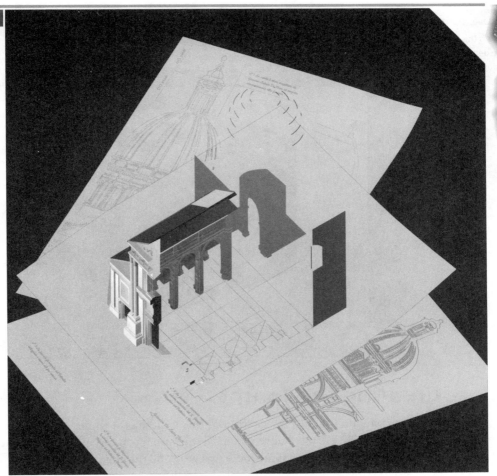

Step by Step: A Three-Dimensional Cube

The following is one of our favorite exercises for new users or those getting their first exposure to creating the illusion of depth and dimension. The cube shown in Figure 12.4 is made up of three rectangles and three letters. The sense of perspective in this drawing is produced by distorting the rectangles and the letters.

FIGURE 12.4

Does this cube really
have depth and dimen-
sion, or is DRAW just
fooling us?

Creating the Frame

You wouldn't build a house without first building the frame, and the same principle
holds for little cubes. Once you have the frame, you can literally snap the objects
onto it. Get ready for some more dragging and duping.

NOTE   There are three different places where you can enter this exercise. You
can easily start from scratch, or you can download cube.cdr from the Sybex Web site.
Page 1 of that drawing includes the basic elements and Page 2 shows the finished
drawing.

1. In an untitled drawing, drag one vertical guideline onto the page by clicking and
   dragging on the vertical ruler. Save the drawing, giving it any name you want.

2. From View, check the status of Snap to Guidelines. If it is not checked, then turn
   it on.

3. With the Rectangle tool, create a perfect square by holding Ctrl while dragging.
   Position the square so that its right side is touching the guideline.

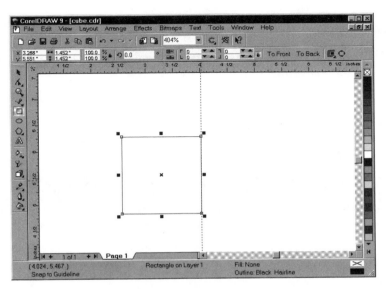

4. Switch to the Pick tool and click a second time on the square to see its rotation handles (you might have to click right on the outline).

When you select an object and click on it again, DRAW takes you into a "rotation mode" in which you can rotate or skew an object by dragging the handles that are around the periphery.

5. Click on the middle-left rotation handle (the vertical arrows) and drag up approximately 20 degrees. The rotation value in the property bar will tell you after each action how much skew you have introduced; you want it to read approximately 340. You don't need to be exact.

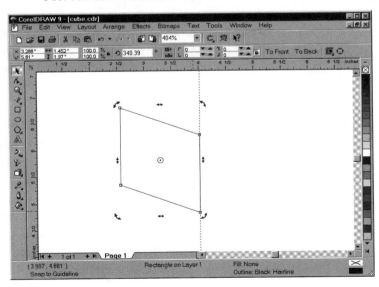

You have now created one side of the cube, and now you'll use the first side of the cube as the basis for creating the other two sides. Here goes:

6. Click again on the square (it's now actually a parallelogram); the regular selection handles return.

7. Click on the same middle-left handle, hold Ctrl, and drag the square across the guideline to the other side.

8. While still holding down Button 1, tap Button 2 once.

9. Now release Button 1.

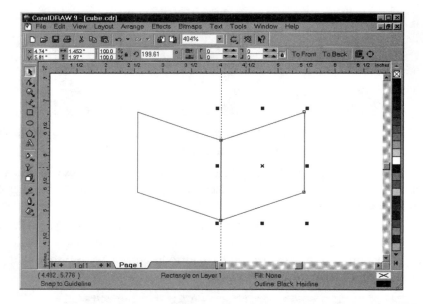

This is a variation of the drag-and-dupe maneuver that we introduced in Chapter 3. We guess it would be called flop-and-dupe. Anchored by the right side, the duplicated square flopped right over across the original, leaving two perfectly symmetrical parallelograms.

Next, to create the top side, you will follow the contours of the first two sides, and that means you need another type of snap: Snap to Objects.

10. Go to View ➤ Snap to Objects and click on it if it is not already activated.

11. Activate the Freehand tool from the toolbox (or press F5) and place your cursor near the top-left corner of the left square. Because of Snap to Objects, all you have to do is get close.

12. Click once and follow the square to the bottom-right corner. As you move nearer, your cursor should snap to the corner. When it does, release the mouse.

13. Click on the Pick tool (or press the spacebar) to select your new line segment. Because it follows the contour of the square precisely, you'll only see the line's selection handles, not the line itself.

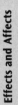

Now you want to perform half of the flop-and-dupe—just the flop part—to mirror this line above:

14. Hold Ctrl and drag the lower-middle handle above the line until it snaps into its mirrored position. Then release the mouse.

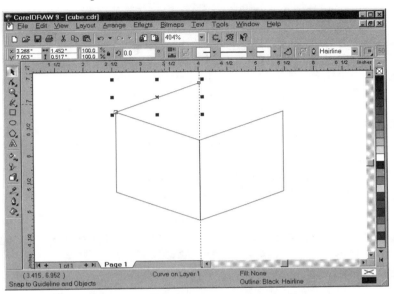

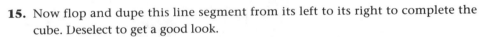

15. Now flop and dupe this line segment from its left to its right to complete the cube. Deselect to get a good look.

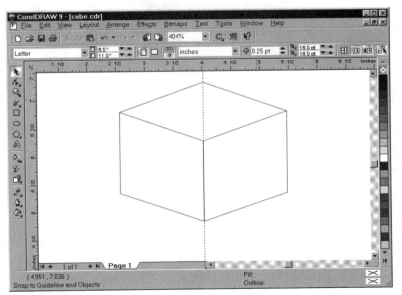

You know that this cube is proportionally correct because the second and third faces were created from the shape of the first side. Drag-and-dupe and flop-and-dupe were the featured performers.

16. Drag a marquee across the entire cube and go to Arrange ➤ Combine to turn them all into one curve.

Creating the Sides of the Cube

The three sides to the cube are nothing more than squares with letters inside of them, and we doubt you need to be led step by step through this part. Create the first one (hold Ctrl to ensure that it is a perfect square), assign a color to it, and remove the outline. Now use drag-and-dupe to create a second, and Repeat (Ctrl+R) to make a third. Don't worry about their positions; any empty part of the screen will do. Finally, make each square a different color.

Next, create three separate text strings, each with one letter. (We used A-B-C and chose three totally different typefaces.) Size each letter so that it fills out the square. Finally, group each letter with its square. Here is what ours looked like.

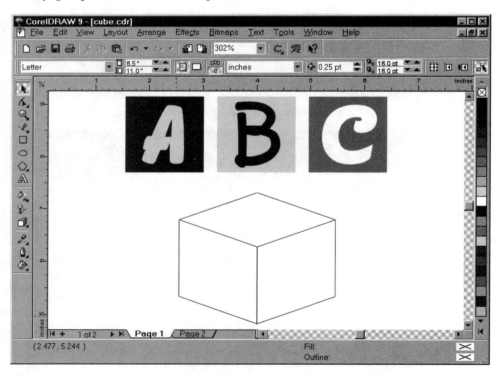

You'll note that we turned off the guideline (View ➤ Guidelines) as we no longer needed it. We also could have simply selected it and deleted it. Now follow these steps to assemble the cube:

1. Make sure that Snap to Objects is still activated.

2. Select the first square and move it next to one of the sides of the cube.

3. Go to Effects ➤ Add Perspective. When you do, the selection handles around the square will give way to four nodes, one at each corner, just as you saw previously in this chapter.

4. Take one of the nodes and drag it until it snaps to the corresponding corner of the cube. As you do, the square and letter will distort severely. That's okay. In fact, it's expected.

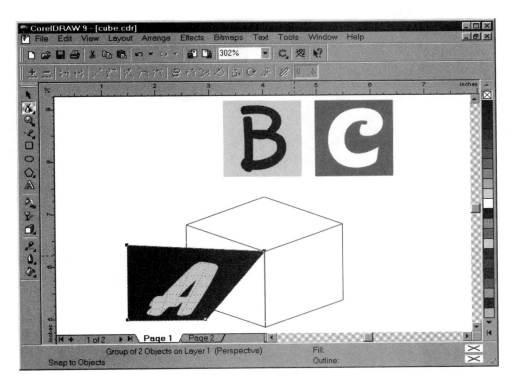

5. Snap the other three nodes onto the corners of the same side of the cube. To snap the fourth one into place, you might have to drag it all the way into the middle first, so you can see the corner, and then snap it to the corner.

6. Repeat steps 2 through 5 for the other two sides of the cube.

7. When you are done, you may want to delete the frame or change its outline to a light shade of gray, or to another color.

We consider this to be one of the ideal uses for the Add Perspective command. With it, you can take simple shapes and figures and add realistic dimension to them.

THE ENVELOPE, PLEASE

Featuring

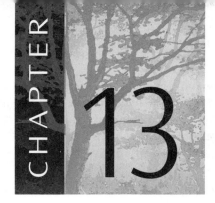

CHAPTER 13

THE ENVELOPE, PLEASE

lthough DRAW's Envelope command is similar to Perspective, you are likely to find it more interesting and versatile. Like Perspective, Envelope reshapes objects without actually adding new elements to your drawing. When you apply an envelope to an object, the object becomes elastic. You can then stretch the envelope, and the object stretches with it.

Envelopes can be applied to any object or group—even to open curves and text. Shaping text is probably one of the most common applications of envelopes, and you observed in Chapter 10 how both artistic and paragraph text can be enveloped, with strikingly different results.

NOTE Chapter 10 is required reading for anyone wishing to learn about the Envelope command. We covered quite a bit of material there, and the technique for enveloping text is the same as for enveloping other objects.

But first, an interesting question, to which we're not sure we know the answer. At last year's CorelWORLD User Conference, the subject came up in one of the presentations: Why is it called Envelope? Our lead author fumbled his way through an explanation about how an envelope implies that you put something inside of something else, and if necessary, you fold the contents to have them fit in the envelope. It was somewhat underwhelming.

Then a woman stood up, and with one sentence, turned the light bulb on within all of us. "I think it would be better," she said, "if you thought of the word as a verb, not a noun. This command creates a container that *envelops* the object."

"So the name of the feature is actually a misspelling?" Rick responded.

"Exactly," she said. "Corel made a typo!" Everyone laughed.

Actually, our theory gained additional credence when we learned that *envelope* is the Canadian spelling for the verb *envelop*. So Corel didn't misspell the word after all, and maybe its creative team really did want the effect to be known as a verb; the other special effects are all active verbs—Blend, Extrude, Contour, etc.

Consider this your useless piece of information for the day, and if you care to, start pronouncing this the *Envelop* command.

Creating an Envelope

As with most of DRAW's tools, learning the mechanics of enveloping is not difficult; mastering the tool is. In its gradual, and now completed, move away from roll-ups, Corel has contained all of Envelope's functionality on the property bar. You won't find an Effects ➤ Envelope command on the menus (although you can build it back in if you want; see Chapter 34).

Figure 13.1 shows the battlefield we will use for exploring envelopes in this chapter. The first thing you must do to apply an envelope is select the object or group of objects you want to envelope (you can envelope multiple objects as long as they're grouped or combined or welded into one object). Then choose the Envelope icon (fourth one on the Effects flyout, looks like a double-jointed rubber band). We show you the cursor in the image so you can see how DRAW cues you that you are about to apply the effect.

Your creative options with Envelope are virtually unlimited, but your choice of controls is well defined. The four buttons that are active on the property bar represent the envelope-editing modes. To their right, the drop-down box and the Keep Lines check box both serve to further define the enveloping effect. The first three modes—Straight Line, Single Arc, and Double Arc—allow you to change the shape of one side of an object or group. The fourth button, the so-called "unconstrained mode," is a Shape tool look-alike, and for good reason: this mode lets you work an envelope as if it were a curve. With this mode, you are quite literally node-editing an envelope; you can select and move several nodes at once, adjust control points to change the curvature of the nodes, and change the node type to line, cusp, smooth, or symmetric.

FIGURE 13.1

Can these simple objects show you everything there is to know about the Envelope tool? Stick around.

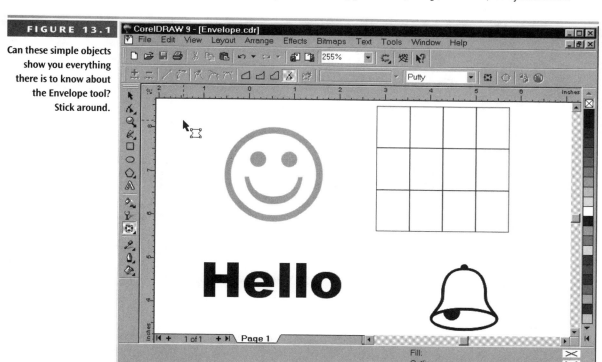

Because this mode can create any type of envelope shape, it is the default mode when you invoke the effect. We polled the members of our team, and most never change from unconstrained mode.

Enveloping Fundamentals

In the age of the interactive tools, clicking on Apply buttons is largely a thing of the past. When you invoke the tool and select an object, you're ready to go: start pulling and tugging on nodes and watch the enveloping begin.

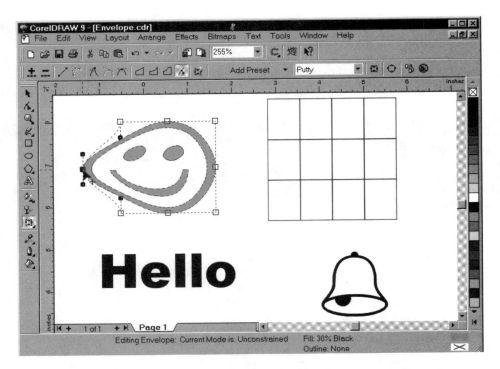

Notice that while in the unconstrained mode, all of the node-editing tools are available.

N O T E   Do you miss the conventional controls, with the Apply button? They are still there; they're just hiding. Corel did not place the Envelope docker on the Effects menu, but you can customize it back in, or just press Ctrl+F7. While the engineers kicked Envelope off the menu, they didn't take away its hotkey.

Once you have enveloped a shape, conventional node-editing is not possible without first converting the object to curves. Were you to click the Shape tool with an enveloped object selected, DRAW would promptly transfer you to the Envelope tool. This is actually quite handy, because it means you can simply press F10 (the hotkey for the Shape tool) to continue work on an envelope. You can also double-click an enveloped shape, and DRAW will promptly switch you from the Pick tool to the Envelope tool.

If you do convert the object to curves, using Ctrl+Q or the button on the Envelope property bar, DRAW leaves the shape as is, but "turns off" the Envelope function (not unlike the Separate command). Once done, you can then use the Shape tool to node-edit.

That is all you need to know to begin experimenting with Envelope, except perhaps the far-right button on the property bar, which removes the Envelope from an object. The next few sections explore the options.

The Four Modes

We've already seen how the unconstrained mode allows for free-form enveloping, with techniques identical to conventional node-editing. Figure 13.2 shows the effects of the three constrained modes. In all cases, the action is very simple: the right-middle node has been dragged to the right.

FIGURE 13.2

The different effects of the three "constrained" modes

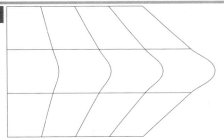

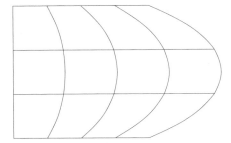

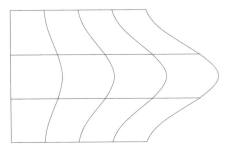

When you're shaping an envelope in the Straight Line, Single Arc, or Double Arc mode, you move the center handles either directly toward or away from the object's center. (These handles will not move laterally.) Corner handles can be moved either vertically or horizontally, and here it gets weird. You *can* move these handles diagonally, but not all at once. First you must move them up or down, then release the mouse, and then start dragging again, this time side-to-side.

Keep in mind, though, the difference between shaping an envelope and directly shaping an object. In Figure 13.3, you can see the three steps that constitute node-editing and envelope-editing, respectively. The motions are the same—select a handle, drag the handle, and release—but the effect is considerably different. With node-editing, you change one node—end of story. With envelope-editing, you change the shape of the container that houses the object, which in turn changes the shape of the entire object.

FIGURE 13.3

Node-editing and envelope-editing are two very different operations.

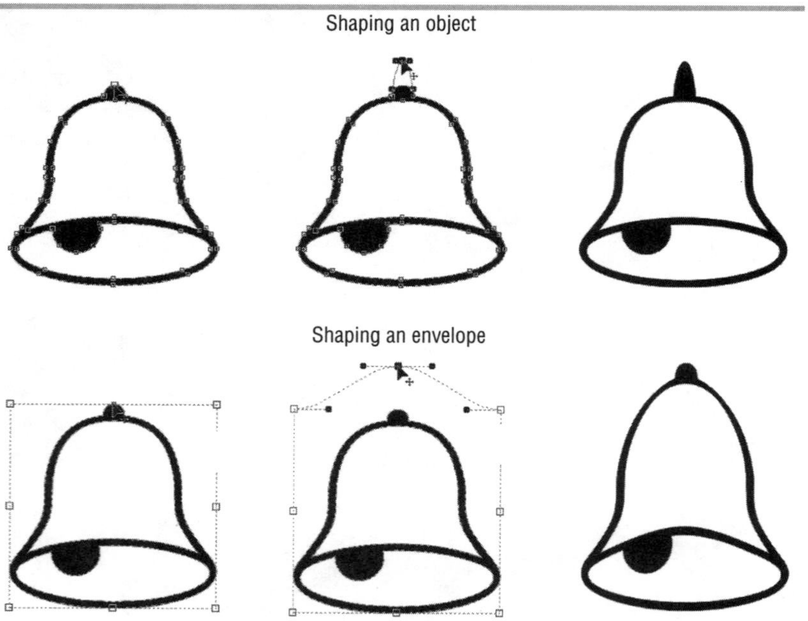

Shaping an object

Shaping an envelope

All about Mapping Options

Envelope mapping is one of the more arcane operations you'll ever perform in DRAW. In rough terms, the mapping options control the way a selected object is shaped to fit into the envelope. There, don't you feel better?

Figure 13.4 shows some examples. In the top image, the Putty map stretches the objects uniformly, as if they were made of putty and you grabbed them and yanked them up and over to the right. In the middle image, the Vertical map, the objects appear to be folded down one side, right at the point where the right-side handles were originally located. And in the Horizontal map (the coolest one, in our humble opinion), the objects are folded over the top—again, right at the original position of the handles. You can see how the top-left handle is functioning as an anchor for the shape.

FIGURE 13.4

Envelope mapping in action

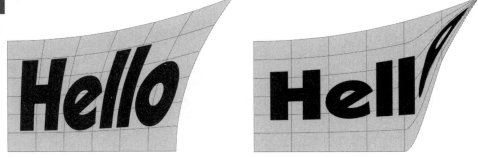

Putty

Vertical

Horizontal

You will probably use Putty most of the time. There is a fourth, seldom-used, mapping option, called Original. It maps the corner handles of the bounding box of the selected object or group to the bounding box of the envelope, so that…oh, never mind. Just follow these rules of thumb and forget about all of the gibberish:

- If an object doesn't conform well to an envelope you are trying to apply it to, clear or undo, switch to the unconstrained mode, and add nodes in places where they can act as hinges for the envelope.

- For single lines of artistic text, vertical mapping usually produces a result that is more readable and less distracting than horizontal mapping.

- If you plan to envelope multiple lines of text, create them as separate strings with an envelope applied to each, rather than a single envelope applied to one multiple-line string.

Keeping Lines As Lines

When you envelope an object, you are asking an otherwise orderly shape to radically distort itself to fit into another shape. Usually, this involves some intense curvatures of the original elements. You can disallow this, however. DRAW offers a "line-item veto" for enveloping shapes. When you click Keep Lines, just to the right of Mapping Modes on the property bar, you tell DRAW to go ahead and distort any shape that is a curve, but lay off any part of the object that is a straight line.

Figure 13.5 illustrates this quite vividly with the letters in *Hello* that have straight lines. In the top image, all of the characters are flopping around inside of this crazy envelope. The bottom envelope is just as crazy, but the *H*, the two *l*s, and parts of the *e* are maintained as straight lines, producing a more jagged look.

If you're looking for a study in futility, try this: create a rectangle, activate the Interactive Envelope tool, enable Keep Lines, and then drag one of the center handles anywhere you want to. You will get no result, because you have issued two conflicting commands—one that says, "Try to bend this rectangle," and another that says, "Okay, fine, but don't bend any of the straight lines."

FIGURE 13.5

Lines will be lines... as long as you say so on the Envelope property bar.

Automatic Envelopes

DRAW offers two ways to automate the creation of envelopes, and a method of constraining them. In many cases, the easiest way to create an effective envelope is to go the prefab route, and then modify it from there.

Add Preset

Like so many other parts of DRAW, the Envelope tool includes several ready-made shapes for your enveloping pleasure. To use one of them, select an object, click Add Preset, and choose the shape from the drop-down list. Your selected object will instantly inherit that shape as its envelope. Figure 13.6 shows a perfectly fine string of text getting manhandled by a preset.

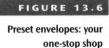

FIGURE 13.6

Preset envelopes: your one-stop shop

 N O T E   One automatic function you can no longer enjoy is Create From, the quick method of creating envelopes from existing objects. Enthusiasts of this function are none too happy about Corel's decision to excise it, and those that asked why during development never received a satisfactory response. If you miss this command, you have our permission to yell at Corel about it.

Copying Envelopes

If you have an existing envelope and you want to use that envelope for another object, you can copy it. Select the object to which you want to apply the envelope. Then choose Effects ➤ Copy Effect ➤ Envelope From and click on the enveloped object. Note the difference between this and Create From—Create From creates an envelope from an unenveloped object; Copy Envelope duplicates an existing envelope.

Keyboard Constraints

As you would expect, Ctrl and Shift provide several quick ways to constrain envelopes. Ctrl forces equivalent action on the side opposite to the one you are shaping, Shift forces symmetrical action, and the two together make all sides act in concert. Figure 13.7 illustrates this.

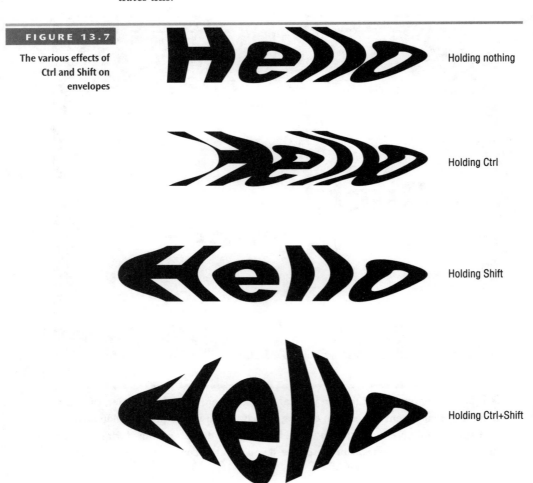

FIGURE 13.7

The various effects of Ctrl and Shift on envelopes

Holding nothing

Holding Ctrl

Holding Shift

Holding Ctrl+Shift

Envelopes and Text

Return to Chapter 10 for a complete discussion and tutorial on applying envelopes to paragraph text. If you have already worked through that section, the discussion here is meant to drive the point home: enveloping paragraph text works the same as enveloping artistic text or any other object. But you are not actually modifying the forms of the letters; you are modifying the frame in which the text flows.

When you select a frame of paragraph text, the only mapping mode available is Text. You can use any of the techniques already described (the four envelope editing modes and Add Preset). However, you can't apply more than one envelope to paragraph text, as you can to other objects. If you apply a new envelope, it replaces the old one, rather than compounding the effect of the first one.

Step by Step: Using Envelope to Create a Reflection

Regular readers of Mastering CorelDRAW will recognize Figure 13.8 from previous editions. While we regularly rotate the artwork we use for tutorials, we are bringing this one back for a curtain call because of its creative use of Envelope. This exercise will take you through its creation; to follow along, you'll need to download Evening Sky.cdr from the Sybex Web site.

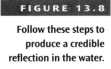

FIGURE 13.8

Follow these steps to produce a credible reflection in the water.

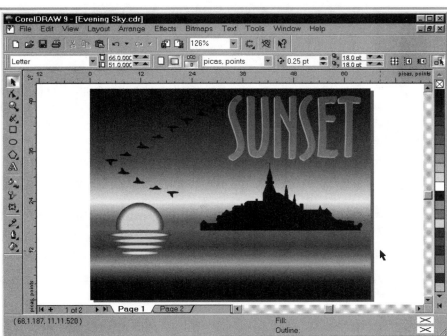

While this drawing isn't trying to be completely lifelike (after all, there are letters in the sky and a bird is flying through one of them), it would certainly look a bit more realistic if the buildings created some reflection on the water. The setting sun has reflections; the buildings should, too. Here goes:

1. Select the buildings and perform a flop-and-dupe to create a mirrored copy below. Make the copy about 75 percent of the size of the original. (You can approximate by eye, or use the property bar's Scale Factor.)

2. Zoom in on both sets, as shown here.

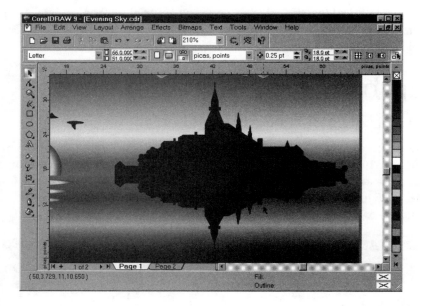

If this were a small pond on a very still night, you might accept that the reflection could be this perfect. But to be more credible, it needs to shimmer on the water. You need to warp it a bit, and as you've seen from this chapter, DRAWspeak for warp is Envelope.

3. Switch to Wireframe view (it's often easier to see and manipulate objects when you don't have to look through their fill patterns and those of the objects behind them).

4. With the reflected buildings selected, switch to the Interactive Envelope tool.

5. Select the unconstrained mode and the Horizontal mapping mode.

6. Marquee-select the top-left node and the one below it.

7. Press the plus key twice, so you have eight nodes running up and down the left edge.

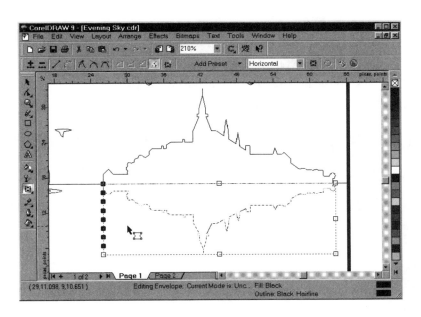

8. Check the View menu and make sure that all snaps are turned off.

9. Click inside the graphic to deselect the nodes (this is not required, but it might be easier to work around the nodes when they are not selected).

10. Click on the path between the top two nodes and drag it to the right, toward the inside of the reflection.

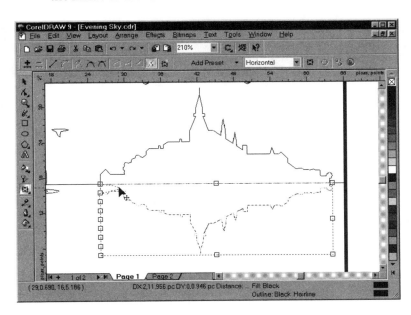

When you release the mouse, the object will distort. Don't be alarmed, there's nothing wrong with your set; no need to adjust your horizontal or vertical.

11. Click on the next path and drag it to the left.

12. Click on the next path and drag it to the right.

13. Continue this until you reach the bottom of the row of nodes.

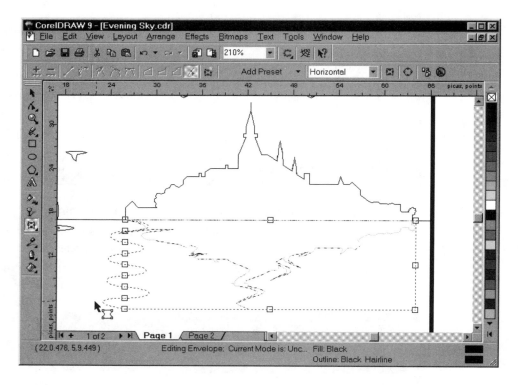

We want you to notice two things about this procession. First, we did not try to stretch each path equally. The physics controlling water reflections are not for us mortals to fathom, and virtually any type of distortion will look credible. Second, the image distorted as soon as you began tugging on the nodes—quite a departure from the old roll-up days.

To repeat this process on the right side of the image, perform the same steps as above, except start by marquee-selecting the lower and middle nodes, instead of the upper and middle ones.

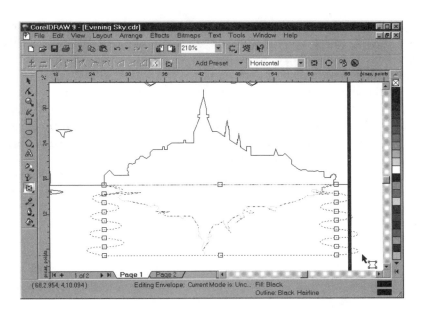

The final image, shown in Figure 13.9, was taken in Enhanced viewing mode, not Wireframe, and with the reflection filled with a dark gray tint.

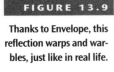

FIGURE 13.9

Thanks to Envelope, this reflection warps and warbles, just like in real life.

We'll return to this drawing in Chapter 17, "Through the Looking Glass." You can download Evening Sky.cdr from the Sybex Web site. The first page of that drawing has the reflection omitted, so you can try your hand at creating it, and the second page shows the completed effect.

We'll conclude by reiterating the main point about enveloping objects: when you apply an envelope to an object, you are not actually reshaping the object; you are shaping the container in which the object is placed. Think of an envelope as one of those fun-house mirrors that stretches and distorts the appearance of the person in front of it, without actually changing that person.

chapter 14

BLENDING IT ALL TOGETHER

Featuring

BLENDING IT ALL TOGETHER

Though it's no longer novel, *morphing* remains one of the hot special effects in the movie industry, thanks largely to modern computing and Arnold Schwarzenegger films. To morph means to change from one shape to another. CorelDRAW has its own set of tools for metamorphoses, and though they might not be quite worthy of Arnold and the Big Screen, they can produce stunning effects on your computer display. This chapter focuses on Blend, DRAW's tool for taking two objects and turning them into many.

Blending Objects

Blending is suspiciously easy to both explain and visualize. You take a vector element, be it a single object or a group of objects. Then you take another vector element. Then you tell DRAW to go from one to the other. Then you tell DRAW how many steps the transformation should take. Okay, in our next chapter...

Well, perhaps it's not quite that simple, but like so many of DRAW's tools, the mechanics of blending are easily understood. And unlike some of the other effects, there are very few restrictions imposed upon blending. You can blend between nearly any two objects, including grouped objects and complex curves (text being a good example). The only objects that cannot be blended are paragraph text and imported bitmap images, although in some instances—like extrusions, contours, and pattern fills—the results are poor and the effect not worth attempting.

A blend starts with two *control objects,* which DRAW refers to as the *start* and *end objects.* When you ask DRAW to create a blend between the two control objects, it produces a series of intermediate objects, or *steps,* that represent the transformation from the start object to the end object.

The transformation involves every component of the two control objects—their shape, fill, and outline—as each of these components is modified by a certain percentage in each step of the blend. If you ask for just a few steps, the amount of change within each step is significant. With more steps, the amount of change is smaller, usually resulting in a smoother, less obvious transition (and a more complex drawing).

For the simplest of all blends, as shown in Figure 14.1, do this:

1. Create a rectangle near one corner of the page, choose a light fill or shade, and remove the outline.

2. Use drag-and-dupe to create a copy of the rectangle in the opposite corner of the page. Color it dark.

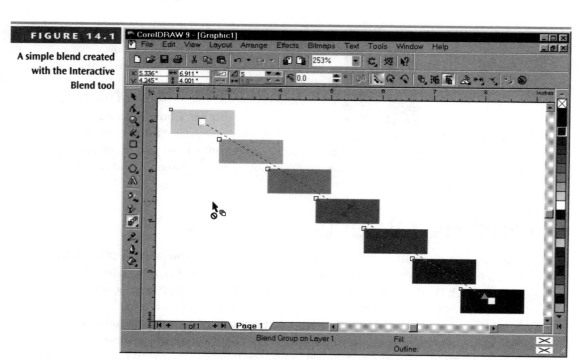

FIGURE 14.1

A simple blend created with the Interactive Blend tool

3. Select the Interactive Blend tool, the first icon on the Effects flyout. With it, click on the interior of one of your rectangles and drag to the interior of the other.

4. On the property bar, change the Steps to 5, then click back on the page.

This is the interactive way to create a blend. It was introduced in DRAW 8 and stands as the method almost all of us will use, what with the Blend docker being relegated to almost complete obscurity. Notice the arrow from the start object to the end object, and the interactive cursor. The cursor shows the "No Action" symbol when it's not hovered over an area of the blend where it can do anything. When you move into an object that can serve as a control object for a blend, the circle-and-line icon changes to a miniature blend arrow.

All of the controls for a blend are on the property bar, and you should take a tour of them by hovering your cursor over each one. You can also effect several changes to a blend just with your cursor, like repositioning or recoloring the control objects, or "accelerating" the blend.

The Anatomy of a Blend

If you followed the directions above, your status bar should now read "Blend Group on Layer 1." This is obviously a group of objects, but not in the conventional sense (as if you had selected them and pressed Ctrl+G). The two control objects remain semi-independent from the blend group.

We say "semi-independent" because you can move the blend group as one, size it, rotate it, skew it, copy it, and so on, and the entire group adjusts. But you can also select the control objects and change them. Press Tab repeatedly and you'll see that you can bounce between the two control rectangles, and the status bar will verify that. Move one of the controls, and the blend adjusts. Refill it, rotate it, skew it, resize it…in all cases, the blend adjusts dynamically.

As you experiment with blends, take note of one important characteristic. It doesn't matter which control object you select first when creating a blend with the docker, and it makes no difference which direction you drag when using the Interactive Blend tool. The start object is always the one that is further down, or further back, in the stacking order of the blend. The ending object of the blend is always the one nearer the top or front (so think of blends as going from the middle of your monitor, where the tube is, to the edge of the glass).

If you want to reverse the direction of your blend, select the end object and send it to the back with Arrange ➢ Order ➢ To Back, or use Shift+PgDn. For more precise control, use the Object Manager as described in Chapter 32. What would happen if you did that to the blend in Figure 14.1? *Absolutely nothing*—none of the objects overlap, so it doesn't matter which of the two controls is on top.

The Science of Selection

One of the most confusing aspects of working with blended objects is supposed to be one of the simplest: selecting objects. But with three distinct parts of a blend, all of which are often overlapping, this seemingly simple task can become difficult and frustrating.

Superceding all other advice, watch your status bar! It is there where DRAW notifies you of what you have selected—the blend group or a control object. That way, if you select the wrong thing, at least you know it right away.

Beyond that, here is a two-step process that will always work for selecting groups or control objects:

1. To select the blend group, draw a marquee around the entire group.
2. From there, press Tab or Shift+Tab to alternate between the controls.

We wish we could tell you which one to press, but it all depends upon the stacking order of the objects nearby. We guarantee it will be one of the two…

A blend stays alive until you kill it, and you do that with the Arrange ➤ Separate command. Once separated, a blend becomes three elements—the two controls and a group of objects that make up the intermediate steps. For normal blends, there will only be two controls, but there could be any number of objects in the group between them, depending upon the number of steps used for the blend. You can go on to ungroup the intermediate steps or leave them as is, but either way, these objects are now just a collection of elements, no longer related.

What Makes a Good Blend?

Blending can be performed between two objects that are quite dissimilar. For example, an object with no outline and a fountain fill can be blended with an object that has an outline and a uniform fill. But beware—there are almost no limits to the types of objects that can be blended, and you can create hideous mutations if you're not careful.

Figure 14.2 shows several different blends, including a few techniques yet to be discussed. The first four are credible efforts: the letter that mirrors itself, the happy-to-sad face, the neon circle turning into a square, and the double-blended squiggle. The polygon shuffle and the square that inherits three extra sides might have you wondering "But is it art?" but at least you'll wonder. The skeleton that mutates into a bomb earns a spot on any user's ugly list.

FIGURE 14.2

The first five blends share "node agreement," but the last two do not.

Neat

Cute

Cool

Interesting

Unusual

Weird

Ridiculous

Regardless of your opinion of the first five blends, they all share one important attribute: they are blends between objects that have the same number of nodes, and that is an important consideration. The last two morphs violate this principle. In the weird square-to-polygon transformation, DRAW gets a bit confused in the middle, trying to give the objects extra sides en route to becoming a heptagon. But because these shapes are not too dissimilar, the effect isn't too bad.

The last one, however, speaks for itself. The disfigurement of the skull and cross-bones is the result of DRAW not knowing what to do with nodes that have no counterpart on the other side of the blend. There is probably some formula that determines where those soon-to-be-orphaned nodes are placed, but you can be sure it has nothing to do with art.

Blending is possibly the single most important tool in DRAW's arsenal for creating realistic effects. It is no coincidence that, year after year, the award-winning illustrations that garner the most attention make constant use of blended objects. We'll show you some before this chapter ends.

The Blend Controls

Here is a tour of the Blend property bar.

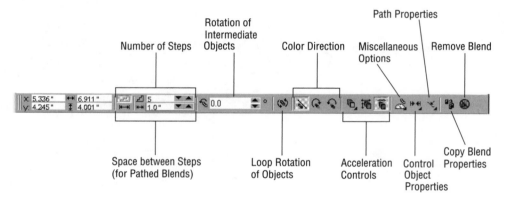

Steps and Spaces

Almost all of the time, you will stay within DRAW's default mode of controlling the number of intermediate steps within a blend, the default being 20. If you choose to fit a blend to a path (discussed in this section), another choice becomes available—space between objects. When blending to a path, the distance between control objects is not fixed—it could go the entire length of the path, or stop somewhere in between. Therefore, the space between objects becomes a variable that you should be able to control. With this check box, you can.

Rotation

By entering a degree in this box, you can set intermediate objects to rotate on their axes as they transition from one control object to the other. By clicking the Loop button, you force the objects not to rotate themselves, but to rotate as a group along an imaginary arc. Both are shown in this graphic, below the standard blend.

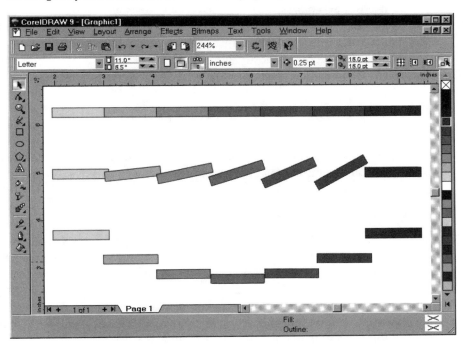

Color Direction

These controls are identical to the options in the Fountain Fill dialog that bear the same name. When a blend involves the transition of one color to another, there remains the question of what route DRAW should take to get there. The direct route goes through the heart of the color spectrum, involving the most abrupt shifts in color. The other two choices take a more leisurely route around the color wheel, in either direction.

Acceleration

These arcane controls will be ignored by most, and to the other two percent of you, we will likely frustrate you by not doing justice to the topic. Acceleration allows you to concentrate the blending operation near one end of the blend or the other. You can choose to accelerate the amount of space between objects, the color shift between objects, or the size of the objects. We could bore most of you with largely unintelligible examples; instead, please bore yourself, uh, we mean please experiment with this for yourself.

The third acceleration control allows you to link your Objects and Colors accelerations, so the two slider controls move as one. Here again, you will need to experiment to determine its practical uses; we're not sure there are many.

One good thing about acceleration: it is very easy to control, thanks to the on-screen control for it. In Figure 14.1, it is the little midpoint handle that looks like a butterfly. Again, we're not sure how relevant acceleration is, but if you think you need it, it's easy to manipulate.

Miscellaneous Blend Options

It is commonly said that when a program offers "miscellaneous" options, it means that its developers painted themselves into a corner or couldn't find the right way to organize a set of functions. That seems the case with this mish-mash collection of controls. Here are the significant ones.

Mapping Nodes

When creating a blend, DRAW associates nodes on one control object with those on the other. Most of the time, DRAW figures out for itself how to match them up. When it doesn't, or when you want to create an unconventional blend, you can remap the nodes—you tell DRAW which node on one control should match up with which node on the other side. This can have a profound effect on the blend, as Figure 14.3 shows. The normal blend, shown on the left, follows one rectangle's metamorphosis into another. And in so doing, the nodes on one control correspond with those in the same position on the other control.

The image on the right is the product of telling DRAW to map the node on one side with the node on the diagonal corner of the other side.

Split

When you split a blend, you turn it into two blends, with an object in the middle acting as the control for both blends.

Fuse

Once you split a blend, you can fuse it back together by holding Ctrl, choosing a spot along the blend, and then clicking on Fuse Start or Fuse End. We have yet to see any user or any .cdr file make use of this, so we won't bother you with it.

Blend along Full Path

When you choose to fit a blend to a path, this control forces the blend to extend the entire path, from beginning to end. DRAW does not adjust the Steps value to do this; it simply moves the control objects to the edges of the path, forcing the intermediate objects to adjust to fit.

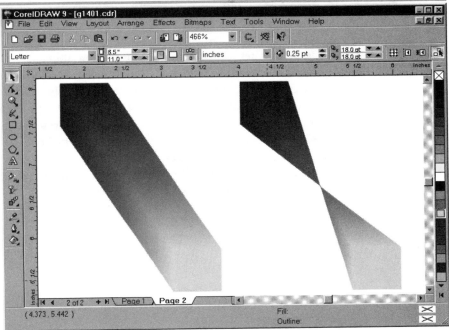

This control, the Path Properties button, and the option to measure a blend in distance instead of steps all should be on one flyout together. The fact that they are in three different locations further indicates that this property bar needs to be better organized.

Starting Points

Usually, when you create a blend, you know what to use as the two control objects. If you change your mind and want to use a different object to start or finish a blend, you can substitute for either one using the button entitled Start and End Object Properties.

From the flyout you can choose to designate a new start, a new end, or show the current start or end. Note that the start object must be behind the end object. If you try to designate a replacement start object that is in front of the end object, DRAW will yell at you.

Paths

The coolest of all the controls, Path (the button with the curved line), lets you set your blend to a path, the same way that Fit Text to Path works on artistic text. The only extra ingredient needed for a pathed blend is a third object, the one that determines the new path. Once you have created your blend, click on the Path button, choose New Path, and click on the object on screen.

For an exercise in this, return to Chapter 11 and follow along in the creation of the gear. There, you create two small circles and blend them around a larger circle.

Most DRAW users wouldn't think of reaching for the blend-to-path technique for such pedestrian projects as an organization chart, yet Figure 14.4 was created in about 10 minutes, using a total of 15 steps. The drop shadows are clones of the foreground boxes, so they move when and where the others do. All of the boxes are tied to the lines. Not only is this org chart quick to create, but it is even quicker to modify. If a position must be added or deleted, it's only necessary to change the Steps value for that blend, and the cloned drop shadow will follow suit.

FIGURE 14.4

This org chart uses the blend-to-path technique for a high degree of precision and flexibility.

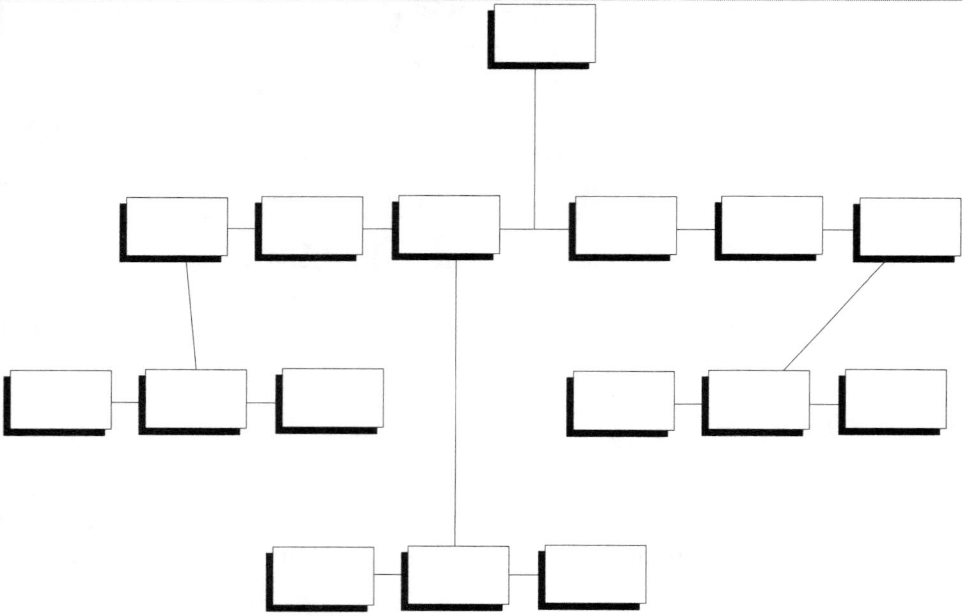

The Art of Blends

Blend is truly an artist's tool, capable of creating spectacular realism. Figures 14.5 and 14.6 show off some of the more celebrated pieces of CorelDRAW artwork. Each uses blend to show shape, dimension, reflections, shadows...all of the elements that can add depth to a flat drawing. Also, check out Hedy Lamarr and Contemplation in the Color Gallery.

FIGURE 14.5

Clipart, this ain't. This fountain pen jumps off the page, thanks to the intelligent use of blended objects.

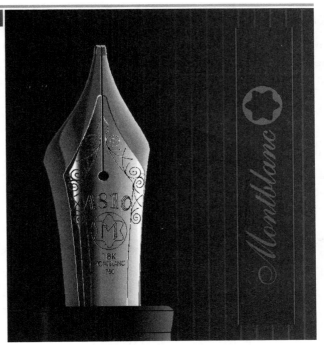

FIGURE 14.6

Most of us would be lucky to get the black keys black and the white keys white. This gorgeous piece practically plays the music, too. Notice all of the intricate blending in the broken glass and in the light that reflects from the keys.

The Science of Blends

Blend is also a technician's tool. We pedestrian users can take advantage of its ability to automate the creation of many objects and/or intricate ones. Watch how this exercise makes swift work out of a watermark that would otherwise be a nightmare to produce:

1. On a blank page, create a frame of paragraph text and type a bunch of text (**asdf** and **jkl;** copied dozens of times will do fine.)

2. Format the frame to two columns.

3. Import a piece of clipart from Corel's library, and scale it up to about half the size of the page. We chose a falcon.

4. Send the clipart to the back with Shift+PgDn.

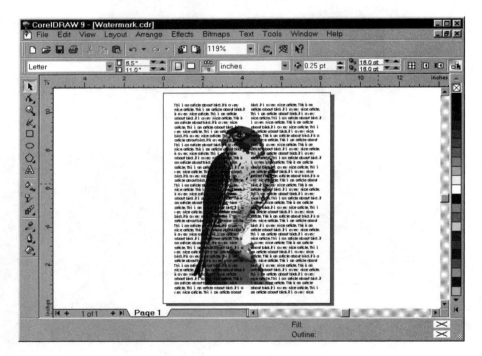

The problem here is obvious: the falcon is way too dark to act as a watermark or a soft background to the text. Each part of the bird needs to be tinted back so the text can be read on top of it. But there are over 300 objects in this bird—that would take hours. And how much do you tint it? Fifty percent? Seventy-five? What if you go through the pains of tinting it, only to discover you didn't tint it enough?

You could throw a lens over the whole thing, but as you'll learn in Chapter 17, transparent objects can become very complex in a hurry. In fact, we reached for the Interactive Transparency tool and DRAW promptly informed us that we had too many objects selected. This problem needs a more creative solution, and the answer lies in Blend. Watch:

5. Select your graphic (you might have to press Tab to get to it) and copy it to the Clipboard.

6. Move to a new page and paste it.

7. Size it down and then drag and dupe a copy to the other side of the page.

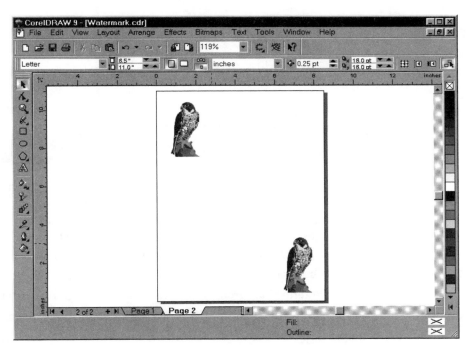

8. Using the on-screen palette, set the fill and outlines for one of the graphics to white. Not hollow, but white. Once you do, it will become invisible, but you can still see it by its selection handles.

9. Select both the full-color artwork and the all-white one.

10. Blend between them with about five steps.

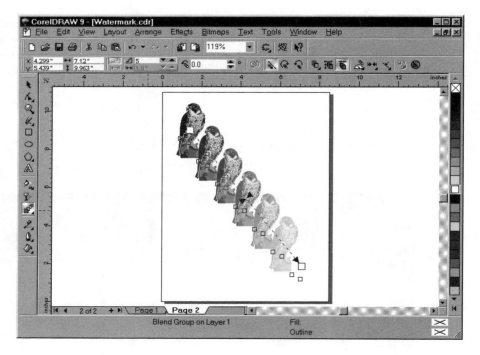

In about five seconds, Blend has done what would have taken us an hour or two. In transitioning between a full-intensity version of the graphic to an all-white version, DRAW created intermediate graphics with varying tints. And all 386 objects are tinted back. You just need to pick which one of the five would be right. If you need more choices, increase the Steps value. When you find one you like:

11. With the entire blend selected, go to Arrange ➤ Separate.

12. Select the intermediate group and go to Arrange ➤ Ungroup (Ctrl+U).

13. Pick the graphic that you think is tinted just right and copy it to the Clipboard.

14. Return to the first page, remove the original graphic, and press Ctrl+V to paste the new one.

15. Size it to taste and move it to the back.

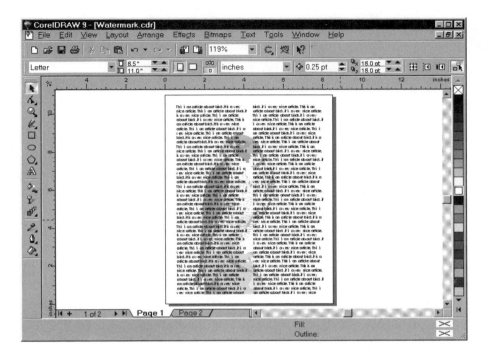

You can find this drawing as `Watermark.cdr` on the Sybex Web site.

In this case, we haven't used Blend to create artwork; we have used it to solve a problem. We have used it to automate a procedure that otherwise would have been virtually unthinkable. Because of its high appeal with both the artists and the technicians, we think Blend is the most versatile and most powerful of all of CorelDRAW's tools.

chapter 15

THE ENIGMA OF EXTRUDE

Featuring

The Enigma of Extrude

We'll start this chapter by admitting our bias. We're impressed with Extrude, but our regard for it is a mix of awe and loathing. Extrude is very powerful and, when used wisely, allows even the artistically inept to produce impressive art. But we draw a sharp distinction between artistic ineptitude—as in "incapable of drawing straight lines and round circles"—and aesthetic insensitivity—as in "incapable of recognizing good art from bad art." If what you lack is good taste rather than good skills, Extrude will only help you dig a deeper grave for yourself. On that cautionary note, we invite you into this chapter.

Faking Out Reality

Our bias notwithstanding, adding an extrusion to an object stands as one of DRAW's most clever functions. With Extrude, you can select any simple object and instantly turn it into something three-dimensional, as either a *perspective drawing* or an *isometric drawing*. To produce a 3D appearance, Extrude creates new surfaces that are dynamically linked to the original object. It does this by projecting the edges and corners of the object and then connecting those points to form closed surfaces. Like all of the other depth-defying effects in DRAW, this one is a fake, but it's a darn good one.

To create an extrusion, do this:

1. Create an ellipse or rectangle.

2. Choose Extrude from the Effects flyout (the fifth icon over).

3. Click and drag from the interior of the object to the exterior, in any direction. As you do, the object will sprout sides.

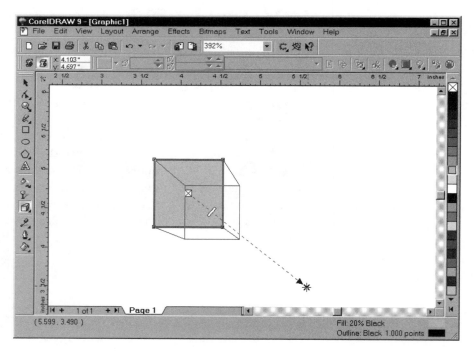

4. Release the mouse to complete the extrusion.

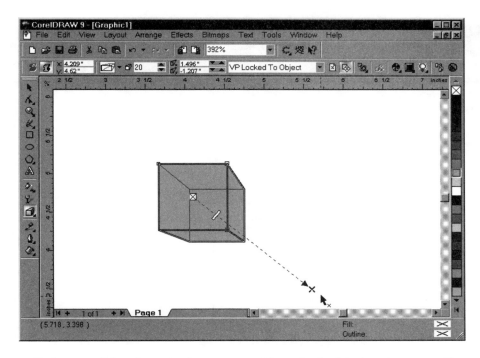

To be a candidate for extrusion, you must be a single object, not a group. You can be a multipathed object and you can be text. But you can't be multiple objects selected or grouped. Text that is extruded is still editable, and the extrusion will update automatically to reflect the edits. Similarly, other control objects can be stretched, skewed, rotated, and so forth, and the extrusion will be updated following the changes.

N O T E Perspective and Envelope also provide depth to an object, but they both do so without the addition of other objects. Extrude takes one object and adds others to it.

Perspective vs. Isometric

Figure 15.1 shows the difference between a perspective drawing and an isometric illustration. Perspective drawings reflect the fact that objects appear to get smaller the farther they get from the viewer; in that respect, they more closely mimic reality. Isometric drawings do not recede, and therefore they are useful for technical drawings, where a viewer can make accurate length measurements parallel to any axis. DRAW refers to an isometric extrusion as a *parallel extrusion*.

Will a perspective drawing or an isometric illustration better suit your needs? Extrude can create either one.

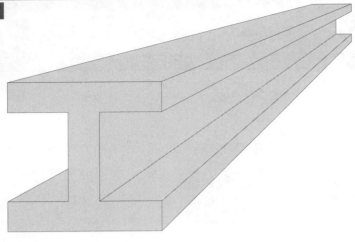

Perspective

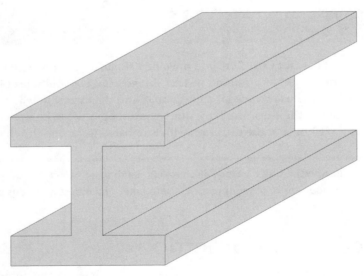

Isometric

WARNING   When you go to select an extrusion, pay attention to the status bar: it will tell you whether you have indeed selected the "extrude group," or just the control object. In many cases, it won't matter—move a control object and the entire extrusion moves with it. But if you select only the control object of an extrusion and duplicate it, only that object is duplicated; it will not be part of any extrusion. If you select the extrude group, then the entire dynamic group gets duplicated. To edit extruded text, you must select just the text, not the entire extrude group.

Controlling an Extrusion

As with the other effects, Extrude has its own property bar, which comes alive anytime you select an extruded object or reach for the Extrude tool. Figure 15.2 shows the various controls that relate to the extrusion, some of which you'll reach for regularly, and some about which you will never have a clue nor will care to.

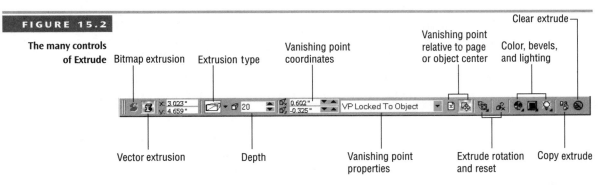

FIGURE 15.2

The many controls of Extrude

For the following section, we created a very simple extrusion to act as our laboratory animal:

1. We created a perfect circle.

2. We made a copy and shrunk it toward the center.

3. We combined them. That created a donut shape—solid on the outside, with a hole in the center.

4. We filled it with a medium color.

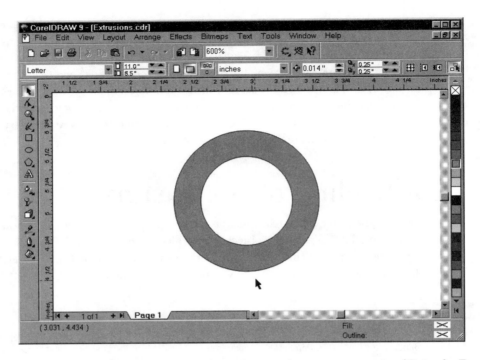

We'll turn our donut loose on the more prominent components of Extrude. To learn about all of them, consult DRAW's online Help: search for "extrusions" in the index.

 TIP   If you have selected an extruded object and you want to edit its extrusion settings, double-click the object. That promptly toggles the Extrude tool and provides all of the on-screen controls.

Extrusion Type

There are four perspective choices and two isometric choices. In all cases, the distinction arises in the direction of the extrusion. In the following graphics, we have included a simple light source, to help you observe depth.

Small Back

This is the default—most users want to create 3D objects that recede into the distance. The lines of this type of an extrusion move away from you and grow smaller as they do.

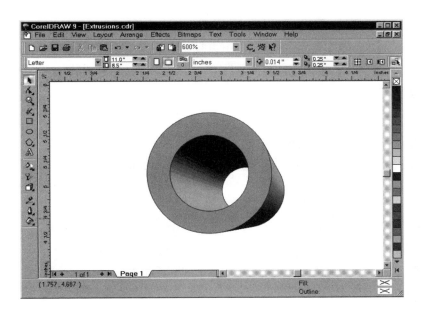

Small Front

This extrusion sends the object toward you. As it is now receding and growing bigger at the same time, your eyes won't believe that the object has a single circumference. It makes the object look more like a cone.

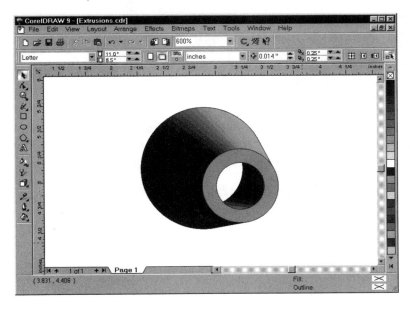

Big Back

This produces the same effect as Small Front, except the back side is expanded, rather than the front side reduced. Therefore, the entire object is larger.

Big Front

This is the same as Small Back, except the resulting object is larger.

Back Parallel (Isometric)

The lines of this extrusion move away from your line of sight, but they do not recede; they remain the same size. This does not reflect reality, but it makes it easier to determine object dimension.

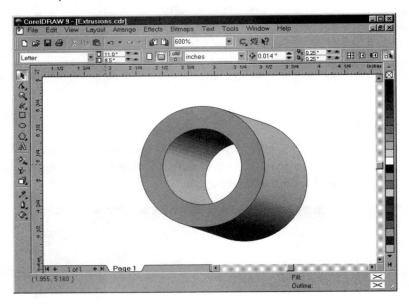

Does the back of this extrusion look bigger than the front? It does to us, even though it's not. We think this is because we are accustomed to seeing it as much smaller as it recedes; when it doesn't recede, it appears big.

Front Parallel (Isometric)

The lines of this extrusion type head toward us.

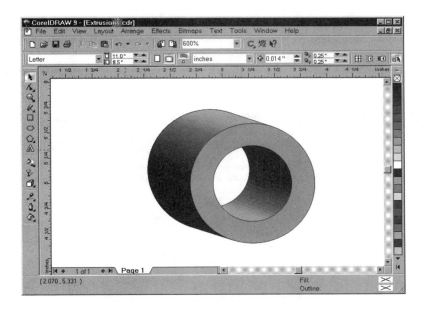

Depth

This is a simple measurement of the length of the extruded shape. The higher the number, the more the shape heads toward its theoretical vanishing point (discussed next). The following graphic gives you a good idea of how depth affects a simple backward-moving extrusion.

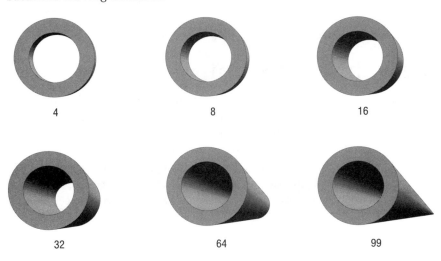

4   8   16

32   64   99

In the six objects shown on the previous page, we changed only the Depth setting. The maximum depth is 99—that indicates the object is all the way to the vanishing point.

You can change the depth of an extrusion by using the property bar or by sliding the thin bar on screen. We're pointing to it here.

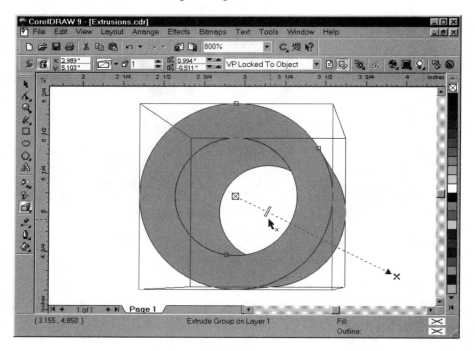

And now you know how to make a conehead...

The Vanishing Point

This is an artist's term to describe the point on the horizon where parallel lines appear to meet. By controlling the vanishing point, you determine in which direction the extrusion recedes. You can adjust this from the property bar or by moving the big × that emanates from the object when you activate the Extrude tool.

In an isometric form, the × has a slightly different function. You still manipulate it on screen with the mouse, but since isometrics don't "vanish," the × is used to determine the depth *and* angle of the extrusion. Wherever you place the × is where the center of the extruded face will appear. For this reason, parallel extrusions have no numerical depth controls.

The tricky thing about the vanishing point (Corel uses VP for short on the property bar) is your option to make it relative to the object, or relative to the page itself. Here's the difference.

VP Locked to Object

This setting indicates that the vanishing point is determined with respect to the object itself. It doesn't care about other objects on the page. If you move this object, its extrusion looks the same; the vanishing point moves with it.

VP Locked to Page

This setting holds a vanishing point to the same place on the page, irrespective of the object's position. If you lock the vanishing point to the page and then move the object, its extrusion changes—it adjusts to continue extruding out to the same position on the page.

You can also use the vanishing point of another object. You can copy the vanishing point from another object, or establish that two or more objects share the same vanishing point. Copying a vanishing point is not the same as sharing—after copying a vanishing point, objects are not tied to the same destiny. But when they share a vanishing point, they are. Copying and sharing vanishing points are performed via the Vanishing Point Properties drop-down list from the property bar. Remember the order: (1) Select the object whose vanishing point you want to change. (2) Choose Copy or Share from the drop-down. (3) Click the object whose existing vanishing point you want to use.

N O T E   If you copy a vanishing point, you are not also copying its orientation (i.e., Locked to Object or Locked to Page). That remains a separate setting.

Figure 15.3 shows nine extruded cylinders, all sharing the same vanishing point—that of the cylinder in the center. If we were to change the vanishing point of the center cylinder, the other eight would promptly follow.

If you want to stop sharing a vanishing point, just select the desired object and choose VP Locked to Object.

FIGURE 15.3

Nine objects, one
vanishing point

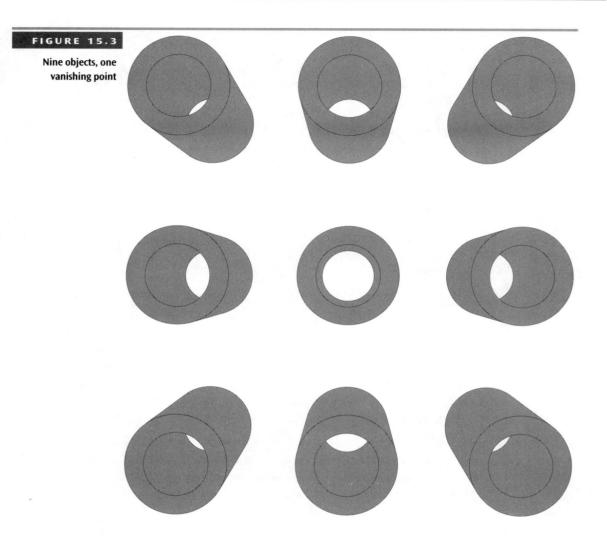

Rotation

Rotating an extrusion produces some of the most dramatic effects of all. Once you create an extrusion, DRAW extrapolates what the objects on the other side would look like. When you rotate the object, you see what DRAW has conjured up.

To watch rotation in action, we're going to return to the gear that we created with the Trim tool in Chapter 11. You can download Gear.cdr from the Sybex Web site. To refresh your memory, we created lots of little circles, used the Blend tool to distribute them around one big circle, and used Trim to cut into the big circle.

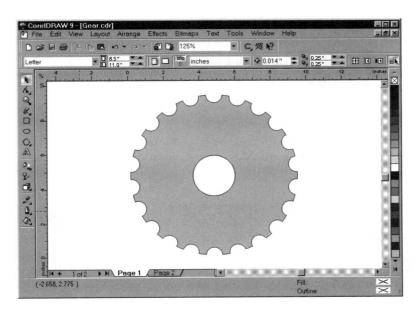

We also drew a medium-sized circle and combined it with the big circle to create the hole in the middle. Here we go:

1. Select the gear and activate the Extrude tool.

2. With your cursor somewhere inside, click and drag out from the interior, in any direction.

3. Set the depth to about 5.

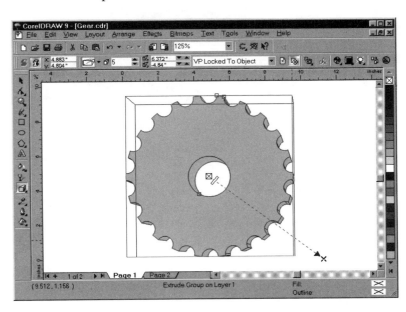

There are rotation controls on the property bar, if you need to rotate an object to a precise angle, but otherwise, it's easier to use the on-screen controls.

4. With the gear selected, click a second time on it.

In rotation mode, you will see two different cursor shapes:

- The one that looks like a horseshoe is for spinning the object around its center—the so-called z-axis. You get this if your cursor is outside of the dotted red circle.

- The one that looks like an atom and an electron is for rotating the object on any and all of its three axes. You get this if your cursor is inside of the dotted circle, as shown here.

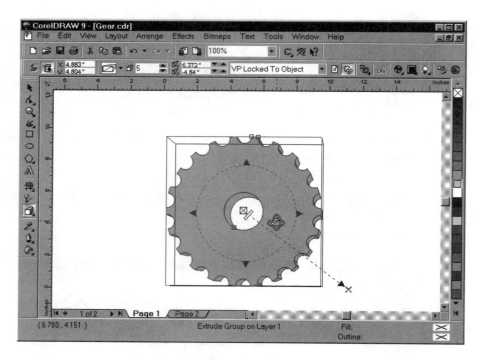

5. Move inside the red circle and begin rotating. The effect is instantaneous; whenever you stop, DRAW recalculates how the object would appear from that position.

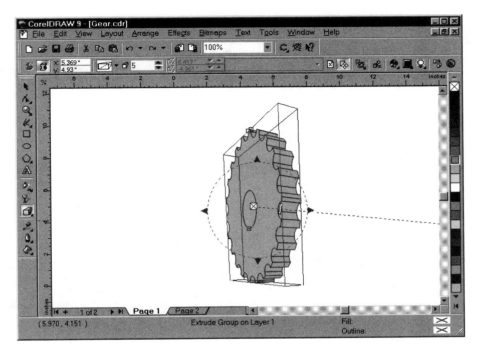

Here are the rules for rotating extrusions:

- You cannot rotate an isometric extrusion—only the ones created with perspective (Big Back, Small Front, etc.).

- You cannot rotate an extrusion whose vanishing point is locked to the page. It must be locked to the object.

- Once you rotate an extrusion, you can no longer adjust its vanishing point. So make sure the vanishing point is set correctly first, then rotate.

You can always use the controls on the property bar to see what kind of rotation you have set, and to communicate precise values to others, if necessary. For instance, you could duplicate exactly the extrusion we produced in the graphic above. You can see the Depth and the Vanishing Point type and values (although the vanishing point values are grayed out, because the rotation pre-empts further use of them); the rotation coordinates are:

x: 3

y: -44

z: -1

Applying Color and Lighting

The default method of filling extruded surfaces is to match the fill of the control curve. In the case of the gear, we filled it with a medium-gray color and so the extrusion took on the same color. You have many other options—you can adjust the color of the extrusion, and because you have created a 3D object, you can also consider the phenomenon of light hitting each surface differently.

To access the color controls, click the color wheel on the property bar. From there, you have three places to go.

Use Object Fill

This simple choice sets the fill of all extruded sides to the same as the original object. We interpret this as the absence of coloring, and we think it should have been its own button on the property bar, similar to the Reset Rotation button.

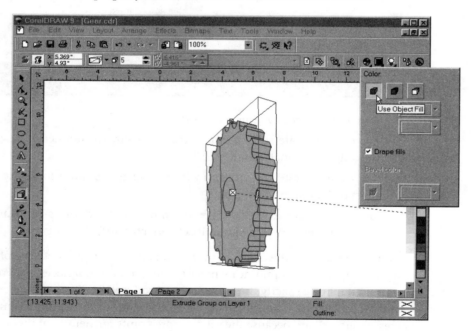

Pulling Drapes

There is one scenario in which the Object Fill setting could produce widely varying results. It has to do with the Drape Fills option. On by default, this option treats an extrusion as a whole when filling it, instead of filling each face of the extrusion individually. In the case of solid fills, this is irrelevant, but if you were to fill the control object of an extrusion with a fountain or texture, this option would play a significant role in the result.

The graphic below, for instance, shows an identical extrusion with identical shading controls. The control object is colored with a fountain fill, and as a result, so is the extrusion. But the one on the left uses the Drape Fills option, and therefore each side of the gear gets the fountain fill treatment. The one on the right does not use the Drape Fills option, and so the fountain fill covers the entire extrusion.

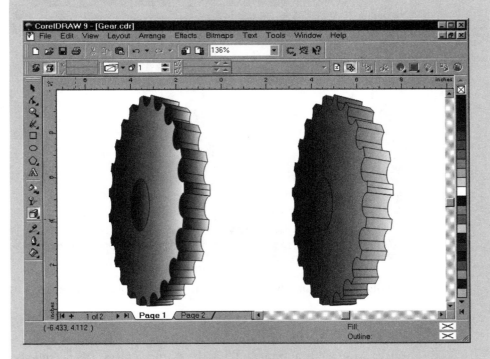

The one with the draped fill looks a bit more dramatic, but as for which is more realistic... well, frankly, the whole thing is a bit silly—who ever heard of filling a gear with a pattern?? Read on for how you can cast the gear in realistic lighting.

Solid Fills

As its name implies, this option allows you to select a solid color from a flyout palette to apply to the extruded faces. Once it's chosen, the faces will retain that color, independent of how you choose to fill the control object.

The color selection button opens whatever custom palette you currently have loaded. You can click on the Other button to mix or select any solid color from whatever color model you want. Here, we have chosen a different solid color for the extrusion.

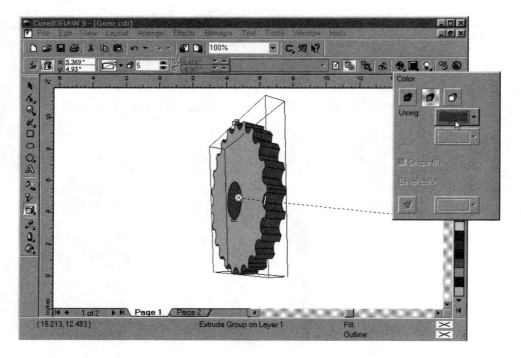

This would be handy for highlighting a certain side of an object, but it's not very realistic.

Fountain Fills

You can also apply a fountain fill to the extruded faces. The default choice graduates from the control object's color to black, and actually doesn't look too bad.

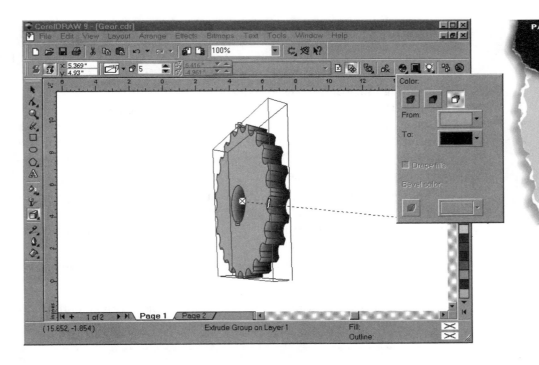

With light approaching from the object's face, the colors could plausibly fade to dark in the back. But as soon as you start messing with different start colors, you instantly leave the realm of plausibility.

NOTE   Remember, these color options affect only the parts of the object added by Extrude. There are two distinct elements to address: the original (or control) object and the extrusions. You can color the control object as you would any other vector object, but the extruded faces must be colored by the color settings on the property bar.

Beveling

This control lets you carve the corners of the extrusion, which otherwise would make 90-degree turns at their edges. This option was used mostly to make buttons on Web sites, and has become such a cliché that we'd rather not show it to you at all! Instead, we'll stall, because beveling looks best when lighting is applied, so stay tuned…

Better Illusions through Better Lighting

For realism, this is the place to go. Forget about fountain fills, drapes, and all of that nonsense—when an object has depth, it reflects light in different ways. That is what the Lighting controls are all about.

The first thing to know about Lighting is that you can create more than one light source, just as would be the case in real life. You determine the intensity of each source (maximum of three). The next thing to know is that DRAW determines where the object would reflect brightly and where not (for instance, which face of the extrusion faces the light sources). This mandates your doing two things for best results:

- Use Object Fill for the extrusion, ignoring all of the fancy nonsense. You might want to apply a light fountain fill to the control object itself, to show the variance of light on the face of the surface, but don't get fancy with the colors of the extrusion. Let the lighting handle that for you.

- Remove the outline from the object—the light that you cast will show the edges. You no longer need a hairline to do that.

So here's your starting point—a solid-filled object with no outline. Attractive, isn't it?

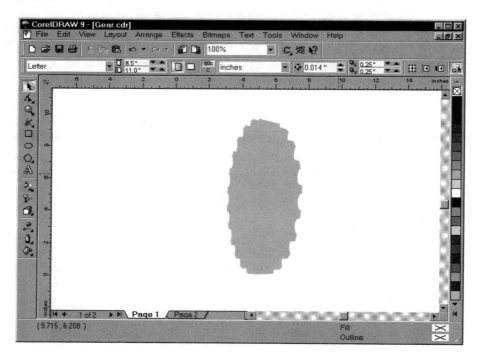

Stop laughing. Now do this:

1. Select the control object of the extrusion and press F11 to enter the Fountain Fill dialog. Go from a very light yellow or gray to a medium tone. For our black-and-white rendition, we chose white to 40% gray. Then angle it at about 25 degrees, so the lighter color is at lower-left gradually darkening as it moves to top-right.

2. Click the light bulb on the property bar, and from the dialog, turn on light source 1.

3. Note how you can move it to many different positions around the object and how you can vary the intensity.

4. Set the source to the lower-left and the intensity to 45%. Here's what ours looks like.

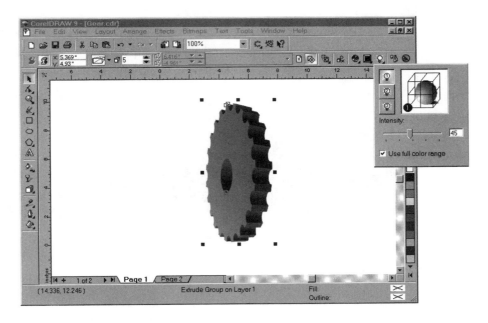

5. On your own, add a second light source, move them both around, and vary their intensities.

WARNING Be prepared to do a lot of experimenting with Lighting. You are likely to discover that turning on the light will often darken object faces, unless the intensity is 100 and the light source is facing the surface directly. You may have to start with the object fill at a lighter color to get the desired effect. A small amount of backlighting often helps also.

Now try adding a beveled edge—you'll meet with much better results.

Figure 15.4 shows our gear being examined closely on a table. We have placed it on a pedestal (although we have absolutely no idea why anyone would want to do this) and are shining two lights upon it. The lower-left light is bright and directly in its face, while the one at right is dimmer, casting ambient light.

FIGURE 15.4

Two light sources,
a beveled edge, and
a bit of rotation creates
a faithful rendition
of our gear.

Study the areas where the gear is dark and where it is light, and you'll likely agree that DRAW has created a plausible object in three-dimensional space. You can find this on the Sybex Web site as Gear on Display.cdr.

P.S. Are you wondering how we got the gear to be sitting inside of the stand? That's not possible in two-dimensional space. Answer in Chapter 19.

P.P.S. We used DRAW 9's new Mesh fill to scatter light and dark areas around this drawing.

TIP   As with DRAW's other dynamic effects, you can use Arrange ➢ Separate to freeze an extrusion. Separate breaks the extrusion into two components: the original control object and a conventional group made up of all the surfaces generated by the effect. If you want to edit an extruded face beyond the norm—apply transparency, create a cutaway, distort it, zoom in on it—you will need to separate it first. And remember, Separate kills the dynamic effect, so make sure the object is the way you want it to be first.

The (Not So) New Bitmap Extrusion Tool

This used to be called Text Extrusion, and Corel had a decision to make: kill it or expand its breadth. They chose the latter, much to the dismay of its team of beta testers. While Corel's vision for DRAW 9 is cohesive and refined, the one glaring exception is its handling of 3D. Corel removed Dream 3D from the CorelDRAW box, and in its place expected to offer a tool for creating 3D renderings directly in DRAW. The Text Extrusion tool offered in DRAW 8 was the precursor, and we were supposed to be treated to a more robust tool in 9, and the whole enchilada in 10.

This was the plan...on paper. When development compromises became imminent (as they always do), this tool didn't get the attention it deserved. We completely understand the realities of application development, and we're fine with Corel concluding that it couldn't develop it the way it wanted to. But instead of removing the feature altogether, Corel has left it in its semicomplete state and pretty much buried it on the Extrude property bar.

Only time will tell if DRAW 10 will bring this feature to fruition. Until then, we are not placing much stock in it, nor devoting any further space to it. If you want to experiment with the tool, you can search for "bitmap extrusions" in Help for more information.

Final Thoughts on Extruding

We already told you up front that we are not completely warm to Extrude, and then we proceeded to show you how wonderful it is! No question that Extrude can be useful in any situation in which you need to render an object with height, width, *and* depth. We certainly made that gear look more realistic.

Our angst is over its misuse. Users tend to get infatuated by, obsessed over, and ultimately in trouble with Extrude. The thought process typically goes something like this:

I think I'll extrude this headline for a bit more punch...looks cool...but now it is extruded and nothing else is...now everything else looks flat...better add a few more...

And before you know it, your drawing is a train wreck. Objects appear to be floating in space, all sense of perspective is lost, and the drawing shouts, "Look at Me!" before there is any chance of getting its intended message across. (Maybe "Look at Me" was its intended message, but that's another sore subject.)

We can't think of any work among the renowned fine artists that includes use of Extrude. When capable CorelDRAW artists want to render depth, they actually create the objects that produce the depth and dimension, they don't rely on an automatic fabricator. We asked one of our resident artists, Shane Hunt, for a sample of his work with Extrude, and indeed, he had to devise one for us, as he also doesn't use it much in his work. Nonetheless, his impromptu effort, shown in Figure 15.5, offers a nifty example of how Extrude could be tastefully used.

FIGURE 15.5

The use of Extrude on the headline adds drama and vitality to this design. The paragraph is being shaped with Perspective.

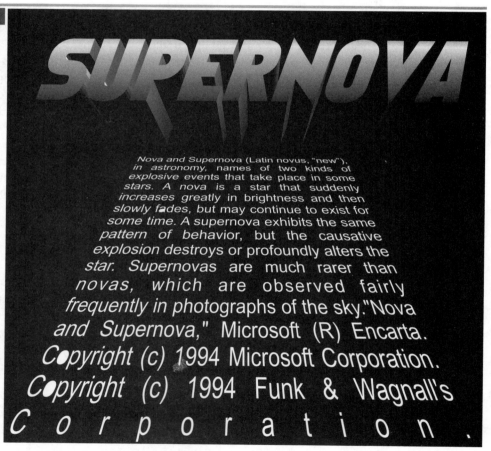

By and large, Extrude will prove to be not an artist's tool, but a technician's tool. If the entirety of the CorelDRAW community understood that, we would be fine with the tool. But they don't...so we're not. If you, dear reader, learn to use it in the right situation and for the right purpose, that will be a step in the right direction.

chapter 16

The Different Faces of Contour

Featuring

THE DIFFERENT FACES OF CONTOUR

ontours are second cousins to blends and fountain fills, with similarities and dissimilarities to each. A contour begins as one object (unlike a blend, which requires two objects) and involves gradual transitions from a start to a finish (like a blend or a fountain). Contours are a series of discrete steps, usually traversing a range of colors (like a blend). But the steps of a contour are based on just one object (like a fountain), rather than a metamorphosis from one object to another (like a blend). Each contour step maintains the same general shape as the start object. The steps get either larger or smaller by an amount you define, while maintaining the shape of the start object as closely as possible.

Like practically all of DRAW's effects, Contour has taken up residence on the Effects flyout, with its accompanying property bar. This chapter's brevity reflects the relatively specialized use for Contour.

Concentric? Say What??

If you understand that word, you understand Contour. Contour creates concentric objects, emanating from the original. Each concentric object is either a little bit smaller or a little bit larger than the original, depending upon the direction you set. The dictionary defines *concentric* as "having a common center," and you could think of two objects as concentric if one fits entirely within the other.

Concentric objects are not always easy to create. If you are talking about two rectangles, then it's cake—you simply make one smaller than the other. But what if you needed to create two concentric versions of the word *Hello*? Figure 16.1 shows our folly in trying. You can't just shrink down a duplicate, as we naively tried with the top image. And even breaking the word into individual letters won't do the trick. We succeeded only with the two *l*s—in other words, the simple rectangles.

FIGURE 16.1

Creating concentric letters is very tedious without Contour.

Again, you might not have many needs for creating concentric objects. But when you do, you'd better know about Contour.

N O T E Contour can be applied to single objects, not groups. The object can have multiple paths, meaning text can be contoured.

Innies and Outies

There are three ways to create a contour:

- As a collection of concentric objects that move outside the control object, by a specified amount, and with a specified number of steps.

- As a collection of concentric objects that move inside the control object, by a specified amount, and with a specified number of steps. Because the area inside an object is finite, you must enter values that make sense. For instance, you cannot contour five steps to the inside, at an increment of 1 inch, if your control object is only 3 inches in radius.

- As a collection of concentric objects that move to the center of the control object. For inside contours, there is no Steps value for you to choose; Contour notes the amount to move (the "offset") and does so all the way to the center, taking however many steps it needs.

Figure 16.2 shows these three types of contours, applied to a square.

PART 4

Effects and Affects

FIGURE 16.2

These three contours have similar instructions, just different sets of driving directions.

Contour to the inside
4 steps, offset of .25

Contour to the center
Offset of .25

Contour to the outside
4 steps, offset of .25

In all three cases, the original object is shaded a medium gray and the Contour color (i.e., the color that the newly created objects gradually become) is white. In all three cases, we have set the offset to .25 inch—that means that each step toward white spans a quarter-inch. And we have defined four steps for two of the three contours. The center contour disregards the Steps value, as it journeys all the way to the center, taking as many steps as needed.

To see the dynamics of contour with its new interactive personality, try this simple exercise:

1. In a new drawing, draw an ellipse.

2. Activate the Contour tool, second icon on the Effects flyout. Note the changed appearance of the cursor.

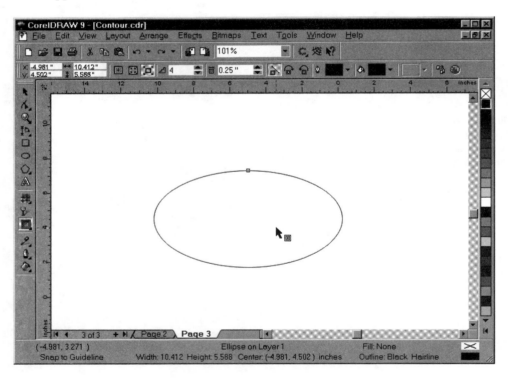

3. From a point inside the ellipse, click and drag to any other position, either inside or outside of the ellipse. We dragged to the inside.

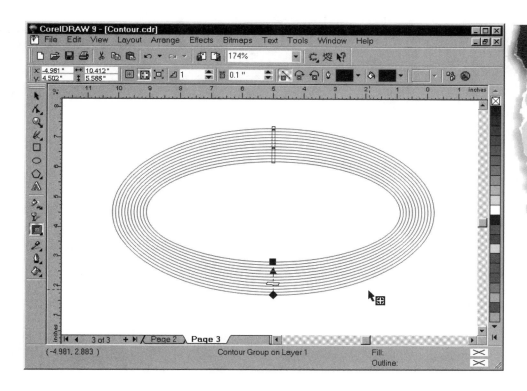

PART

Effects and Affects

The factory default creates a contour with an offset of .1 inch. DRAW watches how you drive the cursor and determines whether to contour inside or out, and how many steps to use (the further you drag, the more steps DRAW uses). If you drag all the way to the center, DRAW creates a centered contour.

While these concentric rings would be easy enough for you to create without Contour, think back to our simple word and how hard it was for us. With Contour, it's easy:

1. Type the word and fill it with a medium color.

2. Switch to the Contour tool, move inside one of the letters, and click and drag a very small distance to the inside (see the graphic on the next page).

 T I P   If you know the precise settings you want, instead of clicking and dragging, head straight to the property bar and work the controls. As soon as you press Enter or choose a color in one of the drop-down palettes, the contour will be applied.

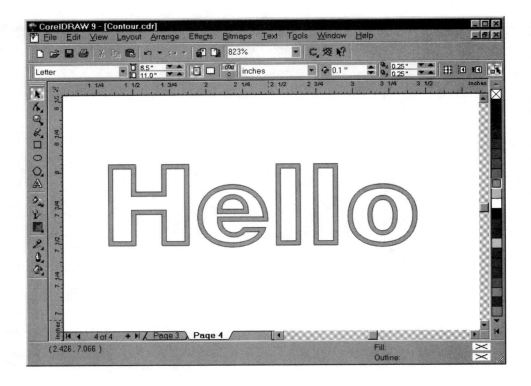

Working the Controls

Thanks to the new on-screen controls, you'll get a feel for Contour much more quickly than with prior versions. Figure 16.3 shows a close-up of the on-screen controls:

Drag the white box to adjust the Steps value. Move it all the way to the center, and DRAW creates a center contour.

Drop a color on the white box to change the color of the contour. This does not change the color of the control object; it changes the color that DRAW uses to transition away from that original color.

Drop a color on the diamond to change the outline of the contour. This is only relevant if the control object has an outline.

Drag the white horizontal slider to adjust Steps and Offset together. We're not sure exactly what the formula is here, but we note that DRAW makes sure to adjust both values in such a way that the contour effect remains smooth and gradual.

FIGURE 16.3

Creating contours is much easier with DRAW 9's new on-screen controls.

We have already discussed the three types of contour, and Steps and Offset. The remaining property bar settings, visible in Figure 16.3, are as follows:

Direction of Contour Colors Just like with fountain fills, you tell DRAW what route to take as it traverses colors. It can take the shortest distance between the two points on the theoretical color wheel, go around the wheel in one direction, or go in the other. As you can see below, you can get significantly different results.

Color Choices   There are three places to go to address color choices, and a drop-down palette for each: (1) setting the outline color; (2) setting the fill color; and (3) if the control object is a fountain fill, setting both the start and end colors.

Remember, these three drop-down palettes *do not* change the outline or fill color of the original control object. Instead, they determine how the color shifts away from the control object as the contour proceeds.

Finally, there is a button for copying contours and one for clearing the effect altogether.

Better Outlines with Contour

If precision is your game, forget about using standard outlines around objects. Why? Let's say you're creating a schematic according to an ultraprecise specification. The plan requires that you create your widget to be 54mm by 48mm, with a 4-point, 40% gray outline placed precisely 48mm in from the schematic's left edge and 24mm from the top. Setting the page in millimeters is no problem, and establishing guidelines at 48mm and 24mm is a piece of cake. You can use the Transformation controls to size your object to the exact spec, and you can snap it precisely in place along the two guidelines.

Calling for a 4-point border is no problem, either, right? So you use all of DRAW's precision controls, you place your object just so…and you are promptly fired from your job. Figure 16.4 shows the reason for your dismissal. By default, DRAW places half of an outline's thickness inside the object boundary and half on the outside. Therefore, 2 points of this object's outline are outside of the boundary.

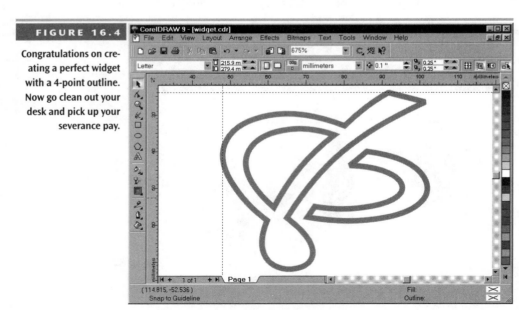

FIGURE 16.4

Congratulations on creating a perfect widget with a 4-point outline. Now go clean out your desk and pick up your severance pay.

If you'd used Contour, you'd still be employed. Try it this way:

1. Create the widget without any outline, using the guidelines for precision placement and the property bar for precision sizing.

2. Fill the widget with 40% gray.

That 40% gray is the color of the object's outline, but in this case, you need to think backward. What color are you starting with and what color continues in the interior? The start color may only last for 4 points, but you define it by setting the main object's fill color. The rest of the object is filled white, but the contouring takes care of that.

3. Activate the Contour tool and set the following from the property bar:

   • Contour to the inside

   • Steps to **1**

   • Offset to **4pt** (enter that precisely, and DRAW will accept it, even though the page is measured in millimeters).

   • Color to white

4. Ask for, and receive, a raise.

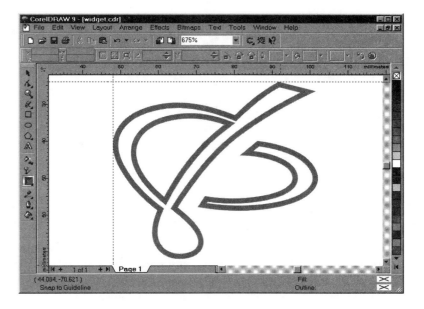

Because you are contouring to the inside, the object begins precisely at its edge. No outlines hang over, upsetting your precision.

Open Contours

You can apply a contour to an open curve to give it a filled look, and the results can be striking. When you select an open curve, Contour only allows you to step to the outside, because there is no inside.

Figure 16.5 illustrates the technique, using the initials of our lead author. The top image is the original, drawn with straight lines; the bottom image is a 10-step contour of it. Rick's initials were a good example, because they could be created entirely with straight lines instead of curves. Keep reading to find out why curves aren't a contour's best friend…

FIGURE 16.5

Contour can turn drab into interesting.

Create a Contour, Take a Coffee Break

You've seen the beauty of contouring; now it's time to reveal its dark side: contouring simple objects like lines and rectangles is quick and easy, but objects that are more complex can send DRAW into a coma.

Figure 16.6 offers the chilling details. Each of the objects in the figure has had a 25-step contour applied to it. The first five objects, consisting of mostly straight lines, contour quickly. Even the letter *A*, a compound shape, takes the contour in short order because it is made up entirely of straight lines.

FIGURE 16.6

Contouring simple objects is fast and easy; contouring complex objects is the computer equivalent of water torture. (Times rounded to nearest quarter second.)

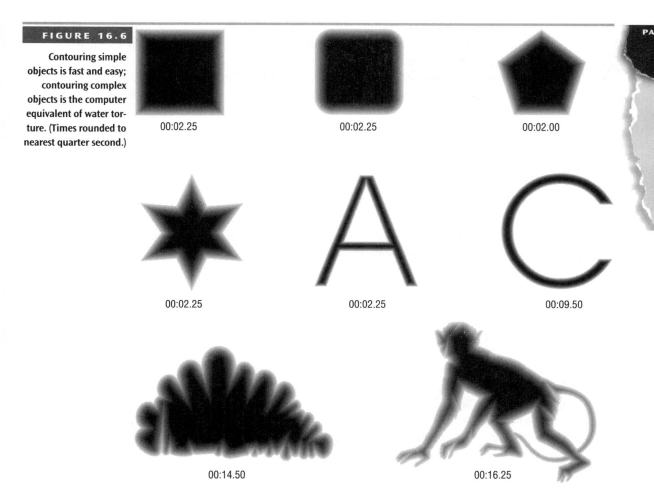

00:02.25   00:02.25   00:02.00

00:02.25   00:02.25   00:09.50

00:14.50   00:16.25

SUPERCALIFRAGILISTIC

02:45.50

The big drop in performance came with the letter *C*, composed entirely of curves. We sunk deeper into the abyss with the cloud (the one that looks like an armadillo with a thyroid condition), the monkey-cum-devil, and the string of text. Would you believe it if we told you that these times are all significantly better than DRAW 8? A year ago, Supercalifragilistic took almost two hours.

When an object is a continuous curve, like the cloud, you can turn to Blend instead of Contour. For instance, we sized and duped the cloud, creating a tiny duplicate inside of the original (a concentric cloud, if you will). Then we shaded it, selected both objects, and blended using 25 steps. Blend has the luxury of control objects on both sides, so its job is much easier than that of Contour, which must painstakingly determine how each step is to be created. The blended cloud was created in less than two seconds.

But it would be unthinkable to try to create a concentric monkey (with its tail forming a subpath) or the long string of text. So our best advice to you, if you don't feel like waiting almost three minutes for contoured text, is *don't contour text.* (Patient: "Doctor, my head hurts when I bang it against the wall. What should I do?" Doctor: "Stop banging it against the wall.")

 T I P   Once you have an object contoured to your liking, group it. We know this sounds strange—to group what is already a group—but hear us out on this one. When you resize a contour, DRAW detects that the control object has changed and so it signals Contour to recalculate the object. In the case of the cloud, you've just bought yourself a 14-second delay. But if you group it first, DRAW treats it differently. It becomes one grouped object that is simply being scaled, without need for any recalculation. The contour is still alive and well, and you can always select it within the group and change it dynamically.

Whither Contour?

We're wondering for how much longer we'll see Contour as part of DRAW's special effects team. Two of the most popular applications for it have been usurped. While Contour was the go-to tool for creating drop shadows, the relatively new Interactive Drop Shadow does a better job. And while Contour once was the only way to simulate an outline that had a pattern or fountain fill, DRAW 9 allows you to separate the outline from the fill and treat it like a closed shape.

We don't know of any other tool that can turn a cloud into an armadillo, but we're not entirely sure how many users appreciate this unique capability. And on that sarcastic note, we'll finish this chapter, wondering if it might be for the last time...

THROUGH THE LOOKING GLASS

Featuring

THROUGH THE LOOKING GLASS

his stop on our tour through DRAW's special effects might be the highlight of the trip for you. It features one of DRAW's most celebrated attributes: its ability to create transparent objects. Unlike effects such as Envelope and Extrude, which influence how an object is shaped, DRAW's transparency tools determine how we *see* an object.

DRAW splits its transparency tools into two categories, each with different functionality: the Interactive Transparency tool and the Lens docker. We suspect that Corel still wants to evolve these features, because there is no apparent reason why the Lens effects couldn't be an interactive set of tools with a property bar, like all the others. This chapter is similarly divided into two; we'll start with the lenses.

New Lenses on Life

Lenses have historically been responsible for more oohs and aahs at trade shows and product demonstrations than any other feature of CorelDRAW. The Lens docker provides access to 11 different camera-like lenses that can be applied to an object. When you apply a lens, the object *becomes* the lens, filtering your view of all objects that are beneath it. Thus lenses allow objects to become, in essence, transparent—an effect that was impossible prior to their debut in DRAW 5.

In the past, to qualify to be a lens, objects had to be combined into a single curve, but no longer. Now any group of objects—even a multiple selection of separate objects—can act as a lens. An artistic string of text can also be a lens; paragraph text cannot.

You control the Lens effect with the Lens docker, shown in action in Figure 17.1. You get there from Effects ➤ Lens or by pressing Alt+F3. Here, an inversion lens is being applied to the ellipse in front of a collection of graphics.

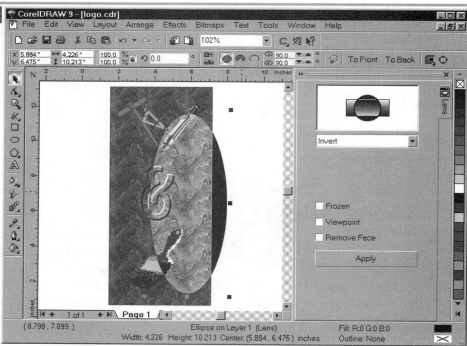

This lens studies the colors of objects underneath and converts them to the colors that are on the opposite end of the CMYK color spectrum. Red becomes cyan, green becomes magenta, and white becomes black. We intentionally drew the ellipse to hang over the edge of the graphic so you could see that it even turned the white page black.

To help you see the effects of the Lens tool, we have placed a file called Lenstour.cdr on the Sybex Web site for you to download. In this file, you'll find several rectangles with different fill types and patterns, and then a simple ellipse placed on top. The bars on the left are created from a rainbow blend, and the four rectangles on the right are (from top to bottom) a fountain fill, a two-color pattern fill, a full-color bitmap

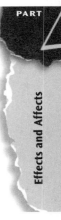

fill, and a fractal fill. Figure 17.2 shows the effect of one of the standard lenses: a 50% transparency. In other words, the ellipse in front is set to allow half of the color intensities from the objects underneath to show through. Meanwhile, the ellipse itself is filled with red. You can re-create Figure 17.2 by following these steps:

1. Open `Lenstour.cdr` and select the ellipse.

2. Fill it with red.

3. Invoke the Lens docker (Effects ➢ Lens or Alt+F3).

4. In the Lens drop-down window in the middle of the docker, choose Transparency as the type of lens.

5. Set the Rate to 50%.

6. Click Apply.

FIGURE 17.2

The red ellipse is 50% transparent, allowing half of the colors underneath it to show through.

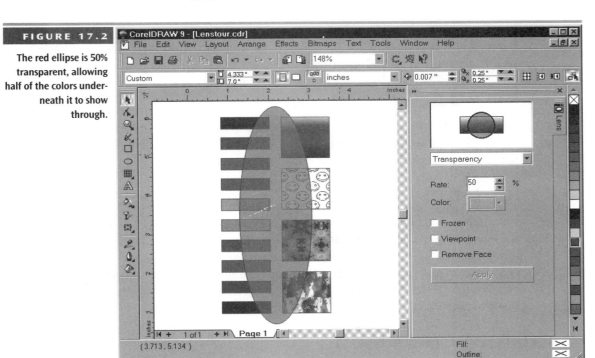

With `Lenstour.cdr`, you can experiment with all of the different lens effects. Try applying each style of lens and refer to the descriptions in the following sections. When a particular lens has additional settings for rate, color, and so on, try varying them over a wide range to see the results. Also try changing the color of the ellipse that is acting as the lens—that can have a significant impact on the result.

Here are descriptions of the lenses.

Transparency

This is likely to be the most used effect but the least used lens, and we'll explain what we mean in a moment. As you saw in Figure 17.2, Transparency causes the colors of the objects under the lens to mix with the lens object's color, creating the illusion that you've placed a piece of transparent film over the object. In the Rate box, you enter a transparency rate from 1% to 100%. The greater this value, the more transparent the lens object; at 100%, the lens essentially disappears, allowing 100% of the underlying object's color to show through unchanged.

However, while transparency is a popular effect, you probably won't reach for Lens to apply it, thanks to the Interactive Transparency tool, discussed later in this chapter.

Brighten

This lens brightens the colors under it by the factor you specify in the Rate box, between –100% and 100%. At 100%, the colors are nearly white; at 0%, the lens has no effect at all; and at –100%, the colors approach black.

Color Add

The Color Add lens mixes the colors of overlapping objects, adding the color of the lens object to that of the underlying object. This lens has no effect where it overlays white objects, because white already contains 100% of every color.

Color Limit

Color Limit works much like a color filter on a camera, filtering out all colors under the lens except the one you specify in the Color box. For example, if you place a green lens over an object, all colors except green will be filtered out within the lens area. You can also control the strength of the filter by specifying a value in the Rate box. For the green filter, a rate of 100% will allow only green to show through; a lower setting will allow other colors to show through.

Custom Color Map

This lens maps colors using a range that you define. The controls are similar to fountain fills—you choose From and To colors, and specify the direction that the mapping should take. You can map directly between the two specified colors or start with the From color and go through the colors of the rainbow, forward or backward, to the To color.

Fish Eye

Just like the camera lens of the same name, this lens magnifies and distorts the objects behind the lens. Figure 17.3 shows the process of creating a fish eye effect. The Fish Eye lens works when the objects it is distorting are objects drawn in DRAW, but it has no effect on bitmaps.

FIGURE 17.3

Better vision through electronics—and DRAW's Fish Eye lens

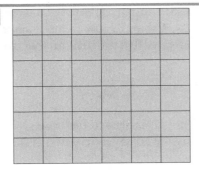

1. A grid created using the Graph Paper tool

2. A circle drawn and placed in the middle of the grid

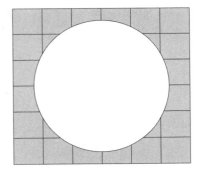

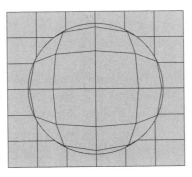

3. The Fish Eye lens applied to the circle

Heat Map

This lens is DRAW's contribution to the electronic psychedelic community. It maps colors to other colors in a predefined palette, creating a *heat map* or infrared look. Bright (or hot) colors are mapped to other hot colors (yellow, orange, and so on), and dark (or cool) colors are mapped to cooler colors (blue, cyan, and purple). The palette Rotation value determines where the color mapping begins. For example, a value of 0% or 100% causes mapping to begin at the start of the palette (at white) and move to the right (through cyan, blue, and so on). A value of 50% causes mapping to begin halfway through the palette (at red) and move to the right, and then go back to the start of the palette.

Invert

With Invert, you can switch the colors under the lens to their complementary colors, based on the CMYK color wheel. We used Invert to create Figure 17.1.

 T I P   Once a lens is applied, you can select colors from the on-screen color palette or the Fill docker to change the lens tint. That way, if the docker is closed, you don't need to reopen it to change the lens.

Magnify

This lens causes the objects under the lens to be magnified by the factor you specify in the Amount box, so it looks like you've placed a magnifying glass over the drawing. The maximum magnification factor is 100. Be careful when using this lens with bitmaps; at twice or three times the magnification, most bitmaps will look very jagged. However, with a vector object, like the coin shown in Figure 17.4, the effect is useful and realistic.

Tinted Grayscale

Objects under this lens appear to have had a tonal scale setting applied—the underlying objects appear in monochromatic tones of the lens color. Colors under the lens are mapped to an equivalent tone of the color of the lens. For example, a blue lens over a light-colored object creates light blue; the same lens over a dark-colored object creates dark blue. This lens is very handy for decolorizing a drawing or imported bitmap, for proofing, or for actual printing. To do this, simply cover the entire object with a rectangle or other closed curve, choose Tinted Grayscale, and set the color to Black.

FIGURE 17.4

Creating a magnifying glass is easy with a Magnify lens.

Wireframe

This clever lens is like switching to Wireframe view, but for just a portion of your screen. Try it on Lenstour.cdr and you'll see instantly how it works. All objects are reduced down to one fill and one outline color, both of which you designate from the Lens docker.

No Lens Effect

Selecting None removes the lens from the selected object and returns the object to its normal state.

Frozen Lenses

Another remarkable weapon in DRAW's lens arsenal is the ability to freeze and even extract a lens effect. Figure 17.5 is a continuation of Figure 17.3, where we created the fish eye effect. After creating the lens, we froze it by checking the Frozen option on the docker. Then the image that is seen through the lens no longer needs the object behind it. You can see in step 3 in the figure that removing the grid behind the ellipse doesn't phase the fish-eyed circle at all.

Frozen lenses work with bitmaps, as well.

FIGURE 17.5

Thanks to the Frozen option, a lens can stand on its own, without the aid of the background object that gave it its appearance in the first place.

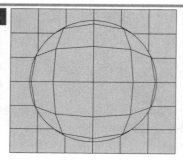

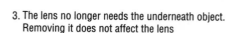

1. The Fish Eye lens applied to the circle

2. The Fish Eye lens frozen in place

3. The lens no longer needs the underneath object. Removing it does not affect the lens

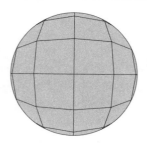

4. The lens is now just a group of objects that can be edited (or destroyed), just like any other group

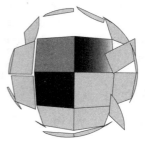

T I P With a frozen lens, DRAW has essentially given us another method to crop objects and images. For instance, a Brighten lens at a rate of 0% creates a lens with no filter or affect whatsoever. Freeze this lens, and you have essentially cropped the object or image behind it.

Changing Your Point of View

An interesting enhancement of the lens effect, debuting in DRAW 6, enables you to change the viewing angle through a lens. When you click the Viewpoint check box in the docker and then the Edit button, an X appears on screen, similar to the one that you adjust to change the perspective of an extrusion. This X allows you to choose an area or object to be visible in the lens, other than whatever is directly behind the lens.

Figure 17.6 shows this in action. On top, a circle is placed over a portion of the drawing and fish-eyed at 175%. By activating the Viewpoint check box and designating another part of the drawing (middle), a different view is seen through the lens (below). This is a great tool for those who need to create blow-ups of an illustration to show detail. Actually, you could accomplish the same thing by placing the lens over the area you want to show, freezing it, and then moving the lens object—but changing the point of view is more convenient, and allows you to couple it with another effect, in this case a fish eye.

Astute readers will note that we performed a similar effect in Chapter 11 with Intersect. Lens has two advantages: it can apply an effect in addition to the perspective change and work on bitmap images.

Combining Lenses

As you experimented with DRAW's lenses, you may have noticed for yourself that you can overlay one lens on another. For example, you might want to both magnify and brighten an object underneath a lens. When you apply a new lens, you replace any existing lens; they are not added together. However, you can *stack* lens objects on top of one another. Make a quick copy of a lens object, which effectively duplicates the lens effect. Then change to a different lens effect, and you create a compound lens effect.

W A R N I N G Lens effects move into the high rent district in a hurry. DRAW creates lenses by duplicating the objects that are underneath. Thus a compound lens effect requires the *quadrupling* of objects, and in the case of a color bitmap image used underneath a lens, the end result can be crippling. In Chapter 23, we detail one solution—converting lens effects to bitmaps.

FIGURE 17.6

With Viewpoint, a lens
object can act like a
movable window.

Learning to Use the Lenses

Having experimented with the effects produced by each lens type, your head might already be swimming with ideas of how to use them. Here are a few.

Tinted Grayscale for Cheap Color

If you want to add a bit of color or take away color, the Tinted Grayscale lens is your answer. We mentioned earlier that you can import a full-color photograph or drawing and apply a Tinted Grayscale lens to it, to convert it to grayscale. You can also colorize a black-and-white image by adding a Tinted Grayscale lens. Despite this lens's name, you can choose any color for it, making it easy and affordable to add some color to a project.

Heat Map

Like Tinted Grayscale, Heat Map is most effective when used with grayscale photographs. Try importing a photo and applying this lens. The result is an effect that has become very popular in Generation X publications. If you are planning to publish a magazine dedicated to heavy-metal music, this is definitely the lens for you.

Using Brighten to Create Text Backdrops

Another popular technique used in many publications is to brighten or "wash out" part of an image to place text over it. The Brighten lens makes it easy to accomplish this, as Figure 17.7 shows.

PART

Effects and Affects

FIGURE 17.7

By brightening this photograph, regular-sized text can be placed in front and be easily read.

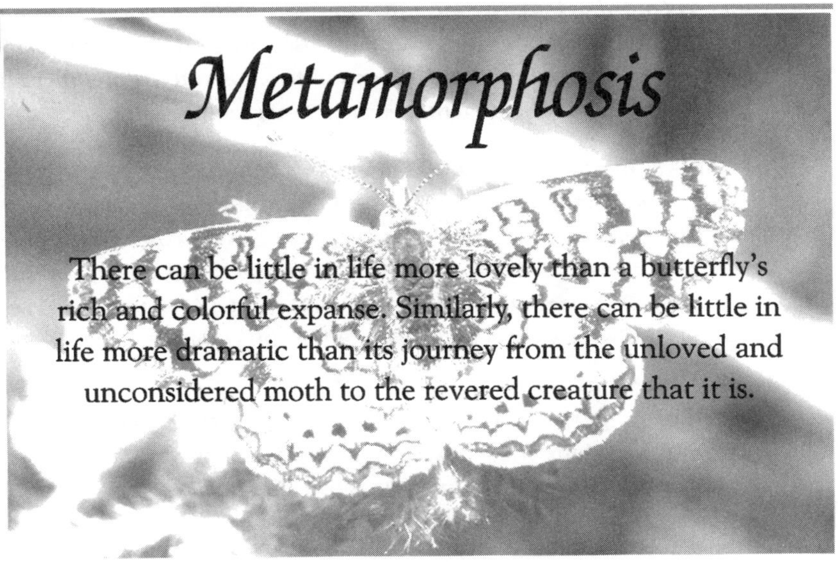

Metamorphosis

There can be little in life more lovely than a butterfly's rich and colorful expanse. Similarly, there can be little in life more dramatic than its journey from the unloved and unconsidered moth to the revered creature that it is.

N O T E   In Chapter 14, we showed you a clever trick for creating a background image, severely tinted from full intensity (we used a falcon behind a page of text). This technique produces similar results, and although we prefer the Blend strategy for its simpler instructions and reduced number of objects required, you cannot use Blend with photographs. When working with bitmap images, you need to use a lens to produce this effect.

The Miracle of Interactive Transparency

Our lead author relates a recent experience at a California seminar:

> *I was on a tour of six cities, in which I met over 300 CorelDRAW users. Most everyone exhibited symptoms of Version-itis, an uncommon, but rarely fatal, condition in which software users develop the inability to recall which version brought about which new features. I am not immune to this epidemic, regularly failing to remember if PowerClip was introduced in version 4 or 5, and when DRAW began supporting page sizes over 30 inches.*
>
> *CorelDRAW users are the most susceptible, given the dizzying pace with which Corel Corp. develops new versions. I was particularly struck by the amazement that greeted me from regular version 7 users who attended these seminars to learn more about version 8. They encountered several features they had never seen before...only to learn that version 7 sported them also.*
>
> *This was most widespread with Interactive Transparency. At each city, when I melted one image into another—an effect normally reserved for PHOTO-PAINT users—legions of users began gasping and taking frantic notes. "And how much RAM does version 8 need to do this?" was one of several typical queries. "No more than you have now—this effect is available within version 7." Stunned silence was often the last word of this exchange.*

Here it is version 9, and we suspect that many of you are still just getting to know this incredible tool. It does not produce as many effects as Lens, concentrating instead on the one lens effect, transparency, used by most users. As an interactive tool, it offers several usability advantages over the docker; and as a more refined tool, it offers functionality that Lens can't touch.

Interactive Transparency, the tenth icon in the toolbox, operates like all of the other interactive tools that you have read about:

1. Select an object.
2. Activate the tool.
3. Work the controls on screen or on the property bar.

To use Interactive Transparency effectively, remember the following three points.

No More Docking and Applying

You can dispense with the Lens docker for standard transparency effects, as Interactive Transparency works straight off of its property bar. No more having to fetch the docker, and no more incessant clicking of an Apply button.

Just Like Filling an Object

Interactive Transparency works just like the Fill tool in its range of possibilities. But instead of applying a color, shade, or pattern to an object, you are applying a degree of transparency to it. (Technically, the same engine is used: when you apply transparency to an object on top, DRAW creates the effect by changing the fill pattern of any objects underneath.) Forget the nerdspeak; the essential point to take away is that you can create transparencies that are themselves fountains, patterns, or textures. The latter two are risky and carry a very high ugliness quotient, but fountain transparencies are very useful and potentially dramatic.

To that end, we promised a return to two graphics that we created in earlier chapters. In Chapter 10, we introduced you to text wrapping with a nice, clean graphic of an article wrapping around a globe. Figure 10.1 shows the image, made a bit more dynamic by the presence of the transparent text. We set the text in Futura ExtraBlack, filled it white, and stretched it out to fit the space. Then we used the Interactive Transparency tool to apply a "fountain transparency" to it—the degree of transparency changes gradually, like the degree of color of a fountain fill.

When first applied, the default fountain runs from opaque on the left to transparent on the right. We changed the angle, using the on-screen handles, so that the fountain went from transparent on top to opaque on the bottom, as shown in Figure 17.8.

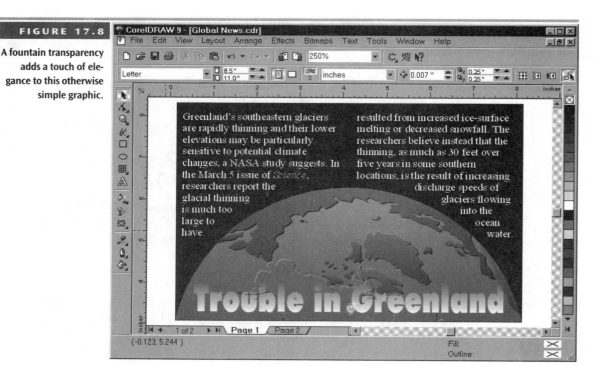

FIGURE 17.8

A fountain transparency adds a touch of elegance to this otherwise simple graphic.

The second graphic we promised to finish for you is from Chapter 13, where we created a ripple effect in the water, using Envelope (see Figure 13.9). With the sun setting behind the cityscape, the reflection would not be opaque; it would be transparent. So after applying the envelope to the reflection, we applied a fountain transparency to the reflection, running at an angle away from the sunset (in other words, most transparent closest to the sun, least transparent away from it). Figure 17.9 shows the effect.

Transparent Anything

Prior to version 7, you could only apply transparency to vector objects created in DRAW. In addition to its interactive qualities, version 7 also introduced the capability of applying transparency to any object on a page, including imported bitmaps (thank you, Xara, the diminutive drawing program that scared Corel so much, the company bought the licensing rights to it). Simply put, if you can select it, you can apply transparency to it, the lone exception being an imported placeable .eps file.

FIGURE 17.9

This fountain transparency is set at an angle—the further from the sun, the darker the reflection.

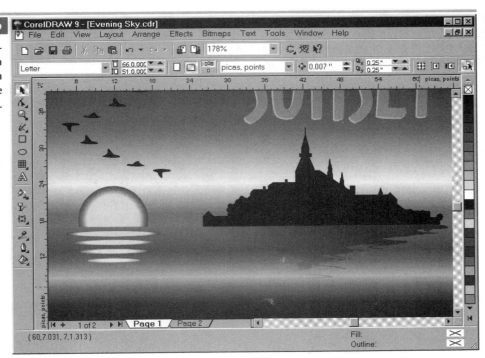

Thanks to Interactive Transparency, amateur and semiproficient DRAW users can create effects that they would never have dared to attempt in the past. We include our lead author in that category. "Producing surreal effects has always been well outside of my artistic resume," he says, "requiring expertise with image-editing software or the wherewithal to be able to communicate my vision to the camera people at my printer. But now that DRAW can do it...I can do it."

Figure 17.10 is a relatively simple example—one of countless advertisements that attempts to mix baseball with patriotism. You are looking at two distinct imported photographs; the flag's background has been removed. With the flag selected, the Interactive Transparency tool can apply any degree of transparency to it, in this case 75% transparency.

This entire effect can also be produced in PHOTO-PAINT. In fact, some would argue that it's easier to do it there. We won't participate in that argument because it is a moot point to many. Despite the big upswing in PHOTO-PAINT interest, many DRAW users feel more comfortable in the vector environment. The fact that this effect can be produced in DRAW is front-page news to these users.

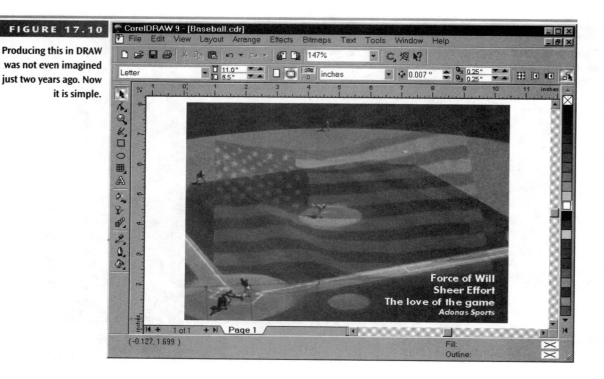

FIGURE 17.10

Producing this in DRAW
was not even imagined
just two years ago. Now
it is simple.

Step by Step: Making Dreams Come True

The following discussion walks you through the creation of another mosaic of two photographs, one merged into another. At the 1998 CorelWORLD Conference, this practically brought down the house, even though it is not terribly complicated. But given the specter of producing the effect with any other set of tools, traditional or electronic, this is nothing short of miraculous.

While the photos we used are not available for free distribution, you can still work with us through these steps by using any two digitized photographs. They will work best if one of them is a background image and one of them is a portrait.

Figure 17.11 shows the three elements—the background photo, the foreground photo, and a string of text, all for a brochure about a timeshare opportunity. ("This could be your backyard," proclaims the cover of this brochure.) Given the message in the text and the romantic look the couple is sharing, our objective is to give a dreamy quality to this image.

FIGURE 17.11

Watch these two photographs become one...

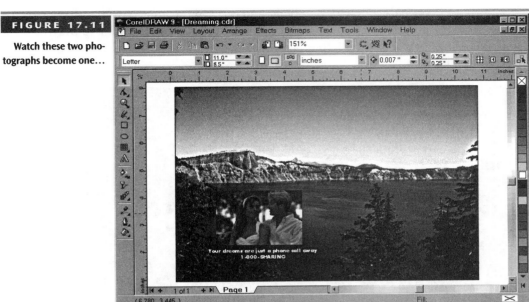

We zoomed in and first applied a simple envelope to help frame the photo of the couple. We chose a single curve envelope, and held Ctrl while dragging down to create the clean arc.

Next, we selected the photo of the couple and invoked the Interactive Transparency tool. From the property bar, we chose Fountain as the transparency type, and DRAW responded by applying a default fountain of 100% opaque on the left to 100% transparent on the right.

This is like a fountain fill, except the color is not changing—the rate of transparency is. And you manipulate a fountain transparency as you do a fountain fill: you can move the handles on screen to adjust the direction, move the mid-point slider to change the rate of transition, and apply shades by dropping colors on the end points or on the line in the middle. There is one essential difference: With a fountain transparency, you don't change the color when you drag and drop from the color palette; you change the degree of transparency. White equals no transparency, black equals full transparency, and gray tones are degrees in between.

To set the transparency, you can either drag and drop colors onto the control handles, or select each handle and use the slider control on the property bar.

Just like a fountain fill, there are four different types of fountain transparencies, and they are represented by the four prominent icons on the property bar. After activating it, we changed from a linear transparency to a radial one, as shown in the top graphic of the facing page.

Now the effect is precisely the opposite of what we had in mind. It is opaque around the outside and transparent in the inside. To reverse the effect, we selected the left handle and dialed transparency all the way down to 0, and then dialed the right handle all the way up to 100, as shown in the bottom graphic of the facing page.

We're close, although we can still see a distinct edge around the photo. Our objective is to completely remove any visible edge to the photo, giving it the appearance of melting into the background. We did this by dragging the right handle in toward the center and nudging the left handle around until we could see no edge.

With the selection handles removed, you can see that we succeeded in producing the image of a young couple realizing their dream of owning a vacation home.

Now the Downside...

As with all of DRAW's effects, transparency can be dangerous if it falls into the wrong hands. First off, if you place transparent objects on top of bitmaps, you can end up with gigantic files (particularly if the transparent object is itself a bitmap, as is the case with our dreamy couple). DRAW might lull you into a false sense of security if you save the .cdr files with bitmap compression turned on; when you create your print files, be ready for the dam to burst. Transparency is a complex effect, and aside from large print files, they are a leading cause of RIPing problems at service bureaus. If you encounter this, try converting the transparent effect into a bitmap. This might sound strange—converting a bitmap into a bitmap—and removing the intelligence from DRAW's tools is not exactly what you had in mind when you adopted the program.

But a little bit of dummying down CorelDRAW can be a good thing. When you convert a transparent bitmap effect into a static bitmap (done by selecting the objects and going to Bitmaps ➢ Convert to Bitmap), you essentially freeze the effect in time—you are taking a snapshot of what the effect looked like at that moment. In so doing, you greatly simplify the work; now it's just a bunch of pixels, and any old Mac-myopic service bureau can RIP a bunch of dumb pixels.

We regularly employ the following routine when preparing print files that might contain troublesome effects:

1. We save.

2. We convert any suspect effects to static bitmaps.

3. We create the print file.

4. We close without saving.

Now any changes that need to be made to the effect can easily be done, as the effect is still live. Once we make the change, we repeat the four steps.

N O T E   DRAW 9 adds a print option to rasterize an entire page, essentially converting all elements to bitmap. This is more convenient because it doesn't involve your converting any of your elements (it's done transparently at print time), but its downside is that it converts *all* elements, including your text. For more information, see our opus, "Print, Darn You!," Chapter 26.

The second major risk to all of this is ugliness, and there we have no quick fixes to offer, except to suggest that you try to avoid it. As with all of DRAW's effects, transparency will haunt you and taunt you into using it just for the sake of using it. You must resist with all your might the use of transparency simply because it's there.

But when it's used at the appropriate time, it can be terrific. It is one of the tools that can truly take you to another level of design, as it allows you to create effects that you might have envisioned but never knew how to create.

Now you can...

DROPPING
SHADOWS

Featuring

DROPPING SHADOWS

If we had to pick one aspect of computer-based drawing that has progressed the most in the last two years, it would have to be the drop shadow. We remember the bad old days all too well, when creating soft shadows behind objects never looked quite right. Of course, it's still easy to mess up drop shadows, or use them in the wrong situations, and we will not let that subject go undiscussed in this chapter. But when you need a clean, soft drop shadow, the interactive tool introduced in DRAW 8 is without peer.

Hard vs. Soft

Let's start by defining a few terms, because there are lots of ways to create shadows in DRAW and in the real world. Figure 18.1 shows a simple drop shadow being applied to a headline for an article about timesharing. This is a very common technique, easily created:

1. Create the headline and shade it as desired.

2. With it still selected, press the plus key to make a copy right on top of itself.

3. Press Tab to switch to the original headline in the back.

4. Fill it black.

5. Use your keyboard arrow keys to nudge down and to the side.

Is this really the way that a shadow would be cast if the lettering were raised and light were shone on it? Probably not, and some in the CorelDRAW community would scoff at the use of a so-called "hard shadow." We wouldn't. We view it as a perfectly credible technique to create a clean and unpretentious graphic effect. By using this, you're not trying to fool anyone into seeing the headline floating above the page. You're not trying to create a realistic shadow. You are simply using an age-old, but still effective, technique of calling a bit more attention to a headline. It is also a very good way to ensure contrast if you are not certain about the color qualities of the background. With light text and a dark drop shadow, one of the two will definitely show up against a medium-colored background.

We think this is perfectly fine; tell the purists to go jump in the lake.

However, we're not so satisfied with Figure 18.2. By moving the headline into the photo, we are implicitly hovering it over the image of the lake (Lake Shasta in California, for anyone who cares), and now the shadow does not pass muster. If we are trying to create the effect of a raised headline, then the shadow cast by the letters would not be a hard shadow, but a soft one. It would show dispersion of light and areas of transparency. It would have to be a real shadow.

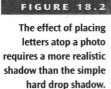

FIGURE 18.2

The effect of placing letters atop a photo requires a more realistic shadow than the simple hard drop shadow.

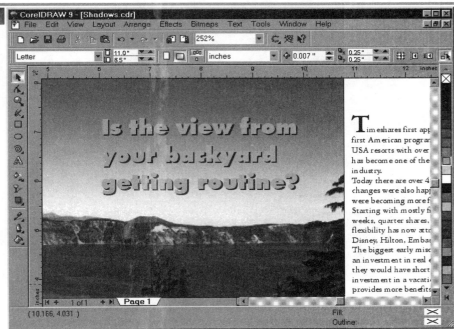

Shadows and Vectors Don't Mix

Trying to create realistic shadows in DRAW has been an unhappy experience for many. Smart DRAW users prior to version 7 would send this image and its lettering into PHOTO-PAINT for a "real" shadow. DRAW versions 6 and below had no such capability, and DRAW 7 offered it only as an undocumented and intricate bitmap effect.

So DRAW users resorted to trickery with Blend and Contour, but the results were usually unacceptable. Figure 18.3 shows our best effort to create a soft shadow behind the headline, using Contour. The results aren't too bad on the bottom of the third line of type, but above that, where the sky is darker, the lighter shade is too light. Were we to compensate up top, the lower part would be off. Were we to try to create a gradient contour, we would have to separate each line of type; it would be very time-consuming, and we would probably give up and redesign the piece.

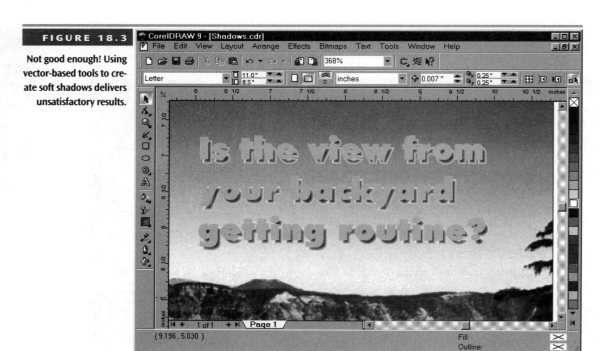

FIGURE 18.3

Not good enough! Using vector-based tools to create soft shadows delivers unsatisfactory results.

This is clearly outside of the domain of vector tools, even with DRAW's recent capability of applying transparency to objects. Vector objects are sharp, clean, and well-defined—that is their undying virtue. But shadows are supposed to be fuzzy, dull, and somewhat undefined. Therein lies the dilemma.

Shadows and Bitmaps Are Made for Each Other

A realistic soft shadow has bitmap written all over it. Pixels must fade to the colors underneath, and the transition needs to be gradual and somewhat diffuse. Vector objects are simply not capable of such effects without undo toil on your part.

As a result, one of the truly cool discoveries back in DRAW 7 was learning we could convert an object to a bitmap and apply a blur to it. It was a bit unwieldy and had its share of bugs, but we made it work. This was the beginning of a new era for DRAW.

Enter the Interactive Drop Shadow

With DRAW 8, soft shadowing hit its stride. Corel introduced its arsenal of interactive tools, including the Interactive Drop Shadow tool. This now stands as the recognized method for creating soft shadows.

Watch how easily and how credibly we can create a soft shadow to the headline above the photo. To follow along, import any photo into DRAW and type a string of artistic text on top of it. Try to find a photo that has a varying background, like the sky in our photo. Then do this:

1. Select the text.

2. Activate the Interactive Drop Shadow tool (the last icon on the Interactive Tool flyout on the toolbox).

3. Place your cursor inside the lettering and drag out in whatever direction you want to cast the shadow. DRAW creates an outline to show you where the shadow will go when you release the mouse.

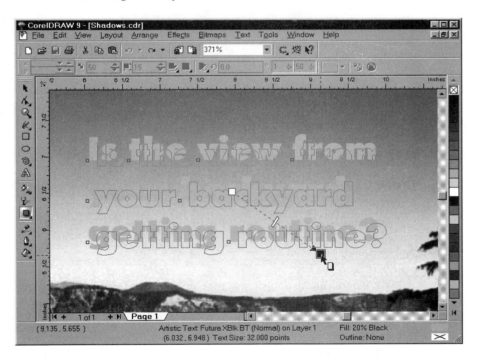

4. Release the mouse.

Now DRAW will think for a while. Internally, it is creating a copy of the text, converting it to a bitmap, and applying a transparent blur to the bitmap. With a simple rectangle, this won't take more than five seconds, but for a three-deck headline, you might be watching it churn away for 30 seconds or more. The result is worth it, though.

While we're not done with this shadow, notice that it already is satisfying the crucial requirements of a realistic shadow:

- It goes from more opaque directly below the letters to more transparent away from the letters.

- Its transparency is true, irrespective of the color beneath it.

To illustrate this last point, we drew an object, filled it with a totally incongruous color, and placed it behind the headline. As shown on the facing page, the drawing suffers from having a bright yellow ellipse with a red outline in it, but the shadowing remains credible.

Behind the sky, the shadowing is a light blue; behind the ellipse, the shadowing is light yellow. Try doing that with Contour.

Once around Drop Shadow

We're beginning to sound like a broken record: "The interactive controls are easy…just play around on the property bar for a bit."

We think this is another one of those times, but in the interest of keeping our page count in the required range, here is a bit of detail on Drop Shadow that you may or may not need.

Direction

This variable is referred to as the Drop Shadow Offset on the property bar, but you'll probably never use those value boxes to adjust this setting. You'll just grab the control handle and move it, as you did to create the shadow initially.

Opacity

This setting determines how translucent to make the drop shadow, with lower numbers being more transparent and higher numbers being more opaque. Figure 18.4 shows the simple effects of this control; a setting of 15 is much fainter than a setting of 76. Note the on-screen slider control—you can adjust opacity from the property bar or from this slider.

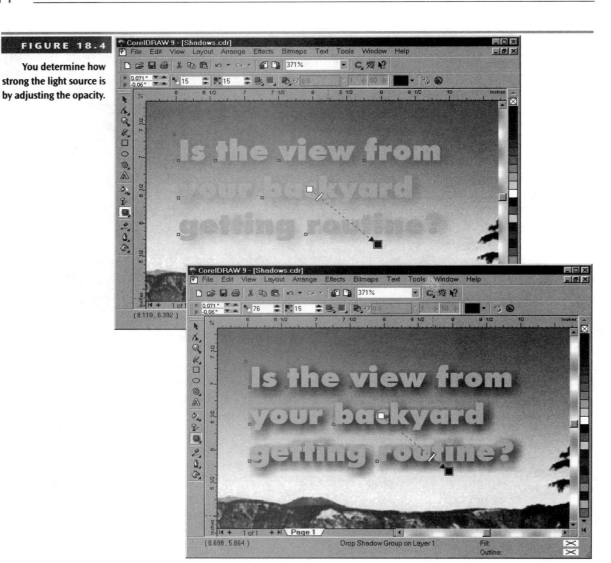

FIGURE 18.4

You determine how strong the light source is by adjusting the opacity.

Feathering

Corel does not define this setting very well, so think of it as the distance between the object being shadowed and the surface below it. With lower numbers—i.e., with less feathering—the shadow is more defined and less diffuse.

For realism, you need to make sure that the feathering and the direction are set in concert. If the text were just barely off the surface, you would have very little feathering, and also very little offset. If you set Feathering to 2 and then set a large offset, the effect would not be credible. We often set Feathering to 5, as shown here.

You can also set the Feathering Direction and the Feathering Edges, two more deficiently explained controls. These are conceptually similar to the direction of a contour and the handling of corners of an outline; adjust them for yourself to see how they operate. Feathering Edges is only active if you set Direction to something other than its default, and odds are you'll rarely move Direction off the default of Average.

Drop Shadow Perspective Type

This wild and crazy setting, new to DRAW 9, lets you cast a shadow off of any one of the four surfaces that might surround the object. Instead of the default of Flat, you can designate a shadow to be cast from the top, bottom, left, or right. With the sun behind and to the left of the extreme skater pictured on the next page, the shadow would be cast off to his right.

And here is a golfer getting one last hole in before the sun sets, compliments of a bottom-casting shadow.

The final three controls, Angle, Fade, and Stretch, all affect the perspective. In the graphic above, we set a high Fade value.

T I P   You can create perspective shadows initially if you pay attention to where you first click on the control object. Click in the middle and drag to get a flat perspective; click on the left and drag to get a left perspective shadow; click on the bottom and drag for a bottom shadow, etc.

Drop Shadow Color

You can determine the color of the shadow—or to be more precise, the color of the light shining on the object—by working the color drop-down on the property bar, or by dragging and dropping colors from the on-screen palette to the solid control handle (the one furthest from the control object).

Caveat Flashlight: Don't Get Carried Away!

Now that soft drop shadows are so easy to create, we fear the worst. We fear that we'll see them showing up all over the place, even when they are completely uncalled for. To that end, we recite the battle cry of all amateur designers:

Do not use an effect just because you learned how.

Remember, a soft drop shadow implies that an object is raised off of the surface. This has implications…

- What if only one object of a drawing is raised off the surface, but others aren't? Would that look weird?

- And what if you decide for the sake of consistency to apply a shadow to all objects? Wouldn't that look ridiculous?

In advance of the 1999 CorelWORLD User Conference, we held a contest to design the cover of our brochure. We took many fine entries…and some not-so-fine ones. Figure 18.5 shows one well-intentioned entrant who just didn't know when to stop.

Everything in this brochure cover is raised off the page, except for the second line of type. So why doesn't it rate a shadow? No fair! Perhaps worse, amid the four elements shadowed, there are four distinct types of shadows used—as if four different lights were shining on this one piece of paper. The shadow at the bottom is a hard shadow, which in this case serves only to make the text more difficult to read. (We're also not too crazy about the use of five different typefaces on one page, but that's another story.)

This is the age-old warning about what happens if you set all type on a page to bold. Answer: you make nothing bold. In a situation like this brochure cover—where everything is two-dimensional and no object would really have a shadow—we would prefer to use a shadow to denote prominence. And to avoid competing with the shadowed object, we would want to see everything else be subordinate to it. Figure 18.6 shows the results of a five-minute makeover, although it was more like a teardown: we chose just one typeface and one object to be shadowed.

FIGURE 18.6

When you limit your use of shadows, the ones you use have more impact.

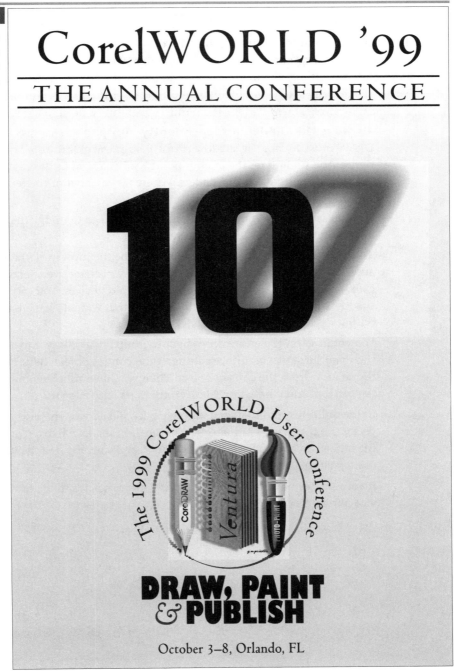

Separation Anxiety

In parting, we want to remind you that a drop shadow—like all of DRAW's special effects that involve compound objects—can be separated, leaving you with a control object and the bitmap shadow. Once you do this (with Arrange ➤ Separate), the visual effect is still active, but the dynamic aspect of the effect is eliminated.

There are two primary reasons to consider separating a drop shadow.

To Move the Shadow Independently   Perspective shadows are tricky, as DRAW must anchor the shadow to one part of the object (top, bottom, left, or right). And sometimes the anchor point is arbitrary, as in the case of a bottom shadow of text that has descenders. Where do you anchor the text—at the baseline or at the descender??

If you disagree with DRAW's decision, you will need to nudge the shadow manually, which requires that you separate it first.

To Ensure Proper Imaging   This might be the most important piece of advice with reference to drop shadows. DRAW's interactive effects are complicated—sometimes too much so for some output devices. You can tame a drop shadow by converting it to a static bitmap—that way, all you are asking of your output device is that it print pixels.

You could select the entire drop shadow group and convert it to a bitmap, but then you surrender all future editing of the control object. Better to separate the shadow from the control object. Then you have your shadow as a transparent bitmap, and your control object still in its native form.

In the unlikely event that your output device still chokes, the next thing to suspect is the transparent bitmap effect of the drop shadow. To overcome that, select the bitmap and any object that is behind it, and convert all of them to a static bitmap image (Bitmap ➤ Convert to Bitmap).

If your service bureau still can't output your image, it's time to find another service bureau...

THE POWER OF THE CLIP

Featuring

THE POWER OF
THE CLIP

his last stop on our tour through DRAW's special effects features what many consider the most useful tool of all. PowerClip is the super-duper cropping tool that enables you to place an object or image inside another object. This feature first appeared in DRAW 5, and it has become a favorite of many.

Like Lens and Interactive Transparency, PowerClip doesn't change an object; it determines how we *see* an object.

The "Stuff Inside" Command

While the technical term for the operation is the creation of a "clipping path," we prefer to think of PowerClip as simply stuffing one object into another. But to better understand what PowerClip does, we'll start by telling you what PowerClip does *not* do.

For starters, PowerClip does not work like Trim. While you can achieve similar results with both tools, Trim literally removes unwanted parts of an object, while PowerClip only hides them from view. Trim's appetite is increased from the days when it could only digest one object at a time, but it still has its limits; PowerClip, however, can spin its magic on hundreds of objects at once, if necessary.

Finally, do you remember the Pepsi-Cola commercial of two years ago? The boy at the beach who draws so hard on the straw that he sucks himself entirely into the bottle? That, too, is not how PowerClip works, because PowerClip introduces no distortion at all as it stuffs one object into another.

Instead, PowerClip crops one object (or group of objects) to fit within a shape. Anything that doesn't fit is ignored. Free-form cropping has long been a feature of painting and image-editing programs such as PHOTO-PAINT, but bringing this operation into DRAW was not so easy. With PAINT, it's a simple matter to create a "mask" and erase all pixels that fall outside of the mask. But unlike a paint program or a manual trim job—both of which delete the portion that is outside of the desired area—PowerClip maintains the integrity of the original object. If you decide to undo a powerclipped object, just extract the contents—it's as if nothing had ever happened to them. Try doing that with a paint program.

If you followed along with Chapter 10, "Advanced Text Handling," you saw a good example of powerclipping in action, where a picture of a sunset was placed inside the word *Sunset*. PowerClip effectively trims the object to fit within a shape. Anything that falls outside the boundaries of the powerclip *container* is simply hidden from view. (We'll explain containers shortly.)

PowerClip Basics

Creating a powerclip is simple: select one or more objects to be clipped, go to Effects ➤ PowerClip ➤ Place inside Container, and then click on the container object. The objects to be clipped can be literally anything—even an imported bitmap, as you saw in Chapter 10. The container can be anything created in DRAW, with the exception of paragraph text. That also rules out bitmaps, but as far as we can tell, anything else is eligible, including multipathed objects, groups, text, envelopes, extrusions, even another powerclip.

Try this exercise on for size:

1. In a new drawing, go to the Symbols docker. From Plants, drag the palm tree (symbol #33) onto the page. From Animals1, drag in an elephant (symbol #52). (This assumes you installed both the Plants and Animals1 symbol fonts when you installed DRAW. If not, you can either install the fonts before continuing, or just select other symbols to use for this exercise.)

2. Shade the palm tree dark and the elephant light, and then select and group them together.

3. Draw an ellipse around the group, using the Ctrl key to make it a perfect circle. Remove the fill and then position and size the circle so parts of both the palm tree and the elephant are outside.

4. Reselect the group, and go to Effects ➤ PowerClip ➤ Place inside Container.

5. Carefully position the arrow cursor on the outline of the circle. That's how you tell DRAW that you want the circle to be the container for the two selected objects.

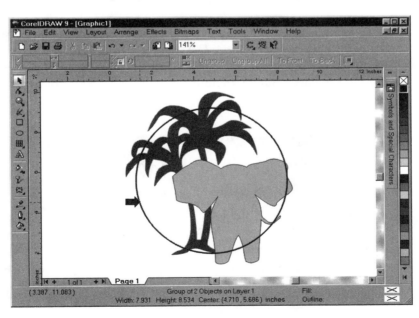

6. Click on the circle and watch DRAW stuff the tree and the elephant into the circle. Whatever fits, you see; what doesn't fit, you don't see.

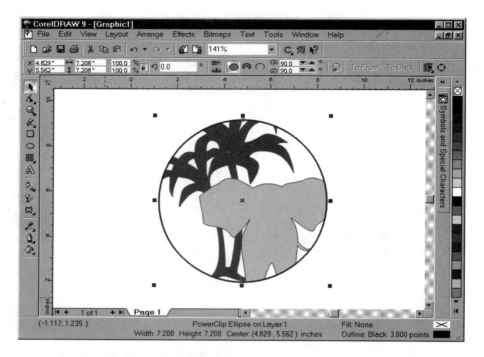

From such a simple set of commands comes such a powerful effect! Notice what the status bar calls this new object. The circle used as the container in the exercise above is hollow, but it could also be filled. The fill color would act as the background for the clipped objects. Any type of fill pattern would work, tempered with reason and constraint, we hope.

Interactive Powerclipping

While using the menus is the most intuitive way to powerclip, there is an interactive way you can do it, too. Try this:

1. Select the object you want to clip.

2. Click and hold Button 2 and drag it into the desired container.

3. Release the mouse, and from the pop-up menu, select PowerClip Inside.

DRAW will automatically clip the object in the container.

PowerClip in the Field

Here are just a few of the many ways that you can put PowerClip to use on everyday projects.

Creating Motion

Figure 19.1 shows a variation of the article we created in Chapter 14 (where we showed a trick for tinting back an object, using Blend). The only change we made was to powerclip the falcon to the edge of the page. The simple act of moving the bird slightly off the page breathes new life into this otherwise unadorned flier. It's amazing how differently we react to an object that is entering or exiting a drawing, half in and half out, than to one that has already arrived. PowerClip is the key to hanging objects over the edges of your drawings. To do this, just create an invisible rectangle at the border of the page, and clip the object into the invisible rectangle.

FIGURE 19.1

Clipping an object adds tension and interest to just about any simple drawing.

Ancient hunting With the Falcon

Hunting with birds of prey probably originated with the nomadic peoples of the Asiatic plains. The nomads used their tame falcons to help procure the food necessary for survival, in perhaps one of the first methods of hunting ever used by man.

Later, falconry developed into a sport, and this fascinating co-operation between man and bird is one of the oldest of all open-air pastimes.

Falconry has long been regarded as a noble art. The falconer was seen as a figure of authority - mounted on his horse, surrounded by his hunting companions and with his falcon descending from the sky to rest on his hand. As he controlled his falcon, so he controlled his territory.

Throughout history the falcon has been the symbol of high birth and luxury, and its care and training have always been given particular importance. It is known as a superlative hunter, and is particularly valuable in the desert, where climatic conditions are extreme and no protection from the elements is available. Here, the falcon can pursue its prey from a great distance, and with a speed and accuracy second to none. It is no wonder that the desert nomads have always appreciated the stamina and hunting instincts of the falcon. The Bedouin people in particular used this bird to hunt game, which provided

an important and nutritious addition to an otherwise monotonous diet.

Today, the Arabian Peninsula is one of the last places in the world where falconry remains an important sporting activity. Although falconry clubs do exist in America and in almost all European countries, it is in the Gulf region that the sport is held in truly high regard and commands the greatest interest. The people of the Gulf have a strong personal commitment to falconry and ensure that it is practised in the correct manner, with the proper respect due to Islamic customs.

The chief falconer is highly respected, as he is responsible for the birds' daily training and care. The falcon requires much human contact and careful attention on a daily basis, or it will quickly grow wild and therefore unreliable. When hunting, an experienced falconer drives his bird ahead to pursue the prey, following at speed to ensure that he is on the spot within a few seconds of the falcon's landing of the game. It is essential that the falcon's talons are well placed in the prey before it lands.

The falconer also needs to ensure that there is no fighting between the falcon and its prey, to avoid injury to either bird. The falcon is less skilful on the ground than it is in flight and may lose its courage when confronted with a larger bird.

Finally, the falconer must be present to ensure that the game is killed according to Islamic custom.

Montages with Flair

Thanks to the World Wide Web, it is easier than ever to publish photographs, and we find ourselves working with scanned and imported photographs much more often than just two years ago. Whether you are publishing to the Web or to paper, your photo layouts can get a real shot in the arm with PowerClip.

The following graphics show the progression of steps for a photo montage. This collection of photos, taken from the Digital Stock library, makes up a theme of dynamic and healthy living. But, as you can see, it's not easy positioning them in such a way that their edges are smooth. They meet in the middle in ragged and haphazard fashion.

The first step is to turn to the first cousin of PowerClip, the bitmap cropping tool. When you invoke the Shape tool with an imported bitmap image selected, you can crop and shape the image (you are essentially node-editing the *boundary* of the photo). As with PowerClip, you are not actually trimming the photo; you are just hiding parts of it from view.

Now the photos align nicely in the middle. The outside edges are still rough, but we don't care about that because the whole thing is getting clipped inside of an ellipse. Remember, anything can be placed into a powerclip, including a collection of photos.

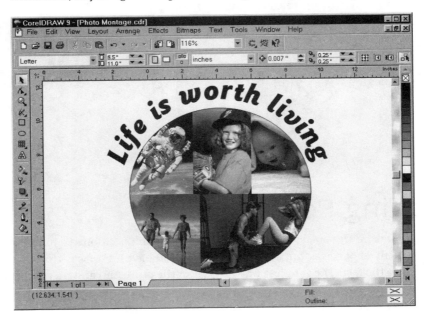

To add the fitted text, we chose the powerclip itself as the path, and then raised the lettering up by a half inch.

Lots of Containers

As the montage demonstrates, you can place anything into a container. As for the container that holds the clipped objects, the requirements are hardly more stringent: any vector-based object (i.e., any object you create with DRAW's tools) can act as the container for a powerclip. What's more, your container can be a group of objects and this opens up myriad possibilities. At the top-left of Figure 19.2 is one of the many cartoon characters available in Corel's library of clipart. The lower-left image shows a series of squares created on top of it, and once grouped, those 30 squares can become a single container for a powerclip. Before clipping, we introduced a bit more hilarity into the scene by selectively rotating some of the squares, as shown in the final version at right.

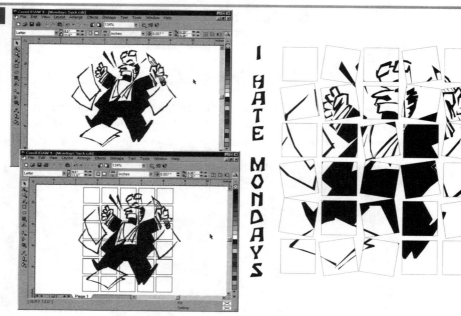

FIGURE 19.2

By powerclipping this poor man into 30 squares all at once, Mondays seem all that much worse...

Editing Powerclips

Your palm tree and elephant group probably wasn't positioned within the powerclip exactly as ours was, but adjusting it is easy. You have lots of ways to modify powerclips after the fact. The simplest way is to select the powerclip and then select Effects ➤ PowerClip ➤ Edit Contents. DRAW shows you only those objects inside the powerclip, with a convenient circle showing where the powerclip container is, and it allows you to edit them any way you like. When you are done, reach for the Effects ➤ PowerClip ➤ Finish Editing This Level command. (It's so named because DRAW allows you to nest

powerclips within other powerclips, and if you were editing a nested powerclip, you would be modifying just that one level.)

T I P When a powerclip is selected, you can right-click to reach the Edit Contents and Extract Contents commands. When done editing a powerclip, the context menu offers the Finish Editing command.

Following are some things to keep in mind as you edit powerclips.

Avoid Auto-Centering

We like PowerClip's clean and intuitive design—with one exception. In its factory condition, DRAW sets a default that automatically centers all objects within their containers. Most DRAW users don't like this, for two reasons:

- Users rarely want objects exactly centered in the container, so making the default *no* centering would make better sense. It is more typical and more logical to position the objects first and then clip them.
- The control for turning centering on and off is out of place. You have to go to Tools ➤ Options ➤ Workspace ➤ Edit and look for the awkwardly named Automatically Center New PowerClip Contents check box.

We suggest that you find this check box, uncheck it, and leave it that way. If you ever do want to center objects within a container, you can turn it back on for the moment—or better yet, just select both objects and press C and E to center them before you clip.

Use the Lock Contents Option

The Lock Contents to PowerClip option is also somewhat hidden, but it is more useful than the auto-center option. When you create a powerclip with this option on (the default), the contents are initially locked to the container, so that the whole powerclip is treated as a single object. This means that the contents move, rotate, and scale along with the container.

Most of the time, you will want to keep this lock on, but sometimes you'll need to change the relative positions of the container and the clipped objects. You can always do this with the Edit Contents command on the PowerClip menu, but that is cumbersome for simple adjustments. That's when the time is right to unlock the contents. Right-click and uncheck Lock Contents to PowerClip. The container then acts as a movable window, letting you view different parts of the objects inside. When you are done repositioning everything, relock the contents to ensure that the powerclip again moves as a unit.

Group while Editing

In the simple exercise earlier in this chapter, you grouped the palm tree and elephant before clipping them. You could have just as easily marquee-selected the two objects and clipped them without grouping, but we wanted you to see that grouping simplifies your powerclipping tasks.

You can ungroup, regroup, combine, and delete elements, change fills, or do anything else to the contents of a powerclip. When you use PowerClip ➤ Edit Contents, think of the contents as a separate drawing that will eventually be cropped by the container outline. Nearly anything you would normally do to objects in a drawing can be done at this point. Then, when you select Finish Editing This Level from the flyout, the powerclip is reapplied to the contents. The only things you cannot do with the Edit Contents command are import elements (paste yes, import no) and reposition the container itself. Repositioning is easily done before you create the powerclip or afterward (by unlocking the contents).

Faking 3D with PowerClip

Figure 19.3 is a close-up of the silly drawing from Chapter 15 in which we placed a gear on a pedestal. In that chapter, we asked you to consider how we did this.

FIGURE 19.3

Can an object be resting inside of another object in two-dimensional space? Not really...

In a two-dimensional drawing program, it is not possible to place an object through another. Consider this simple drawing below.

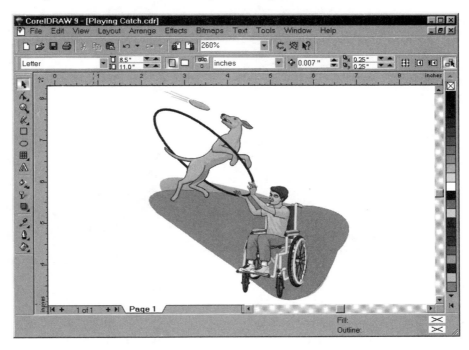

In CorelDRAW's world, the dog can either be in front of the hoop or behind the hoop; it cannot be going through the hoop. Yet to any reader's eye, this acrobatic canine is making this circus catch while jumping through the hoop held by his master.

PowerClip is responsible for this illusion. To follow along, create an ellipse and then find a dog or other animal from Corel's clipart library (we used `dogwfris.cdr` from `\Clipart\Animals\Pets`). Place the animal in front of the ellipse. Then do this:

1. First, go to Tools ➤ Options ➤ Workspace ➤ Edit and uncheck Auto-Center New PowerClip Contents. This first step is crucial to the entire operation—you don't want any auto-centering of your powerclips to occur.

2. Draw a rectangle over one half of the dog, making sure that the rectangle is inside of the hoop, as shown here.

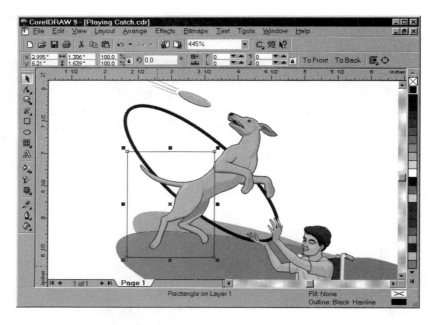

3. Select the dog and copy it to the Clipboard with Ctrl+C. From this point forward, make sure not to move the dog. If you do have to reposition it, then press Ctrl+C again afterward.

4. PowerClip the dog into the rectangle: select the dog, go to Effects ➤ PowerClip ➤ Place inside Container, and then click on the rectangle.

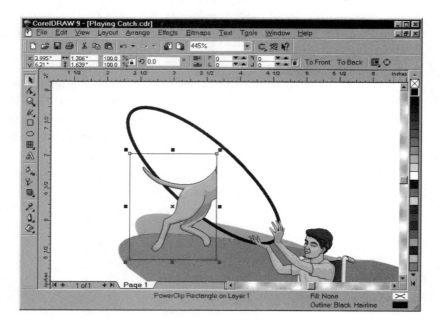

5. Remove the outline of the rectangle, and if there is any fill pattern to it, remove that too. You want the rectangle that contains the dog to be completely invisible.

6. Press Ctrl+V to paste a copy of the dog back into the picture.

7. Press Shift+PgDn to move the copy to the back. And *voilà…*

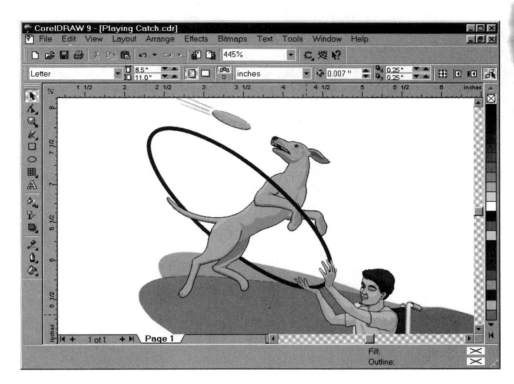

Let's recap. You essentially have cut the dog in half, placing one half in front of the hoop and one half in back. Because they are exact copies, one goes right atop the other, and the half that is in front is powerclipped. So the stacking order is:

- Half of dog in front of hoop
- Hoop
- Copy of dog behind hoop

That is what creates the illusion that he is jumping through. You can download Playing Catch.cdr from the Sybex Web site to see our version of it.

Better PowerClip Access for Advanced Users

PowerClip is very easy to use, thanks to the intuitive nature of its controls. However, once you begin using PowerClip regularly, you will likely grow tired of all of the incessant clicking. Your mind will say, "Select this and clip it to that," but your fingers will still have to say, "Effects...PowerClip...Place inside Container..."

This is a job for a custom hotkey, discussed at length in Chapter 34, "Your Very Own Interface." Create a hotkey for the Place inside Container command—Ctrl+1, for example—and now your fingers can move at the speed of your brain:

1. Select object to be clipped.
2. Press Ctrl+1.
3. Click on container.

When you learn the commands, you don't want the user-friendliness, you want speed. That's where customized hotkeys and icons will become your best friends.

DRAWING FOR CYBERSPACE

THE BASICS OF CREATING WEB GRAPHICS

Featuring

THE BASICS OF CREATING WEB GRAPHICS

or those of you who are fearful, nervous, or even intimidated about the World Wide Web and what it takes to design for it, we start this chapter with some good news: creating graphics for the Web is easier than creating graphics for traditional output. There are fewer rules to follow, there is less chance of major screw-ups, it is less expensive, and much of the time, it is more fun.

Now, don't you feel better?

If you're nervous about Web publishing, it's probably because you are encountering an entirely new terminology outside the friendly confines of .cdr files, .eps files, standard color separations, and film. You know how to create print files and send them off to your service bureau, but sending .htm files and strangely named graphics to who-knows-where is an altogether different experience, largely devoid of the warm fuzzies that traditional designers get from watching their work go from concept to film to print.

Consider this chapter to be the cyber-equivalent of Bonehead English. This is Web Graphics 1A, where we cover the concepts, terminology, and basic methods for using CorelDRAW to create graphics for the World Wide Web.

N O T E   It's all too easy for authors to bite off more than they can chew when covering the vastness of the Internet, so it is important for us to be clear on what we are not covering, as well as what we are. This chapter assumes that you already have a connection to the Internet—either a permanent one, such as a company network, or a dial-up connection from a provider such as AOL, Earthlink, ATT, or a local or regional provider. This chapter also makes assumptions about your involvement with HTML, the language of the World Wide Web. It assumes that you have a basic understanding of HyperText Markup Language (HTML) files and how they define the look of a Web page, or that you don't need to know all that because someone else in your organization does, and your job is specifically to create the graphics.

Web Page Basics

Traditional artwork typically includes a combination of text and graphics, and the same is true of pages that you design for the World Wide Web. Nevertheless, while a CorelDRAW file can contain both types of elements, the ingredients for a Web page are handled differently. The text for a Web page is contained in the HTML files, but the graphics are all external, with pointers in the HTML code that identify them. For instance, here is a sample piece of HTML code from our lead author's home page. It shows the code for the title of the page, the blue background, Rick's logo, a headline, and a paragraph, including a hyperlink.

```
<html>
<head>
<title>Complete services for the Corel graphics community</title>
</head>
<body background="bg.gif">
<img src="logo.gif">
<h1>June 1999</h1>
<b>CorelWORLD News: </b>The first 100 people to register for the conference
will receive a Super 10 Pack of professional photos on CD. Over 1,000
royalty-free, high-resolution images. Click <a href="corelworld.htm">
CONFERENCES</a> for all the details.
</body>
</html>
```

The picture (logo.gif) was created in DRAW and exported as a GIF file, one of the two universal formats that the Web understands. Note that the graphic is not contained in the HTML file; it is only referenced in it. Figure 20.1 shows how this code would look in Microsoft Internet Explorer (or Netscape Navigator).

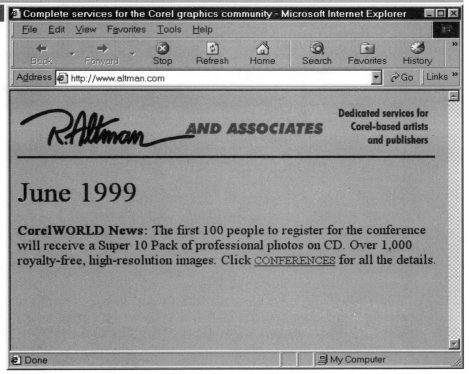

FIGURE 20.1

The lines of code above appear as this simple page when viewed in a Web browser, such as Internet Explorer.

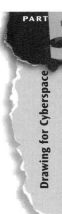

Note how the hyperlink is coded, with the HREF="_____" syntax. You can also make a graphic be a hyperlink. The Sybex Web site has numerous examples of HTML files with graphics identified both as static images and hyperlinks, and we will be referring to them throughout this chapter and the next two.

As we mentioned earlier, in many important ways, creating graphics for a Web page is easier than for traditional media. Here are a few reasons why.

Color Is Cake

Creating four-color printed material is a very demanding process, involving choosing color models, creating film separations, and enduring an expensive and time-consuming printing process. But creating color graphics for the Web is easy: you just do it. Today, everyone has a color monitor, and if you create a picture in color, your audience will see it in color. End of story.

No Dots to Deal With

The second big headache in traditional printing is determining the resolution of the final output device and how that will affect the graphics and photographs you use. This issue is almost entirely moot with Web pages. There is little point in creating graphics beyond 100dpi when final viewing will take place on a display monitor. There are issues involving the pixel resolution of monitors (640 × 480 vs. 800 × 600, for example) and also the color depth (16, 256, 64000, or 16 million), but these are more easily resolved than traditional print issues.

Instant Feedback

If you wonder how a graphic will look on the Web, you don't have to go very far to find out. Open your browser and load the graphic. No need for color keys or Iris prints, or conducting a press check. You create it and you view it.

In all three of these points, the common factor is this: the output device is a computer monitor, not a piece of paper. No toner or ink is involved, only rays of red, green, and blue light emanating from a cathode ray tube.

For example, Figure 20.2 represents the annual appearance of our lead author's two young daughters, Jamie, who turned three in early 1999, and Erica, six and a half by the summer of '99. This picture was scanned at high resolution and prepared for printed output. As such, the scanned image required 7.3MB of disk space, and when prepared for color printing, created almost 15MB of print information. We also needed about 30 minutes of test prints to ensure its quality.

FIGURE 20.2

Scanning this picture and printing it in this book required over 7MB of storage space and many tests to make sure it was prepared properly.

In stark contrast, preparing this photograph for display on the Web required five minutes and less than one diskette's worth of data. We could sample the photo all the way down to 600 pixels wide and 100dpi and save it in a Web format with very high compression. Figure 20.3 shows how the photo appears when viewed in a browser. You can download `Jamie & Erica.jpg` from the Sybex Web site and see for yourself. It is only 26KB in size, but is perfectly adequate for on-screen viewing.

FIGURE 20.3

Preparing this picture for Web viewing requires only 26KB of space, and you can see immediately how it will look.

The Flavors of the Web

If you were producing traditional artwork with DRAW, you would create a `.cdr` file and do one of two things with it: you would either print it out, onto paper or film, and be done with it; or you would export it to be incorporated into another drawing or a document created in another program.

Veteran exporters are quite familiar with the standard export formats of EPS, TIFF, and WMF. (These formats are discussed in Chapter 30.) The World Wide Web introduces two entirely different graphic formats: GIF and JPEG. The following sections offer some background and a few of the finer points about both formats, but if you want to cut to the chase, you can't go wrong if you observe the following:

- The JPEG format is for displaying photographs and graphics with fountain fills or other multicolored patterns.
- The GIF format is for all other graphics.

Granted, we're painting with a broad brush, but you will find these rules of thumb to hold true most of the time.

At its core, creating Web graphics involves exporting your DRAW artwork (or saving your images from PHOTO-PAINT) in one of these two formats. These are both bitmap formats—the Web doesn't understand vector graphics yet, although by the time you read this, we might be there, so swift is new development in Web graphic formats.

You should also have a browser up and running—either of the two mainstream browsers (Microsoft Internet Explorer or Netscape Navigator) will do.

The GIF Format

The GIF format was developed by the CompuServe Information Service (CIS), one of the original online services, and most programs (including DRAW) still refer to this file type as "CompuServe GIF," even though its reach now extends far beyond CIS. GIF stands for Graphic Interchange Format (so "GIF format" is redundant, but who cares). At least DRAW 9 has renamed it to GIF-CompuServe Bitmap so you can press G to find it in the list of file types.

You will use the GIF format to display simple graphics that you create in DRAW. It is highly compressible and, though it is limited to 256 colors, is more than adequate for a majority of artwork created for the Web.

What is significant is not that the GIF format is limited to 256 colors, but that it can contain any number up to 256. In other words, you can create GIF files with fewer than 256 colors, and that means even smaller files. Do we seem obsessed about small file sizes? We are, and so, too, should you be. Indeed, this promises to be the No. 1 issue throughout your Web-designing career, as you embark upon a never-ending quest to keep your Web site as compact as possible. Most Web sites don't charge any money for visitors to browse, but your potential audience measures the cost of a visit in a different way: waiting time. How long will they be willing to wait for your graphics to load and display? Web surfers have fast trigger fingers; your mission is to present enough of your page to deliver your message before they pull the trigger and press the Back button on their browsers.

Creating a GIF File

For this series of exercises, you will need three programs running: CorelDRAW, your Web browser, and Notepad (or some pure text editor). You are going to create a graphic in DRAW, export it to a GIF file, and view it in your browser. Here goes:

1. In DRAW, create a thin rectangle as shown below. Apply a fountain fill to it that uses relatively light colors, like orange to cyan, or yellow to red. Set the fountain fill to move from side to side, instead of top to bottom, and remove any outline from it.

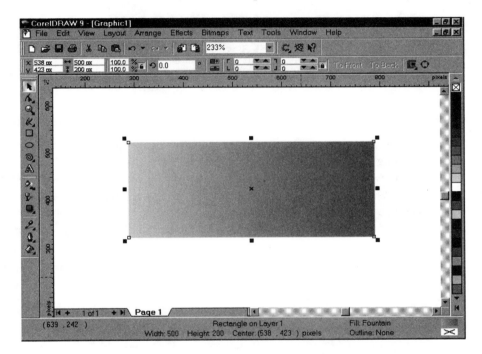

NOTE In the graphic above, we have set our global unit of measure to pixels (note the rulers) and you can see on the property bar that our rectangle measures 500 by 200 pixels. As monitors are the official output device of the Web, pixels are the official unit of measure. To change your unit of measure, deselect all objects and use the **Drawing Units** drop-down on the property bar.

2. Export this rectangle using the GIF-CompuServe Bitmap format. Name it anything you want, like **rectangle.gif**, and remember where in your system you created it. When you reach the settings dialog, use the graphic on the next page as your guide. Notice in particular that the color depth is set to 16 and anti-aliasing and dithering are both unchecked.

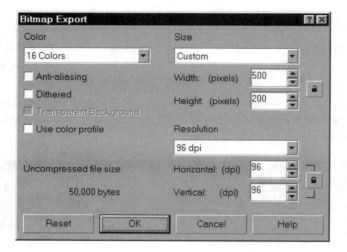

3. At the next screen, set Transparency to None and ignore all other settings.

The settings we chose for you describe a low-quality graphic, and that's intentional. By using a palette containing only 16 colors, the pretty fountain fill you created in DRAW won't look very pretty by the time it gets to your Web browser. The resolution is set for 96dpi, because that is all you would need when creating a graphic for display on a computer monitor. Finally, we had you fix the size at 500 × 200 pixels just for the purposes of this exercise, so that your browser screen would look similar to ours.

4. Switch to your text editor and create a simple HTML file, like the one below. Save the file with any name you want, but make sure to do two things: use an extension of .htm or .html, and save the file in the same location in which you exported rectangle.gif.

5. Switch to your browser and use File ≻ Open to retrieve the HTML file you just created. (Alternatively, you could find the file with My Computer or Windows Explorer and double-click it.)

Figure 20.4 shows the result, and it is likely to be quite different from what you imagined. As mentioned above, 16 colors can't do justice to a fountain fill. This is Lesson No. 1 of Web page creation: you can never control all of the variables, as you can with traditional publishing. Every person who visits your Web page will be influenced by the type of computer they have, the grade of monitor and video card, and the way they have configured their browser. In fact, some people might opt to show no graphics at all.

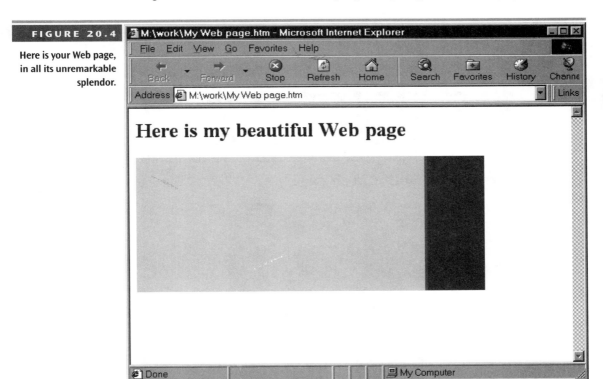

FIGURE 20.4

Here is your Web page, in all its unremarkable splendor.

PART

Drawing for Cyberspace

Fine-Tuning Your GIF File

At this point, you have set up a mini-laboratory for spinning Web graphics. You have DRAW opened to your main source of artwork, you have the Web page opened in Notepad, and you have your browser running and loaded with that same Web page. From this point on, changes are going to be easy, immediate, and even fun. Any time you make a change to the graphic or to the HTML file itself, you can switch to your browser and see those changes by issuing the Refresh or Reload command (F5 in Explorer, Ctrl+R in Navigator).

Your first objective is to rescue your fountain fill from the evil clutches of the 16-color empire.

Dithering

Dithering is the process by which DRAW essentially airbrushes a graphic to give the illusion of more tones or a smoother transition between colors. In truth, it's a fake.

1. Return to DRAW and export the rectangle again. Make sure to use the same name, `rectangle.gif`; you want to replace the previous version.

2. At the Export settings dialog, check the Dithered box. Leave all other settings the same.

3. Switch back to your browser and refresh the display.

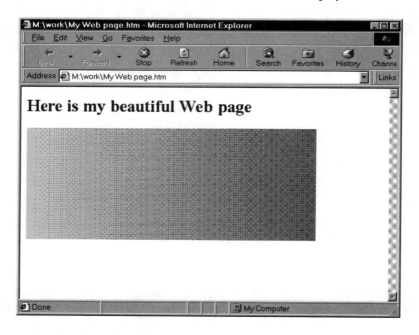

This is still a paltry 16-color graphic, but DRAW has given the illusion of more colors by infusing white dots throughout. The transitions between colors appear smoother. It pales in comparison to the original, but it is an improvement over your first effort.

Paletted Images

This change will be more significant, as you will be able to use more colors to render your fountain fill. Return to DRAW and re-export the graphic, this time choosing Paletted (8-bit) and no dithering (everything else the same). "Paletted (8-bit)" is a fancy term for 256 colors, but there is an important distinction between DRAW 8 and 9's handling of larger color palettes and that of earlier versions. If you create a 16-color graphic, the palette that is used to render the image includes white, black, cyan, magenta, yellow, red, green, blue, purple, orange, and four percentages of gray. That palette will never grow or shrink—if you export a 16-color graphic, those are the 16 hues that will be used to render your image, whether or not they will be sufficient.

The next step up is a 256-color palette, and indeed, that was the choice offered to users of DRAW 7 and earlier versions. And no matter how many colors were actually used in a graphic, the palette contained all 256 of the colors.

DRAW 8 and 9 are smarter. When you choose Paletted as the color palette, DRAW studies the colors actually contained in the drawing and creates a subset of the 256-color palette from them. You may only use a few dozen colors from the 256-color palette. You may only use 16...or four...or two. But that doesn't mean that you could get away with the 16-color palette, because those wouldn't necessarily be the correct 16 colors. When you choose Paletted, you are permitting DRAW to determine the size of the palette, based on the colors you are actually using in your drawing.

With all of this said, re-export your rectangle—this time as a Paletted image instead of a 16-color graphic—and see if your browser doesn't show you a clean and smooth fountain fill, like ours in Figure 20.5.

FIGURE 20.5

As a Paletted image, the subtleties of this fountain fill are rescued.

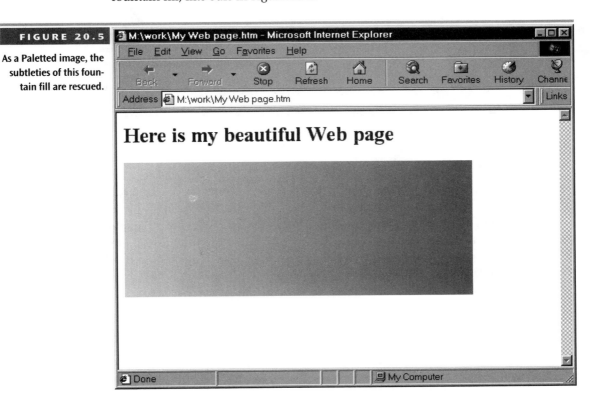

PART

Drawing for Cyberspace

Creating Transparent Graphics

One of the most important aspects of creating GIF files is the ability to control which parts of the graphic will be visible and which will be transparent. Follow these steps:

1. Return to DRAW and round the corners of your rectangle. (You can do that with the Shape tool and the rectangle's on-screen selection handles, or with the slider on the property bar.)

2. Export it again, same settings as before.

3. Switch to Notepad, where your HTML file should still be loaded, and change the file as follows (changed line is highlighted).

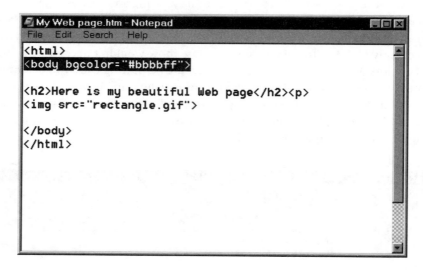

This code defines a light blue background color.

4. Save the file and switch to your browser.

When you refresh the display, it should look similar to Figure 20.6, and that's bad. You rounded the corners of the rectangle, but DRAW still uses a rectangular area to define the space of the graphic (as it does for all exported graphics). The unsightly white spaces are because neither DRAW nor your browser understands that you only want the graphic to display, not the rectangular area in which the graphic sits.

FIGURE 20.6

Here is your not-so-beautiful Web page.

FIGURE 20.6

Here is your not-so-beautiful Web page.

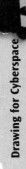

Fortunately this is easy to fix:

1. Return to DRAW and export the graphic again. Confirm the first Export settings dialog (where you have been adjusting the colors) and stop at the second one.

2. In the Transparency section, change None to Image Color.

3. At this point, DRAW gives you an opportunity to define a particular Color to be transparent.

4. Click on the Eyedropper tool on the right side of the dialog.

5. Carefully click on the white regions in the thumbnail display labeled Original. If you did it correctly, the color white becomes the chosen color in the palette of colors, as well as the larger swatch.

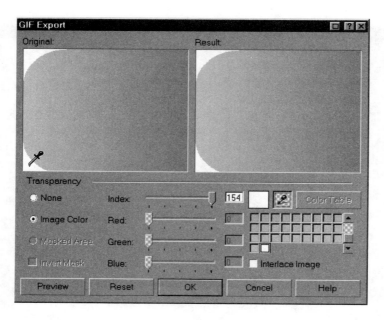

6. OK the box to create the file and switch to your browser. When you refresh, you should no longer see any white in your graphic. You have set white to be transparent.

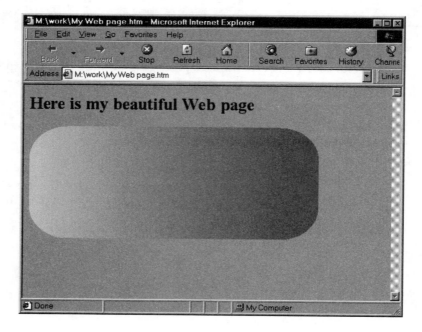

TIP   What would happen if the foreground of your graphic contained white and you set white to be transparent? This could be hazardous to your career as a Web designer. When you choose a transparent color, you need to first ensure that the color is not part of the drawing. If it is, you must choose a different background color: draw a rectangle behind your artwork and assign it a color that you haven't used. When exporting, choose that color as your transparent color.

Creating Interlaced Graphics

As we have already said, and will say several more times, the display speed of a Web page is critical to its success. Graphics are the most common reason for a Web page being slow to load...too bad they are also crucial to your page's appearance. You can help matters by creating interlaced GIF files for your larger graphics (graphics over 50KB in size).

You might be familiar with the term *interlaced* if you have recently bought a display monitor for your computer. One of the important qualities of a professional monitor is that it be "non-interlaced." An interlaced display does not draw every scan line in succession from top to bottom; instead, it draws every other or every third and then goes back and draws the others. This is easier for manufacturers to produce and makes for a cheaper monitor. A non-interlaced monitor is greatly preferred, as it draws your screen much more smoothly and crisply.

With Web graphics, though, an interlaced graphic can be a very good thing. An interlaced graphic does not draw itself completely from top to bottom, but instead first appears as a very rough representation. Then on the second pass, it fills in a bit more detail. Still more on the third, and more on the fourth and fifth. If you're visiting a site and don't need to see the entire graphic, you'll appreciate getting a low-resolution glimpse of it so you can decide whether to click on it or move on. That is the idea behind creating interlaced GIF files: you let your visitors have a quick look at a graphic without forcing them to sit through the whole show.

There is nothing to creating interlaced files. On the same dialog where you defined transparency, simply check the Interlace Image box, and you're done.

The ABCs of Anti-Aliasing

Anti-aliasing can spell the difference between a great Web graphic and an ugly one. Anti-aliasing is like dithering, in that it adds other colors to smooth out harsh transitions. Dithering adds white to colors to soften transitions, while anti-aliasing smoothes jagged edges by adding an intermediate color, be it white or another color. Figure 20.7 shows the anti-aliasing effect with a very simple graphic—a rounded letter. You don't

PART

Drawing for Cyberspace

need any labels to know which is which—the one that is noticeably smoother and cleaner is the one that was created with Anti-aliasing checked during export.

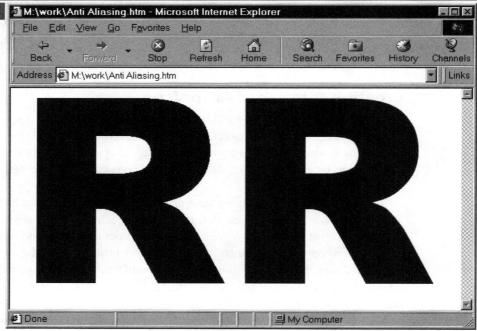

While it is obvious which looks better, it is not at all obvious why. You would need a much closer inspection to understand what anti-aliasing is actually doing, and Figure 20.8 offers the pixel's eye view. In this close-up of the curved portion of the letter, you can see that the anti-aliased version on the right adds gray pixels to smooth out the journey around the curve. So it's not rocket science—it's the simple introduction of intermediate-colored pixels at the edges of objects.

WARNING   By adding intermediate colors, anti-aliasing requires that a broader color palette be used, and that will increase the size of GIF files. This is a trade that you'll probably take every time, but you should be conscientious of the price that anti-aliasing exacts.

We will have a lot more to say about anti-aliasing in Chapter 22.

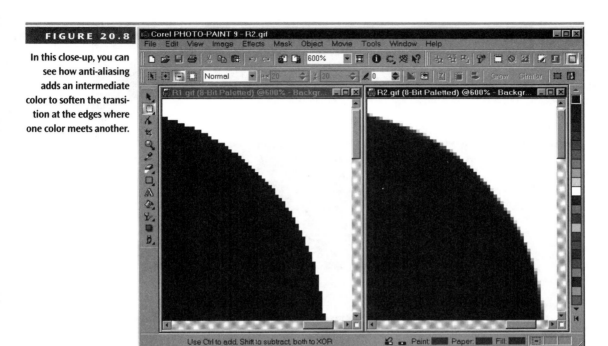

FIGURE 20.8

In this close-up, you can see how anti-aliasing adds an intermediate color to soften the transition at the edges where one color meets another.

PART

Drawing for Cyberspace

The JPEG Format

The JPEG (Joint Photographic Experts Group) format is ideal for displaying photographs or full-color graphics because it supports palettes of up to 16 million colors (and even beyond, although there is no point in using deeper palettes for Web graphics). JPEG is also very aggressive in its compression. Unlike with the GIF format, though, this compression comes at a price: JPEG files lose their fidelity as they are compressed. You do have control over how much compression you use, and therefore how much fidelity loss you introduce.

The other compromise you must deal with is the absence of the transparency control you have with the GIF format. This is rarely an issue with photographs, as they are usually rectangular, but there will be times when you will wish for a transparency feature for JPEG images.

Figure 20.9 is the starting point for our exploration into JPEG file creation. It is the same rectangle used before, but it is filled with a bitmap pattern fill instead of a fountain fill.

FIGURE 20.9

These stones have more shades and colors than can be faithfully reproduced with 256 colors. That makes it a good candidate for the JPEG format.

Here's what you need to do to prepare for our next laboratory test:

1. Switch to your text editor and open the HTML file you created for working with GIF files (we called ours My Web Page.htm).

2. Make the following change.

Save and close the file—now you're ready to begin. Switch to DRAW and replace the fountain fill in your rectangle with a bitmap pattern fill (you can use the stones as we did, or pick another one).

1. Export the rectangle, this time choosing the JPEG Bitmaps format. Call the graphic `rectangle.jpg` (the name you have already designated in the HTML file) and make sure that it is being written to the same directory.

2. Choose RGB Color for the palette, set the Size to 1 to 1, and the Resolution to 96dpi.

3. OK this dialog, and you will be taken to a subdialog.

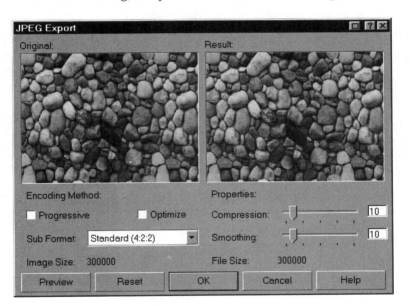

The two key elements here are Compression and Smoothing. As you move those sliders to the right, they each affect the display of the image and the resultant file size. You can click Preview to see a dynamic representation of each adjustment, as well as an approximation of file size.

4. Set both sliders to 0 and OK this dialog to write the image.

5. Switch to your browser and refresh the page. It should look like Figure 20.10.

If the picture of the rocks does not display, it means that the name you designated in the HTML file is not the same as the one you just used when you exported the image from DRAW, or you did not export `rectangle.jpg` into the same location.

FIGURE 20.10

When exported at the lowest compression level, these rocks look as good as they do in DRAW.

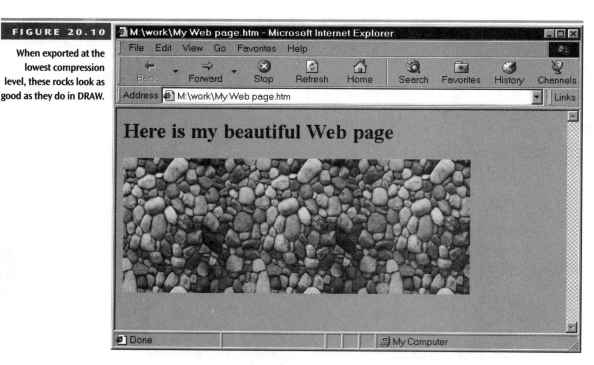

The stones display at the highest possible fidelity, and they also consume over 130KB of disk space. As you have probably already guessed, when you move those controls to the right, the image size shrinks and the quality of the image is reduced. Small increases in compression are not likely to be noticeable, and every image will have its own threshold—the point beyond which increases in compression do result in image degradation. The responsibility is yours to find that threshold, and you can practice the routine with these stones: export the image with different compression and smoothing values, and then switch to your browser to see the difference.

Two other controls are found on the compression and smoothing dialog. The JPEG format has its own version of the interlace control, and it's called Progressive. It is much more subtle than the Interlaced effect on GIF images, and in fact, we don't use it very often. The Optimize check box instructs DRAW to use the most efficient encoding method possible. This check box is a bit ahead of its time; in fact, we suspect that 95 percent of the time that you arrive at this dialog, you will address Compression and Smoothing and ignore all else.

N O T E   As with all types of publishing and "printing," nothing takes the place of trial, error, and observation. In that spirit, we have created a comprehensive Web page whose sole purpose is to demonstrate the various controls and settings discussed here. It is located on our lead author's Web site at www.altman.com/webgraphics. This page uses four independent frames so you can make side-by-side comparisons of images with different color depths and settings. It is ideal for developing a feel for the controls and how they affect image quality. You can either work this page from altman.com, or download all of the files and open them from your own hard drive for better performance. If you do, make sure to place them all in the same directory.

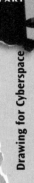

PART

Drawing for Cyberspace

Animated GIF Files

We approach this topic with fear and trepidation. Please raise your right hand and repeat after us:

I will not abuse the power of Animated GIF files. I will not use them inappropriately, and I will resist all urges to use them on every page that I create.

Okay, with that out of the way, we can now explain to you that the GIF format is capable of containing multiple images in a file, each in its own frame. When the file is read from a Web page, each of the images is displayed in rapid succession. This gives the appearance of animation, much the way that Saturday morning cartoons are displayed on television. The alternative is to resort to complex script programming using Java or CGI—a fate on par with watching a dishwasher operate from the inside.

DRAW does not know how to create animated GIFs, but PHOTO-PAINT does. Using its movie feature, PAINT stitches multiple images together into an animation. PAINT's movies can be saved as AVI files or animated GIF files, and the current versions of Internet Explorer and Navigator support animated GIFs.

Creating an Animation

The steps for creating an animated GIF file are beyond the scope of this chapter, but to the rescue comes the companion page on the Sybex Web site. From there, open flight.htm to see a simple animation in action. From that page, you can also take a tour of how it was built, complete with step-by-step instructions and illustrations.

Continued on next page

And once again, please keep in mind the potential distraction that animated GIF files can cause if they are used frivolously (not to mention the fact that they take longer to load than conventional graphics). If you expect your visitors to spend several minutes on the same page, nothing could be worse than making them watch something constantly blink, or flash, or scroll. If, on the other hand, you want to highlight a special offer on a page designed to be a launching point (meaning that viewers won't spend much time there), then creating a button that changes from one color to another might be an effective way to do it. But make sure to not set it for an endless loop—one or two cycles will be just fine.

Remember our admonition from Chapter 18: if you make everything bold, you have made nothing bold. If you animate in the wrong places or for the wrong reasons, you doom your original purpose.

CREATING A
WEB GRAPHICS
LABORATORY

Featuring

CREATING A WEB GRAPHICS LABORATORY

While some of you turn to DRAW to create complete Web pages, most users have other tools to do that. Most cyber-designers have CorelDRAW in their software arsenal to produce the graphics that will make their way onto a Web site. The following chapter will explore DRAW's more exotic features; this one focuses on what we consider to be the meat and potatoes of Web graphics creation.

This chapter assumes you read or understand the basics covered in Chapter 20.

Think Pixels

It's not enough that you know how to export your graphics as GIF or JPEG files. Setting up a good laboratory for Web graphics requires a deeper understanding of the essence of Web sites. You need to understand that:

- The final output device is a computer monitor, and computer monitors don't understand the concepts of inches, picas, or points. They only know pixels.

- You may have the coolest 1200dpi printer in the land, but a computer monitor produces output that is equivalent to only about 100 dots per inch. Ninety-six to be exact.

- You may know every export flavor in the world and be a whiz at producing scalable .eps files, but every graphic that goes up on a Web site is a bitmap, and as such, it must be created at exactly the right size.

- When it comes off the press, everybody will see your gorgeous brochure the same way, excepting factors out of your control, like severe myopia or hallucinogenic substance abuse. But everybody will see your Web pages a different way. Your ability to limit that variable will be key to your success.

Setting the Stage for Web Creation

With these points in mind, here is how we think you should set up your laboratory. Follow these steps:

1. From a blank screen, go to Layout ➤ Page Setup.

2. From this dialog, click Landscape and set the unit of measure to pixels. As soon as you do that, the Resolution list becomes active.

3. Set the resolution to 96.

4. Set the width of the page to 610 pixels. Set the height to something similar.

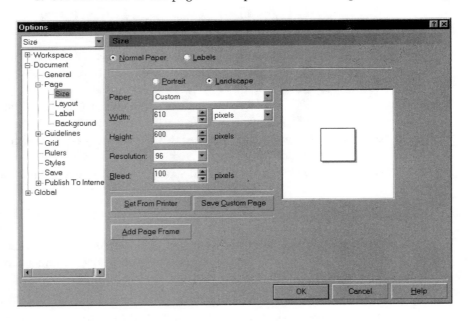

5. OK the dialog. On the page, click and drag the intersection of the two rulers and move out to the page.

6. Take this intersection to the top-left corner of the page and release. That sets the 0,0 point of the ruler to the top of the page instead of the bottom.

The PostScript printing language measures a page from the bottom up, which explains why DRAW's default page measurements are that way. But on the Web, there is no bottom of a page; it could go on forever. Better to measure from the top.

7. Drag a horizontal guideline down and place it approximately 330 pixels down the page.

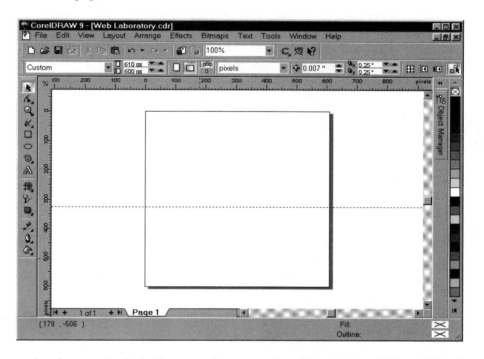

So where on Earth do these numbers come from? Resolution of 96...width of 610...a guideline at 330. Here is why we recommend this configuration.

How Many Pixels Fit in an Inch?

As we have already established, there is no sense in exporting Web graphics at high resolution when their intended output device is low resolution. Monitors today render graphics at the equivalent of 96 dots per inch. You can change the resolution of a graphic during export, but setting the page to this same resolution of 96 before you begin makes your life easier. Once you do this, you can create all graphics at precisely the same size as they are to appear on a Web page.

Set the page resolution at 300 and you'll see what we mean. The Export dialog is no longer very cooperative, and you'll have to override the resolution and/or the size settings. Establishing agreement between the object resolution and the page resolution is the smart way to go.

How Wide Is Too Wide?

This point gets debated often. Most computer users today use a screen resolution of at least 800 × 600, but there are still plenty who stay at the standard resolution of 640 × 480. (Furthermore, just because you run at 800 × 600 doesn't mean you open your browser full screen.)

We think there is nothing wrong with scrolling down a Web page, but we don't like to scroll over. There is no Intellimouse scroll button for that and no keystroke—just a cumbersome scroll bar. Therefore, it's a courtesy to design Web pages that do not require horizontal scrolling. If you are able to design within that, your visitors will appreciate it, even if they aren't conscious of the favor you are doing them.

So why 610? Because if a browser is running full screen on a standard display, the program window on the left and the scroll bar on the right consume 30 pixels. The maximum viewing width is 610 pixels.

Over at altman.com, our lead author takes this argument even further. His comments:

> *Web pages are not as easy to read as a book, and anything that we Webmasters can do to help, we should. By keeping text widths relatively narrow, it improves readability. On our Web site, we design all of our pages with widths of 500 pixels. At first, I thought that was going to be stifling. It's not. It is a very comfortable constraint; I've come to enjoy designing within it.*

Figure 21.1 shows a page from altman.com running on our screen, whose resolution is 1152 × 864. We certainly appreciate how small we can keep our browser window and still be able to read everything.

How Long Is Too Long?

We are not nearly as concerned with the length of a Web page. In fact, designers who chop up a long article by turning it into multiple pages with hyperlinks go through a lot of extra work and anger those readers who don't want to do all of that clicking, or more importantly, who wish to print the article.

That's why we didn't specify a depth of the page in DRAW. If you set the page too shallow, the page border gets in the way, and if you set it too deep, pressing Shift+F4 to see the entire page becomes kind of useless. A square page in the vicinity of 600 pixels has been a comfortable workspace for us.

FIGURE 21.1

Keeping the width of your Web pages down makes your site friendlier and more accommodating.

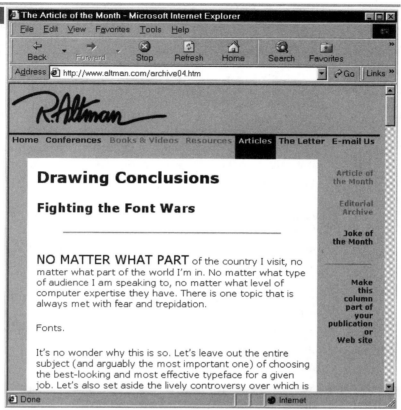

The guideline at 330 pixels represents the viewable depth of a full-screen browser running at standard resolution. The menus, toolbars, command line, and scroll bars consume a hearty 110 pixels. So if you are designing a page on which it is crucial that certain elements always appear (the cyber-equivalent of "front page, above the fold"), this guideline shows you where the boundary is.

But Remember...

It's important to keep track of your objective. In this laboratory, you will probably not create complete pages with flowing text. It is unlikely that you will place elements all over the page and send the whole thing out as a Web page. If you do, you'll want to read the next chapter carefully, but most of you will be creating individual graphics or groups of graphics.

This is your drafting board, your electronic sketch pad. The height and width parameters are there for visual aids. And we won't complain if you set your page to

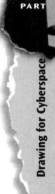

PART

Drawing for Cyberspace

a different size. However, if you change the resolution to a setting other than the one at which you export your graphics, we will send you SPAM mail about bogus viruses, pyramid schemes, and long distance scams every single day until you switch it back.

Building a Better Background

Do you watch the evening news? How about the Tonight Show? The Sunday morning political talk shows? Why do you prefer to watch the news on Channel 4 instead of Channel 7? Of course, you'd like to answer that you think the programming, commentary, reporting, and overall coverage is superior. However, many viewers respond to talk television on a different level, a level of which they may not even be consciously aware.

Many choose a news program or a talk show because of the studio design, and if you doubt this for a second, consider the untold millions of dollars that networks and local television stations pay to determine the most effective backdrop, color scheme, furniture arrangement…right down to the pattern of the ties worn by the sports reporter.

Receiving written and graphical information across the Internet is still a new experience, and as such, the entire look and feel of a Web site contributes greatly to the experience. On most Web sites, the background paints first on screen—the ubiquitous first impression in cyberspace.

Read This First!

If you take away nothing else from this chapter—indeed, from this entire part of the book—please know this: your background must make it possible for the foreground to be read and viewed. Otherwise, forget it. Pack it in. Retire. Switch professions.

Plain black text in front of a plain white background is a hundred times better than a mauve background behind peach-colored text. Dark text on a dark background…light text on a light background—they declare to all of your visitors, "I don't know any better, or I just don't care—either way, I'm going to make you work to read this page." Typical Web surfers are not unlike television channel surfers, and your Web site is like one channel on a 10-million-station cable system. They won't stick around for long if you abuse then.

So take the Hippocratic Oath when it comes to backgrounds: Above all, do no harm. It is now safe for you to read on…

Using Graphics As Backgrounds

Just about any JPEG or GIF file can be used as a background for a Web page. The only mechanical difference between using a graphic as a background instead of in the foreground is a bit of simple HTML coding. The important thing to remember is that when you assign a graphic to the background, it automatically tiles to fill the entire screen. Whatever pattern you create as a background will be repeated from the top-left corner of the browser screen down to the bottom-right.

You can use this to great advantage in your continuing quest to keep your graphics compact. If a pattern is going to repeat all the way down and across the page, you can keep your original image small. You can also use this to your peril if you do not consider the range of monitor types that might be used to view your page. Here are some examples of both. To follow along, you'll want to do four things:

1. Open DRAW.

2. Open your Web browser of choice.

3. Create a simple HTML file with Notepad or any text editor, containing the following lines of code:

```
<html>
<body background="bg.jpg">
<h1>Hello World
```

4. Save it as `Background.htm`, or some such descriptive name, in any directory you want. Remember its location though, because you will be creating graphics in DRAW and saving them in the same place.

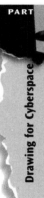

All about Tiling

Your screen at work might be a 17-inch monitor with an 800×600 resolution. At home, you might visit the Internet on a 640×480 notebook. Your colleagues might surf at 1024×768, and the untold thousands who visit your page might do so at any one of these resolutions. How do you create backgrounds to accommodate all of them? Let's have a look.

Figure 21.2 is a composite image of DRAW and Internet Explorer running side by side. On the top-left, DRAW shows a simple rectangle with a fountain fill, ranging from yellow on the left to blue on the right. It has been exported as `bg.jpg` and is displaying as the background in Internet Explorer.

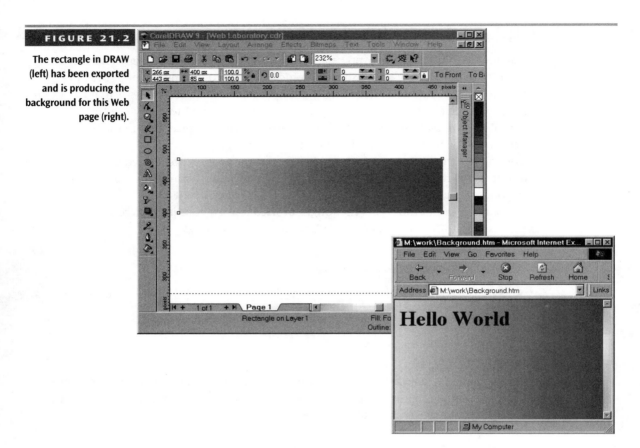

FIGURE 21.2

The rectangle in DRAW (left) has been exported and is producing the background for this Web page (right).

What we have here is a happy coincidence. The rectangle that we drew in DRAW is wide enough to cover the entire width of the browser window at its current size. But the browser window is not very wide—less than 400 pixels. Figure 21.3 shows what happens if we widen the browser window. The original graphic was not created with enough width, so the image repeats on the right side.

A mistake like this is quite insidious. Not only is your Web page representing you in a potentially embarrassing fashion, but you might never be aware of it because your own display looks fine. It is critically important that you understand how backgrounds are created and how they behave when placed on a Web site.

The simple definition of a tiled graphic is an image that repeats. It isn't stretched or distorted to fill the space; it simply repeats itself as often as is needed in order to fill the space. Therefore, the ending of the graphic needs to flow smoothly into the beginning, otherwise there will be a visible seam.

FIGURE 21.3

If your browser window is wider than the background graphic, the graphic repeats itself.

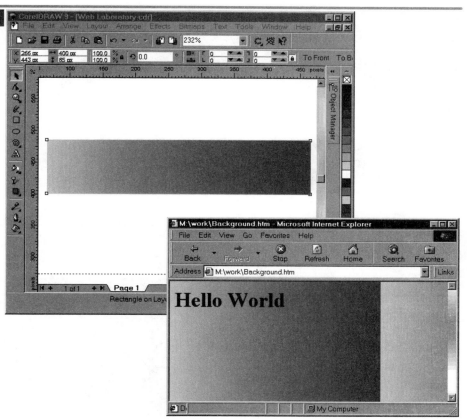

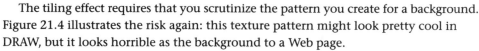

PART

5

Drawing for Cyberspace

The tiling effect requires that you scrutinize the pattern you create for a background. Figure 21.4 illustrates the risk again: this texture pattern might look pretty cool in DRAW, but it looks horrible as the background to a Web page.

If you have set up your laboratory, you can explore this quite easily. As you create different graphic effects in DRAW, continue to export them as bg.jpg. Then switch to your browser and refresh the display (F5 in Internet Explorer, Ctrl+R in Navigator).

You might be tempted to circumvent the whole tiling issue by simply creating your graphics large enough so that they won't need to tile. Resist this temptation with all of your might, for two reasons: (1) You would have to create very large graphics, thereby saddling your visitors with intolerable wait times, just to see your background; and (2) How large is large? To accommodate all viewers, you would have to create the graphic at 1600 × 1280 pixels, which further exacerbates reason No. 1.

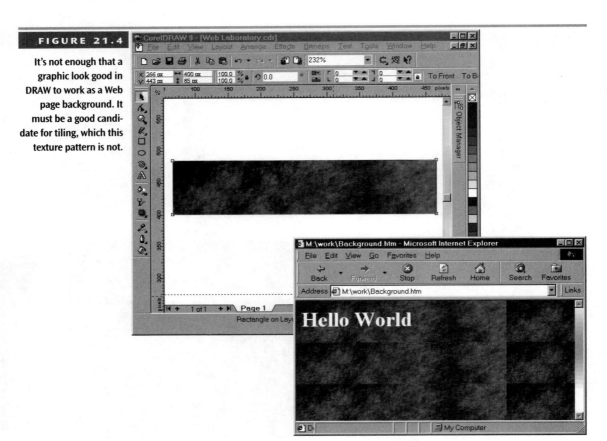

No, better to focus intently on graphics that tile properly, and fortunately there are
many sources for creating and acquiring them, including your own creative vision
and your new Web laboratory within DRAW.

Figure 21.5 shows a very simple and effective tiled background for a musically
oriented Web page. The graphic in DRAW uses a symbol from the Musical typeface
and the offset between the two symbols makes for nice visual variety. The symbols
are also just barely darker than the background, ensuring a soft, even background that
maintains a high readability quotient. At the very least, this background contributes
to the theme of the page, does not inhibit readability, and achieves absence of ugliness, the latter being the minimum, yet oh-so-important, requirement for an effective
Web page.

Note the size of the graphic in DRAW—a scant 150 × 165 pixels. The resultant GIF
file was less than 2KB.

FIGURE 21.5

This graphic has a pattern that will tile nicely in a Web browser. If the screen were deeper or wider, the musical symbols would simply repeat in either direction.

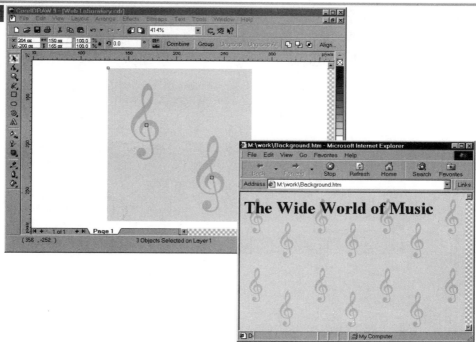

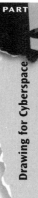

And just so you don't get soured on the prospect of using DRAW's popular Texture Fill engine to produce Web backgrounds, Figure 21.6 shows one that works nicely. The difference between this one and the one in Figure 21.4 is all in the seams: the pattern in Figure 21.4 does not repeat effectively because the image is too defined; it has a distinct seam. But the one in Figure 21.6, the Fiber Embossed texture, has no visible seams. Study it in DRAW and in the browser and you can see that the pattern repeats over and over again, but without a visible seam. That is the litmus test for any background graphic. Again, create a few textures and save them one after the other as bg.jpg, each time switching to your browser to have a look. Experimenting with Web designs is so immediate and interactive, it is almost intoxicating.

Creating Borders

One of the more popular forms of backgrounds is the vertical border, a stripe or pattern that runs down the left side of the page. The rest of the page is left white or set to some other background color and the bulk of the text and graphics is placed there. The border serves as a simple graphic element, or can be used to place navigation links or other special elements.

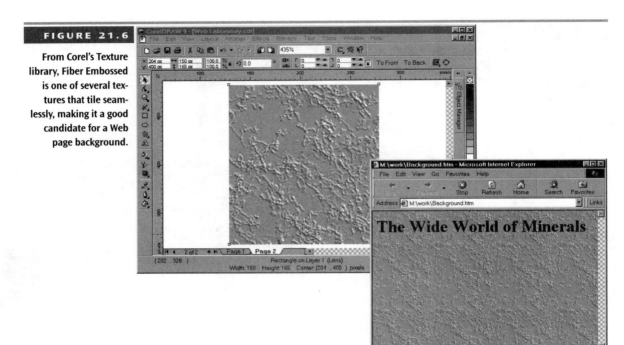

FIGURE 21.6

From Corel's Texture library, Fiber Embossed is one of several textures that tile seamlessly, making it a good candidate for a Web page background.

Quick, how come you see lots of left-hand borders on Web pages but very few right-hand ones? Give up? Because it's impossible to know where the right-hand border will be. All left borders will begin at pixel No. 1, but the right border could be at 400 pixels, 640, 800, 1000, 1280, or really any number at all. There is no telling where the right edge of the screen will be, unless you make clever use of a table with relative sizes assigned to the columns.

The second question is this: how can you prevent the left border from repeating itself at some point across the screen? Remember, all backgrounds tile, so what's to stop the border from showing up again and again? The answer is you. You stop the border from reappearing by creating a background that actually is much wider than it appears. Follow these steps:

1. Create a small square approximately 100 pixels wide and about 50 pixels high. (You can approximate both, or enter precise values from the property bar.)

2. Fill the rectangle with any color, let's say red, and remove the outline.

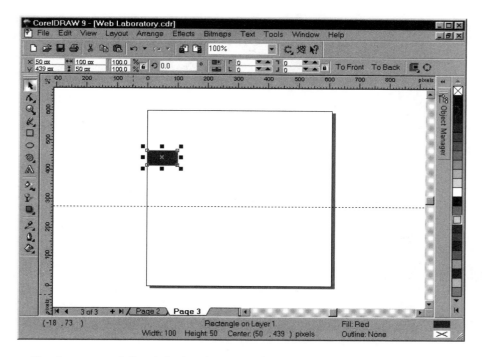

You have now defined the border stripe that will run down the left side of the screen. To prevent it from tiling, you need to fill all of the space to its right. This is a job for flop-and-dupe:

3. With the rectangle still selected, take the left-middle handle and drag it across the rectangle to the right side.

4. Before you release mouse Button 1, click Button 2 to leave behind the original.

5. Color it yellow or cyan or some other uniform color other than red.

Now, how wide should this yellow rectangle be? To prevent the red border from repeating itself, how much white space do you need? Would 1024 pixels be sufficient? What if some of your readers run at 1280 × 1024? What about the one or two percent of users who are at 1600 × 1280?

It costs you so little to cover all contingencies, you might as well set the rectangle so that the entire graphic spans 1600 pixels.

6. Stretch the yellow rectangle so that it reaches the 1600-pixel mark. You'll need to scroll quite a bit to get out that far (and DRAW should do that for you).

PART 5

Drawing for Cyberspace

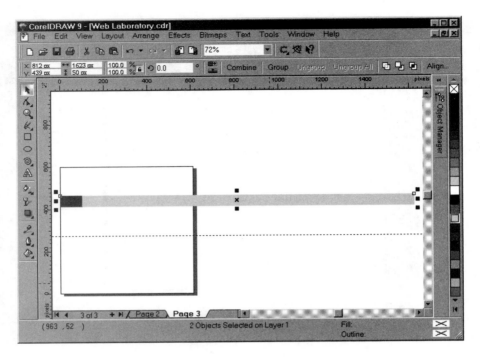

7. Select both rectangles and note their combined sizes, which should be at least 1600 × 50 pixels.

8. Export the graphic as bg.gif.

9. When you reach the Bitmap Export dialog, select Paletted for the color depth to allow DRAW to find the optimum palette size (which should be just three—red, the second color you chose, and white, which is included in all palettes).

10. Verify that anti-aliasing and dithering are both unchecked.

11. Verify that Resolution is set to 96.

12. Check to make sure that the size fields are the same as the values you noted in step 7. With the page set to the same resolution of 96, and 1 to 1 chosen from the Size drop-down list, DRAW should automatically pick up the size of the objects. If not, then choose Custom for the size and enter the values manually.

13. OK this dialog and at the next screen, click Image Color under Transparency.

14. Choose the second color as the transparent one, either using the Eyedropper or by clicking on the color in the palette.

15. OK this dialog to create the file. Here is how it would look in a browser (after editing the HTML file to reference bg.gif instead of bg.jpg).

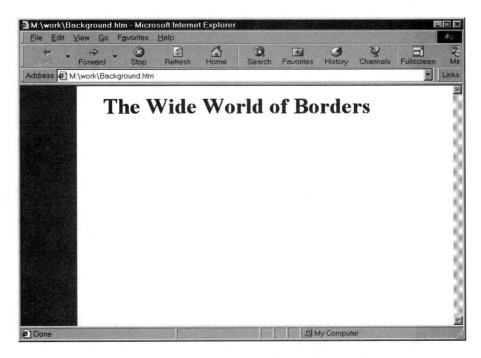

Do you see the role that the yellow rectangle plays? It simply consumes space—all the way out to the 1600-pixel mark if necessary, thereby preventing the red strip from showing up again. You didn't have to make it yellow. You could have filled it white in the first place and then not had to have applied transparency. But we have found that working with invisible objects in DRAW is a leading cause of early retirement.

Of course, if you want a colored background, or even a patterned one, you would use a color or pattern for the wide rectangle and not apply transparency.

The Cost of Being Fastidious

You may think that creating a 1600-pixel-wide graphic is overkill, but it costs you virtually nothing to be so fastidious. If you want hard numbers, the 1600 × 50 pixel graphic you created for your background consumes a grand total of 781 bytes. Creating it with a width of only 1024 pixels would probably suffice for 95 percent of your viewing audience, maybe more. That graphic consumes 659 pixels. So it costs only an extra 122 bytes to make your background effective for all users.

Continued on next page

These numbers might seem like they come from a different universe, after spending 300MB or so to install CorelDRAW. But consider this:

- You are rendering for the screen, so the graphic only needs to be 100dpi at most.
- There are only two colors, so DRAW creates a very small palette when you choose Paletted for color depth.
- The graphic is very short, only 50 pixels high. The height is inconsequential because your browser is going to tile it to the bottom of the screen. The truth is, the only reason to give the graphic any height at all is so you can select it in DRAW.

These are the factors that work in your favor when creating backgrounds and other Web graphics. The more you take advantage of them, the happier you will make visitors to your site.

Step by Step: A New Background for *Altman.com*

Our lead author's semi-annual Web site redesign will be publicly aired in these pages before being unveiled to the general Web populace (so if you don't like it, send your hate mail to webmaster@altman.com). And as always, the first step is the background. Here are the steps we took:

1. First, we inserted Corel's CD No. 3, where all the photos are stored, and went to Tools ➢ Scrapbook ➢ Photos.
2. We navigated to Webart, then Backgrds, and then Design.
3. As each thumbnail image displayed, we took a liking to bluewall.jpg.

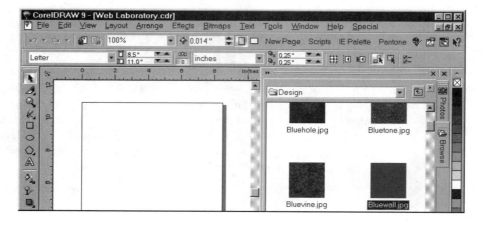

4. We dragged it from Scrapbook onto the page and then closed the Scrapbook docker.

The native image is 240 pixels square, which is needlessly large. Also, we prefer to have the surface contours and textures be smaller.

5. So we went to Bitmaps ➢ Resample, and reduced the image by 50%.

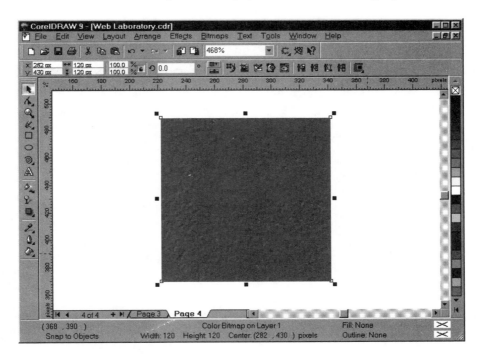

There are a few things to point out about this graphic. First, note its size of 120 pixels square, a result of the Resample command. Resample is the responsible way to size a bitmap image when pixels are involved. Sizing a bitmap with its handles has inherent risks of image degradation, and you are asking a pixel to do something it inherently doesn't know how to do: change its size. Resample is a more sophisticated process whereby pixels are actually adjusted.

Second, note that we are on page 4 of `Web Laboratory.cdr`. We are using these pages as a sketch pad—each page containing graphic elements, experiments, or just idle doodling.

6. We activated Snap to Objects with View ➤ Snap to Objects and then drew a rectangle directly on top of the image.

7. We removed the outline of the rectangle and went to Effects ➤ Lens to open the Lens docker.

8. We chose Color Add, found a medium blue tone, and accepted the default rate of 50%. Upon clicking Apply, our image looked much lighter and softer.

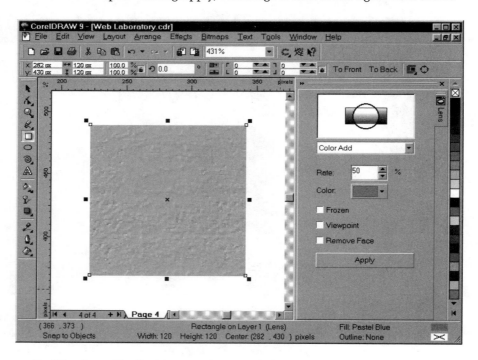

9. We selected both objects and grouped them with Ctrl+G.

10. We saved.

11. We exported the image as `bg.jpg` and immediately went to look at it in the browser. Figure 21.7 shows what we saw.

The `bg.jpg` file consumes 13KB. That's not a lot for an element as crucial as our background, but if we could get it smaller, we would in a heartbeat. So we exported the graphic many times, with different compression and smoothing values. Each time we exported, we switched to the browser to have a look. We concluded that a Compression value of 20 did not visibly affect the graphic, yet took the size down to 8KB.

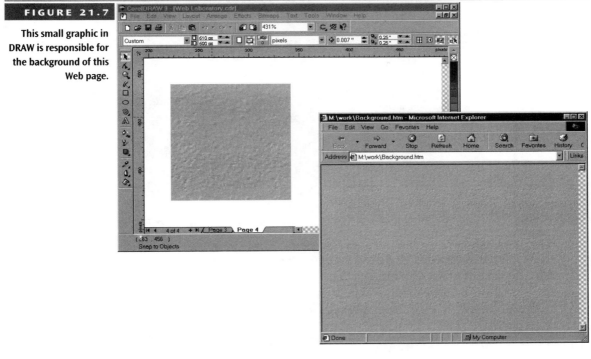

FIGURE 21.7

This small graphic in DRAW is responsible for the background of this Web page.

Drawing for Cyberspace

Finishing the Laboratory

Now that we have chosen the background for our Web site, we can finish the laboratory. If it is going to serve as a place to create graphics for a Web site, we need to know how those graphics will appear against the site's background.

This used to be a 20-step process, involving careful grid-setting, dragging and duping, powerclipping, and layer management. Now it is six simple steps:

1. Go to Layout ➤ Page Setup.
2. Click Background from the menu tree at left.
3. For Background, click Bitmap, and click Browse.
4. Find the file you have created for your Web site.
5. Uncheck the Print and Export Background box.

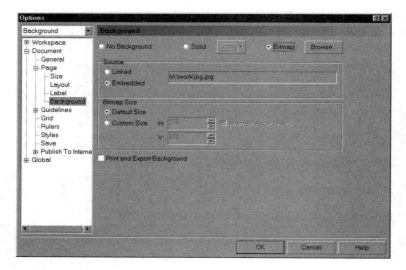

6. OK the dialog and note that your background image now fills the entire page.

You won't be able to select or move the background, and anything you draw appears on top of it. That is precisely what you want—it is behaving just like a Web site's background. Now you can create elements and get an immediate sense of how they would look. In Figure 21.8, we see that the headline stands out nicely and the text is quite readable. However, we think we'd better lose that fountain-filled rectangle...

FIGURE 21.8

By flipping one switch, you now have an electronic tracing pad for your Web graphics.

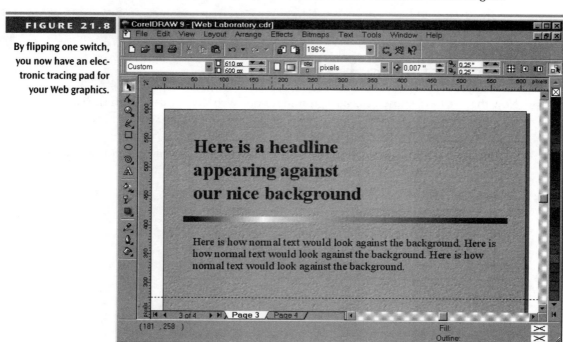

NOTE If you want to make printouts with your background, return to the Backgrounds page and check Print and Export Background. Then to export a graphic, make sure to select it and choose Selected Only in the Export dialog. Regardless of the status of the Print and Export Background box, the background will appear when you press F9 to get a Full Screen Preview.

Start Designing

When you begin creating and compiling elements, you can—and should—do everything precisely to size. Your page is showing you the optimum width, your background is in place, and you can get immediate feedback on what looks good and what fits.

Figure 21.9 shows two variations of the altman.com logo being tested. By creating it in our laboratory, we see that it fits within our ideal 610-pixel width, and there is sufficient contrast between the lightest and smallest elements and the background. When it comes time to export, we will do so at the exact size we created these elements.

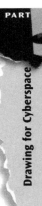

PART

Drawing for Cyberspace

FIGURE 21.9

Thanks to our laboratory setup, we see that these logos will fit and they will be easily visible.

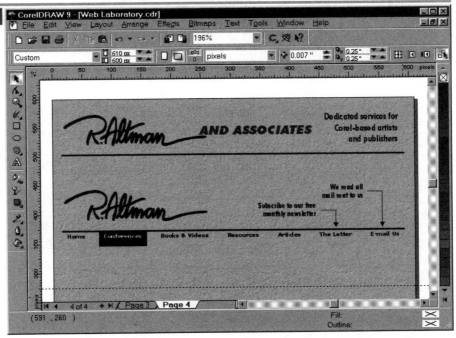

As we build solid-filled objects, we will make sure to use one of the browser-friendly color palettes, like the one shown in Figure 21.9. These browsers are RGB-based, and contain the 216 colors that are guaranteed to display without dithering on any display using SVGA or better. With fountain fills, texture patterns, and full-color photographs, it's not as easy to guarantee color accuracy down to SVGA, but you can't lose sleep over that. There is only so much you can do to cater to the lowest common denominator. Assuring that solid colors display accurately is a reasonable expectation and worth the effort. Limiting all colors in all graphics to the 216...that's asking too much.

WARNING   Before creating Web graphics in DRAW, make sure that you turn color correction off. Go to Tools ➤ Options ➤ Global ➤ Color Management and uncheck Calibrate Colors for Display. Otherwise, DRAW will display all colors based on how it thinks they will print, and the colors you choose for your graphics will display entirely differently in a browser. This is the one time when you don't want DRAW to correct for printed output. So turn off color correction, and for once, what you see really will be what you'll get.

Start Exporting

We wish that the process of exporting were as straightforward as the design process, but as we'll detail in the next chapter, DRAW's export engine has some fundamental and potentially significant flaws that might require a diversion through PHOTO-PAINT. Stay tuned for this and many other spellbinding topics in our anything-goes concluding chapter on creating Web graphics.

STRATEGIES FOR WEBMASTERING

Featuring

STRATEGIES FOR WEBMASTERING

T his chapter explores two distinct paths, and the one that will be most salient to you has to do not only with the kind of Web site you want to create, but also your very philosophy about the World Wide Web.

The distinction comes down to this: are you turning to DRAW to create graphics for Web pages, or do you want DRAW to create the Web pages themselves? DRAW can handle either task, and each strategy will get airtime in this chapter. But to many, this question cuts right to the core of the essential nature of a Web page. Is a Web page a single entity, like a brochure, or is it a collection of elements? Do you design a Web page, or do you program one?

Ultimately, you do a bit of both, and that is one of the reasons why millions of DRAW users have turned their creative energy to the Web with such zeal. This chapter explores with more detail the ways that DRAW can best be used to create Web graphics and Web pages, before concluding with some general and wandering commentary. It is not for beginners.

Exporting Graphics: Can DRAW Pass Muster?

The two previous chapters explored in-depth how and why you create your artwork in DRAW and export it to one of the two popular Web formats, GIF or JPEG. In this chapter, we will look at why you might *not* want to do that. And we'll spoil the punch line and just tell you this:

All by itself, DRAW might not be good enough.

Your eyes will ultimately be judge and jury, but if you're like most discerning graphic designers, you are likely to find DRAW's output deficient with certain types of graphics. Fortunately, the solution for this comes in the box, in the form of Corel PHOTO-PAINT, but first, the problem.

Figure 22.1 shows a close-up of a logo used at `altman.com`. We want to point out three things about it:

- The background is one uniform color—there is no outline.

- The bar at the bottom is also a solid color, and there is no shading or tinting intended between the two. One color meets the other.

- The white lettering is small but sharp and readable.

FIGURE 22.1

This simple logo has uncovered some not-so-simple issues with DRAW's GIF export.

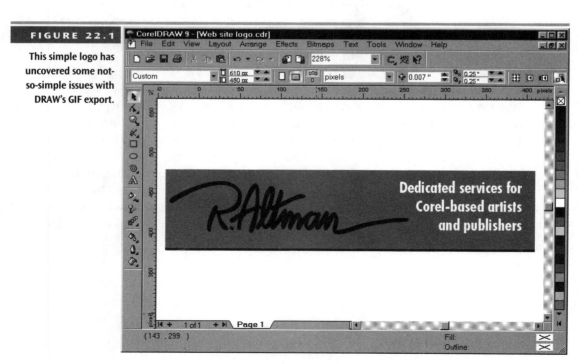

We exported this file as an anti-aliased GIF file and opened it in PHOTO-PAINT. Here is what we saw when we zoomed in:

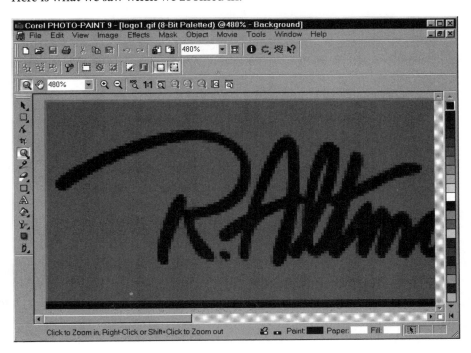

If you're not used to seeing close-ups of anti-aliasing, you might be startled at the appearance of the lettering, but actually, DRAW does a pretty good job of rendering it. (At the correct size, the jagged lettering will look smooth.) Our concern is what we see along the perimeter of the graphic: DRAW added anti-aliasing all the way around the edges, and above the dark bar spanning the bottom—as if there could be jaggies along straight lines!

This sparked quite a debate during development. When we complained about DRAW's propensity for blurring the straight lines of our test images, Corel's engineers defended their position. "It is true our anti-aliasing will anti-alias straight lines also," responded one of them. "That is the correct method for anti-aliasing lines. Horizontal and vertical lines do not always lie on a pixel's edge or on a pixel's center and our anti-aliasing is actually more accurate because it indicates exactly what percentage of the pixel it occupies.

"The blurring in these cases is not just to handle fractional pixel positions. The process of rendering anything to a bitmap involves starting with the continuous, mathematical representation of the object, low-pass filtering it, and sampling. Therefore, a correctly anti-aliased image will never have infinitely sharp edges in it, even in cases where a line is exactly on a pixel center.

"I call it a feature and not a bug."

We can't speak to this issue in such technical terms; it is beyond our comprehension and probably most of our readers. We only know what our eyes tell us: when we visit professionally created Web sites, we see clean and sharp graphics that have effective anti-aliasing around curves, but not along the four edges of the graphic. If Corel is right about the rules of anti-aliasing, a lot of Webmasters are breaking the rules, and many in their audience prefer it that way.

In Pursuit of Cleaner Graphics

First off, you may not find Corel's interpretation of anti-aliasing to be objectionable. (It is much better than in previous years—last year, DRAW would place a white dot in the corners of GIF and JPEG files.) It's possible that your graphics will be shown at a small enough size to make the blurred lines insignificant.

Nonetheless, you should know how to make them better. And Corel's claims to the contrary notwithstanding, we find PHOTO-PAINT to be a smarter tool than DRAW for exporting bitmap graphics.

Here are various DRAW-to-PAINT strategies that you can try in search of this electronic holy grail. Our instructions here assume that you either know your way around PHOTO-PAINT or have already read Chapters 24 and 25.

Use PAINT for Clean-Up

If you are not satisfied with the appearance of the graphics you create in DRAW, open them in PAINT and clean them up. In the case of unwanted lines produced by the anti-aliasing effect, you can embark on what we like to call the Search and Destroy mission:

1. Open the graphic in PAINT.

2. Zoom way in so you can see, and easily click on, the pixels that make up the lines of unwanted colors.

3. Use PAINT's Eyedropper and Color Replacer tools to replace the unwanted color with the color of the graphic. This is like using Search and Replace, but in PAINT instead of in your word processor:

   - With the Eyedropper tool, click on the unwanted color, then Alt+click on the correct color.

   - Switch to the Color Replacer tool and click and drag across the unwanted color—it will turn into the correct color.

In the graphic on the facing page, our cursor is heading down the left side, removing the unwanted color.

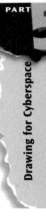

 T I P You can toggle between Eyedropper and Color Replacer with the spacebar, so you can easily define new search and/or replace colors. And when replacing, you can hold **Ctrl** to keep your cursor headed along a straight path. With PAINT's auto-panning, this makes replacing a continuous line of color fast and easy.

4. Save the file from PAINT.

To reiterate, we don't think that this operation should be necessary, but then again, Corel argues that its GIF export interprets anti-aliasing correctly. So this becomes a matter of taste and development philosophy.

Chapter 25 discusses the find and replace operation in considerable detail.

Export from DRAW, Import to PAINT

This next strategy takes advantage of Corel's private file format, CMX.

1. Export the graphic from DRAW in CMX format (Corel Presentation Exchange).

2. Switch to PAINT and open the CMX file. Because this file needs to be converted to a bitmap, PAINT asks you how to do so. Choose Paletted, check Anti-aliasing, set the resolution to 96, and set the sizing to 1 to 1.

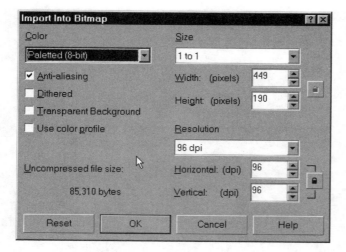

3. Use PAINT's masking tools to surround the graphic with a mask. For the graphic shown here, we used the Lasso Mask tool and simply drew roughly around the outside of the graphic. PAINT figured out what we meant and created a mask around the logo. If necessary, we touched up with the Magic Wand tool.

N O T E For more information and instructions on using PAINT's masking tools, see Chapter 25.

4. Go to Image ➤ Crop ➤ To Mask to remove all unwanted white space from this graphic.

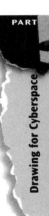

5. Go to Image ➤ Resample and scale this graphic to the desired size (return to DRAW to check the size, if necessary). Set the resolution to 96dpi, if it isn't already set that way. Here were the settings for our graphic.

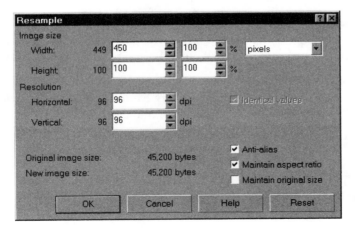

6. Go to Mask ➤ Remove (or press Ctrl+Shift+R) to remove the mask (and the annoying moving line). Then zoom way in. You'll see the unwanted anti-aliasing around the edges of the graphic, and maybe applied to interior straight lines.

7. Remove the unwanted lines, using the search-and-destroy technique described earlier.

8. Export the file in GIF format.

Use the Clipboard

The first cousin to the export-import shuffle is to transfer the image across the Clipboard. This involves the following:

1. Zoom in as tight as you can on the objects to export. The easiest way to do this is to select them and press Shift+F2.

2. Press F9 for a full-screen preview.

TIP   To get the cleanest look, go to Tools ➤ Options ➤ Workspace ➤ Display and check Use Enhanced View and uncheck Show Page Border.

3. While in preview, press Alt+Prtsc to capture the image to the Clipboard.

4. Switch to PAINT and go to File ➤ New from Clipboard to paste the image into PAINT.

5. Repeat the steps described above to mask the logo, crop to it, resample it, and export it.

The Super-Export Strategy

You can often get better results by exporting from DRAW at two or four times the size desired and then resampling it down in PAINT.

To do this without permanently altering the graphic in DRAW, do this:

1. Select the graphic.

2. Use the sizing controls on the property bar to increase the graphic by 200% or 400% (most users will have enough RAM to try for 400).

3. Export as CMX.

4. Press Ctrl+Z to undo the resizing operation.

In PAINT, you would follow the same steps above, resampling the graphic down to its original size and exporting it.

Judge for Yourself

The following table shows the results of our tests with a simple logo. As the native medium for these graphics is the Web, we have also prepared a comprehensive Web page with the specs and visual results of the test. You'll be better able to scrutinize the appearance of each graphic on the Web, so visit www.altman.com/logotest to judge for yourself.

Method of Creation	File Size	Time to Create	Result
Direct export from DRAW	4.3KB	10 seconds	services for used artists
Original export, refined in PAINT	4.0KB	75 seconds	services for used artists
Graphic exported as CMX file, refined in PAINT	3.9KB	125 seconds	services for used artists
Full-screen preview image captured to Clipboard, pasted to PAINT, and refined	4.6KB	95 seconds	services for used artists
Graphic exported at 400% original size, refined and resampled back down in PAINT	5.3KB	125 seconds	services for used artists

From the Web site, it is obvious that the expand/compress strategy yields the highest fidelity, especially in the all-important category of fine text. It is also the most time-consuming, so only you can evaluate this for your own needs and purposes. The other one we like is the Clipboard route, because it's fast, it doesn't involve the creation of CMX files that then become superfluous, and it renders text very well.

Meanwhile, we hope for the day that DRAW can export Web graphics as cleanly as PAINT, so we won't have to bother with any of these workarounds.

All about Image Maps

In this section, we assume you already know the "click here to go here and click there to go there" dynamic of the World Wide Web. You probably also know that you can turn a graphic into a hyperlink just as easily as you can turn a string of text into one.

Image maps bring another dimension to that dynamic. An image map is a graphic coupled with HTML instructions that describe how it should behave when clicked. Essentially, image maps have multiple hotspots, so that clicks on different places produce different results.

PART

Drawing for Cyberspace

At its core, the graphic for an image map is no different from any other exported graphic (so we refer you to the previous strategies for good output). It's the integration of the hotspot instructions that turns it into a more interesting creature.

WARNING   Image maps are not unanimously acclaimed in the Internet community. They are usually robust graphics with significant download times, and sites that neglect to provide a text-based alternative anger those who choose to navigate without graphics. If you are considering their use, avoid unnecessary file bloat as much as you can, and make sure to provide a text-based alternative.

One of our favorite image maps is devoted to Beatles trivia, and it is shown in Figure 22.2 (with the correct URL for fans who want to visit it). Each of the song titles, and the other parts of the label, represents a topic of discussion or interest, and clicking on any one of them takes you there.

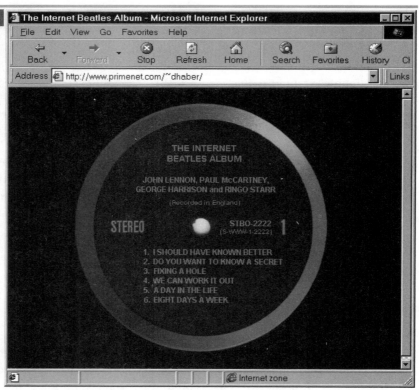

FIGURE 22.2

This image map offers lots of fun clicks for Beatles enthusiasts.

This graphic is about 35KB, and that's not chump change in Web currency, but it's bytes well-spent, because it's clever, effective, and provides excellent navigation.

Building an Image Map in DRAW

Again, an image map is a graphic with a set of instructions. It's not magic or voodoo, and we nonprogramming mortals can look under the hood on this one and understand what's going on. Keep the following key points in mind when creating an image map:

- Make sure the graphic lends itself to an image map. In other words, make sure that the areas representing links to other places are graphically distinct. Many image maps include words that spell out the hotspots, and that is preferred over a vague graphic that would confuse your visitors.
- Know the exact URL address of each hyperlink, whether it is another Web page on your own site or one somewhere out on the Internet.

Figure 22.3 shows the graphic elements for a simple image map that a high school might create for its students. The cork board is one rectangle inside of a rounded rectangle, filled with a texture pattern called Oatmeal (we changed the color from that lumpy white to a corky yellow). The notices are just two more stacked rectangles, the one in back filled black and the one in front skewed ever so slightly. The thumbtack came from Corel's clipart library. Finally, the text is Corel's Technical.

FIGURE 22.3

This is a good candidate for an image map because it is obvious where to click and what happens when you do.

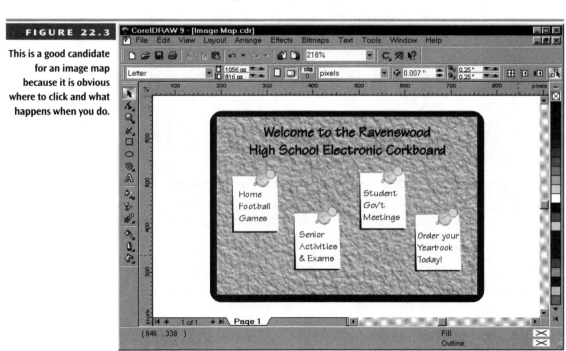

PART

Drawing for Cyberspace

In the following exercise through the creation of this image map, we have fabricated the URLs; if you want the hotspots to function, substitute ours with real ones. Here goes:

1. Select the elements of each notice—in this case, the white rectangle, the black rectangle, and the thumbtack—and group them. This is not required, just recommended.

2. Go to Window ➤ Toolbars and check Internet Objects. At your option, either float this toolbar or dock it.

3. Select one of the notices and place your cursor in the Internet Address field of the toolbar (the far-left drop-down list).

4. Type a URL as we have done here.

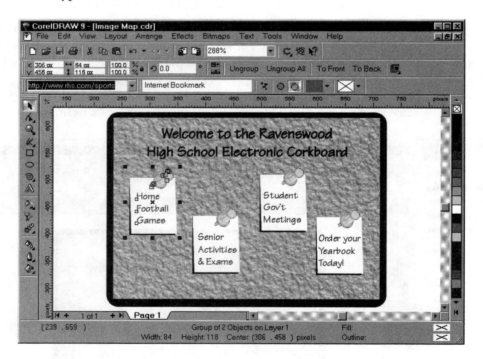

5. Press Enter to attach the URL to the selected object(s).

The next drop-down list is for creating a hyperlink to an element or page within your drawing—that is not relevant here. But the next five options are useful, and one of them is crucial. Here are descriptions of those options.

Show Hotspots

By clicking this, DRAW highlights the areas that have been defined so you can easily see them on screen, without having to laboriously select each object and consult the Internet Address window.

Use Object Shape to Define Hotspot

Conceivably, you might create an image map with very precise graphics for hotspots and you might want the object shape itself—and not the rectangular area it sits in—to be the hotspot. Most of the time, however, we recommend against this option (too bad it's the default). If the object shape is unusual, DRAW will have to plot the entire shape, spinning out dozens of kilobytes of HTML code. This is classic file bloat.

Use Bounding Box to Define Hotspot

Choosing this option instead of Object Shape makes DRAW's job much easier, and the jobs of those who visit your page. All DRAW has to do now is define a simple rectangle for each hotspot, which it can do in about six words of HTML. Only an extraordinarily shaped graphic would truly need more than a rectangle to have its hotspot defined, and most of the time your visitors will appreciate being able to click a bit more lazily.

With our high school corkboard, using the object shapes as hotspots resulted in an 18KB HTML file. Using the bounding box brought that number all the way down to 4KB.

Foreground and Background Colors of Hotspot

Only relevant if Show Hotspots is clicked, this determines how the hotspot appears. Choosing a background color seems only to blanket the entire hotspot with a solid color; choosing a foreground color makes more sense, as we have done here.

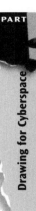

PART

Drawing for Cyberspace

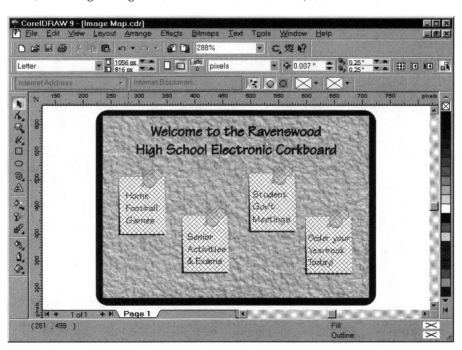

Select each notice on the bulletin board and enter a URL for it. We used `http://www.rhs.com/` for the main address and `sports`, `seniors`, `government`, and `yearbook` to complete the URL for each of these four links. You can use any URLs you want to, including `corel.com`, `altman.com`, `sybex.com`, or your own Web site.

Ready to Export

Corel has defined a Grand Central Station for sending pages to the Internet, and it is the File ➤ Publish to Internet command. This command can be driven as a Wizard or a series of dialogs; either way, you get the same choices. Here's how the Wizard works.

What's Your Name, What's Your Line?

On this page, you determine what type of HTML file DRAW is to create, what it will be called, and where it will be created. In the graphic below, you can see the four layout method choices; Single Image with Image Map is selected.

Above that, we have chosen a folder on our local G: drive. If we wanted to place the graphic in a subfolder underneath that—like Pictures, for instance—we would enter it in the line below. We could also check Use HTML Name for Image Folder and DRAW would create a subfolder using the `.cdr` filename. We have left it blank, indicating we want all graphics (in this case, only one) to simply be written to the same folder as the HTML file, `g:\rhs`.

The Use Internet Dialog button toggles you between this hand-holding Wizard and the less interactive dialog. In the graphic below, that button is obscured by the drop-down list of layout methods. Trust us, it's there.

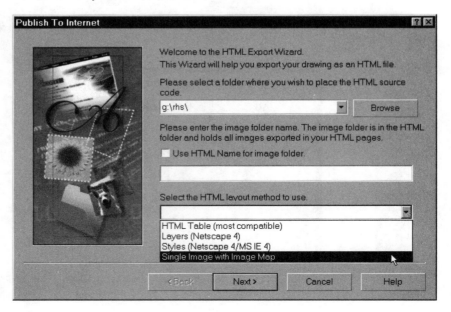

Image Is Everything

This page asks you about how graphics are to be handled, starting with the fundamental choice of JPEG vs. GIF. If you choose the former, the JPEG Options button takes you to the export subdialog to choose compression and smoothing. There is no GIF Options button, and we'll talk about the implications of that soon.

If your drawing has imported bitmaps, you can opt to have them created as separate files, as opposed to the drawing being one big image. And the Resample Bitmaps to Screen Resolution option is a good idea in theory, but we have objections with its implementation. DRAW uses 72dpi for screen resolution, even though many monitors today achieve 96dpi. Anyway, if you have set up your laboratory correctly, as discussed in Chapter 21, you would never need it because you have already set screen resolution properly.

Finally, the Render All Text As Images option is occasionally useful, and will be discussed in the next section.

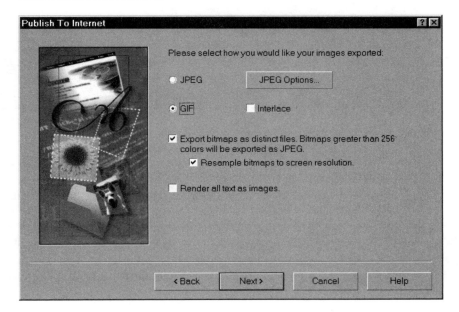

Pick a Page, Any Page

The final stop on the Wizard is to choose the pages to export, what to call them, and how to display them. In this case, there is only one page in the drawing; if there were more, you could choose which ones to export, or click on Export All Pages and be done with it.

Of the three check boxes on the right, the first two are obvious (View Page in Browser invokes whichever browser is identified on your system as the default). The third one, Create Statistics Page, is a nifty little option that tells you how the page is structured, what links are present, and how long the page will take to display at various Internet connection speeds.

When you click Finish, DRAW creates the file, and your image map is done. In our case, DRAW created two files:

Image Map.gif   The graphic created in DRAW

Image Map.htm   The HTML file containing the hotspot definitions

N O T E   Even though this image map was created on your local system, it is perfectly capable of opening Web sites out on the Internet. As long as your browser finds an Internet connection, your image map will be fully functional, from any location.

Image Map Caveats

We think that image maps are a fine navigational technique, but we have some reservations about creating them solely with DRAW. Here are some of the reasons for our reservations:

Limited Graphic Options   The Publish to Internet tool does not offer the same range of choices as the GIF and JPEG export functions do. We would like to be able to determine for ourselves what size the graphic should be and if a particular color should be transparent. And as noted earlier, graphics are exported at 72dpi, not the more correct 96.

N O T E If you use the dialogs instead of the Wizard, DRAW offers an Options button that includes a page for graphic export. It offers the additional choices of palette type and anti-aliasing. We think those choices should also be present in the Wizard.

No Selected Only Option We tore our hair out over why DRAW continued to create our image map with so much white space around it. Then we realized that it was exporting the entire page from DRAW. To fix this, we had to size the page to be the same size as the graphic and then make sure the graphic was positioned properly on the page. DRAW exports the page, the whole page, and nothing but the page.

No Hyperlink Options We like having the choice of creating our hyperlinks so that they open in a new window. This is a standard capability in a Web page editor, but DRAW doesn't offer it.

And this last point is the most salient: DRAW is simply not as robust at Web page creation as a program like Microsoft FrontPage, NetObjects Fusion, and the like. For this reason we tend to shy away from creating our image maps in DRAW. A sports analogy is in order here, because image mapping is a team effort, and any good coach tries to find roles for his or her players that match up well with their skills. In the case of image mapping, we see it this way:

- Use DRAW and PAINT to create the graphics, using any of the strategies outlined earlier in the chapter. Note where you want the hyperlinks to go, but don't create them in DRAW. Just use the Export command to create the graphic.

- Use a Web page editor to create the hotspots. It is more adept, offers the option to open the hyperlink in a new window, and ultimately is more convenient. We say this because, usually, an image map is part of a Web page; it isn't the Web page itself. That means you would have to open the page in a Web page editor and then insert the image map that DRAW created. You might as well just create the hotspot info in the Web page editor to begin with.

When we placed this team strategy into action, it paid immediate benefits. First, we reduced the size of the graphic from 54K to 35K without suffering loss of image quality. Second, while we told DRAW to use the bounding box—not the object shape—for the hotspot, it didn't really listen to it. It created little bounding boxes for each of the objects in the group. The thumbtack alone had seven!

We took the file into FrontPage and used one simple rectangle for each of the hotspots. The HTML file went from over 4KB to barely 1KB. We made a mental note to ourselves that were we to create image maps in DRAW, we would create a rectangle with no outline or fill and cover the hotspot objects. Then we would assign the URL to that rectangle.

DRAW is fine for quick-and-dirty image maps. But when you want clean image maps, think like the coach of a basketball or football team and match up the skills of the players with the jobs that need to be done. Use DRAW for the graphics and a Web page editor for the HTML part.

 WARNING   Image maps tend to involve large graphics, and testing the graphic that DRAW creates can be very misleading. Please don't think that a graphic that loads swiftly from your hard drive will load just fine from a Web site. That thinking is akin to the belief that (warning, another sports analogy coming) because you can hit a golf ball 250 yards off the tee on a nice summer day, you could also do it in a rainstorm with a 30-mile-per-hour wind in your face.

From DRAW Straight to the Web

Image mapping is just one example of CorelDRAW's ability to produce HTML files. In fact, DRAW can create complete Web pages and even sets of Web pages, with all hyperlinks in place. Before this section is out, we will debate the usefulness and application of this, but not DRAW's ability to do it. For a drawing program, its skills in this department are without peer.

The engine for all of this is the Publish to Internet command introduced in the previous section. It acts like a one-stop shop for Web content creation. From it, you can publish image maps or complete pages created one of three distinct ways: tables, layers, or styles.

Figure 22.4 shows a replica of our lead author's home page at altman.com. We have replicated the background, the logo, and the positioning and typeface of the main text. (Not hard to do, since he created the graphics in DRAW to begin with.) There are a few things to know about this screen:

- We removed the Standard toolbar to have sufficient working room.
- The background image was not imported and placed on the page; it was loaded through Page Setup, as described in Chapter 21.
- All of the artistic text strings underneath the logo are hyperlinked.
- The text in the body of the page is paragraph text and has been made "HTML compatible." We'll discuss that in this section.
- The date is centered.
- Two hyperlinks are assigned to selected words in the body of the text.
- A white square is dropped behind the text.

FIGURE 22.4

This page in DRAW can be sent out as one complete Web page.

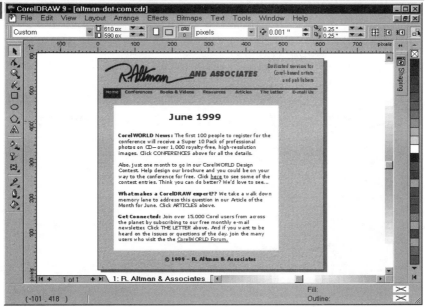

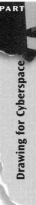

The steps to creating this Web page are the same as for the image map, and if you want to follow along with us, you can download altman-dot-com.cdr from the companion page of the Sybex Web site.

1. Go to File ➤ Publish to Internet. This time, we will navigate through the single dialog, instead of the Wizard; to get there, click Use Internet Dialog.

2. Choose HTML Table for the HTML Layout.

3. Pick a drive, a folder, and optionally, a location underneath that for images.

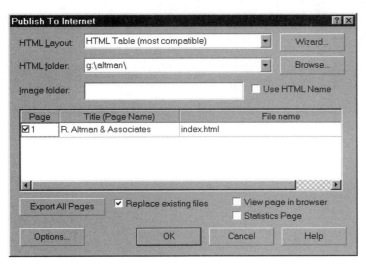

4. Decide for yourself on the three check boxes, and if you feel like it, snoop around behind the Options button. We'll cover it next.

5. Click OK to create the page in the folder you specified.

By opening the HTML file in a browser, you can see how DRAW performed in Figure 22.5.

We'll analyze and comment on this image in the section called "A Question of Purpose." But first, we'll discuss some of the options and factors to consider when you are creating HTML pages.

What Is HTML Compatible Text?

For text in DRAW to be treated as text in a Web page, you must do two things:

- Set it as paragraph text.
- Make it HTML compatible by going to Text ➤ Make HTML Compatible (or use the command on the context menu).

When you do this, DRAW treats it as other Web page editors would, by offering formatting options that are distinctly HTMLesque. Text sizes are measured on a scale of 1 to 7; spacing, leading, and kerning controls are unavailable; and only the most basic of styles can be used.

But the payoff occurs when you open the page in a browser and encounter real text that can be selected and saved off. The alternative would be for all text to be treated as graphic images—imposing potentially crippling slowdowns on the display of the page.

Options has a page that controls the handling of text, and you can see the three choices in the dialog below. The third choice, TrueDoc, is an exciting technology that is not quite ready for prime time yet, in our view.

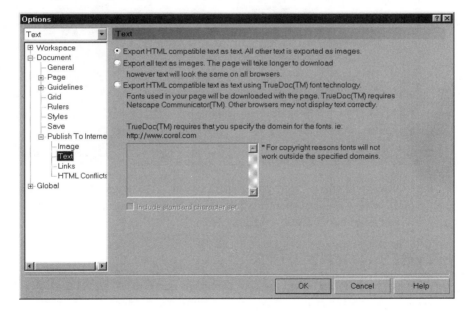

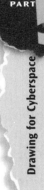

Warning, Warning…Danger…Conflict

DRAW has a funny way of telling you about problems that it encounters in creating HTML. First it notifies you of a conflict, offering you the choice of ignoring the conflict or fixing it. If you answer no, DRAW creates the page, and you'll never know what the conflict was. If you answer yes, DRAW halts the creation operation and opens the Conflict docker. To resume, you have to start over in the Publish to Internet dialogs.

Nine out of 10 times, the conflict arises when DRAW cannot make a string of text HTML compatible, and most of the time, it is text that you had no intention of converting in the first place (like an artistic headline or text that is part of a logo).

You can tell DRAW not to be so persnickety about this by clicking Options during the Publish to Internet process and clicking off the check box for HTML compatibility, as shown below.

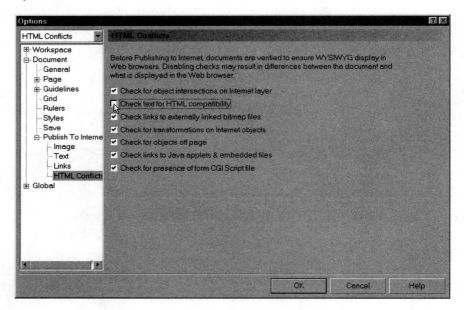

DRAW will still convert paragraph text into HTML text, but it will no longer notify you if (when) it encounters a string of artistic text or a frame of paragraph text that has not been made HTML compatible.

Layers and Styles

These two layout choices are less universal than the HTML Table choice. Layers are used only with Netscape Navigator, making it suitable only for tightly controlled circles of users (like an intranet at Netscape Corp).

Styles are more widely used but DRAW does not create an external Cascading Style Sheet (.css) file by default. So before you go any further, we suggest you return once more to Options and check Use CSS File for Text Styles.

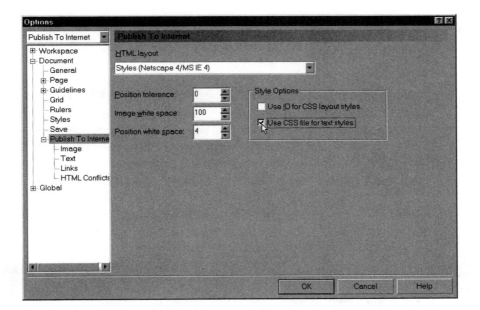

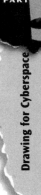

PART

Drawing for Cyberspace

With this option active, DRAW creates an external file that governs the formatting of the HTML page, and any others that you want to be controlled by it—potentially an entire Web site with hundreds of pages. To adjust the formatting of a page or an element on the page, you edit the .css file.

We are glad that DRAW has adopted support for CSS, as we see its use becoming nearly universal very soon.

A Question of Purpose

For the most part, DRAW has produced a credible replication of this page. The logo appears clean, text is readable, and all the links are in place, including the one in the text that we are pointing to in Figure 22.5.

But who would want to create a page this way, and we don't mean for this to be a rhetorical or sarcastic question. Earnest Webmasters would use a Web page editor, and anyone thinking of becoming one would receive unanimous advice to do the same. Why would one turn to DRAW to create a Web page?

We'll answer this question shortly, but first let's see why people would *not* choose DRAW. While the page looks fine in a browser, it is not without its flaws, both obvious and subtle:

- The date is not centered.

- The white background is gone altogether.

- Even though the background in DRAW was created by a JPEG file, DRAW chose to export it as a GIF during HTML page creation. As a result, it is visibly grainier than it should be.

Most notable, however, is what you don't see—the structure that DRAW uses to create this page. To be frank, it's a mess. We asked for HTML Tables as our layout—boy did we get a table...

Figure 22.6 shows the actual home page for `altman.com`, opened in a Web page editor (this is an ideal way to see how a page is actually constructed). The thin dotted lines represent the rows and columns of the table used to position these elements: the first row is the logo; the second row contains the seven main departments of the site; and the third row is the body of the page, with one blank column at the left for positioning, and the second column set with a background of white. The size of the HTML file is 2.7KB.

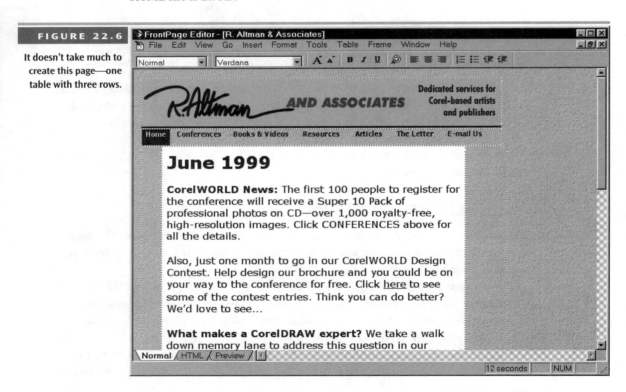

FIGURE 22.6

It doesn't take much to create this page—one table with three rows.

As pages go, this one is pretty simple. But the same cannot be said for DRAW's rendition. Figure 22.7 shows it in all of its, uh, voluminosity.

FIGURE 22.7

This page might look similar to the original home page, but behind the scenes, it is quite different.

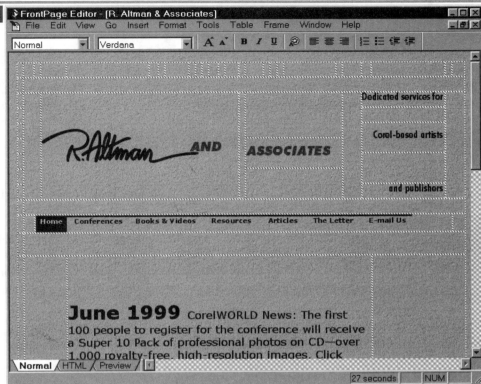

DRAW has gone completely table-happy, scattering little rows and columns everywhere. The logo has been broken up into five sections all by itself. This HTML file is almost 9KB.

So who would use DRAW to create Web pages? People who don't care about the purity of an HTML file. People who want to communicate the look of a drawing in the most universal way. People who won't have any interest in editing the page after the fact. We would argue that PDF would be a better choice, but not everyone has Acrobat Reader—almost everyone, but not *every*one. But today, everyone has a browser.

This is a narrow application for a feature that Corel has touted mightily. During development, several beta testers were even calling for the removal of DRAW's HTML creation features. We're glad they are there, if for no other reason than to expose users to HTML files. But none of the members of this book-writing team uses it for Web page creation, and as a collective, we don't place too much stock in an illustration program trying to double as a Web page creation tool.

We would prefer to see DRAW stick to what it does so well—making the graphics—and concentrate its efforts on making the GIF and JPEG export as clean as it can possibly be.

Miscellaneous Musings about Web Pages

We enter the home stretch of this chapter with a free-for-all. Here are some thoughts about working on the Web, delivered to you in no particular order except as we thought of them. When you reach Chapter 22 of a book, you are entitled to ramble…

On-Screen Proofing Is Hazardous to Your Job Security

Do you remember when you first began using a computer at work? Our lead author does.

It was 1981 and I had just begun as the managing editor of Inside Tennis *magazine in Oakland, California. I bought an Osborne 1 to use as a word processor. I loved using WordStar; it was incredible to be able to make edits on screen without having to retype everything. My copyediting speed increased ten-fold.*

And you know what else happened? I became a worse writer. This was not a good trade. I found that editing on screen was so convenient, I wouldn't bother to print my articles before turning them in. I would just read them once on screen. It was bad enough when I wrote that "Jimmy Connors uses a toe-handed backhand," but I knew something had to change when I had intended to report that Bjorn Borg had never won the U.S. Open, but wrote instead that he had never won at Wimbledon (where he had just won his fifth consecutive title). I had become better at correcting errors, but worse at spotting them.

I learned then what I have since concluded to be gospel: people don't read as effectively from a computer screen as they do from a book or a piece of paper.

Let's set aside the obvious, like the fact that even with today's notebook computers, you can't curl up on the couch with a really good Web site. And let's also set aside the fact that you can't take a Web page with you into the, uh, into the…no, let's not go there, either.

There are other implications to the Web revolution. When you are reading online, your speed is down, your comprehension is diminished, and your reading enjoyment quotient might be lower, as well. Webmasters who appreciate this create pages with narrower columns, they keep the type size at a readable level or a bit beyond, and they pepper the pages with tasteful graphics.

As writers, we have ardently believed that content should always prevail over form. However, we must acknowledge how frantic a place the World Wide Web is. We have to admit that if a little bit of eye candy will make somebody feel more comfortable at our Web site, then we stand a better chance of having our riveting and incredibly insightful prose read.

The Ongoing Struggle for Smaller Graphics

Until all houses and small offices come equipped with cable modems or DSL service, Webmasters must fight a never-ending battle to keep Web sites as compact as possible. In almost all cases, this boils down to the handling of graphic content. Here are some thoughts and advice on fighting graphic bloat.

When you create Web graphics, you must always play the FSRC game: format, size, resolution, color depth. Let's take each of these in turn.

Format

The rules of thumb for choosing between GIF and JPEG formats are well-established: use JPEG for photos and fountain fills, GIF for simpler graphics. The criteria for this advice is image quality, not file size, and sometimes you can shave a few bytes by going against the grain. Specifically, you should experiment with the JPEG format, along with a high compression value, in situations that would normally call for a GIF file. We have found that compression values in the 50 to 60 range will often result in no visible degradation with simple graphics or ones that use pure colors. Yet those JPEGs might end up as much as 50 percent smaller.

There are others who argue that JPEG files do not compress as much during download and are therefore slower even though smaller. It's true that JPEGs aren't as efficient during downloads, but statistical data on this is very elusive. As always, this is an ideal opportunity to experiment for yourself.

Size

When you export vector graphics for printed documents, size is relative. The Encapsulated PostScript format is designed as a scaleable format, and so is Windows Metafile. Vector graphics are all mathematical, so they scale freely without extra overhead.

Not so with bitmap graphics. The size of the original graphic in DRAW or the scanned photo or bitmap in PAINT is crucial to the entire process, and that's why we hit this point quite hard in Chapter 20. The HTML language offers commands to size graphics, but we don't want you depending upon them.

Figure 22.8 shows two seemingly identical graphics that were created in DRAW and displayed in a Web browser. The one on the left was created at exactly the right size, while the one on the right was created larger than needed and scaled down. The codes in the HTML file look like this:

```
<img src="image1.gif">
<img src="image2.gif" height=325 width=320>
```

FIGURE 22.8

Are these two graphics identical? Hardly—the one on the left is 5KB, the one on the right almost 14KB.

While it is possible to show a large graphic at a smaller size, it is not a good practice. The image on the right is almost three times larger than necessary, and unless you get the proportions just right, image quality suffers (how's that for irony). That is another classic case of needless file bloat.

You must also guard against the reverse situation—that of creating a graphic too small and enlarging it with the height and width commands. That is likely to result in poor image quality. There are Webmasters who insist upon using them so that the *picture well*—the space that the picture will consume once it draws—is the correct size, but to that we say, "Big deal." That's not worth the risk of mis-sizing your graphics; focus on creating your graphics the right size in the first place.

Resolution

This one is simple. Unless your graphic is very, very small, do not use resolutions higher than 96dpi. The only exception is if you are making a photo or graphic available for downloading, in which case you would handle it an altogether different way and wouldn't need to display more than a small thumbnail of the image.

DRAW helps you out by allowing you to define a resolution for your drawing in Page Setup. Set the value there to 96 to complement the same resolution setting during export, and the export engine will accurately pick up the dimension of the graphic. This is discussed in detail in Chapter 20.

Color Depth

Do you really need 16 million colors to render a graphic? If yes, then choose JPEG and go for it—at least you made a conscientious and responsible decision. If not, though, you have a valuable opportunity to reduce cyberspace congestion. By exporting your graphics as paletted images, you can potentially reduce the number of colors in graphics (and therefore file size).

Then there is another level of aggressiveness you can take for your graphics, previously only available by going through PHOTO-PAINT. You can convert your graphics into paletted images and then apply any type of palette you want to the image, including one that has very few colors. This is a more radical process than just choosing "paletted" during export, and because it involves converting the object(s) to a bitmap, you'll want to use a copy of the graphic.

The feather in Figure 22.9 is a good guinea pig, because it has well-defined solid colors as well as a soft shadow made up of many shades. We intentionally created a graphic with a component that is a good candidate for palette reduction (the feather) and a component that can't do with much less than a full-color palette (the shadow).

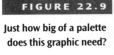

FIGURE 22.9

Just how big of a palette does this graphic need?

PART

Drawing for Cyberspace

DRAW does reduce the palette when you export as a paletted image, but it is fairly conservative. You can be more ambitious, by following these steps:

1. Select the graphic and make a copy for safe-keeping. Then go to Bitmap ➤ Convert to Bitmap. Accept all of the defaults; they will all be overridden by later conversions or exports.

2. Go to Bitmap ➤ Mode ➤ Paletted. You will meet a scary dialog with multiple tabs and many words that you won't understand. Fortunately, you can ignore most of them.

3. Pull down the Palette menu and browse the choices. Click on the Preview button after each one. Try some of the different Dithering choices.

4. Choose Optimized and enter different values under Colors, all the while clicking the Preview button for any obvious loss in color accuracy.

The magic potion in this brew is the Optimized choice, because without it, you would have to decide for yourself which colors to keep and which to remove (and starting with a 256-color palette, that could take hours). But the Optimized choice studies your image and determines the color tones that are used.

How low can you go? Every byte helps your Web site's traffic flow, but beyond that, the answer lies in image quality. We suggest that you export your image at full color and then create renditions with color values running all the way down to single digits. Create an HTML file that displays the full-color graphic next to the experimental ones, and see for yourself when you can see a significant difference.

We conducted an exhaustive test, the results of which are available at `http://www .altman.com/feather`. Here are our conclusions:

- The shadow needed the full color of a JPEG file or a GIF file with no palette reduction at all, the latter resulting in a bit of image loss. As soon as we played with the palette and reduced the number of colors used, the shadow was ruined. The JPEG file consumed 12.7KB (with a compression value of 20) and the paletted GIF file 17.6KB.

- The feather needs far fewer colors, and with each palette reduction we performed, the file became smaller and smaller. Even down at eight colors, the feather looked sharp. Too sharp, in fact—the concession being that there were not enough colors available to anti-alias as much as DRAW normally would have. With eight colors, the file was only 4.7KB.

To reiterate, this palette reduction is performed by converting the objects to a bitmap and then applying optimized palettes with varying numbers of colors present. It cannot be done at the time of export. The paletted choice in the Export dialog implies that DRAW will either use a standard palette with vector objects, or honor an optimized palette that has already been created and applied.

PART

Drawing for Cyberspace

Repeat Graphics Whenever Possible

If your Web site has many pages, seek out opportunities to repeat background and foreground graphics. Not only will this strategy serve to unify the graphic theme of your site, but it will help out your visitors immensely. Once they download a graphic, it is stored in a data cache on their system. If that graphic is called for on different pages, the cache supplies it (at hard drive or even RAM speeds) instead of the Web site (at Internet speeds). Once a visitor to your site has downloaded and viewed a graphic, it will not need to be downloaded again during that visit (or maybe not even during future visits, depending on how often the cache fills and is emptied).

Hide Large Graphics

There are many situations in which displaying a large photograph or graphic is necessary and unavoidable. For example, if you have created an online photo gallery, you have to display them in some way. But there are right and wrong ways to do it, and your strategy will spell your success or your failure.

Figure 22.10 shows the strategy we employed to display entries in the CorelWORLD Design Contest. We used a small image that would be sufficient to give judges and other visitors an idea of the illustration. This small image is hyperlinked to a larger image, and when you, the visitor, hover your mouse over it, the bubble help announces how big the larger image will be. That way, you can decide for yourself if you want to spend the download time or move on. And if the thumbnail displays all that you needed to see, so much the better.

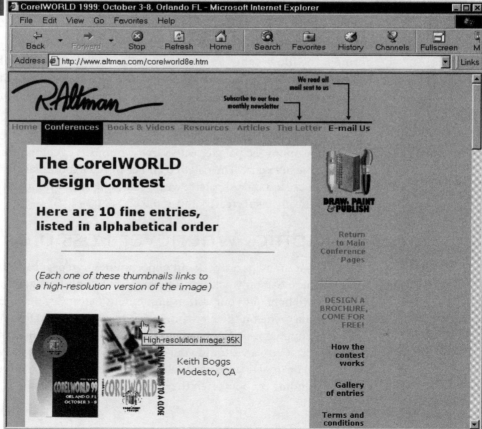

FIGURE 22.10

Responsible Web design includes making large photos an option rather than a required download. If you don't want to download it, don't click on it.

Can You Achieve Absence of Ugliness?

We turn once again to the words of our lead author:

> *I make no bones about it: I am an amateur designer. I do not have formal schooling in the arts, and I don't believe I have any true feel or natural flair for creating eye-catching designs.*
>
> *Once in a while I get there by accident, but most of the time, I spend my creative energy trying to get my point across with a design that doesn't get in the way. I try to avoid being ugly.*

Unfortunately, for our lead author and others like him, the World Wide Web is dreadfully fertile ground for ugliness. Consider the following:

- Learning HTML is much easier than learning other languages.
- There are very few limits on the use of graphics or color.
- You can place an HTML file on the Web with very little effort.

So what can we do to avoid being ugly? Here are some points to ponder.

Don't Overtool

The majority of sins on the Web are ones of commission, not omission. Most come from trying to do too much, usually for no other reason than because it is possible. This dynamic works on the aesthetic level as well as the technical level. While the overdesigned Web site is as common as the computer crash, plenty of well-designed Web sites are ruined by the temptation to build in too much functionality. Frames… image maps…multiple navigation tools…search engines…indexes…tables of contents. Most sites don't need all of these tools, but when a Web builder learns about them, it's irresistibly tempting to place them into service.

There are some sites that really need multiple levels of navigation aids. But let's face it, many sites, perhaps most, don't need all of the infrastructure that they offer. We recommend the one-one-one rule of thumb:

- Use one graphic-based navigation tool as a central design element.
- Use one text-based navigation tool for ease and swiftness of navigation.
- Use one other navigation tool for quick access to a special place, be it back to the top of the site, to an index, or to a page with a special product, offer, or announcement.

If you can show off the technology within that constraint, you will have scratched your gee-whiz itch, and at the same time very likely will have achieved absence of ugliness.

PART

Drawing for Cyberspace

Resist the "Because It's There" Syndrome

Do you remember the first time you were embarrassed by a computer? Our lead author does.

> *I created an advertisement in the 1985 version of Ventura Publisher and placed three solid lines below the headline. It was ugly. U-G-G-L-L-Y. Why did I do it? Because as I was investigating the dialogs, I noticed that the Ruling Line Below dialog supported the creation of up to three rules and a thickness of up to 12 points.*
>
> *If it could do it, I had to do it. I fell victim to the "Because It's There" syndrome: use of a feature based on availability, not need or appropriateness.*

The Web is full of opportunity to succumb to this dreaded disease, with the following zingers lurking behind every cybercorner.

Stop the Music   Did you know that one of the elements you can define as a background is a WAVE or MIDI file? When the background loads, a song or other sound plays. This would be mildly tolerable if the browser knew to only play the sound once for each visit to the site, but it doesn't. Instead, any time you refresh the page or return to it after visiting another page, it plays again. One colleague used a WAVE file of Daffy Duck saying, "This time, you push a button." This was very clever and amusing…the first time. But to hear it every time you hit the page is enough to compel you to rip the sound card out of your PC. And don't forget, a 45KB WAVE file (which would be a very small snippet of sound) requires just as much download time as a 45KB graphic.

We are not making a blanket condemnation against the use of sound, but if you have designed a page that is likely to serve as a frequent landing point (like many home pages), remember that any sound embedded on that page will play every single time that a visitor returns to it.

Eat at Joe's   When you see a scrolling banner on a Web site, does it not remind you of that time a few decades back when you first saw a bi-plane flying over the coastline with a trailing sign telling us all to buy a truck, listen to 103.7, or yes, eat at Joe's? Like the use of sound, a scrolling banner can be an effective way to announce a genuinely significant event that would interest visitors to your site. Microsoft used a scrolling banner to announce the introduction of Office 2000. It included the number of copies that had been sold that day. That was an impressive use of a scrolling banner because it got the point across while also providing potentially interesting information.

Many times, however, scrolling banners feel more like the old bi-planes with that schlocky message about something we should buy. If you consider the use of a scrolling message, make sure it conveys properly the value of your product or service as well as your image as a marketer.

You Are Visitor No. 5!

Why is it so important for Web sites to advertise their traffic? We can think of two reasons: to show potential advertisers the value of sponsoring the site, and to tell us how much company we have. Okay, fair enough—we'll set aside the fact that jimmying these meters is easier than rebooting a computer. So now the question is this: Why is it so important for these same sites to notify us in the most ghastly and ostentatious way? Why must it be done at headline size and with ornate graphics flanking both sides of a digital odometer that looks like it belongs on a billboard?

The height of embarrassment, of course, is when these obnoxious announcements tell us that we are the fifth visitor to this site since its inception 10 months ago.

Read This, Read This, Read This, Read This

There is no polite way to say this, so we're just going to say it. If you create a page with blinking text, you deserve to have a virus eat your hard drive.

The Whole World Is Watching

As we conclude this chapter and this part of the book devoted to the World Wide Web, we must make one parting admonition. When you experiment with Web designs and you place them on your server, you are essentially practicing in public. We have addressed the pros of the Web's immediacy; this is one of the cons. It is so easy to publish on the Web that you have to guard against displaying pages that are not yet ready. You need a tangible checklist for completing projects:

- Are your pages as well written as they can be?
- Do they use graphics appropriately and as efficiently as possible?
- Do they require hardware that your target audience is likely to have?
- Are you sure that your pages will open quickly enough when they are placed on the Web?
- Have you chosen an effective background? Is there sufficient contrast? If the page has a lot of text, have you considered black text on a white background?
- Have you avoided ugliness by playing it safe when in doubt?
- And once again for good measure, are your thoughts and ideas communicated as effectively as possible?

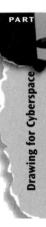

PART

Drawing for Cyberspace

Until all of these conditions are met, your pages should remain in your laboratory, not on the Web. Start by building them on the PC that you are most comfortable working on. If possible, move your pages to a lesser machine, like a notebook with limited resolution and colors. The next step is to place them on your Web server (whether it is on a local machine or the one that houses your Web site at your Internet Service Provider). But don't locate them where the public can see them yet. Create a private directory whose name nobody else knows. Connect to the Internet and browse to that private directory to see how your pages look and how quickly they open.

Now you are ready to place your Web pages in their rightful homes. Now you are ready to proudly represent your business in cyberspace.

PART VI

THE BITMAP ERA

THE BITMAP ERA IS HERE

Featuring

THE BITMAP ERA
IS HERE

t has crept up on all of us gradually. First, there was the desktop scanner that allowed DRAW users to integrate favorite photos into electronic artwork. Then there was DRAW's ability to import those same photos into vector-based projects. Soon thereafter, PHOTO-PAINT became more than a toy, forcing earnest DRAW users to take seriously the abilities of a professional-grade image-editing program. And now, with a slew of new special effects generously lifted from PAINT and dropped right on DRAW's menu line, CorelDRAW 8 and 9 have become even more powerful. This chapter explores the capabilities available to you within DRAW that previously required a trip to PAINT.

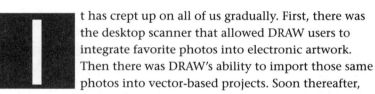

NOTE   This chapter focuses on the Bitmaps menu and the special effects that can be applied to bitmap images within DRAW. For an exploration into PHOTO-PAINT, see the next two chapters, and for information about importing and exporting bitmaps, see Chapters 29 and 30. Finally, bitmap graphics are an integral component of World Wide Web pages, and for that we refer you back to Part V, "Drawing for Cyberspace."

Why Bitmaps?

There was a time when DRAW users disparaged bitmap images because of their potential lack of fidelity when compared to vector-based objects (see the Introduction for a synopsis of the difference between bitmap and vector objects). And indeed, it's true that bitmap images, such as scanned photographs or the screen renderings of this book, are created at a fixed resolution, and no amount of coaxing will make a 72dpi screen shot look any better when it is printed on a 600dpi printer. One of the values of vector objects is their ability to print at low resolution one minute and ultra-high resolution the next. They are programmed to do their mathematical gyrations and produce themselves at the highest fidelity possible.

But in the case of bitmap images, we would argue that the glass is half-full, not half-empty. One of the intrinsic values of bitmap images is that they are *not* capable of changing themselves. They are fixed, set in stone, destined to look the same regardless of the output device (allowing for the obvious, of course, like printing to a color printer and then a black-and-white printer).

This can pay off in huge dividends for you, and we'll share with you a production experience we had with this book. Figure 23.1 shows one of our experiments: three photographs overlaid one on top of the other—each with decreasing degrees of transparency—and then a string of transparent text on top. Because each layer of objects carries an intricate set of instructions on how to render the objects underneath, this became an extraordinarily complex drawing.

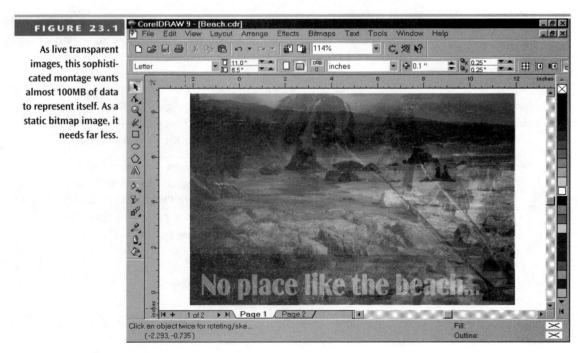

FIGURE 23.1

As live transparent images, this sophisticated montage wants almost 100MB of data to represent itself. As a static bitmap image, it needs far less.

At first, we created this graphic in the usual way—by creating an encapsulated PostScript file. In so doing, DRAW studied all of those complex instructions and created the code necessary to display this labyrinth of overlaying transparent graphics. When it was done, the .eps file measured over 96MB!

That seemed like quite a bit of code for a graphic that was ultimately going to be rendered in 8-bit grayscale, not 32-bit color. DRAW's EPS Export dialog has an option to render full-color bitmap images as grayscale, and that did take the file down almost in half. Still, that was too much.

This struck us as the perfect opportunity to test-drive DRAW's bitmap controls, so we converted the entire graphic to a bitmap. Instead of having a group of objects, each of which contained all of those sophisticated instructions, we converted them to one composite image that represented how they looked at that particular moment. In other words, we converted a very smart graphic into a collection of stupid dots. But don't misunderstand: stupid is good; stupid is exactly what we wanted. We had already created the picture; now we just wanted to freeze it and render it. Here are the essential statistics:

Type of File Exported	Size of EPS File
Original image	96MB
Converted to CMYK bitmap	25MB
Converted to RGB bitmap	19MB
Converted to grayscale bitmap	7.5MB

To render the image for this book, we got away with under 8MB, instead of 96MB.

From Vector to Bitmap

On the subject of format conversion, the world still waits for the miracle of bitmap-to-vector conversion. Despite the best efforts of tracing programs, like the OCR-TRACE module in the CorelDRAW box, taking a collection of clueless dots and converting them into intelligent shapes remains equal parts art, science, and black magic. But converting in the other direction is cake: reducing intelligent shapes into a morass of dots is one of the easier tasks you can give to DRAW.

To see this for yourself, create any simple shape, like the fountain-filled ampersand shown in Figure 23.2. As a character of text, DRAW identifies this object very efficiently. It tracks its nodes, its shape, its kerning information (were there to be a character beside it) and its fill pattern, all according to numeric values.

But when you convert it to a bitmap image, DRAW is only concerned with what color and what size to render all of the dots that will team up to make you think you are looking at an ampersand.

PART

6

The Bitmap Era

FIGURE 23.2

DRAW relies on color
and resolution to
convert images from
vector to bitmap.

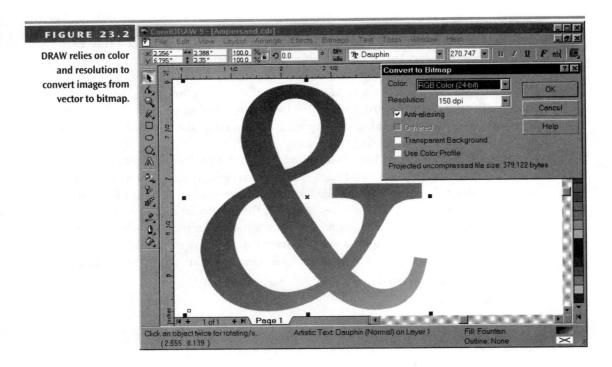

Resolution and Color

As Figure 23.2 shows, the Convert to Bitmap command offers several options, and the two key questions are resolution and color depth. Here, the ampersand is being converted into a 150dpi bitmap, meaning that each "screen dot" will be 1/150 of an inch tall and wide. This is in contrast to the "printer dot," which is dependent upon the actual output device (1/300 for a standard laser printer, 1/600 for a modern laser printer, and 1/1200 and smaller for film-making equipment). This topic is a constant source of confusion for all but the more advanced users of graphics software. Suffice it to say that if an object is going to be rendered only in terms of dots, the software needs to know what size to make those dots. The larger each dot, the less opportunity there is to render detail; the smaller the dot, the more opportunity and the larger the file size.

The second question is the number of colors that will be used to render the object, and in the case of this rainbow-filled character, it is the more urgent one. Theoretically, millions of colors would be needed to traverse from the dark northern regions of this character to the lighter shades in the south. If converted to a 24-bit (or 16-million color) image, most human eyes would not be able to tell the difference between the original and the bitmap. But as soon as you drop down to 256 colors, you are asking

DRAW to render this pattern with fewer colors than it needs to do the job correctly. And if you were to convert this to a 16-color bitmap, the results would be more hilarious than useful.

Dithering

If you intend to convert a full-color object into a bitmap with 256 colors or fewer, DRAW gives you the opportunity to cheat. In the world of color, cheating is referred to as *dithering*. It describes the process of approximating colors that don't exist in the current palette. In the case of the ampersand, you would need more colors than 256 to smoothly depict the color shifts that take place. If you tried to render it at 256, the result would be a blunt transition between colors that would not do the image justice. Dithering is kind of like airbrushing—it glosses over the colors at their edges so that your eye is fooled into seeing a smoother transition. It is a mere illusion, and a close look will show how dithering is nothing more than a clever scrambling of dots.

Figure 23.3 illustrates this with two conversions of our ampersand to 16-color bitmaps. The same amount of colors are present in each, but by infusing the lower one with white pixels and interspersing the other 16 colors, the illusion exists of more colors present. The magnified portion shows how the trick is performed, with lighter and darker colored pixels sprinkled about.

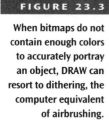

FIGURE 23.3

When bitmaps do not contain enough colors to accurately portray an object, DRAW can resort to dithering, the computer equivalent of airbrushing.

PART

6

The Bitmap Era

We're not trying to imply that either of these images looks very good—imposing a 16-color palette on this nice fountain is a misdemeanor at least. Dithering is a last resort, needed only when you are stuck with palettes well below 256 colors, which is, hopefully, very infrequent.

Backgrounds

The other option in the Color section determines how the background is to be handled. Normally, when DRAW converts an object to a bitmap, it defines a rectangular area (a "bounding box") for that shape and treats that area as the object. As Figure 23.4 shows, this can create undesirable results. The top ampersand has been converted to a bitmap with a visible background. The lower one was converted with the Transparent Background option checked, producing much better results. We suspect that you will want your background transparent more often than not, and recommend turning this option on as your default. Once you check it, it remains checked until you say otherwise.

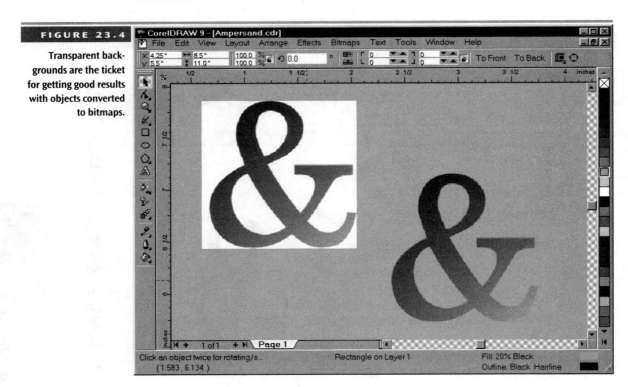

FIGURE 23.4

Transparent backgrounds are the ticket for getting good results with objects converted to bitmaps.

Anti-aliasing

A second cousin to dithering, the anti-aliasing process seeks to remove jagged edges from bitmaps, and is most noticeable at lower resolutions. Anti-aliasing is covered at length throughout Part V, "Drawing for Cyberspace."

From Bitmap to Bitmap

Vector objects aren't the only things that can be converted to bitmaps from within DRAW. You can also convert bitmaps to bitmaps. In other words, you can take an existing bitmap and change it into another kind of bitmap.

We found this to be extremely handy throughout the production of this book, as we took many pictures of the DRAW screen. Our video adapters are set for 24-bit color or higher, but the pages of this book are all black, white, and gray. So once we captured an image and pasted it into a drawing, we quickly converted it from 24-bit color to 8-bit grayscale. We estimate that this procedure saved over 500MB of storage space, without sacrificing quality at all. Here are the menu choices that come alive when you select a bitmap image.

Edit Bitmap

While DRAW can now wield considerable control over your bitmaps, it cannot actually add, remove, or change their pixels. For that, you would need to return to PHOTO-PAINT or your preferred image-editing program. This menu choice loads PAINT and opens the bitmap image in it.

Crop Bitmap

This takes the idea of cropping one step further than DRAW normally does. So for the sake of this discussion, there is cropping and there is CROPPING—the latter making the operation permanent, like the Trim command. As you may already know, you can crop a bitmap by using the Shape tool, but the area made invisible is still there, and you can bring it back by performing the reverse procedure with the Shape tool.

Once you crop a bitmap, you can CROP a bitmap by going to Bitmap ➤ Crop Bitmap. It chops away the unseen parts, leaving you with a smaller bitmap.

Trace Bitmap

This new command is a direct hook into CorelTRACE, the venerable auto-tracing application. When you invoke it, TRACE works on a copy of the graphic, and

PART

6

The Bitmap Era

automatically saves the vectorized version when you close it and return to DRAW. TRACE adds a few nice touches, like the Mosaic effect shown here:

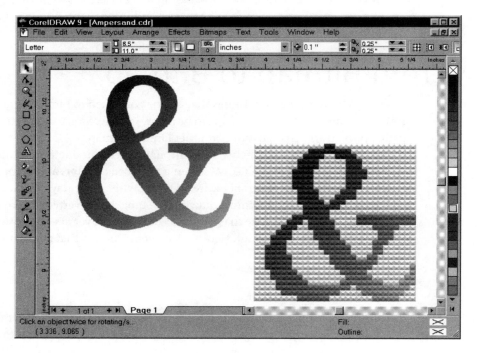

Resample

This term refers to the process by which DRAW changes the size or the resolution of a selected bitmap. You have probably heard the warning against grabbing the selection handles of a bitmap and arbitrarily sizing it. When you perform that seemingly innocuous task, you are asking DRAW to do something that it is fundamentally incapable of doing—fiddling with the size of the pixels that make up the image. (Remember, once you create a bitmap, the size of its dots is fixed. Scaling the bitmap doesn't change the resolution, it only distorts the placement of the dots.)

Resampling is the responsible way to size bitmap images. You can resize the bitmap by absolute values or by percentages, and as you do it, DRAW automatically corrects for any possible distortion that would have occurred had you merely sized the image on screen.

As you can see in Figure 23.5, you have an anti-aliasing option. The Maintain Original Size option forces the bitmap to remain at its original size, even if you ask for a change in resolution. Finally, checking Maintain Aspect Ratio is a must, unless you intentionally want to create a distortion.

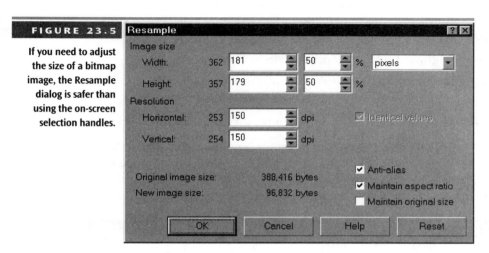

Sampling a bitmap down in size or resolution is generally a safer course to take than sampling up. It is better to create your bitmap too big, with too much resolution or too many colors, and then sample down.

Mode

This used to be called the Convert To command, and we think that had more flair than Mode. This menu provides you with all of the available color depths to which a selected image can be converted. You can also use this flyout to determine the current value of a bitmap by looking for the choice that is grayed out. The Mode command only adjusts color depth. For changes in size or resolution, return to Resample.

Inflate Bitmap

Added in DRAW 8, this command allows you to change the size and aspect ratio of your bitmap graphics. The dialog shows you the original size of the object and gives you the choice of inflating by a percentage or to a particular size. This is a valuable command any time an effect increases the size of the bitmap. Prior to having this command, the effect would get clipped off, and this angered a whole lot of users who were becoming enamored with drop shadows. This command simply accounts for the increase (the inflation) of the bitmap's shape when certain effects are applied to it.

PART

The Bitmap Era

Bitmap Color Mask

This docker allows you to make specific colors transparent (or to "mask out" specific colors—hence its name) in a bitmap image. It is particularly helpful in removing unwanted backgrounds. The process is quite easy with a bit of practice:

1. Select a bitmap image and open the Bitmap Color Mask docker.
2. Click the Eyedropper on the docker and move out to the image.
3. Click on a certain color of the image.
4. Click Apply and watch that color, and any other similarly colored pixels, disappear.

With the Tolerance slider, you can determine how exacting to be. In the image below, we changed the fountain fill to a radial fill, so when DRAW masks out a particular color, it searches the entire graphic for other pixels. In this case, all similar pixels lay in a circle.

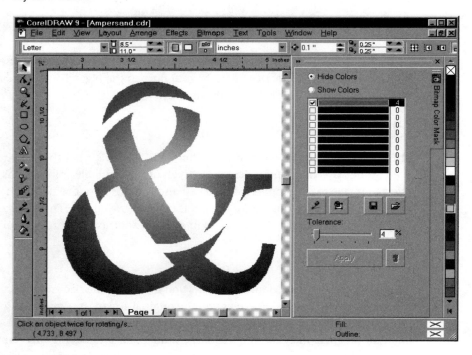

Resolve Link/Update from Link

DRAW 9 can import bitmaps by reference—in other words, it will not swallow them up within the .cdr file, but instead keep them external. You'll find this option on the Import dialog. Resolve is another word for *embed*—it takes the externally linked bitmap and makes it an internal graphic. Update goes out and checks for a newer version of the file.

Importing a bitmap by reference is terrific if several drawings use a logo that is subject to change. Change the external graphic and then update the drawings—much easier than deleting and reimporting. The Link Manager will show you a list of all external graphics and provide various tools for keeping them organized and current.

Those Wild and Crazy Effects

Tread lightly, dear readers—you're about to once again enter the CorelDRAW Danger Zone. The Danger Zone is the place where unsuspecting users destroy perfectly good drawings with overproduced and purposeless special effects. The Danger Zone now has one more entrance: the bitmap effects. While we could probably write an entire book on these effects, we will resist the temptation, just as you should resist using them when not appropriate.

Taking over the entire lower half of the Bitmaps menu, these effects will be familiar to PHOTO-PAINT users, who have had access to them for years. Corel's engineers have ported most of them to DRAW, and you can apply them to any bitmap image.

Keeping in mind our repeated warnings about life in the Danger Zone—not to mention the prospect of being arrested for high crimes against a sitting president—follow along with us as we have a bit of fun with a photo of our country's leader. Here is the original photo.

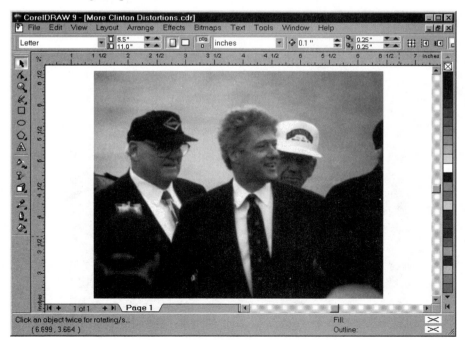

PART

6

The Bitmap Era

A bit fuzzy, but we'll get to that later. Here's a sampling from each category. Oh, and we performed an Undo after each one of these.

1. Choose Bitmaps ➤ 3D Effects ➤ Emboss.

2. Bump the Level up to about 150.

3. OK the dialog.

1. Choose Bitmaps ➤ Art Strokes ➤ Pastels.

2. Choose Oil and OK.

T I P   Each dialog has a Preview button, and by default, the previews work on the actual image, not a little window. If you want to use a preview window (for better performance), click the two small icons next to the Help and Close icons at the top-right of each dialog. The lock next to the Preview button forces the preview to be interactive, eliminating the need to click it after each adjustment. Finally, these effects are not cumulative within one session with a dialog. If you preview five different effects, the prevailing effect will be the one set before you say OK. If you then re-enter an Effects dialog, the effect *will* be cumulative.

1. Choose Bitmaps ➤ Blur ➤ Radial Blur.
2. Click the centering button (the one with a cursor and a plus) and click on President Clinton's face.
3. Set a blur amount of 25.
4. OK the dialog.

1. Choose Bitmaps ➤ Color Transform ➤ Psychedelic.
2. Set the Level to 220.
3. OK the dialog.

PART

The Bitmap Era

1. Choose Bitmaps ➤ Contour ➤ Edge Detect.
2. Set Color to Black and Sensitivity to 5.
3. OK the dialog.

1. Choose Bitmaps ➤ Creative (as if the others aren't?) ➤ Weather.
2. Set Forecast to Snow.

3. Set Strength to 15 and Size to 10.

4. OK the dialog.

 TIP Each of the Effects dialogs has a small triangle in the top-left. Click it and all of the other effects on the Bitmaps menu will drop down. This makes it easy to experiment with different types.

1. Choose Bitmaps ➤ Distort ➤ Ripple.

2. Set the Period and Amplitude both to 65.

3. Set the Angle to 0.

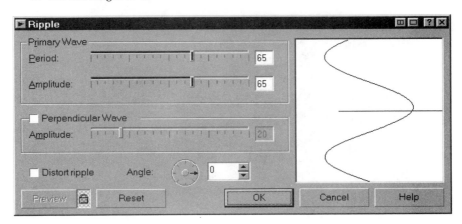

PART

The Bitmap Era

4. OK the dialog. Notice how the ripple in the photo matches the graph in the dialog.

1. Choose Bitmaps ➤ Noise ➤ Add Noise.

2. Set Noise Type to Uniform.

3. Set Level and Density to 100.

4. OK the dialog.

1. Choose Bitmaps ➤ Sharpen ➤ Unsharp Mask

2. Set Percentage to 400.

3. Set Radius to 2.

4. OK the dialog. Compare this image with the original a few pages ago.

 N O T E   Unsharp? Say what?? This term is taken from traditional photography, whereby edges of an image are toned down (unsharpened) while other pixels are sharpened. DRAW and PAINT determine edges by looking for areas of high contrast. So the image is sharpened by toning down the edges. Oh, forget it…

When Soft Meets Hard

One of the ideal situations for using a bitmap effect is when you want to soften the look of an object, and the following exercise shows the creation of a simple logo that blends vector and bitmap elements.

This came about by accident when our lead author was working up a simple logo for a presentation focusing on the combined use of DRAW and PAINT. He wanted to show traditional tools for drawing and painting. We pick up the action midway through the first half, with the drawing tools already in place (you can follow along

by downloading `Bitmap Logo.cdr` from the companion page of the Sybex Web site). Figure 23.6 shows the starting point, and there you can see:

- A background created from one of DRAW's Bitmap patterns
- A collection of drawing tools taken from the CorelDRAW clipart library
- An ampersand embossed into the background (for details on how the embossed effect was created, see Chapter 10)
- And a paintbrush, also taken from the clipart library. The brush is actually two groups of objects—the handle and dry hairs are one, and the hairs with paint another.

FIGURE 23.6

Nothing here but us vector objects.

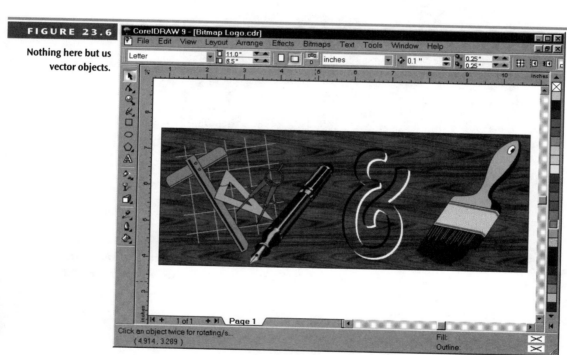

Now follow these steps:

1. With the first part of the paintbrush selected, go to Bitmaps ➤ Convert to Bitmap.
2. Choose 24-bit for the color depth, and 300 for the resolution.
3. Check Transparent Background and Anti-aliasing.
4. OK the dialog, at which point the paintbrush won't look much different (you have chosen high resolution and high color depth, so the paintbrush has maintained most of its original fidelity).
5. Repeat for the second part of the brush.

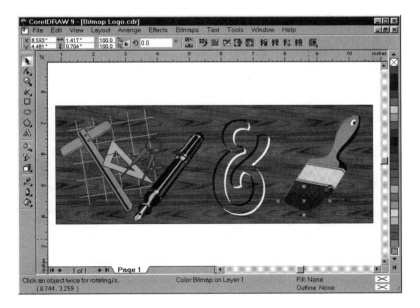

Notice how the status bar now identifies the paintbrush—as a color bitmap.

6. With the top part of the brush selected, go to Bitmaps ➢ Art Strokes ➢ Crayon.

7. Set Size to 10 and Outline to 25.

8. OK the dialog.

9. Repeat for the lower half of the brush.

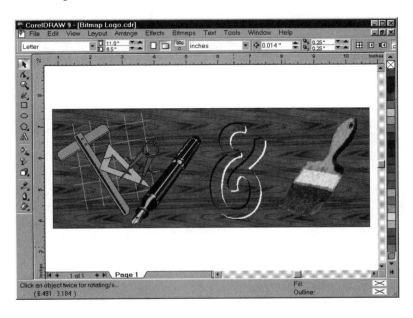

10. With the lower half still selected, go to Bitmaps ➤ Distort ➤ Wet Paint.

11. Set Wetness to about 42 and Percent to 100.

12. OK the dialog.

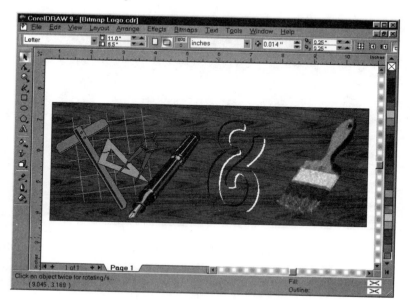

We note that the Wet Paint effect tends to shift the object a bit, so at this point you might have to nudge the lower part of the brush a bit, and you might have to move it to the front with Shift+PgUp. We decided to do so, and so our finished piece looked like this.

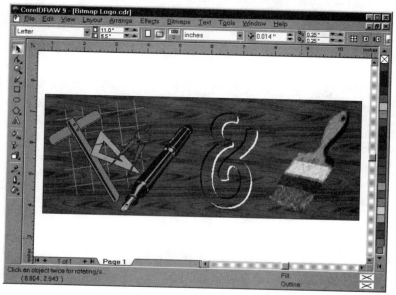

This use of bitmap effects works for two reasons. First, the effect is appropriate to the topic. The subject is a "painterly" seminar, so a painterly effect is in order. Second, the effect does not overwhelm the image. It is still clearly a paintbrush. It is very easy to apply effects that make the original object unidentifiable (witness the Ripple effect applied to our president).

The best way to learn DRAW's bitmap effects is to experiment with them and try them on for size, remembering all the while that you are driving right through the Danger Zone.

The Bitmap Era

An Introduction To Photo-Paint

Featuring

AN INTRODUCTION
TO PHOTO-PAINT

I f you are like most Corel users, you have spent a majority of your time in DRAW, watching with a mixture of eagerness, excitement, and fear as PHOTO-PAINT (that other program in the box) makes its move. First slowly, with a few good magazine reviews...then with more momentum, as talented drawing specialists try their hand at more painterly effects...and finally—how would Ross Perot describe it?—like a giant sucking sound funneling in users from all corners of the graphic community.

As we said in the previous chapter, the bitmap era is upon us, whether or not we are ready for it.

Why does PHOTO-PAINT evoke such a range of emotion? Because it is the closest thing to painting that electronic media knows, and painting is (gasp) real art. Drawing with vector objects is a different experience, and while not to imply that it is something less than art, the tools of its trade are rooted in mathematics and science, not paintbrushes and canvas. When you work in PAINT, you have ownership of every dot that makes up an image. One brilliant move and your painting shines. One false move, and it could be destroyed. Thank goodness for Undo...

We are at the same time delighted and guilt-ridden about offering these two chapters on PAINT. In previous editions we have ignored PAINT altogether, and in the face of such growing popularity, that is a literary capital offense. Yet, PAINT really needs a book all for itself. We are glad to reintroduce coverage of it here, but we will not pretend to do it justice.

Our quest is to expose you to the foundation and concepts that underlie PAINT, and the ways that you can use it to help you in your work. In continuing the theme of this book, we're not going to teach you fine art; you either have those skills or you don't, and either way, no book is going to help you. And we are not going to just throw a bunch of special effects at you. We flirted with that in the previous chapter, and all of the effects we showed you there (and more) are available from within PAINT.

However—and this is a large however—PAINT can perform a wealth of services outside of the "fine art" arena, and we will identify many of them in this chapter and the one that follows.

PAINT or DRAW?

Here is the most important fact to remember about the two programs:

> *CorelDRAW is vector-based and PAINT is pixel-based.*

Remember that and recite it like a mantra. While you can apply effects and filtering to bitmaps in DRAW, you wouldn't turn to it to work on pixels, and you wouldn't turn to PAINT to create typographically accurate text or other "smart" vector objects.

We have discussed in previous chapters the fundamental difference between vector- and bitmap-based applications, but it bears repeating here. A vector is a mathematical description of a curve or shape. Vector objects can be filled with a certain color and stroked with a certain line thickness. DRAW provides you with the tools to create and arrange vector objects as well as different methods of filling those objects with color.

A pixel is a solitary square of color. Pretty boring by itself, but you can make a grid of multiple pixels to create an image. The fun begins when you use the tools of PAINT to change the appearance of those pixels in ways that mimic traditional tools. "I used to spend a great deal of time using DRAW to create photo-realistic images," says Ron Richey, our resident PHOTO-PAINT expert. "But then I came to realize that my technique was too mechanical and didn't allow me to expressively follow my creative desires. I now use DRAW to plan and set up images that will ultimately be completed in PAINT."

The Many Faces of PAINT

What do you want to do with PAINT? If you can name it, you can probably do it. The only limitations you will encounter are your own because PAINT has the tools to create a veritable dream studio. Paper, pencils, pastels, oils, acrylics, canvases, watercolors, airbrushes, darkroom—they're all available on the PAINT desktop. PAINT offers you:

- A professional darkroom with a retouching assistant always on call. You'll find capabilities for image editing, collage, special effects, and other techniques that can't be done in a traditional darkroom.

- An art studio with pencils, pastels, oils, acrylics, watercolors, airbrushes, and a few tools unique to computer software, such as the Image Sprayer. If you've never sprayed an image before, you're in for a treat...

- Complete services for creating Web graphics.

- Many special effects such as drop shadows and theatrical lighting.

- Enough filters to make you go blind.

A Quick Tour of PAINT

The next chapter offers more detail about various PAINT tools and techniques. Here are some prominent ones that all users should know about, regardless of their level of artistic skill.

The Professional Darkroom

Do you like to restore old photographs? You can remove wrinkles, scratches, and dust, as well as discoloration and stains. Figure 24.1 is an old photo of our lead author's grandmother, and you can see how PAINT was able to restore it.

PAINT 9 offers several new sets of image-editing tools, including a very impressive set of all-in-one sharpening tools. There are so many ways to sharpen a photo (including one called "unsharp"—go figure), it takes an expert to know the difference. The Tune Sharpness dialog, shown in Figure 24.2, shows you previews of four sharpening functions at once, so you can better determine which one to use.

Channel operations wizards will be in ecstasy with "Split Channel To." HSB channels are only a distant fantasy for PhotoShop users, and that is only available on a Mac with a special plug-in. PAINT can split an image into component channels for RGB, HLS, YIQ, Lab, and CMYK, the latter shown in Figure 24.3. When you finish work on a particular channel, you can combine them back to their original state.

PART

The Bitmap Era

FIGURE 24.1

Photo retouching, compliments of PAINT's Clone tool

FIGURE 24.2

Sharpening a photo is often black magic, but the new Tune Sharpness dialog helps.

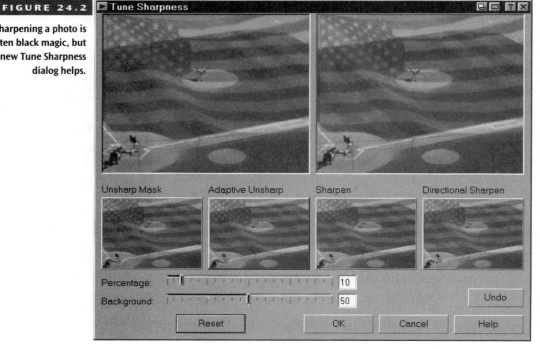

The Art Studio

While someone like our Ron Richey would never give up the experience of learning a multitude of artistic tools while in art school, affording all of those tools is another matter. PAINT offers them all in one package. About the only extra hardware you are likely to need is a drawing tablet—while driving DRAW with a mouse is plausible, creating in PAINT requires a more precise instrument. And with said instrument in hand, you can really let your imagination go. Here is a sampling.

Spraying Images

Once you create an image, you don't need to keep creating it over and over. You can create an *image list,* and then *spray* an image. On the following page, for instance, is an image list for creating snowflakes.

PART

The Bitmap Era

And then by using this list, "spraying" the following artistic backdrop was simple.

"After painting a zillion trees," says Richey, "I finally figured out that I could paint just six or seven as individual objects, select the whole bunch of them, and then save them as an image list. Suddenly, creating a forest takes five minutes."

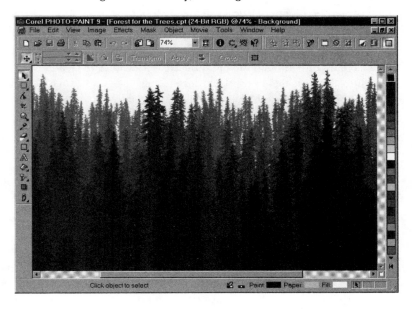

Once you get going, there's no end to the ideas you can come up with. What, you have to create a creepy background for an Indiana Jones story board that features a heaving mass of little crawlies? Don't run off to Industrial Light and Magic just yet.

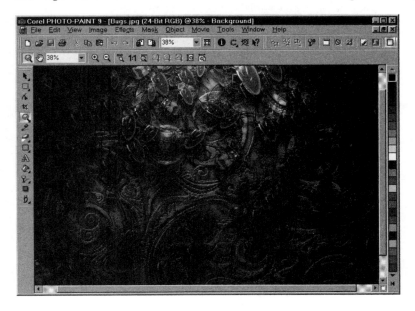

PART

The Bitmap Era

Thinking Laterally

While Chapter 25 is quite practical, we asked Mr. Richey to get a bit ethereal about his use of PHOTO-PAINT. Here is what he had to say…

A solitary skill (like pencil sketching) can achieve great results up to a point. But the artist who adds to his or her repertoire of skills is able to synthesize creations that are always greater than those created by artists possessing an insular (or singular) technique. I characterize these two ways of thinking as vertical and lateral.

Artists who desire only to learn a step-by-step process to re-create a specific effect, like a neon glow around neon light shaped letters, are vertical thinkers. Vertical thinking and vertical techniques tell you that a screwdriver is only used for driving screws into blocks of wood and that the neon effect is only for electric neon signs. Instead, try thinking laterally—look at each technique as a basic skill that can be used in infinite ways. With lateral thinking, the neon technique allows you to apply luminous qualities to any image you wish to create.

A great number of graphic and commercial artists learn specific, step-by-step methods without making an intuitive leap that sees that method being applied to something new. In other words, synthesis. The successful artist is a person who successfully manipulates symbols in such a way that the intended viewer of the image will make a predictable response. That person must be a master of both the message and the medium.

What can you accomplish with PAINT 9 and lateral thinking?

- Instead of creating an image as a flat layer while at the same time carefully trying to avoid mistakes and countless Undo commands, use objects to their fullest potential. You can even create a copy of your entire image, floating as a separate object above or below the one you want to apply an effect to.

- One of the biggest vertical thought traps with most PAINT users is that crazy rodent they use for drawing. A tablet is too expensive you say? Spend five hours creating a custom mask with a mouse and ask yourself that question again. Don't tell yourself that tablets are only for fine artists. Replace your mouse with a tablet and you'll discover a thousand other things you never knew you could do. I dare you to prove me wrong.

- There is more than one way to create a mask or selection. Very few PAINT users know the difference between the Scissors Mask tool, Magic Wand Mask tool, and the Lasso Mask tool. Do you?

Continued on next page

- And they are not the only way to create a selection. Why not just paint a mask with any of PAINT's artistic brushes? Also, masks and selections can be altered and fiddled with in any manner you can imagine as well as many ways you never dreamed of.

- How much do you use keyboard shortcuts? Have you tried customizing yet? I hate programs that don't offer shortcuts for the most basic of tools. I'm even more surprised when I find artists who refuse to use shortcuts for the strangest reasons (any reason not to use a shortcut is strange). PAINT users can change every last keyboard command to their heart's desire and even create new ones for menu commands without any. Add powerful and fully editable scripting to the mix and look out!

Surviving PAINT

While Ron will likely pooh-pooh the tone of the next chapter, that provides a good yin-yang dynamic for our treatment of PHOTO-PAINT. For those who have had the privilege of seeing Ron present his work at the annual CorelWORLD User Conference, you undoubtedly came away with a happy case of Easy-itis. As most professionals can do with their crafts, he makes his look so easy. And what's more, he'll insist that it is easy for you, too.

Well, we wish we could agree. For the unenlightened (like your lead author, and the others on the writing team), learning PAINT is—to use Ron's metaphor—a vertical experience. We learn all we can about a particular function, in the hopes that we can recognize the next time we need to use it and remember how. Maybe one of these years, we'll come to realize how that tool fits into the overall scheme of PHOTO-PAINT expertise, but we'll settle for learning how the darn thing works. With apologies to Ron, we think that most PAINT novices approach the software that way, and so that's the way we'll cover it in the next chapter.

In the upcoming chapter, we will uncover what we believe are the essential functions and skills that must be learned in order to use the program effectively. Once you do—once you learn them vertically—then you can spread your wings.

PART 6

The Bitmap Era

chapter 25

PHOTO-PAINT SURVIVAL SKILLS

Featuring

CHAPTER 25

PHOTO-PAINT
SURVIVAL SKILLS

W e need to begin this chapter by reiterating our mea culpa from Chapter 24. PHOTO-PAINT cannot be covered in two chapters. We know PHOTO-PAINT authors who claim that it cannot be covered in an entire book! We could lie and claim that this chapter is the authority on PAINT, and with it, you will learn all that there is to know about the program, but then you'd get mad at us and we wouldn't be able to sleep at night.

The safe alternative is to tell you exactly what we hope to do with this chapter, and what we won't attempt with it.

This chapter will not try to:

- Turn you into painters and fine artists.
- Teach you about gratuitous special effects.
- Pretend to be able to tackle the sophisticated issues surrounding equalization, tone curve, or gamma, to name a few.

This chapter will attempt to:

- Identify the essential skills and techniques that all PAINT users should know.
- Help you with simple clean-up jobs, like cropping, color replacements, and cloning.
- Make it easier for you to get in and out quickly by creating a friendlier work environment.
- Give you a good handle on masking and creating objects.

As with DRAW, PHOTO-PAINT is not just a medium for professional artists—it can also be a very handy technician's tool. That will be the focus of this chapter, and we have chosen four topics that we think represent the requisite skills for effective use of PAINT.

Converting Images

We could retire if we were paid a nickel for every graphic project we encountered that included a gorgeous full-color photograph…but was printed in black and white. Or the fabulous image embedded in a PowerPoint presentation…ruined by the projector that could only muster standard VGA.

In the case of the former, the perpetration is merely wasted hard drive space, excessive use of system resources, and perhaps the risk of print failure. In the case of the latter, a project is ruined. In either case, PAINT can help you with an armament of conversion choices.

Figure 25.1 is a photo from Corel's collection—we picked it from the Cityscps folder on CD No. 3, and you can open it directly in PAINT to follow along. It is clear and has good contrast—making it suitable for a wide range of applications, including a full-color brochure, a budget-minded flier, a one-color book, and a Web site.

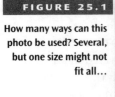

FIGURE 25.1

How many ways can this photo be used? Several, but one size might not fit all…

If you were to export this as a TIFF file, it would consume nearly 7MB of space—not at all unreasonable for a four-color photograph. Yet in the pages of a black-and-white book, that would be a waste. And if destined for an on-screen presentation with old equipment, you direly need to know how the image will reproduce with a smaller color palette.

The place to go for these answers is Image ➤ Mode. There, you will be presented with an entire menu of choices.

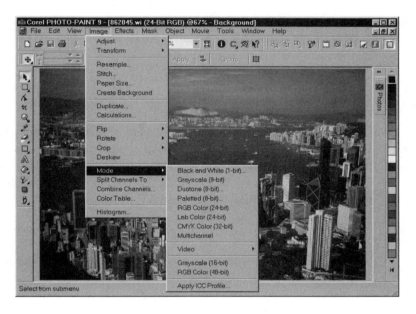

NOTE   Corel used to refer to these functions as Convert To, but in version 9, they are now under a menu called Mode. We liked the old name better...

Here are some of the conversions that DRAW and PAINT users commonly need to perform.

Grayscale

If you are creating an image for a one-color book, converting the image to grayscale could save you up to 10 times the disk, RAM, and RIP space. We converted our cityscape, and the resulting file was less than 700K.

In addition to digital economy, the other reason to convert the image would be to see how well the image fares with all of its color gone. Contrast is a tricky thing when you only have grays to work with, and some colors—red, most notably—will often

become very dark or very light. By converting the image ahead of time, you'll know if there are any trouble spots.

And the reason not to convert? If you want to use the same image in different media—like a book and a Web site—and you plan to create both from the same document. Then it's best to keep the image in 24-bit RGB and let the colors map to gray during imaging. It's still wise to perform a test conversion to check for contrast.

N O T E   PAINT 9 offers a 16-bit Grayscale choice, and images stored that way can be composed of 65,000 shades of gray, instead of the standard 256. It might be overkill, and your partnering software might not support it, so you'll want to experiment with this first.

Black and White

This stark treatment to a photo forces every pixel to be black or white. There are several patterns to choose from and various ways of determining which pixels become white and which ones become black.

As you can see below, you would never use this type of conversion when you intend to show detail of a photo, but for abstract work, it is a nice choice:

- It retains its identity—you still know what it is.
- Line art affords a generic quality to a photo.
- With nothing but white and black pixels, it will print or render to any device.
- It's tiny—only 86K in this case!

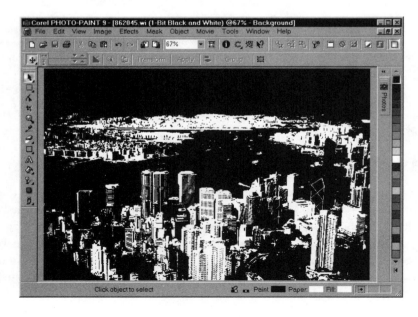

Duotone

This describes a process whereby an image is rendered with two different colors (three for a tritone, four for a quadtone). A duotone is quite unlike a conventional color photo, where certain pixels are colored differently to create the hues and tones of the image. It is closer to a grayscale image than a color image, and in fact, a duotone must start out as a grayscale image (PAINT 9 converts it for you automatically).

Think of a duotone as two identical copies of a single-color photo placed one atop the other. One is typically rendered in black and the other in a second spot color. You determine how each ink color is rendered by adjusting the *tone curve,* and PAINT does a good job of showing you the final result. This is an economical way of adding color to a budget-minded project.

Paletted

This describes an image whose color depth is controlled by a fixed palette, instead of by a virtually unlimited number of colors. Using any palette smaller than 16 million colors was once thought of as inferior, but today that is hardly the case. PAINT can create palettes made up of precisely the colors that are represented in an image, and can use dithering tricks to compensate for colors that fall outside the palette.

This is an excellent conversion choice when preparing files for the Internet or for out-of-date projection systems. While most Webmasters will create full-color JPEG files and not bother with palette reduction, if you face a requirement to create GIF files or otherwise limit your use of color to the 216 browser-friendly colors, you can make good use of this conversion choice.

Likewise, if you have to give a presentation in an auditorium with old equipment, you might think twice about using a full-color photo. Indeed, this photo would look pretty dreadful when displayed on a standard VGA monitor or projector.

PART

6

The Bitmap Era

However, with PAINT and its conversion to fixed palettes, you can at least try it out before conceding. And who knows, you might be able to apply a bit of dithering (the electronic equivalent of airbrushing) and make the photo acceptable.

The water and the sky are broken up, but otherwise, this photo holds up surprisingly well, considering that only 16 colors are being used to render it.

RGB

The default mode for new images, this renders images in the three colors (red, green, and blue) that computer monitors project.

PAINT 8 and 9 offer a 48-bit RGB mode, used mostly for precision scans. However, many devices do not support it, and that includes your monitor—you won't notice any difference on screen when viewing a 48-bit image.

Lab Color

The Lab color mode is a sophisticated color scheme designed to offer "device independence" to an image. A Lab-colored image contains the same color values when displayed on a monitor or printed to a printer or output device.

But as for what those color values are, you'll need a degree in something and we don't have it. To quote Corel's online Help: "The Lab color mode creates color based on luminance or lightness (L) and two chromatic components: 'a' and 'b.' The 'a' component consists of colors that range from green to red, and the 'b' component consists of colors that range from blue to yellow. You can use the Lab color mode to edit the luminance and color values of an image independently."

Aren't you glad you asked?

CMYK

If a photo is destined for film separations, it is best to describe the photo in terms of the four process colors that will be used by conventional printers. When you issue this conversion, the image will change on screen, as PAINT attempts to apply color-correction to the display image to more closely depict how the image will appear in print.

Multichannel

This is similar to making a color separation, except the software does it in real-time, not just in print-time. Applying this command to a photo converts to separate channels the various colors of the current model (red, green, blue for RGB; cyan, magenta, yellow, black for CMYK, etc.).

The images are converted to grayscale, and the shade of gray reflects the color values of the pixels in each channel. Just like when you separate for film.

Once separated into channels, you can view each channel from the Channels docker. Like DRAW, all dockers are listed at Window ➤ Dockers.

Searching and Replacing Pixels

We take for granted the find and find/replace commands in our word processor, but as writers, we'd be lost without them. DRAW can offer a Find and Replace function

PART

6

The Bitmap Era

because elements that you create in DRAW are objects with specific identities and properties. What about PAINT? All it has are colored pixels.

As it turns out, that's enough. And as with our word processors, finding one element and replacing it with another proves to be one of the most powerful and important of all capabilities. We use it all the time for cleaning up simple-colored images like computer screen images. It's not glamorous, we know, but it is oh-so valuable.

Figure 25.2 is a close-up of one of the screen images for this chapter, opened in PAINT. It shows a menu with several commands that are available, and a few that are grayed out. This is an interesting dilemma for us computer book authors—what to do with images that have grayed-out choices—and we confess to occasionally opening them in PAINT and magically bringing those commands to life. The alternative of restaging the screen exactly as it was is inconvenient and sometimes impossible.

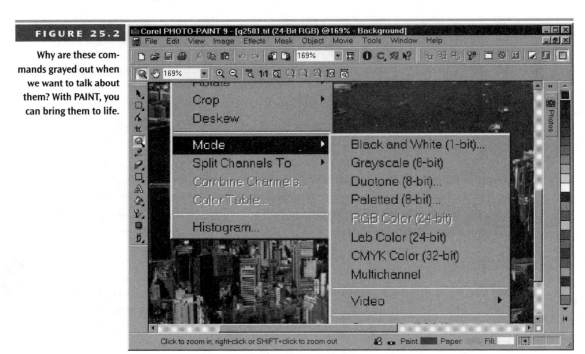

FIGURE 25.2

Why are these commands grayed out when we want to talk about them? With PAINT, you can bring them to life.

Identifying the Colors

The first step in this procedure is knowing how to identify the color you want to find and the color you want to replace it with, and PAINT does you no favors:

- You use the fill and the paper colors, which have little or nothing to do with searching for and replacing colors.

- In every version since 6, Corel's developers have seen fit to change the way you identify these colors on screen. They did it again for 9.

So remember this: Click, Ctrl+click.

That is the key to unlocking search and replace in PAINT. Click, Ctrl+click.

Commit it to memory. Write it down. Sing it in the shower. Ally McBeal enthusiasts should imagine John Cage telling the jury to say it out loud with him.

Click, Ctrl+click.

So what does your new mantra mean? It is the way you use the Eyedropper tool. It is the way you tell PAINT which colors you want it to find and with which color you want to replace it. Click, Ctrl+click.

To follow along, open DRAW, PAINT, or any program that has on-screen icons that are grayed out. Press Alt+PrtSc to take a picture of that application, switch to PAINT (if you're not already there), and go to File ➤ New from Clipboard. Then press Z and zoom in on a part of the screen that has grayed-out icons. As in DRAW, you can zoom out gradually with F3 and zoom to the entire image with F4, but the key for marquee-zooming is a plain old Z. (PAINT makes liberal use of one-key accelerator keys—we wish that DRAW used as many.)

Now follow these steps:

1. Zoom in as close as necessary to be able to click on the gray color of the unavailable icons.

2. Activate the Eyedropper tool from the toolbox, or by pressing E.

3. Carefully click on the gray part of the text or icon. Your status bar should indicate the color next to Paint.

The Bitmap Era

Note the Eyedropper tool clicking on the C in Channel. You have just defined the Paint color—the color that results if you use one of the drawing or painting tools. By definition, it is also the color that PAINT will seek out during a search and replace operation.

Now, what is the color you want in place of the gray? Answer: solid black, and ideally, this color is present somewhere in the image.

4. Find a patch of black in the image and Ctrl+click on it with the Eyedropper. As you do, the status bar will respond by setting the Paper color to black.

There it is—the Click, Ctrl+click. The click sets the find color and the Ctrl+click sets the replace color.

T I P   If the color you want to use as the replacement is not present in the image (meaning you cannot Ctrl+click on it to define it), double-click the Paper swatch on the status bar to invoke the Paper Color dialog. From there, you can dial in any color you want.

Using the Color Replacer

Defining the colors is the challenging part; replacing them is easy. You just smear across them, like this:

1. From the Undo Tools flyout (right below the Eyedropper tool), choose the Color Replacer tool. In the future, you can simply press Q, but in the future, don't ask us why color replacement is considered an undoing—we don't know.

2. From the property bar, set both Transparency and Soft Edge to 0 and disable Anti-aliasing. You don't want any ambiguity in this operation—you want to find every pixel that qualifies for replacement, and you want to replace it completely.

3. Set the size of the tool so it is comfortable to operate. You can do this interactively by holding Shift and moving the mouse up or down. You can also use the slider or the value box on the property bar.

4. Start dragging across the grayed-out area and watch how the pixels that are of the find color convert to the replace color.

You are halfway there. Now you need to remove the white pixels, or to say it more correctly, you need to turn the pixels that are white into the same color as the background.

   5. Switch back to the Eyedropper tool.

   6. Click on white and Ctrl+click on the gray background.

   7. Press Q to return to the Color Replacer tool and have at it.

Strategies for Successful Replacing

There is a technique to replacing colors effectively, and once you find your rhythm, you'll be able to move quickly. Here are some things to think about.

How Similar?

You can tell PAINT how particular you want it to be when it looks for colors to replace. For instance, you can tell it to find only pixels that are *precisely* the color that you defined, or ones that are close. The property bar offers a value box called Color Similarity, and you can either use the default of Normal or click HSB, which lets you set separate values for hue, saturation, and brightness. The lower the number, the more exacting PAINT is, and the higher the number, the more forgiving it is.

We like to play it safe and use a very low number. That means that we might have to make two passes over an area, if there are patches of pixels that are slightly different (like an area that has been anti-aliased), but we prefer that to the risk of changing pixels that we didn't mean to change.

Take Several Trips

When you are replacing, there will likely be nearby pixels that match the find color but are not supposed to change. In the examples above, the separator lines on the menu are the same color as the one we are seeking out, but they should not change.

It is inevitable that at some point you will accidentally pass over an area you didn't mean to and change pixels that were not supposed to change. The easiest way to correct this is to issue the Undo command, Ctrl+Z. But how does Undo know what to undo? It watches your mouse clicks, not your mouse motion—it will undo your most recent click-and-drag operation in its entirety. Therefore, it's a good idea to replace colors with lots of little click-and-drags, instead of one big one. That way, if you have to use Undo, you will only lose a bit of work.

Local Undo

If you did manage to make one little mistake in the middle of a very long replace operation, and you don't want to undo the entire thing, turn to Local Undo. The first icon in the Undo Tools flyout, Local Undo allows you to pick and choose parts of your last operation to undo. It won't go further back in time than the last operation, but its value is not in how far back, but just the opposite: you can undo specific portions of the last operation instead of simply all of it.

Comfortable Constraints

You can constrain the motion of the Color Replacer, and the other two Undo tools, by holding Ctrl. If you are moving along one axis, say vertically, and you want to switch to the other, press and hold Shift.

Clone: The Quicker Fixer-Upper

To the extent that PHOTO-PAINT is associated with photo restoration, you could make a good case that the most valuable tool in the program's arsenal is the one that speaks to that task.

PAINT does not have a Fix Scratches tool, per se; it is not yet intelligent enough to study a photo, identify where it has been marred, and fix it—although program developers speculate that such a feature is not out of the question.

Instead, the tool that contributes the most to photo restoration is the one that lets you take pixels from one part of the image and duplicate them elsewhere. It is called the Clone tool, and in so far as it can repair visible scars and flaws, you would do well to think of it as a grafting tool: it takes good skin and places it over bad skin.

Figure 25.3 is a photo of our lead author's younger daughter, and it is in peril, with a big scratch across it. But because there are other areas of the photo that have the same colors and tones as the damaged area, there is hope. You can graft from the good areas—you can clone.

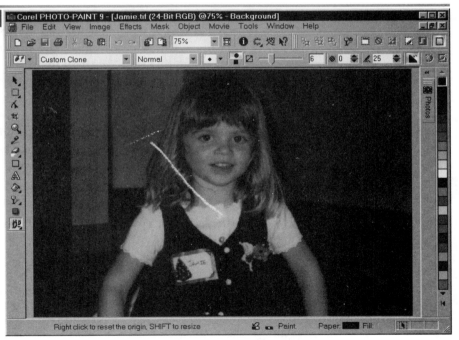

FIGURE 25.3

Jamie was wounded in this photographic mishap, but we can repair her...we have the technology.

The Clone tool has some similarities to the Color Replacer tool:

- There are pixels that get changed and pixels that determine the color to change to.
- You click and drag to effect these changes.

- Settings on its property bar determine how the cloning takes place and how drastic the action is.

As with PHOTO-PAINT in general, we won't quite do justice to the Clone tool, as there is considerable depth to its capabilities. But the points that we cover here represent the fundamentals of the tool.

 N O T E   You can download Jamie.tif from the companion page of the Sybex Web site to follow along.

Clone Fundamentals

Working the Clone tool involves little more than knowing your left button from your right. Any time you click the right button, you are defining the grafting position—the place where pixels will be taken from. A plus symbol (+) marks the spot on the screen. As you click and drag, pixels under the + are cloned at the cursor position (which will either be a circle or a square).

The important point to note as you experiment with this tool is that the + moves with you. As a result, you will need to regularly redefine the "clone from" position. So get used to right-clicking to place the +. This is both a benefit and an annoyance, and you will undoubtedly experience both during your time with the tool.

As with Color Replacer, you can use Undo to remove your last operation, so it pays to perform lots of little click-and-drags instead of one big one.

You can also choose between a circular or a square cursor (we find the circle is easier to dab with), and a host of other controls on the property bar. The drop-down list near the left of the property bar holds many preset configurations, but you can always work the various controls manually. The ones you will probably use the most are:

- Nib size (a fancy word for the cursor), which can be adjusted with the slider, the value box, or by holding Shift and clicking and dragging.

- Transparency, which paints transparent pixels atop the existing ones, the degree of which you set.

- Soft Edge, which controls the blending of pixels along the edges. This is generally more useful than Transparency.

Finally, cloning usually involves a lot of zooming, so familiarize yourself with the shortcuts for zooming:

F4	Full image
F2	Zoom in gradually
F3	Zoom out gradually
Z	Marquee-zoom

Repairing Jamie

Parts of this repair job will be easy, but other parts will be challenging. In almost all cases, the prevailing factor is the background: what is supposed to be behind the scratch?

Figure 25.4 is a close-up of the scratch, and we have divided it into four sections:

- The tip of the scratch at the top-left will be easy, because the background is diffuse, undefined, and insignificant.

- The part that goes through Jamie's hair will be much more difficult, because her hair is full of highlights and contours.

- Across her neck won't be as challenging as the hair, but imperfections will be more noticeable.

- Removing the scratch across her shirt shouldn't be difficult, but we'll need to be careful with the neckline and the subtle vertical stripes.

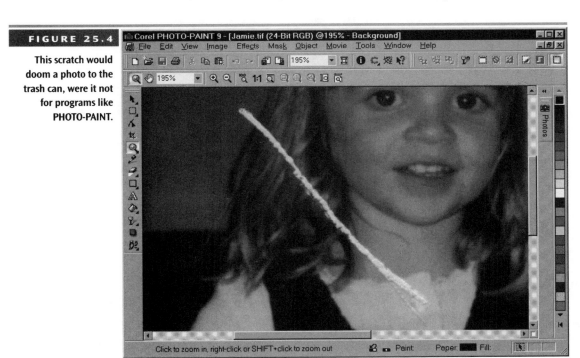

FIGURE 25.4

This scratch would doom a photo to the trash can, were it not for programs like **PHOTO-PAINT**.

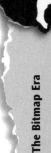

PART

The Bitmap Era

Start at the top-left, where you can get your feet wet with the easy part:

1. Zoom way in on the scratch.

2. Invoke the Clone tool by pressing C and move out to a point away from the scratch.

3. Set Transparency to 0, Soft Edge to about 25, and set the nib size to any size that feels comfortable to you.

4. Right-click the mouse to set the cloning position.

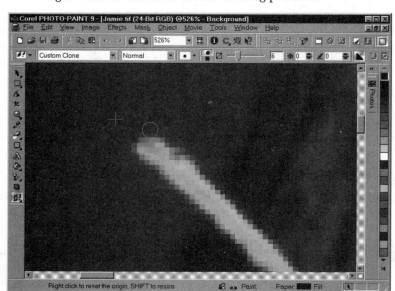

5. Now drag across the scratch. As you do, note the grafting action, and keep an eye on the +, to make sure that it remains in the background area. If it begins to intrude on Jamie's hair, or the scratch itself, reset it.

6. As you successfully clone a region, remember to release the mouse frequently, even if only to continue immediately where you left off. That makes undoing friendlier.

7. Work carefully as you approach Jamie's hair.

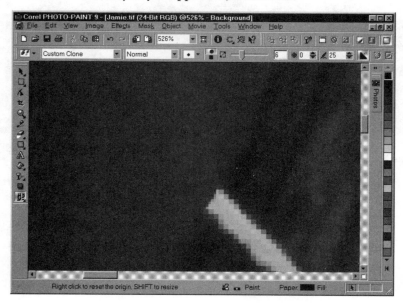

Repairing the hair requires that you define and then carefully follow the contours and the patterns of Jamie's locks. As you can see in the preceding images, there are rivers of color running down her hair, and that describes the course you will need to take as you paint cloned pixels across the scratch. Here goes:

1. Draw an imaginary line down one of the rivers, and place the + at the bottom of your imaginary line.

2. Set the nib size just a bit smaller than the width of the river, and increase the Soft Edge to about 50. You're not going to be able to replicate her hair perfectly—the Soft Edge is like a fudge factor.

3. Start cloning, moving your cursor *down* the river. It's important to keep the + in the river as you clone, otherwise, you'll start picking up pixels of a different color. As necessary, reposition the + as you proceed. When finished with the first river, your screen should look something like this.

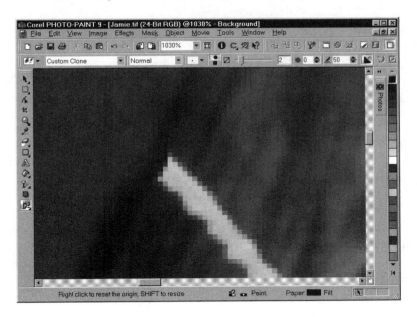

If some patches are too dark, you could increase the transparency and clone the area from lighter-colored pixels. If you find that you are creating small lines of color within the river, increase the size of the nib.

Continue through Jamie's hair—defining, plotting, and traversing through the rivers of color. Zoom and pan as necessary; position the + as necessary; undo as necessary; touch up as necessary. Figure 25.5 shows what our screen looked like after a first pass through her hair—it should be obvious to you where we had success and where we failed.

FIGURE 25.5

Some of Jamie's hair
was easy to clone,
while other parts
were trickier and left
some rough edges.

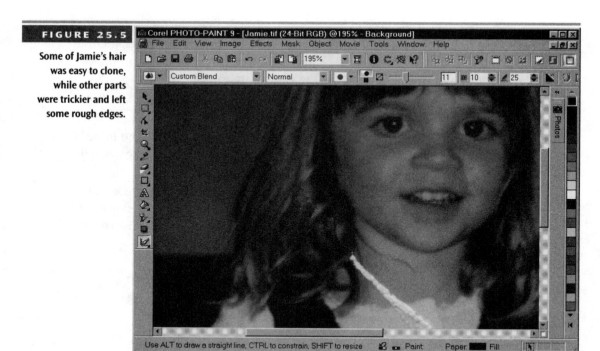

The left portion was much more defined, and we had a relatively easy time follow-ing rivers of color. But the part closer to her face has more curls, more abrupt color changes, and we couldn't find many rivers to help us clone. Now the photo doesn't look scratched; it looks folded and mutilated. (Make a note, to create a fold in a photo, use the Clone tool, and try to do a poor job...)

You could probably fix this with the Clone tool, by zooming in ever more closely, and cloning very small portions, and then painstakingly moving over by a tiny amount, continuing to clone tiny sections. But really, it's better to turn to another tool for the finishing touches. While clone can pick up pixels from another area, and while the Soft Edge setting can help smooth over edges with intricate and overlap-ping areas of color, it is ultimately a flawed proposition to weave old and new pixels together perfectly.

So it's best not to try. It's better to gloss over the entire area, and that is the job of the Blend tool. Blend mixes different colors to make the transitions between them less pronounced. Furthermore, that is the problem that we have with Jamie's hair—difficult transitions.

Two other of PAINT's tools sound as if they would be relevant here, as both Smear and Smudge address how colors interact. But we find that Smear *really* smears colors, and Smudge is often too subtle. Both are worth trying, but we predict that you'll choose Blend. Here's how you would use any of them:

1. From the Brush Tools flyout (the same one that houses Clone), choose the Effect tool.

2. From the Effects drop-down list on the property bar (far-left), choose the desired effect:

   - Smear, the top-left effect
   - Smudge, one to its right
   - Blend, lower-left

3. From the property bar, set the Amount to about 50 and the Soft Edge to about 75.

4. Then just work the area. Drag over it until you can't see the harsh edges—the places where it is obvious that you are looking at pixels, not hair. As before, do it in small steps, so you can use Undo.

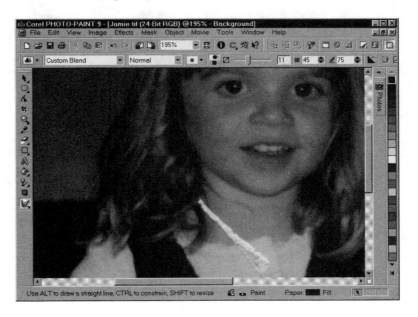

Better?

We spent about 15 minutes on the rest of the recovery process. We had to redirect one of the curls below Jamie's neck, but we're confident that she'll forgive us. And in the white shirt, it was virtually impossible to recreate the very subtle vertical strokes in the pattern, so we just smudged over it to suggest that the shirt is a bit wrinkled in that spot.

PART

The Bitmap Era

Figure 25.6 shows the finished image, sans scratch. How you judge the success of this process depends entirely upon your point of view. If you compare the photo to the original, expecting that they will look identical, except for the scratch, you will be less than satisfied. And if you study the area of the scratch, you will probably be able to see evidence of the cloning and blending.

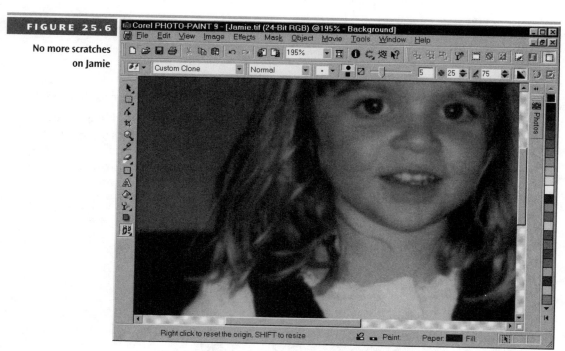

FIGURE 25.6

No more scratches on Jamie

But if you didn't know that the photo was scratched...if you had nothing to compare it to...if you were just looking at this photo on its own merits...you probably would never know that it was retouched.

Our lead author decided to embellish the photo by achieving that which he has otherwise been incapable: cleaning Jamie's face. So much for realism...

The Magic of the Mask

In Chapter 23, you saw a few of the many effects that can be applied to a photo, in DRAW or PAINT. While the same Effects engine is used in both programs, PAINT enjoys a big advantage in its ability to effect changes to an image: it can change a portion of an image. It does this through the concept of a mask, and mastery of the mask is the gateway to advanced usage of PHOTO-PAINT.

Masks are easy to understand—just think about what you do before painting a room: you tape the window sill so when you paint near it and your brush inevitably touches it, the paint goes on the masking tape, not the sill. To be precise, the masking tape analogy is really the opposite of a mask—the paint is applied where you *do not* mask (and that is relevant, because you can reverse masks in PAINT). So instead, think of those old-fashioned stencil sets, where you could happily mark all over the cardboard, safe in the knowledge that the only part that would make its way to paper was through the cutouts of the letters.

That is how a mask functions in PAINT. When you mask off an area of an image, you can then draw, erase, distort, color-adjust, or otherwise create mayhem on screen, and the effect will only take place in the masked area.

You can see this for yourself in about 30 seconds.

1. Go to File ➢ New and accept all of the defaults.

2. Activate the Rectangle Mask tool, second from the top in the toolbox.

3. Create a rectangular mask in the image, any size, any shape, anywhere.

4. Now activate the Paint tool, last icon in the toolbox. It doesn't matter what the current effect is—any one will do.

5. Start painting on the screen with it, and notice how you can only paint within the mask.

The Basics of Masking

Open the Mask Tools flyout from the toolbox and you will see seven tools specific to masking. In order, they are:

Rectangular Mask   The simplest of all, it creates rectangular masks.

Circle Mask   A misnomer, because it makes ellipses, unless you hold Ctrl.

Freehand Mask   Creates any shape you want.

Lasso Mask   Creates an irregular selection surrounded by pixels of similar colors. In other words, it attempts to make intelligent choices about how it creates its shape, and while it has limited appeal, it works well in some situations.

Scissors Mask   This largely ignored tool detects edges of elements and masks along the edge. This tool just isn't friendly enough for regular use.

Magic Wand Mask   This tool is the chief reason the Scissors and Lasso aren't used very often. It lives up to its name, creating masks that include all adjacent pixels that are similar in color to the pixel you click on. One click with this tool can sometimes create the entire mask for you.

Mask Brush   This one is just like a brush, but instead of painting pixels with it, you paint masks.

All of these tools have controls on the property bar that affect their operation. Some use controls that change color tolerances, and others use transparency and soft edges like the Clone and Color Replacer tools.

Effective masking will often involve using more than one masking tool, and a good mask-maker starts by studying the image and the area to mask in order to determine the best course of action.

The other important point about masking is that you can use any of these tools to:

- Replace the existing mask
- Add to an existing mask
- Take away from an existing mask
- Create holes in a mask

These controls are at the left side of the property bar, as well as on your keyboard (Ctrl to subtract from a mask, Shift to add to), and again, knowing when to use which is often the key to the masking puzzle.

WARNING   A bug throughout the development cycle was not fixed in Corel's final versions. The Mask Brush functions backwards: Ctrl adds to a mask and Shift subtracts from it.

Create some masks on your own, using any image at all. Try adding to an existing mask by holding Shift, and then taking away from a mask with Ctrl. Click on various parts of the image with the Magic Wand, and then do some mask sketching with the Freehand Mask tool. Then grab a brush and draw on the image. Change the color values. Apply some far-out effects.

Real-World Masking

The following examples show how you would create masks in various scenarios, and why you would want to. While these are not step-by-step tutorials, we have chosen photos from the collection on CD No. 3, so you can follow along with us.

N O T E   All of the images used in this section are in subfolders below the Photos folder on CD No. 3. You'll also notice that in all of the screen images shown below, the Mask Tools flyout has been torn off of the toolbox for easier access to the individual tools.

Lassoing and Colorizing

The keyboard shown in the graphic below has a deep blue tint to it, and as such, it doesn't pop out of the background very much at all. This is as the photographer intended, but if you wanted a different look, you could easily achieve it.

This is 845039.wi from the Business folder, and in order to mask this keyboard, the Lasso is the best tool. There is such a distinct contrast between the keyboard and its background, the Lasso will easily see the edges. Meanwhile, while you could try the Magic Wand, you would have to click on each key, or increase the tolerance. Either way, it would be about five or six steps. The Lasso is barely three:

1. Activate the Lasso Mask tool and start outside the keyboard.

2. Create a closed shape around the keyboard. The only requirement is that you stay outside the keyboard and you not touch the headphones.

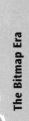
PART

The Bitmap Era

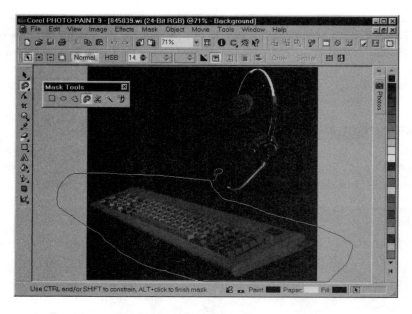

3. Double-click to tell PAINT to create the mask.

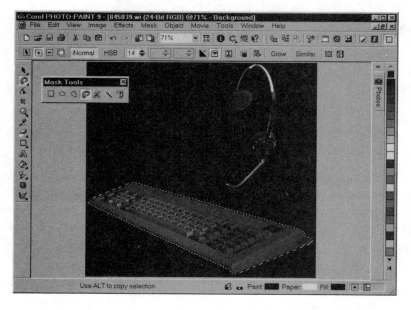

You can see how the Lasso created the mask perfectly around the keyboard. We created the finished image, Figure 25.7, simply by adjusting the "tone curve" (Image ➤ Adjust ➤ Tone Curve) to lighten the keyboard. As with all of PAINT's effects and controls, when a mask is present, the operation is applied only to the masked area.

FIGURE 25.7

This keyboard comes alive with a different tonal quality applied to it.

Waving a Wand and a Feather

Figure 25.8 shows a very lonely boy (885060.wi from Child), and he is made even lonelier by his dark clothing and the dark shadows cast upon his face. This might have been intentional, but again, that doesn't mean that we can't change it. We'd like to brighten the boy up a bit.

FIGURE 25.8

A mask and a brightness adjustment can make this scene a bit less depressing.

PART

6

The Bitmap Era

As we study this photograph in search of masking strategies, we note that there is quite a bit of sameness to the boy's tones, and even better news, those tones are distinct from the wall behind him. That cries out for a session with the Magic Wand tool.

If you follow along, you'll want to make sure that you are masking in "Additive" mode (with the plus selected on the property bar). That way, each click with the wand will grow the mask, not replace what was previously done.

With a Tolerance setting of 12, we were able to mask most of the boy in just five clicks.

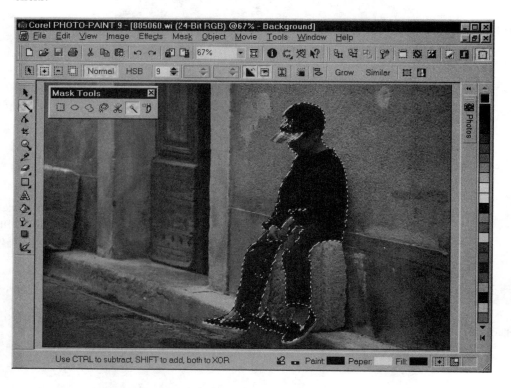

You can see that we didn't get all of him, and we got a bit of the sidewalk (the dark parts). Also, the bill of his hat is too much pattern for the Magic Wand to handle, but these flaws will be fixed in clean-up with the Mask Brush tool—an inevitable part of the process. By zooming in and drawing around the periphery of the boy, we reached this stage in a scant five minutes.

You'll notice that there are plenty of little holes in the mask, and we did that intentionally. We only concerned ourselves with the perimeter of the child—we went around the bill of his hat, got his shoes, removed the sidewalk between his feet, and made sure his neck made it within the mask. We did not worry about filling in the entire mask, and here's why:

Mask ➤ Shape ➤ Remove Holes

This command does just what it promises to do—it removes any holes that are inside of a mask. That one command can shave hours off of a project, and we use it so often, we created a hotkey for it from Tools ➤ Options ➤ Customize ➤ Shortcut Keys.

PART

The Bitmap Era

Now that our boy is masked, we can do something to him, like brighten him up. But when we first did so (by going to Image ➤ Adjust ➤ Brightness-Contrast-Intensity and setting a Brightness value of 15), we didn't like what we saw around the edge of his body. It was as if he was no longer part of the photo—eerily floating above it.

That's when we turned to the Feather command. There are several commands in PAINT called Feather; the one that pertains to masks applies a bit of blending to the edges of a mask to help it integrate with the background. That is precisely what we wanted, so we added 10 pixels of feather, and that made all the difference in the world.

Finally, we carefully masked the boy's face and applied five percentage points of additional brightness to it. Compare Figure 25.9, the finished image, with the dark original shown in Figure 25.8.

If you remember nothing else from this exercise, remember this:

Mask ➤ Shape ➤ Remove Holes

Focusing Attention

Just like we brightened the boy, we can also affect the background of an image. In Figure 25.10 (879035.wi from Nature), the grapes and the leaves share the same color and tone, and the grapes don't stand out very much. Also, the photographer used a fairly wide depth of field, so the background leaves are almost as focused as the grapes.

FIGURE 25.9

A brighter child, thanks
to a mask and the
Brightness controls.

FIGURE 25.10

This is a pretty photo-
graph, but if a vineyard
wanted it for an ad, it
might want the grapes
to stand out more.

PART

6

The Bitmap Era

We can't change the color of the leaves (although we suppose purple grapes would not be out of the question), but we can blur the background a bit, calling more attention to the grapes.

There is good news and bad news with respect to these grapes. The bad news is that there is no automatic way to mask them—too much detail and not enough contrast. You will have to use the Freehand and Brush tools. But the good news is that you do not need an exact mask; in fact, it's better if you don't. When you apply most of the blur effects, it's better if you not define such a sharp edge around the foreground and background.

Therefore, masking the grapes was a 30-second operation with the Freehand Mask tool, and then one trip to Mask ➤ Shape ➤ Smooth to fix any excessive bumps that we made during the trip around the grapes.

Now we have the grapes masked…precisely the opposite of what we want. To switch things around, go to Mask ➤ Invert—now the background is masked.

We chose a subtle Radial Blur (Effects ➤ Blur ➤ Radial Blur ➤ Amount of 3), as it brought a bit more energy to the photo—as if the background was revolving around the grapes. This proved more dynamic than the conventional Gaussian Blur. The final effect, Figure 25.11, doesn't look like an actual untouched photograph, nor is it supposed to. It would be used to call particular, and exaggerated, attention to the foreground object.

FIGURE 25.11

When you really want an object to stand out, blur everything else...

Local Motion

Today's cameras are so sophisticated, they can capture a moment of time with utter precision—making it seem as if the entire world has stopped. That is the case with Figure 25.12 (869077.wi from Sprt_Fit). On this nice bright day, the shutter speed is so fast that the bikers are motionless, and yet the camera lens is stopped down so much that the entire foreground is in sharp focus, and even the clouds and the mountains in the distance are almost in focus.

The more artistic effect would be if you, as photographer, were to use a slow shutter speed and follow the bike riders with your camera—keeping them in a constant position in your lens and allowing all other elements to pass from left to right. This is tricky to do with the camera, but easy to do in the digital darkroom.

PART

The Bitmap Era

FIGURE 25.12

Are they moving or
standing still?

Our mission, therefore, is to mask the hill that the riders are on and apply a
Motion Blur to it. We could mask the hill manually, but we'll introduce you to a different technique. This mask begins as a rectangle, covering the width of the image
and the highest point of the hill.

Then we reached for the Mask Transform tool, which for reasons entirely unknown,
resides on the Object Tools flyout (the first one on the toolbox), not on the Mask Tools

flyout. With that tool, we could shape the mask as if it were a vector object, so we grabbed at the top-left corner and dragged it down until it flattened out. That was the quickest way we could think of to get to this point.

To shave the mask down to fit the hill, we turned to the trusty Mask Brush tool, but before heading out to the image, we stopped at the property bar to toggle Subtractive mode, turn the nib square, flatten it, and rotate it to the approximate angle of the hill. Now we could shave the mask just by sliding down it.

PART

6

The Bitmap Era

Now for the blur. The bike riders are heading to the left, and we are following them in our camera lens, as if the hill they are on is moving to the right. That is easily achieved with Effects ➤ Blur ➤ Motion Blur and setting the direction to the right and a distance of 20 pixels.

The screen image above was taken with the mask marquee turned off (Mask ➤ Marquee Visible toggle) so you can better see the effect. The problem is the bicycle tires—they are blurred also, as they reside within the masked area. (They make it look like the riders are riding on sand…a nice effect only if you want it.)

This is a job for Local Undo. With a close zoom, and the Local Undo tool activated, we traced over the bicycle tires with a round nib the size of the tire. Here we have finished the first two tires, but not the third.

You can see a distinct line where the tire meets the ground, and we'll need to apply a bit of blend to it, if it is noticeable at normal magnification. Figure 25.13 is our final product, and it included the following:

- 10 minutes of blending and cloning to refine the meeting of tire and ground.
- About 20 minutes with the Smudge tool, when we realized that the spokes of the wheels would be turning very quickly and would not be frozen in the photo. At high speeds, they create a propeller effect, partially obscuring anything behind them.

FIGURE 25.13

Motion, brought to you by Motion Blur

A Woman Gets a Companion

The woman in Figure 25.14 came from People and the dog from Pets. Her feet look like they are getting cold and the dog looks like it is dying to curl up next to them. Here is how this little operation will come down…

First, the dog. Masking her is a study in backward thinking. As always, we look first to see if the Magic Wand could work because it is by far the swiftest of the masking tools. Using the wand on the dog would be problematic, what with all of the highlights and color shifts throughout her coat.

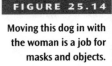

FIGURE 25.14

Moving this dog in with the woman is a job for masks and objects.

The background is much more consistent, even though it is the foreground that we want. We could mask the background and then invert the mask, but we have a better idea:

Unmask the background.

How, you might ask, could we unmask that which isn't masked in the first place? Don't ask—just do this:

1. Activate the Magic Wand tool.

2. Click the minus symbol on the property bar to enter Subtractive mode.

3. Begin clicking on the background, adjusting the Tolerance setting as necessary.

In other words, you are telling PAINT: Take the mask away from any place I click—start with a mask everywhere and remove it from pixels that look like *this* (click). This is the digital equivalent of the sculptor's advice about how to sculpt an elephant: remove everything that doesn't look like an elephant.

With a Tolerance of 25, one click removed the entire blue background. Two minutes of clean-up later, we had this.

You'll surely notice that the mask is inside the edge of the dog; this was intentional. We didn't want any of the blue background to come with the dog on her journey, and the dog is so hairy and shaggy that, frankly, she won't miss a little if it gets cropped out.

Masks can be turned into floating objects several ways, and the simplest (especially when moving between images) is to copy it to the Clipboard:

1. Press Ctrl+C.

2. Switch to the image with the woman.

3. Press Ctrl+V.

PART

6

The Bitmap Era

As a floating object, the dog can be sized, moved, and most importantly, *feathered*. By feathering five pixels, she integrates nicely into the photo with her new master, as Figure 25.15 shows.

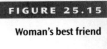

FIGURE 25.15

Woman's best friend

More on Masking

We said at the beginning of this chapter that PHOTO-PAINT needs its own book. Well, masking could practically have a book onto itself. Here are a few other topics to explore on your own with respect to masks.

Like a Mask, Save a Mask

Masks can be saved in several ways. First off, if you save your work in PAINT's native CPT format, any mask that exists in the image is maintained. When you reopen the file, you will see the familiar mask outline, or "marching ants," as our friend and PAINT specialist Peter McCormick likes to call them.

You can also save just a mask, for later use in the same image or a different one. Go to Mask ➤ Save and then choose Save to Disk or Save As Channel. The former will save the image as a monochrome bitmap in any file format at all, with white pixels identifying the masked region and black pixels covering the rest. You can then load that mask into any image to activate it. Saving a mask as a channel keeps it internal to the file.

Any image can be loaded into PAINT as a mask, even one that was not created for that purpose. When you do this, PAINT uses the image as a stencil—pixels that have color can be drawn on or filled, while pixels that do not are protected.

Figure 25.16 began as the photo of Jamie being loaded in as a mask. Then we sprayed clouds on top of her. The sunburst at the top is also courtesy of the image sprayer, but we just clicked once.

FIGURE 25.16

We're not quite sure how we got to here, but we started by loading Jamie.tif as a mask and then we spray-painted clouds on top of her.

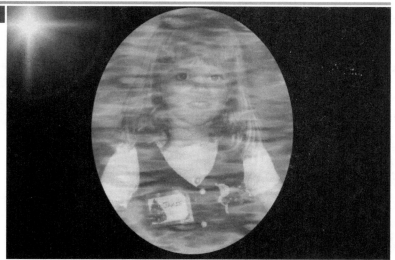

Mask All

Double-click any of the mask tools and you instantly mask the entire image.

Now You See It...

If the marching ants are bothering you, turn them off at Mask ➤ Marquee Visible (or Ctrl+H). The mask still functions. To remove the mask altogether, go to Mask ➤ Remove Mask (or Ctrl+Shift+R).

PART

6

The Bitmap Era

Quick Copies

A masked area can be easily used elsewhere—a click and a drag is all you need. Just make sure that the mask tool—any mask tool—is still active, and drag the mask to another area. The hole left behind will show through to the paper, taking on whatever color is defined for Paper.

If you want to copy the masked region, hold Alt as you drag. To turn it into a floating object, you can either use the Object ➤ Create command, or just do as we do and copy it to the Clipboard and then paste it right back down. As we did with the dog and the lady, you can also switch to another image and paste.

If you want to move a mask but not upset the image underneath it—in other words, adjust the mask boundaries—then use the Mask Transform tool.

Bézier Drawing in PAINT?

Yes, it's true—the third icon on the toolbox is the Path tool, and it functions just like DRAW's set of Pencil tools. You can create paths with the Bézier tool or the Freehand tool. Once you create a path, you can convert it to a mask.

The two primary advantages to drawing paths instead of creating conventional masks are precision and editability. While you forego the intelligence of the color-sensing mask tools, you get inordinate control over where each node goes—just like in DRAW. And once you place the nodes, you can do anything with them that you would in DRAW. You can relocate them, convert them to and from lines and curves, change their direction, everything.

How would you like to mask this face?

No thanks—this is a job for the Path tool, and you can see that we are well on our way to a precision mask around this unruly pup.

Out the Door

We conclude this chapter with the assumption that many of you, perhaps most, will head for PHOTO-PAINT to create an image that will then be used elsewhere—DRAW, VENTURA Publisher, Adobe Illustrator, Microsoft PowerPoint, or of course, a Web page.

We have good news for you—Export has grown up. In earlier versions of PAINT, the Export command ranged from useless to frustrating. In PAINT 7, exporting required special plug-in filters, and almost nobody used it. We had to use Save As all the time, and then try to remember (or decide arbitrarily) which image was the original.

Later, in PAINT 8, you could only export to a file format if the elements on your screen could be supported by that format. We developed a deep loathing for the error message: "Image must be converted to 8 bit [sic] or less before saving as GIF." So save the &%$#@ thing as 8-bit for me!

In version 9, Export is as robust as it is in DRAW, and that has many positive implications for you. Now you can (and should) save your work in PAINT's native CPT format, knowing that you can export it to another format at any time. CPT tracks all of your nonpixel elements, like masks, paths, channels, and objects—elements that the conventional bitmap formats would not hold onto. And if you need a quick GIF file for a Web graphic, when exporting, PAINT offers you palette choices for the 8-bit conversion that must take place. You can keep the original image at full fidelity.

This will prove of particular interest to those who regularly handle JPEG files. With a compression scheme that results in the elimination of pixels, saving JPEG files repeatedly results in gradual image degradation. Much better to save your image in a nonlossy format—again, CPT being the best—and then export it as a JPEG file when you are ready.

One more advantage of using Corel's CPT format: using floating objects in DRAW. When you bring a CPT file with separate objects into DRAW, they come in as a group. When you ungroup, each object is its own bitmap, and the background is a separate bitmap. This is the easiest way to bring an irregularly shaped bitmap with a transparent background into DRAW.

After having made it through this chapter, we deem you officially armed and dangerous. For our part, we deserve something, too. It's not easy covering in one chapter a topic that needs an entire book. We think a vacation is in order...

PART

The Bitmap Era

A well-prepared perspective and a strong sense of motion and energy earned acclaim for this piece in Corel Corporation's annual World Design Contest. Mr. Thornton went to enormous lengths to add detail to the train—we suspect that he liked to play with them as a kid. Maybe as an adult, too…

WAKE-UP CALL

Doug Thornton

Camarillo, CA

This lovely piece is distinguished by its lavish use of pastels and, once again, a strong sense of perspective (you can practically draw a line down the rooftops to the vanishing point). Artists turn to many techniques to create ripples and reflections in the water; Mr. Kardinal used flopped duplicates of the original objects, and then painted streaks of color across them. While not completely realistic, it contributes to the colorful imagery that is this illustration's signature.

ST. TROPEZ HARBOR

Hans Kardinal

Berlin, Germany

We can only imagine the fun that Mr. Rose had while creating this fresh piece. You can practically taste the irreverence, both in the use of the scribbles and in the mischievous devil-may-care expression of the young artist. From this unusual perspective, you really feel like the parent, and we could only hope to be this patient if it were our child who expressed his creative side quite this way. We hope that Mr. Rose got a free tablet from Wacom for his effort...

NEW TOOL

Mark Rose

Moorhead, MN

Image courtesy Corel Corporation. Copyright 1999, Mark Rose. All rights reserved.

The eyes alone are worthy of an award. The attention to detail is unmistakable in this clean, precise drawing. We note the deft use of transparency in her goggles and the blending to create the shine on the propeller and the jet engine. Sometimes vector tools can actually be too sharp, and we think the woman's lips and the hair that has escaped her helmet are examples of this pitfall. The lines on lips and hair are rarely that well-defined in real life. With DRAW introducing so many bitmap effects, such as blurring and softening, we expect to see even more realism on the parts of talented artists like this one.

THE STAMP

Ljubomir Penov

Sofia, Bulgaria

The two words that come to mind as we view this piece are soft and serene. It looks like an oil painting! The choice of colors provides a soft contrast, the windless conditions as depicted by the water whisper serenity, and the sky hints at a fragile warmth of a spring or early-summer morning. Mr. Intakidis used a different technique to create reflections than that used by Mr. Kardinal in St. Tropez Harbor. This kind of warping can be done either by DRAW's Envelope tool (as shown in Chapter 13) or by the Motion Blur filter in DRAW or PAINT.

VISION

Panagiotis Intakidis

Athens, Greece

Who says computer-generated art has to be complicated? This wonderfully simple piece is a glorious example of the artist's vision counting for so much more than the powerful effects possible within a program such as DRAW. The most elaborate element of this mosaic is the drop shadows, and we wonder if they are even necessary. Any one of us could have produced the simple shapes and curves that make up this drawing; the genius is in the imaginative way they are used and combined.

KINDERGARDEN

Tomasz Wawrzyczek

Rybnik, Poland

K I N D E R G A R D E N

PLAYGROUND

GYMNASTIC HALL

CLASSES

EMERGENCY EXIT

GREENHOUSE

KITCHEN

Depth and spatial relationships are often the most challenging elements to depict in two-dimensional illustration programs. This artist makes it look easy. All of our senses tell us that the leaves are right over our heads, the water is a few hundred feet below us, the nearest neighbor is a mile or two away, and the mountains in the distance would require an all-day sail. Is that a rhinoceros doll on the ledge? We can only wonder about its significance...

VIEW ON THE BAY

Yves Lanthier

Boca Raton, FL

Awarded Best of Show in 1996, Mr. Corkery's stunning depiction of 1940s film star Hedy Lamarr stands as one of the most heralded and recognized CorelDRAW efforts ever. The artist's quest was to use DRAW to create a photographic look, and he succeeded beyond all expectation. Virtually all observers' first impression is that he used PHOTO-PAINT. But no, with an exquisite mixture of blends, powerlines, and fountain fills, he stayed completely within the vector object domain to create this haltingly lifelike drawing. Unfortunately, it became the face that launched a thousand lawsuits—Mr. Corkery made sure that the photograph he used was outside of any copyright protection, but Corel did not actually seek permission from Ms. Lamarr to use her likeness. Corel had to settle out of court with the actress on various charges of infringement, unlawful use of image, pain and suffering, etc.

HEDY LAMARR

John Corkery
Silver Spring, MD

Another piece that exudes realism from all of its electronic pores, Señor Santos won Best of Show honors in 1998 for his depiction of this deep thinker. While not quite as photographic as Mr. Corkery's, this drawing perhaps tells more of a story about the person doing the thinking (although, ironically, we are not altogether sure of gender). We see wisdom, experience, understanding, philosophy, and many other qualities etched into a well-worn and comfortable face. While use of tobacco products tends to polarize Americans and could influence one's reaction to this piece, we note with amazement the delicate transparent effect given to the smoke in front of the subject's face.

CONTEMPLATION

Adauto Santos

Aracaju, Brazil

When we announced a contest to design the cover of our CorelWORLD Conference brochure, we received over 75 entries from all over the world! This effort won Mr. Downey free travel and admission to our October event in Orlando, Florida. He found a photo that captured the flowery nature of the Sunshine State, used a PHOTO-PAINT effect along the right side, dropped a fountain transparency in front of it in DRAW, and then added the lettering. This is another example of a seemingly complex effect actually being a series of simple steps.

CORELWORLD '99

Doug Downey

Niagara Falls, Canada

Learn the
Secrets of the
Corel Experts

Corel
WORLD '99

**Five days of in-depth
seminars and workshops**

➤ *Learn hundreds of
undocumented tips*
➤ *Create winning
logos and designs*
➤ *Automate your workflow*
➤ *Produce great output*
➤ *Manage color like a pro*
➤ *Tame huge publishing jobs*
➤ *Create dazzling
Web effects*
➤ *And meet fellow users
from around the world*

**The Conference for DRAW, PAINT, and VENTURA users
OCTOBER 3–8 • ORLANDO, FLORIDA**

From the lifelike, almost photographic efforts of Corkery and Santos, we journey to this totally surreal image that would make any pianist's heart skip a beat. And there must be many keyboard aficionados among DRAW users—this is the fourth award-winning illustration that we know of since 1995 to use a piano keyboard as its central focus. We're not sure what it means, what it signifies, or what kind of structure has risen from the ocean floor. And we don't care that we've never seen a moon quite this big and that the moon would not be capable, from its current position, of casting the type of shadow depicted to the right of this stairway to heaven. We just know that we like it, and that's good enough for us.

MOONLIGHT SERENADE

Giovanni Re

Rome, Italy

One of the most popular themes in computer-generated art is the new meeting the old—traditional tools encountering the electronic ones. We appreciate that mix, and we also enjoy the mixing of bitmap and vector elements to depict humankind's continual search for its creative outlets. This piece might be finished, but the work in progress that the artist refers to is never-ending.

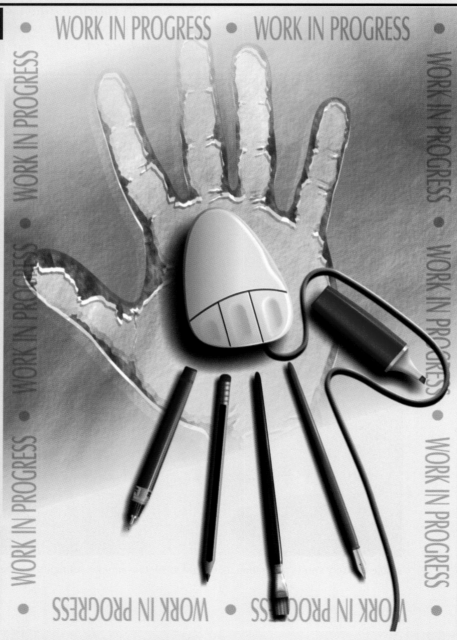

WORK IN PROGRESS

Flavio Fanchini

Mantova, Italy

At first glance, we thought this piece was too dark. Perhaps Mr. Maul used the wrong filter, we wondered. But then we found that we just couldn't take our eyes off of it. We had never before seen such detail given to electronic woodwork. And the predominant darkness serves to make even more conspicuous the area that is cast in light—the fallen king. Chess is never this dramatic when we play it...

CHECKMATE

Wolfgang Maul

Edmonton, Canada

Image courtesy Corel Corporation. Copyright 1999, Wolfgang Maul. All rights reserved.

Whoever said that CorelDRAW acts like a narcotic was probably well-acquainted with the Effects menu. While we don't mean to pick on this skillfully executed piece, and we will sing its praises before we're done, what we see first is special effects run amuck. The bubbles are finely crafted…but what are they doing coming out of the mask and fin? And we suspect that the curling image is used here more because of the tool that can create it automatically than for its suitability to the image. The sense of being underwater is spellbinding and expertly described by the dancing light on the sides and bottom of the pool and by our view of the water surface from below it. We think the artist should have stopped right there, as that alone would make the piece worthy of our highest appreciation.

POURING THE WATER IN

Carlos Bastian Pinto

Rio de Janeiro, Brazil

Image courtesy Corel Corporation. Copyright 1999, Carlos Bastian Pinto. All rights reserved.

We are not entirely sure what Mr. Crook meant when he named his piece, but we have had an absolutely marvelous time guessing. This kitchen is so beautifully adorned and attended to…the randomness with which the light hits the counter tops…the subtle reflection off of the spotless floor…the deftly cast shadows on the ceilings and walls…the exquisite detail of the cabinets, sink, flowers, and window (the scene outside the window is a work unto itself). By gosh, this kitchen is just so perfect…it would have to belong to somebody else!

SOMEONE ELSE'S KITCHEN

Paul Crook

Knowbury, England

If light is the ingredient that all fine art needs, then Valerie Kuleshov is truly a master of the arts. The artist's ability to mix brilliantly radiant objects with muted, almost dull ones contributes to the appeal of this illustration. We love how lifelike the water in the glass appears, and how the brushes and the ink bottle shine with ambient and direct light. Contrast that with the burlap, which was seemingly put on this Earth to absorb light. We would have to make a large leap of faith to accept that you could actually paint on burlap as is depicted here, and in fact, we would be perfectly fine if the central text element of this illustration were removed altogether.

PROFILE

Valerie Kuleshov

Moscow, Russia

The commentary on the 16 color images included in this section and the techniques used to create them are solely the opinions of the lead author.

PART VII

THE CORELDRAW FREEWAY

chapter 20

PRINT, DARN YOU!

Featuring

PRINT, DARN YOU!

So you've created some great designs or a dynamite page layout in CorelDRAW. Now what? Most likely, you want to print your handiwork. Even if you create art solely for placement in other applications, you are likely to want print proofs along the way. We know many Web designers who print their work, because they proof better on paper.

DRAW has helped create a collective reputation among illustration software for focusing more on what can be produced on screen than what can be produced on paper or film. Let's just say that the range of work that can be printed is a subset of that which can be produced. Workarounds have helped, but one goal in each DRAW version has been to improve the print functions, minimizing the need for workarounds and troubleshooting. DRAW 9 furthers those efforts.

In terms of "features"—things that Corel's marketing department could latch onto—there might be only one: the Mini-Preview option shown in Figure 26.1. This nice addition allows you to quickly get to the most frequently used print settings while also previewing the result.

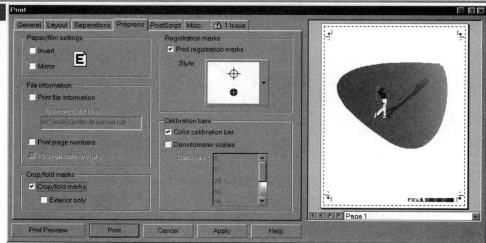

FIGURE 26.1

DRAW 9's Mini-Preview
is certain to be an
instant hit with users.

By default, Mini-Preview is hidden, but you can unhide it by clicking on the new double-arrow button at the upper-right corner of the dialog. The last state of Mini-Preview will be remembered for future files and sessions of DRAW. The traditional Print Preview and additional imposition and prepress options are available by clicking the Print Preview button at the bottom of the dialog.

We welcome the return of Mini-Preview (it left the scene at DRAW 5) as it makes the entire print operation more intuitive. Working in traditional Print Preview can be trying at times, because there are so many portals into and out of it, you can easily get lost. For instance, once in Print Preview, who would guess that clicking Options returns you to the general multitabbed Print dialog? And if you click Close, what are you closing, the Print Preview or the entire Print dialog? For most operations, using the Mini-Preview will be an easier experience.

Some tasks still require the traditional Print Preview, and we'll devote an entire section to it later in this chapter.

Beyond Mini-Preview, Corel's engineers have been busy making printing in DRAW 9 more intuitive, and they have reduced the number of dialogs you must navigate to get where you want to go. This is not to say that prepress printing is easy—it's not. But DRAW 9 goes a long way toward reducing its stress quotient. With that in mind, we can say with confidence that most of the print features in DRAW 9 are relatively easy to decipher—and most work as advertised. This chapter explores all that is old and new in DRAW's print engine.

Before moving on to DRAW's printing controls, let's take a look at DRAW 9's page setup mechanics.

A Word about PostScript Printers

Throughout this chapter we will refer frequently to *PostScript printers* and *non-PostScript printers*. PostScript is a very powerful page-description language developed by Adobe Systems Incorporated. A PostScript .prn file is simply a program for the PostScript printer—nothing more than a recording of the various commands that would normally be sent directly to the printer from the application.

One big plus for PostScript is that its command language is written as ASCII text. That means people knowledgeable in PostScript can find useful troubleshooting information in the file, should something fail to print correctly. And even less savvy users can check this file to see that all fonts are properly downloaded. You simply look for lines like the following:

```
%%BeginFont: AachenBT-Bold
%!PS-AdobeFont-1.0: AachenBT-Bold 003.001
```

Non-PostScript printers utilize a variety of command languages, typically Hewlett Packard's PCL (Printer Control Language). These languages have their own strengths but are generally less robust than PostScript. And many high-end output devices won't use anything but PostScript.

You Can't Print What You Can't Set Up

The Page Setup dialog is available from Layout ➢ Page Setup or by going the scenic route through Tools ➢ Options ➢ Document ➢ Page. You can also get to Page Setup by double-clicking the page border on screen. The jury is still out on what we affectionately refer to as the Options Gorilla—the single clearing house for all options, controls, and settings across the program—but at least in DRAW 9 access to and through the Gorilla is faster.

DRAW Does BIG

One of the significant changes introduced when DRAW moved to a 32-bit operating system was the increased maximum page size you can design and print. In prior versions, the maximum drawing page was 30 by 30 inches. That limit has increased to a truly unimaginable 150 by 150 feet. So feel free to design as large a page as you want. The bigger problem may be finding a device that can print it. Today's market offers an increasing number of devices to handle large output, and later we'll show you how to print BIG using even your humble little desktop printer.

Page Setup: The Basics

Page Setup has five (well, four and a half) pages. Here, we'll summarize the more fundamental steps of defining your document settings and cover some of the changes in DRAW 9.

Page Settings

There are only three items on this page, and two of them can be toggled from the View menu. There is no direct access to this page, and an easy way to miss it is to open Page Setup from the Layout menu and expect to be taken to the top of the tree. Instead, you have to conscientiously click on Page to get to the dialog shown here.

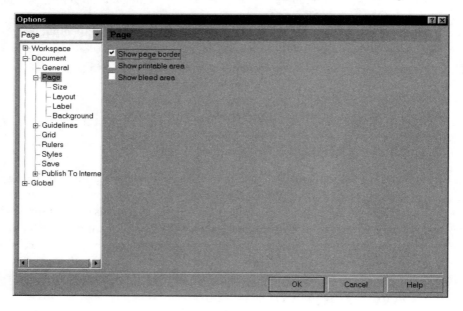

Show Page Border   This option is on by default, and adds a nonprinting frame for the page you have defined—which is quite different from adding a printable page frame (described shortly). This nonprinting border will also be visible if you switch to

full-screen preview. You will normally want to keep Show Page Border turned on. In rare instances (when page size is irrelevant), you may benefit by turning it off to unclutter your work area. In fact, for many of the screen images in this book, we turned it off.

Show Page Border does have a pronounced effect on two of DRAW's other features:

- When Show Page Border is on, the area outside the border serves as a virtual pasteboard, a special drawing layer called the Desktop in DRAW's Object Manager. In multipage documents, objects on this Desktop layer are always visible on all pages, and you can drag objects from one page to another. With Show Page Border turned off, you can still put objects on the Desktop layer, but it means a more tedious trip through the Object Manager to accomplish it.

- Fit to Page prints all objects regardless of page border visibility.

Show Printable Area   Have you ever designed a page, printed it out on your desktop printer, and wondered why the edges of your design were cut off? Then this option is for you. Printers are designed with some amount of an unprintable region, generally done to prevent the spillage of toner inside the printer. The printer driver reports this nonprinting area to DRAW; by turning on the Show Printable Area option, you will see a visual representation (a black dashed line marquee) of the true printable page border *before* you start your design. The orientation will match that set in the printer driver itself.

Show Bleed Area   An option new to DRAW 9, Show Bleed Area works in conjunction with the Bleed setting on the Size page of Page Options. When you have set a bleed, this region will be represented on screen by two black dashed line borders around the page. The bleed setting will update automatically when you create multipage files with multisize pages within the same file. (What? Multisize pages within one file you ask? Read on.) For more on page bleeds, see the "Layout" section under "Printing...At Last!" later in this chapter.

This page of Page Setup remains a curious example of over-designing, and we had hoped that Corel would streamline this a bit. Maybe version 10...

Size Settings

As shown in the graphic on the following page, the radio buttons at the top of this dialog allow you to switch between the Normal Paper and Labels pages. The Paper choice itself—size and orientation—is a fairly straightforward endeavor. The most significant change DRAW 9 brings to page settings is the ability to assign multiple page sizes and orientation within the same multipage file.

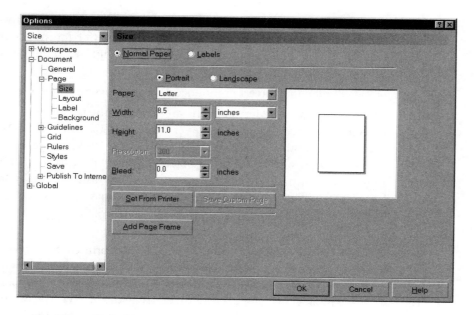

The Paper drop-down list offers a variety of standard US and international paper sizes. The size and orientation you choose here or from the property bar while the Page Size and Orientation button is in "default mode" determines the defaults for your file. Any new pages added to your file will take on the properties you have set for the default page.

In addition to the standard sizes, you can enter custom page sizes. There is even a choice in the drop-down list called "Custom," but we find that it's much easier to simply enter the desired page dimensions into Width and Height. DRAW will automatically change the Paper value to Custom. As you enter a custom page size, the Save Custom Page button will become available.

TIP   If you think you might use your new custom page again, click the Save Custom Page button and give it a name. Your new page information will now be available from the property bar and at the bottom of the Paper list. Unfortunately, Resolution is not saved with a custom page, requiring an extra step for Webmasters who want to customize a page for creating graphics.

It is important to understand that the Page Size settings determine the *drawing's* page sizes, and this may or may not be the same size as the paper or other media you print on. For example, perhaps you need to create a drawing page that is based on a newspaper ad specification: 27 picas, 6 points wide by 42 picas tall (about 4.6 inches

by 7 inches). You can easily specify this as a custom page by changing the units to picas, points, and then typing in the values and setting the orientation to portrait. Now you can merrily lay out your ad, knowing exactly where to place objects in relation to the edges of the ad space. We'll cover imposition and tiling large drawings to smaller media later in the chapter.

One of the page sizes available in the Paper drop-down list is for creating slides. It generates a page size that has the same aspect ratio (height to width) of a standard 35mm slide, obviously not the physical size of the slide. (You could set up a page size identical to a slide's actual dimensions, but working at a normal page size is more convenient.) This way, settings for nudge and text sizes and so forth don't have to be altered. Once your slide is prepared, you use a special print driver to create a file for a slide-imaging service bureau.

Set from Printer   This button simply sets the page size to match the current paper size setting of the Windows default printer.

Add Page Frame   When you specify a page size, you are defining a nonprinting bounding box that indicates the edges of your drawing. (It appears on screen as a rectangle with a drop shadow.) A handy option in the Page Setup dialog—the Add Page Frame button—lets you create a printable frame the size of your document page. It simply creates a rectangle on your active drawing layer that is exactly the size of the page you have defined. The rectangle will initially appear with whatever default fill and outline you have set for graphic objects. Because it's merely a rectangle, you are free to change the fill and outline as you would for any other object.

T I P   The easier way to create a page frame is to double-click on the Rectangle tool. It does exactly the same thing as the Add Page Frame button in the Page Size dialog.

Layout Options

This page controls how printing will be handled in relation to the kind of document you are creating. This is very handy when you are publishing a newsletter for the local fishing club or custom calendars to keep track of business meetings.

Regardless of the actual dimensions of the page size you define, more often than not you will work with a full-page layout. This is the default option in the Layout drop-down list. In the graphic below, you can see all of the options, and a thumbnail preview of the one chosen. Each specialized layout has its own specific usage, but all share one common characteristic: essentially, they subdivide the full page into a series of smaller frames.

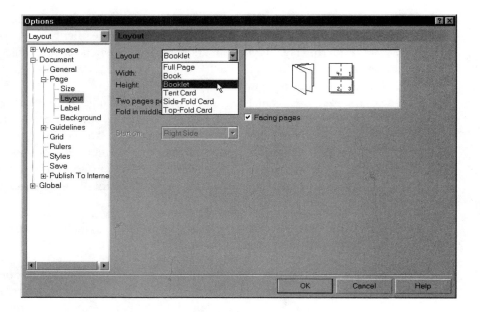

 N O T E   A key to understanding how to use these layouts is to realize that each subdivision is represented as a separate document page in your file. For example, if you are making a side-fold card and want to print on all four panels, you must create four pages in the file. In this layout, each multiple of four pages in the file defines another card.

Books and Booklets   These two layouts look similar—both subdivide the full page into two halves—but they behave differently at print time. We're going to focus on the Booklet layout, since it is often the more useful of the two. As with the other layouts, the Booklet layout requires that you create pages in multiples of four in your file (minimum four pages for one booklet). You can edit each page in the normal sequence of the assembled booklet, and even flow paragraph text from one page to the next. At print time, the pages are printed in the proper imposition—for instance, in an eight-page booklet, pages 1 and 8, 2 and 7, 3 and 6, 4 and 5. You reproduce the pages as two-sided sheets, then fold and staple them to create completed booklets. If you don't have a two-sided printer, the Duplexing Wizard can help you with two-sided printing.

Card Layouts   The three card-style layouts—Tent, Side-Fold, and Top-Fold—can all be accomplished manually by subdividing a single full-page layout with guidelines, then rotating all elements in the upside-down panels 180 degrees. By using one of the Layout options, though, you can easily edit each individual panel because you can work right-side-up on all of them. Then, at print time, DRAW will do the thinking for you and make the appropriate rotations as it prints the full page.

Certainly it's easier to create cards this way, but it's also a bit more limiting than doing it manually. Let's assume you want to create a birthday card and you want some elements to span the front and back frames of the card. Easily done using the manual method, but next to impossible using Layout's card options.

Facing Pages The Facing Pages check box is a handy application in a multipage document. Turning on Facing Pages allows you to view what would normally be the pages that face each other in a book or booklet.

The Facing Pages option serves another very practical function in setting up books and booklets. You can create objects that span two facing pages (known as a *spread*). When you print the book or booklet, these objects are split in half over the printed pages. In assembly, the two halves are reunited to a single object, just as you designed them with Facing Pages turned on.

Figure 26.2 illustrates how this would work with an eight-page booklet. Pages 2 and 3 are designed as a spread, and even though they won't be printed together (page 2 would go with 7 and page 3 with 6), DRAW will make everything right during printing.

FIGURE 26.2

With Facing Pages turned on, DRAW prints spreads correctly.

How it appears on screen

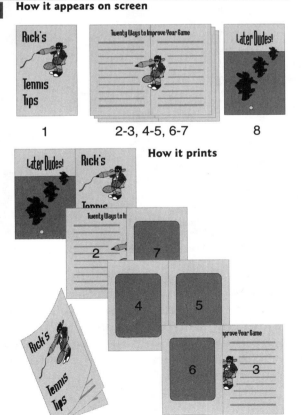

PART

The CorelDRAW Freeway

Start On: (Right or Left)   One other Page Layout option used in conjunction with multipage files is the Start On setting. Books and other multipage files normally start on the right-hand (recto) page. Occasionally, however, the book's cover is produced elsewhere, or for some other reason the data in a file must start on the left-hand (verso) page. DRAW gives you the option to do so. Unfortunately, this option is unavailable for booklets. If you are creating a booklet with preprinted covers and want printing to begin on the inside of the cover, you're out of luck, unless you include blank pages in the layout.

Labels

Unchanged from DRAW 8, from the Labels page, you can select the kind of label you want to print to, and customize it in just about any conceivable manner. Many manufacturers are listed, and as you can see from the graphic below, you can pick the label by product identification number.

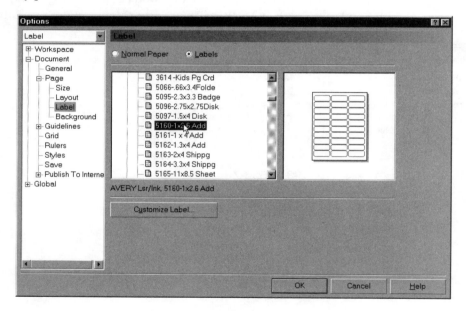

It has always been possible to construct a sheet of labels in versions of DRAW prior to 7—it just wasn't very easy. You had to do a good deal of measuring, calculating, and pasting, and you were limited to sheets of duplicate labels. If you wanted to print a series of changing labels to a single sheet, it was manual-city.

But by providing this Labels page in Page Setup, you can either create a sheet of labels from one "page" in DRAW, or you can create a string of different labels just by

adding pages to the file and making each one different. The information is fed directly to DRAW's print engine. You can see this for yourself by choosing a label, creating an element on the page, and then going to File ➤ Print Preview to see how DRAW behaves.

Custom Labels   If the Labels list doesn't have what you want, click the Customize Label button and have at it. As a starting point, this dialog reflects the values for the last label you chose, and we find that very handy. Figure 26.3 shows the way we use this feature—to avoid wasting a partially used sheet of labels. By increasing the left margin and knocking off the bottom, we can just print onto certain labels.

FIGURE 26.3

The Customize Label dialog is good for the environment...

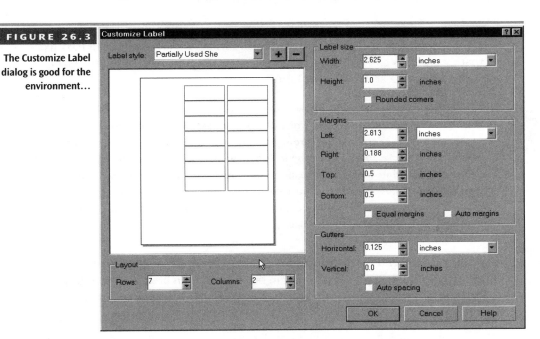

As you can see in Figure 26.3, there are many options for positioning labels. Most are self-explanatory, but watch out for the Equal Margins check box. If you turn on this option and play with the top or left margin, it won't appear that anything new is happening. Equal Margins functions only in conjunction with the Auto Spacing check box in the Gutters section. Unless you tell DRAW to auto-space the labels based on your margins (equal or otherwise), then the top and left margins and the manually set gutter widths will define the resulting right margin; thus Equal Margins will have no effect. With *both* Equal Margins and Auto Spacing turned on, however, the net result is that the block of labels is distributed symmetrically on the page.

Background

This powerful feature, new as of 8, eases the process of adding backgrounds to your drawings. This is not a can't-live-without element, and many of you have probably ignored this setting entirely. But while its use is specialized, it is oh-so-valuable, especially to those who create Web pages from DRAW.

No Background   Pretty easy. This option applies absolutely nothing to your document. When creating Web pages directly from DRAW, selecting No Background will give your Web page the default white background color.

Solid   This option is useful for visualizing your final product if you plan on printing to colored media, since it allows you to simulate what your document will look like on that media. This choice has absolutely no effect on printing (unless you enable Print and Export Background at the bottom of the dialog).

 W A R N I N G   On screen, any white or lightly tinted objects will appear completely opaque against your colored background. If you were actually to print these objects on colored stock, white objects would be invisible against the paper (unless, of course, you are using a spot white ink), and the paper color would leak through a lightly tinted object, changing the actual appearance of its color. Using a colored background lets you quickly and easily experiment with various color schemes without having to print samples, but before printing, change back to No Background.

Bitmap   Adding a bitmap as a background has never been easier in any version of DRAW. Simply click on the Bitmap option button and then browse to your bitmap file to add it. When you have selected your file, you have two options to call on.

- You can tell DRAW whether you would like to embed the graphic into your document or link it to the document. Embedding the graphic is fine if you don't plan to modify it later. Linking the bitmap to your document allows you to make any changes to your background and see it reflected in the linked file immediately.

- You can retain the original size of your bitmap background or size it to fit your needs. Click on the Maintain Aspect Ratio check box to smoothly scale the bitmap without losing much of its original fidelity.

Print and Export Background   Check the box to do just that. If your output medium already has the background on it, you will want to turn this off. In this fashion, you can preview what your printed document will look like. If you plan on printing the

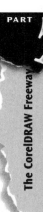

background with the document's contents, make sure this option is checked. Additionally, if you are creating a Web page using Publish to Internet, checking this option will add your background color or bitmap to your Web page *as a tiled background*. See Chapter 21 for details.

Printing...At Last!

We've finally made it to the heart of the matter: actually printing your work. So to print your drawing, you go to File ➤ Print and click OK, right? Right??

Would that it were that easy.

For basic proofing on a laser printing, perhaps it is. But if you rely on CorelDRAW for professional output and accurate communication of your work to a service bureau, you'll need to know about more than just the OK button. Here is a tour of the six tabs of the Print dialog (or seven, if you're printing to a PostScript device).

General

Again, for commonplace print jobs, this might be the only stop you'll need to make, as Corel has done a good job of placing the most common controls on the first page of the dialog.

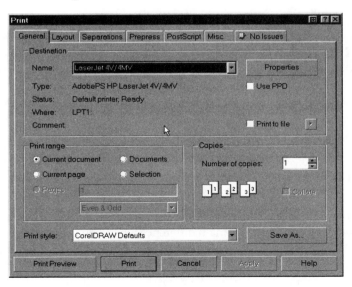

Destination

This section of the General page describes the current output device and/or method. Initially, this is your system default. Changing the selection at this point is simply a matter of choosing another from the drop-down list. From the list, you can select any other installed printer or output device (such as a fax/modem driver) or the new DRAW 9 option of Device Independent PostScript File. The other fields will change to reflect related settings. Most of this information is self-explanatory. The Status field is probably most useful in a shared-printer environment, when you need to know if the printer is available. The Where field is the output destination (either a physical port such as LPT1 or a logical port such as FILE or a directory or filename).

When you select Device Independent PostScript File for output, DRAW will control the device setup instead of a driver. You can select any media size defined in the page size settings of the Options dialog, including any custom definitions you have added to this list. Device Independent PostScript offers a way to output completely DSC-compliant PostScript files with no interference from device-dependent operations. This is especially desirable if you are sending PostScript files to post-processing applications like TrapWise, PressWise, etc.

If you select a different printer and cancel without printing, your selection is promptly forgotten and the default printer is again selected. If you proceed and print a document, the printer and other options you chose are retained for subsequent printing of that document during the current session.

 WARNING   DRAW's multiple-document capability allows each document to retain its own print settings. Generally, this is a good thing; it will reduce the required steps each time you print. You need to be careful, though, if you're working on several documents at once. If each document uses different page sizes, printers, and so forth, you may lose track of which file goes to what printer and with which settings. (We know this from personal experience!)

Properties

This button takes you to your printer's own driver settings. Here you can control many printer settings that would normally be accessed from the printer's Properties dialog in the Windows Control Panel. The main difference when you change the settings from within DRAW is that they will only stick with the document for the duration of your session. Open another application or a new DRAW document, and everything reverts to the default printer and its settings. So if you find yourself entering Properties and making the same change over and over again, you should make one trip to Start ➤ Settings ➤ Printers and make the change there. That way, it will become the default.

Use PPD? Isn't That Illegal??

No, not PCP—PPD! If you have selected a PostScript device as your output method, the brand new PPD check box will be available. A PPD is a PostScript Printer Description file. It describes the fonts, paper sizes, resolution capabilities, and other features that are specific to your PostScript printer. Using the correct PPD files ensures that your printer's features will be available when you print.

If you choose to use a PPD file, DRAW generates all of the PostScript code. If you choose not to use a PPD file, Windows relies on information in the print *driver*, which is more generic and not always as up-to-date as the PPD file. For this reason, we applaud the new support for PPDs and recommend you use them for jobs that are destined for unknown or sophisticated output devices.

After you check the PPD check box, you will be presented with a dialog from which to locate the PPD file itself. Usually, PPD files are installed into the Windows ➤ System folder, but if you downloaded the Adobe PostScript driver, it comes with dozens of PPD files that do not get installed. If you cannot locate the PPD file for your device, first check at www.adobe.com, then with the manufacturer or your service bureau. Once you have selected the PPD file, it will remain selected for that particular device anytime you enable the PPD check box. To change PPD files, click the Properties button in the DRAW Print dialog and then browse to the new PPD file.

Think of PPD as the opposite of Device Independent PostScript. PPD describes the things that are unique to a printer, while Device Independent PostScript represents generic PostScript that is common to all.

Print to File

The Print to File option allows you to create a file that can later be downloaded to the selected output device. You can install drivers or PPDs for remote devices or select the new Device Independent PostScript File output method, and record the printer command code in a print file (usually with a .prn or .ps filename extension) for later output.

Print to File is especially useful for creating files destined for output at service bureaus. That means you don't need to own a $50,000 imagesetter, and the service bureau doesn't need to have CorelDRAW or your chosen fonts in their shop—or even a DOS/Windows computer, for that matter. Print files can be created for both PostScript and non-PostScript output devices. However, most devices found at service bureaus are PostScript.

Next to the Print to File check box is a new flyout arrow giving you access to even more options. Included on this flyout are three toggles for controlling the final file. You can choose to have all pages in multipage files sent to one file, each page to a separate file, and even each color separation (plate) sent to its own file.

This brings us to the For Mac option. If you are preparing files for a Macintosh-based service bureau, you will want to select this option when you create a print file. It tells DRAW to strip out a start/end control character (Ctrl+D) from PostScript files. This character is informative to DOS-based printers, but it tends to choke Mac networks.

Look for details on preparing files for service bureaus throughout the rest of this chapter.

 TIP   You can also instruct your printer to strip this control character for all printing under Windows. To do this, go to Start ➤ Settings ➤ Printer, choose the desired printer, and press Alt+Enter to get its Properties sheet. From there, go to the PostScript page, click Advanced, and find the options for sending the Ctrl+D character.

Other Uses for Print to File

You may find the Print to File option useful even if you do not use a service bureau. Use it whenever you need to print on a device not attached to your computer.

For example, perhaps you have a notebook computer that you take on the road, sans printer. You prepare some artwork for your office, which has a color printer. No one else in your firm uses DRAW, so it is installed only on your notebook, along with a driver for the office printer. You print to file, and at the office, entering a quick DOS copy command:

```
copy filename.prn LPT1 /B
```

will produce your masterpiece! In this command, *LPT1* refers to the port to which the printer is connected. Typically it will be either LPT1 or LPT2, but you should substitute the port to which your printer is attached. The */B* tells the printer that you are sending binary information, so it won't treat the file as ASCII text.

There are fancy Windows utilities that do this also, but sometimes there's nothing cleaner and simpler than a good old DOS prompt.

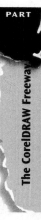

Print Range

With these options you tell DRAW what objects, pages, or documents you want printed.

Current Document   By default prints all objects that fall within the document page borders—recall the discussion of the Desktop layer. You can print the Desktop layer contents and guidelines by making these layers printable through the Object Manager docker. Gridlines are not printable. If there is more than one document window open, the Current Document is assumed.

Current Page   Prints whatever page you are viewing when you invoke printing. This is useful when you're proofing multipage documents. Current Document is the default, but there is an option to set Current Page as the default. Go to Tools ➤ Options ➤ Global ➤ Printing and place a check mark in the box to print only the current page by default.

Pages   Prints your specified range of pages—all even, all odd, both even and odd, specific pages, or a combination thereof—within a multipage document. You can, for example, combine choices to print only even pages in the range 4–10. For a quick reference to the range options, click on the question mark at the top of the dialog and then click on Pages.

Documents   Available if more than one document is open. Place a check next to the documents you wish to print, and uncheck the box for those documents you do not want printed. Except for page orientation, the options chosen in the Print dialog will be applied to all documents.

Selection   Prints the objects you have selected with the Pick tool prior to printing, on the current page or Desktop (if a printable layer). This is a great productivity booster; you can print small sections of a complex drawing instead of the whole page.

Copies

This one's fairly obvious: it tells your printer how many copies of each page to print. Just remember to reset it for every print job; like Print Range, the number of copies always reverts to its default value between document sessions.

PostScript printers and some non-PostScript printers can print multiple copies at the maximum rated speed of the printer, regardless of the complexity of the original image. (Typical ratings are 4, 8, or 12 pages per minute for laser printers.) The image is created in the printer's memory once, which may take a while, and then is duplicated as you've specified in Number of Copies. Other printers may require DRAW to regenerate the page for each printed copy and will be noticeably slower.

Collating

The handy Collate option allows you to tell DRAW and your printer to produce collated sets from a multipage document. There's a disadvantage, though: you may lose the speed gain mentioned in the previous section. It depends on what type of printer you are using and the nature of the document.

Layout

You can use this page to ensure that the elements of your drawing fit, and if they don't, to force them to. To experiment with, we created a frame of paragraph text and intentionally skewed it so that it hangs off the page.

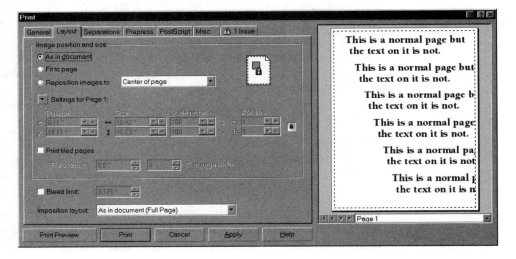

Size and Position

While one option for printing this page properly is obviously to cancel Print and resize or reposition the text, maybe it's positioned that way for a reason—perhaps as part of a multipage spread. If you don't want to change the original artwork, you can use some of the adjustments in this section of Layout.

From Layout, there are three ways to treat the position and size of what will be printed:

As in Document   Makes no adjustments at all.

Fit to Page   Scales all objects up or down to ensure that they fit at the largest possible size.

Reposition Images To   Offers a list of choices, like center, top-left, bottom-right, etc. As soon as you click here, the Settings controls below it come alive.

Note what happens in preview when we click Fit to Page.

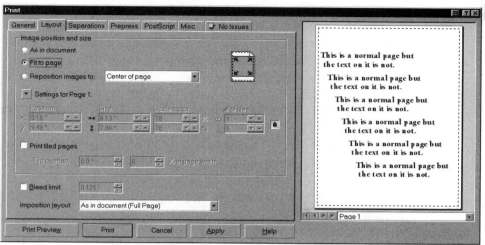

If you wanted to print just a portion of a drawing and size it to the page, you could choose Selection for the print range and then choose Fit to Page. This would work even if the object is way off the page, like on the Desktop.

T I P   In most cases, Fit to Page works correctly. With some printers, however, the assumed print margins do not quite match the actual unprintable area, and small portions of your image will get clipped. An easy solution: turn on Fit to Page, note the resulting scale factor in the % box, and turn it off again; then select Reposition Images to Center of Page and manually enter a scale factor a few percentage points less than what was determined by Fit to Page.

If you check Reposition Images To, you can then adjust the Position, Size, and Scale values below it. Note that Height is initially grayed out, because Maintain Aspect Ratio is on by default. Set this way, adjusting the width will automatically adjust the height to maintain the proper ratio. Click the little lock box to the right to disable proportional sizing, but be careful...

T I P   If you mess up the settings and louse up the page, just reselect As in Document to return to default settings.

Tiled Pages

Despite its usefulness, the Print Tiled Pages option is consistently ignored by many DRAW users. This feature lets you print artwork that is larger than the printable page. Tiling is great for creating do-it-yourself posters and banners, and for proofing at full size work that is destined for a large output device.

As its name implies, choosing this option gives you a series of printed tiles that, when trimmed and pasted together, form the full-size image. Tiling takes into account your printer's unprintable margins by creating a certain amount of overlap on each tile.

Figure 26.4 shows a poster that was made for our lead author, who celebrated a big birthday in 1999. Note the size of the page—48 inches wide.

FIGURE 26.4

This drawing is destined for one of the large printers at the print shop down the street, but how would you proof it from your laser printer?

Preview would tell us that a normal print job would be absurd, as the image would be way too big.

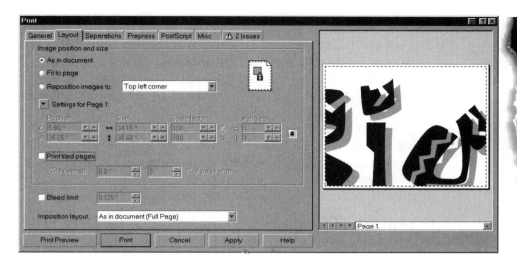

And we could certainly just click Fit to Page to get a one-page proof. But to proof at actual size, we need to click Print Tiled Pages. Once done, Preview shows us exactly how this poster would print.

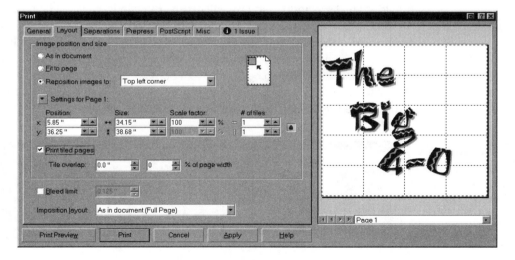

 T I P The Tiling engine is not very environmentally conscious, and it won't think twice about adding an entire row or column to accommodate a sliver of an object. Therefore, if exact size isn't crucial for your proof, you could use any or all of the Position, Size, Scale, or # of Tiles settings to reduce and position the printout of the drawing. We saved eight sheets by reducing the poster shown above by eight percentage points.

Bleed Limit

A *bleed* is a printing term that refers to extending large swatches of color, as in a rectangular background, past the physical borders of the document page. You do this so that the block of color will extend all the way to the edge *and a little bit beyond*. That way, when the page is printed and trimmed, the ink is sure to go all the way to the edge, as intended.

Normally, a bleed extends as far off the page as determined by the objects you created and where you created them. But sometimes you may not want this—for instance, when printing multiples of objects on a single printer page, as in label printing. Perhaps you drew the bleed so large that it overlaps into the next label. Bleed Limit lets you specify the maximum amount of bleed for the entire drawing.

Imposition Layout

Up to this point, we've been discussing print options in terms of a full-page layout, with one or more pages. The Signature and N-Up options from DRAW 8 have been combined into one drop-down list in DRAW 9 called Imposition Layout. The Imposition Layout drop-down list offers quick access to more commonly used layouts and impositions. Additional imposition options and the ability to save custom presets are available from the full Print Preview window, and we will discuss these in more detail later in the chapter.

You can get a good sense of how Imposition operates just by scrolling the list and watching the Mini-Preview. We created a simple four-page booklet, but in DRAW we were lazy—we just created each page as a standard page, without regard for how they would have to be placed to be printed as a booklet. As you can see in Figure 26.5, DRAW forgave our laziness, thanks to the Side-Fold Card imposition, which automatically created the proper "signature" for these four pages.

FIGURE 26.5

We didn't create these four pages as required for proper signature printing, but DRAW did it for us.

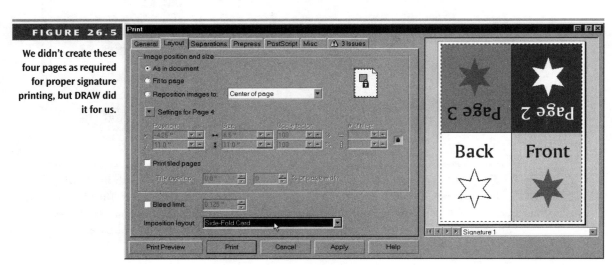

PART

The CorelDRAW Freeway

Printing Signatures

Signatures are commonly used for high-volume book and magazine printing. Pages are ganged together on a single sheet—much like our side-fold cards, but the sheet is printed on both sides. After printing, the signature is folded and trimmed, producing a set of pages ready for binding in the book or magazine. Layout Styles are typically used for production of camera-ready masters for output to an imagesetter, but you can use it with any output device. Thus, you might use a laser printer to proof signatures before sending the project to film.

You begin, as always, by defining the document page size in Page Setup. Choose the size of one regular page (not a full signature). Next, create the document, making sure to use the right number of pages, be it 4, 8, 16, etc.

Printing signatures works something like creating a side-fold card. In the example shown here, the signature has four pages, so each block of eight pages in the document will represent the front and back of a single signature sheet.

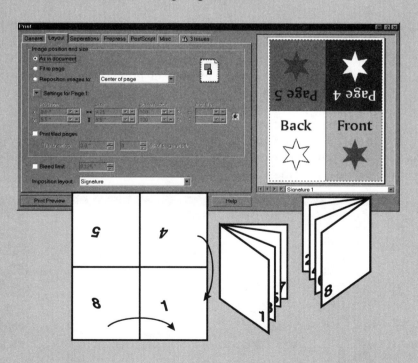

WARNING   DRAW gets very confused if you try to print multiple copies of a two-sided signature. If you are proofing signatures on your desktop printer and need more than one set, it's better to do just one and then simply repeat the process. Either that, or take a trip to your neighborhood copy shop.

Separations

This page of the Print dialog is devoted to the needs and requirements of creating film for conventional printing. Making film requires that each color used in a drawing be represented separately from the others. And while it may seem obvious to some, color separations themselves are not printed in color. Each separation is black and white, usually negative film, from which your printer burns a plate for the printing press. That's when the specified ink color for each plate is applied, resulting in the composite color product.

If you are serious about color work, sooner or later you will need to create color separations—usually image-set film destined for the commercial printer. You can also print color separations from a desktop laser printer, but the quality is not sufficient for commercially printed process-color work. Six hundred dots per inch is fine for many applications, but making negatives requires that a whole lot of toner be put down, and we have yet to meet a laser printer that can do it solidly and uniformly.

Silk-screeners sometimes use desktop printers for process separations, because they typically don't require high resolution and halftone frequencies (more on this later). Simple spot-color separations are not as demanding as process-color work and can often be handled by a good laser printer (as long as you avoid extensive use of subtle blends and fountain fills). But whenever you want commercially produced process-color printing, you are destined for a trip to a service bureau, and you'll become quite familiar with the Separations page shown below.

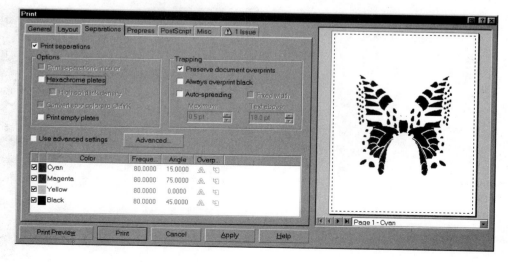

The Value of PostScript

Nearly all imagesetters are PostScript devices, as are many of the high-end color proofing devices. So if you are likely to be using service bureaus frequently, it's advisable to own a PostScript laser printer (or at the very least read Chapter 28, "Publishing to PDF," to learn about using PDF files as a PostScript preflight option).

At $10 or more per plate, mistakes at the service bureau can be very costly. Proofing on a PostScript laser printer cannot eliminate all possible errors, but it can help minimize them. For instance, after we prepare a .prn file using a Linotronic print driver, we often copy the prepared file to a desktop laser printer to verify the condition of all our plates. The pages look clipped and sometimes rather ugly, but at least we know all the pieces are there.

Without a PostScript printer, we wouldn't know this. We could print separations, but they would not be fully representative of the .prn file bound for the service bureau.

To create separations, you simply check the Print Separations check box. When you issue it, many elements of this page come to life and you will be faced with numerous decisions.

The most important part of this dialog is the bottom portion, where the colors that are used in the drawing are shown. If nothing else, this dialog is an excellent troubleshooting tool: if you are creating a two-color job—Black and Pantone 342—and Magenta and Yellow appear when you click Separations, you know that there is some object hiding somewhere with wrong color assignments. The preview can help you isolate them, because you can preview each color separately. In the graphic on the previous page, you are seeing the parts of a full-color butterfly that will be printed in Cyan.

Normally you will print all separations at once, but you have the option of deselecting any colors you don't want printed. You can also tell DRAW to print a plate for every color, even if it is empty for a given page (using the Print Empty Plates option).

Here are some other notable options on the Separations page.

Print Separations in Color

Only available if your target printer is capable of printing color, this option prints each plate in its specified color. The value of this feature is for visualization, and it is particularly useful if you print to transparencies. You can create a home-grown color key, wherein you overlay the transparencies to see how the composite image will look. This has limited usefulness compared with the professionally prepared color keys or matchprints provided by service bureaus, but it may help you catch certain glaring problems. If one color doesn't look right overprinting another, for example, it isn't likely to look right when printed commercially.

Most of the time, you will be printing separations to a print file or to your laser printer, and this option will be unavailable.

Hexachrome Plates

DRAW can create color separations for the six-color hexachrome printing process as well as for traditional four-color separations. By using six inks instead of four, hexachrome printing is capable of reproducing a wider range of colors. Of course, the additional negatives, plates, and press impressions make it more expensive than traditional four-color printing, and there aren't too many print shops offering the service; but at least DRAW makes the option available if you need it and can get it. Choosing the Hexachrome Plates option will automatically convert any spot colors in your document to hexachrome colors.

High Solid Ink Density

If you choose to create hexachrome plates, you'll also have the option of choosing High Solid Ink Density. Consult with your service bureau or print shop to determine whether your job will print better if you use this option.

Convert Spot Colors to CMYK

This feature is specifically for use with the Pantone Matching System of spot colors. Turning this option on tells DRAW that you do *not* want a separate plate for each spot color in the document. Instead, you want DRAW to approximate these colors with a CMYK equivalent. This can simplify the project and reduce printing costs.

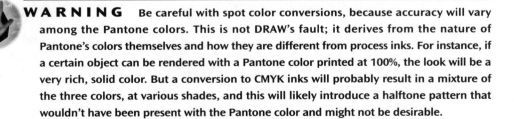

WARNING   Be careful with spot color conversions, because accuracy will vary among the Pantone colors. This is not DRAW's fault; it derives from the nature of Pantone's colors themselves and how they are different from process inks. For instance, if a certain object can be rendered with a Pantone color printed at 100%, the look will be a very rich, solid color. But a conversion to CMYK inks will probably result in a mixture of the three colors, at various shades, and this will likely introduce a halftone pattern that wouldn't have been present with the Pantone color and might not be desirable.

Print Empty Plates

Checking this option tells DRAW to print a plate for every color, even if it is empty for a given page, and is a means of minimizing confusion when a job is passed from you to service bureau to printer. This method of tracking can prevent the printer or someone else from erroneously thinking there are missing plates and holding up your job.

Bear in mind, however, that you will be charged for each plate imaged on film at your service bureau, even if there is nothing on that plate. A solution might be to supply a set of laser proofs that include empty plates for reference. Then prepare the film without the empty plates.

Trapping

Trapping itself will be discussed at length in Chapter 27, but let's take a look at the three auto-trapping functions here in the Separations page. They can help you in lieu of manually created color traps, for many situations.

Preserve Document Overprints   If you have deliberately set overprints in a document, you must enable this check box, or DRAW will ignore them. Fortunately, this option is checked by default; otherwise there would be a lot of angry DRAW users, whose carefully overprinted objects did not overprint on film.

Always Overprint Black   This option does exactly what it says. It tells DRAW not to create "knockouts" where a black object sits on top of objects of other colors. If you have a lot of black text in paragraph size, this would be a good option to have on. But if your drawing contains many large black headlines or objects, your printer might advise you to keep this off.

Knockouts are the opposite of overprints. They are areas on a color plate that are left empty, in anticipation of a shape on another plate going in that space. Head to Chapter 27 for a more involved explanation of both overprints and knockouts.

Using Pantone Colors in Fountain Fills

In some prior versions of DRAW, objects with a fountain fill or blend going from one Pantone spot color to another would be automatically converted to CMYK color at print time. There was a workaround in DRAW 5, but it required editing the Corelprn.ini file. DRAW 9 normally separates such a fill to the appropriate Pantone plates, as long as you don't turn on the Convert Spot Colors to CMYK option.

By the way, watch out—printing Pantone fountain fills is risky business. Though we've occasionally done this successfully, muddy-looking fountain fills happen a lot. Best results come from using lighter Pantone colors, or colors that are not too dissimilar. If you do attempt a Pantone fountain fill, use two different halftone screen angles. A logical choice might be to use one of the CMYK standard angles (0, 15, 45, or 75 degrees) for each overlapping Pantone color.

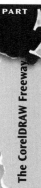

PART

The CorelDRAW Freeway

Auto-Spreading   This option is a method of automatic color trapping. It takes an object that is *not* to be overprinted (an object under which the color is knocked out, instead) and adds an outline of the same color that *does* overprint. This technique can work quite well but has limited applications. The object in question must have a uniform fill, no outline of its own, and cannot already be designated for overprinting.

The Maximum value determines the largest spread, in points, for any object. The extent of trap is determined by the darkness of the object. Lighter-colored objects will have a larger spread because they cause less visible shift where colors overlap. And the Text Above value determines the minimum size of text to which auto-spreading is applied. Spreads applied to very small text cause blurring and illegibility.

Advanced Settings

The Use Advanced Settings check box is available only if you have chosen a PostScript output device. Most of the so-called advanced controls can be adjusted on the Separations page, with a few reserved for the Advanced Separation Settings dialog hiding behind the Advanced button. Most users won't need to touch these complex options, and we'll get to that momentarily.

When you initially enter the Advanced Separations Settings dialog, the Screening Technology field is set to Standard Defaults. These are the normal halftone screen angles and frequencies for your output device. The angle settings have long been conventional in the preparation of color separations: 0, 15, 45, and 75 degrees. They will be common to any output device you choose. The frequency defaults will vary depending on the output device and selected resolution.

This dialog provides several ways of changing the default settings, though that will seldom be necessary. One way is to select a color and then type specific values in the Frequency and Angle boxes. Or choose from the drop-down list of industry-standard screening technologies; these assign the values for all four CMYK plates at once. Any Pantone color plates present will initially take on the same screen settings as process black (unless you have specified a custom screen angle from the PostScript options in the Color dialog). For most spot-color work, this is perfectly acceptable—though not if you have areas where tints of several Pantone colors are going to mix. In that case, you can and should alter the angles.

Overprint Color   In DRAW 7, each CMYK color setting could be modified in the Current Selection area. DRAW 8 changed that and continuing in DRAW 9, you make your modifications in the list itself. To overprint color, click on the icon to the far-right of the color you want to overprint (the icon changes are very subtle). This is the same for the large *A*, which indicates Overprint Text. These settings give you the option of overprinting objects (graphics, text, or both) that are filled with the color you select. This can be especially useful when working with Pantone colors. It's much faster than having to overprint object by object.

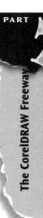

Have the Advanced Settings Lost Their Audience?

If you prepare print files for high-resolution output at a service bureau, talk to your service bureau before you venture into the Advanced Separations Settings dialog. One of the larger service bureaus in our area told us that typically, throughout the industry, virtually any angle and frequency choices you make in this dialog for CMYK plates will be ignored when the file is output. Although such screening technologies are used, the settings are made on the imagesetting system itself. When you submit your file and indicate the resolution and nominal screen frequency you want, the service bureau operators will set these values directly on their hardware, overriding the global settings in your file. One of Corel's engineers confirmed this and recommended the DRAW defaults. Before you invest a lot of time experimenting with these settings, realize that in most instances they won't be used.

One scenario in which fiddling with the defaults might be useful is when you are outputting directly from DRAW to your own imagesetter or another device. Instead of constantly resetting your hardware, leave any custom screening turned off and simply set the desired frequency and angle values for each document as it is printed.

We asked our informative Corel engineer whether one might be able to use custom screening settings in a .prn file destined for a Brand X imagesetter that doesn't incorporate similar technology. The answer was no. Without the technology, the device can't produce the proper halftone dots required by the custom screen and frequency settings. So there would be no advantage over the standard screen settings.

We've already mentioned that you can control the halftone settings individually for each color plate, including any Pantone plates that will be made. But what happens if you have some areas filled with only a 15% tint of the dark Pantone color? You certainly wouldn't want that to overprint. DRAW recognizes that, and has an inherent minimum tint of 95%, below which objects will not overprint.

Halftone Type The option to choose the halftone type is seldom used but can help you create some interesting special effects. Your choice determines the shape of the halftone object (usually a circular dot, but there are other choices available). You might, for example, choose to print a fairly coarse screen frequency for each color, while using a line or diamond halftone type to create an interesting texture.

No discussion of printing and separations is complete without an exploration of color theory and practice, and that makes Chapter 27, "Color for the Color Blind," required reading for those who want a good grasp on driving DRAW in color.

Halftones for Skin Tones

An engineer at Corel told us that selecting an elliptical halftone type can improve skin textures in photographs. Although mainly used in PAINT, the same technique is possible when printing photos from DRAW. It did, indeed, improve the skin tone in a photo printed to an HP-4M laser printer. Halftone types may adversely affect the vector objects in the artwork, so you'll need to experiment with specific choices for every project.

For your own experiments with the halftone pattern on your laser printer, throw a Tinted Grayscale lens over full-color art before printing. Set the lens color to black. Then print your file, opening the Separations page and selecting Print Separations—but print only the black plate. You can then experiment with the angle, frequency, and halftone type settings on your composite image to see what interesting effects you get.

Prepress

The options on this page are relevant when you are making film or paper separations from your DRAW document. The various prepress marks are turned on automatically when you enable the Separations check box on the previous Separations option page, and these marks will print outside of the page margins. This means that if your DRAW document page size is the actual size of the media used to print on, the marks will not be visible. Why would you want to print something that's not visible? To that question, we pose another question: imagine if it were visible—imagine if all of those marks printed *within* your page.

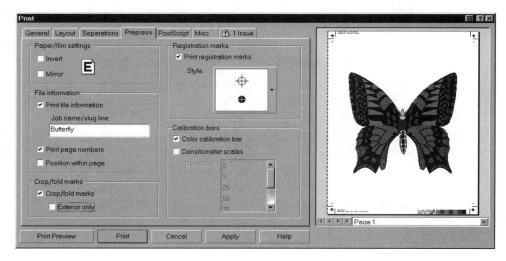

No, the idea here is that the paper or film you are imaging onto is larger than the size of your drawing. That way, you can accommodate all of the important marks that this dialog offers, and more importantly, objects that must bleed. So you will either need to use one of the oversized pages supplied by the printer driver, or set the page size in DRAW to be smaller than the standard $8^1/2$ by 11. (And if you have to fit printer marks to the current paper size, stay tuned...)

Paper/Film Settings

With the Mini-Preview active, all you have to do to learn these is click them and watch. While most film is created as negatives and many jobs are inverted, most service bureau operators will ask you not to use these controls in your software. They would rather do it themselves.

TIP Have you ever printed T-shirt transfers? If so, you know that text will transfer backward unless you manually flip or mirror it on the page itself. Instead, choose the Mirror option on the Prepress options page and let DRAW do the work for you. Your text will remain in a human-readable form on your DRAW page and still print correctly for transfers.

File Information

This option prints information about the plate, at the top and bottom of the separations, near the left-side crop marks. It identifies the color of the plate, the color profile used (if any), the halftone screen angle and frequency for that color, the filename, the date and time printed, and the plate number.

Page Number

This number identifies an individual document page, as opposed to the plate number. As we see it, the feature has little value, except for the prepress operators who need to keep document page numbers straight when preparing the plates. If you want to see page numbers on a laser proof, check Position within Page so they will appear within your laser printer's printable area.

Crop/Fold Marks

These standard marks indicate to the press operator where cuts need to be made to take your job down to its intended finished size. We've never heard them called "fold marks," but booklet printing does indeed involve folding, so having marks to show where the folds are to go would be helpful. The Exterior Only choice becomes relevant if you are printing labels, business cards, or similar items, where the choice exists to place crop marks around the entire page or around each label or card.

Registration Marks

Registration marks are used solely for color separations to ensure that the various color plates are in register, or aligned properly with each other. Without these little targets, it would be next to impossible to predict the press adjustment needed to bring the plates into register. You've undoubtedly seen examples of hideously blurred color pages, or pages with unsightly white gaps that result from misregistration. We see at least one of these a week in the local newspaper. You can choose from several different styles of registration marks, including cute little Corel icons.

Color Calibration Bar

This produces a series of rectangles, which will print in the primary colors of cyan, yellow, magenta, black, red, green, and blue. These are used by the press operators to verify the accuracy of the inks coming off the press.

Densitometer Scale

This advanced feature is used in conjunction with a *densitometer*, an instrument used to measure the density of tones. This scale will help verify that the film or printing plates were prepared within proper device calibration limits.

If you are really into density calibrations, you can adjust the density of the individual steps in the Densitometer scale. Make sure the Densitometer Scales check box is checked, and click on a density in the scroll box below. Use the value spinner to the right of the value or type in a new value for each of the densities. As for how well this works…we have no idea.

PostScript

Unless you have a PostScript device selected on the General print options page, you won't see the PostScript page as a choice in the dialog. Most of the features found here existed in DRAW 8, but a couple of new tweaks have been added. Most are geared toward improving the appearance of your output and minimizing the risk of failed pages. Most, also, are advanced and not for the faint of heart. We show it here with the Mini-Preview for consistency, although none of the changes that you could make here would be reflected in the preview—they affect the PostScript code created, and as such lie well outside the purview of a bitmap displayed on screen.

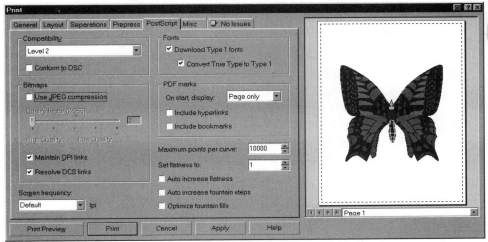

If you are just starting out in DRAW, you won't understand everything we say about this page of the dialog, and we do not use language that will help you understand it. We mean no offense when we say that you'd be better off not trying to mess with these settings too much.

Compatibility

PostScript Levels 2 and 3 support is in both DRAW 9 and the Windows 95/98 PostScript driver. Many newer desktop printers, such as the HP6 PostScript printers, are manufactured with Level 2 support, and a good number with Level 3. Most service bureaus have updated their RIPs to recognize Level 2 PostScript and many more to Level 3. Level 2 PostScript is a rewrite of the PostScript page description language. It has new features and handles complex artwork more quickly and gracefully than Level 1. PostScript 3 offers even more features and enhancements, as well as full support for Adobe's Portable Document File format. The defaults are (a) PostScript Level 1 for Device Independent PostScript, (b) the level reported by the PostScript driver if it is being used, and (c) Level 2 otherwise. If you are using the correct PPD and driver, and have the Use PPD option enabled, the PostScript level will be preset and grayed out. Talk with your service bureau to be sure you choose the correct PostScript level for your device to avoid costly mistakes.

N O T E If you disagree with DRAW's choice of PostScript level, be sure you have selected the Use PPD option and the correct PPD file for your output device.

Bitmap Options

The PostScript options include some choices for working with bitmaps, especially important to graphics professionals.

Use JPEG Compression   This feature of DRAW is available only when the PostScript Level 2 or 3 option is checked. Activating it tells DRAW to send bitmaps to the output device in JPEG format. If you elect to use this option, you can control the degree of JPEG compression with the slider. For instance, you might drag the slider toward the low-quality end to create a small .prn file and fast output for proofs and select a higher quality (with less compression) for final output.

DCS   DCS stands for Desktop Color Separation. Some bureaus can send you a DCS file to act as a low-resolution placeholder if you are using high-resolution OPI (Open Prepress Interface) files. This is helpful since it allows you to work quickly with very, very large files. If you are going to use this in conjunction with your bureau, make sure to disable Resolve DCS Links in the PostScript page.

Maintain OPI Links   Certain bitmap formats—.tif, .cpt, and others—can be used to create OPI (Open Prepress Interface) links. You can import one of these images into DRAW with the OPI option turned on, as explained in Chapter 29. If you do, you are telling DRAW that there is another, higher-quality version of this bitmap that your service bureau will substitute at print time. The obvious advantage here is that you can edit using a lower-resolution bitmap for your design and avoid the memory overhead of a high-resolution color bitmap that could easily consume tens of megabytes.

At print time, you have a choice. In the PostScript Preferences dialog, leave Maintain OPI Links checked (the default), and DRAW will place a reference to the path and name of the high-resolution version in the .prn file. For proof printing, you can turn off the check box and print the low-resolution bitmap instead.

Screen Frequency   We've already covered screen frequency as it applies to color separations. The value set in this box is an *overall* frequency setting. It is used for composite output, or as the default setting for separation plates unless you modify it in the Advanced Separations Settings dialog.

The Default setting for Screen Frequency uses the screen frequency for the device via the Windows Printer settings. If you reset this value, it will stick throughout your session for subsequent printing of the document.

Font Handling

The first font option, Download Type 1 Fonts, tells DRAW to download either to the printer or to a .prn file any fonts required to reproduce the text in your document. With a .prn file, you don't have to worry about whether your service bureau has the right fonts. Many DRAW users, including most of the members of this writing team, prefer to work this way, even though an increasing number of service bureaus accept .cdr files.

Type 1 fonts are the only flavor that PostScript devices actually recognize. That's why Type 1 is the primary option in this dialog—and it's also why the second option, Convert TrueType to Type 1, exists. When Download Type 1 is on (which it is by default), the second option is also automatically turned on. This allows you to utilize either Type 1, TrueType, or both in your document and still have it print correctly on a PostScript printer.

You might be wondering what happens if you choose not to download fonts. Does your text not print? Does it print, but in the wrong font? The text prints correctly, but it is changed when it is reproduced. At print time, DRAW converts the text to graphic objects, either vector curves or (for smaller text) bitmaps. This works fine for small amounts of text but is highly inefficient for large text blocks, particularly paragraph text. Converting text to curves slows the printing process and can produce very large and unwieldy .prn files, and that can mean added expense at the service bureau.

When would you not use these options? Actually, there are situations where DRAW ignores font selection anyway. Any time you envelope artistic text, extrude it, or do some other artistic transformation, the text will be converted to curves at print time. And sometimes it's preferable to convert text to curves. In a page containing many short strings of artistic text using a large variety of fonts, the .prn file might be smaller if the text is converted, rather than downloading all the required fonts. Another reason to convert to curves: too many different fonts can choke a PostScript device because only a limited portion of its memory is allocated to fonts. Most of the time, however, you will want to leave both these options on.

Figure 26.6 shows a large block of copy and a single character. We created print files from these two elements, alternating between choosing to download typeface information and to treat as curves. As expected, rendering a single character as a curve resulted in a smaller file than defining an entire character set just for it. If the typeface was one of the standard 35 already resident in printer ROM, the difference was small—30KB as opposed to 32KB. If we chose a typeface that had to be downloaded in its entirety, consumption rose to 91KB.

Treating the long block of copy in the customary way, as text, also resulted in a 32KB file. But asking DRAW to render the copy as curves sent it off into PostScript code hell—871KB. So you'll need a very good reason to treat blocks of copy as curves, and frankly, we don't think such a reason exists.

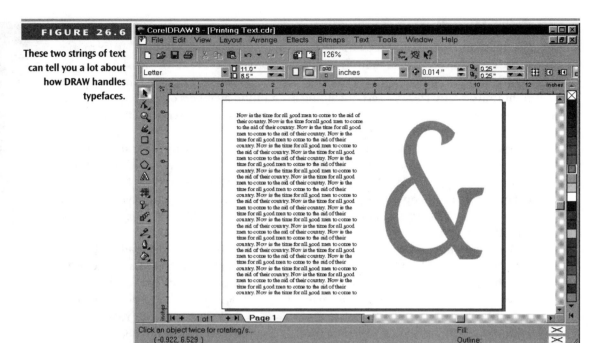

FIGURE 26.6

These two strings of text can tell you a lot about how DRAW handles typefaces.

Type 1 vs. TrueType

The issue of which fonts are better is always a source of debate. Many service bureaus claim they always have difficulty with TrueType fonts, but there really is no inherent reason that their conversion and printing would cause trouble. Many DRAW users have been quite successful using TrueType fonts, and you will find font aficionados supporting both sides of the debate. TrueType fonts do account for more print problems, but they usually stem from the individual fonts, not the font format.

Most Type 1 fonts on the market have been carefully crafted by well-established digital font vendors. The same can be said for many but not all TrueType fonts. Quite a few "cheapie" font packs exist, and they are almost always TrueType. Most shareware fonts, as well, are TrueType. Some obey the rules of font-mongering, others don't—and those are usually the ones causing print problems.

Most of the fonts supplied with DRAW are properly crafted, and either format should work. However, we admit a bias toward Type 1, because it is the language spoken by PostScript devices. Why do a translation if you can supply the real thing?

PDF Marks

The options here are used when creating PostScript files destined for Adobe's Acrobat format, also known as Portable Document Format (PDF).

On Start, Display   These settings control how Adobe Acrobat displays a PDF file. To be more precise, these settings affect the PostScript code that DRAW creates, which in turn is run through Distiller.

Full Screen is a good choice if you are creating PDF files for screen presentations, as the PDF is displayed without the Acrobat menus and toolbars. Page Only is the standard display, with menus and toolbars, and the Thumbnails option instructs Acrobat to open the PDF file with Mini-Previews in a separate window to the left of the main PDF contents window.

Include Hyperlinks, Bookmarks   The Include Hyperlinks and Include Bookmarks check boxes are used in conjunction with the Links and Bookmark Manager dockers so that any paragraph text you have formatted as a hyperlink or bookmark will be formatted as such in the final PDF file. Formatting objects as hyperlinks and bookmarks will create clickable hotspots in the final PDF file.

These new settings here in PostScript are part of Corel's big commitment to supporting the PDF format. We have details on these and all of the other aspects of creating PDF files in Chapter 28.

Maximum Points per Curve

This option reduces the maximum number of "control points" PostScript uses to generate curves. Contrary to the implication, reducing control points is not at all like reducing nodes in an object. A processing function only, reducing control points will not degrade the quality of the output, but it may increase output time significantly. If you are getting limitcheck errors, this is one option you can try. It is a sticky option that will remain set for each document during your DRAW session.

Another alternative is to simplify the objects. If you have an idea which objects are causing limitcheck problems, you might break apart complex elements into several less-complex components (converting stylized text to curves, for example). The advantage of this approach is in avoiding drastically increased print time. And it's permanent—you won't have to remember to set an option every time you open this drawing and print.

Set Flatness To and Auto Increase Flatness

Unlike setting Maximum Points per Curve, adjusting flatness is a bit like removing nodes from an object. It simplifies printing but may also reduce printed quality. When a PostScript device creates a curve, it generates a series of small, connected line segments. (Using many small segments generates a smoother curve than using fewer large segments.) Keeping track of all these little lines also increases the demand on the output device's memory.

So, one way to simplify a drawing is to increase its flatness. Increasing flatness means producing fewer, larger line segments. You can do this up to certain levels with no noticeable degradation in quality. How much increase you can get away with will depend on the artwork in question and the results you want.

DRAW provides two ways to control flatness. One way is to type a specific value in the Set Flatness To box. This value will apply to all objects, and the default is 1.00. Figure 26.7 shows some reproduced samples that were originally printed on a laser printer. To make it easier for you to detect the change on the object, we've used extreme flatness values. (Even so, you may need to examine the figure with a magnifier to fully appreciate the effect.)

FIGURE 26.7

The phenomenon of flatness

Draw

Flatness = 1

Draw

Flatness = 10

Draw

Flatness = 100

The other way to adjust flatness is with the Auto Increase Flatness check box. This option only kicks in when your output device encounters an object that will cause a limitcheck error. PostScript then retries the object with flatness increased by 2. It continues increasing until the object prints successfully, or the flatness value reaches 10 over the Set Flatness To value. The advantage to this method is that it increases the likelihood of getting every object to print. The disadvantage is that the flatness value required to get past the error may produce unacceptable results.

TIP Here's how to determine if you are likely to encounter limitcheck errors on an imagesetter. Before you burn up expensive film, set an artificially low flatness value and print to your desktop laser printer. How low? Divide your laser printer's resolution by the destination imagesetter's resolution, and use a setting slightly lower than the result. For example, divide 600dpi (for the laser) by 2540dpi (for the imagesetter) for a resulting flatness value of 0.24. This method isn't foolproof, but if your artwork gets a limitcheck on the laser printer, it almost certainly will on the imagesetter.

Smart Control of Fountain Steps

Determining exactly how many steps to use for optimum fountain fills is a difficult process—practically an art form. There is a lot of math involved, based on the output resolution, halftone frequency, range of color in the fill, and length of the filled object. You'll have to make trade-offs, and sometimes banding will be inevitable, depending on the selected halftone frequency and resolution. Once these two controlling parameters are chosen, DRAW gives you a couple of options for avoiding the calculator and, we hope, fountain-step banding. These two options can be used alone or in concert, and both options will stick for the duration of the session with that particular drawing.

Auto Increase Fountain Steps looks at your output settings (resolution and halftone frequency) and determines the maximum number of steps that can be effectively reproduced. This may not eliminate banding, but it will give you the best possible results with the selected print settings. Note that this option will never reduce the number of steps. It can only increase them, and it will override any low values you may have chosen for an object in the Fill dialog.

Optimize Fountain Fills is the mirror opposite of the Auto Increase option. It looks at your print settings and automatically reduces the number of steps for any fills that are set higher than the target printer can actually produce with those settings. Mirroring its counterpart's action, it only reduces the number of steps, never increases them.

When you use both options in conjunction, all other settings for fountain steps will be overridden. This generates the best optimization of your printing, producing as many steps as necessary to minimize banding, while not creating more steps than are useful. Bear in mind that this will override any values you may have set via the Fill dialog.

What? More Options?

If Corel's engineers had tried to separate the remaining settings into neatly compart-mentalized pages, we would all surely go button happy. So even though they don't all relate to each other, we are thankful for the Miscellaneous page, whose unifying theme is more or less "What did we leave out?"

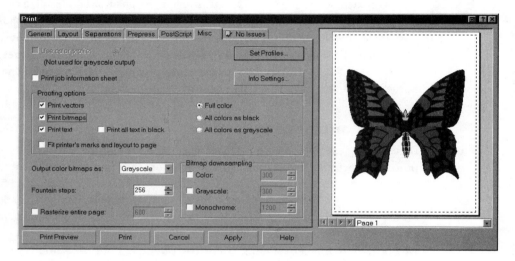

Rest assured, for much of your day-to-day printing needs—especially if you rely mainly on desktop printers—you may never need to access this area. But there are some interesting and useful features here. Some will help you with your color separa-tion work, others just with composite artwork.

Use Color Profile

If you are printing to a color device, you can choose to map the output colors through a specific (or generic) color profile. You can select a different color profile by clicking the Set Profiles button. The active profile is shown below the Use Color Profile check box. We will comment on the use of DRAW's color management in the final section of this chapter, "Tips for Reliable Printing."

Print Job Information Sheet

This check box lets you send an informational sheet to a selected printer, to a text file, or to both. Just click on the Info Settings button to open the Print Job Information

dialog shown in Figure 26.8. This information will be useful for troubleshooting a problematic file, for job tracking, for reproducing the same settings at a later date, and for getting a handy list of fonts used in the drawing. Printing the information sheet is quite straightforward, and the various options can be understood simply by studying the figure.

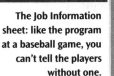

FIGURE 26.8

The Job Information sheet: like the program at a baseball game, you can't tell the players without one.

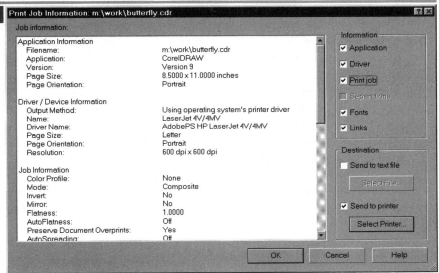

Proofing Options

Three of these options allow you to specify which general categories of objects you wish to print: vectors, bitmaps, and/or text. These can be useful when proofing complex layouts. You can also speed up the proofing process in general by printing only those elements you are concerned about at any given time. Use these proofs to verify the integrity of each category of object, or to help isolate troublesome objects.

When you print only the text from your drawing, you may find it necessary to use the Print All Text in Black option. In a layout that has white text on a black background, for instance, the white text would not be visible without its contrasting black background object. Printing in black would also be preferable when you have light-colored text that would ordinarily map to very light grays. If you needed to fax this to someone, the light text might not be legible. Happily, the Mini-Preview will respond to these changes on the fly, so you can get instant assurances that you have chosen the right settings.

The three options on the right side of the Proofing Options group apply to composite (not separation) printing. Full Color does nothing when printing to a standard laser printer, and the All Colors As Grayscale option is equally pointless, as that is the only thing that it knows how to do. On the other hand, if your only printer is a desktop color model with a separate black ink cartridge, printing everything in grayscale could save costs if you only want to proof the layout for position and balance.

All Colors As Black does what its name implies—it renders all colors as black. This option might be useful to generate line art from color or grayscale drawings—for faxing, perhaps.

Fit Printer's Marks and Layout to Page is a welcome proofing option. Unlike the Fit to Page and scaling functions found on the Layout page, which only affect the artwork itself, this option scales everything that you've designated to print on the chosen page, objects and prepress marks.

Suppose your printer page is the same size or smaller than the document page; with Fit to Page you wouldn't see any printer's marks. When you have a large document that you need to proof on a laser printer, and you need to see everything that will ultimately appear on the film yet maintain the actual proportions of the document page, this is the option to choose.

Why it is here and not on the Prepress page is an annual mystery. We suppose it is because it addresses the prepress marks *and* drawing elements, but that's a weak explanation, because it is only relevant when you turn prepress marks on (otherwise, Fit to Page from the Layout page would suffice).

Output Color Bitmaps As

Normally, colors are either separated to CMYK plates or printed to a composite color device that uses CMYK colors. Some devices, such as slide makers, use RGB colors just as your monitor does. The Output Color Bitmaps As option tells DRAW to store information in a .prn file or send it to an output device using the selected color component information, rather than converting it to CMYK components. This option can also be used with printers that lack black ink and use only the three primary colors, CMY, to produce composite color. Apparently, the translation from RGB to CMY is easier and more accurate than the reverse. The grayscale option is a nice way to save ink when printing quick proofs.

Fountain Steps

When you create a fountain fill in a vector graphics program, it is displayed and printed as a series of discrete bands of color hues and shades. The more bands, the smoother the fountain fill appears, but the longer it takes to redisplay or print. How many bands your screen displays can be set in the Tools ➤ Options ➤ Workspace ➤ Display dialog. However, that has *no* bearing on how many steps are printed.

The value in the Fountain Steps box determines how many steps are printed, subject to two restrictions. First, the setting applies only to fountain fills that you left

locked (the default) when creating them. As described in Chapter 6, you can unlock the steps setting for a particular fountain-filled object, and set a value independently for that object, which overrides what you set with this print option. Why set separate step values? Perhaps you're after an effect that requires a coarse fill and thus fewer bands. Or you may want a few objects to have more fill steps than others.

Use this option to create specialty fill patterns, not to solve print problems. The Auto Increase and Optimize settings on the PostScript page are better for that.

Rasterize Entire Page

This new option is the ultimate safety net for problem-prone pages. It forces the entire page to be converted into a bitmap at the resolution specified in the number box next to the option. The minimum resolution is 72dpi and the maximum is 1000dpi. If you have a lot of bitmap effects in your document, such as lenses, transparencies, bitmap objects, etc., you may want to experiment with this option to reduce print times and complexity, especially when printing quick proofs.

Keep in mind, though, that "entire page" means entire page and any text will also be converted to a bitmap. We do not recommend this option for commercial print jobs and advise instead that you manually "flatten" bitmap objects and effects to simplify PostScript output.

Bitmap Downsampling

The Bitmap Downsampling options are also new for DRAW 9. Use these options to decrease print file sizes and output time, especially when preparing quick proofs.

N O T E   The Rasterize Entire Page and Bitmap Downsampling options can both be enabled at the same time. If you do enable both options, bitmaps would first be downsampled to the selected resolution and then rasterized (or re-rasterized) to the resolution set for Rasterize Entire Page. As a result, the effective resolution of the bitmap would be the lower of the two settings, but the amount of data sent to the printer would be determined by the Rasterize Entire Page setting.

The Preflight Page

The DRAW 9 Print dialog has a new page: Issues (or, if you're lucky, No Issues). The Issues page offers alerts and warnings that can help reduce the number of failed or unacceptable pages you may produce. Or this page can just get in the way—that's up to you.

You can instruct DRAW to check for overly complex objects, banded fountain fills, too many spot colors, too many fonts, or many other potential problems. In the default print style, all of the warnings are active, but you can specify only those warnings you want to see (or none at all) and save your preferences as a new print style.

In previous versions, when PostScript warning messages were enabled, DRAW would issue warning messages after OKing the Print dialog (and then leaving for lunch, coming back, sitting down, and seeing the message on your screen instead of the printout on your print tray). The alerts were issued for each potential problem encountered during the print process. In DRAW 9, every time you issue the Print command, DRAW will "preflight" your document, to borrow the phrase used by pilots to make sure their planes are flight-worthy.

Potential problems will be flagged and the Issues tab will have a yellow warning icon and a tally of the issues you should review. Problems are now caught and can be corrected prior to actually printing the document—a much less intrusive solution in our opinion.

When you select the Issues tab, you will see two panes of information. At the top is the list of potential problems found in your document. These issues will be divided into three categories: high-risk items that will likely result in output problems, shown in red; legitimate but less-severe problems, shown with a yellow warning icon; and potential problems or advisories, marked with a blue information icon. As you select the items from the list in the top pane, helpful context sensitive information and troubleshooting tips will appear in the bottom pane.

You can choose which issues DRAW checks for. For example, if you have a design that incorporates three spot colors, you don't want to see a warning about many spot plates. Click the Preflight Settings button and uncheck this option. Then from the General page of the Print Options dialog, click the Save As button to create a new print style. You may wish to name the print style to reflect the job, the client, or some other naming convention that will be recognizable. (More on print styles later.)

You'll also begin to get in rhythm with the Issues page. If you regularly use TrueType faces, you'll always see "1 issue" appear on the tab, unless you tell DRAW never to notify you about it. But we like being told about that—we know that "No Issues" means that we are using no TrueType faces and "1 issue" or more means that we are.

From the Issues page, click Preflight Settings to see the entire list of situations that DRAW could warn against, and decide for yourself which ones are worth being bothered about and which ones are not.

The Fine Art of Previewing

We have already discussed the value of the reintroduced Mini-Preview window and how we expect it to be used most of the time. (Remember, to toggle the Mini-Preview, click on the new double-arrow button near the top-right of the dialog.) That being

said, there are some controls that live only on the more robust Print Preview screen. While most users won't need to reach for them very often, if you expect to find them on the pages of the Print dialog, you'll tear your hair out.

In the Mini-Preview, you scroll through each page of your document or each separation either by clicking on the arrows at the bottom of the preview window or by accessing a specific page directly from the drop-down list. In Print Preview, you cycle through the pages and separations of your document by clicking the tabs at the bottom of the window. In either case, the printable area is represented by dotted margin lines near the edge of the page. Any objects that reside beyond those margins are clipped off of the preview, just as they would be clipped on the printout.

N O T E For some devices, including imagesetters, you will not see any margins in the preview. The output media used with such devices is actually larger than the size of the declared print page; thus, the entire page area is printable.

To reach Print Preview, you can either go to File ➤ Print Preview or, if you are already in the Print dialog, click the Print Preview button that is present at the bottom of all pages. The image below shows the notable commands that can be found only in Print Preview.

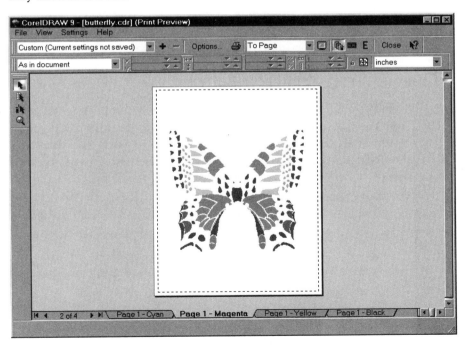

Print Preview's most notable capability is object selection. You can reach right into the preview window, select the objects (as one), and relocate and resize them. With the Print dialog and the Mini-Preview, you must work the controls to achieve the same effect. Here is a tour of the other notable parts of Print Preview.

The View Menu

Most of the items here explain themselves, the notable one being the first: Show Image. If you tire of waiting for a large file to load into the Preview window, you can deselect the Show Image toggle. In its place, DRAW shows a bounding box with an × inside to indicate the actual size of your graphic.

The next two items, Preview Color and Preview Separations, are also handy, as they save you from having to navigate your way back to the various pages of the Print dialog. If you're like most, you might have spent an hour the first time you tried to find your way back to the Print dialog, until you realized that the Options button was the secret password.

The Settings Menu

Gee, what do you know?—more ways to reach the Print dialog that most people never knew existed. This menu also opens the Printer Preferences dialog, where you can quickly and easily adjust print style settings and troubleshoot driver problems, and the Duplexing Wizard, for assistance with double-sided printing.

The Standard Toolbar

Starting from the left end of the toolbar, you will find the Print Style pull-down list. From here you can select a print style to apply to the print job. If you have created a custom style, you can save the style by clicking on the big plus button and entering the style name and related options. Likewise, the big minus button will delete the selected style. The other items here are:

- Options, the ill-named button that takes you to the Print dialog. Hmm, if the menu with the same access is called Settings, why isn't the button?
- The printer icon, which is equivalent to a "Print Now" button.
- Zoom settings in a drop-down menu, and next to it, an icon for previewing full-screen with no screen elements in the way. (Press Esc to return from it.)
- Toggling icons for Print Separations, Invert, and Mirror.
- The Close button. This does not close DRAW, just Print Preview. In fact, think of Print Preview as its own application—you can also press Alt+F4 or use the Close button at the top-right corner of the window.

The Toolbox and Its Property Bar

Here is where things get interesting, and for us author types, very trying. Many of these controls have to be used to be understood—no amount of rambling on our parts can help the learning curve. Not that it's steep, but there is really only one way to learn these things—by working them.

Pick Tool

With the Pick tool selected, the property bar allows you to select several options: preset image positions, top-left corner position, width and height for the selected object, whether to maintain the object's aspect ratio, units of measurement, and tiling options.

Imposition Layout Tool

The Signature Layout and N-Up tools from DRAW 8 have been melded into one and renamed the Imposition Layout tool. With this tool selected, you can choose an imposition layout from the list of preset imposition standards, create and save a custom imposition, delete an imposition, preview a template or document, set the number of pages across and down, toggle the double-sided layout, set gutter spacing, set sheet order, set the page sequence number, and define page rotation.

You can also select N-Up format, save a new format, delete an existing format, preview a template or document, set the number of rows and columns, toggle clone frames, maintain document page size, define gutter spacing, toggle auto-gutter spacing, set top and left margins, set bottom and right margins, and choose from equal margins or auto margins. And, if that wasn't enough, in DRAW 9 you can now set bindery options, custom gutters, fold and trim options, and edit page placement. Whew!

This new Imposition Layout tool is quite powerful, and there should be no imposition that you cannot create and save either directly through the input boxes on the property bar, or interactively using the Imposition Layout tool on the preview pages themselves.

Marks Placement Tool

This is a subset of the Prepress page, with buttons for toggling all of the various and sundry marks that can be scattered around the page. One control not found in the dialog is the ability to move the marks up and down and left and right. Why you would want to do this is beyond us, but hey, we just write about it...

WARNING   If you're printing butt-cut business cards or some similar layout with no gutters, remember to turn the Page Number button off. If you don't, the page number will print within your card. Not good!

Zoom Tool

These buttons in order are: Zoom In, Out, To 100%, To Selection, To Fit, To Page, To Width, To Height, and Open the Zoom Dialog.

Putting It All Together: Creating a Print Style

You can save settings by name and recall them for use at a later date by creating a master print style. Your style can include just about every option covered in this chapter—the only exceptions being the choices you make from the General page of the Print dialog.

The process of making a print style is quite simple. From the General tab on the Print dialog, after selecting the desired options, click the Save As button. Or, from the Print Preview window, again select all the options needed to properly print your document and then, before exiting back to your drawing or to the main Print dialog, go to File ➤ Save Print Style As. Either of these methods then opens the dialog shown in Figure 26.9.

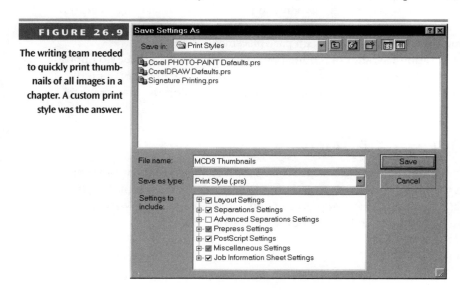

FIGURE 26.9

The writing team needed to quickly print thumbnails of all images in a chapter. A custom print style was the answer.

Certain settings, such as Layout style, are not automatically included in a print style. It is a simple matter to add the ones that aren't saved by default (or, for that matter, to remove some settings from the style). You work this tree-structured menu like you would DRAW's main Options dialog, or the Windows Registry, or just about any application setup program that offers installation options.

To include every possible setting in a category without reviewing them, just click on the little check-box icon until it is checked and unshaded.

Once you determine the settings, enter a name for your print style, and it is saved for posterity. You can also delete it by choosing File ➤ Delete Print Style in the Print Preview window.

You can also save and delete print styles in the full Print Preview window by clicking on the big plus and minus buttons at the left end of the Standard toolbar. The pull-down to the left of these indicates which print style you are using. Curiously, you cannot delete print styles from the Print dialog—only from Print Preview.

WARNING   A saved print style will remember that you turned on separations, but it will not remember if you activated only some of the colors. All of the colors in the drawing will be activated when you initially turn on separations.

Once you have defined a print style, its settings are there for you whenever you need them, at the click of the mouse. You can verify or change the settings as needed by going through the Print Options dialog. When you want to use the style, just select it right from the main Print dialog, and all the options in the style are implemented automatically for that print job.

Print Styles Go Portable

In DRAW 9 each print style is now saved as a separate file, making your print styles portable between systems and users. In Figure 26.9, the print style we created for this book is safe and sound in the Corel90 network of folders. We would find it in Custom\Print Styles, named MCD9 Thumbnails.prs. Other writers on the team, upon receiving the file, would need only to place it in the same folder on their systems to be able to load it.

A print style is less than 1.5KB in size, and it is all ASCII. We didn't need to be rocket scientists to identify PrintEmptyPlates=0 as the line that disables the imaging of empty color plates during separation printing. Advanced users might find it easier to open the file and change the 0 to a 1 than to wade through the dialog, make the change, and then resave the print style.

This is a very popular feature with those who do a lot of repetitive printing. For example, a company that uses DRAW to design and produce packaging labels could make efficient use of print styles. And if you add in a Corel or VBA script, the label project could be almost completely automated.

TIP   You can also save custom impositions for later use or for sharing with others. Impositions are stored in .cly files, located in Custom\Layouts.

Tips for Reliable Printing

Recent versions of DRAW have made significant progress toward making the print process as fail-safe as possible. Inevitably, however, problems arise, some beyond DRAW's power to control. These will generally fall into two categories: hardware problems and poor design choices.

In the first category, you should realize that PostScript code and PostScript printers can be cantankerous beasts. If you are having trouble getting pages to print and no descriptive error messages are being produced, the first thing to do is turn your printer off, then back on again. You might want to clear the print queue as well, and start completely fresh. One bit of bad code can ruin a PostScript printer's whole day. This is the quickest and easiest way to set things right. And it can work for non-PostScript printers, as well. They are less susceptible to the type of error that brings PostScript crashing down; but if you are having problems, try the same procedure. Clear the print queue, restart the printer, and try again.

The second issue—problematic designs—can be overcome with some forethought and informed document preparation. It is forever possible to create things in DRAW that tax or exceed your printer's capabilities. In the first case, you may encounter very slow printing. In the second, you'll get a printed error sheet, or perhaps nothing at all.

Here are a few specific suggestions.

Simplifying Vector Objects

We've mentioned several ways to overcome limitcheck errors produced by overly complex objects. You can either break the object up into smaller components, or try reducing the Maximum Points Per Curve in the PostScript page of the Print dialog. Something else to try is increasing the flatness, from the same page.

You may find that an object cannot be broken into smaller components, yet it is still too complex. Try increasing the Curve Smoothness from the Node tool property bar (the old Auto-Reduce function) to eliminate unnecessary nodes from the object. In many cases, the same curvature can be achieved with fewer nodes. (Refer back to Chapter 4 for advice about using the fewest possible number of nodes.)

Handling Bitmaps

Since bitmaps are already just a collection of dots or pixels, there is nothing particularly complex about them. However, the *number* of dots in a bitmap can run into the millions, and PostScript is not very efficient about handling them. Your biggest problem is likely to be speed, or rather the lack thereof (and potential surcharges at a service bureau).

Make the best of the situation by using every trick possible to minimize the amount of data in your bitmap that will still produce the results you are after.

Line Art, Grayscale, or Color?

Color images can be 8-bit (256 colors) or 24-bit (16.7 million colors). It's nice to have that many colors available, but 24-bit image files can be huge. A 5-by-7-inch image with a pixel (ppi) resolution of 300dpi will weigh in at a hefty 9.5MB! Will reducing the palette to 8-bit color suffice?

And what about when you are printing black and white? Is grayscale a requirement? All else being equal, a grayscale (8-bit) image has eight times as much data as a comparably sized line-art (pure black-and-white) image.

What about Size?

More often than not, you really don't have much choice as to the type of bitmap to use. The next best alternative is to see about reducing the size (in pixels) of the image. The first tactic to try is to consider the bitmap's final printed size as compared to its original size. If you're including a 300dpi image in your artwork but plan to reduce it to half-size in the printed piece, you should scan it at 150dpi.

Resolution is really a relative value for bitmaps. Though it's expressed as dpi (dots per inch), it's actually a measure of pixels per inch—something quite different from a printer's dot. We tend to think in terms of the resolution of a bitmap, since this defines the quality of output. But the absolute measure of a bitmap is how many pixels it contains. When we set a scanning resolution for a given size, we are in fact determining the number of pixels in the bitmap.

For example, an image 500 pixels wide by 700 pixels tall contains 350,000 pixels. If it's an 8-bit image, the file size is about 350KB. If you size this image in DRAW to 5 by 7 inches, it will have an output resolution of 100dpi. The same image, when sized to 2.5 by 3.5 inches, will be 200dpi. Conversely, it would only be a 50dpi image if sized to 10 by 14 inches. Ideally, you would use Corel PHOTO-PAINT to create (or edit) your bitmap images to the exact size, cropping, and resolution you need before bringing them into DRAW.

Output resolution should not be confused with *printer resolution*—they are two separate but related things. One is an expression of the image in pixels per inch (though we use the term dots per inch). The other is an indirect expression of the smallest size dot a printer can produce.

What Resolution Is Absolutely Necessary?

So, what resolution do you need? For line art, it will depend on how free of jaggies you want it to be, and what the printer's resolution is. There is a direct mapping of pixels to printer dots, since no halftones are involved. If a printer can print 600dpi, you could utilize an image with a resolution as high as 600dpi.

For color and grayscale, the halftoning process changes the applicable rules. The rule of thumb is to make sure the bitmap's output resolution, expressed in dpi, is at least 1.4 but not over 2 times the intended halftone screen frequency, expressed in lpi. A common halftone frequency for Linotronic output is 133 lines per inch. At this value, there's no need to create any image with a resolution higher than 266dpi, and you'll probably get acceptable results with as low as 186dpi.

Optimizing the bitmap size can speed the printing process, liberate valuable disk space, and save bucks at the service bureau.

N O T E   If you don't want to permanently change the resolution of images in your document, make use of DRAW 9's new Bitmap Downsampling options on the Miscellaneous page of the Print dialog. And don't forget about using OPI links. (See the "PostScript" section earlier in this chapter.) This won't ease printing, but it will certainly speed your design process and save disk space, if the service bureau stores the image.

Fonts and Fills

There is really only one thing to say with regard to typefaces: try not to use too many at once. This is important from a printing efficiency standpoint, but is also simply good design policy. As mentioned in the "Font Handling" section earlier in this chapter, if you must include a lot of fonts, with small bits of text set in each font, you should probably let DRAW convert the text to curves at print time, instead of downloading the fonts.

From the same perspective, don't get carried away with special fills. Effective art makes judicious use of these—use too many and they lose their impact. Specialized fills also can affect print efficiency. They take longer to print than objects filled with uniform color, and some are worse than others.

Fountain fills print fairly fast. The only caution here is regarding quality. Are you seeing a lot of banding in the result? See "Smart Control of Fountain Steps" earlier in the chapter about handling fountain fill steps.

The various pattern fills are quite another story. Whether they print quickly or bog the printer down depends on various parameters. We printed a solid-filled pentagon, created with the Polygon tool, to a PostScript laser printer in a few seconds. Then we filled it with a simple two-color pattern set to a large tile size, and it took just a wee bit longer to print. Next, we changed the tile size to small. Whoa! Print time shot up to almost two minutes.

Other Tips for Printing

Bitmaps usually print trouble-free on most non-PostScript devices. Laser printers do have finite memory in which to image your work, so the foregoing advice to optimize the pixel size of bitmaps holds here, as well. If you find printing is frequently very slow or you often get messages such as "Print Overrun" or "Mem Overflow," you might need to invest in additional printer memory.

On some non-PostScript printers, notably laser printers that use or emulate HP's PCL language, fonts and vector objects can be handled in one of two ways. The printer can treat these objects as vectors and do its own rasterizing, or you can tell the computer to send a rasterized image to the printer. Using vectors is faster but can cause problems. If you get errors, try switching this option for your printer (look in the Properties ➤ Graphics options).

For those who encounter trouble even after taking all of the above measures, Corel's developers have included options for overcoming operating system, printer, and driver problems. Open the Print dialog and click on the Print Preview button. From the View menu in the full Print Preview window, select Printing Preferences. This dialog is divided into three sections and contains a plethora of options for both PostScript and non-PostScript devices that you can enable (or disable) so that your prints are trouble-free. Look in the Help files under Fine Tuning a Print Job for explanations for these options.

Tricks with Color Substitutions

Always keep in mind that separations are produced in black and white. The colors that actually get printed are determined solely by what color inks are used at print time. Armed with this knowledge and a little creative thinking, you can sometimes work around a few sticky situations, especially when working with spot colors.

We've often found it beneficial to use process-color substitutes for preparing Pantone spot-color print pieces. Say you're going for a final result printed in a specific Pantone orange and pale green. Instead of designing with these two colors in DRAW, use process black and process magenta to represent them. It's harder to visualize the finished artwork this way, but it opens a few doors.

PART

The CorelDRAW Freeway

For example, you're confronted with a project for which only black-and-white or grayscale artwork is available, but you want to print it in a Pantone color. Rather than attempting to recolor it, you simply let the black plate represent the actual printed Pantone color. If the job requires its own separate black plate for text or other elements, you could create these in process magenta. This juggling of plate definitions won't harm your final product as long as your printer knows which ink to use with which plate.

Duotones offer another opportunity for color substitution. Duotones are black-and-white photographs enhanced by application of a single tint. If you're importing a photograph into a two-color layout and want to create a duotone out of it, the obvious choice would be to apply a Tinted Grayscale lens in one of the two spot colors. Though Pantone colors can be selected for this lens effect, they're converted to CMYK at print time. Substitute a process primary color as the lens color and for all other instances of that Pantone color, and your problem is solved.

We started this chapter by saying that printing can be a simple affair. So how come we just killed a tree? An old proverb speaks about how the first 90 percent of any acievment is easy and the last 10 percent is difficult, and that seems apt here. Ninety percent of the time, printing will be easy; you really will be able to click Print and go. Ten percent of the time, you'll have to think about it, and tweak, fiddle, adjust, and hopefully not swear too much.

We like to think that this book is a good read, and we take it as very high praise when readers tell us that they read it page by page. But we have no illusions about how this chapter should be used. It's a reference; it's not a good read. Come back to these pages when you encounter a challenge or a problem; return here for a refresher on creating good film; use this chapter to create killer print styles.

The new proverb says that if you can't print, it's just a video game.

chapter 27

COLOR FOR THE COLOR BLIND

Featuring

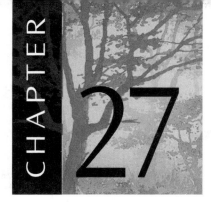

COLOR FOR THE COLOR BLIND

t our ongoing series of CorelDRAW seminars, we routinely ask the audience for a show of hands: "Do you think you have a good understanding of color publishing?" In a crowd of 100, it is unusual for more than a dozen to raise their hands. Despite the proliferation of color scanners and affordable desktop color printers, the realm of color publishing continues to give DRAW users a case of the heebie-jeebies (to use the technical term).

Don't expect this chapter to be the ultimate treatise on working with color. Dozens of books dedicated to the subject are readily available to you from the usual sources. This chapter should serve as your launching pad. Once you've read it, you'll be able to recognize the terms, understand the concepts, and above all, be able to translate it all into effective use of DRAW as your front end for color publishing projects.

Do You See the Light?

When creating the heaven and the earth in those first six days, God also created two ways that humans perceive light. We see light that is *directly transmitted* from a source (from the sun or a light bulb, for instance), and we see light that is *reflected* (from the moon, the clouds, the walls in your house, and the pages of this book). Why should you care about this self-evident fact? Because as a computer user, you deal with both types of light, so it's important to understand how they are different.

Like the sun and a light bulb, your computer monitor is a light source, and the light it uses to display images is transmitted directly to your eyes. On the other hand, your computer produces a printed piece that reflects light but does not transmit it. This is a very important point that we will return to throughout this chapter.

You have probably heard these terms before—RGB and CMYK. They are the color models that most distinctly represent these two kinds of light.

The ABCs of RGB

So you've probably heard of RGB, and maybe you sort of know what it is—a way of defining colors—and that the initials stand for Red, Green, and Blue. (Maybe you've also heard the term "RGB monitor," which is a bit superfluous, because there can be no other type of monitor than an RGB one.) Although most light sources in the physical world emit white light, which is made up of all the colors of the rainbow, the human eye perceives only red, green, and blue light. In other words, all the colors that the human eye can perceive are registered by the eye as combinations and varying intensities of these three colors. That's why color monitors and TVs, which emit only red, green, and blue, can simulate the full spectrum.

Figure 27.1 shows a woman looking at a computer monitor. In this black-and-white drawing you can't tell that she is seeing a monitor with a yellow screen, but she is (although it looks as if her eyes are closed, but we'll overlook that). What forces are at work that cause "yellow" to register in her brain?

N O T E   Here we are faced with our annual frustration: how to present a chapter on color publishing in a book printed in black and white. Thank goodness for the companion page of the Sybex Web site—there you'll find all relevant drawings, named according to their figure numbers. For instance, Figure 27.1 is file f2701.cdr at the Web page.

Like all color monitors and TVs, hers emits RGB light, which means little rays of red, green, and blue light emanate from the monitor. In fact, if you held a magnifying glass up to your own display, you would see hair-thin lines of red, green, and blue. In Figure 27.1, the monitor is emitting red and green light, the two colors that combine to produce yellow. Why yellow, you ask? Because that's what red and green do. It would take too much time and ink to explain the science of RGB light, so let's just accept the fact that when red and green light are combined, they form yellow.

FIGURE 27.1

This monitor is transmitting red and green light, and those two colors combine to form the yellow screen seen by the woman.

RGB is the most straightforward of the various color models, not only because it depicts the behavior of light in the real world, but also because it is easy for humans to visualize. Imagine a bunch of red, green, and blue flashlights shining in various directions in a darkened room. When the rays of light overlap, they form other colors. By varying the intensities of the rays (pretend you have very sophisticated flashlights), you can create all the colors that the human eye can perceive.

When combined at full intensity, red, green, and blue form white, although you might have been tempted to guess the opposite, remembering your crayon-drawing days when using all of your crayons at once gave you a nice black mess. But black is actually the *absence* of light—a point that is obvious to anyone who has walked into the coffee table in the middle of the night.

The RGB color model is called an *additive model,* because those three primary colors combined in various intensities produce the spectrum of visible colors.

Reflections on CMYK

You probably know that CMYK stands for Cyan, Magenta, Yellow, and Black (K for Black because B could also be for Blue). And you probably also know that those are the four ink colors used in conventional four-color printing. What you may *not* know is that CMYK is worlds apart from the RGB color model. RGB represents the *transmission* of colors, but CMYK represents the *reflection* of colors.

The light you see from a printed piece is reflected light. This book, for instance, is not a light source (although we hope it is illuminating); rather, the black ink on this page absorbs light and the white paper reflects light. Colored inks and papers each absorb some portions of the light striking the surface and reflect others, allowing you to see particular colors.

Figures 27.2 and 27.3 demonstrate the process of reflected light. In Figure 27.2, a man is looking down at a book illuminated by white light and he sees red. Why? What forces are at work here that cause him to see red?

FIGURE 27.2

Red, green, and blue rays of light are hitting this page. Why does this man see only red?

The page he is reading is not like a computer monitor—it transmits no light of its own. So to read the page, the first thing he needs is a light source. Like all white-light sources, his emits red, green, and blue rays of light. In Figure 27.2 the desk lamp is flooding the book with RGB light.

The question now becomes this: If the light hitting this page is full-spectrum white light, how come the only light that bounces off the page is red? What ink colors are present on the page to make this so? Figure 27.3 has the answer: yellow and magenta (best seen from f2703.cdr on the Web site). When the light hits this book, the yellow ink absorbs colors at the blue end of the spectrum. Why does this happen? Again, we could write another book entirely about this topic—it's called the "subtractive" theory of color. That's what yellow does—it absorbs blue light. And the magenta absorbs the

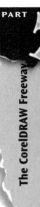

green, because that's what magenta does. So with all of the blue and green light absorbed by the ink on the page, the only color that reflects off the surface is the red.

FIGURE 27.3

The ink on the page absorbs most of the color spectrum, but allows the red to pass through and be reflected off the white paper.

This man sees red because the page contains yellow and magenta ink. Though you might be tempted to say that yellow and magenta combine to make red, that's actually RGB-speak. Rather than combine, they each filter out one of the other two colors, resulting in red. It may seem like this is just a semantic distinction, but it helps to better digest the whole color thing when you think of CMYK inks in terms of what they take away, not what they add.

You don't need to understand the intricacies of additive and subtractive color theories, but you should grasp the moral of this story so far: color from your monitor is totally different than color from a printed piece. We will return to that point later in this chapter.

The Two Kinds of Ink

Now that we have distinguished between monitor colors and ink colors, let's focus on the difference between the two types of inks. The two primary methods of designating inks invoke names that are probably familiar to you: *spot color* and *process color*. There are many criteria for choosing one printing method over the other, not the least of which is the amount of money you are willing to spend. Here is a quick overview.

Spots of Paint

The simplest and most affordable way to introduce color into a drawing is to use one primary color and another color for accent. This is called *spot-color printing,* so named because you typically choose a few spots here and there to add the accent color. A drawing that uses black and one spot color will only require two passes through a conventional printing press; a full-color print job, using CMYK inks, requires four passes.

Spot colors are premixed, ready-made inks that you use when you want to introduce one or two colors into a drawing. Cornering the market of spot colors is Pantone, whose Pantone Matching System and corresponding color swatch books show every color in a 1,000-plus palette. Once you find a color you want to use, you can ask for it by name in DRAW's Fill dialogs.

 WARNING   Choosing a Pantone color because it looks good on screen is a tragedy waiting to happen. Choosing a Pantone color because it looks good in the Pantone Color Formula Guide is the way the professionals do it.

You will pay less for a print job that requires black and one spot color rather than four colors, but price is not the only consideration for using spot colors. Sometimes you must use a color that cannot be reproduced by process colors. The color range of CMYK is a subset of what the human eye can perceive, and it is possible to create a specialty color that cannot be reproduced with CMYK inks. If you've ever asked your neighborhood quick-copy store for a fast print job employing Reflex Blue, for instance, you used a color that has no CMYK equivalent. The classic example is the red—known only as Coca-Cola Red—that the Coca-Cola Company uses for its soda cans. No combination of cyan, magenta, and yellow can create it faithfully, and printing runs at Coca-Cola require an extra pass through the printer, using the company's proprietary spot color.

Spot colors do not mix if you overlap them, and indeed, you are not supposed to. They are opaque. Think of them as paint: you dab them in specific places in your drawing, but you don't overlap them with other colors—unless you really do want to produce the color of mud. (The exception is the creation of *duotones,* which is a conscientious process involving two identical images, rendered by mixing two spot colors at different screen angles.)

The Process of Transparent Ink

The other printing method, *process color,* is very different from spot color. Just four distinct colors—the familiar cyan, magenta, yellow, and black—team up to produce all the colors and shades that you might want to have in a drawing. This requires four separate passes through the press, but in return you get printed pieces in full color.

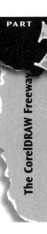

But let's back up for a minute. We just finished telling you that you can't mix and overlap spot colors. Why can you do it with process colors? How come you can take cyan, magenta, and yellow and just throw them together to create other colors? How come they don't create mud?

The answer is in the ink. The inks for these colors are not like regular ink; they are like transparent gels. Light passes through them and is either absorbed or reflected off the surface. For the red page in Figure 27.3, it didn't matter which ink was laid down first, the yellow or the magenta. The yellow absorbs the blue and allows the red and green to pass through, and the magenta catches the green—regardless of which one receives the light first.

Separation Anxiety

This one word, *separation,* is responsible for a lot of gray hair among desktop designers, but it's a necessary evil for anyone who wants to print large projects in color. As you may know, creating separations is how you prepare a drawing for color printing. You produce separate pieces of paper or film, each one representing a specific color—spot or process—used in the drawing.

Figure 27.4 shows a simple drawing of a postage stamp, created in DRAW. It is made up entirely of the four process colors and, as such, is perfect for a color-separation exercise. If you want to follow along, open f2704.cdr from the Sybex Web site.

FIGURE 27.4
All four process colors are used to create this postage stamp.

Element	C	M	Y	K
32¢	60	40	0	40
Left semi-circle	40	0	40	0
Middle	0	100	100	0
Right	20	60	0	20
US Postage	60	0	60	20
Border	30	20	15	40

Making a Proof

First, you create a proof for your desktop laser printer.

1. Open the drawing and choose the Print command from the File menu.

2. On the General page of the dialog box, choose your desktop printer from the drop-down list of printers.

3. Click the Separations tab to turn to that page of the dialog.

4. Click on the Print Separations check box, and notice that the colors window becomes available, listing the colors used in the document. Each color is checked, indicating it is to be printed.

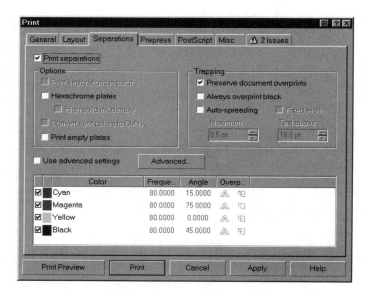

5. Click Print to print the file. Your laser printer will deliver four pages that look a lot like Figure 27.5.

TIP   You can click on the Print Preview button in the Print dialog box to display a preview of the image as it will print. If you've told DRAW to print separations, you can preview the separations color by color. Use the tabs along the bottom of the preview window to select which color to display. Click on the Close button to close the preview window and return to your drawing.

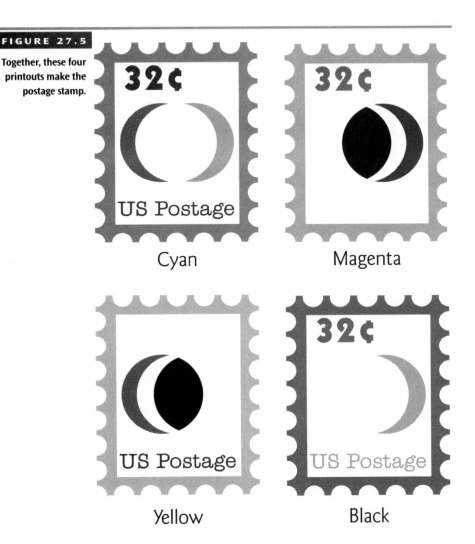

FIGURE 27.5

Together, these four printouts make the postage stamp.

Cyan

Magenta

Yellow

Black

Making a Print File

When your proofs are satisfactory, you are ready to move from dress rehearsal to live performance: you are ready to create print files. The procedure is the same as the five steps above, but instead of printing to your laser printer, you ask for all print information to be stored in a file that you can transport to your service bureau (assuming you don't have one of those large and expensive imagesetters in your office). The details of creating print files are in Chapter 26.

If you have a color laser printer, you can check the Print Separations in Color box below Print Separations. Each page will be printed in the actual color of ink to be used. This is handy for demonstration purposes—especially when you use transparencies—to create an actual color key; the printed pages, however, will bear little resemblance to what you deliver to your print shop. Those folks aren't interested in color; that part comes when the ink is loaded onto the press. Your objective in the print file is to tell your print shop where the color goes, and that is done in plain black and white. The areas that are printed in full intensity indicate that the particular color is to be printed at 100%, and the areas that are tinted represent the corresponding tint of the color.

So to get this postage stamp printed in color, you would deliver to your print shop four pieces of film or paper that look like Figure 27.5, right? *Wrong!* As part of the process of making the metal plates that go onto the press, the operators at your print shop don't want positive images, they want negative ones, like the ones shown in Figure 27.6. They want film negatives, so that is what you'll be asked for when you send the print files to your service bureau.

N O T E   If you are creating "camera-ready" artwork for small print jobs, t-shirts, or other projects where laser-printed art is acceptable, then you would send positive images.

N O T E   DRAW offers an option to create negative output (Invert) on the Prepress page of its Print dialog, but most service bureaus would rather do it themselves. So check with your service bureau first. Chances are that you will be asked not to check the negative option, but instead give them a positive print file.

Unless you have a lot of experience studying film negatives, they are difficult to use as proofs because they are quite different from the image that you see on screen. That's why it's crucial to make proofs and trial separations on your laser printer. Don't worry if you don't own a color printer and can't proof in color. In some ways, it's better to proof in black and white, because that's how the film will be made. At the proof stage, your job is to make sure there are no copy errors (obviously) and that all the colors that you intend to use are correctly represented on the separated printouts. Print Preview can do this for you, as well.

FIGURE 27.6

Now we're getting somewhere. These negative images are just what your print shop wants as it prepares your work for press.

Cyan

Magenta

Yellow

Black

Trap Your Colors Before They Trap You

In the previous section, we discussed the importance of proofing your color work before sending it off to your print shop. But one thing your proofs won't show you is whether you need to apply *trapping* to your work. This word typically strikes fear in the hearts of experienced, well-intentioned designers—we're even afraid of writing about it. Color trapping defies a simple definition, so bear with us here.

Print shops do their best to make sure that a sheet of paper running through a high-speed press will come out with all the layers of colored ink placed in exactly the right places. The degree of accuracy in this process is called *registration,* and one of the options when you print in DRAW is to enable registration marks—little bull's-eyes that print on every piece of film for a given project. Despite their best efforts, print shops can't align the paper perfectly on the press every time. Truth is, registration errors are common in color-printed work, but the degree to which they harm your finished work depends upon the nature of your drawing and the extent to which you can prepare for these errors. This section is a qualitative introduction to color trapping—why you need it, how you can apply it, and in some cases, how you can best avoid it.

N O T E   Color trapping is not required when printing to a desktop color printer, slide processor, or other single-pass output device. Trapping is only required for printing on a traditional printing press, where the various colors will be applied to the paper in separate passes.

Where Colors Touch

Figure 27.7, also available on the Web site, is a rendition of a cube along with a list of the colors used. If you were to print it in color, the cube would require three distinct pieces of film and three individual passes on the press (there is no black in this cube).

Understanding registration and trapping issues begins with an analysis of the areas in a drawing where colors meet, because that is where registration errors can hurt you. For instance, the top face of the cube is made up of 20% magenta, and the left face is 100% yellow. Let's assume that there is a registration error when printing the yellow—it is not lined up exactly where it is supposed to be. If this error causes the yellow to be placed too high (and in terms of registration errors, we're talking about errors of less than 1 point), then the yellow will bang into the magenta. By all accounts, this is a "friendly" error. A tiny bit of yellow overlapping the magenta will probably be unnoticeable. Even if you could see it, you wouldn't react negatively to it because your eye is expecting to see both yellow and magenta in that vicinity. There would be about a quarter-point of space where the magenta is a bit redder than it should be, and that's okay.

But what if the registration error is such that the yellow is placed too low, so that it doesn't actually reach the magenta? Again, we're talking about less than a quarter-point, but now instead of an overlap of colors, there would be a small area without any color. You'd see a streak of white (or whatever color the paper is) which, though tiny, would be both noticeable and objectionable.

FIGURE 27.7

Can you find the places on this cube where color trapping is required?

Element	C	M	Y	K
Left face	0	0	100	0
Letter A	0	100	0	0
Right face	100	100	0	0
Letter C	100	0	0	0
Top face	0	20	0	0
Letter B	0	100	100	0

There is no way for you to know whether a registration error will be a friendly one or not, so you have to "trap" against all possibilities. (Hence the term *trapping*, and this is about as close as we can get to definition—nobody seems completely sure where the term came from.)

Trapping will also be needed for the big *A* that is inside the yellow face. Here there is no possibility of a friendly registration error because any error will result in a white streak somewhere. This becomes clearer if you stop and think about how this cube is actually printed. Figure 27.8 offers a depiction of the process. Notice how the yellow face has a large *A* cut out of it, right where the magenta *A* is to go. This is called a *knockout,* and it is necessary in process-color printing. If the *A* weren't knocked out of the yellow, then the two ink colors would overlap to form red (remember, process-color inks are transparent). The knocked-out area where the *A* is to fit must not have any ink color at all, except for the magenta, the intended color.

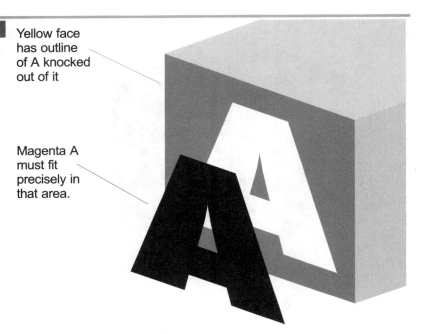

Yellow face has outline of A knocked out of it

Magenta A must fit precisely in that area.

In Figure 27.8 we have tried to make it look like a jigsaw puzzle, which seems a pretty good way to think of this knockout dynamic. You can see why it's so important for the registration to be accurate; the magenta A needs to fit precisely into the hole in the yellow face. But again, you can't always count on perfect accuracy, so you must take matters into your own hands.

Eight Ways to Deal with Trapping

Because registration issues have been around for as long as there have been color presses, numerous strategies have evolved to ensure good-quality color output. Here are the most common ones.

1. Use Trapping Software

These days you can choose from a collection of sophisticated software whose job is to study a PostScript print file, determine the areas where colors butt against one another, and apply trap to those areas. The program will then create a modified version of the PostScript print file, which you can in turn send to the imagesetters at your service bureau. The software that runs on PCs, called TrapWise, is marketed by Luminous Technology Corporation. This is not typical, run-of-the-mill software—it costs nearly $4,000. Some businesses can justify that type of investment, but it's more likely you would seek out a service bureau that has purchased TrapWise and will apply it to your work for a usage fee.

2. Find a Smart Imagesetter

Well-equipped service bureaus may use a special imagesetter made by Scitex. This machine reads composite print files (that is, ones that are not separated), separates the colors, and applies traps where needed. Then it sends output directly to a raster image processor that creates the film. Using the Scitex machine costs close to twice the usual $12 to $18 for a piece of film produced on a standard imagesetter.

3. Choose Common Colors

If your drawing's color scheme has any flexibility, you can avoid trapping errors by choosing your colors with that in mind. When two objects share at least 20% of the same color, you have effectively eliminated the risk of registration errors.

For instance, let's say that the big *A* on our cube doesn't have to be pure magenta, but instead could have a slightly red tint of 100% magenta and 25% yellow. Now think about how the yellow ink would be laid down in that area: it would be at 100% intensity around the face of the cube and at 25% in the space where the *A* is to go.

Now when the *A* is laid down, it still needs to be placed in the knockout area, but because that area already contains yellow ink, a registration error is not going to be too unsightly. Remember, a bad registration error is one that produces white streaks where there is no ink present at all. In this case, though, the entire face has yellow ink, including the knockout area for the *A*. As you can see in Figure 27.9, the knocked-out area of the face has a small amount of ink coverage—enough to keep a small registration error from being too objectionable.

FIGURE 27.9

This knockout area of the cube is effectively trapped by using a common color. The entire face of the cube has some amount of yellow, eliminating the possibility of the paper color showing through.

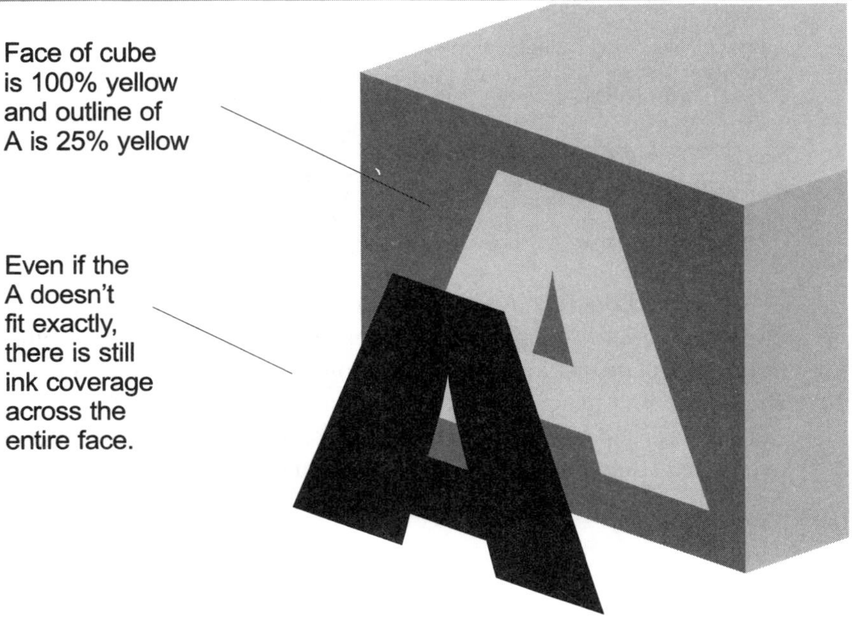

Face of cube is 100% yellow and outline of A is 25% yellow

Even if the A doesn't fit exactly, there is still ink coverage across the entire face.

Incidentally, the top face of the cube and the red *B* need no trapping because they share a common color—the *B* has yellow and magenta, and the top face also contains magenta. The same is true for the right face and the *C*, which share cyan.

4. Overprint Small Objects

Applying trap to your drawings can be a daunting task, but there is one situation that is easy to handle. When you have small text or other objects on a colored background, the trapping strategy is simple.

Figure 27.10 shows a two-color drawing with black body copy placed on a colored background. The simplicity of this piece belies the trouble it will cause when it goes on the press, and Figure 27.11 shows why. By default, DRAW creates separations using knockouts, as described in the preceding section. Imagine the registration nightmares of printing this piece, what with all of those fine serifs and thin ascenders in the 9-point text. This job would be virtually impossible to register properly.

We remember it as if it were yesterday: the day that CorelDRAW was first released. Up until then, the closest things to illustration software were unremarkable paint programs and non-graphical applications that required a degree in programming to run. CorelDRAW was one of the first Windows-based drawing programs to take hold.

Today, over ten years later, CorelDRAW remains one of the leaders in Windows-based graphics, both in terms of its customer base, its stature, and the sheer volume of programs that are included in this one product.

It is no mystery to us why this is so. From its inception, CorelDRAW became known as the most approachable, the most inviting of the drawing and illustration programs, and its stable of users covers virtually all corners of the graphics community. Fine artists…illustrators…technical artists…freelance designers…logo creators…desktop publishers…book publishers…sign-makers…t-shirt designers…newsletter editors…converted secretaries…department managers…and even the lead author's six-year-old daughter. Becoming proficient with CorelDRAW might be a daunting task; however, hundreds of thousands of users will attest to the fact that playing around with, developing a feel for, and even getting the hang of the program is not difficult at all.

This project offers an ideal opportunity to use *overprinting* of your black text. Overprinting is the opposite of knocking out. Instead of creating white holes on the other color plates, you tell DRAW to ignore the black text on all other plates and pretend that it isn't there. Let's back up one step. Earlier in this chapter, we established that some objects had to be knocked out of other objects. Otherwise the transparent inks overlap, creating an unwanted color. But that doesn't apply to black, because it absorbs all light. When you mix black with another color, you get black. Therefore, you don't need to knock out small black text; instead, you can ask for it to be overprinted.

PART

The CorelDRAW Freeway

FIGURE 27.11

How would you like to try to line up these two plates on the press?

We remember it as if it were yester released. Up until then, the closest um able paint programs and non-graphi gramming to run. CorelDRAW was grams to take hold.

Today, over ten years later, Corel dows-based graphics, both in terms volume of programs that are include

It is no mystery to us why this known as the most approachable, th programs, and its stable of users co munity. Fine artists…illustrators… creators…desktop publishers…book ers…newsletter editors…converted the lead author's six-year-old daught might be a daunting task; howeve fact that playing around with, deve the program is not difficult at all.

We remember it as if it were yester released. Up until then, the closest um able paint programs and non-graphic gramming to run. CorelDRAW was grams to take hold.

Today, over ten years later, CorelD dows-based graphics, both in terms of volume of programs that are included

It is no mystery to us why this is known as the most approachable, the programs, and its stable of users cove munity. Fine artists…illustrators…tec creators…desktop publishers…book ers…newsletter editors…converted se the lead author's six-year-old daught might be a daunting task; however fact that playing around with, develop the program is not difficult at all.

Color separation with black text knocked out

Black separation

You can ask for overprinting in DRAW in two different ways:

- On an object-by-object basis, you can instruct that outlines or fills be over-printed by clicking mouse Button 2 on the object and choosing Overprint Fill.

- Globally, you can turn on the Always Overprint Black option in the Separations page of the Print dialog. With this option set, any object that contains at least 95% black will be set to overprint.

Figure 27.12 shows the effect of asking for text to be overprinted. By eliminating the knockout, you have also eliminated any registration issues.

Purists argue that black overprinted on another ink color produces a different type of black—referred to by some as a "juicy black." Technically, they're right, but the point is not really worth arguing for any but the most demanding of print jobs. Certainly, if you ask for a 72-point headline to be overprinted, you're laying down a whole lot of black ink on top of other ink colors and that would be noticeable. This is why the Always Overprint Black option should be used carefully, and overprinting should only be used for small objects. Nevertheless, when you are working with smaller text, fine hairlines, rules around boxes, and other small black objects that are to be placed on top of other colors, overprinting is the answer to your trapping needs.

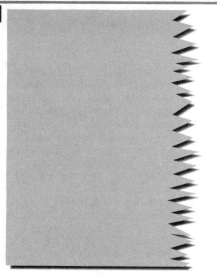

FIGURE 27.12

Bye-bye registration errors. With over-printed text (on the left), there are no fine serifs and other small objects to align.

Color separation with black text overprinted

Black separation

5. Let Your Print Shop Take Care of Trapping

The next option in the trapping gambit is to do what designers and publishers have been doing for as long as there have been color presses: send your film to your print shop and ask them to trap your colors for you. The operators there will place your film under a powerful camera, study the areas where there might be problems due to misreg-istration, and apply tiny amounts of a common color to those areas. If your print shop employs skilled camera operators, this option is the friendliest of all, though not neces-sarily the cheapest. You'll be charged from $30 to $150 or more per page for this service, but it's usually the most reliable trapping option—and it's not so terribly expensive when you factor in the hassles of doing it yourself and the cost of your time.

6. Do Nothing

Believe it or not, thousands of professional DRAW users take this route. They decide that they don't want to be bothered with the specter of trapping, and they turn their film over to their print shops and hope that the job comes out okay.

7. Tell DRAW to Trap for You

Since version 4, DRAW has offered an option called Auto-spreading, found in the Separations page of the Print dialog. This option will spread, or expand, certain objects by minuscule amounts, thus providing the tiny overlap needed to prevent registration errors. Three criteria must be met before Auto-spreading can be applied to an object: (1) it must contain a uniform fill, (2) it must not be set to overprint via the pop-up menu, and (3) it cannot have an outline.

Approach DRAW's Auto-spreading feature with caution. In theory, it's a credible tool, but many DRAW-using color professionals don't trust it in actual implementation.

8. Do It Yourself

We've already discussed how you can trap black text by having it overprinted. With a bit of careful thought, you can use a technique based on the overprint strategy to trap all the objects in your drawing. This technique is called a *trapping outline.*

For example, in the discussion of the cube, you learned that the boundary between the yellow face and the magenta face is a danger zone in the event of a registration error. This is because there is a risk of a white streak appearing if the yellow face is placed too low. The same issue applies to the vertical boundary between the yellow and the blue face. A trapping outline applied to that area is the answer. This thin, yellow rule will nudge into and overprint on top of the magenta and blue faces. Here are the steps to make it happen:

1. Apply a half-point yellow outline to the yellow face. (Rule of thumb: When you have a choice, apply the trap to the lighter-colored object.)

2. Click mouse Button 2 on the face, and choose Overprint Outline.

When you apply an outline to an object, half of its thickness is on the inside of the object, and half on the outside. In our example, therefore, a half-point outline will encroach upon the magenta face by a quarter of a point—a fairly typical trapping amount. With a normal outline, the yellow would merely begin knocking out the magenta a quarter point higher than otherwise, and you would have accomplished nothing. But to apply the trap, you set the outline to be overprinted, and that's the key to the entire puzzle. In that quarter-point space, the magenta will be laid down underneath the yellow, and both ink colors will be present in that area. Now if a registration error causes the yellow face to be placed too low, the magenta ink will still cover that area. You have set a trap against registration errors, thanks to one little overprinting outline. Now, you'll need to repeat the process for every potential trapping problem area in your drawing.

N O T E   One implication of the trapping outline: it has added one-quarter point of thickness to only one face of the cube. This will likely go unnoticed by many of your audience—but you'll know it's there. If it bothers you, you can add a corresponding half-point outline to the other two faces, in the name of consistency.

The other area in this drawing that needs to be trapped is the magenta *A* and the yellow face of the cube. Once again, a trapping outline is the solution, this time applied to the *A*: use the same color as the character itself, set it for a half-point thickness, and designate it to be overprinted. As Figure 27.13 shows, the outline will be placed on top of the yellow ink, ensuring ink coverage all the way around the *A*.

PART

The CorelDRAW Freeway

FIGURE 27.13

The trapping outline around this character prevents a white streak in the event of registration errors.

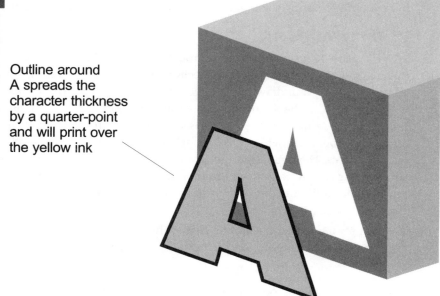

Outline around A spreads the character thickness by a quarter-point and will print over the yellow ink

Incidentally, Figure 27.13 is heavily exaggerated. First of all, the outline color is supposed to be the same as the fill color (good for actual trapping, bad for demonstrating same). Second, the actual outline is supposed to be very small, not the bulky 3-point outline that we have applied here. When you trap for real, the outline won't be seen because all you are adding is a tiny outline colored the same as the object itself. The thickness of the trapping outline will vary depending on the screen frequency you use and the press registration. Check with your print shop for the appropriate thickness of the trap for your project—or better yet, let the specialists at the print shop handle the necessary trapping.

How CorelDRAW Lies to You

If you took a color print of your postage stamp and held it up next to the same drawing on screen, how would the two compare? Would they look:

(a) The same?

(b) Close enough?

(c) Quite different?

(d) Ridiculously different?

If you did this comparison 100 times, it's likely that the result would be (a), the same, approximately zero percent of the time. It's equally likely that the answer would be (d), ridiculously different, more often than (b), close enough. In other words, *forget about accuracy when using your display monitor to view print colors.* And now that you've read this far in the chapter, you know why that is: you can't expect an RGB device—one that's made for transmitting red, green, and blue rays of light—to be able to depict how light will reflect off a surface filled with cyan, magenta, and yellow inks.

Hyperbole aside, there might be hope for your poor monitor yet. And the timing is right, because color printing has never been more approachable. The last two years have seen great strides in alternate methods (other than conventional film-to-plate-to-press printing) for achieving color output. Many service bureaus and quick-copy shops now offer high-end color copiers. Connected to a Fiery RIP (raster image processor), they can directly image your computer files in impressive, continuous-tone (photo-realistic) color.

Today's desktop color printers cost less and produce much higher quality work than their predecessors. Most are still being used for proofing purposes, but even some inexpensive models can now be used for certain commercial projects. It is amazing how well photographs and complex DRAW objects reproduce on, say, a budget-priced Epson inkjet printer with the right kind of paper loaded.

Color output is a far more common goal today for average DRAW users. It's not only the graphics professionals who must confront the complex world of color. Which brings us to the issue of Corel's color management system—overhauled in DRAW 6, improved somewhat in DRAW 7 and 8, but still not quite perfect. In fairness, though, is there such a thing as perfect color matching? Not a chance, and DRAW's system is as good as any other—better, perhaps, because of all of the device profiles it supplies.

When Blue Is Purple

The custom DRAW palette has a color called, simply, Blue. As viewed on your monitor, Blue is an entirely apt name—it looks absolutely and undeniably blue to all but the color blind. (Actually, our color-blind lead author says that it looks blue to him, too.)

But what happens when this simple color is printed? The so-called color Blue is produced by combining 100% cyan with 100% magenta, and unfortunately, this will always look purple.

What Is Color Management And Why Should You Care?

What can color management do for you? Does it adjust the printer to match what you see on the monitor, adjust the monitor to approximate the printer, or a bit of both? Corel's philosophy is to adjust the monitor to more closely approximate what is normally printed, and we applaud this decision. The printer is not only the limiting factor (you can see on your monitor more than you can print), but the *critical* factor. It's far more important for your printouts to be an absolute reference of a color model than a relative one. We think, and Corel agrees, that the printed color models should be the ultimate authority. So the emphasis is to tweak display colors to more closely represent what actually prints.

But there are still lots of variables and conditions to consider. For instance, do you want your color desktop printer to attempt to match the output of a traditional print job? If so, then should it be color-corrected? And if not, then what should your monitor try to reflect—the output of an offset press, or the output from your desktop printer. Indeed, this can all get complicated…

Color profiles (ICM files) try to normalize output devices to meet certain print standards, established by the International Color Consortium (ICC), an organization that sets standards for device characterization. The profiles of some output devices get more adjustment than others. For example, it wouldn't make any sense to color-correct Pantone spot colors when producing film separations on an imagesetter; Pantone inks are already premixed and standardized.

On the other hand, a desktop inkjet printer might need a good deal of correction in this area, because it must use process inks to simulate Pantone colors. That correction comes from the ICM file that instructs the device as to what adjustments to make in order to match its output to the ICC standards for color.

If you're able to understand this mess, you're smarter than most. We asked one of the specialists on our writing team, Debbie Cook, to try to translate this into English. She rolled her eyes, sighed in exasperation, and then tried to have a bit of fun with it.

"Okay," she says, "the ICC says chartreuse should print like A. But we printer manufacturers have to tell our XYZ printer to do B in order for its printout to look like A. And the monitor people say, OK, ICC says chartreuse should display like C, so we monitor makers have to tell our monitor to make adjustment D in order to display chartreuse the way ICC says. DRAW uses the monitor profile for display, and if you choose the Simulate Printer option in Color Management, it also matches the monitor profile to what the printer profile tells DRAW how it (the printer) will print the file. Can I go now?"

Yes, Debbie, right after you tell people that even by default, some form of color conversion will occur on screen when you are viewing drawings destined for print. Whether you choose to stick with Corel's generic settings or you would rather have more control over the process by calibrating your system is up to you.

Corel's Color Management System

The friendly Color Profile Wizard takes you step by step through development of color profiles. You can find it in Tools ➢ Color Management ➢ Profiles or click on the

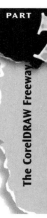

PART

The CorelDRAW Freeway

Set Profiles button in the Miscellaneous page of the Print dialog. Even if you find it necessary to customize the device profiles supplied, the Wizard-like procedure is a more straightforward process than in earlier versions of DRAW. For one thing, you only need to create profiles for each device you use; you don't have to build separate system color profiles for every combination of devices you might use.

Your color profile comprises up to five device-specific components: a scanner profile, a monitor profile, two output options (composite and separations), and an internal RGB profile. What your profile contains and the complexity of creating it will both depend on your needs and system capabilities. At its simplest, you will choose predefined profiles for each of the device types. Corel provides quite a few, and most hardware manufacturers supply ICM files. If you have a choice, use the ones that the manufacturer created.

After selecting the devices you are using, you can choose to have your monitor simulate the results from either the composite or separations output device. You can take it further by beginning with an existing device profile and then using various built-in calibration options to adjust for the unique characteristics of your own equipment. In fact, if you are going to use color profiles at all, you might as well do a bit of calibration. Even devices from the same manufacturer have characteristics that vary from one unit to another and may change over time, as well.

The Bad News and Good News On Color Management Settings

You will likely need to use more than one color management configuration. Let's say you always use a scanner and a particular monitor, but sometimes you print to a desktop color printer and sometimes to a .prn file for a Linotronic imagesetter. Other times your .prn files are destined for color match prints. In theory, you would need different color management settings for each combination of devices you use. And, you would need color management settings for output to different media from the same device—plain paper vs. coated paper, for example. That is a lot of profiles.

Changing color management settings is not devoid of start-up headaches. As you calibrate your various devices, you'll need to do some adjusting and testing. This can be time-consuming and, depending upon how precise you want to be, expensive if you are trying to calibrate to a commercial printer's offset presses.

Once the device profiles are created, you can open the appropriate combination of device profiles in the Color Management section of the Options dialog (go to Tools ➤ Color Management ➤ Profiles). Once chosen, the device profiles are used by all applications in the CorelDRAW suite.

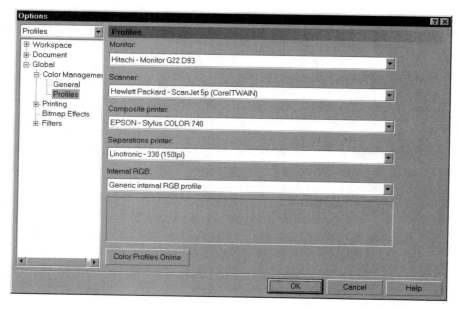

Once you choose the device profiles from the drop-down lists, you select how to use the profiles to color-correct your monitor. At the bottom of the dialog, you can choose to have your monitor simulate the colors you will get from either the Separations or Composite output device. At print time, a check box in the main Print dialog on the Miscellaneous page determines whether the selected profile will be used to color-adjust output.

Color profile files can be gathered from many sources:

- Windows supplies some in `Windows/System/Color`.

- Most vendors keep them on their Web sites.

- Corel keeps a reservoir of them at

  `www.corel.com/support/ftpsite/pub/coreldraw/colorprofiles/index.htm`.

- The Profiles dialog includes a button entitled Color Profiles Online, but at press time, this link was not yet activated.

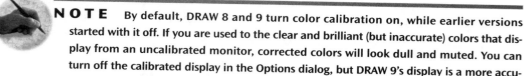

N O T E   By default, DRAW 8 and 9 turn color calibration on, while earlier versions started with it off. If you are used to the clear and brilliant (but inaccurate) colors that display from an uncalibrated monitor, corrected colors will look dull and muted. You can turn off the calibrated display in the Options dialog, but DRAW 9's display is a more accurate representation of your final printed output. If your work is entirely screen related, you can safely disable the option.

But Does It Work?

Simple question, complex answer. If you're going to be working with color, your best investment will be a set of Pantone and TruMatch color swatch books. No matter how evolved color calibration has become, we reserve 100 percent trust only for the swatch books.

Although we were very careful in preparing the device profiles for the printer and monitor and spent hours experimenting, the results were far from completely accurate. It is only with experience that graphics professionals can judge what they see on screen vs. final output, and even then, they all still refer to their swatch books when possible.

After considerable testing and calibration, screen output with the calibrated monitor profile matched our Epson Stylus Color printer's corrected output surprisingly well—a definite aid in predicting how selected colors will print. Blues were actually blue and purples were actually purple. Vivid reds, on the other hand, suffered in the translation. The screen-corrected reds looked duller than the printed ones; an uncorrected screen rendered truer reds. On balance, though, the monitor/printer correlation was acceptable...almost good.

Unfortunately, monitor/desktop printer correlation is not the litmus test for color management systems. It may suffice if you're only going to print color on desktop printers, but the true test for commercial printing is how well the monitor and the desktop proof conform to the end product. The results of our color management experiments weren't bad, but we'll hang on to our swatch books, anyway, thank you very much.

A well-calibrated color profile can help improve the design process by making on-screen colors look more like the colors that you have already chosen for a project. But note the careful choice of words here: *colors that you have already chosen*. We don't want to give you the impression that using Corel's color management, however improved it is over past incarnations, makes it safe to pick colors based on how they look on screen. That would be a serious, potentially expensive, and embarrassing mistake.

The only reliable way to choose colors for a print job is to pick from printed samples. Base your choices on jobs that you have already done, or use a swatch book, such as the Pantone Color Formula Guide for spot colors, or the TruMatch Colorfinder for process colors. Once you have chosen the colors and assigned them to parts of your drawing, then you can turn on Corel's color-correction feature and hope that the colors' on-screen appearances will be more accurate. But if they are not—if your screen looks radically different from the printed color—take comfort in the fact that you have chosen your color scheme responsibly. You have picked colors from printed samples, not from your screen.

Only one situation is an exception to this rule, and that's when you're using DRAW to produce artwork for an on-screen slide show, Web page, or other online presentation. In those cases, the monitor *is* your final output device, and you can choose any color that strikes your fancy.

PUBLISHING TO PDF

Featuring

PUBLISHING TO PDF

ou have probably heard all of the hype about the Portable Document Format (PDF) being the ultimate prepress solution for professional publishing. Maybe you have even contributed some of it; we have. That's why we were particularly interested when Corel announced its intention to include in DRAW 9 a Publish to PDF function. We received this information as half-skeptic and half-fan, and we adopted that same posture for this chapter. At least we tried to; however, we found ourselves getting bowled over by this terrific new functionality.

According to the PDF buzz, in the very near future service bureaus won't need any program but Acrobat, since all artwork will be converted to PDF for output. That's a nice thought, but anyone who is familiar with desktop publishing or service bureaus knows that you need more than an automated "print button" to achieve success in the prepress world. PDF will not replace knowledge and experience, because the minute something goes wrong—and it always does—that "print button" is not going to help.

With that in mind, there are a lot of advantages to PDF, and if you haven't already, you will want to consider adding it to your box of tools. It is likely to become a big part of service bureau and other cross-platform workflows in the coming years. Here are some of PDF's strengths:

- Fonts are included with the file, eliminating that last-minute mad dash to gather and send fonts with the job followed by that lurch in your stomach as you view the match prints where all of your text has reflowed and is now presented in your favorite typeface of Courier.

- You can create one document for multiple destinations (print and screen, for example) by publishing the same DRAW file to PDF using different publish options.

- You can embed or attach "job tickets" from which the service bureau can view your instructions on a per-file basis.

- You get live PostScript previews of your documents right on your own screen, using Adobe Exchange or Reader, the public-domain version.

- You (or the service bureau) can make last-minute in-place edits to the PDF file, and print only one page out of many in the file. Try doing that with a PRN file…

And now that Corel has included an extremely robust PDF tool, you won't have to shell out a couple of C-notes to Adobe Corp. to take advantage of all of this.

Not Your Father's PDF Tool

If you experimented with DRAW 8's Export to PDF feature, you may well be thinking once burned, twice shy. That PDF export filter was—how shall we say—awful! If your document contained text or complex objects, you never really knew what you were going to get. Export to PDF was just like using the PDF Writer of Acrobat—it did barely more than take a screen shot, and it had no clue what embedded files were all about.

But the Publish to PDF engine in 9 is different. It is not a rewrite of the DRAW 8 filter, but a completely new engine built by Corel *for* Corel from the ground up. Corel knows that it needs to fight down a reputation, just or unjust, for being less reliable at the service bureau than Adobe and Quark products. Publish to PDF rings a very loud bell for that cause: it is fast, accurate, and from all indications, bug-free from the start.

OK, It Works. But Why Should I Use It?

Although PCs are making headway in the Macintosh-dominated desktop publishing arena, the fact is most service bureaus, and many designers, are still predominantly Mac-based. Those who have made serious investments into equipment and personnel training aren't about to abandon a system that is working just because some of their customers bring them PC files. More likely, forward-thinking service bureaus will add a PC or two to their network and buy some Windows software—maybe even Corel-DRAW—but they still won't have the years of experience behind these products that their Mac-based customers rely on.

The Man and the Muse Behind the PDF Decision

Championing the CorelDRAW print cause for over seven years has been once-engineer, now Development Manager, Rus Miller, one of the most notable PostScript specialists around. It was he who pushed forward the Publish to PDF cause. Before unveiling the new PDF engine, he spoke to us about its issues and opportunities, as well as Corel's decision to not integrate Publish to PDF with the main print engine.

"Like it or not," he said, "Corel has an image problem in the prepress industry. We know this. We also know our printing capabilities have come a long, long way since the days when they were the cause of this problem. Now they are second to none. The Publish to PDF functionality is going to be awesome as well. We're hoping to gain quick acceptance in the professional market with our PDF capabilities in DRAW 9. I believe, in order for us to achieve that, we cannot associate it with the print engine at all, at least not in its first incarnation. We must let it stand alone and gather its own glory.

"I think it is our second chance at the prepress industry, and it puts us in an excellent position to ride the wave of the two biggest keywords therein today: *PDF* and *workflow*. If we ship perfect composite PDF output, that service bureaus can fit seamlessly into their existing and emerging PDF workflows, we will start to gain that trust and exposure we need in order to be able to lead the edge."

That's where PDF helps you. It is entirely cross-platform across Windows, Macintosh, and Unix systems, and it is now completely painless for you to create from DRAW 9. You can avoid the driver search and checklist for creating PostScript print files destined for the service bureau. You'll be able to trade files with your Mac-based colleagues. You'll be the envy of your kids' carpool. OK, so maybe not that last bit, but your workflow *will* be easier and you'll have more control of your files.

With DRAW 9's Publish to PDF (and the right disk-formatting utility), the service bureau operator that peers down his nose at the mere mention of DRAW or Windows will never even have to know where your files came from.

If you already use Adobe Acrobat, don't stop reading. DRAW's PDF engine offers several advantages over creating PostScript files and pumping them through Adobe Distiller:

- You can eliminate the step of generating a PostScript file before starting Distiller.
- DRAW knows better than any other application how to render its patterns, textures, and transparent objects, and now, so does its PDF engine.

A PDF Torture Test

Figure 28.1 shows the drawing that we put together to test PDF creation. It contains all of the various elements that have been notorious for creating havoc with output devices. Here is a tour:

- The rectangles at top-left are each filled with colors from a different color model (and the text describing them is a mix of artistic and paragraph text). The two on the right are created with a dotted outline pattern and a contour, respectively.

- The stars running down the left side contain a mesh fill, texture, pattern, and fountain.

- The text in the middle is a paragraph set in a TrueType face.

- At right is a blend and an arrow, the latter created automatically with an arrowhead from DRAW's Outline tool (these have been known to render as straight lines, not arrows).

- The red rectangle below the text is the backdrop for an imported color bitmap, set with 25% transparency.

- Below that are two strings of artistic text, one set in TrueType, the other Type 1.

- To their right are a CMYK photo and a whisk from the Artistic Media tool.

- And to their right is a drop shadow.

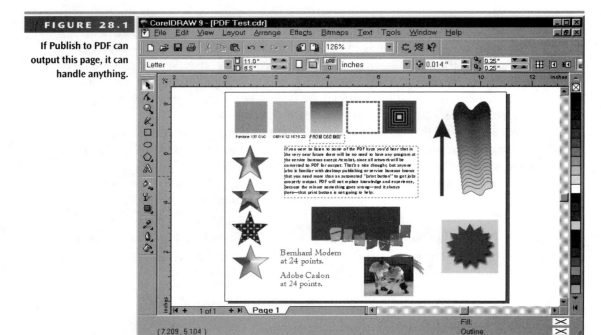

FIGURE 28.1

If Publish to PDF can output this page, it can handle anything.

For a fair comparison, we generated a PDF file from DRAW 9 and then compared it with the same document printed to file using the Adobe Distiller 3.01 driver and PPD as well as DRAW 9's new Device Independent Postscript. We then ran the PostScript files through Distiller 3 and viewed all three in Acrobat Exchange.

The Envelope, Please

Figure 28.2 shows the result, and in a word—perfect. The output was perfect. Acrobat was able to render every one of the elements that we have come to identify as problematic.

FIGURE 28.2

From DRAW straight to PDF, the new Publish to PDF passes our torture test.

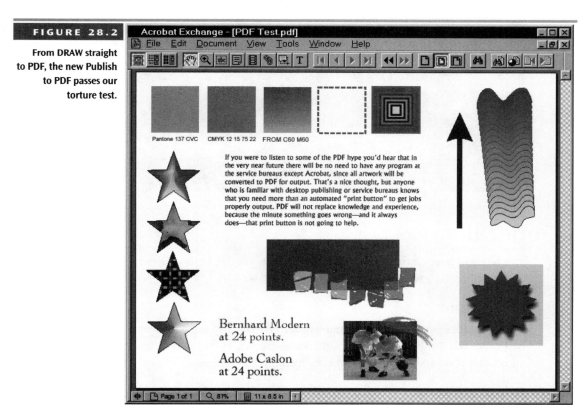

While we have uncovered some limitations in the PDF engine (which we will detail later in this chapter), we have yet to find an object or effect that we couldn't output to PDF.

The Options

To open the Publish to PDF dialog, you must have at least one object on the DRAW page. Go to File ➤ Publish to PDF and you will see this dialog.

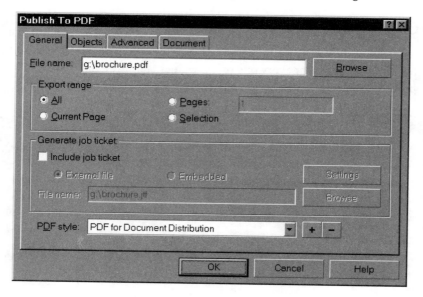

General

The General page of the Publish to PDF dialog is similar to its counterpart of the Print dialog, but with fewer options.

File Name

As it indicates, this is where you name your PDF file and select the path to which it will be saved. If the prefilled path and name are not to your liking, just change them. Of course, you can click Browse and navigate to the desired location.

Export Range

The Export Range area is where you pick which pages of your current document will be published to PDF. You can choose All pages of the document, the Current Page, selected Pages, or the current objects selected on the page.

Generate Job Ticket

Job tickets are files containing important pre- and postpress information about the PDF files. You submit these to the service bureau outputting your job. Because the service bureau must have job ticket editing software in order to read the .jtf file, you should make certain they can read the job ticket information. Job tickets can be a separate .jtf file or they can be embedded in the PDF file itself. Again, check with your service bureau for their preference.

Include Job Ticket   If you will be generating a job ticket for your PDF file, check the Include Job Ticket check box and select either the embed or external file options. If you choose the external file option, either type in or use the Browse button to designate the path to which the .jtf file will be saved.

Settings   The good news about the Settings dialog, shown below, is that it is sticky between DRAW sessions; the bad news is that job ticket information is not saved with PDF style information and will have to be re-entered should the information change.

Job Ticket Settings		? ✕

Customer Info | Delivery | Finishing

Account #: [   ] Job Name: [   ]

● Creator/Submitter   ○ Primary Contact   ○ Billing Address   ○ Shipping Address

Creator/Submitter

Name: [   ]

Company: [   ]

Address: [   ]

City: [   ] Zip/Postal Code: [   ]

State / Province: [   ] Country: [   ]

Telephone: [   ] Fax: [   ]

Email: [   ] Mobile/Pager: [   ]

[OK] [Cancel] [Help]

For Customer Info, that would generally be you, as the customer of the service bureau. If this information remains the same, you should only have to update the

Job Name for each new job. There are four radio buttons: Creator/Submitter, Primary Contact, Billing Address, and Shipping Address. Again, this information may change on a job-to-job basis, and you should always check to be sure the information is still valid before sending the job ticket to the service bureau.

The next tab is for Delivery information once the service bureau has completed your job. The drop-down list has a number of preset delivery methods, but we think it was an oversight not to include an option for the customer (you) to enter a custom delivery method. If a delivery method is not on the list, use the Delivery Instructions section below, which is also a good place to include billing information should your instructions include "bill recipient." Enter the number of copies to be delivered in the number box at the top.

Finally, you can include Finishing instructions with the job ticket information. These should be self-explanatory, and any custom instructions required can be keyed into the bottom Job Note window.

PDF Style

DRAW 9 includes four preset PDF styles:

- For Document Distribution
- For Prepress
- For Editing
- For the Web

We're not sure we agree with some of the options selected for these presets, although they are a reasonable starting place from which to create your own PDF styles. These are similar to Print styles, covered at length in Chapter 26. As you read more about these options, you'll be able to make choices that fit into your particular workflow.

PDF styles differ from Print styles in that they are not saved as separate files. To create a custom PDF style, make your selections throughout the dialog, click on the plus button, and then type in a name for the style. To delete a style, scroll to the style in the list and then click on the minus button.

WARNING   All PDF styles, the four that ship with DRAW and any that you create, are stored in one file, corelpdf.ini in the Config subdirectory. We wish that Corel used separate files for each style; instead, you'll want to back this file up methodically and be careful with off-line editing.

Objects

As its name implies, the second page of the dialog is where you determine how DRAW handles the various objects in your document.

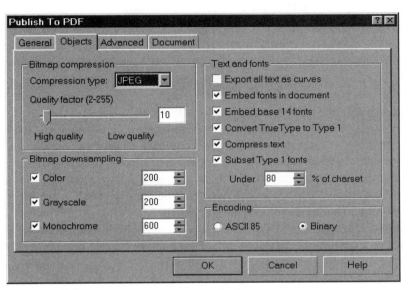

Bitmap Compression

DRAW offers three choices for how to handle embedded bitmap images: None, which is, well, none; LZW, a *lossless* compression algorithm; and JPEG, a *lossy* method.

You can probably guess what the difference is between these two curious-sounding options. With lossless compression, DRAW will compress bitmaps as much as it can *without throwing away any data*. Lossy, on the other hand, will generally return the smallest file sizes, but data will be removed. Depending on the amount of compression, the result could be a visible loss of quality.

Weighing the benefits of small sizes vs. high quality is up to you, and the final resting place of the PDF file is perhaps the most important consideration. For example, files destined only for onscreen viewing do not require images with fidelity as high as if they were to be used for generating film and plates for commercial printing. A general rule of thumb is to use JPEG compression for screen and Web files, and LZW for everything else. (We can't think of a reason to choose None, unless you're entered in a contest to create the largest possible PDF file.)

PostScript files through Adobe Distiller to PDF are marginally smaller than DRAW 9's PDF files, due to the differences in compression methods. DRAW 9 uses JPEG for lossy and LZW for lossless. Adobe also uses JPEG, but instead of LZW, it employs ZIP compression, which does generate somewhat smaller files. In either case, however, when you choose lossless compression, you will see no degradation of bitmap images.

Bitmap Downsampling

Bitmap Downsampling gives you the option to reduce the resolution of any bitmaps in your document, which in turn reduces the overall size of the PDF file. You can downsample all color, grayscale, or black-and-white bitmaps; only color, grayscale, or black-and-white bitmaps; or any combination thereof. The Downsampling and Compression options sound related, but technically speaking, they are not. A downsampled image might not look as good as the same one at full resolution, but it is not due to the arbitrary removal of pixels. It is the result of the entire image being converted to a lower resolution. If both options are enabled—downsampling and compression—bitmaps will be downsampled before being compressed.

As mentioned earlier, the PDF format allows true one-document-multiple-destination output. Bitmap Downsampling is one of the options available to you to achieve this end. If you have created a document originally destined for commercial printing, any included bitmaps will be high resolution—overkill for screen graphics. The solution is to keep your original DRAW file intact and only adjust Bitmap Downsampling as appropriate.

N O T E   Some of the preset styles include bitmap resolutions we disagree with. For example, the Web style has Bitmap Downsampling set to 120dpi. We would change this to 96dpi. And, we see no reason for most prepress work to ever downsample to more than 200dpi.

Text and Fonts

Another intimidating list for the uninitiated, but don't worry, your eyes will uncross with a few simple explanations and recommendations.

Export All Text As Curves   Choosing to export all text as curves means first and foremost that the text in your PDF file will not be editable. Since one of the benefits of the PDF format is the ability to make minor adjustments and edits on the fly, and to copy and paste text from PDF files into other documents, we do not recommend using this option except for extreme circumstances of unusual text characters. Converting text to curves will also increase the complexity of the file, resulting in larger file sizes and increased RIP time. However, if you are using a customized typeface, or some strange TrueType face, exporting as curves ensures that it will be seen the way you intended. This is not unlike the Separate or Convert to Bitmap commands that freeze DRAW's effects in their tracks.

Embed Fonts in Document   Embedding fonts in the file means that What You Want to Give Them Is What They Get. Without embedded fonts, the PDF engine substitutes what it thinks is the closest match to the font you used to create the text. Often the substitution is not even a close match, and your design integrity is lost. Embedding fonts is the best choice for generally all PDF files you will publish. Exceptions can be made if you are absolutely certain that the recipient has exactly the same fonts loaded on their system, but you know what?—it's not worth it. Just embed them.

Embed Base 14 Fonts   All PostScript output devices have 14 base fonts (PostScript, of course) available at all times. However, over time some of these fonts have evolved into slightly different versions. If you use one of the base 14 fonts in your document but do not embed the base 14 fonts into the PDF, the PostScript device will recognize the call to the font in the PDF and will substitute its version. Chances are you will never notice a difference, but, for example, if your copy of Helvetica is slightly newer than the Helvetica resident on the service bureau's imagesetter, your letter spacing may change and your text may reflow.

Again, don't take the chance—it's not worth it. Embed the base 14 fonts when you are heading to a service bureau for film or high-resolution output. For Web output, font embedding is a moot point, and you should uncheck this option and save a bit of file space.

Convert TrueType to Type 1   If you use TrueType fonts in your document but do not check the option to convert them to Type 1, they will be converted to curves when you publish to PDF. While you will not notice a difference by looking at the final output, the inclusion of many TrueType fonts converted to curves will substantially add to the complexity of the file, and the recipient will not be able to perform any edits to that text in the PDF file.

Converting TrueType to Type 1 means that the fonts will be embedded in the PDF (if you choose to embed fonts) and the recipient will be able to edit the type. However, it also means that file size will increase substantially if you have used a lot of TrueType fonts. If file size is of less importance than file integrity and editability, then enable this option. We recommend always using this option.

Compress Text   Compressing text will not result in any data loss and will decrease the size of your PDF files. Depending on the amount of text in your DRAW document, the decreased file size may be substantial. As with the None option for Bitmap Compression, we see no reason *not* to enable this option. It is lossless compression.

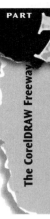

PART

The CorelDRAW Freeway

Subset Type 1 Fonts   This speaks to the strategy of sending only the needed portion of the character information, instead of the entire character set. You determine the threshold for subsetting—the percentage under which DRAW will use a subset of the font information.

The arguments for and against subsetting Type 1 fonts are almost as vigorous as those for and against TrueType fonts, or Macs vs. PCs. We'll try to stay out of the fracas and just relay the facts.

Argument 1: Subsetting reduces the file size.   Sometimes yes, sometimes no. Any file size decrease depends on how much text is in the original document. If there is a lot of text that uses the same font, however, subsetting may be ignored depending upon the percentage threshold you entered.

Argument 2: Subsetting makes it difficult to combine PDF files.   True. If you expect to do this, do not choose to subset typefaces.

Argument 3: Subsetting hinders in-place editing of PDF files.   It's a gamble all right. If you accidentally spelled it "ozymoron," and you want to fix it, you had better hope that somewhere else in the file you used a lowercase *x* of the same face. Otherwise, that letter won't be available for use. If there is any possibility that someone, somewhere, sometime will edit the PDF, do not subset fonts.

Argument 4: Subsetting is risky with printer-resident fonts.   If a font of the same name is already resident on the output RIP, that font will be substituted for the one you used, often with disappointing results. If you are using a base 14 font, do not subset fonts. Instead choose to enable the Embed Base 14 Fonts option to avoid this potential problem.

Well, we thought we were neutral, but after reviewing our own prose, our bias shows. We recommend unchecking the Subset Type 1 Fonts option unless none of the above applies to your files.

Encoding

Binary encoding is the default because the compression is greater, resulting in smaller PDF files. Under most circumstances, you will not run into any trouble with Binary Encoding and, in fact, it is also the default for Distiller/Acrobat. But, if for some reason the recipient of your PDF is having trouble reading your files, try ASCII 85 encoding instead.

Advanced

If you've opened the Print dialog or read through Chapter 26, most of the options on the Advanced page will be at least vaguely familiar to you. But, just in case memorizing

Chapter 26 wasn't high on your list of fun things to do, we'll cover the options again here (as well as those not available from the Print dialog).

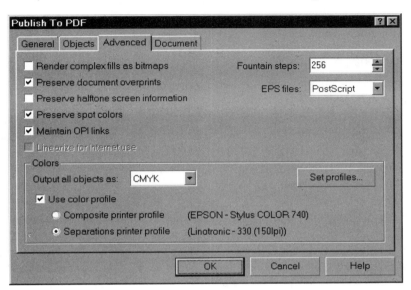

Render Complex Fills As Bitmaps

What qualifies as a "complex fill"? Texture fills, fountain fills, pattern fills, lenses, and transparencies are all complex fills and objects of one sort or another which can bring a RIP to its knees and give imagesetter operators more gray hair than they already have (to say nothing of your own condition, should they report back to you that the job failed). Checking this option will reduce the overall complexity of the PDF file. If your service bureau rep grumbles every time you walk in the door, you may want to enable this option. And, if you are creating a PDF for the screen, you *should* enable this option.

This is a recurrent theme throughout the book, as Chapter 23 and several of the special effects chapters discuss the viability of converting complex objects to bitmaps. This is a very handy option to have here, because should you decide to use it, you don't need to convert your objects, perhaps permanently. Instead, you can just do it when it's time to output.

Preserve Document Overprints

DRAW 9 lets you manually set overprint options on a per-object basis. Checking this option will preserve those overprints. However, third-party trapping software may override your selections, and we advise communicating with your service bureau before choosing this option.

Preserve Halftone Screen Information

DRAW 9 also allows you to set custom PostScript halftone screens for objects filled with spot color. Again, consult with your service bureau before checking this option or you may find it has been overridden by the RIP.

Preserve Spot Colors

Most service bureaus now have the ability to generate color separations from composite PDF files, either directly in-RIP via PostScript 3 devices, or with third-party PDF separation software. Checking this option will generate separate plates for the spot color inks defined in your original document. If the option is unchecked, spot colors will be converted to CMYK, RGB, or grayscale, depending upon your selection for Output All Objects As.

Maintain OPI Links

Certain bitmap formats—.tif, .cpt, and others—can be used to create OPI (Open Prepress Interface) links. You can import one of these images into DRAW with the OPI option turned on, as explained in Chapter 26. If you do, you are telling DRAW that there is another, higher-quality version of this bitmap that your service bureau will substitute at print time. The obvious advantage here is that you can edit using a lower-resolution bitmap for your design and avoid the memory overhead of a high-resolution color bitmap. Such bitmaps can easily be larger than 20MB. When creating the PDF, you can check Maintain OPI Links and DRAW will place a reference to the path and name of the high-resolution version in the PDF file. Check with your service bureau for their instructions on how to handle OPI links and images.

Fountain Steps

When you create a fountain fill, it is displayed and printed as a series of discrete bands of color hues and shades. The more bands, the smoother the fountain fill appears, but the longer it takes to redisplay or print. The value in the Fountain Steps box determines how many steps are printed, subject to two restrictions:

- The setting applies only to fountain fills that you left locked when you created them.
- The output device has its own limits, based on its resolution. A very high number would be ignored on, say, a 300dpi printer.

EPS Files

EPS files are comprised of two parts: the actual PostScript code describing the file contents and a low-resolution preview header. Choose the PostScript option if the PDF will be output on a PostScript device. (Note that a placeholder indicating an embedded EPS file will be placed in the PDF preview; however, the PostScript portion of the EPS file will print to a PostScript device.) Choose Preview for screen output and proofing.

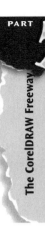

Colors

As with other output methods from DRAW, you have color conversion choices for Publish to PDF. Color management for print output is discussed in detail in Chapter 27, as are DRAW 9's Help files, and this information is applicable to the Publish to PDF feature as well. But here are a few simple rules of thumb.

Output All Objects As This option controls the color conversion of all objects in the original file, unless Preserve Spot Colors is checked at the top of this dialog page. If the Use Color Profile option below is unchecked, and you choose to output as RGB, all document colors will be converted to DRAW 9's currently active default RGB profile. Use the Set Profiles button to set DRAW's internal RGB profile. If you choose output as CMYK, all CMYK objects will be untouched; all other objects will be converted to CMYK through DRAW's default colorspace. For grayscale, objects will be converted to grayscale based on their RGB values.

Use Color Profile If you check this option, you have two choices for color conversion: the active composite printer profile or the active separations printer profile. To make another profile active, click the Set Profiles button and browse to the ICM file you wish to activate.

Document

The settings on the sparsely populated Document page are for PDF files created as the final destination: screen presentations, Web pages, and archives, for example. You should disable all of these options if your PDF will be output to a PostScript device.

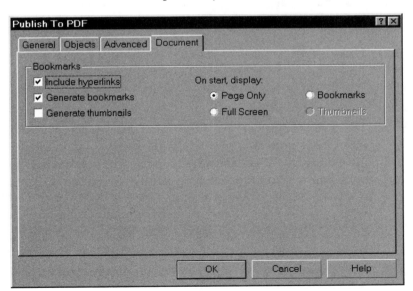

The CorelDRAW Freeway

Include Hyperlinks

In DRAW 9 you can assign URLs to artistic and paragraph text, as well as graphic objects (which can be managed through DRAW 9's Link Manager docker). Enabling the Include Hyperlinks option will create a clickable "hotspot" in the PDF file which will open your Internet browser to the Web page assigned to the link.

Generate Bookmarks

Generate Bookmarks is similar to Include Hyperlinks, except that the bookmarks generated will jump to and from page locations within the PDF file itself. DRAW 9 includes a Bookmark Manager docker to manage these links. In addition, Adobe Acrobat will display the bookmarks as a table of contents next to the main PDF window.

Generate Thumbnails

If you check this option, DRAW will create thumbnails of each page in the PDF file. When you view the file in Adobe Acrobat, you can view the thumbnails in a separate window and use them to navigate through the PDF file.

On Start, Display

These four options—Page Only, Full Screen, Thumbnails, and Bookmarks—control how the PDF file initially displays in Adobe Acrobat. Page Only will show you only the main page of the PDF file, regardless of whether thumbnails have been generated. Full Screen will display the PDF without the Adobe Acrobat standard toolbars and menus (the Esc key returns the application window). The Thumbnails or Bookmarks options will direct Adobe Acrobat to open the PDF file and display either the thumbnails or bookmarks generated for the PDF. (You must select the option to generate thumbnails or bookmarks for this display option to be available.)

Should You Dump Distiller?

If you haven't already purchased Acrobat Exchange and Distiller, you may no longer find a compelling reason to do so. If you already own it, you should be aware of some of its features not yet implemented in DRAW's Publish to PDF engine.

- With Distiller, you can generate preseparated PDF files. However, by preseparating PDF files you give up some of the biggest reasons PDF is becoming so popular: editability, soft-proofing, fast and efficient transfer, and the benefits of in-RIP functionality. There are better tools available to separate PDF files at the right point in the workflow, such as CrackerJack and PostScript 3 RIPs.

- If you cannot live without preseparated files but still don't wish to invest in Distiller, you can take the long way around by creating preseparated PostScript files, importing each separation back into DRAW and publishing separate PDF files. Hey, where there's a will, there's a way.

- In Acrobat Exchange you can "combine" multiple PDF files into one. Again, you can also do this in DRAW, by taking advantage of its excellent PDF import filters and then publishing the whole enchilada to PDF. Still, it's easier to do it with Exchange if you own it.

- Acrobat Exchange allows you to set various levels of file security, such as password protection, printing rights, etc. We've found no workaround for these options in DRAW 9.

- Distiller allows "watched folders" for automatically generating PDF files from using preset options. Of course, with Publish to PDF, you create the PDF file automatically.

- And the most conspicuous limitation, jobs that require bleeds are not as easily produced with DRAW and Publish to PDF. With Distiller, you create a print file, and therefore it is simple to define a page size larger than the actual page in DRAW. But Publish to PDF concerns itself only with the page, not any elements that hang over it. To create a bleed and output it with Publish to PDF, you would need to adjust the page size in DRAW first.

Aside from the above, we haven't seen much that Acrobat Exchange and Distiller can do that you can't do directly with DRAW's Publish to PDF engine. And with it, we've seen some things that Acrobat Exchange and Distiller can't do. The best news for you, though, is if you need to create solid PDF files, you won't have to leave home to do it.

We think DRAW 9's Publish to PDF is the Rookie of the Year for 1999.

chapter 29

SNEAKING OVER THE BORDER: IMPORTING FILES FROM OTHER SOURCES

Featuring

IMPORTING FILES FROM OTHER SOURCES

f you own CorelDRAW (and since you're reading this book, it's a good bet that you do), there will come a time when you will need to import or place a file in DRAW that you created elsewhere. Corel has historically provided a very robust set of import and export filters, indeed much better than its two main competitors. You won't encounter too many file formats that you cannot bring into or export out of DRAW.

This chapter is your roadmap for getting to your destination—that being the comfortable confines of a CorelDRAW graphic. We're in the passenger seat giving directions so you don't miss any important turns. After this chapter, the next marker on the highway is the Exit ramp—getting your work *out* of DRAW by exporting.

Why Import?

Is this a dumb question? We think not. While importing clipart stands as the prototypical reason to import, there are several other methods and reasons to import graphics into DRAW:

To edit an existing graphic A graphic that is in a standard vector format (such as AI and WMF) can be imported into DRAW and then edited. Once you import it into DRAW, you can then change it, and it will be integrated into your final DRAW file.

To incorporate an existing graphic   We've chosen our words carefully: *edit* in the paragraph above, and *incorporate* here. Some graphic formats cannot be taken apart or edited by DRAW, but they can still be imported and printed by DRAW. These include all of the bitmap formats (which can now be transformed with effects within DRAW, but still not actually edited at the pixel level) and placeable EPS files. EPS files imported via the PostScript Interpreted filter are an exception; we'll discuss them later.

To create a hot-link   DRAW is a willing party to the Object Linking and Embedding phenomenon (you know it as OLE), in which graphics and other formats are sent across the Clipboard and are able to retrace their steps back to the original program that created them.

Importing linked or embedded objects is not done through the File ➤ Import command, but rather with the Edit ➤ Paste Special or Edit ➤ Insert New Object commands. However, this operation qualifies as an import, and we'll treat it as such. In broad categories, incoming graphics are either vector or bitmap format, and imported vector art can be taken apart, while bitmap art cannot.

Importing Clipart

Getting clipart files remains one of the top reasons that DRAW users reach for Import. Whether these images come from an external source or from Corel's vast library of clipart, DRAW's defining characteristic for tens of thousands of users is its ability to ingest and digest clipart images from many different sources.

Our surveys show that most clipart is used for layouts no more complicated than the one in Figure 29.1, showing several game pieces, stored in Corel's CMX format, integrated into one composite drawing.

The clipart images that make up Figure 29.1 were not changed in any way, except for a bit of resizing and shading. But most vector art that is imported into DRAW can be taken apart and edited, *just as if you had created the objects in DRAW initially*. This last point is important: DRAW uses its filter to translate all incoming objects into elements that it understands. Therefore, all objects are of a type that *you* understand—curves, lines, and text characters, with and without fills and outlines. Figure 29.2 shows one of the pieces of clipart from Figure 29.1, in its original condition (top-left) and mercilessly broken up into its component parts, at the hands of the Arrange ➤ Ungroup command.

FIGURE 29.1

These simple pieces of art can team up to create a nice, attractive flier.

Raw Materials

Source: Corel Gallery Magic 200,000

Finished Product

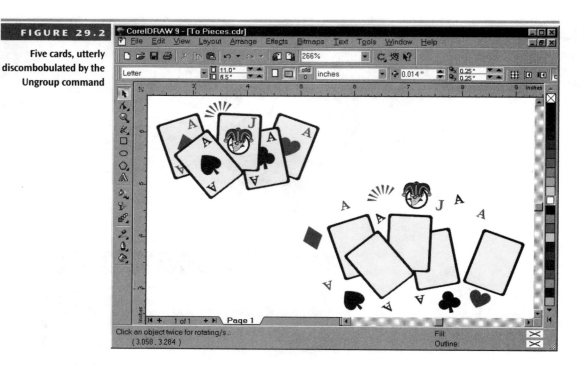

FIGURE 29.2

Five cards, utterly discombobulated by the Ungroup command

What Happens When You Import?

Importing (or pasting) graphics is not a one-size-fits-all proposition, although in all cases DRAW uses a *filter* to perform the task. Filters act as translators. They enable DRAW to convert vector information from other file formats into its own internal object format and to translate bitmap art into printable images. The key word here is *translate*, and it has implications for you: if DRAW has to translate graphic information from a format you can't read, how do you know whether DRAW got the translation right?

Until the last few years, the answer to this question might have been, "Cross your fingers, don't forget your mantra, and only import on Tuesday nights, when atmospheric conditions seem to be more favorable." Before today's file format standards were adopted and implemented, exchanging graphics information was all too often one big crapshoot. It required both parties (the exporting program and the importing program) to be on the same wavelength, and even then, elements such as hairlines, typeface names, and color mixes carried long odds of being interpreted correctly.

Today your prospects of accurate graphics exchange are much brighter. Corel is now writing many of the import and export filters itself and working very closely with the third parties that write the others. The Windows Metafile (WMF) format, and its older sister, Enhanced Metafile (EMF), have taken hold and are recognized as accurate and reliable formats for translating graphical information. This bodes well for users of non-PostScript devices, as well as for those who have had to resort to the often treacherous waters of OLE.

Placing and Interpreting

We hold these words to be self-evident...but they're not! PostScript files—in all their various flavors, like PS, EPS, or PDF—can be imported to DRAW one of two ways. But first, allow us two paragraphs of background.

PostScript is a set of instructions, stored in plain ASCII text, that make sense to printers and other output devices having the ability to interpret it. PostScript instructions have one common objective: to describe a page. In fact, PostScript is referred to as a *page description language.* PostScript is really a programming language, similar to Pascal, Turbo C, and the various flavors of BASIC, but there is one big difference. With few exceptions, PostScript doesn't live inside your computer; it lives inside your printer. When PostScript instructions are sent to a PostScript printer, the printer begins building an image of the page. To get output from a service bureau that utilizes PostScript devices, you deliver a file made on your computer containing the PostScript instructions your bureau's imagesetter needs to interpret and image your pages.

Encapsulated PostScript is a rigidly defined subset within the PostScript language. An EPS file is not designed to be sent directly to the printer (although, if you know how to manually modify the file, you could do it). Rather, it is intended to be incorporated into another document and then sent to the printer from there. An EPS file can be scaled up and down like any other graphic. Many of the output samples in this book were produced as EPS files and imported into a page layout program for final publishing and printing.

Now, as for the two ways that EPS files can be imported:

They can be placed. DRAW's instructions are to keep its lousy hands off of it, and when it comes time to print, just send it to the printer. If there is a preview, fine—show it. Otherwise, DRAW is to do nothing except...*place it on the page.*

They can be interpreted. Here, you tell DRAW to do just the opposite—you tell it to sift through all of the PostScript code of the incoming file and build the image on the page, using its own vector tools or any bitmap images it finds in the code. This is an ambitious undertaking, at which DRAW has gotten much better since version 7.

The criteria, therefore, are obvious: If you want to incorporate a finished piece of artwork into a drawing and you don't need to change it at all, *and you are printing to a PostScript device,* then use Placeable EPS. If you want to convert the artwork to editable objects, use Interpreted PS.

We elaborate on this later in the chapter.

Adobe, Corel's closest competitor in the graphics field, has also been making big strides with the Portable Document Format (PDF), and Corel has not ignored these important developments. Beginning with the Rev B patch to DRAW 8, and in cooperation with Adobe itself, DRAW includes both placeable and interpreted PDF filters. With DRAW 9's improved filters and Publish to PDF feature, cross-platform file transport has never been easier or more reliable.

Some graphics formats tax DRAW's filtering to the max. The CGM and GEM file types are notorious for being unruly with fills and outlines, and AI files often get typeface names wrong, although Corel has made improvements to many filters since earlier versions of DRAW. Other formats, such as CDR and CMX, need very little translation. The clipart from Figure 29.2 was stored in Corel's own CMX format.

N O T E   In previous versions you could only use File ➤ Open to retrieve CDR files. Beginning with DRAW 8 and continuing into DRAW 9, all *vector* formats which have import filters may also be opened. There is a subtle difference between *opening* and *importing* files. Using the Open command will start a new drawing, while using Import will add the incoming file contents to your currently active drawing. We repeat: File ➤ Open starts a new file; File ➤ Import adds one file's contents to another.

Imported art always arrives on the page as one group of objects. We're not sure whether this is an engineering requirement or just a decision on the part of the developers, but we like it. Generally, the first thing you want to do with imported art is to move it and resize it, and these two operations are eminently easier to do with a group. Although, as we explain later, you can now place and resize the incoming art before it lands on your page, you'll probably end up moving and resizing anyway. Remember that you can get to objects without ungrouping them; just hold Ctrl when you click on them.

Wash and Wax: Importing Details

In DRAW 9, the Import, Open, and Export dialogs received an overhaul. We'll cover the first two in this chapter, and discuss exporting in Chapter 30. Was the overhaul worth the effort? Unequivocally, yes. Extension sorting options that previously required a trip to Options are now accessible directly from the Import and Open dialogs. And in usual Corel fashion, more options were added to the import and open functions themselves. We start this section with a few general rules of thumb concerning bringing files into DRAW, then follow with dialog specifics, the Scrapbook, and one or two other details we affectionately refer to as Other Ways to Get Stuff into DRAW That Don't Fit into a Specific Category, but we'll call Miscellaneous here to keep the editors happy.

Let DRAW Figure the Flavor?

When you import (or open) a file, you can either tell DRAW explicitly, via a dialog, the format of the incoming file, or you can let DRAW figure it out for itself. In fact, the default choice in the Files of Type drop-down window is All File Formats. In that state, DRAW shows you every file in a given folder or directory and promises to be able to determine for itself which filter is needed for any given file.

This is a promise that DRAW used to break regularly. What's more, many users believed the loathsome message that resulted, proclaiming that the file that you asked to be imported had become corrupted, or was unsupported, or even better, that your TEMP drive was full. "After all," DRAW would seemingly say, "it couldn't possibly be I who made the mistake." In fact, it was. DRAW used to be chronically incapable of figuring out the format of some files, leaving unsuspecting users to believe that their graphic had gone bad or DRAW itself had gone bad.

DRAW is much smarter now, almost never failing to recognize the format of the file you have selected. In the rare instance that DRAW can't tell (or doesn't support) the file type, it won't blame the graphic. Instead, it now returns a reasonable error message, shown below, and that is your cue to simply try again, this time specifying the format of the file, to check that the specific filter is actually installed, or to check if the format is even supported by DRAW. More on that later.

N O T E   Another difference to be aware of in newer versions of DRAW is that in the case of certain file types such as EPS or PDF, the default filters may be different. For example, when the dialogs are set to show All Formats, an EPS file *opens* as Postscript Interpreted, but *imports* as a Placeable file. If the file that lands on your page is different from what you expected, be sure to select the specific import filter from the Open or Import dialogs.

The Import Dialog

Figure 29.3 shows the new DRAW 9 Import dialog. We resorted to a bit of PHOTO-PAINT trickery to make every option look available, even though that is probably an impossibility (no format would offer you *every* choice). Depending upon the format you are opening, your options may vary. Void where prohibited.

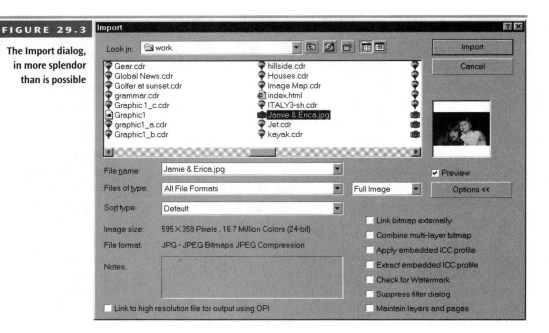

FIGURE 29.3

The Import dialog, in more splendor than is possible

The Basics

The upper portion of the DRAW 9 Import dialog is similar to Windows 95/98/NT dialogs in most other applications, as these dialog are written to specifications set down by the Almighty Operating Systems Gods in the American Northwest (for the geographically challenged, that would be Redmond, Washington).

From this dialog, you can browse to any location on your hard drive, toggle details and list views of the contents of those drives, create new folders, rename folders, and cut, copy, and paste between the current folder and to any other you browse to within this dialog...essentially all the things that you could do in an Explorer window.

The lower half of the dialog is all DRAW. These are the options we will describe in more detail. There is one thing about file selection you should note: by holding the Ctrl key as you select files, you can select multiple files for the same import sequence. More on this later.

File Name

While at first glance you may wonder why we didn't lump this section of the Import dialog into the Basics section above, upon closer observation you'll notice that this box now appears in DRAW 9 as a drop-down list. So what, you say? Well, have you ever been frustrated by the "stickiness" of DRAW's Import dialog? If so, you know that it always remembers the most recently used (MRU) folder. Because imported art and other files usually come from a variety of sources—a clipart CD, a ZIP disk from a client, another folder on your hard drive, for example—it's quite common that the MRU folder is not the one you want to use.

DRAW 9's Import dialog takes a big stride toward helping to alleviate this seemingly minor, yet time-consuming, frustration. The Import dialog now remembers the last five imports, complete with full path information. You might not want to import that very file, but you might want another one in the same folder. By selecting an MRU file, DRAW sets the file window to that folder. This will result in a significant reduction in click-click-clicking your way to and from those other locations on your hard drive. In fact, with a bit of folder organization, coupled with the use of the Scrapbooks (discussed later), you may forget how to use those Explorer-like browsing features at the top of the dialog!

PART

The CorelDRAW Freeway

Files of Type

Here is where you select a specific import filter by name if DRAW has trouble identifying a file format. More likely, you'll change from the default of All File Formats to make the file window easier to manage.

Filter Madness

If you're wondering why that one format you used to import all the time isn't listed, chances are you did a Typical install and the filter, while still included with DRAW, simply was not installed. The first thing to check, however, is whether the filter has been deactivated. To do this, go to Tools ➢ Options ➢ Global ➢ Filters.

In the right-side pane of this dialog is a list of all currently active filters. If you can find the format you seek by expanding the various trees on the left pane, highlight it and click Add. If you still don't see the filter list, dig out CD No. 1 and perform a Custom install. Expand all the trees for all the options (yes, we know there are a lot of them) and deselect everything *except* that filter. Unchecked items will not be removed, and you'll save reinstall time by only selecting the missing options for install.

And while you're in the Filters area of the Options dialog, now would be a good time for you to note this as the place to go to associate or disassociate file extensions with DRAW 9. Simply go down one level in the Options tree to Associate. Place a check mark next to those file extensions you want to associate with DRAW 9 or remove the check mark next to those extensions you want to disassociate from DRAW 9. The next time you double-click those file types in Explorer, DRAW 9 will (or will not, if you disassociated) launch and open the file.

Sort Type

To perform any type of intelligent sorting of the import filters in DRAW 8, you had to make a special trip to the Options dialog and manually move filters up and down in the list. New to DRAW 9 are preset sort options:

By Extension   Sorts the filters alphabetically by the file format extension. This means that AI will come before BMP, BMP before CDR, etc.

By Description   Sorts the filters alphabetically by their descriptions. For example, PSD is an Adobe PhotoShop filter. The file extension is .psd. The description, however, is "Adobe PhotoShop." This filter will be sorted by the *A* in Adobe.

By Most Recently Used   A good option for your workstyle or even a particular job if you find yourself importing just a few types of files, but don't want to give up access to the complete filter list. If you're importing a lot of PCD files, a sort by either extension or description will still put this format at the middle of the list, and you'll probably find yourself scrolling that list for every import. A temporary switch to By Most Recently Used will put PCD at the top of the list for fast access every time.

Vector, Bitmap, Text, and Animation   Sort all the filters alphabetically by extension, but place the filters specific to those sorts at the top of the list in their own "mini sort." The other remaining filters will appear below the sort line.

Default   Sorts the filters as in DRAW 8, where you can still make a custom arrangement from the Options dialog by changing the order manually. Although this will now be a "custom" sort, the dialog will still refer to the sort order from the Options dialog as "default." Don't ask.

Image Size

This option applies to bitmap formats only, and will show you information about resolution and color depth of the selected bitmap file. Sometimes you'll see Image Size information for nonbitmap formats, but only when that format has a bitmap preview (such as EPS or PDF). The information reflects only the preview, not the file contents.

File Format

If you are using the Windows Explorer defaults, chances are you are not seeing file extensions when viewing files in Explorer or Explorer-like dialogs such as DRAW's Import dialog. (In which case, that little discussion just above on sort order meant nothing to you!) Or, maybe a Mac-based colleague has given you a file which doesn't have an extension (very common). Or, maybe you even goofed during a save or export and assigned a file the wrong extension (perish that thought). The file format information listed here will reflect the actual contents of the file by format. This can be a very helpful bit of information should you receive an error when importing a file using a specific filter. In this case, try switching to the All File Formats option or renaming the extension to match the information DRAW is reporting.

Notes

Some formats, when saved, allow the insertion of user notes along with the file content. If notes are present, they are reflected here. Refer to Chapter 30 to learn how to include your own notes in files saved and exported from DRAW 9.

OPI

No, that's not a reference to the Sheriff of Mayberry's red-headed son. OPI stands for Open Prepress Interface. Certain bitmap formats—TIFF, CPT, and others—can be used to create OPI links between low-resolution files and their high-resolution counterparts. Generally, your service bureau will supply you with the low-resolution file when performing drum and other scans. You can import one of these images into DRAW with the OPI option turned on. If you do, you are telling DRAW that there is another, higher-quality version of this bitmap that will be substituted at print time. The obvious advantage here is that you can design a layout using a lower-resolution bitmap and avoid the memory overhead of a high-resolution color bitmap that could easily consume tens of megabytes. However, your service bureau must have OPI software that will perform the substitution and must also have the high-resolution file stored on their system. Because there may be instructions specific to your own service bureau, we advise communicating with them before checking this option. For more on how to print with this option enabled, refer to Chapter 26.

Preview

Checking the Preview box will bring up a bitmap header representing the contents of the actual file, as you can see back in Figure 29.3. Some formats do not support previews, in which case this option would be grayed out and you'd see an × in the preview window. For other formats (including, *finally*, WMF), DRAW will build a preview "on the fly" by reading the contents of the file. Depending on the size of the file, this may take a few seconds. If you have already selected a file, you're stuck. You'll have to wait until the preview is built before you can uncheck this option. Finally, the presence of a preview in no way relates to the integrity of the actual file contents. Plenty of otherwise corrupt—and unusable—files will display a preview. This means only that during the last successful save, a preview was created and the file looked like this at that time. Sadly, oftentimes a corrupt file will still have a working preview. If this happens to you, you will never feel more teased and tantalized.

Full Image

This box does not have an official name, so we refer to it here by its default value. When importing bitmaps, three options are available in the drop-down list. Full Image, the default, has no effect on the image. Choosing either the Crop or Resample option will open another dialog, and we'll detail those later when we discuss importing bitmaps. As the names imply, Crop allows various cropping options to be applied, and Resample allows resampling (redistributing pixels). Both of these options work on the bitmap before the file is imported, but you perform both actions after import, as well.

Options Button

The Options button is a simple toggle on and off for the bottom half of the Import dialog. When the arrows point toward the word Options (<<), the dialog is opened fully. When the arrows point away (>>), some of the dialog is hidden.

Link Bitmap Externally

With this option checked, a placeholder (or proxy) image is placed on the page after import, reducing file size overhead. The original bitmap file is externally linked, which means that any changes made to that file are tracked by DRAW and reflected automatically by the placeholder image. When printing, the original bitmap file is substituted for the proxy.

This was introduced in DRAW 8 and will surely be warmly received by VENTURA Publisher users, who have been working with externally linked graphics for years. Just remember, however, that the original bitmap must remain in the location you imported it from, otherwise DRAW will have a cow. (Make a note…first time in six editions of this book that we used the expression "have a cow.")

Combine Multi-Layer Bitmap

Another option new to DRAW 9's importing function, you can now "flatten" layered bitmaps upon import. This option, which has no effect on the original source image, is automatically enabled when importing linked bitmaps.

Apply Embedded ICC Profile

Color management and ICC profiles are discussed in more detail in Chapter 27. Color profiles can be embedded directly into some file formats, including DRAW 9 CDRs, PHOTO-PAINT 9 CPTs, and Adobe PhotoShop 5 PSDs. If this new option is checked, DRAW will read the embedded profile and convert the values relative to DRAW's active display options. Applying embedded profiles means accurate color reproduction across systems and platforms using the same profiles.

The CorelDRAW Freeway

Extract Embedded ICC Profile

In addition to applying an embedded ICC profile, DRAW 9 can extract the profile and save it to disk. This option is also extremely useful when you are preparing artwork across multiple systems and platforms. One color profile can be used by multiple users, helping to ensure that What Everyone Sees Is What Everyone Gets.

Check for Watermark

Various third-party software will place a digital "watermark" in a file in an effort to protect against unauthorized use or outright theft of original works. With the easy access to a multiple of images on the Internet, digital watermarking is gaining in popularity. Enabling this option will scan the file for such a watermark. You can obtain information about the watermark by reading the embedded information.

Suppress Filter Dialog

Some file formats will open additional dialogs upon import into DRAW. If you always accept the defaults for these imports, you can safely enable this option, and the secondary dialogs will not appear.

Maintain Layers and Pages

Self-explanatory, this option applies to vector formats which (a) support layers and formats and (b) for which DRAW supports layers and formats. Corel's own CMX format, which saves layers and pages, is one example—AI, CGM, DXF, and EPS are a few more.

The Import Cursor

Although technically not a part of the Import dialog itself, once you have selected a file for import and set all the options, the cursor shown in Figure 29.3 appears before a file is actually placed in your document. You can select a specific area on the page to place the imported file by moving the cursor to that location and clicking on the page. You can resize the incoming object or text before it lands on the page by simply dragging a bounding box with the import cursor. By default, the bounding box is constrained to proportionate resizing. To apply disproportionate (or freeform) resizing to the incoming file, hold the Alt key while you drag. We would rather not tell you that, however—pretend you didn't read it.

In Figure 29.4, the actual cursor is accompanied by the name of the file selected for importing. As mentioned before, you can import multiple files at once by holding the Ctrl key as you select files within the same folder. This filename feedback can be quite helpful in such cases.

Curses, it's the
import cursor.

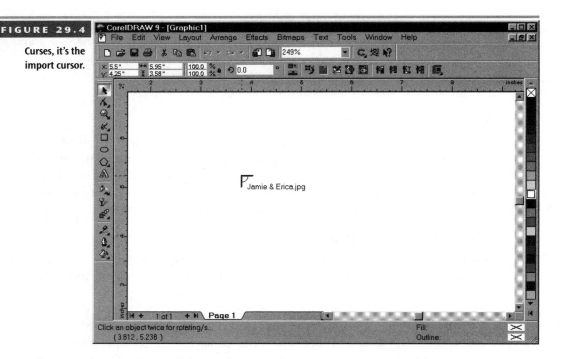

 TIP   But what if you liked the previous method for importing, when you could count on every imported file landing in the direct center of the current page? DRAW 9 has you covered as well—just hit the spacebar or the Enter key when you see the Import cursor, and file placement will behave exactly that way.

Dragging and Dropping

Mouse-savvy Windows users can import into DRAW without even bothering with the Import or Open dialogs. They can find the file they want to import using the Windows Explorer or their file manager of choice, drag it to DRAW, and drop it. This is the equivalent of performing an import with the file filter set to All Files: DRAW figures it out for itself.

If you like dragging and dropping from Explorer, then you're going to love the Scrapbook. Four Scrapbooks were first introduced with DRAW 7 as roll-ups. In DRAW 8, the roll-ups migrated to docker windows, where they stay for DRAW 9 along with a couple of new Scrapbooks. That's semantics; the functionality hasn't changed much, if at all, since DRAW 7. To open any one of the Scrapbooks, go to Tools ➤ Scrapbook

and choose a Scrapbook from the flyout. In Figure 29.5, we've opened the Scrapbook in its docked state at the right side of the screen.

FIGURE 29.5

Easier import and export through the Scrapbook

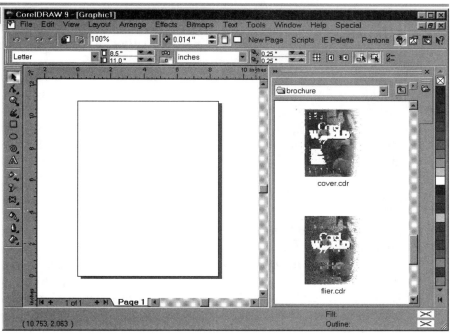

Scrapbooks are a gateway from DRAW to Windows Explorer. Some Scrapbooks are hardcoded to look first in one location, such as the Clipart, Photos, and 3D Objects Scrapbooks. When you open one of these Scrapbook dockers, DRAW is expecting a CD in the drive from which DRAW was first installed. If the CD is missing, or in another location, you'll receive an error message and be asked to redirect to the appropriate drive or to load the CD into the drive DRAW is expecting.

When a Scrapbook is open, you can select a file and import it into the current DRAW document by dragging from the Scrapbook to the main DRAW window. This action mimics an import from the Import dialog in that the file contents arrive onto the DRAW page as a group. You will not have the opportunity to specify any import options, nor to resize beforehand; only the defaults will be used. However, if you have a library of artwork or text that you repeatedly add to your DRAW documents—such as credit card icons when creating advertisements—the Browse Scrapbook is an excellent method of on-the-fly access, with the added benefit that by using it, the most recently used list of imported files on the Import dialog will not be affected. Likewise, the Clipart, Photos, and 3D Objects Scrapbooks provide fast and easy access and previews to the art included with DRAW 9.

The FTP Sites and Favorite Fills and Outlines Scrapbooks work differently from the other Scrapbooks. The default Favorite Fills and Outlines are CorelSCRIPT presets that Corel created by scripting fills and outlines applied with the more conventional methods available in DRAW. To apply one of the preset fills or outlines, select an object on the DRAW page and double-click the preset from the Scrapbook, or drag a preset onto an object on the page. You can add your own custom scripts to this Scrapbook docker, and we'll tell you how in Chapter 33.

The FTP Sites Scrapbook is a hybrid FTP client and import method. The Help files provide step-by-step instructions on setting up new sites, either with anonymous or password-protected logins. Our opinion: We think you're better off with a true FTP utility, such as WS_FTP or Cute FTP, since the FTP Sites Scrapbook is only one-way—you cannot use it to upload files to an FTP site. This strikes us as Internet marketing gimmickry—it's a "Web feature," so it must be good. Pass...

The Road Test

As usual, Corel has been busy at work tweaking its filters. We see significant improvements to many of the more popular formats, but the proof is in the pudding. We created a torture test in DRAW for the next chapter on Exporting (see Figure 29.6). We then re-created it as closely as possible in DRAW's main competition—Illustrator and Freehand—to test DRAW 9's import prowess for this chapter. The test file included a spot color object, CMYK objects, text using both PostScript and TrueType fonts, an object with a dashed outline, a filled open curve, a 30-step blend, a linear fountain fill, a line with an arrowhead, a transparent object, a mesh fill, a contour with a hairline outline, and both an RGB and a CMYK bitmap. Some effects, such as mesh fills, transparency, and contours, were not available in all applications. To test some of the other more popular formats, we begged original application files from various sources or created our own, outside of any Corel software.

How did DRAW handle this racetrack? Read on...

The Vector Interchange

Because vector art can be dissembled, it remains the most versatile form of clipart. The following paragraphs offer brief descriptions of the more popular flavors along with their shortcomings and ways to work around them. For further notes on these and other formats, get assistance by choosing Help ➤ Technical Support. Select the Import and Export File Formats topic, and then search under the List of Import File Formats for the individual format name.

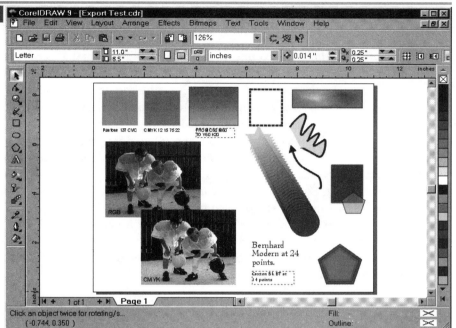

FIGURE 29.6

The torture test

Adobe Illustrator Files

Few things are more frustrating while teaching or lecturing on these topics than having to try to explain how EPS files created by Adobe Illustrator are different from standard EPS files (even though Adobe created the EPS format in the first place). The standard Encapsulated PostScript file was designed to be included in another container document, such as a VENTURA, PageMaker, or QuarkXpress. The original concept was to provide a way to get the highest quality output from a printing device. Unlike the Illustrator brand of EPS, standard EPS was never intended to be opened and edited in a drawing program.

The Adobe Illustrator format, on the other hand, is a special subset of the PostScript format. When you examine an Illustrator file (which may have an .ai or .eps extension) in a text editor, it looks like an EPS file—it is stored in ASCII, and you can find in it a lot of the same unintelligible syntax as in standard EPS files (*gsave, annotatepae, grestore*, and *packedarray*, for instance). However, unlike regular EPS files, Illustrator files can be imported and placed into DRAW as a group of editable objects. Though they generally produce highly refined, extremely accurate art, Illustrator files confuse the heck out of unsuspecting users who are led to believe that *all* EPS files can be imported and edited the way that AI files can.

To make matters even more interesting, DRAW *can* import standard EPS files, but not in the way it imports other vector formats (more on this shortly). To minimize confusion, in this chapter we will refer to Adobe's special flavor of EPS as *Illustrator format*, or as *AI files*. For your own sake, think of this format as completely distinct from standard EPS files.

So, how did the test file fare? In the past, the correct translation of color models from AI files to DRAW was unreliable. Adobe and Corel used different flavors of Pantone naming conventions, intermediary colors in fountain fills would be off, bitmaps would always be RGB, and text was a major headache. Those of you who regularly work with other designer's Illustrator files or who have many tools in their illustration arsenal will be happy to know that DRAW 9's Illustrator imports are the most solid yet. The only caveat is that Illustrator 8 files are not supported directly; version 8 files must be saved down to version 7 for the best import.

With the exception of mesh fills (which is an Adobe export problem), all objects and fills imported into DRAW 9 with very little editing necessary afterward. Color models were retained, and typefaces translated easily. (If you must import an Illustrator mesh fill into DRAW, convert the object to a bitmap in Illustrator 8 before saving to Illustrator 7 format.)

Recommendations Export from Illustrator in Placeable EPS or Placeable PDF if the import requires no editing; AI7 for best translation; EPS to Postscript Interpreted if you have no choice.

Avoid Do not use PDF Interpreted for bitmaps and stay away from CGM and EMF at all times. We tested Illustrator's PDF export in Acrobat 4 and, as expected, it looked perfect. Illustrator's CGM and EMF exports never imported correctly when tested in various other applications.

Freehand

Imports from Freehand did not fare as well. DRAW has no direct Freehand import (or export) filter, and we're not sure why, but Freehand 8 has at least four distinct EPS export filters. We tried them all and could find no differences between them when importing our test file using DRAW's PostScript Interpreted filter, including Freehand's DCS export. All typeface and font information was lost, as all text was converted to DRAW's default artistic text properties. Spot fills and RGB bitmaps were converted to CMYK. As expected from PostScript, fountain fills imported as multiple distinct objects, as did contours and blends. At least mesh fills were not a problem—Freehand 8 cannot create them to begin with!

Knowing that DRAW handles Illustrator files fine, we tried exporting from Freehand that way, but every Illustrator format available from Freehand (there are five!) was rife with problems, from mysterious visible text bounding boxes to the complete loss of included bitmaps. Spot colors were converted to CMYK, and some outline properties

were slightly altered (width, style). Illustrator 8 opened four of the five flavors of Freehand 8's AI exports, so we have to point the finger at DRAW on this one.

Recommendations   Use placed EPS or PDF imports only; take a side trip through Illustrator if possible; otherwise, pick any of the EPS formats as Interpreted PostScript.

Avoid   Do not use WMF or EMF, and avoid AI if you don't have Illustrator.

Windows Metafile

The WMF format is a good third choice to AI and EPS for transporting files between Windows applications. It is not a choice for cross-platform compatibility as the Macintosh does not recognize this format at all. It is also not the best choice for press work as all colors are converted to RGB. Although WMF is a "standard" across many Windows applications, there is certainly nothing standard about any of these applications' WMF exports. For example, DRAW imports PowerPoint 97 WMF files flawlessly, but the same file contents from Freehand die a slow, painful death. Your best option for applications that don't speak WMF clearly is to export to EPS. If that is not available, you can install a PostScript printer driver and connect it to FILE. Create a PostScript file by printing to this device and then use DRAW's PostScript Interpreted import filter to bring the contents into DRAW.

AutoCAD

AutoCAD's DXF and DWG files can be imported into DRAW with relatively little fuss. Like Illustrator files, AutoCAD files are stored in ASCII format, making for an easier conversion. However, there are numerous features of AutoCAD that are not supported by DRAW's AutoCAD filters, not the least of which is three-dimensionality. DRAW will force an incoming DXF file into 2D confines by simply stripping the 3D information out and discarding it.

AutoCAD continues to add features to the DXF format, and you will find that DRAW's filter may not be able to handle DXF files from recent releases of AutoCAD, although our text files from various corporate sources imported perfectly. If you encounter this problem, try saving AutoCAD files as EPS. For a complete discussion on the AutoCAD/CorelDRAW connection, use DRAW's online Help. Choose Help ➤ Technical Support, select Import and Export File Formats, then List of File Formats, and choose AutoCAD DXF.

CorelDRAW's CDR Format

The CDR file format will forever be your friendliest, because it is DRAW's native tongue. Whatever is in the file—fountain fills, blends, unique typefaces, layers, pages, guides, and so forth—will survive the trip into your current drawing unscathed (assuming you have installed the typefaces required by the incoming CDR file). Some CDR files created in earlier versions of DRAW might show some differences from the original; typical variations include excess character and word spacing, which require some fine-tuning.

CorelDRAW's CMX Format

The CMX format is an alternative to the full-fledged CDR file. If you export a drawing to CMX format and then re-import it, the integrity and quality of your drawing will be maintained. However, special effects such as contours, blends, and extrusions will be separated into their basic components and will no longer be dynamically editable (i.e., you can still change the objects, but not the effect itself). CMX supports layers upon import, while CDR does not—a good thing to keep in mind. The CMX format is intended to be an intermediate format that all Corel applications can read. Corel has seized upon this as a good strategy for distributing its clipart on CDs.

Importing EPS Files

You'll read it here and again in Chapter 30: if you want the cleanest possible form of data transfer, then turn to Encapsulated PostScript. End of discussion. For users of a PostScript printer, there is no safer way to transport graphic information than as an EPS file. There is no filtering or interpreting required by DRAW, because—and this is key—*DRAW doesn't even try.* When you tell DRAW to import an EPS file, it says to itself, "Ah, an EPS file—good, I don't have to try to digest all of that PostScript code. I'll just read the bounding box information (the values that define the size of the graphic), drop the whole thing into a square of that size, and forget about it until it comes time to print. I see that the file has an embedded image for preview, so I'll show that to the user."

You'll notice with your very first import of a Placeable EPS graphic that it looks different from the original object—it probably looks worse. And don't bother reaching for the Ungroup command; this graphic cannot be ungrouped, taken apart, or edited in any way. Why? Again, DRAW's EPS import filter doesn't really apply a filter to translate all the PostScript code contained in the file. It just places it on the page (hence the name) and lets the printer worry about interpreting the actual code in the file.

Inquiring minds will want to know, therefore, if DRAW doesn't try to read the file, how come it can display the image on screen? The image you see on the screen is a low-resolution, bitmapped rendition of the file's contents. Sometimes DRAW can't even show you that much—that depends upon the application that created the file and whether it has the capability of embedding a *header* or *preview* into the file. You might be met with nothing more than a gray box, showing you the area that the graphic will occupy. In either case—low-fidelity image or dull gray box—you can rest easy, knowing that the EPS file will print at the highest possible resolution of the output device.

The catch to all of this, of course, is that EPS graphics will only print to PostScript output devices. If you print a drawing that contains EPS graphics to a non-PostScript laser printer, the PostScript data will be ignored and the only thing that will print will be the image header...or the gray box.

The CorelDRAW Freeway

Interpreted PostScript

Now here is the wrinkle that we mentioned earlier: in addition to the Placeable EPS format—where DRAW places the file on the page without trying to edit its components—DRAW offers another import choice called PostScript Interpreted. When using the PostScript Interpreted filter, DRAW will try to do what your printer does—interpret the data and construct the image, using DRAW's native elements.

This becomes a sophisticated and ambitious undertaking for DRAW, as it effectively becomes a PostScript image processing engine to translate the language of PostScript into the language of DRAW. The program is a testament to the adage that when at first you don't succeed, try, try again. Early versions of the PostScript Interpreted filter were awful, with version 6 it became credible, and in versions 7 and 8, reliable and useful.

Figure 29.7 shows a chart produced in Microsoft PowerPoint, a program that does not have a simple Export As EPS command. Instead, we issued a print command, as if we were going to print to our PostScript laser printer, but instead instructed PowerPoint to direct all data to a file. We then took this file and imported it into DRAW, using the PostScript Interpreted filter.

FIGURE 29.7

Getting this chart into DRAW is not so easy in the absence of an export command in PowerPoint.

Microsoft PowerPoint - [chart.ppt]

File Edit View Insert Format Tools Slide Show Window Help

Will this chart import properly??

| | 4th Qtr | 3rd Qtr | 2nd Qtr | 1st Qtr |

0 20 40 60 80 100

Slide 1 of 1   Blank Presentation.pot

Unlike the conversation that DRAW had with itself with the EPS file, this one will be a bit more daunting: "Okay, I see a bunch of PostScript data. Uh-oh, this time that blasted user wants me to translate all of the data into objects, instead of just dropping the thing on the page. Okay, let me get my dictionary and thesaurus out and get to work. I'd better cancel all of my appointments for the next few hundred milliseconds because this will take all of my attention."

The first thing DRAW does is ask if you would like it to convert text—as editable text or as curves that resemble the typeface. Translating text to curves carries a much better chance of successful replication of the *appearance*, but the text becomes uneditable. In this case, we chose text because we wanted to preserve the typefaces, or at least be able to edit it once in DRAW.

Our experience with this operation was typical: a bit of failure and a bit of success, the success ultimately prevailing. First off, the entire chart came into DRAW rotated 90 degrees. This was easily fixed with the rotation controls. But then we noticed that the text down the x-axis, set in a TrueType face, did not make the trip through PostScript. When we set it in a Type 1 face, it survived the trip...but it suffered from multiple-personality disorder.

Furthermore, the text along the bottom was out of position, as was the headline. Figure 29.8 shows the result, after we rotated everything.

FIGURE 29.8

Mixed results at the hands of Interpreted PostScript

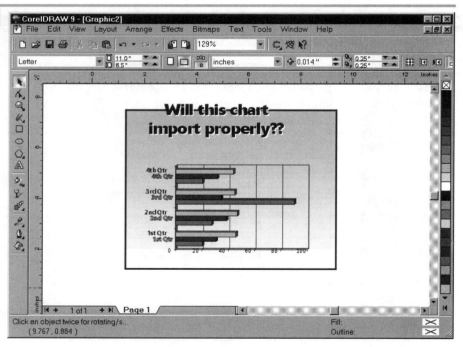

Now, a perfect solution this is not. You can see the text out of whack, and the fountain-filled background is not really a fountain-filled rectangle. Instead, it is a series of long and thin rectangles, each one a hair lighter in color. This is not a

mistake that DRAW made; that is exactly what the PostScript instructions said to do—create a bunch of razor-thin rectangles to produce the effect of a fountain fill. DRAW is not smart enough to say, "Those little rectangles make up a fountain fill, so instead I'll create one big rectangle and apply a fountain fill to it."

But you know what?—this wasn't such a bad starting point for producing this chart in DRAW. The typefaces came across (once we made sure to use Type 1), the bars and the graph itself are correct, and the background is the right color. We were able to delete the duplicate text and reposition the headline in about three minutes. If you do not have an original file—if all you have is a PostScript file of an illustration—trying your luck with an Interpreted PostScript import is better than the alternative of creating it from scratch.

Adobe Acrobat PDF Format

DRAW 9 has enjoyed huge advances in this department—not surprising, seeing how it has developed a whole new engine for exporting PDF. We got sensational results with the chart from PowerPoint: text was text, the background was perfect (although still not a fountain fill), and there was no mirrored text or 90-degree rotations. We would show you a screen image of it, but instead just look at Figure 29.7, the original in PowerPoint. It looks exactly like that.

DRAW also offers a Placeable PDF import choice, which also yielded great results. We especially like the intermediate dialog offering us a choice of pages to import and a preview resolution.

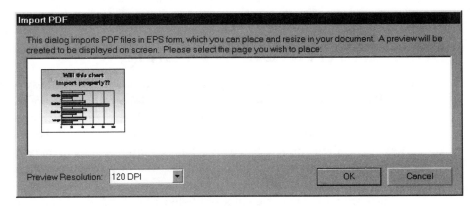

If we didn't say it enough in Chapter 28, we are so impressed with the robust and accurate support for handling PDF files, both incoming and outgoing.

Using the Clipboard

If you have a graphic in another program that needs to make its way to DRAW, another viable option is to employ a copy-and-paste maneuver across the Clipboard. Our chart in PowerPoint once again serves as a good example. We had great success selecting the objects in PowerPoint, copying them to the Clipboard, and switching to DRAW for the corresponding paste. First, we used the Edit ➤ Paste Special command and chose Enhanced Metafile as the format. (That is our standard operating procedure for pasting graphics. In fact, we redirected the Ctrl+V hotkey to be Paste Special instead of the straight Paste command that carries out the default choice without presenting us with the other options.)

Much to our surprise, the results were awful. So we tried it again, this time choosing the standard Metafile format, and the results were dead-solid perfect. (Again, we aren't even bothering to show you the picture; it's identical to the source.) We had figured that Enhanced Metafile would do better than Standard, and have no idea why that wouldn't be the case (in fact, like most users, we really have no idea what the Metafile format is all about). But again, the moral of this story is to go to Paste Special and try all the choices there, in the hopes that one of them will produce a winner.

 WARNING   While we are fans of the Clipboard, we are not so keen on the use of hot-linked graphics across the Clipboard. We used to wax on about the potential of creating live links with graphics files, but we have crashed too many times, run out of memory too often, and encountered too many instances of inaccurate renderings to recommend the use of linked graphics. We know how cool it would be to include a pretty chart from your spreadsheet program that includes live links back to the original data, but we just don't trust the process. We prefer to keep our data dead but accurate.

Slow, Bitmaps Crossing

DRAW can import many different bitmap formats, including the heavyweights: TIFF, PCX, JPEG, and Kodak Photo CD. In addition, DRAW can handle the popular online formats GIF, JPEG, PNG, and a list of other specialized formats such as Scitex, Targa, and MacPaint. Color, black and white, gray—DRAW doesn't care. For the most part, DRAW treats these formats as it does EPS files, simply passing them on to the printer.

But DRAW does speak a bit of bitmap. It can show your imported images in considerable detail. If an imported bitmap contains 16 million colors, DRAW will show you an image with an impressive range of life-like colors and fine detail. It also allows you to apply untold special effects to imported bitmaps, details of which can be found in Chapter 23. Many of the caveats that we have issued in past editions have been eliminated with recent versions:

- We used to warn you about rotating bitmaps, because redraw time would slow to a crawl, but that is no longer the case. Output will slow down, but on-screen rendering does not.

- We used to point out that bitmaps could be overlaid onto other objects, but not layered. Well, not only can bitmaps be made gradually transparent, but PHOTO-PAINT (and, yes, PhotoShop) images that are saved with layers will import to DRAW that way.

- We used to warn you about scaling bitmaps, and we still will! Bitmap images are made up of dots, which are quite size-sensitive. Although you may get away with reducing a bitmap, enlarging a bitmap could be hazardous to your career.

Lots of Dots, Lots of Data

Imported bitmaps can get big—in a hurry. Even if the file size isn't large, DRAW might need to move a mountain or two to import and display certain bitmap images. For instance, a TIFF file stored in the now-common compressed format might take up no more than 100K on your hard drive. But when you import it, DRAW uncompresses it, and the space requirements balloon to many times the original size. The CDR file containing this bitmap will grow quite large, and DRAW will swipe an equally large chunk of space from your Windows Temp directory. Here are two functions that speak to that.

Cropping upon Import

As we touched on earlier when describing the Import dialog, you have three options when you import a bitmap. First, there's Full Image, which does nothing to your file. This is the default. Next is Crop Image, which, when you select it, will open the dialog box shown below. Here you'll see a preview of your image and you can enter the crop amounts numerically or use your pointer to drag the bounding handles interactively. The Select All button will reset the dialog.

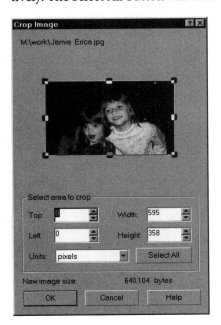

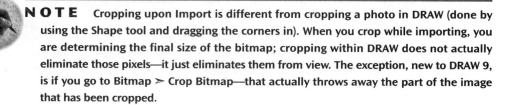

N O T E   Cropping upon Import is different from cropping a photo in DRAW (done by using the Shape tool and dragging the corners in). When you crop while importing, you are determining the final size of the bitmap; cropping within DRAW does not actually eliminate those pixels—it just eliminates them from view. The exception, new to DRAW 9, is if you go to Bitmap ➢ Crop Bitmap—that actually throws away the part of the image that has been cropped.

Also, remember that you can apply a powerclip to a bitmap, essentially stuffing it inside any other object. Powerclipping a bitmap inside of an irregular (nonrectangular) shape or inside of a piece of text is an effective cropping effect, and you can see it in action in Chapter 10.

Lightening Your Load

The last choice in the nameless drop-down list of Import options is Resample. From the dialog that opens when you choose this option, you can scale the bitmap up or down, or simply redistribute the pixels. We recommend redistributing (maintaining file size) or resampling down only, as resampling upward means that DRAW is guessing where to add pixels, and the results could be quite unpleasant. Each of these options is sticky and the last used will still be selected the next time you import a bitmap.

DRAW can also resample once the image is on the page, from the Bitmaps ➢ Resample command. This procedure is not like a crop or a lens; you are actually changing the basic qualities of the bitmap.

Importing Text

Realizing that text can be imported into DRAW using any number of methods, we felt this topic deserves its own section in this chapter. Although some of these methods produce better results than others, don't expect any of them to win awards for intelligence.

You can bring text into DRAW by going through the Import dialog or by dragging and dropping from an Explorer window. Don't expect formatting or extended symbols to appear correctly, although Corel WordPerfect formats perform better than Word formats, as you might expect. In general, if you have a choice over file format and desire formatting to be preserved as closely as possible, choose the Rich Text Format (RTF). If you are looking to strip formatting, save the original text as ASCII text or use Edit ➢ Paste Special ➢ Text. Keep in mind, however, that the overall integrity of the original format depends on the format itself—some import filters just plain work better than others.

If you do not have a choice over formatting, we recommend this strategy for preserving the most formatting while allowing the best placement options:

1. With the Text tool, drag a paragraph text frame to the size you want.

2. With the text cursor planted inside the frame, go to Text ➤ Edit Text (or click the Edit Text button on the property bar).

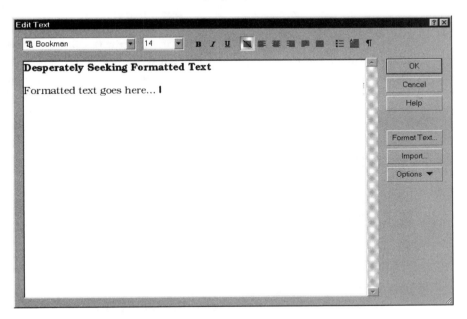

3. Click Import, select your text file, and OK.

This strategy allows you to choose how additional text frames flow; other methods automatically create additional pages in your DRAW document and then flow spillover text into full-page paragraph frames on those pages. Automatic page creation can be a convenience for creating a multipage, threaded document, but a pain in the hind quarters if you simply wanted to incorporate a chunk of text into a single-page drawing.

Here is the rub when it comes to importing text: do you want the formatting of the original word processing file maintained, or do you want the text to take on the formatting of DRAW's styles? That one question will determine the approach you take:

- To maintain the most amount of original formatting possible, use the conventional Import command.

- To maintain typeface and style information, but not page information, use the Edit Text dialog as described above, or use the Clipboard, choosing RTF as the format.

- To force the text to adhere to DRAW's prevailing format, paste the text as Text.

For more on working with text, see Chapters 8 through 10.

Digital Cameras

Although not strictly an import, we thought this topic belongs alongside of the other methods for bringing artwork and other files into DRAW. The new digital camera support means that you can plug your camera into a serial or USB port on your computer and add digital photographs directly into DRAW.

The first step after you've physically connected the camera to the computer port is to tell DRAW that it's there. To do this, go to File ➢ Digital Camera ➢ Select Camera. Enter the appropriate information about your camera and the port it's connected to.

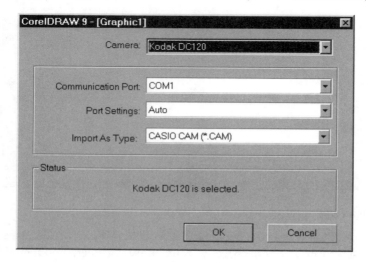

Once DRAW is aware of the camera connection, you can use File ➢ Digital Camera ➢ Get Image to transfer images into DRAW or, for those cameras that support two-way file transfer, File ➢ Digital Camera ➢ Send Image to upload images back onto the camera's memory card.

Only the most popular cameras are supported. If your camera is not listed, you'll have to rely on the camera manufacturer's recommended method for image acquisition. But, frankly, we're not impressed with hooking the camera up directly via a serial port; too much battery drainage and the transfer can be excruciatingly slow. For less than $80, you can purchase a card reader which will hook up to a parallel or USB port and your keyboard port for power. Your computer will see the card reader as another hard drive and you'll have full—even network—access to it at all times. Just pop in the memory card and open or import the photos just as if they were clipart.

Now that we have explored the entrances to the CorelDRAW freeway, it is time to get to know the exits.

Exit, Stage Left: Exporting Files to Other Formats

Featuring

EXIT, STAGE LEFT: EXPORTING FILES TO OTHER FORMATS

hose of you who produce and print your artwork entirely within DRAW won't be interested in this section. The other 99 percent of you regularly, perhaps constantly, produce work that is designed to be incorporated into something else: a letter in your word processor, a brochure in PageMaker, a logo in VENTURA Publisher, a background for a chart, a button on a Web page, or one of hundreds of other types of drawings that will find their way into other documents.

This is your exit ramp as you leave the familiar home territory of DRAW and head out into the rest of the known universe. Without doubt there will be some speed bumps along the way, so we're here to provide travel advice so you can prevent your work from becoming road kill on the illustration highway.

Choosing Your Weapon

What format should you use to export your work? That depends entirely upon your purpose—the range of projects that involve exporting from DRAW has widened significantly in the last few years. There used to be only one reason to export: to place a drawing in a document that was ultimately to be printed. Today, you can export (or publish) from DRAW to the Web, to a portable document, to a presentation, or of course, to print. Each has its own rules of thumb, and we'll be exploring some choices in more detail, but first let's have a look at...

The Export Dialog

The Export dialog shown in Figure 30.1 is very similar to its Import counterpart; therefore, our recap here will be brief.

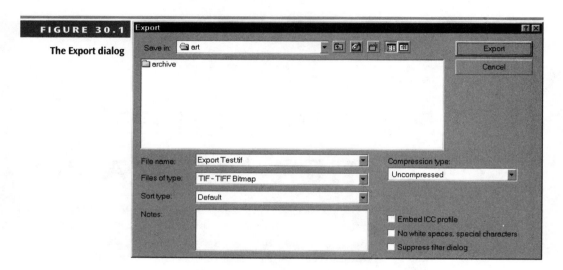

FIGURE 30.1

The Export dialog

The Basics

As with the Import and Open dialogs, the upper portion of the DRAW 9 Export dialog box is similar to Windows 95/98/NT dialogs in most other applications, meaning that from this dialog you can browse to any location on your hard drive, toggle details and list views of the contents of those drives, create new folders, rename folders, and cut, copy, and paste between the current folder and to any other you browse to within this dialog...again, essentially all the things that you could do in an Explorer window. The lower half of the dialog is where you'll choose your exporting options, and we'll discuss those next.

File Name

As you've probably already guessed, this is where you name the file to be exported. By default, this box will be prefilled using the name of your current drawing and the last-used export format. New to DRAW 9, the File Name box is also a drop-down list of your five most recently exported files. While this proves handier for importing and opening files, you may find this option an easy way to jump between recent export locations.

Files of Type

This is the list of all currently installed export filters. If you think you're missing something, read the "Filter Madness" sidebar in Chapter 29. You'll notice that CDR is not on this list. You cannot export a DRAW file to the CDR format; you must use Save (or Save As). Select the export format from this list.

Sort Type

New to DRAW 9, the export filter list can be sorted in eight different ways: By Extension, By Description, By Most Recently Used, Vector, Bitmap, Text, Animation, and Default. We refer you back to Chapter 29 for details.

Notes

Here you can add notes about the file you are exporting, which may be helpful to the recipient of that file. Not all formats support included notes, and the box will be grayed out for those that don't.

Compression Type

Some export formats, notably bitmaps, include one or more compression options. If you know that the receiving application is compatible with the compression method, go ahead and choose one. Otherwise, we recommend the defaults.

Embed ICC Profile

Another new export option in DRAW 9, this allows an ICC color profile to be embedded into the file information. If the receiving application cannot use the information, it would be discarded. For more on ICC profiles, see Chapters 27 and 29.

No White Spaces, Special Characters

When exporting graphics created for the Web, you should not overlook this new feature. Spaces and other characters not supported on the Internet will be replaced by underscores. `My Pretty Web Button.gif` would become `My_Pretty_Web_Button.gif`.

Suppress Filter Dialog

Some file formats will open additional dialogs upon export from DRAW. If you always accept the defaults for these formats, you can safely enable this option, and the secondary dialogs will not appear. We recommend you do not check this box until you are familiar with the various export options.

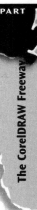

Road Test Revisited

If you've read the last chapter on importing, our test file in Figure 30.2 will look familiar. This drawing contains examples of many different types of objects, including those with known tendencies to trip on their way out the door. The test file includes a spot color object; CMYK objects; text using both PostScript and TrueType fonts; an object with a dashed outline; a filled open curve; a 30-step blend; fountain, pattern, and texture fills; an arrowhead; a transparent lens; a mesh fill; a contour with a hairline outline; a powerclip; and both an RGB and a CMYK bitmap.

FIGURE 30.2

How well can DRAW export this demanding test file? That depends upon the export flavor...

As we explore the more popular export formats, we'll explain what to choose and when, and tell you how our test file fared so that you'll know what to expect on your own road trips through file exports. While we don't have the space to explain every option available, we note here, and again during discussions on specific formats, that Corel's online Help files have been updated and are a good resource for a filter's features and limitations. If we don't list it here, we don't recommend it, having found other formats that do the job better.

Traditional and Other Printed Media

What is "traditional" media in these days when Web pages and graphics are so prevalent? It includes books, magazines, and other materials printed using commercial presses. The Internet may be everywhere you look, but it is not yet considered "traditional." Here are the formats that speak to these traditions.

EPS

When it comes to exporting graphics to traditional media, the discussion is very brief: if you are outputting to a PostScript device, create EPS files. For all of the same reasons that we liked the EPS import, this is one of your safest and cleanest avenues out. This goes double in today's environment, where the integration of bitmap images into drawings is commonplace, because EPS is one of a few formats that can reliably handle both types of graphics at once. It is also one of the few reliable cross-platform transport formats. Figure 30.3 shows how EPS aced our test.

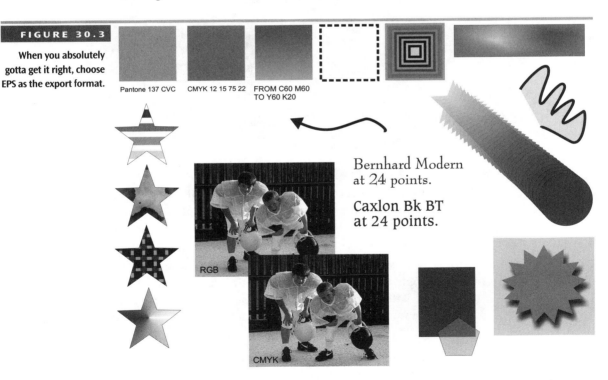

FIGURE 30.3

When you absolutely gotta get it right, choose EPS as the export format.

Pantone 137 CVC CMYK 12 15 75 22 FROM C60 M60 TO Y60 K20

Bernhard Modern at 24 points.

Caxlon Bk BT at 24 points.

RGB

CMYK

The contents of EPS files cannot be edited by the recipients (unless their software has a PostScript interpreter, like DRAW does). Most likely, they will simply drop your EPS file into their layout, using the preview header as a placement guide. When the entire layout is printed to a PostScript device, the PostScript information contained in your EPS file is included in the stream of PostScript instructions for the output device.

Exporting to EPS will invoke a separate export dialog (shown below), which shares many options with the Print dialog, and we refer you to Chapter 26 for those details.

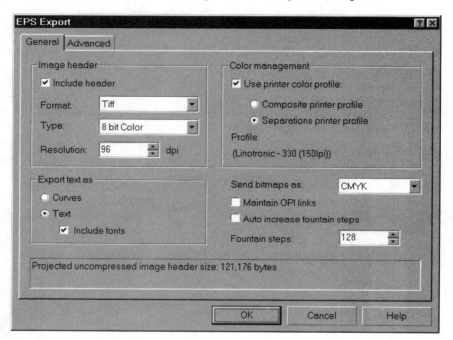

Options that are unique to EPS export include:

Include Header   A choice between TIFF and WMF. Choose TIFF when delivering files cross-platform, and keep the header resolution to a minimum to avoid bloated file sizes (although this bloat will not affect print integrity or print times—only the display of the graphic).

Bounding Box   Here you choose whether the bounding box seen by the receiving application will represent the entire page size or only the objects in the file. The latter is the default and the one you'll use most often, but if you need to show an entire page, margins and all, you'll want to choose Page. This option is on the new Advanced page of the dialog.

If you need a bit more help, right-click on a dialog item and choose What's This from the pop-up menu or click the Help button.

Test Results   The EPS file we created printed perfectly to an Epson 1520 Level 2 printer, to a Linotronic imagesetter for film output, and it displayed perfectly in Acrobat Reader, versions 3 and 4.

Recommended For   Preserving file integrity across PostScript output devices and the software used to create it; when creating files for inclusion in other documents; when creating files for cross-platform delivery.

Avoid When   The contents will have to be edited as individual objects and graphics, as chances are the receiving application will not have the means to interpret the PostScript information correctly.

N O T E   Although we stand by our previous advice, we've relaxed a little bit and include PDF alongside of EPS, provided, however, that you use DRAW 9's new Publish to PDF feature. Read Chapter 28 for the scoop on Publish to PDF details, especially if you are providing files cross-platform.

WMF

The obvious exception to the EPS rule is if you must create graphics that will ultimately be printed on a non-PostScript printer. We suggest you try two formats: Windows Metafile, covered here, and TIFF, discussed later. The WMF file will not handle bitmaps or powerclips reliably, and will break down fountain fills into tiny bands of shades. Yet of all of the common vector formats, it is the closest pursuer to EPS, provided the receiving application's own import filter is up to speed.

Test Results   Our results were varied, owing to the differences in receiving WMF filters themselves. Freehand and (surprisingly) WordPerfect 7 and 8 imports were close to unusable. Illustrator 8, Xara 2, and Microsoft Office 97 products opened the WMF test file with very little discrepancies, telling us that DRAW's WMF export does indeed work. Figure 30.4 shows the WMF file DRAW created, imported, and displayed in Word 97. Those good results proved to be a pleasant surprise for us, revealing that DRAW's WMF export capabilities are improved over previous versions. The powerclip stayed inside of its boundaries (previous versions would simply ignore the clipping path entirely), and while complex patterns and other fills were rendered as bitmaps, they looked perfect. Text remained editable and showed up in Word 97, Illustrator 8, and Xara 2 with all of the correct typefaces. Fountain fills had the least favorable results, and we would recommend converting any such filled objects to bitmaps in DRAW before a WMF export.

Recommended For   General compatibility between most Windows applications; non-PostScript output.

Avoid When   EPS, PDF, or native formats are options; if your file contains complex fills that cannot be simplified.

The CorelDRAW Freeway

PART

7

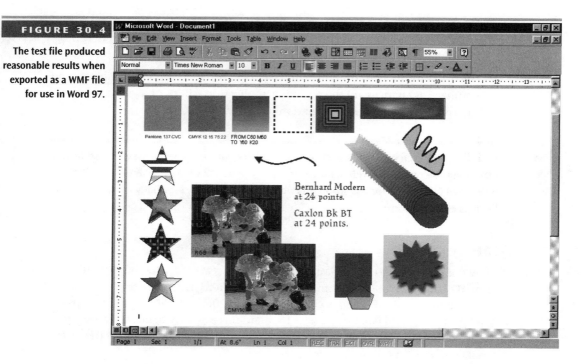

NOTE   A general comment about exporting transparent bitmap effects: transparencies
are rendered in RGB. For exports for print output, we recommend separating any bitmap
effect from the control object and either converting it to CMYK or "flattening" the effect
with any underlying object layer by selecting both and converting to one bitmap.

Illustrator (AI)

One of the first things many users try when testing the integrity of their Illustrator
exports is to immediately reimport the AI file back into DRAW. Big mistake. DRAW's
Illustrator import and export filters are two separate beasts. The only true test of DRAW's
AI exports is to open the resulting file in Illustrator itself, which we did. DRAW's AI
export filter has been written from the ground up by Corel, and we are happy to
report perfect results with Illustrator 7 and 8, as shown in Figure 30.5. With DRAW 9's
improved AI import filter, moving your work between these top illustration applications has never been easier. Choosing the AI format will open an intermediary dialog,
presenting numerous options to create the most compatible export.

Test Results   Perfect, with one limitation: because nonlinear fountain fills
will be converted to objects, we recommend converting nonlinear to linear,

when possible, and re-creating the fill in Illustrator. Also note that mesh and other bitmap fills will be converted to bitmaps. Pattern fills were retained.

Recommended For   Working between DRAW and Illustrator, and other later Adobe products.

Avoid When   Never—when transferring files to Illustrator or output devices that require AI format as input, it is the best way to go.

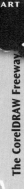

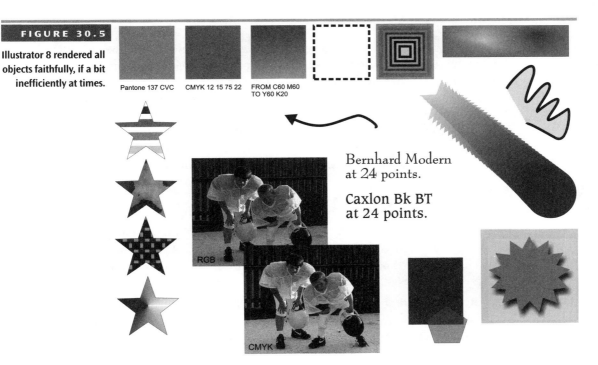

FIGURE 30.5

Illustrator 8 rendered all objects faithfully, if a bit inefficiently at times.

CMX

CMX is Corel's own format. This format—which stands for nothing at all, as far as we can tell—is an efficient version of the CDR format. It contains only the information necessary to render a drawing, but not the elements that helped you create it, like grid information, styles, or guides. Much of Corel's clipart is stored in CMX format.

There are two ways to work with this format. The most obvious is to export drawings as Corel Presentation Exchange (the CMX format, which upon further scrutiny, should have been named the CPE format). Once done, you'll be able to import the file into any Corel application that supports CMX. The second approach is less obvious: when you save your drawing for the first time (or issue a Save As command with an existing drawing), the Advanced button takes you to a screen of secondary options, one of which is called Save Presentation Exchange. With this option enabled, you embed the CMX data directly inside the CDR file. With this extra data, you can import the CDR file into other Corel applications that support CMX.

Corel itself has watered down the usefulness of CMX by offering direct support for CDR in most of its other applications. Still, this export option is useful for delivering a "just the facts" version of a drawing to another user, without all of the frills that might get in the way.

HPGL

HPGL is initially a command language for plotters of Hewlett-Packard. Because all CAD systems support plotters, it becomes a simple way to send data from CAD systems to 2D systems like word processors or imaging tools. When printing in HPGL(/2), the printer will define points "a" and "b" and then draw a line between them. Consequently, if your image contains a lot of points or nodes, the plot file will have a harder time connecting the dots. This will result in larger file sizes and slower plots. The HPGL format is recommended for simple line art or text, and should be avoided if your file contains complex fills, bitmaps, or multiple multinode line segments.

WPG

As you probably expect, DRAW's WPG exports are quite reliable, subject only to the limitations of WordPerfect itself. Some bitmaps are broken into separate pieces, complex fills are rendered as bitmaps, all colors are converted to RGB through who knows what conversion method, and fountain fills are broken into multiple lines. On the up side, text remains editable and the correct typeface and format is retained.

Recommended For   Simple files, such as logos, destined only for WordPerfect.

Avoid When   Using complex fills and bitmaps.

Portable Documents

In one of the sleeper moves of DRAW 8, export support for creating Adobe Acrobat or Portable Document Files (PDF) was included. These filters didn't meet any of our export standards, and in version 9 have been dropped in favor of the excellent new Publish to PDF engine. Read all the details about Publish to PDF in Chapter 28 to learn how to create highly accurate and transportable files from your DRAW documents.

Exporting to Bitmap Formats

Exporting to a bitmap format is not unlike converting a graphic to a bitmap within DRAW—all of your clean, intelligent curves are transformed into an army of unintelligent dots. The advantage of exporting to a bitmap format is that you have not

permanently dummied down your drawing—when you're done exporting, your drawing still contains all of its curves. Furthermore, you might be surprised at how good a 300dpi TIFF file can render your work.

N O T E   For the details on Web graphics, we send you back to Part V. In general, DRAW can create GIF and JPEG files, and the newer PNG and Wavelet formats. It also offers a Wizard for turning a finished page into an HTML file, with all formatting and positioning maintained.

The Dialog

The Bitmap Export dialog has been updated in DRAW 9. The new dialog, shown below, is smaller, arranged more logically, and offers a few new choices.

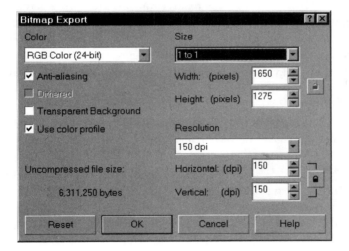

Color

The usual suspects: Black and White, 16 Color, Grayscale, Paletted, RGB, and CMYK. If your chosen format does not support one of these color depths, that choice will not be on the list.

Anti-aliasing

Anti-aliasing is a process that simulates smoother transitions between contrasting colors by creating pixels of intermediary colors between the transitions. Choose this option to reduce the appearance of jaggies. For graphics with small text or straight lines, you will probably see better results without anti-aliasing. We offer chapter and verse in Chapters 21 and 22.

Dithered

Check this box to create the illusion of more color in paletted and other low-color images. A second cousin to anti-aliasing, dithering simulates a greater tonal range with dots of color instead of solid blocks. This option will create larger compressed files and should be used carefully when creating Web graphics, since large areas of color which compress easily are eliminated. For examples of dithered graphics, consult Chapter 21.

Transparent Background

If an image format supports "alpha channels" (such as TIFF, PNG, CPT, and PSD), this option will be available. An alpha channel is another channel like the RGB channels. This extra "alpha" channel defines the relative transparency of the pixel. It is an 8-bit (256-level) grayscale representation of the image and is used to "mask out" the color of the underlying pixels. By checking it, you are telling DRAW to create an alpha channel for any background area contained in the final image's bounding box. This is an easy way to banish those pesky white backgrounds on the fly, without ever leaving DRAW.

Use Color Profile

Check this box to enable your active color profile when image colors are translated. For more on color management, see Chapter 27.

Uncompressed File Size

This tells you information about the expected size of the export, before compression. If this number is incredibly high, you might need to decrease Resolution, but export the file first and judge for yourself. We have learned not to blindly trust DRAW's estimates.

Size

You will usually want to keep this option at its 1:1 default. But for those times you want to change the dimensions of the image disproportionately, this is where you'd do it. We were glad to see the outdated FAX resolutions finally removed. But now we're equally perplexed with the preset monitor resolutions, since choosing one would almost certainly distort the image unless your drawing was created at precisely one of those sizes (in which case, 1:1 would achieve the same results).

Resolution

Choose the size of the export image, in pixels, here. For a detailed discussion on bitmap resolution, consult Chapters 21 and 22.

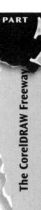

 T I P   In-place bitmap exporting is a new feature for DRAW 9. To see this in action, right-click a bitmap on the page and choose Save Bitmap As from the pop-up menu for a quick jump to the Export dialog.

By Popular Demand

All bitmap exports begin the same way, with specialty options available from the secondary dialog that appears after you name the file. We discuss the most popular formats here; more notes on each format can be found by clicking on the Help buttons in those secondary export dialogs. We're happy to report that DRAW 9's bitmap exports will not discard the corner pixels, as DRAW 8 was prone to do. In fact, with version 9 we have seen some of the cleanest bitmap exports ever.

FlashPix

When exporting to FPX, a secondary dialog will open, as shown below. This format is gaining in popularity, having been designed from the ground up with the Web in mind. FlashPix avoids the long downloads associated with previous generations of imaging technology. Since only the portion of an image needed for the viewing area is downloaded, images appear immediately, and you can quickly zoom in to examine high-resolution details, and zoom out to get the big picture.

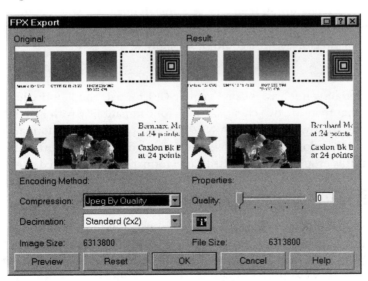

TIFF

TIFF files produce surprisingly credible results—in fact, better than some vector exports, as the page will look exactly the same. (We'd show you the result of our test file exported to TIFF, but it looks just like the original.) The difference is that the image is no longer individual objects but instead a file full of pixels, which limits the amount of editing or resizing options. TIFF offers a number of compression methods with the most popular being the lossless LZW. If you're unsure of compression compatibility with the receiving application, we recommend no compression. TIFF offers true CMYK output and is an all-around good choice if appearance and cross-platform compatibility are important and editability is not.

PNG

PNG is a great bitmap format waiting for wider Web acceptance. It offers excellent compression, true colors, and transparency. But unless you are sure your viewers are using browsers that support PNG, you should limit your exports to other non-Web uses, such as PowerPoint bitmaps with transparency.

BMP

BMP is another good all-purpose format. However, because CMYK colors are not supported, we recommend that you use this format only when preparing files for business-related applications, such as word processors and presentation software, and desktop printer and screen output. If you are creating an image for your desktop wallpaper, this is the obvious choice you would use, and you would want to export the file to the WINDOWS directory, so you could easily apply it.

CPT

Last but certainly not least is Corel's native CPT format. You'll notice in the Files of Type list that there are two choices. One is for compatibility with PHOTO-PAINT 7 and 8; the other strictly for PHOTO-PAINT 9, because of the updated format's ability to embed an ICC color profile. Choose this format only if your export will be for PHOTO-PAINT, as this proprietary TIFF-based Corel format is not supported elsewhere.

The Clipboard and Other OLE Matters

In a word, don't. DRAW has many reliable methods of transferring your work to other applications, and the Clipboard is not one of them. This is especially true if you choose to create a hot-link back to DRAW instead of a static paste. This is not DRAW's fault, but the limitations of the Clipboard itself. Transferring files via the Clipboard is essentially the same as a WMF or EMF export, except that text and other vector objects are usually converted to bitmaps, powerclip containers are dropped, and many other unwanted conversions occur. Save yourself a headache and actually export to WMF (or a more appropriate format) instead.

As for OLE (Object Linking and Embedding), if you paste your DRAW file as a link into another application, that link will be broken as soon as you transfer that application's file to a system without DRAW 9. Even if that system does have DRAW 9 installed, chances are the link will still be unreliable and may even corrupt the container document. OLE is just not a reliable enough feature to trust with safekeeping all of the hard work and time you've put into creating your DRAW documents.

We can't end on such a downer note when the prevailing theme of this chapter should be one of triumph. DRAW's export capabilities have never been more robust and more clean. When Corel's engineers said that their focus for DRAW 9 was on clean output, they meant it, and the proof is in the exporting.

PART

7

The CorelDRAW Freeway

TAKING CONTROL

USING STYLES

Featuring

USING STYLES

Time is a luxury those in the graphics business usually aren't allowed. When the big client wants the slides done tomorrow, you order some take-out and settle in for a long night. As the clock ticks on, you can't afford to waste time repeating commands over and over while formatting text and graphics. CorelDRAW's styles and templates are the answer: you can store frequently used formatting attributes and reapply them later with a click of the mouse. Who knows—with a little help from styles and templates, you might be able to catch your favorite late-night talk show after all.

This chapter is divided into three sections. The first focuses on creating and applying text and graphic styles. The second section discusses templates, which store styles and other page-layout information. The third section deals with color styles. And because we're here in the back of the book, in a part entitled "Taking Control," we assume that you know your way around the program.

What Is a Style?

A *style* is a collection of formatting attributes, such as color and font, which can be applied to text or graphic objects quickly and easily. Rather than assigning each of the attributes individually (selecting the color, choosing the face, adjusting the outline width, and so forth), you can apply a style that defines all these attributes in one quick step.

Styles are saved in the .cdr file and, if you choose, in a DRAW template file. Saving styles in a template allows you to use the styles with other drawings. How styles and templates work together is discussed in detail later in this chapter.

Desktop publishing and word processing applications have long been able to create text styles, and so can DRAW—but DRAW lets you create styles for graphics as well. For instance, the attributes of a graphic style might be a texture fill with a 3-point outline. DRAW's text styles are separated into artistic text and paragraph text styles.

The power of styles goes beyond speed—styles also help you achieve consistency in design. They help guarantee that every title in a project uses the same font, style, and color, adding to the overall appeal and professional appearance of your work. You can also establish a dynamic connection between all objects using a particular style. This connection allows you to change the attributes of the style—the fill color, for instance—and thus affect the fill color of every object that uses that style.

Suppose you are in charge of producing a weekly sales presentation. By creating styles for the presentation's graphic objects and for the title and body text, you're giving yourself a head start on building the next presentation. The styles are saved in a *template*, and the template is used to build the next presentation. (As you'll see, templates can even store objects such as the slide background and a company logo.) Say you get halfway through the project and realize the body text needs to be smaller. Simply change the body text style, and all text with that style also changes. Suddenly, that weekly task doesn't sound so bad.

N O T E   The Copy Attributes From command is another way to apply formatting to several objects in a drawing. In this case, however, the objects are not linked, so changes made in one object do not affect other objects with the same formatting. When you use styles, any change to a style affects all objects using that style.

Using the Styles Docker

In DRAW 8 and 9, styles are managed with the Styles docker. To open it in 9, you have three choices:

- Go to Tools ➤ Graphic and Text Styles.
- Go to Window ➤ Dockers ➤ Graphic and Text Styles (every docker across the program can be opened from Windows ➤ Dockers).
- Press Ctrl+F5.

As you can see in Figure 31.1, graphic, paragraph text, and artistic text styles appear on the Graphic and Text page of the docker.

FIGURE 31.1

Press Ctrl+F5 to quickly
display the Styles
docker.

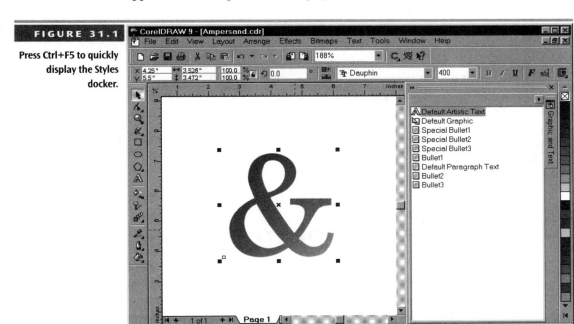

PART

Taking Control

We have several things to point out about this docker:

- On our screen, the names of the styles might appear smaller than on yours. The default is to show large icons, but we prefer small ones. We right-clicked on an empty portion of the docker and chose View ➤ Small Icons.

- The small triangle at the top-right of the docker provides access to many of the commands relevant to styles, but you can also get there by right-clicking white space in the docker. We find that to be easier—a much bigger target.

- For as long as we can remember, these nine styles have been present in Corel's default template. We see no reason for having six bullet styles in a program whose emphasis is graphics and we see nothing that warrants three of the bullets to be called Special. Yet it has been that way since DRAW 3.

- Also for several years now, the hard-coded sort order has Default Paragraph Text being placed between Bullet 1 and Bullet 2. But hey, we don't develop it, we just write about it...

Unless you have loaded another template, the styles that appear in the docker are those of DRAW's main template, `coreldrw.cdt`. You can load a different template of styles, make modifications to the default template, or pay no attention to templates whatsoever. We'll talk about templates soon.

The icons attached to each style name indicate the type of style. As you can see, the *A* denotes an artistic text style, the document icon marks a paragraph text style, and the square and triangle icon is the symbol for a graphic style. DRAW lets you decide which types of styles are displayed in the docker. By default, all style types are shown, but if you never create paragraph text, you could instruct DRAW to only show you the artistic text and graphic styles, and then you'd never see those special bullets again. You can do this from the context menu (right-click on the docker).

T I P   Select the Auto-view option to see only styles for the type of object selected. For instance, when a block of artistic text is selected, only the artistic text styles are displayed in the docker.

Creating and Applying Styles

The first step in creating a style is to build an object with the formatting attributes you want saved in the style. Figure 31.1 on the previous page shows the colorful ampersand that has appeared in other chapters. It's set at 400 point Dauphin, with a blue-to-yellow angled fountain fill. If you think that you might want to create other characters like this one, then it is your "prototype" for creating a style, in this case, a text style.

Don't worry if you're not certain about all the formatting—you can always make changes later. After the prototype is formatted, you're ready to save the style:

1. Right-click on the object and select Styles ➤ Save Style Properties. The Save Style As dialog appears.

2. Enter a style name and choose which attributes are to be saved as part of the style.

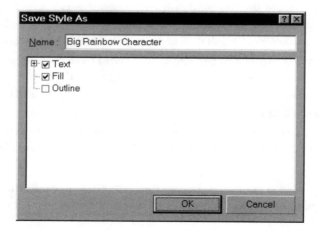

Notice that we unchecked Outline—we might want to apply this style to some ornate text that has its own outline. We want to be able to apply all of the other formats of the style to the text, but not lose the outline we'd already created for it.

TIP You can also create a style with drag-and-drop. If the Styles docker is open while you create the prototype, drag the object into the docker. The new style will join the list and be given a generic name. Click the name twice to rename it to something better. When you use this method for style creation, the style contains all possible attributes.

Now to apply the style to a new element:

3. Create a new string of artistic text. It starts out like all others—as drab 24 point AvantGarde.

4. With the new string of text selected, you have four choices for applying it:

   • Double-click the style in the docker.

   • Right-click the style and choose Apply Style.

   • Drag it and drop it onto the text (for this choice, you do not need to select it first).

   • Right-click the text, go to Styles ➤ Apply, and choose the desired style from the flyout.

There should be a fifth choice—use the Styles drop-down menu. But to our chagrin, Corel opted not to place Styles on the Standard toolbar or any of the property bars, except the one that appears when your cursor is in the text (showing once again a lopsided emphasis on paragraph text activities). Three chapters from now, that will be one of the first things we'll do as we redesign the interface. Please remind us in case we forget…

Styles can be saved in templates, and we'll discuss the advantages of that strategy soon. For now, just remember that you don't need to save a new style in a template. If you don't, then it lives only within the .cdr file in which you created it, but it does live.

WARNING When you use the context menu to save a new style, DRAW places the Default _____ Style name in the save field (Artistic, Paragraph, or Graphic). If you aren't paying attention and you don't enter a new name, you will have changed the default style, and any similar element that hasn't been given a different style will immediately change. We wish that the Save Style dialog began with a blank field, but at least there is Undo.

PART

Taking Control

The process for creating graphic styles and paragraph text styles is the same. In the following sections, you'll find step-by-step instructions for creating graphic, artistic text, and paragraph text styles. Since the styles created with these instructions are used as examples as you work through the chapter, you may want to create them as you read each section.

N O T E   Creating a style saves the attributes of an object, but not the object itself. If you wanted, for instance, to save the entire ampersand, formatting and all, then you would turn to the Scrapbook (Tools ➤ Scrapbook), not Styles.

Graphic Styles

Any attribute applied with the Fill or Outline tool can be saved in a graphic style. For instance, fountain fills, two-color pattern fills, arrowheads, and dashed lines can all be attributes in a graphic style.

Graphic styles are useful when all graphics in a project need to use a specific spot color. Suppose you're creating a piece using black and Pantone 192 Red. When it comes time to output color separations to film, it can be a real mess if some objects use Pantone 192 Red and others use Pantone 185 Red (you'd get an extra separation for the 185 Red). Creating a graphic style with the desired Pantone color guarantees you'll always apply the right color.

Furthermore, if you know that you'll be using a second spot color, but you're not sure which one, then you'll be grateful for using styles. Name the style "Pantone Color," assign the most likely color to it, and apply it to all appropriate objects. If the color gets changed down the road, you need only update the style to change all of the elements to the new color.

Artistic Text Styles

Styles that you create for artistic text can contain the following attributes:

Font   Typeface, type size, and type styles such as bold and italic

Alignment   Left, center, and right, plus full justification or forced justification

Spacing   Between characters, words, and lines

Lines   Underlines, overlines, and strikeout

Text effects   Superscript, subscript, and capitalization

Each of these can be included or excluded from a text style.

We haven't made much of an effort—here or back in Chapter 8, "Working with Text"—to hide our disdain for Corel's decision to make the default text face be AvantGarde. During the beta-testing cycle, we asked publicly, "When is the last time that anyone here has ever used AvantGarde intentionally?" Nobody could remember.

So with every new version of DRAW, we waste no time changing the default for artistic text to something more useful, like FuturaBlack, ErasUltra, or...well, just about anything would be better! There are several ways to do this:

- Format a string of text to your liking, and use the context menu to update Default Artistic Text.

- Right-click on the style name in the docker, choose Properties, and click the Edit button next to Text (you're at Tools ➢ Options ➢ Document ➢ Styles).

- Drag the correctly formatted text into the docker and rename New Artistic Text as Default Artistic Text, saying yes to the overwrite query.

However you do it, at this point you have defined a new artistic text default *for this drawing only.* To make it permanent for all drawings, right-click in the docker and choose Template ➢ Save As Default for New Documents.

For a deeper discussion about defaults and permanent conditions, see the sidebar in Chapter 34 entitled "Making Things Permanent."

TIP DRAW allows you to share attributes across style types. For instance, if you have created a rectangle and you want to give it the nice rainbow you created in an artistic text style, you can select the rectangle and apply the style, even though it was created for text. Similarly, you can apply a graphic style to a string of text to change its fill and outline. As long as the attributes are shared between the styles—like fill and outline—DRAW allows it. To do this, however, you must apply the style using the docker. The Apply command on the context menu only shows a list of styles for the type of object.

Paragraph Text Styles

Paragraph text carries several more attributes than artistic text, and all of them can be saved to a style. You already know about bullets, thanks to all of those bullet styles in the default template. You can also include tabs, indents, hyphenation, large first characters, and all spacing controls. You cannot, however, include columns in a style. Essentially, styles can be applied to the text within a frame of paragraph text, but not to the frame itself. So elements like frame size, rotation, skew, or column alignment are not part of a paragraph text style.

PART

Taking Control

We either do not understand how paragraph text is supposed to work, or there has been a bug associated with it for several versions. The following is a typical encounter for our lead author:

> *I'm working on a brochure, with lots of copy. My frame of paragraph text has several headlines and lots of body text. I create a style for the headlines, using one of them as a prototype, and begin applying it to other headlines. But the prototype that I used to create the style never got the style name applied to it. My cursor was blinking away inside that headline, yet DRAW still refers to it as Default Paragraph Text. And those asterisks...they never go away!*

We feel the pain of our leader—it's happened to all of us. Indeed, DRAW's behavior with paragraph text is unconventional, to say the least. You'll probably need to tell DRAW more than once to apply or update paragraph text styles.

And the asterisks of which he speaks with such angst refer to DRAW's way of telling you that an object has been formatted outside of the style's format. The asterisk appears in the Style list, which is only visible when your cursor is planted in text. In theory, you make the asterisk go away by reapplying the style to the element. In other words, you say to the text, "Whatever exception format you have applied to you, lose it—adhere to the format of the style." Unfortunately, we regularly encounter instances where we could reapply the style all day, and the asterisk never disappears.

We sure sound like curmudgeons in this chapter, but we're also not real wild about the defaults that Corel chose for paragraph text. We've already vented about the choice of AvantGarde; further to that, the size for Default Paragraph Text is 24 points, with 28 points of interline space. We don't know about you, but we usually create paragraph text at about 10 or 12 points, not 24. We frequently draw a nice little frame in a particular area of a drawing, only to find that the 24-point cursor won't even fit!

So again, we recommend that you quiz yourself on the ways that you usually use the Paragraph Text tool and then adjust the default style to reflect that. When you have it to your liking, use one of the techniques mentioned above to make it permanent.

And if you are setting a lot of copy and you need uniformity, you might want to consider doing what we do: use VENTURA Publisher.

Applying Styles

There are numerous ways to apply styles, including the Styles list that is present for text editing. Other than that, you can:

- Double-click the style name in the docker.
- Right-click the style name and choose Apply Style.
- Right-click on the object, go to Styles ➤ Apply, and then pick the desired one.

Applying Styles with Hotkeys

As if the three previous methods weren't enough, you can also set up hotkeys (keyboard shortcuts) to speed up the job.

The easiest way to assign a hotkey to a style is to right-click the style in the docker and choose Edit Hotkey. From the Shortcut Keys dialog, enter a hotkey combination in the Press New Shortcut Key box. In Figure 31.2, we chose Ctrl+H, and DRAW immediately informed us that Force Justification owned that keystroke. We were able to take it away, but we had to conscientiously click Delete Conflicts before the Assign button would function.

With that hotkey defined, we can turn a paragraph into a headline by pressing Ctrl+H. Chapter 34 offers further detail on custom hotkeys.

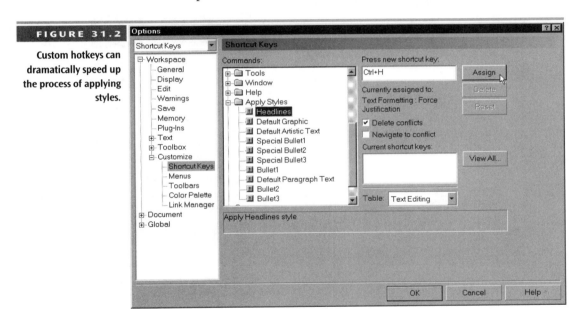

FIGURE 31.2

Custom hotkeys can dramatically speed up the process of applying styles.

Changing Style Attributes

As you've seen, applying styles is easy, and so is changing a style's attributes. In fact, changing a style can be done by simply repeating the routine for creating the style in the first place: once you have reformatted the object to your liking, right-click, go to Styles ➤ Save Style Properties, and save the style. The dialog that appears is just like the one used to create the style.

If the Styles docker is open, you have two more ways to change the style's properties to that of a particular object. You can right-click the style name and choose Copy

Properties From. Then use the bold pointer to click on the object whose properties you want to use to update the style. Because this method skips the Save Style As dialog, you do not get the opportunity to omit some of the object's properties from the style.

As mentioned earlier, you can also change a style by choosing Properties from the context menu, which takes you to the dialog shown in Figure 31.3 (yet another page in the seemingly endless network of Options settings). This doubles as a style checker—you can go here to see at a glance what the attributes are. In the case of Figure 31.3, we see that the style calls for a solid fill of a medium brown tone, and a black hairline outline.

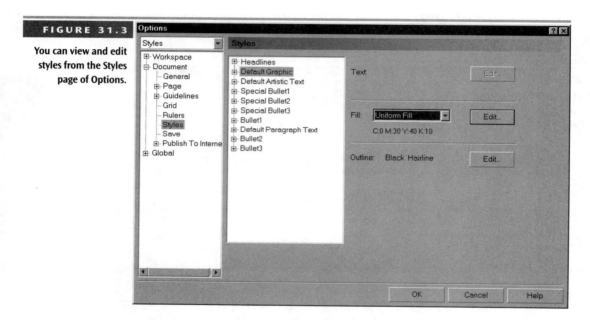

FIGURE 31.3

You can view and edit styles from the Styles page of Options.

DRAW offers no preview for style changes, but you can undo them once you get back to the page if you don't like the results.

Overriding Style Attributes

The idea behind styles is, of course, to make your formatting tasks more efficient. Being able to apply consistent fill, outline, and font attributes to objects is an important element of that efficiency. Nevertheless, there will undoubtedly be times when you wish to format one object independently, and despite our earlier rant about the dreaded asterisk, overriding styles works as expected with graphics and artistic text.

In Figure 31.4, all of the objects use the Fountain Graphic style, but we filled the circle in the center with white. We overrode the style.

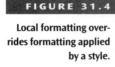

FIGURE 31.4

Local formatting over-rides formatting applied by a style.

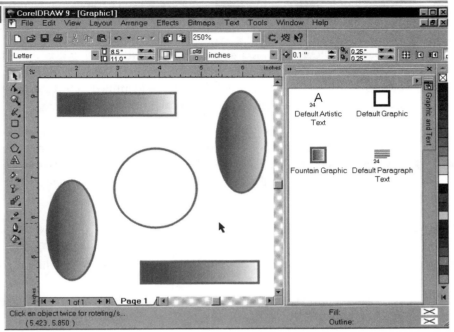

Any change we make to the fill of the style will not be applied to the center circle, because we formatted it "locally"—apart from the style formatting. It is still attached to the Fountain Graphic style, and if we updated the outline settings of the style, all of the objects would change, including the circle in the center. The so-called "local formatting" takes precedence over the object's fill, but the other attributes are still getting their instructions from the style.

The circle in the center retains its local formatting (in this case, the fill) until another style is applied or the original style is reapplied.

Renaming, Deleting, and Finding Styles

After creating a style, you can rename or delete it using the docker. You cannot rename or delete the default styles, however.

- To rename a style, right-click it and choose Rename, or click twice on its name (not a double-click, but two clicks in slow succession).

- To delete a style, right-click it and choose Delete, or just select it and press Delete.

PART

Taking Control

If your drawing contains a lot of elements, it can be tough to remember which style is applied to which object. You can find objects with a specific style using the Find command. To find occurrences of a style, right-click the desired style in the docker and choose Find. DRAW will select the first object to which the style is applied. Choose Find Next to select the next, and keep going until you've located all the objects using that style. Objects that have local formatting will be identified in this search—they still have the style applied, even if they also carry local formatting.

 TIP   If you're looking for more than a couple of objects with the same style, DRAW's Find Wizard is more efficient than the Find feature described above. You can open the Wizard from Edit ➤ Find and Replace. For more details, see the next chapter.

When and When Not to Use Styles

Styles are designed to save you time. Here are some tips for deciding if you need to create a style:

- **When you want to manage the attributes of many objects.** A style's greatest value is the collective control it gives you over the appearance of multiple objects. You never have to worry about one of them being wrong—they're either all correct or they're all wrong.

- **When you have several attributes you want to apply at once.** Simply make the changes to one object, save the changes to the style, and all objects using that style will automatically display the new formatting.

- **When you anticipate that you might be changing all instances of one color, fill, or outline in a complex drawing.** With styles, tracking down and changing all occurrences of a particular attribute gets done in one or two steps rather than 10 or 20 or more.

- **When you want to control elements across multiple pages or even multiple files.** Styles can be saved in templates (described in the upcoming section), so they can be used with various projects, like a monthly publication or newsletter.

Sometimes, other tools will work better than styles. Here are situations where you may want to choose another strategy:

- You already have a custom palette created, and you want to quickly assign colors to objects. Though you could create several styles containing these colors, using a palette is a better method.

- You want one or more objects to look *exactly* like an original; this is a job for the Clone command. Clones don't need to be applied or updated; they automatically and instantly take on all the appearance attributes of the master object.

- You want to borrow just one attribute of a formatted object and are not interested in maintaining a direct connection to that object with a style. Though you could apply the style and then strip off the attributes you don't want, it's wasted effort. A better way is to use either Edit ➤ Copy Properties From, or Effects ➤ Copy. Both commands let you choose the particular attribute you want to copy from an existing object. This is better than using a style when all you want is a piece of the style.

And finally, some situations call for yet another CorelDRAW efficiency expert: scripts. We'll get to them in Chapter 33.

Working with Templates

Templates help you organize and manage styles. You can store a group of styles in a template designed for a specific type of drawing, such as a slide presentation or a sales brochure. Template files store more than just styles, though; they can also save page-layout information and text and graphic objects. A template for a slide presentation could include the page setup and the company logo, as well as styles for bullets and titles. A template for sales brochures might contain the graphic elements that appear in every brochure. In addition to the templates you create yourself, DRAW includes several hundred predesigned templates for everything from announcements to box designs.

Templates are separate files with extensions of .cdt instead of .cdr. They contain all of the formatting and styles you choose to store in them. This is convenient for your regularly recurring projects, because you can keep all the styles you use for a particular project or client in a template, safely protected from your day-to-day activities. DRAW always starts with the default template, coreldrw.cdt, loaded, but changing to a different template is easy.

N O T E When you create styles, you don't have to save them in a template—DRAW stores them directly in the drawing (the .cdr file). If you don't save the styles in a template, the styles are loaded in the Styles docker when you open the .cdr file that you saved them in. But unless you save the styles in a template, they'll only be available to the drawing you created them in. The advantage to saving them in a template is that they are available in other DRAW drawings, as well.

The Default Template

The coreldrw.cdt template includes default styles for graphics, artistic text, and paragraph text. You can modify this template by adding styles or changing the default styles, following the procedures already outlined in this chapter. After making style changes, if you want the changes to be available in future drawings using this template, you must save it. If you don't, the new and modified styles are only saved in the .cdr file—they do not become part of the template.

To save changes to the default coreldrw.cdt template, select Template ➤ Save As Default for New Documents from the docker's context menu. You can also use Template ➤ Save As to explicitly save over the top of coreldrw.cdt—these two actions would have the same result of altering DRAW's default template. And for good measure, you can achieve the same result by going to Tools ➤ Options ➤ Document, checking Save Options As Defaults for New Documents, and then browsing the list of settings whose current conditions you could choose to be defaults.

 N O T E   Coreldrw.cdt is a plain old file, residing on your hard drive like all other files. Therefore, before you start any wild experiments with your default settings, you might want to back up this default template first. You'll find it in the Draw subdirectory under the main CorelDRAW 9 directory.

Creating a New Template

Instead of filling up coreldrw.cdt with all kinds of different styles, you may find it more effective to save particular groups of styles in individual templates. Then, when you're ready for a certain set of styles, you can just load the desired template.

As mentioned earlier, DRAW's templates can contain more than just styles; they can contain any element that would normally go into a drawing. With templates, you can give yourself a major-league running start toward the completion of a repetitive project. You can create the template before you've made style changes, before you've laid out the page, and before you have created objects; or you can do it afterward. In fact, it's probably more practical to save the template after making these changes to a drawing, so you don't have to continue to tweak it as you refine your work.

You must use the Styles docker (Ctrl+F5) to create templates because the object context menu does not provide access to template creation (only style creation). So to create a template, you select Template ➤ Save As from the docker's context menu and name the template. If you just want the styles from the current drawing, you're done. If you want the page layout and the elements on the page also, click the With Contents option to save the page setup and any text and graphic objects that may be in the document you plan on making a template.

In Figure 31.5, we are about to save the current lineup of styles as a template for newsletter creation. Note that we have created several new artistic text styles and that we have eliminated all of those dreadful bullet styles. Note two other things:

- We have checked With Contents, so the elements on the page will be part of our starting point for creating newsletters.
- We are saving the template in the Draw directory, where `coreldrw.cdt` is located. We note this because it is not the factory-defined location for saving templates. We tried saving templates in the Template subdirectory, but we didn't like it, because that is not where `coreldrw.cdt` resides. Alternating between `coreldrw.cdt` and ours in another subdirectory became annoying. We prefer to keep them all in one location, so DRAW can continue to look in the same place. If Corel's engineers wanted us to use the Template subdirectory, they should have put `coreldrw.cdt` there.

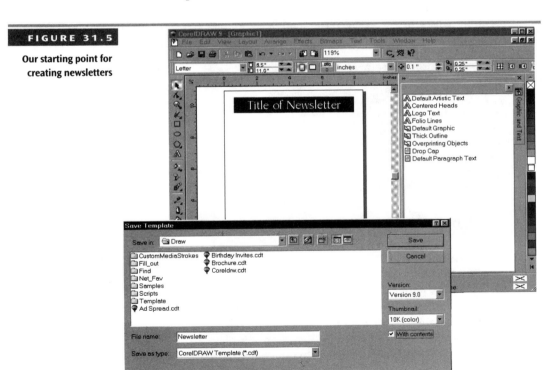

FIGURE 31.5

Our starting point for creating newsletters

The Newsletter template in Figure 31.5 is quite sparse, to be frank, making it suitable for newsletters that might take radically different forms each month. For a more structured publication, the template could be quite specific, with many fill-in-the-blank elements already in place.

TIP   You can also save a template by issuing a conventional File ≻ Save As command, changing the file type to CDT, choosing the location, and saving the file. When you do this, the contents automatically get saved as part of the template.

Using Your Templates

When you're ready to use the styles and objects stored in a template, you have two choices: choose a template when you begin a new drawing or load a template during work in a drawing. We'll look at both methods here.

Creating a New Drawing from a Template

This is the route to take if you intend to begin a project with a template that includes contents. To do this, go to File ≻ Open, select CDT as the file type, and navigate to the subdirectory where you saved the template. Double-click it, and a small dialog appears.

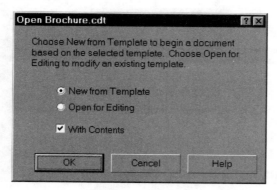

Since you want to create a document based on the template, be sure New from Template is selected. Check or uncheck With Contents, then OK the dialog. DRAW places the entire template on your page. This remains an untitled drawing—DRAW uses the generic Graphic 1—and you can save and name as you wish. You don't have to worry about altering the contents of the template or any existing file.

If you choose Open for Editing in the Open Template dialog, the template file will be opened like any other DRAW file. Changes you make will be saved to the template and will be incorporated into future documents you create based on that template.

N O T E   DRAW did us no favors with the naming of its template functions. Raise your hands, how many of you went to File ➤ New from Template, expecting to be able to load a .cdt file? No, this command starts the Template Wizard, letting you select from nearly 500 PaperDirect templates stored on CorelDRAW CD No. 1. The Wizard does its job nicely, but it should have been called something else, because it doesn't allow you to load your own templates without jumping through enormous hoops. If you really want to jump through those hoops, click the Wizard's Help button, then the How To button in the upper-right corner of the Help window. This will open a set of instructions for running the TempWiz script to add templates to the Wizard.

Loading Templates

To load a template after you've started a document, select Template ➤ Load from the Styles docker context menu. The With Contents option is not available when you load a template this way—it's as if you are importing the template into an existing drawing, so adding contents would probably be unwelcome.

Loading a new template this way will swap out all of the old styles for new ones, but it will not change the formatting of existing objects in your drawing. Whether this is good or bad news depends upon your point of view. It would be very powerful if you could load a new template and instantly change the formatting of objects that had the same style name as one in the newly loaded template.

And it would also be dangerous. Corel played it conservatively here, and we think that's wise. Save that functionality for VENTURA. Instead, when you swap in a new template to an existing drawing, all objects keep their formatting but are all reassigned to the default styles. Newly created objects take on the formats of the new defaults.

Succeeding with Styles and Templates

DRAW's styles can be enormously powerful when used to help you reach your productivity potential, so ask yourself some questions about your work: Do you regularly need to assign 2-point outlines with round caps? Create a style for them. How about a custom Calligraphic Pen? Create a style. You can have all of these styles immediately accessible every time you start the program. Just park them right in coreldrw.cdt.

To summarize, here are some important points to remember as you gain skill in the use of styles and templates:

- Keep the default styles simple. They won't be of much help if they give all objects a texture fill and a thick outline, or if they put all artistic text in 400 point Crazy Creatures. Save the fancy formatting in new, separate styles.

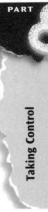

- All styles that you create are stored in the .cdr file itself. By saving styles in a template, you make it easier for new projects to use the same styles.

- Install the AvantGarde BT and Common Bullets typefaces. Many of DRAW's templates and sample files expect to find these two typefaces. Although you can use the PANOSE font substitution utility to make your own substitution, we have found that even ardently anti-TrueType users have capitulated and installed these two faces, just to make life easier.

The Color Styles Idea

Color Styles were an entirely new feature in DRAW 7 that promised to speed the work of artists who produce the same designs in a variety of color schemes, or who are sometimes confronted by last-minute color changes. These handy color styles can be created as you work, either manually or with assistance from DRAW. Additionally, DRAW can create color styles from a finished drawing or object.

Graphic and text styles are an excellent aid to maintaining consistency. They enable you to change any shared attribute (such as fill, outline, font, or spacing) incorporated in the style. This includes, of course, fill and outline colors.

Now consider a different situation: your client wants an image of a hot red sports car, a drawing that will use several shades of a basic color, red. This design calls for realism, so you, the skilled artist, will be using several shades of the basic color for areas of shadow and highlight, based on the direction and intensity of light on the subject.

You painstakingly finish the drawing and your client admires your work. He shows real appreciation for your rendering skill...nods approvingly...and then decides he wants the car in green.

In the era of hand-drawn artwork, you would have had to redraw the image from scratch. In past versions of DRAW, you would at least have had to select each object in the drawing and apply a new color to it—a tedious and time-consuming task. In either case, there was little you could do in advance to reduce the workload, even if you had foreseen the problem.

DRAW's Color Styles feature offers ways to automate this work. The color change can be virtually instantaneous if you prepare for this situation in advance, and can be accomplished quickly even if you are caught by surprise.

If you used a color style to relate your shadow and highlight colors to their basic hue, you can simply turn to the Color Styles docker. Find your basic color, called a *parent color*, and change it to the new color, perhaps with a bit of experimentation. All the related colors, called *child colors*, change accordingly, and you're done.

If you didn't set your drawing up with color styles, DRAW can create them automatically. You'll probably have to make some adjustments, but the task should still go quickly.

The next day you tell your client you were up half the night, and the new art is ready. The client is most appreciative of your dedication, and pays you a handsome fee for the late change—which actually took you all of 10 minutes.

Creating Color Styles Manually

The key to advance preparation for the color change scenario is to create your shadow and highlight colors as members of a color style "family," in which all color variations share the hue of a single parent color.

It doesn't matter whether you prefer to work by filling objects as you create them, or by creating all the objects of a drawing first and then going back to fill them. Either way, begin to create a color style by giving a suitable object a uniform fill of your "base" color, for parts of the drawing that are neither shadow nor highlight. This will be the parent color for the color style.

We will use a brick building as our example of how to go about coloring a drawing using color styles. If you want to follow along, you can download `Brick Building.cdr` from the companion page on the Sybex Web site.

1. The outline is already done, so select the large section of wall at the left end, whose color will be typical. Apply the fill color you want, using the on-screen palette or the Uniform Fill dialog.

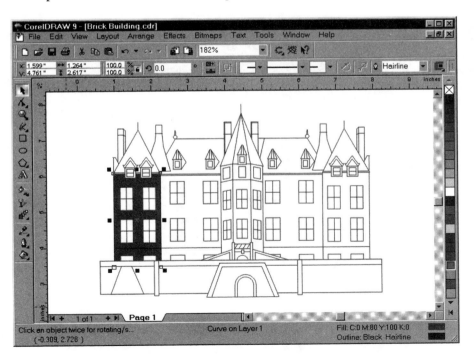

Note that this is not a pure color—it is a percentage of Magenta and Yellow. But it is our "base" color.

2. Now open the Color Styles docker, and with your newly filled wall section still selected, click the Auto Create Color Styles button (the last one on the row of buttons at the top).

3. In the dialog that appears, uncheck Use Outline Colors because you are interested only in the fill color you just created. The other settings in the dialog are not important at this point. Just make sure Use Fill Colors is checked, and OK the dialog.

DRAW will create a color style, using the color of your object as the parent color. That style will promptly show up in the docker.

4. Now you can proceed to fill the other objects in the drawing that get the same color. Just drag from the color swatch in the docker and drop on each object. When you are done, your screen should look similar to Figure 31.6.

TIP   You can also drag a filled object with mouse Button 2 and choose Copy Fill Here from the pop-up menu. That may be quicker than retreating to the docker each time. Also, if you hold Shift while dragging with Button 2, you will copy the fill immediately, without needing the pop-up menu.

FIGURE 31.6

The parent color has been applied to all of the drawing objects that require the same color.

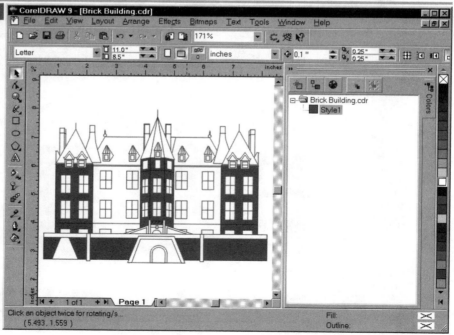

5. Before going any further, click twice on the name Style1 and change it to something appropriate, such as Brick.

6. Now create your first child color. It will be a lighter shade and will be used for the chimneys and for accents around the front wall and the attic window frames. With the parent color selected in the docker, click on the New Child Color button.

7. From the Create a New Child Color dialog, you can change the name of the new color from the default Child1 of Brick to something meaningful like Accent Brick. Then create the color, either by entering saturation and brightness values in the boxes, or by dragging the little square around the selection window. For the accents, try creating a color with lower saturation and higher brightness than the parent color.

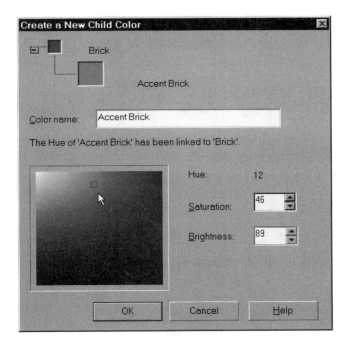

8. Click OK and watch DRAW create the bond between parent and child.

The process is similar to creating a color in the Uniform Fill dialog, with one important exception: you can't change the hue, because the basic requirement of a color style is that all the child colors have the same hue as the parent.

9. Now drag from the new child color swatch and drop it in turn on each object in the drawing that needs that fill. Note the name of the color in the status bar.

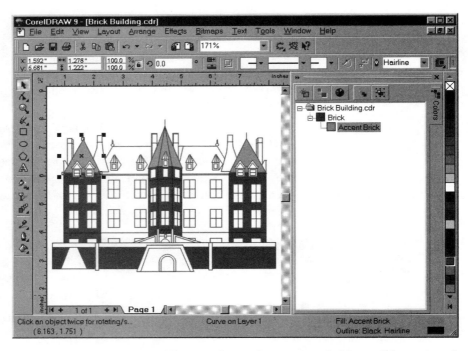

As you please, continue filling in the castle, creating children of the main color for all instances where a variation is called for. Here is what it might look like.

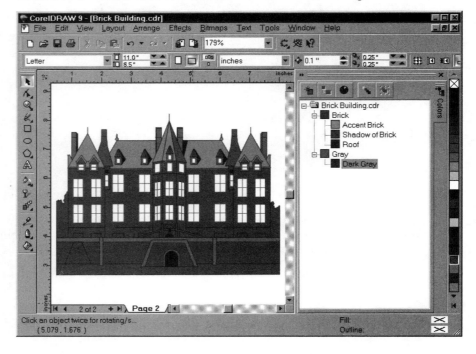

So what's the point of all this? After all, it took extra time to create all of these children, against using one of the standard fill methods. There are two benefits to using color styles:

Consistency through constraint   By using tints and variations of a central color, you bring uniformity to a drawing. An abstract illustration might not benefit from that, but a drawing like this building certainly does.

You can change your mind!   As we noted at the top of this section, should the main color scheme of this drawing change, it would involve one action, not three dozen. You can see this for yourself very easily:

1. From the docker, right-click on the parent color and choose Edit Color.

2. From the Edit Color Style dialog, make a radical change, like changing the hue to blue.

3. OK the dialog and watch what happens to the child colors, and hence, to the entire drawing.

Try changing the brick to a brighter shade of orange, then to yellow. You can also experiment with a weathered copper green roof, or any other color that appeals to you. This is the real power of color styles.

Creating Color Styles Automatically

The demonstration above should have convinced you of the potential power of color styles that you create as you design your drawing. But what about a drawing that has already been created, either by you or someone else, without incorporating color styles? How can you make this excellent idea work for you?

For an example, open `Kayak.cdr` from the `Clipart\Collection\Transpor\Boats` directory of CD No. 2 (the clipart CD). Press F4 to zoom in as close as you can, and if you select it, DRAW will report to you that there are 68 objects that make up this little ship, most of them shades of red. How would you like the assignment of turning this kayak electric blue? We wouldn't either...

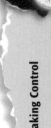

PART

Taking Control

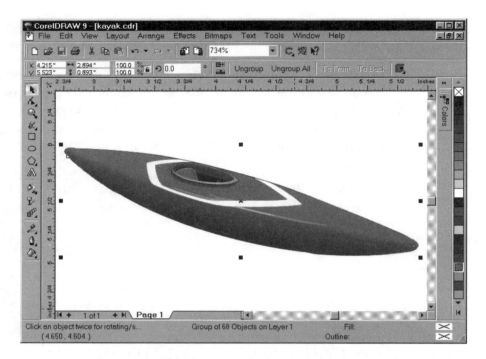

But color styles make it easy. Marquee-select the entire boat, or just double-click on the Pick tool to select all objects in the drawing. Now do this:

1. From the Colors docker, click Auto Create Color Styles.

2. OK the dialog without changing the defaults.

3. Click on the plus beside the drawing name in the docker, then again beside each of the styles DRAW created. DRAW studies all of the colors in the drawing and determines the relationship between them. It defines each shade of red in terms of how it relates to the "main" color of red.

4. Press Ctrl and begin selecting individual objects—as the status bar will verify, each object is filled with a child color.

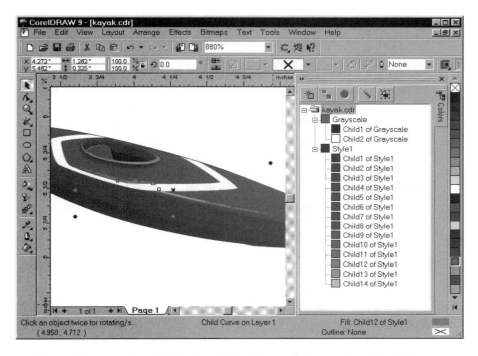

Now making an electric blue kayak is cake: you change the main color.

This kayak is an ideal example because it is almost exclusively drawn with reds, and a bit of gray. Drawings with more hues wouldn't be good candidates for global hue changes.

Controlling Automatic Color Style Creation

Let's take a closer look at the Automatically Create Color Styles dialog, the one responsible for the miracle performed on the kayak. The top portion is self-explanatory: simply choose fill or outline colors or both to be used in creating color styles.

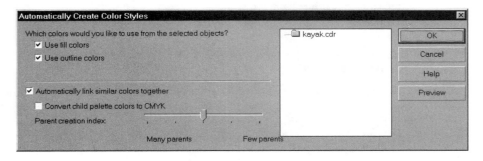

The Automatically Link Similar Colors Together option tells DRAW to group similar colors into a single color style. That is the key to the whole operation, really, because if you uncheck this box, every color in the selected object will become a parent color. This might be desirable if you want to add shading to an unshaded drawing. It would ensure that every color in the original becomes a parent, so you can create appropriate shades for each. In the case of the kayak, though, it was crucial to check this option, and in fact, it is checked by default.

The Convert Child Palette Colors to CMYK option tells DRAW how to handle colors from different palettes. When enabled, colors from other palettes, such as Pantone, are converted to CMYK so they can become part of a color family. If disabled, each color from a different palette is made into its own parent. If a drawing has colors from disparate palettes, and uniformity is the objective (like with the kayak), you would want to check this option.

Perhaps the most useful, but volatile, control in the dialog is the Parent Creation Index slider. Slide it all the way to the left (Many Parents) and instead of one red parent with 16 child colors, the kayak would yield 13 red parent colors with a total of 28 children; 41 shades of red in all! Good for Corel for including a Preview button which would show you exactly how many parents and children would be created at any point along the slider.

The Color Styles Shoe-Horn

Recall that the basis of color styles is that all child colors share the hue of the parent color. When an artist creates a shaded drawing such as the kayak without using color styles, some of the shades are likely to have slightly different hues even if they don't really need to be different. This is simply the consequence of working in an unconstrained environment. Since nothing forces the hues to be the same, the artist is likely to introduce some variation while creating the shade colors.

When you ask DRAW to create color styles from such a drawing, you have to tell the program how much hue variation it should squeeze into a single style. That is what you do when you set the Parent Creation Index slider. Leaving it in the default center position tells DRAW to take objects whose colors are fairly close in hue and give them identical hues so they can fit into a single color style. In the case of the kayak, this allows all the shades of red to fit into a single color style, without noticeably changing the color of the boat.

This is exactly what you want when your task is to change the color of the object without losing the shading. On the other hand, moving the Parent Creation Index slider to the left reduces the range of adjustment that DRAW makes, resulting in more parent colors and less change to the original colors. Therefore, the trade-off is:

- Slide to the left: more accuracy, less global control
- Slide to the right: less accuracy (more lumping of color associations), more global control

Creating Shades

In the last section, we saw the beauty of automatically creating children from an existing drawing. When starting fresh, you might want to adopt another strategy if you think you will want several variations of a main color.

Start by creating a style based on a main color—let's say the rich navy blue color we found in our TruMatch swatch book, No. 36a (70M, 100C). From the docker, click Create Shades to get this dialog.

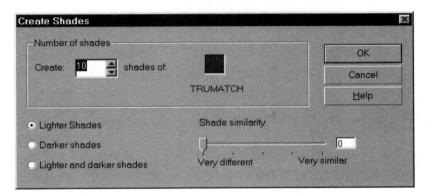

When you request Lighter and Darker Shades, DRAW creates an equal number of each. If your parent color is very light or dark you may not want equal numbers of lighter and darker shades. Just create your shades in two passes, specifying the number of darker shades and the number of lighter shades separately. Figure 31.7 shows the result.

The Shade Similarity slider in the dialog allows you to control the range your set of shades will encompass. Leaving the control at the default setting of Very Different will spread darker shades nearly to black and lighter shades nearly to white. A Very Similar setting will cluster the shades close to the parent color.

N O T E   You can also create shades of a shade. Whatever element is selected in the docker when you click Create Shades is what gets shaded.

Color Styles and Custom Palettes

From the context menu of any parent or child, you can choose to add that color to a custom palette. This allows you to extract a single color from a color family and keep it in your custom palette for future use.

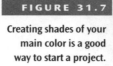

FIGURE 31.7

Creating shades of your
main color is a good
way to start a project.

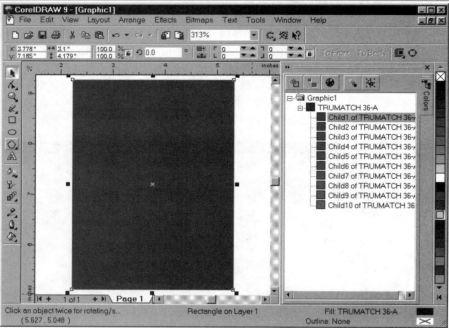

NOTE   A color that is added to a custom palette loses its connection to the color style from which it came. Changing the parent color of the style will not change the color in the palette, nor will it update the fill of objects that have had the color applied from the palette. When you use the color from a custom palette, it's just a uniform fill like any other.

FINDING AND MANAGING OBJECTS

Featuring

FINDING AND MANAGING OBJECTS

This chapter is dedicated to helping you more effectively manage the objects in your drawings: selecting, finding, arranging, grouping, and ordering are among the many methods DRAW provides for organizing the objects you create into a coherent drawing that expresses your vision. None of these concepts is complex, although some of them may have seemed obscure in the past. New tools provided since DRAW 7 make them easier to understand, and therefore easier to use productively.

When Going Nongraphical Is Good

When a drawing begins to get complex—and crowded—it can be difficult to identify objects, let alone select and format them. Sometimes a nonvisual interface works better. (Our lead author remembers when that is all that DRAW had, when it was known as Corel Headline, back in 1988!) That is the idea behind the Object Manager. With it, you can view pages and layers, the former offering a tree-structured view of all objects on each page.

The Object Manager offers brief descriptions of each object present in the drawing. Selecting the object in the Object Manager in turn causes the actual object on the page to be selected. Once an object is selected, you can do pretty much anything to it, so this docker becomes a handy way to navigate a busy drawing.

The Lowdown on Layers

It was right about at version 4 in late-1993 that DRAW users started creating work that was so sophisticated, the simple stacking order of objects (with Move to Front and Move to Back commands) proved deficient as an organizational aid. Corel introduced the concept of a "layer," and that was all intermediate and advanced users needed to restore order to their asylums.

When you begin a new drawing, DRAW creates a default Layer 1 as well as three additional layers: Grid, Guides, and Desktop. The Grid and Guides layers serve as homes for the grid and guidelines that you set up via the Layout menu. The Desktop layer is a handy place to keep objects you want to use repeatedly, because it is always accessible regardless of which layer or page you are working on.

Layer 1 is the default drawing layer, and if you pay no attention to layers (like many DRAW users) all the objects of your drawing are created on Layer 1. For most purposes this is entirely satisfactory, and you won't need to concern yourself with the layer structure or how to create and use additional layers. But when drawings get complex or technical, proper understanding and use of layers becomes essential.

News Flash: Layers Rescued from Object Manager

DRAW 8 will not be remembered fondly for its handling of layers. Corel's engineers decided to combine it with object management, and veteran users screamed bloody murder as their layers were lost in a sea of other extraneous information that they didn't care about. In DRAW 9, layer management is still handled in the Object Manager docker, but one of the new buttons in the docker is called Layer Manager View, and it allows you to work just with layers. This was a very good compromise, as it accommodated the streamlining that Corel wanted and restored the service that the users wanted. Figure 32.1 shows the dramatic difference this one button makes when all you want to get is information about layers. We're pointing to it in the lower image.

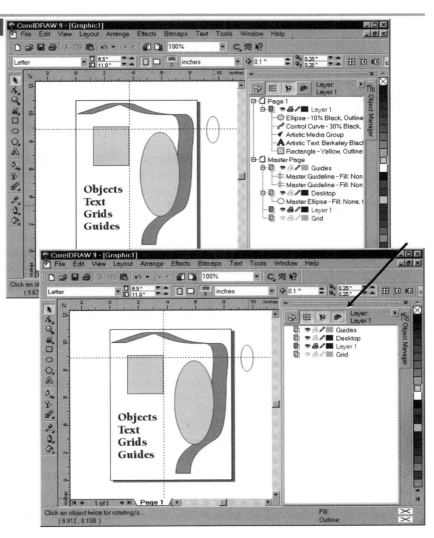

FIGURE 32.1

Just because your page is noisy doesn't mean that the Object Manager has to be. If all you want is layer information, click the Layer Manager View button.

A layer has four basic properties that you can control—for reasons unknown, three of them can be toggled from the docker, while the fourth requires a trip to the layer's context menu. Here are the four properties of all layers:

Visibility Click the eye to make a layer visible or invisible. If the docker is already open, you might prefer to click the eye next to Guides, rather than go up to View ➤ Guidelines. Most importantly, you can make invisible an entire layer, if a big, slow graphic is bogging you down. Objects on invisible layers can still print, provided you have addressed a layer's...

Printability   You determine, with the next icon in the row, if objects on a layer will print or not. By default, only Layer 1 is set as printable, but you could set the Guides and Grid layers to be printable, if you wanted to show someone how you created a schematic or other precision drawing.

N O T E   If a layer is printable, it will appear in a Full-Screen Preview.

Editability   You can lock a layer so no activity can take place on it at all. Click the pencil icon to toggle this setting. If you have intricate guidelines created and you don't want to mess them up, lock the Guides layer. If you create a background for a drawing and don't want it touched, place it on a new layer and lock the layer.

T I P   You can also lock an individual object by choosing Lock Object from its context menu. A locked object can still be selected; a locked layer can't be touched at all.

Masterability   That's not a word, we know, but our editor required a subhead that ended in "ability." With this toggle, you can make objects on an editing layer appear on every page of the drawing. Guides, Grid, and the Desktop are all master layers by default and cannot be altered. Layer 1 and any other layers you create for holding objects are not master layers by default, but can be set that way. This is the one control that doesn't have an icon—right-click the layer and choose Master Layer.

The far-left icon indicates which layer is "active"—in other words, which one will house objects you create from this point forward. You can "draw" on any layer: activate the Guides layer, draw a rectangle on the page, and you have just created a guide in the shape of a rectangle.

W A R N I N G   It's way too easy to inadvertently draw on the wrong layer, so watch the active icon carefully. DRAW doesn't even care if you make a locked layer the active one—it won't yell at you until you actually start to click to create an object.

Creating New Layers

As with styles, the controls for working this docker can be reached one of two ways:

- By clicking on the small triangle at the top-right corner of the docker
- By right-clicking on any open space in the docker

And as we said in the last chapter, we think you'll prefer the latter method—it's much easier on your clicking hand. So to create a new layer, right-click the docker and choose New Layer. It defaults to Layer 2, but you can proceed to rename it however you want.

New layers are placed in front of existing layers, and that is consistent with how DRAW treats new objects—they are drawn on the top of the stack. In the docker, Layer 2 will appear above Layer 1, but you can drag it to any other position.

You can also move the Guides layer behind your drawing layers. On the face of it, this sounds absurd (what good are guidelines *behind* your objects?), but it is actually a good idea if you are using objects as guides. Otherwise, you will find yourself selecting them often when you intend to select objects that overlap them. The best strategy—if your workflow permits it—is to establish your guides and then lock the Guides layer.

Moving Objects between Layers

To move an object to a different layer, you have two choices:

- Select it, right-click the docker, choose Move to Layer, and click on the desired layer.
- Drag the object into the docker and drop it on a different layer.

If you move an object to the Guides layer, it will immediately lose its fill pattern and inherit the outline color that is established as the color for guides (more on this soon). Moving an object to the Desktop layer is ignored by DRAW—the Desktop is defined as the area outside of the page. So to move an object to the Desktop, just drag it outside of the boundaries of the page.

More Layer Properties

Figure 32.2 shows the Properties sheet for a layer, where every control is housed. You can see the repetition of the four main controls—Visible, Printable, Editable, and Master—as well as three other handy controls.

Layer Color   If you want all of your guidelines to be blue, this is where you would turn. Note that as of DRAW 9, you can color guidelines individually, just by applying an outline color to the guideline, as if it were any other object. In fact, as of DRAW 8, guidelines are just objects—you can select them, delete them, move them, and rotate them.

Override Full Color View   This is a deceptively useful control. It will force all objects on a layer to show up as hollow, with an outline color determined by the Layer Color setting. DRAW offers a few avenues of relief from slow-drawing objects, but this might be the best one of all. By forcing all objects on that layer to render essentially in Wireframe view, they will draw very quickly. Sure, you could create an invisible layer for your complex objects, but then you get no

PART

Taking Control

visual feedback at all from those elements. By using a color override on a layer, at least you still see where the objects reside.

Apply All Property Changes to the Current Page Only   Just as it sounds, this instructs DRAW to enact changes on a page-by-page basis.

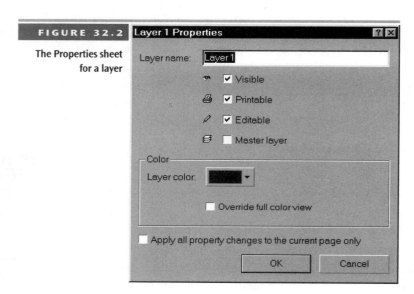

FIGURE 32.2

The Properties sheet for a layer

And finally, another one of the buttons on the docker—Edit across Layers—might be of marginal interest. It is on by default, but conceivably there might be instances where you would want to focus your attention, and thus confine your action, to one layer.

Of all versions, this is the cleanest that the Layer Manager has ever been. In version 8, layers were rolled into the Object Manager in an awkward way, and in version 7, implementation was marred by bugs. If you have shied away from using layers in your more intricate work—either because you didn't understand how they worked or were beset by their faulty operation—you owe it to yourself to try again.

The Object Manager

Figure 32.3 shows a drawing that has several elements in it (we used it to create the enveloped reflection on the water in Chapter 13). The drawing is displayed in the traditional drawing window on the left, and on the right the Object Manager is showing quite a different view of it. Indeed, every element of the drawing is identified in Object Manager.

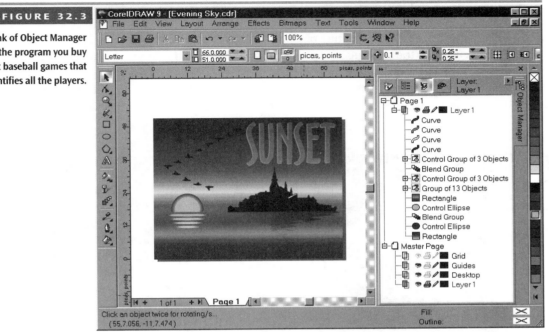

FIGURE 32.3

Think of Object Manager as the program you buy at baseball games that identifies all the players.

According to this hierarchical view of our drawing, we have created one page, and all objects on that page are on a single layer. There are four simple curves, two blends, a group of 13 objects, and two rectangles.

As mentioned earlier, you can select objects in either place, and once selected, adjust their properties either the traditional route or from the docker. Notice that you can expand each group to see the children within that group, and every control object of a more complex effect is identified. For users who have trouble selecting control objects, the Object Manager is a terrific aid.

To alter the stacking order of objects, you can use the conventional controls of Shift+PgUp, Shift+PgDn, Ctrl+PgUp, and Ctrl+PgDn, or you can just drag the object in the docker and move it to another place in the stack. The big advantage this docker has is that it displays for you the precise order of objects—this is practically impossible to decipher from the drawing screen.

T I P Drag-and-drop has another function in the Object Manager docker—drag one object and drop it onto another and you have just grouped them. Your cursor is your cue to the action: as you drag an object, the docker shows you a horizontal line if you are changing the stacking order; the docker shows you an arrow and a group of shapes if you are making a group. You can also ungroup from the docker by dragging a child object and dropping it onto the layer name.

PART

Taking Control

Naming Objects

Perhaps the most useful feature of Object Manager is its ability to name objects. Those four curves in the drawing in Figure 32.3—what are they? "Curve" is not very descriptive. And what about the group of thirteen?

Figure 32.4 shows how much more descriptive the docker can be, once you rename the objects. And notice how DRAW refers to the selected object in the status bar—by its new name.

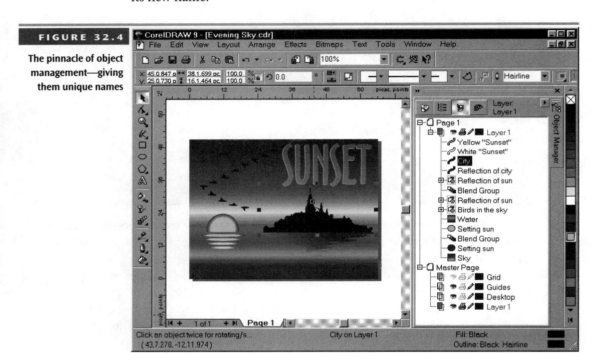

FIGURE 32.4

The pinnacle of object management—giving them unique names

While this is one of the most powerful features of Object Manager, it is also one of the most secret. We can't find any mention of it in the user guide, other books, or online Help, which discusses renaming pages and renaming layers…but not the objects themselves. To tell you the truth, we can't remember how we learned about it—we probably just stumbled upon it. Isn't that how all discoveries are made?

We don't hold illusions that the Object Manager is going to revolutionize the way you work, because to be candid, most projects don't warrant its use. But we do think that all users should familiarize themselves with this docker so they know to turn to it when the need arises. However specialized it is, there is no other service like it in the program.

Finding and Replacing Objects

Veteran DRAW users waited a long time for a workable method of finding and replacing objects. After several false starts, version 7 finally delivered on the promise.

You are no doubt familiar with find and replace operations in your word processor. A sophisticated word processor can find or replace not only text strings but styles, typefaces, and a variety of other formatting characteristics. DRAW does things a bit differently.

In the first place, there are not two operations (find and replace) but four: Find Objects, Replace Objects, Find Text, and Replace Text. And while the text operations are very simple, Find Objects and Replace Objects have such potential for complexity that they are not presented as simple dialogs (or even complex ones), but as Wizards.

DRAW's Find Wizard allows for almost any conceivable combination of object types and properties and lets you save and reuse a complex set of Find specifications after you have created it. As you can see in the graphic below, Corel has anticipated some of the most common searches, placing them directly on the menu.

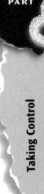

PART

If we were to carry out the above search, DRAW would inform us that there are no Pantone-filled objects to be found in this drawing. We know this beyond any doubt because we accidentally *did* use a Pantone color for the sun, and DRAW told us so when we performed this search the first time. We located the offending object and reassigned a CMYK color to it. Great tool, this Find & Replace—makes up for a multitude of sins...

Let's say that this drawing (which, incidentally, is available from the Sybex Web site as Evening Sky.cdr) is destined for a Web page instead of a picture frame. You originally created it with the process color model, and you know that DRAW will convert the colors to RGB when you export it as a JPEG file. But you want to know what those colors are now, and you might want to adjust some of them. Follow along to see how you would do it:

1. Go to Edit ≻ Find and Replace ≻ Replace Objects.

2. Choose Replace a Color Model or Palette.

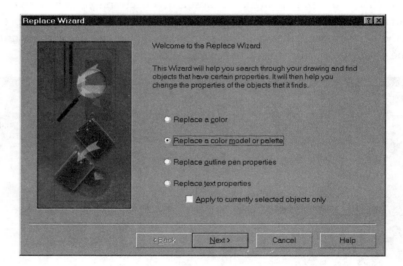

3. On the next screen, check Find Any Color Model or Color Palette. You don't care what kind of models or palettes are present now—you want to change them all.

4. At Replace with the Color Model, find RGB on the drop-down list.

5. At Replace Colors Used As, choose Fills. We don't understand why there isn't a choice to replace both fills and outlines; because there isn't, you'll need two passes to do both.

6. Check all three of the options below that.

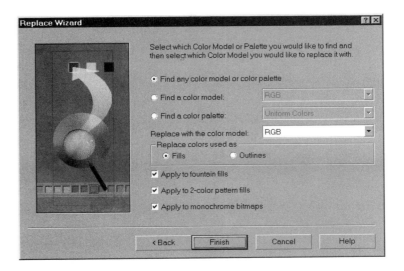

7. Click Finish, and then choose Replace All from the final dialog.

On our system, DRAW only needed about 10 seconds to sift through every fill and convert it to its closest RGB counterpart. Thanks to this exercise, we discovered that Deep Yellow on DRAW's default palette is R248, G196, B0. That's your useless piece of information for the day.

N O T E   We are focusing here on the find-and-replace operation, but curiously, DRAW has built more into the find engine that does not accompany replace. You can edit an existing find, and save and reload finds for later use. We're not sure why all of this delicious functionality is not available with replace, but we wasted no time adding that to the official Version 10 Wish List.

When dealing with text properties, DRAW's Replace Wizard is limited to font, weight, and size. If you need to replace other text properties, remember that the Find Wizard is far more flexible. You will have to perform the replace part manually, but you'll still be ahead of the game.

Finally, the Find Text and Replace Text commands are for seeking out and changing actual strings of text, not text formats.

PART

Taking Control

SCRIPTING SUCCESS

Featuring

SCRIPTING SUCCESS

Are you fond of red text set in 100-point Futura, with a drop shadow offset of 20% black? How about adding perspective and custom fountain fills to objects? Whatever your specialty, repeating the same steps over and over for your favorite effects is not likely to rank as your favorite CorelDRAW activity. DRAW's scripting tool enables you to record transactions and then play them back to quickly format text and objects. Using scripts is like plugging a very efficient tape recorder into your computer, and since DRAW 7, scripts have had a significant impact on how many advanced users go about their business.

Back in DRAW 6 we gave less than two pages to the scripting tool, and we suspected that very few users would use it. We were right: not too many DRAW users had the time or inclination to learn a programming language in order to record repetitive steps. But now everything is different, thanks to the little red Record button in the Script and Preset Manager. It's just like the one on your VCR or cassette recorder—it listens, and then it plays back. As a result, the potential of the tool has increased manyfold.

Scripts: the Evolution

Before there were scripts, there were presets, an awkward way to store an effect for later use. Now that the scripting tool is so much more robust, presets are being phased out. In

DRAW 9, as in 8 and 7, you cannot create a preset for a general effect, although there are other places on the interface where the word "preset" is used—like fountain fills, texture fills, and print styles. But to accommodate users who have created presets from previous versions and still want to use them, the Script and Preset Manager can play them back (hence its name). Our assumption is that the only users who would need to work with presets are those who already know how to create them; in fact, for simplicity, we will refer to the tool as the Script Manager instead of its more verbose name (except where we are indicating the name of the command as it appears on the interface).

DRAW 9 includes several premade scripts—in fact, you may find the very effect you are looking for prerecorded for you. Go to Tools ➤ Corel SCRIPT ➤ Script and Preset Manager to display the docker. The Scripts folder is shown in Figure 33.1, with each script represented by a thumbnail. On the page is a rectangle to which we applied the *fillout* script, which created an artistic outline for it.

FIGURE 33.1

To apply these scripts to an object, double-click the script, right-click and choose Apply, or press the triangular Play button.

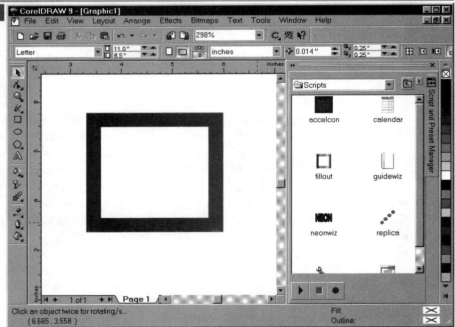

N O T E   In addition to the folder shown in Figure 33.1, ready-made scripts are also stored in the Scripts subdirectory directly below the main CorelDRAW directory. There you will find some generic scripts, including one that turns your CD-ROM drive into a music jukebox. We're sure that DRAW users around the world have been waiting anxiously for that one...

Script Basics

While there is considerable depth to DRAW's implementation of scripts, on the surface, things are simple: you record a script and then you play it back. If you remember those two things, you can't go too far wrong.

Recording a Script

Imagine the following scenario: You have several drawings that need a particular effect applied to them. They each need a rectangle to be placed against a vertical guideline, to be skewed up by 30 degrees, and then to have a 45-degree black-to-white fountain fill applied to it. This is a perfect time to create a script, because you need to automate several actions at once. Styles can't do it, templates can't do it, and the Scrapbook can't do it. Here are the steps to take:

1. Before you begin, turn on Snap to Guidelines (that is the only part of this exercise that can't be recorded in a script).

2. Choose Tools ➤ Corel SCRIPT ➤ Script and Preset Manager to open the docker. Click on the red Record button. From this point, DRAW watches your every move, and stores all "recordable actions" as part of the script.

3. Create a vertical guideline at the 4-inch mark on the ruler. (You can create it somewhere else, but remember its location.)

4. Create a rectangle that snaps to the guideline.

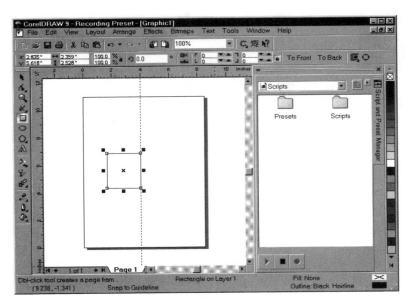

Note two things about the previous graphic: the round Record button in the docker is grayed out, indicating that it has been pressed (that is your only visual cue), and we have backed out one level in the docker. We find it helpful to have a separate place to record personal scripts—away from the prefab ones—and one level up in the directory structure makes sense (so you can easily get to the others).

5. Press F11 to reach the Fountain Fill dialog. Set a fountain fill (the default of black to white is fine) with an angle of 45 degrees. (The script doesn't care how you issue commands—here, you could have pressed F11, or used the Fill flyout, or the Interactive Fill tool.)

6. Switch to the Pick tool and click on the rectangle to get its rotation handles.

7. Hold Ctrl while you drag the middle-left handle up. Release after two "snaps."

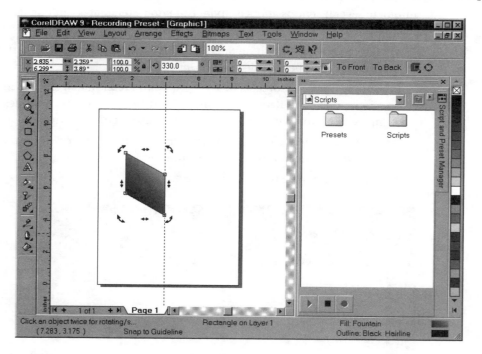

8. Press the black Stop button on the Script Manager to stop recording.

9. In the Save Recording dialog, choose a location, supply a name, and optionally, a description, as shown on the facing page. DRAW will store the script and use the object you created as the thumbnail.

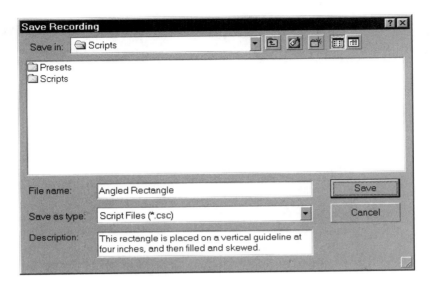

This beats the heck out of all previous methods for creating scripts or presets, as you'll see in a moment. To finish the story, let's play back your script, by following these steps:

10. Get a new drawing by pressing Ctrl+N.

11. Find your newly created script and play it back (double-click, right-click and Apply, or click the Play button).

In an instant, DRAW should create the vertical guideline and the skewed rectangle, just as you did when you created the script (only much faster, and with less effort on your part).

With previous versions of DRAW, automating this routine would have been practically impossible. You could create a style that includes the angled fountain fill, but you would have to skew the rectangle yourself. You could create a preset that skews the rectangle and applies the fill, but it would have been incapable of creating the guideline.

Only a script can perform the entire task, but in early versions of this tool, you had to create the script by coding each line, as if you were a programmer, and Figure 33.2 shows how daunting that task would be. This relatively simple maneuver created over 20 lines of mostly unintelligible instructions.

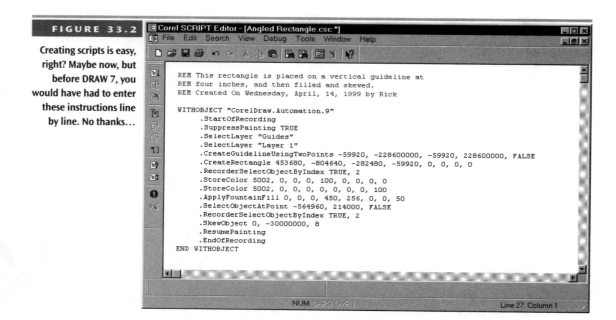

FIGURE 33.2

Creating scripts is easy, right? Maybe now, but before DRAW 7, you would have had to enter these instructions line by line. No thanks…

What You Can and Can't Record

During the recording exercise, we referred to a "recordable action." Not everything can be captured by the Script Manager during the recording process. As far as object creation goes, we have yet to find an object that cannot be captured during a recording. But with respect to interface changes or other types of commands, Script Manager has many limits.

For instance, if you were to toggle Snap to Guideline on or off, DRAW would ignore that. If you were to waive the mouse cursor all over the screen without stopping to click on anything, DRAW would ignore you. If you were to tear off a toolbar and float it on the screen, DRAW would ignore you. By ignore, we mean that the command would be carried out, but it would not be incorporated into the script.

This is not to say that you cannot program many of these commands into a script—the scripting language is immense. But you would have to manually encode them; you can't record them. In this regard, the Script Manager is different from a conventional keyboard macro program or the now-ancient Windows Recorder. Those programs would try to retrace your every move, regardless of context. Script Manager tries to be a bit more intelligent. We wish that there were a "go dumb" feature, whereby you could instruct DRAW to follow your every move—that way, you could make interface changes without having to face the specter of traversing Options.

N O T E   Many actions that used to be unrecordable are now allowed. For instance, most file operations can now be scripted—you can open, save, print, import, and export.

The Corel SCRIPT language, as it's called, supports the creation of custom dialog boxes, so you can turn your scripts into mini applications that run within DRAW. There is also a standalone application called the Corel SCRIPT Editor that helps you with some of the arcanery of scripting without recording. It is beyond the scope of this chapter (and 95 percent of its readers), but you can get a complete rundown of its capabilities from the online Help. From within DRAW, go to Tools ➤ Corel SCRIPT ➤ Corel SCRIPT Editor, and access the online Help for reference about the Corel SCRIPT programming language, syntax, and command set.

And what's more, DRAW 9 supports the Visual Basic scripting language. Essentially, anyone who can program in VBA can now automate procedures in DRAW. Access to it is at Tools ➤ Visual Basic.

Playing Back Your Scripts

If you followed the steps above, you have already played back (or run) a script. There are several ways you can run scripts. Coming up shortly is a set of strategies for managing your scripts, but suffice it to say at this point that playing back a script is as simple as finding it and double-clicking on it. You can do this in one of two ways:

- You can open the Script Manager, find the script in the window, and run it.
- You can go to Tools ➤ Corel SCRIPT ➤ Run Script, and then navigate your way to the desired script.

To continue the VCR analogy, this is akin to walking up to the machine and pushing the Play button. You can also use the remote control, and we'll talk about that later in this chapter. Before running a script, make sure to think about anything you would need to do to set the stage, like opening the desired drawing, moving to the right page, or selecting a critical object. Scripts are smart, but they can't read minds.

Working with Text

The Script Manager is quite adept at handling text, both creating and formatting it. When you record a script in which you format artistic or paragraph text, DRAW tracks the font, its attributes (bold, italic), line attributes (underline, overline, and strikeout), placement (superscript and subscript), and spacing between characters, words, lines, and paragraphs. Try the following exercise to create a script for formatting text:

1. Create a line of artistic text and select it.
2. Click on the Record button in the Script Manager.

3. Using the Text property bar or the Character dialog, change the face, the style, and the size. It doesn't matter what you change them to, as long as you make some kind of change to all three.

4. Click on OK or Apply, stop the recording, and assign a name to your script.

Because you selected a new face, style, and size, this script will apply those attributes to any string of artistic text. If you had only changed the point size, the script would have recorded just that change. For example, suppose the text you are using when you create the script is in 24-point AvantGarde. While recording, you leave the face at AvantGarde but change the color to red and the size to 100 points. When this script is applied to text in Century Gothic, the text will be sized to 100 points and filled with red, but the font will stay Century Gothic. Since you did not select a font while recording, it did not become part of the script.

In other words, the script recording function does not take note of the current settings; it only pays attention to what you *specifically change*. So if you want to create a script that changes text to 14-point Century Italic, left-aligned, you'll have to make sure to click on each of those controls in the dialog or property bar, *even if they are already set that way*. If the dialog already displays Century Italic as the face, click on it anyway. Incidentally, this applies to graphic scripts as well. If you're creating a script for a blue fill and a red outline, make sure you select the blue fill and red outline during recording, even if they are already the current settings.

One other point concerning text and scripts: you can only apply a script to an entire string of text, not a few characters selected with the Text tool. If you have characters selected with the Text tool when you run a script, the entire string or frame of text will be changed. DRAW will issue a message to this effect during the recording process.

Advanced Scripting

If you go no further than the basics covered here, you will be well ahead of the game when it comes to coping with redundant and tedious tasks. Nonetheless, there are many other ways to take advantage of DRAW's scripting tool while still stopping short of learning the programming language. Here are two of our favorites.

Turning a Script into a Command

What is the difference between one of your scripts and one of DRAW's commands? On the surface, you can eliminate any difference at all. You can make one of your scripts look as if it were designed into the program by adding it to one of the menus or toolbars, or by assigning it to a hotkey. The next chapter gives a complete overview of customizing your environment and techniques for creating custom toolbars, menus, and hotkeys. In short, any command, any docker, any style, and any script can be added to the interface as a menu choice, an icon on a toolbar, a hotkey, or all three. This is the remote control of the Script Manager—it provides instant access to any script you create. Figure 33.3 shows the script we created earlier being assigned the hotkey of Ctrl+Shift+R.

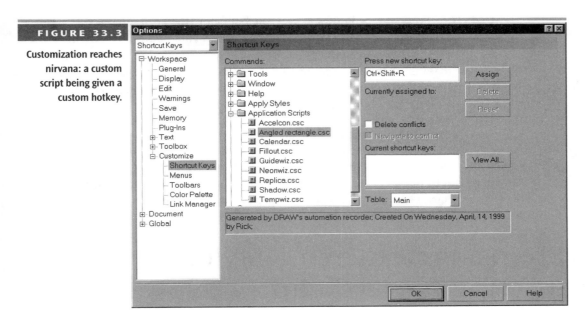

FIGURE 33.3

Customization reaches nirvana: a custom script being given a custom hotkey.

Auto-scripting

You can create scripts that automatically execute whenever you start DRAW, start a new drawing, open an existing drawing, print, or close the program. These are very handy for any housekeeping that you seek to do on a regular basis, like, say, automatically setting guidelines, creating some boilerplate objects or text, or setting defaults. These are things you could store in templates, but it's much easier to press Ctrl+N to get a new drawing than to do the New from Template dance.

The online Help offers a good rundown on auto-scripts, but it is completely buried, so with apologies to Corel, we are borrowing generously from it and including it here.

Auto-scripts are identified by their names and their locations. They must be placed in the Draw directory, not the Draw\Scripts directory. There are six auto-scripts, as follows:

OnStart Runs after DRAW is loaded and supersedes any other startup features that you may have selected. This means that you can write a script that replaces the Welcome to CorelDRAW dialog with a custom dialog, perhaps offering a menu of current DRAW projects.

OnOpen   Runs after you open an existing drawing.

OnClose   Runs before you close a document.

OnNew   Runs every time you create a new drawing. Our lead author uses this one to automatically draw ellipses on the Guideline layer for creating CD labels.

OnPrint   Runs when you start a print job, but before the print job is actually sent to the printer. For example, if you want to insert your name or copyright information in the lower-right corner of every drawing you print, you can write a script that inserts this information and save it as OnPrint.csc. Every time you trigger a print job in DRAW, this script will run before the print job is generated.

OnExit   Runs when you exit DRAW. After the script terminates, DRAW closes.

You can try these out for yourself. Record a simple script, like one that creates a circle, and save it in the Draw directory as OnNew.csc. Then press Ctrl+N for a new drawing and note how that circle will appear out of nowhere.

If you do not want an auto-script to run, you can hold Shift while the particular event occurs (open, close, print, etc.). For instance, if you hold down Shift while DRAW is starting, OnStart will not run.

Choosing between a Style, a Script, and a Scrap

In many instances, styles, scripts, and the Scrapbook can be used interchangeably. If you want to color an object or group of objects blue, you can use any one of these three functions. Here are some tips for determining which tool is best for the task you need to get done.

Situations That Call for Styles

You have already created and formatted an object.   A style works better here, because it can be created from an existing object. With a script, you would have to repeat all of the formatting steps to record them.

You want changes you've made to one object to affect other objects. If you anticipate that additional formatting changes will be needed in the future, you're better off using a style. By changing one object and then updating the style, you automatically change the others. There is no similar global link with scripts.

Situations That Call for Scripts

You want to transform an object.   Use a script here. In a script you can record all of the functions in the Transform docker. A style does not save these transformations.

You want to convert an object to curves.   Again, we are talking about the recording of an action taken on the object, rather than applying a format to it. Styles can't do that, but scripts can.

You want to create objects automatically.   A script can actually create an object as part of its playback. A style cannot create objects.

You want to record a blend between two objects.   Scripts can do that; styles can't.

You like to add descriptions of the effect.   The Scripts Manager allows you to store the name of the script, a description up to nine lines long, and a visual thumbnail of the result. In contrast, the Styles docker offers nothing more than the name of the style. If you find yourself forgetting what a style does and why you defined it in the first place, you might have better luck recording a script.

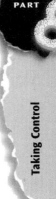

Situations That Call for the Scrapbook

The relatively new Scrapbook feature will take a bit of time to find its way into our hearts, not because it is poorly implemented, but because it is easily forgotten. But we have begun to respect its ability to act as a bone yard for drawings in progress. Use the Scrapbook when:

You want to add several elements to a drawing at once.   You could use a script for this, but it's much easier to just drag them out of the Scrapbook, as many times as you need copies of them. Of course, you need to add it to the Scrapbook in the first place, but once you do, you can create copies rapid-fire.

You realize, too late, that you did something perfect.   Our lead author regularly exclaims, "Look, I did it—why wasn't I recording it!" Then he remembers that he can take his work of art and drag it into the Scrapbook until he wants to use it again.

You're just not sure what to do with it...   Sometimes, it's tedious to create, name, and store a script for an effect whose fate is unclear. But dragging it to the Scrapbook is very painless.

Case Study: Debbie Does CorelSCRIPT

While most of us won't go anywhere near the stuff, one member of our writing team, Debbie Cook, has gotten up close and personal with the scripting language for a series of PHOTO-PAINT plug-in effects that have become very popular among those who have used them (see instructions at the end of this chapter for downloading a trial version). Here is her story…

I'm not a programmer, and I never had any intention or expectations of becoming one. And make no mistake, to a real programmer, I'm no programmer. But I do know DRAW and PAINT, and if programming a script is simply a way to operate those programs more efficiently, then it's worth a bit of code hell to get there.

Because Corel SCRIPT commands were my first introduction to any kind of programming, I'm probably lucky that I first tried recording little scripts in PHOTO-PAINT rather than in DRAW because I might never have explored Corel SCRIPT any further. The difference is that the PAINT recorder returns an immediate list of every recordable action performed, while in DRAW recording is "invisible" right up through when you save the recording. At that point, if you have included a command that is not recordable, DRAW informs you rather unceremoniously.

I slowly became familiar with the Corel SCRIPT commands while watching them as they were being recorded. OK, "familiar" might be stretching it, but at least I was starting to recognize the patterns and general syntax of this foreign language.

Armed with my simple recordings, I opened the Script Editor to have a closer look. I remembered someone telling me once that if you highlight a command in a script and press F1, the Help files will open at that particular command. When I first saw these files, they might as well have been Greek. They assume a certain level of understanding of programming in general, and I had none. Nada. Zilch. But I read through this information anyway and actually began to understand some of it. Then I wondered if there was a rogue geek gene in my DNA somewhere. I was hooked.

I moved on to dissecting many of the sample scripts I found in both DRAW and PAINT, as well as various Web sites. It was a slow process of understanding, but it was better than dissecting that frog in my 10th grade biology class (and a lot less messy). As I continued to experiment, I continued to learn, and soon my scripts were growing into miniprograms that offered options and automation. I was quite proud of the first special effect I created in PAINT, but you know what—I was more proud of the script I wrote that automated that special effect.

When you're ready to try your hand at creating your own scripts, here are some hints and references that I wish I had known when I began.

Continued on next page

Read the Help files   Open the Script Editor Help file (F1), go to the Contents tab, and read the sections in order. The documentation for version 9 has been improved, and most of it now can be understood by nonprogrammers. As you begin to experiment with your own recordings and scripts, go back and read the Help files again. You'll be surprised by how much more you'll understand, and you'll probably learn something new with every review.

Ask for help   Corel's support newsgroups are a wonderful resource for every aspect of DRAW, and there is a separate newsgroup area devoted entirely to scripting: news://cnews.corel.ca/corelsupport.draw-scripting. Chances are you'll have an answer to your question within 24 hours, and we might even run into each other there.

Walk away   When you become frustrated with a script that you just cannot get to work, take a break and clear your head. I used to obsess over uncooperative scripts before I learned to just get up and leave the computer. I was amazed at how much more easily solutions came to me when I returned. Programming is a set of linear and logical expressions, but we humans are not. Double that when you are frustrated and out of patience.

Read the Help files again   This time, though, read through the index portion to learn about commands you might not know even existed. When you see something interesting, read about it and try it out. Many commands have sample syntax that you can cut and paste into your own script files.

Debug   Don't overlook the Script Editor's debugging tools. It's very helpful to execute your first scripts line by line so you can watch them in action. The Script Editor will also check your scripts and return error messages if it finds something wrong. While the error messages may be cryptic, you'll at least be pointed to the line number of the problem.

Use the recorder   There's no need to reinvent the wheel. Record the actual commands, save the snippets, and then cut and paste them into your scripts. You'll save yourself a lot of typing and the error checking that goes with the inevitable typos.

Think modularly   Scripts are executed top to bottom, and the more you can break up what you want to accomplish into separate pieces, the more successful and efficient scripts you'll write. Begin by creating a formal linear outline of what you want to accomplish with your script and then try to write it in that order. And don't forget to save particularly good pieces of code into separate files to copy into new scripts later. The best programmers write code once and use it forever!

Take notes   Don't try to remember what every block of code does. Placing REM at the beginning of a line means that whatever follows on the same line is a remark and will not be executed. This is a great tool for visually separating blocks of code or to simply add notes and reminders to yourself.

Continued on next page

PART

Taking Control

Start small and don't give up   Don't overwhelm yourself with complicated syntax and functions. Start by adding simple options to your recordings with a message box or a simple OK/Cancel static dialog. As your knowledge and experience grows, so will your script functionality.

Get online   Visit the experts' Web sites listed below. Many of these did not exist when I was learning Corel SCRIPT and I would have given my eye teeth for Alex Vakulenko's tutorials! Download the free scripts and open them in Script Editor to see how others organize their scripts and execute various commands and options.

```
http://www.vakcer.com/oberon/script
```

```
http://tfts.i-us.com
```

```
http://www.tld.net/users/mcdesign/downloads.htm
```

```
http://www.richz.com/scr-utl/c-script.html
```

```
http://www.cedesign.com/html/scripts.html
```

`http://www.cedesign.com/cefx` (to download demo of Cutting Edge F/X)

If I can do it, anyone can. This isn't false modesty—I know what I'm good at and what doesn't come naturally to me. Scripts definitely do not come naturally to me, but in that regard scripting skills are unlike actual design and illustration skills. Without some natural design sense, there is only so much you can achieve in the arts. But with scripting, effort, practice, reverse engineering, and a bit of sweat and toil really can spell success.

chapter 34

YOUR VERY OWN INTERFACE

Featuring

YOUR VERY OWN
INTERFACE

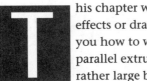

his chapter won't teach you about any new special effects or drawing commands, and it won't show you how to wrap text around a graphic or create a parallel extrusion. In fact, the last chapter of this rather large book does not contain any tips and tricks at all, at least in the conventional sense. We'll even go so far as to suggest that if you are satisfied with the way DRAW presents itself to you and with the overall design of the interface, you can skip this chapter and start reading the Index, line for line.

But if you want to customize DRAW to make it more efficient for what *you* do, you'll want to read every word of this chapter. Corel has given DRAW 9 an interface that is almost completely customizable, and it takes center stage here.

This chapter includes step-by-step instructions, and we start with the basics. But the ramp is short and steep, because we presume that most of you who want to customize the interface are already familiar with it in the first place.

Tool Terminology 101

This chapter will be easier to digest if you start by learning a few terms.

Microsoft's definition of a *tool* is very specific, and Corel has done its best to comply. DRAW has always had a *toolbox* (the one on the left of the work area), and all of the icons on it (Pick, Shape, Zoom, and so on) are referred to as tools. But what used to be known as the Ribbon Bar is now called the *Standard toolbar*—although you'll discover in this chapter that there is nothing standard about it. Also at your command are the *property bar* and various other toolbars—including ones that you can make up to suit yourself.

Flyouts emanate from the nine toolbox icons that have a small triangle in the lower-right corner. When you click and hold on one of these tools, several additional icons "fly out" from there. Flyouts can be separated from the toolbox and floated on the screen like toolbars, and as of DRAW 9, they too can be customized.

The *status bar* is still the status bar; ditto for the *color palette*, the *rulers*, and the *scroll bars*.

To best understand the starting point for customizing DRAW, you should try to keep the following straight in your mind:

The toolbox Its default home has always been on the left of the screen.

The Standard toolbar By default it lives below the menu bar and contains the icons for the Open, Save, Print, Cut, Copy, Paste, and other fundamental commands.

The property bar This is a special type of toolbar whose controls change depending on the tool and object(s) selected. By default, it is located below the Standard toolbar.

Toolbars These ship with DRAW in a certain arrangement, but you can change them and create new ones.

Flyouts Display these by clicking and holding on one of the nine toolbox icons that have the triangle. These flyouts should not be confused with the menus that are available from some dialog boxes, which are also called flyouts.

CorelDRAW's Control Room

Before we begin any conversation at all about customization, you need to understand the architecture that supports this. We wish that Corel were more clear about the relationship between designing the interface and the place where those design changes are kept; we'll clarify it here.

Corel calls this reservoir of interface design a *workspace,* and its job is to store and make available for future recall all of its elements: the size of the CorelDRAW application window…the status of dockers and toolbars (floating or docked)…the folders last used for opening, saving, importing, and exporting work…the value of such items as Nudge, Duplicate, and Constrain Angle…all the way down to when and where to make backup copies of drawings. Finally—and the topic central to this chapter—a workspace tracks any changes you make to the interface from the Customization tools. Figure 34.1 shows the tree structure in Options of all of the elements within the Workspace heading, and we have expanded Customize.

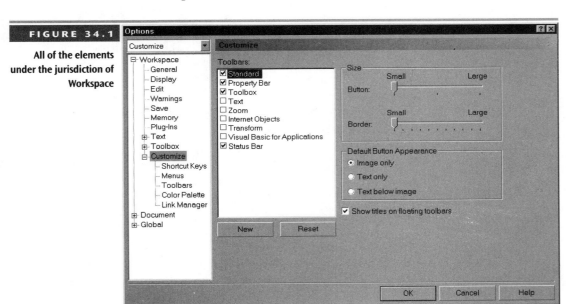

FIGURE 34.1

All of the elements under the jurisdiction of Workspace

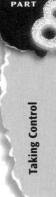

PART

Taking Control

It looks perfectly logical here in the dialog, but in practice, there is little that is intuitive about this, especially when you think back through recent versions to all the disparate ways these settings have been stored and recalled.

Workspace is one of three organizational constructs designed to house DRAW's settings. They are described as follows, in the order in which they appear in Options:

Workspace identifies a collection of settings and conditions that creates the environment (the interface) in which you work. These settings do not change from one drawing to the next.

Document identifies those settings that *do* potentially change from one drawing to the next. In this grouping are elements such as whether to show the page border, the color of guidelines, and the status of the snaps, styles, and HTML settings.

Global settings are on the other side of the spectrum—they are outside of the reach of Document or Workspace settings. So such controls as color correction, preflight controls for printers, and file extensions recognized by DRAW are as sticky as they come: change them once and they will not change again unless you do it.

Making Things Permanent

This question of "how do I make DRAW remember" has become practically age-old. There are so many different aspects of the program that need a default condition, and at the same time, so many different ways to establish those defaults. It's no wonder that DRAW users have always been confused about this. In fact, we're glad that many pairs of eyes read this book before it's published—otherwise, we might blow it ourselves!

First off, there are items that pertain to the interface, like the condition of palettes, dockers, and toolbars. Think of these as the toys in your childhood bedroom: if you leave them on the floor, they'll stay on the floor until you pick them up and put them away. If your home had a housekeeper while you were growing up, then you'll have to come up with another analogy—there are no housekeepers to put your toys away in DRAW.

Then there are elements that pertain to the drawings themselves, like styles, page size, bleed and page borders, units of measure, and the status of the rulers. The condition of these elements change with the wind: every time you open a new drawing, these conditions could change. Kind of like the mood of your older sister when she had to get ready for school and you were already in the bathroom—would she crawl back into bed, or break the door down? (What, separate bathrooms? Another useless analogy.)

While this second group of settings comes and goes with each drawing, there still must be default conditions which DRAW uses for new drawings, and so there must be a way for you to set them. Go to Tools ≻ Options ≻ Document, and click Save Options As Defaults for New Documents. DRAW offers seven general categories whose current condition you can save and use as defaults.

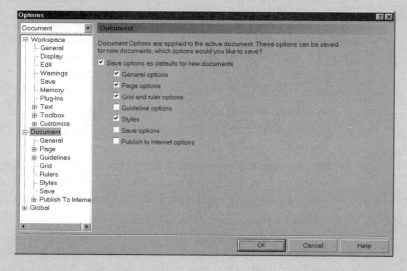

Continued on next page

This subject surfaces most often when users want to change their default typefaces. That is governed by the styles, and they indeed are one of the seven categories that can be saved in this dialog.

This manner of saving is in sharp contrast to the main thrust of this chapter—namely, redesigning the interface and saving those changes in a workspace. If this confuses you, forget that you ever read this little digression—understanding workspaces is more important.

Creating Workspaces

Before you begin any significant remodeling of the CorelDRAW architecture, you should conscientiously create a place to store your work. Figure 34.2 shows the top page of the Workspace tab, including three workspaces supplied by Corel. The one labeled _default is the plain vanilla configuration that we all see the first time we start the program. The next is to help Illustrator defectors make the transition, and the third is for those who prefer the way DRAW 8 looked and felt. And then there is the one that we created to facilitate the writing and production of this book, and the large dot indicates that it is the default.

PART

Taking Control

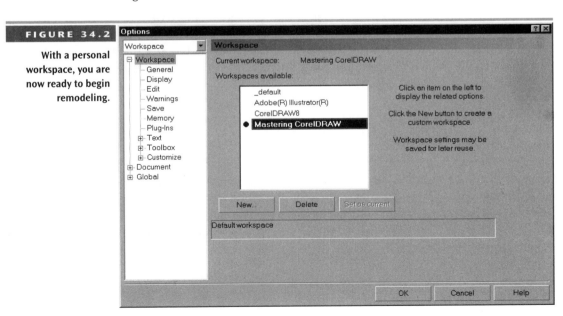

FIGURE 34.2

With a personal workspace, you are now ready to begin remodeling.

Most users never pay attention to this dialog and so they simply use _default (although "use" implies intent, and few users even know these workspaces are here). Any interface changes—even unintentional ones—get stored there.

While there is nothing dangerous about doing this, we recommend instead that you leave _default alone and create a workspace of your own. Even if you don't expect to change the interface—even if you don't know what we're talking about!—go ahead and create a workspace for yourself. It's easy—click New, supply a name, and click Set As Current. To switch between workspaces, just double-click them.

 N O T E   We like leaving _default pristine because that way you have a baseline reference for any changes you make, and for technical support purposes (should you ever need to seek assistance with the program), it's good to know what the factory settings are and how to return to them. If, however, you have made substantial changes to _default, you can return to factory settings by holding F8 while starting DRAW.

Once you have created a home for your personal interface, you're ready to begin building the interface.

Flying Tools

Let's start with a basic technique that works with all of DRAW's toolbars. Look closely at the toolbox. You'll notice that it sits inside of a *region*—our term for this area that is defined by the edge of the screen on the left, the ruler on the right, and small lines at the top and bottom. Once you're aware of this region, you'll notice that the Standard toolbar, the property bar, and the color palette all have defined regions as well. Now do this:

1. Move your cursor anywhere in the empty space around the toolbox, but still inside its region.

2. Now click and drag out to the page. If you did it right, the entire toolbox will up and leave its home and switch to a floating horizontal toolbar.

The now-floating toolbox can be reshaped back to vertical or into a block, just by dragging its edges, and it can be moved anywhere on the Windows desktop. This "floating" of the toolbox is not new, and inquisitive users might have discovered this same capability as far back as DRAW 5. But the way it is done—by clicking and dragging on the region that defines it—is a key characteristic of the modern DRAW interface.

Playtime is not yet over; now try the following.

3. Drag the toolbox to the right edge of the DRAW window. As you do, it should jump back to a vertical arrangement. Release the mouse, and it takes up residence (in Corel-speak, it "docks") on that edge, beside the color palette.

4. Drop the toolbox on top of the status bar, and it docks itself and creates a region just above the bar.

5. Drop the toolbox on top of the Standard toolbar, and they appear to merge, as the toolbox docks itself to one side of the toolbar.

This basic drag-and-drop maneuver can also be used on the Standard toolbar, the property bar, the color palette, and any of the nine flyouts in the toolbox. You can pick them up, move them anywhere, and dock them on any of the four sides of the application. (The status bar can be moved to the top or the bottom of the screen, but not floated or docked on the sides.)

TIP Windows 95/98/NT sees a toolbar as a miniapplication and gives it a title bar and a Close button. If you close a toolbar, you can reopen it one of two ways: (1) by going to Window ➤ Toolbars and checking it; or (2) by right-clicking on an existing toolbar, finding the desired toolbar on the list, and clicking it back on. To restore the color palette, go to Window ➤ Color Palettes and choose the one you want.

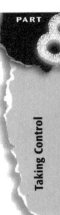

Flying Flyouts

So how do you make a toolbar fly? Go to the toolbox now, click on the Fill tool, and hold for a moment. As expected, the Fill flyout emerges. But study it closely and you'll see that it, too, like the toolbox, has its own region. Pull the flyout away and, you guessed it, it becomes its own little toolbar.

All toolbars behave the same way, so you can float this Fill flyout-turned-toolbar anywhere on your screen, or dock it to one side of the application. Guess what—the Texture Fill dialog can now be one click away instead of two, and it can also be much closer to your cursor and the objects in your drawing. Those two qualities are the enduring virtues of floating toolbars. Icons that used to require two clicks can now be reached in one; icons that used to reside on the edge of the window can now be placed right next to your objects.

In Figure 34.3, we are using two windows: one to view leaves for shading and coloring purposes, and another to zoom in on one of the leaves for a bit of node-editing work. Each window has the appropriate flyout close at hand. You can save a lot of time and mouse effort by keeping the essential tools nearby.

FIGURE 34.3

The toolbars can be positioned right where the action is in the window on the right. No excess mousing required.

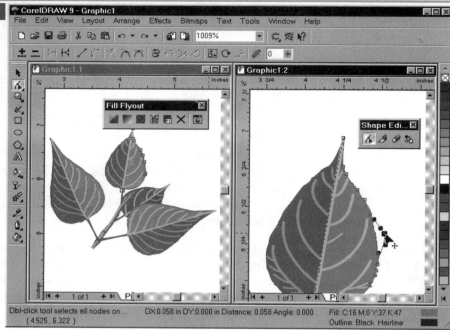

DRAW ships with five additional toolbars that are not on screen by default. As we mentioned earlier, they can be displayed by right-clicking a toolbar and checking off the one you want to see.

Repairing DRAW's Zoom Services

The current DRAW interface has been a work of refinement in progress, but we think that Corel is still struggling to get DRAW's Zoom tools right. By definition, tools are persistent—they stay on screen until you close them. But nobody wants a persistent zooming tool; you want to zoom once and then do something else. We contend, therefore, that there is little to be gained by having a floating Zoom toolbar.

Furthermore, the Zoom tool in the toolbox does not function as it did in earlier releases. Now its flyout offers only the marquee zoom and the seldom-used Panning tool, and when you click on either one, the tool stays active until you change to another tool. This is especially aggravating when you have just marquee-zoomed and, expecting to be once again working with the Pick tool, you go to select an object...only to be surprised by zooming in on it even further.

Continued on next page

Further confusing matters is the curious fact that no less than *five* zooming controls are available to you. Oy vey…read 'em and weep:

- You can click on the Zoom tool in the toolbox and tear it off to get a little toolbar of just those two tools.

- You can right-click the Zoom tool, select Properties, and check Use Traditional Zoom Flyout to return the Zoom function to the way it was back in version 5 and earlier.

- You can right-click on the Standard toolbar and choose Zoom to get a toolbar that consists of all zooming commands.

- When you click the Zoom tool in the toolbox, the property bar offers the same set of zoom commands.

- With Tools ➢ View Manager, you can turn on a full-featured dockable tool for saving and retrieving zoom states in your drawing.

Here are our recommendations. First off, avoid the Zoom tool in the toolbox altogether—whether floating or docked. Unless you change its operation, via Properties on its pop-up menu, it doesn't function the way it used to, or the way that most users want it to. Just ignore it.

Second, as we mentioned way back in Chapter 3, the best way to zoom continues to be with your hotkeys:

- F2 for marquee-zoom

- F3 for zoom out

- F4 for zoom to all objects

- Shift+F2 for zoom to selected objects

- Shift+F4 for zoom to page

Pressing F2 to marquee-zoom is not like clicking on the Zoom tool, and you don't have the problem of it not going away after use. But if you have grown accustomed to using the icons for zooming, we suggest that you activate the Zoom toolbar and dock it below the toolbox. Even with just an SVGA display, there will be enough room for all of the important tools to fit.

Now you have a set of zoom controls that are much better than the defaults—better because you can reach all of them with just one click instead of two and because they go away after each use.

You Say Tomato...

It is impossible to please everyone all of the time, and Corel knows it. Its program designers have created a default interface that they think will please most of the people most of the time. They have thought through which commands and functions should always be available (they would go on the Standard toolbar), and which ones are only needed in certain contexts (in which case, they would belong on a property bar). In these efforts, they have probably succeeded in finding a good middle ground.

But that doesn't mean you have to be satisfied with it, because you can make it perfect. All it takes is a bit of customization know-how and a long interview with yourself. For instance, the on-screen Nudge setting is a wonderful addition to the property bar, saving us countless trips to Options when we want to change it from 1 point to 1 pica, or from 1 point to 1/4 of a point. (We're pointing to it in Figure 34.4.) We love it.

We also hate it. Corel placed it on the so-called "No Selection" property bar—the one that you first see when you start the program, the one that is active when no objects in the drawing are selected. But that's not when we want to change a Nudge setting; we want to change it after selecting an object and getting ready to nudge. But the property bar for selected objects is different and it does not include the Nudge setting. This requires that we deselect the object, change the Nudge, and then reselect. No good!

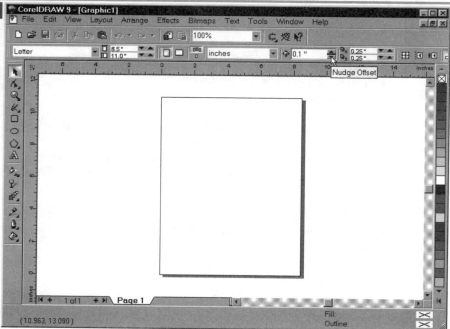

FIGURE 34.4

Great tool, lousy home. We think the Nudge Offset value box deserves a permanent place on the interface.

We want this great little Nudge adjuster to *always* be present. We want it to be visible when we have one object selected, multiple objects selected, a group selected, a bitmap selected. Any time, any place. That means just one thing: Standard toolbar, not a property bar. While some of the maneuvers in this chapter are advanced, this one isn't. Watch:

1. Press and continue to hold Alt until we tell you to stop. By holding Alt, all toolbars become "unlocked" and their elements free to be moved.

2. Place your cursor inside the Nudge box and begin dragging it up.

3. Find a place on the Standard toolbar where you would like its new home to be, like, say, next to the Zoom Levels drop-down list.

4. Release Alt and note that Nudge has left its spot on the property bar and taken up residence on the Standard toolbar.

 TIP To copy an interface element, hold Ctrl during the above operation. To remove an element altogether, drag it away from any toolbar (like to the middle of the page) and release Alt.

Now we're happy. Our Nudge box will always be available, no matter the context, because it now lives on the Standard toolbar, as shown below.

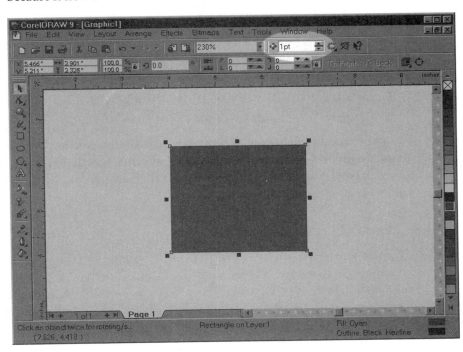

Realigning Alignment

Here is one of our lead author's pet peeves: "I will never understand the logic," he says, "behind having more than one property bar for text. Corel has made a distinction between selecting a string or frame of text, and having your cursor in the text, actually editing. Perhaps there is a reason for this, but c'mon—not being able to align a paragraph unless your cursor is in it? That's crazy!"

Allow us to clarify, with a slightly more diplomatic tone. Let's say you have a headline in a frame of paragraph text and you want to center it. With your cursor in the headline, you can easily head to the property bar for text and choose the Center icon from the Alignment drop-down list. But if you have selected an entire frame or string of text, the alignment controls disappear—DRAW has two distinct property bars for text, depending upon if the cursor is in the text, or not. We think that's, um, silly, and here is how you can fix it:

1. Set some text and select all of it, with no editing cursor in place. In other words, make DRAW show you the property bar that lacks the Alignment drop-down list.

2. Right-click on any toolbar and click Text to invoke the Text toolbar.

This is not a context-sensitive property bar, but instead a static toolbar with the most popular text functions. We're not sure if Corel anticipated that users would want to actively use it, or if they thought it would serve as a storage house for text functions. The latter use is what we are interested in, because it includes the one control we want to have placed on the Text property bar.

3. Press and hold both Ctrl and Alt.

4. Find the Alignment drop-down list (to the right of Underline).

5. Click and drag it up to the property bar and drop it. Release Ctrl and Alt.

6. Close the Text toolbar—you don't need it anymore.

Now you will be able to align text, irrespective of the presence of the text cursor. As these two property bars are a bit different, the control will likely jump from one position to the other as DRAW switches bars, but that's easy to cope with. Not having the control at all is what is aggravating.

Standard? Says Who??

Now that you have a sense of how the Standard toolbar and the property bars behave, you can begin to scrutinize the placement of icons. There isn't that much space on the Standard toolbar—if an icon is going to always be visible, it had better be pretty important. Therefore, we suggest you treat the Standard toolbar as precious real estate and make sure that the icons there are worthy of their positions. Our lead author likes to joke about placing icons on probation: "Every few weeks or so," he says, "I browse the icons on the Standard toolbar. If I haven't clicked one since the last time I checked, I put it on probation. If it doesn't get clicked from now until the next checkpoint, I fire it."

We asked Rick to perform one of his routine checks for us. Here is our ruthless leader's report:

For starters, I would wipe out the entire first section—I use the hotkeys for New, Open, Save, and Print. I can't remember the last time I clicked on any of those four icons. Same with Cut, Copy, and Paste—I've been pressing Ctrl+X, C, and V since my days with an Osborne Computer. They're history, too.

Redo is kind of an awkward keystroke (Ctrl+Shift+Z), so I'd keep the Redo icon there, and for consistency, I'd let Undo live, too. And there are times when I like to use the Import and Export icons if I know I'm going to have to mouse around to find the file.

The Zoom Levels list definitely stays, and so does the What's This Help thingie. But Application Launcher and Corel Community can go bye-bye. When I'm done, there is all sorts of room for good stuff:

With all of that extra space, I think about the controls that I might need to use in many different contexts, or ones that are buried deep in the interface. Definitely the Nudge box. Also, I want permanent access to the orientation controls—Portrait and Landscape.

I also like the automatic Insert Page command that doesn't ask you about before or after, or size, so I plucked that one out of Customize. I record scripts a lot, so I want one-click access to the Script and Preset docker.

I regularly activate the IE and Pantone palettes—no sense in schlepping up to the Window menu every time I want one of them. And turning on and off color correction is a nightmare—thank goodness there's an icon for that!

PART

Taking Control

There are times when I want to see a Properties sheet but don't feel like right-clicking, so I click the Object Properties icon. And while I really like the new interactive controls, I prefer to edit blends with a docker. You know, all of the special effects still have dockers—they're just hidden.

Finally, several of the graphic icons for these commands are hideous, so I changed them to English. Now this is a toolbar that I can sink my teeth into...

Our lead author assumes many facts not yet in evidence, but rest assured we'll cover them before this chapter is finished. Most notable in his little diatribe are the facts that you can set any icon to display in text, and that there are dozens of commands that Corel's interface designers chose not to place on the visible interface. If you didn't know to search for them, you would never know they existed at all.

Interchangeable Parts

This simple technique of dragging items from one toolbar to another is central to your customization strategy, so you should practice it until you get a feel for it, keeping in mind these things:

- Press and hold Alt to unlock DRAW's interface, allowing all icons to be relocated.
- Press and hold Ctrl along with Alt to copy an icon instead of move it.
- To invoke one of the hidden toolbars, right-click on a visible one and pick it from the list. Once visible, you can copy and move those icons, as well.
- To return any toolbar or property bar to its original condition, do this:

  1. Go to Window ➤ Toolbars (or right-click on a bar and choose Toolbars).

  2. Choose the desired toolbar and click Reset.

- Any of the nine toolbox flyouts can be pulled off and floated on screen.
- All of these changes will be remembered from one DRAW session to the next.

All of this type of remodeling falls under the heading of workspace changes. If you created a personal workspace and set it to be current, as we recommend at the top of this chapter, all of these changes would be recorded there. Otherwise, they would be recorded in whatever workspace is current, probably _default.

Building Your Own Interface

For repeated use of a particular tool, there is nothing better than having it right next to your cursor. But the downside to this is the temptation to keep *all* of your tools close by. Give in to that, and before you know it, your screen may look like Figure 34.5—and that's without any dockers!

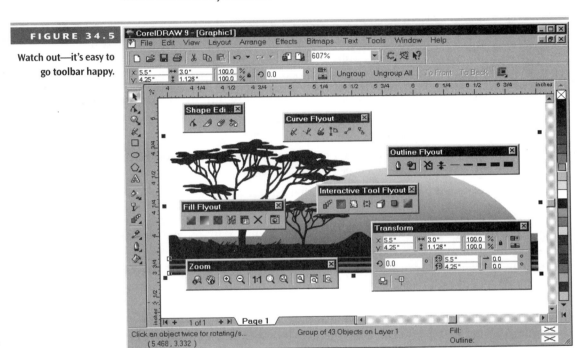

FIGURE 34.5

Watch out—it's easy to go toolbar happy.

Clearly, another strategy is needed to keep a select set of tools within easy reach, and DRAW provides for it. To best illustrate it, consider yourself hired as our new designer.

Special Tools for a Special Project

We have commissioned you to create a floor plan for our new editorial division, in which each member of the writing team will have an office. We want the plan drawn to correct scale, and it must have sufficient detail. We are paying you $365,000 for your efforts, so you'd better do a good job.

As a savvy DRAW user, the first thing you think about are the electronic tools you will need for this project. You write down your tasks and the tools you will need for them:

- You'll need to import lots of objects from your personal home-furnishings library of clipart.
- The Clipboard will be kept very busy with frequent copying and pasting.
- You'll be creating lots of rectangles and free-form objects.
- The Copy Properties From command will be your faithful assistant, helping you quickly take attributes from other finished pieces.
- You can already think of three layers that you'll need for the various objects.
- You'll have to set a grid, and will be regularly turning on and off Snap to Grid and Snap to Objects.
- You expect to be doing a lot of trimming and welding.
- The View Manager, which can quickly zoom you into specific parts of the schematic, will offer a welcome advantage.
- Your preliminary design reveals that certain shapes will need to be distinguished by fill patterns—black, 50% gray, and 20% gray.

With this list in hand, you float a few of the important toolbars and flyouts on your page and quickly conclude that you have no room left to work. To correct this, you move all of these toolbars outside of the DRAW window and hover them over the desktop. But now they are so far away from your cursor that reaching them via the menus would be easier.

Ah, but you have already read this chapter that you are now reading, and so you know what we haven't yet told you: that you can create a work environment ideally suited for this project. Your first order of business is to head to Tools ➤ Options ➤ Workspace, and create a workspace called, say, Floorplan. Once you make it the current workspace, you are ready to explore the buried treasure that is the Customize dialog page of Options:

1. From Customize, click on the Toolbars tab. There you will find every tool, command, and docker that exists on the menus, in the Standard toolbar, and in the toolbox—and even a few tools that exist nowhere!

2. In the middle window, click on the plus sign beside File & Layout, then on File, and then on one of the listed commands. In the Buttons area, 28 icons appear, each one representing a command appropriate to the File menu.

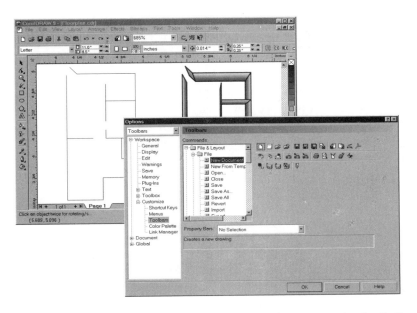

3. Select a command in the list and note that its icon in the Buttons area is high-lighted, and the Description area explains the command. You can also hover your cursor over the icon to get the description as bubble help.

4. Find the button for Import and drag it from the dialog onto the page. As you do, DRAW automatically creates a toolbar to house it.

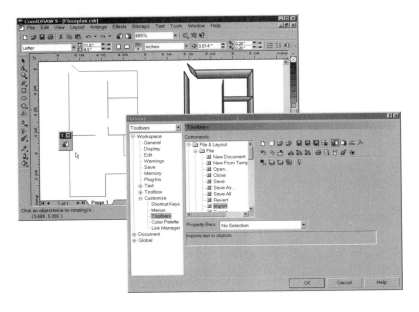

This fledgling toolbar contains only the Import button so far. Assuming this is your first custom toolbar, DRAW has called it Toolbar 1 (although it's so small, the name won't fit on its title bar).

5. Referring to your list of tools and commands, you start moving through the command tree in the Toolbars page. Still under File & Layout, you expand Grid, Guidelines & Snap, click on Grid and Ruler Setup, and drag the highlighted button to your new toolbar. Then you do the same with Snap to Objects. You don't need to take Snap to Grid, because you've been pressing Ctrl+Y for that since version 2.

6. Moving on to Styles, Layers & Object Management, you take the Object Manager button and add it to your toolbar. Your toolbar is starting to grow.

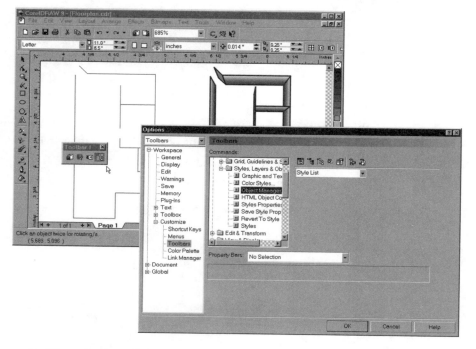

7. Next you go to the Edit & Transform category. From the Editing Commands group, you decline the Clipboard commands because you can press Ctrl+C and Ctrl+V in your sleep. (Your sole criterion in selecting icons is ease of access, and you're a right-handed mouse user, so Ctrl+C is easier than clicking on an icon.) However, you do drag the Copy Properties From button to your new toolbar.

8. Under the View & Display category, you explore the Zoom & Pan group and take View Manager, which is a tremendous help when zooming in and out of many different parts of a drawing.

9. Next, from Toolbars ➤ Toolbox, you take the Bézier tool.

10. Under Fill & Outline ➤ Fill, you scroll the long list and find icons for Black Fill, Gray20 Fill, Gray50 Fill—just what you need. (These icons used to be on the Fill flyout, but they disappeared in DRAW 9.)

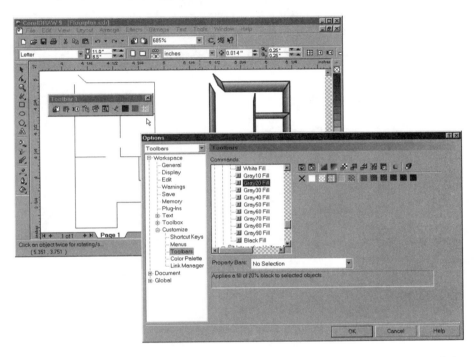

11. For better organization, you place the Bézier tool at the beginning of the toolbar, just by dragging it there. You move a few other icons around, based on whatever divine guidance you possess.

12. You discover, probably by accident, that if you move an icon a tiny bit one direction or the other, DRAW creates a separator. So you waste no time determining logical groupings for functions.

13. A few of the icons have unintelligible symbols, so for each one, you right-click, choose Properties, click Show Text, and type in a short identifier.

TIP When the Customize dialog is open, you do not need to hold Alt to move icons. With Customize open, it's as if the entire interface is unlocked, so you could also drag icons from visible toolbars and place them on your custom one.

14. You resize the toolbar so that it appears as two rows instead of one long one.

15. Finally, you back out to the main Customize page of Options, find Toolbar 1, click on it twice to get a cursor, and rename it to Floorplan Tools. Your custom toolbar is now ready for active duty.

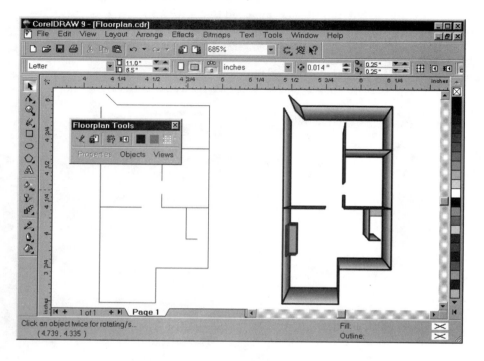

Cleaning Up Your Environment

As you begin work on your floorplan, you soon realize that, thanks to your custom toolbar, you don't need much else on your screen. So, to get more work space, you remove the Standard toolbar.

Occasionally as you work, you zoom way in on an object and find that your custom toolbar is in the way. To prevent this, you simply dock it to one of DRAW's edges. Ultimately, you decide just to place it where the Standard toolbar used to be. For this project, it *is* your default toolbar, and in fact, you decide to dock it below the property bar instead of above it, so it can be as close to the page as possible.

To maintain consistency between types of objects, you have created several styles. You've always disliked having to right-click or go to the Styles docker to apply styles, so you head back to Customize to see what it offers for Styles tasks. Under File & Layout ➤ Styles, Layers & Object Management, you click on each command and check its description. You discover that the last one, simply called Styles, represents a drop-down list box of all styles in your drawing. You waste no time adding that to your custom toolbar, which is now docked at the top of your screen, as in Figure 34.6.

FIGURE 34.6

No more navigating multiple flyouts to assign styles, thanks to the Styles list that you have added to your toolbar.

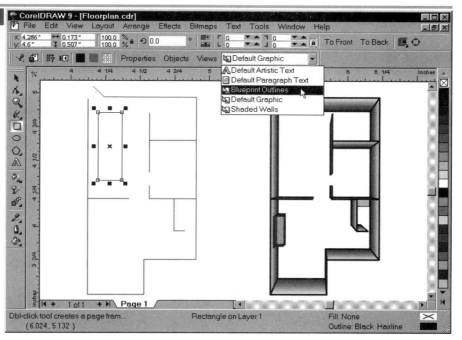

 NOTE   In addition to customizing the Standard toolbar or creating your own custom toolbar, you can also customize each and every property bar that DRAW uses. This would be tedious and exacting work, and you would need to learn what each one is called, but the Customize ➤ Toolbars section includes a drop-down list of every property bar. When you select one from the list, the property bar on the screen changes to the selected configuration. You can then customize it like any other toolbar. And as of DRAW 9, you can even customize the toolbox.

Menu Mania

Toolbars aren't the only thing that you can rearrange in DRAW. Nothing is sacred, including the menus that hold all of DRAW's commands, dialogs, and dockers.

From the now-familiar Customize dialog, click on the Menus tab. You will arrive at the gateway to total control of the menus and their elements.

Adding and Removing Menu Items

While the approach is a bit different, you can add or remove items from a menu just as you did with a toolbar. Furthermore, you can create new menus altogether. The Menus page of Customize has two windows (three, counting the tree of Options): the one in the middle shows all available commands, whether or not they are currently assigned to a menu; the window on the right shows the current configuration of DRAW's menus. Browse the commands in the middle window and add them to the current configuration using the Add and Move buttons.

In the buttons next to the items in the Menu window, exclamation marks indicate commands. Plus (+) signs and small right-pointing arrows indicate submenus that contain commands within menu choices (for example, the set of Order commands for moving objects to the front or back). You can either click on the plus button or double-click on the arrow to drill down to these commands. The <<Separator>> represents the dividing lines that appear in the menus. Once added, you can rename any command, as well as determine its keystroke access. The ampersand (&) designates the underlined letter in the menu command that you would press to invoke that command.

To add or change the keystroke access to a menu, just enter or move the & character while typing. Figure 34.7 shows what the dialog for adding or editing menu items looks like. Notice the minus key next to Bitmaps, indicating that it has been expanded. The plus next to Mode tells you that it is a submenu. Also note the & symbols indicating the keystrokes that would invoke any of these commands. We preferred "Convert" as the name of the command to change color depths to a bitmap, so we are in the process of changing it back to its pre-DRAW 9 name.

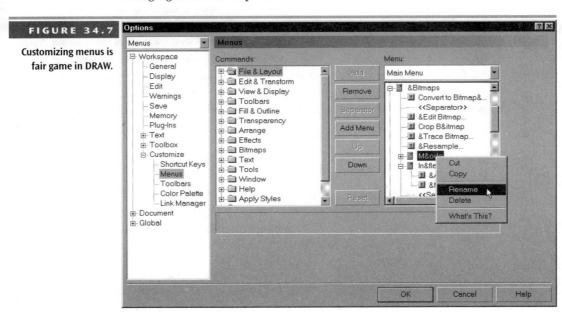

FIGURE 34.7

Customizing menus is fair game in DRAW.

Creating New Menus

The handy Customize ➤ Menus dialog goes beyond the rearranging of menu items—you can also add your own menus. Here is how it's done, and why you would want to.

1. In Customize ➤ Menus, click on the last item in the Menu window, &Help.

2. Click on Add Menu and type **&Special**, or whatever menu name you prefer. Try to give it a letter for keystroke access that is not used by another menu.

3. Browse the command tree looking for frequently used commands that would otherwise require more than one or two keystrokes or mouse clicks. When you find ones you want, simply click on Add. Then, if necessary, rename the items and/or reposition the &. Add as many separators as you deem necessary.

Figure 34.8 shows the Special menu we created for our Mastering CorelDRAW workspace, and we're going to tour most of them here for you. It might be more logical to place some of these commands on other menus (e.g., Snap to All and None on the View menu), but there is a certain simplicity in housing all customized commands under a single menu. You can decide this for yourself.

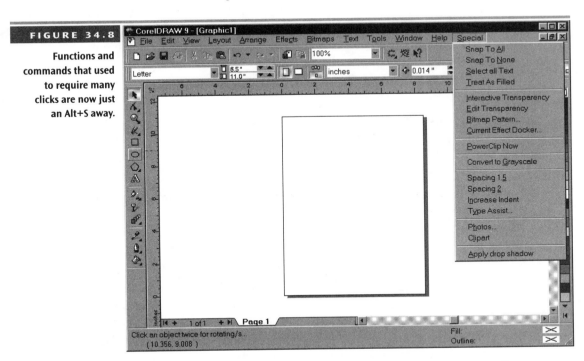

FIGURE 34.8

Functions and commands that used to require many clicks are now just an Alt+S away.

Snap to All and None   We regularly want to ensure that all snaps are on or off. These commands exist; Corel chose not to place them on the View menu with the other snap toggles.

Select All Text   This is the easiest way to accomplish this. The alternative is Edit ➤ Select All ➤ Text. That's too many mouse clicks.

Treat As Filled   There is an icon for this on one of the property bars, but it is so far to the right as to be cut off at many display resolutions. We kept forgetting it was there, so we added it to our Special menu.

Special Effects   The next three items ease access to the tools in the toolbox that we invoke frequently, but are nested in flyouts. And we still like to work "un-interactively" at times with effects, so we were delighted to find that little jewel that opens whatever docker is relevant to the currently selected object.

PowerClip Now   We see this as the prototypical candidate for improved access, the alternative being Effects ➤ PowerClip ➤ Place inside Container. Frankly, the best way to treat this command is with a hotkey, so stay tuned.

Convert to Grayscale   We convert more images to grayscale than any other color depth, so it made sense to promote this command to one-click access.

Text Commands   We'll bet that most of you didn't know that the first two commands of this section existed. Sure, you can dial up any spacing value you want in the Format Text dialog, but these are different—they automatically set spacing to 150% or 200%, figuring out for themselves what that would be, based on type size. These are two of the many commands hiding in the Customize treasure trove.

Photos and Clipart   These are the two Scrapbook dockers that we use most often.

Drop Shadow   Finally, you won't find this command anywhere on your system. It is a script that we wrote for applying a simple drop shadow behind a selected object. Once we saved it as a script file, DRAW made it available for inclusion on any toolbar or menu.

In all of these cases, our chief criterion is obvious: which commands and functions require that we click through multiple menus, flyouts, or dialogs? As far as we're concerned, any command that is nested in a flyout (meaning we would have to click three times, and possibly click and hold for one of them) had better be an item that we don't use often. If we need it regularly, it gets promoted.

T I P   We have focused on customizing the main menu, but DRAW has other menus. Examine the drop-down list in Customize ➤ Menus and you will find every context menu that DRAW offers (the one that appears when you right-click an object). One valuable customization strategy is simply to place the commands you use most often at the tops of each context menu.

The Keys to Happiness

Those who want to drive the CorelDRAW interface as fast as they can will look no further than their keyboards. We decline to debate which method is best—icons, menus, or keystrokes—as it is based on personal preference. But for pure speed, keystrokes will win all the time, and we'll challenge anyone to a race to prove it. Keyboard users have yearned for Corel to provide more hotkeys, even if the developers have to use strange and bizarre ones (such as Alt+F3 for Lens and Ctrl+Shift+A for Copy Properties From). But you no longer have to accept weird key mnemonics or absent hotkeys. From Customize ➤ Keyboard, you have total control.

Assigning and reassigning shortcut keys follows the same path as toolbars and menus: you get a list of every single command in DRAW-land, and then a box to type the shortcut key you want applied to the chosen command. If you choose a keystroke that is already in use, you must click Delete Conflicts in order to continue, and once you do, you then have the option to Navigate to Conflict—meaning DRAW gives you a chance to assign a new keystroke to the command that just lost its original one.

There are two distinct sets of shortcuts—text editing and everything else—and the View All button takes you to a dialog displaying every shortcut key in service, with options to print the list or export it to a file.

The one shortcut key that we think has saved us the most time is our Auto-PowerClip key. Here is how we created it.

1. From Customize ➤ Shortcut Keys, we drilled down to Effects ➤ PowerClip Effects ➤ Place Inside…

2. In the Press New Shortcut Key box, we typed Ctrl+1.

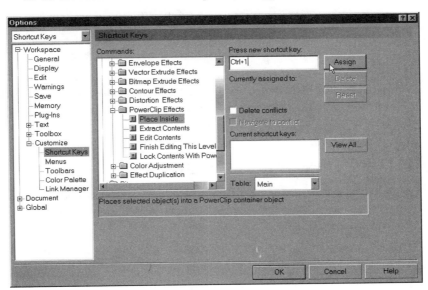

We did not have to deal with Delete Conflicts because no other command or function uses this keystroke. (In fact, we found that Ctrl+1 through Ctrl+0 are excellent places to store custom shortcut keys.)

3. We clicked Assign and then OK.

The reason we like this shortcut so much is that it allows us to operate with maximum efficiency and minimum effort. Imagine that you're about to powerclip one object into another—the final action to be taken is a click with your mouse on an object on the page. That's non-negotiable; there is no way to do that without using the mouse. Even if you know the cool shortcut of right-dragging one object atop another, it's still a mouse-centric operation. So the last thing you want to have to do is traverse off the page to the menus to do a bunch of clicking, only to have to return to the page to click on the container. With the hotkey, it is so much simpler:

1. Select the object to powerclip.

2. Move your cursor to the desired container.

3. Press Ctrl+1 and click.

That's it—you're done. Couldn't be simpler.

Hotkeys for Your Hot Tools

By now it is self-evident, but it is worth reiterating: all of the icons in the toolbox can be given shortcuts. You can create a keystroke for the Bézier tool, the Knife tool, or the Slanted Dimension tool, and for any particular fill type, such as Texture or PostScript. Even No Fill can be customized, which would otherwise require a trip to the × on the color palette.

We wasted little time swapping Uniform Fill with Fountain Fill—we have never understood why the busier Uniform Fill requires Shift+F11, while the more exotic Fountain Fill only needs F11.

You might also be interested to know that all of the node-editing commands are assignable, such as Join, Break, Smooth, Cusp, and so on.

Managing Workspaces

If you have followed along with this chapter, you have created a workspace to store all of your interface design changes, and perhaps thought of more than one workspace you can create:

- Is your computer shared among multiple users? Each can have a workspace.

- Do you have separate projects with radically different needs? Make workspaces for them.
- Do you routinely change screen resolutions? Make a workspace that is better suited for lower resolutions.

All of this can be handled swiftly from the Workspace page of Options, where the New, Delete, and Set As Current buttons perform as expected. But there is another element to workspaces that has not been accounted for: what if you use two computers and you want the same workspace on both of them? We'll need to go backstage to handle this one...

DRAW's Configuration Files

DRAW manages all of your customizations with configuration files that are buried deep in the recesses of the CorelDRAW directory chain. From the main CorelDRAW directory, you'll find them at `Workspaces\CorelDRAW9`, with each workspace having a subdirectory for its files. In each subdirectory, you'll find two `.ini` files, several `.cfg` files for tracking toolbar and menu assignments, and the rather crudely named `.sck` file for storing shortcut keys.

In addition, for each workspace that you create, DRAW creates a small file with a `.cw_` extension. An Explorer window of the Workspace subdirectory would look like this.

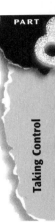

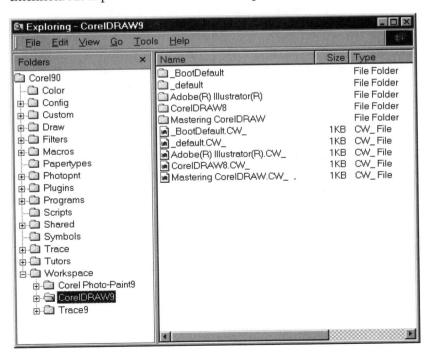

These files store all of the changes that you make to the DRAW interface. When you created the Floorplan toolbar earlier in the chapter and docked it on the top of the screen, DRAW recorded all of that action into cdrbars.cfg. Each time you launch DRAW, it looks in cdrbars.cfg for instructions on how to configure its toolbars. If cdrbars.cfg doesn't exist, DRAW uses its own factory defaults and re-creates cdrbars.cfg from them.

As a result, deleting .cfg files is never fatal. You might lose whatever intelligence you programmed from the Customize dialog, but DRAW can always re-create the file and start up according to its factory defaults. We had quite a fun time experimenting with this, creating all sorts of "accidents" for DRAW:

- We deleted all of the .cfg files. DRAW just re-created them.

- We deleted the entire Workspace directory and all of its subdirectories, just to see if DRAW would complain. It didn't—it blithely opened with factory settings and re-created the subdirectories that it needed.

- We took all of the .cfg files and replaced them with nonsense files—like autoexec.bat, .dll files from the Windows directory, and text files that read "Mary had a little lamb." DRAW issued a message that the files were corrupt and that it was using factory settings instead. That was all—no fireworks. We were halfway disappointed...

Moving Workspaces

So with these files being so small, portable, and ultimately not terribly essential, it is really quite a low-risk proposition to share them with another system. In fact, at the CorelWORLD User Conference each year, we create a workspace for the presentation computers, and disseminate it out to 14 computers. Here is how you move a workspace to a different computer:

1. Using Windows Explorer or your preferred file manager, navigate to the Workspaces subdirectory under the main CorelDRAW directory, and then drill down to CorelDRAW9.

2. Find the subdirectory and the file with the name of the workspace you want to transport. The file will end in .cw_.

3. Copy or archive them. There are lots of methods that would work:
   - Copy the directory and the .cw_ file to a diskette.
   - Create a .zip archive from them.
   - E-mail them to another location.
   - Copy them across a network.

The only requirement is that the files in the subdirectory *stay* in the subdirectory, and the .cw_ file be one level above those files. Consult the Explorer window shown in the previous section for the proper hierarchy.

4. On the destination computer, copy the files into the same location, with the .cw_ file and the new workspace subdirectory residing in the CorelDRAW9 subdirectory.

Two points to make about this. First, if you are unfamiliar with the destination machine, you will need to find where CorelDRAW was installed. If you can find the icon that starts it, you can check its Properties sheet. Second, if there already is a workspace with the name of the one you want to add, you have two choices: overwrite the existing one or rename either one of them. Renaming a workspace is easy, as long as you remember to rename both the subdirectory and the .cw_ file. If DRAW doesn't find both elements, it won't show the workspace in Options ➢ Workspace.

Our choice for transport is a .zip file. WinZip handles nested subdirectories with ease, and carting around one file is much easier than several. We also archive our workspaces this way—after all, these files get written to and updated regularly, so they are at greater risk of having something happen to them. We have invested quite a bit into our workspace, so we treat it like valuable data: we back it up. We copy the workspace to a .zip file, so we can easily retrieve it should something bad happen, like, say, the files ending up with "Mary had a little lamb" all over them.

N O T E Seeing how workspaces are so portable, we have prepared one for advanced users called "Killer Workspace," and have made it available for download on the companion page of the Sybex Web site. Follow the instructions in this chapter for incorporating it into your system.

What's Next

Nothing! Ask any author: appendixes don't count; when you finish the last chapter, you've finished the book. Thirty-four chapters ago, we were discussing nodes, paths, lines, and curves. Now we're talking about custom workspaces, configuration files, and Mary and her lamb. Yup, sounds like we're done, all right…

PART

Taking Control

INSTALLATION

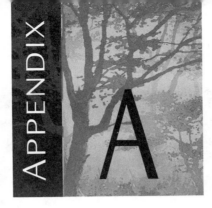

INSTALLATION

orelDRAW 9 is a suite of 32-bit applications that will only run under a 32-bit operating system. As such, it is designed to run under Windows 95, Windows 98, or Windows NT. It will not run under Windows 3.1. Corel will also soon release the Apple Macintosh version of the suite.

Installing the program is not particularly complicated, but it can have a number of options. Begin by inserting CD No. 1 into the CD drive. (You won't need the other CDs—they contain clipart, samples, and other files for use with the modules after they are installed.)

On most systems, the screen shown in Figure A.1 will automatically appear; otherwise, you will need to find `setup.exe` on the CD and launch it. The long-winded but aptly named Install CorelDRAW 9, PHOTO-PAINT 9, and Utilities button starts `setup32.exe`, which installs the suite. (We know advanced users who create a shortcut to the `setup32.exe` file for when they want to add items to their installation.) The next three items install third-party utilities that have been bundled with the suite to enhance its functionality.

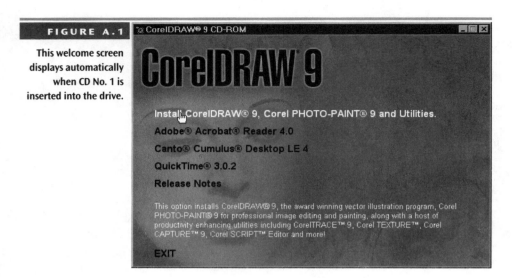

FIGURE A.1

This welcome screen displays automatically when CD No. 1 is inserted into the drive.

Adobe Acrobat Reader 4.0   Acrobat Reader is the software used to display and print Portable Document Format (PDF) files. DRAW 9 offers complete support for creating PDF files, and Corel made sure to include the latest version of Reader.

Canto Cumulus Desktop LE 4   This is part of Corel's ongoing pursuit for a strategy of cataloging media. Cumulus is a third-party replacement for the MEDIA FOLDERS of DRAW 8. It can be used to catalog the Corel-supplied clipart as well as your own. You can generate thumbnails and supply keywords and notes for cataloged media.

If you have a lot of media in varied formats, you might enjoy using Cumulus, but if you stay within the domain of Corel's clipart, then this would prove an overly complex tool that doesn't provide much advantage over our freeware favorite, RomCAT (available from our lead author's Web site, www.altman.com/software.htm). Cumulus offers the ability to print thumbnails and to perform complex searches for cataloged media, but this assumes that you have taken the time to catalog the media in the first place.

QuickTime 3.0.2   This is a multimedia format developed by Apple Computer. PHOTO-PAINT now supports this animation format, but the QuickTime software must be installed to make use of it.

Release Notes   The final option, Release Notes, starts your Web browser and loads a page found on the installation CD. The Web page includes detailed notes on various aspects of both installation and use of CorelDRAW 9. No matter how big a hurry you might be to get CorelDRAW 9 up and running, take a few minutes to at least scan these notes before continuing.

See How They Autorun

Windows has a feature that executes a program called Autorun every time a new CD is inserted. (To be technically precise, a file called Autorun.inf is read from the root directory of the CD, and an executable file is designated there—in this case, intro.exe, the program responsible for the welcome screen in Figure A.1.) Autorun was quite controversial among beta testers, many of whom wanted Corel to remove this "convenience" from their install CD. These detractors made a good argument that users who had already installed DRAW would grow tired of dealing with Autorun when all they wanted to do was install a font, check a Readme file, or perform some other housekeeping task. Corel decided to keep Autorun in place, however.

If you do want to bypass the opening screen, you can instruct Windows to ignore Autorun. To do this temporarily, hold down the Shift key when you insert the CD. You can also get rid of the feature permanently in the Control Panel's Device Manager (it's called Auto Insert Notification), but Autorun can be nice to have for playing audio CDs.

WARNING If you disable Autorun, permanently or temporarily, you must manually execute intro.exe in order to install the third-party utilities, or navigate the CD to find their individual setup programs.

Setup

The Setup program is configured as a Wizard that prompts you through installation options one step at a time. The welcome screen gives you another opportunity to examine the release notes. Next up is the standard license agreement. The first entry screen you encounter asks for your name and company name, if applicable. Following this is a screen that asks you to fill in your serial number. Installation can proceed without filling this in, but doing so validates your license and makes the number available from within the online Help, should you ever need to confirm your license with Corel technical support.

Once you've entered and confirmed the user information, the screen shown in Figure A.2 presents three installation options: Typical, Compact, and Custom. Initially, Custom and Typical require virtually the same amount of disk space. This is because a Custom install begins with the components included in a Typical install. From there, you have the option to select more or fewer components for installation.

APPENDIX

Installation

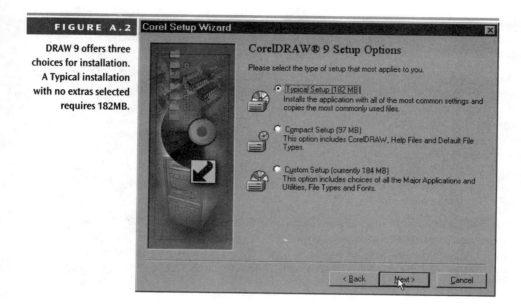

Typical Installation

This installation is the quickest and easiest way to get CorelDRAW installed and running, with the most commonly used features. We recommend doing a Custom installation, for no other reason than knowing exactly what options are available to you. Of course, you can return and add components later. In fact, Corel has specifically provided an option to add components once an install is complete, something lacking in prior versions.

A Typical installation of CorelDRAW installs the following components:

- DRAW
- PHOTO-PAINT
- Graphic utilities: Corel CAPTURE, Corel TEXTURE, and CorelTRACE
- Help files
- Tutorials
- Sample files
- Scripts
- Print Duplexing Wizard

- Commercial label formats
- A selection of filters and TrueType fonts

If you opt for the Typical install, the only choices you'll make are whether to add more languages for use by Corel writing tools, and whether to change the default language from English to something else.

N O T E You can select more than one language for writing tool use. Some languages, like Spanish, support all the tools—spell check, hyphenation, grammar, and thesaurus—while others are more limited in their support.

The next screen prompts you to select locations on your system for the application and shared files. In an effort to conform to Windows standards, these default to sub-directories of the `C:\Program Files` folder, but you can set any destination you wish, including a networked drive. This screen also shows how much space is available on each drive and how much space is required based on your choices, as shown in Figure A.3. You'll get a warning message if there is not enough space for your selections on any of the drives chosen.

APPENDIX

FIGURE A.3

You select the destination for your installation.

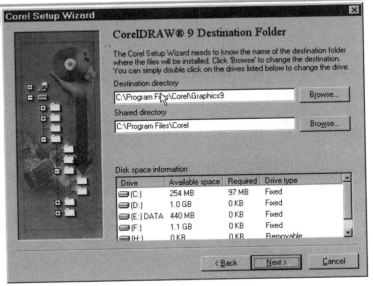

Corel Setup Wizard

CorelDRAW® 9 Destination Folder

The Corel Setup Wizard needs to know the name of the destination folder where the files will be installed. Click 'Browse' to change the destination. You can simply double click on the drives listed below to change the drive.

Destination directory

C:\Program Files\Corel\Graphics9   Browse...

Shared directory

C:\Program Files\Corel   Browse...

Disk space information

Drive	Available space	Required	Drive type
(C:)	254 MB	97 MB	Fixed
(D:)	1.0 GB	0 KB	Fixed
(E:) DATA	440 MB	0 KB	Fixed
(F:)	1.1 GB	0 KB	Fixed
(H:)	0 KB	0 KB	Removable

< Back   Next >   Cancel

Installation

Compact Installation

The Compact installation option provides a bare-bones installation, consuming "only" about 97MB.

A Compact installation installs only the following items:

- CorelDRAW
- DRAW Help files
- Default filters

The other choices are virtually identical to a Typical install.

 NOTE Unlike version 8, neither the Compact nor Typical install allows you to specify which fonts to install or where they are installed. Each installs a minimum set of fonts consisting of AvantGarde and Common Bullets. If you are not already using a font management tool, we recommend you perform a Custom install and add Font Navigator 3.0 to your component list. You can do this during initial installation or at a later date.

Custom Installation

Custom installation begins with the components selected that comprise a Typical install. With Custom installation, you can pick and choose individually from among the following available applications and options:

- CorelDRAW
- PHOTO-PAINT
- Graphics utilities
- Productivity tools
- Filters
- Fonts

Each one of these choices can be expanded to allow you to pick and choose individual subcomponents. Custom installation adds a series of cascading folders to the Start menu, with shortcuts for each application that you choose.

Applications

DRAW and PHOTO-PAINT allow you to install or omit Help files and tutorials. You can also choose vector file types to associate with DRAW (see Figure A.4) and bitmap file types to associate with PHOTO-PAINT. Initially, only CDR and CPT files are associated with DRAW and PHOTO-PAINT, respectively, which is a change from prior versions. There are optional Outlines & Fills, Scripts, and Preset conversions for DRAW that are not part of a Typical install.

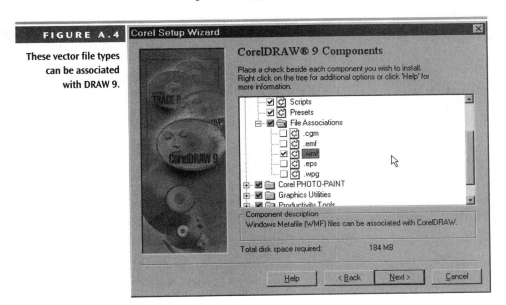

FIGURE A.4

These vector file types can be associated with DRAW 9.

Graphics Utilities

The graphics utilities no longer include CorelMEDIA FOLDERS INDEXER. Instead, Corel has bundled the third-party utility, Canto Cumulus Desktop 4 LE. Cumulus is backward-compatible with MEDIA FOLDERS, but doesn't retain previously assigned notes and keywords. (As noted earlier, Canto Cumulus must be installed separately from the Intro screen.)

CorelTRACE no longer does optical character recognition, but its bitmap tracing is greatly improved. Corel TEXTURE, Corel CAPTURE, CDR/CMX thumbnail displays, and plug-in filters are still included, and have been updated for the new release. DRAW and PHOTO-PAINT 9 are fully compatible with PhotoShop plug-ins, and several manufacturers have supplied filters, which are included with the suite.

Productivity Tools

CorelDRAW 9's productivity tools include a Script Editor, Barcode Wizard, automated label creation in three different national standards, and a Duplexing Wizard.

APPENDIX

Installation

One of the more compelling reasons to use Custom install is to install Font Navigator 3.0 from Bitstream. With this utility, you can install and organize your TrueType and Type 1 fonts. Draw will even automatically install fonts required by a CDR file, as long as they have been cataloged and are available on disk somewhere on your system.

CorelDRAW now fully supports Microsoft Visual Basic for Applications and includes version 6 as part of a Custom install. This provides a much more robust programming environment than does Corel's Scripting language, and also allows for the development of custom programs that can work between applications. By default, when you select this option, you will also install Internet Explorer, version 5. If you choose this item, your system will only do a partial install, restart, then complete the actual CorelDRAW installation.

N O T E   Of the new features of Visual Basic for Applications 6.0, Digital Signatures will be welcomed by many. Digital Signatures describes a method of preventing unauthorized execution of macros from unknown sources. One of its main values is in minimizing the risk of virus transmission. In order to use this feature, Internet Explorer 5 must be installed.

If you do not care about Digital Signatures, do not want to install Internet Explorer 5, but still want to install Visual Basic, you must expand the tree and select only the second item, as shown in Figure A.5.

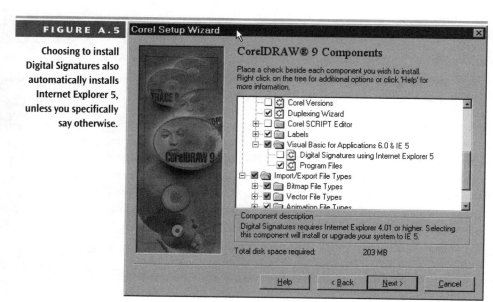

FIGURE A.5

Choosing to install Digital Signatures also automatically installs Internet Explorer 5, unless you specifically say otherwise.

Filters

Default installation includes selected filters in five categories: Bitmap, Vector, Animation, Text, and Internet, taking up a total of 17MB. If you choose to install all filters, the total will go up to 40MB.

Writing Tools

Once you have chosen all the options you want, click Next to reach the Writing Tools screen. Here you can choose what the default language should be, and any additional languages you wish to work in. This is described earlier in "Typical Installation."

Color Profiles

The next screen allows you to choose from color profiles Corel provides for a variety of common printers, monitors, and scanners. These are limited in number, and Corel no longer provides a utility to tune them. However, Corel will be providing more profiles on its Web site, and there are easy links within the program to get to the appropriate page and download the profiles you desire.

Digital Cameras

The next screen allows you to pick from a list of common digital cameras, so that you can transfer pictures directly into DRAW or PHOTO-PAINT from the camera.

Fonts

To Corel's install program, "fonts" means TrueType fonts. However, Corel also supplies all of its typefaces in Type 1 format. If you prefer to use Type 1 fonts, you'll need to take care of it by yourself. First, perform a Custom install and deselect all fonts. Then install the ones you want later with Font Navigator, Adobe Type Manager, or another font manager.

If you don't make any changes, you'll get a default group of 55 TrueType fonts. These can be individually deselected, and other fonts can be added, either individually or by groups. Figure A.6 shows some of the font groupings available. We like to go to that screen for comic relief—some of the names for font categories are quite amusing. If you choose to pick individually, you will be presented with a complete list of all TrueType fonts in alphabetical order.

APPENDIX A

Installation

N O T E   CorelDRAW 9 supplies a set of 33 multilingual fonts. Notes on their installation and use can be found in the release notes.

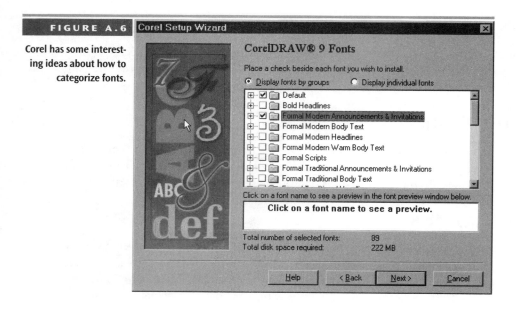

FIGURE A.6

Corel has some interesting ideas about how to categorize fonts.

Completing the Installation

Following the fonts screen, you can choose the destination just as in a Typical install. If you have chosen to install fonts, an additional field lets you to choose the destination for those as well (see Figure A.7). This field will not appear if you don't install additional fonts.

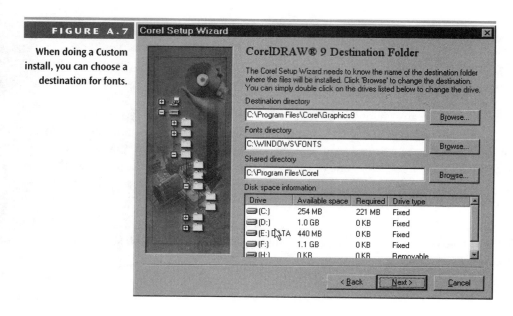

FIGURE A.7

When doing a Custom install, you can choose a destination for fonts.

Moving forward to the next screen, you are given the choice of creating program shortcuts in an existing shortcut folder or by default in a new one called CorelDRAW 9. If you go with the default choice, you can always copy or move the shortcuts later. Click Next, and you are finally at the Install screen. Here you can review the selected components and destinations one last time, or take the plunge and click Install.

Setup displays the progress of the installation with the familiar Windows-style "Percentage Complete" status bar. Various bitmap images appear during the installation, highlighting CorelDRAW's features. Now is probably a good time to go eat lunch or take the dog for a walk. The length of time for the install varies depending on your hardware and the options chosen—we've seen it as short as three minutes and as long as an hour. But hey, aren't you glad you're not installing from diskettes?

At the end of the install, you're offered the opportunity to register online. If you say yes, the Registration Wizard springs into action, presenting you with several screens to fill in and then collecting system information. You'll have an opportunity to see what information was collected and to decide whether or not you wish it transmitted with your registration. If you choose not to register, the application will automatically remind you again in two weeks. Of course, there is always the old-fashioned method of simply filling out and sending the registration card.

Adding Components

CorelDRAW 9 has finally given us an option to go back and install additional components after our initial install, without having to wade through all the various screens of a Custom install. If you run Setup, after an install, you are presented with a dialog that has, as one of three choices, the option to Add New Components. If you select this, the tree structure on the following screen will only display those components that have not yet been installed. Just pick the ones you want to add, and move on to the next screen. From that point on, the install screens will look just like a Custom install, except that your destinations will already be set from your prior install. Depending on which components you add, the resulting process should take far less time than a Typical install.

Uninstall

With the increasing size and complexity of today's programs, the numerous files that are installed in a variety of locations (including the Windows directory and System subdirectory), and the entries added to the Registry by the installation program, manual removal of software is too complex for mere mortals. That's why most Windows programs include an Uninstall utility that is installed during setup.

CorelDRAW's Uninstall can be invoked from the Start Menu folder containing the Corel applications (you'll find it under Setup and Notes), or the Add/Remove Programs

APPENDIX A

Installation

command in the Control Panel. The Uninstall Wizard allows you to select from a list of Corel applications you have installed. You can choose just one or several applications to uninstall, and you can choose to uninstall everything or choose individual components, as shown in Figure A.8.

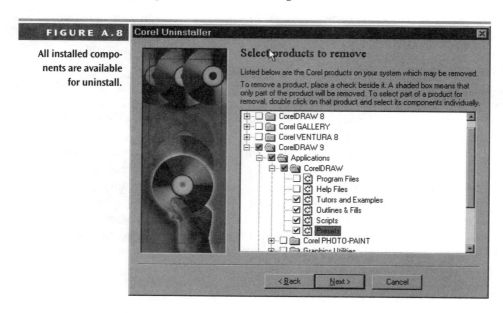

FIGURE A.8

All installed components are available for uninstall.

INDEX

Note to the Reader: Throughout this index **boldfaced** page numbers indicate primary discussions of a topic or the definition of a term. *Italicized* page numbers indicate illustrations.

Numbers and Symbols

3-D cube exercise, **297–304**
3-D effects. *See also* Extrude tool; perspective
   with PowerClips, 432–435, *432*
3D Models tab in Scrapbook, 70
& (ampersand) in menus, 846
* (asterisks) in Style list, 772
… (ellipsis) in menus, 21

A

Acceleration controls in Blend property bar, 331–332
accelerator keys. *See* hotkeys
Acrobat. *See* PDF files
ACSII 85 Encoding option in Publish to PDF dialog box, 706
Add Noise bitmap effect, **544**
Add Page Frame option in Page Setup dialog box, 617
Add Perspective command, 290–292
Add Preset option in Envelope tool, 315, *315*, 317
adding. *See also* creating
   Alignment list to Text property bar, 836
   color styles to custom palettes, 791–792
   commands to menus, 846, *846*
   CorelDRAW components later, 867
   graphic elements to Web page backgrounds, 485–486, *485*
   hotkeys to menus, 846
   Nudge box to Standard toolbar, 834–835, *834*
   Style list to custom toolbar, 844–845, *845*

additive color, **669**
Adobe Acrobat Reader. *See also* PDF files; Publish to PDF dialog box
   installing, 858
Adobe Exchange and Distiller software, 710–711
Adobe Freehand files, importing, 732–733
Adobe Illustrator files (.AI)
   exporting to, 752–753, *753*
   importing, 731–732
Advanced page in Publish to PDF dialog box, **706–709**
   Colors options, 709
   defined, **706–707**, *707*
   EPS Files option, 708
   Fountain Steps option, 708
   Maintain OPI Links option, 708
   Output All Objects As option, 709
   Preserve Document Overprints option, 707
   Preserve Halftone Screen Information option, 708
   Preserve Spot Colors option, 708
   Render Complex Fills As Bitmaps option, 707
   Use Color Profile option, 709
Advanced Separations Settings dialog box, 638–640
advertising banners in Web pages, 522–523
.AI files
   exporting to, 752–753, *753*
   importing, 731–732
aligning
   objects
     hotkeys, 33–34, 128
     overview of, **78–79**, **127–128**, *127*
   text
     adding Alignment list to Text property bar, 836

Align page in Format Text dialog box, 203, 217, *218*, *219*
artistic text, 203
paragraph text, 203, 217, *218*, *219*, 223–224, *224*, *225*
vertical justification settings for paragraph text, 220
Alt key. *See also* Ctrl key; F keys; hotkeys; Shift key
   + F3 (Lens docker), 384
   marquees and, 15, 72
   scrolling with, 9
   Spray mode and, 13
Altman's Laws of DRAW, **61–62**
Always Overprint Black option in Print dialog box, 637, 683
ampersand (&) in menus, 846
animated GIFs, **461–462**
anti-aliasing, **455–456**, *456*, *457*, **535**, **755–756**
anti-virus protection, 864, *864*
Apply All Property Changes to the Current Page Only option in Layers docker, 800, *800*
Apply Embedded ICC Profile option in Import dialog box, 726
Apply to Duplicate option in Transformation dockers, 123
applying
   scripts, 810, *810*, 815
   styles, 769, 771, 772–773, *773*
archiving workspaces, 853
Arrange menu, **121–133**
   Align and Distribute command
     aligning objects, 78–79, 127–128, *127*
     distributing objects, 78, 128–129
     hotkeys, 33–34, 128, 130
     overview of, 78–79
   Break Apart command, 75, 131
   Combine command, *74*, 75, 131

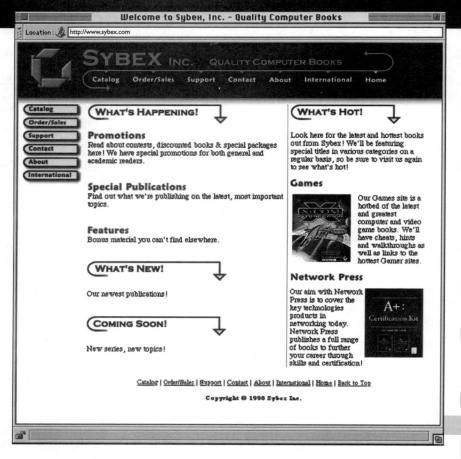